THE MUSIC
OF
CHRISTIAN HYMNS

by

Erik Routley

THE MUSIC
OF
CHRISTIAN HYMNS

by

Erik Routley

Dedicated with affection to my friend and mentor,
JOHN WILSON
our generation's most devoted encourager of fine hymnody

Library of Congress Catalog Card No.: 81-85055
ISBN 0-941050-00-9

Preface

The story which these pages recount is one which has occupied my attention over a period of close on fifty years; indeed, it was fifty-three years before the time when I am writing this that I first became interested in the music of Christian praise. This was when, at the age of not quite nine, I was translated from my home, which used one hymn book in church, to school, which used another.

This is not the first time I have attempted to tell the story. I presented to two long-suffering examiners in the University of Oxford a thesis, hopefully aimed at the degree of D.Phil., which was so long that I feel it must have defeated those worthy men, and that they passed it in a sort of helpless despair. Those who have time to waste will probably still be able to locate it in the Bodleian Library, but I should advise them to find something else to do. This appalling monster was abridged to about 40 per cent of its length and published in 1957, seven years or so after it was first written, as *The Music of Christian Hymnody*, by far the most tedious of the books I have written and the least typographically inviting. This went out of print years ago, and that is another sleeping dog which readers would be well advised to let lie.

Now I have done it again, and if this is in any sense an improvement on the previous efforts, that will be due to the fact that a sober sixty is being substituted for a hopeful 35. Especially it will be due to the fact that I have since had the privilege, first of visiting, then of living in, the United States. I think I may be a shade less paralytic in my appreciation of American hymnody than I was in those earlier days.

I ought to take my reader into my confidence at least to the extent of indicating that this is an awkward subject to handle, largely because there is no single source to which my reader can be referred to check what I am talking about. Hymnals continue to proliferate, and I cannot expect my reader to possess more than one or two. My own collection, which is nothing out of the way for a hymnologist, numbers at this moment about 525, and that is a tiny fraction of those that have been published. So I must at the same time apologize for the necessity of providing abundant examples to illustrate my text, and give notice that the reader will get along pretty well if he or she has either the *English Hymnal* (1933 edition) or the *Hymnal-1940* of the Episcopal Church. I select these because they represent, in Britain and the USA respectively, the best all-round selection of texts and tunes to be found in single volumes. But the *Hymnal-1940* is not as readily available in Britain as the *English Hymnal* is in the USA, so I have been obliged to rely only on the *English Hymnal* as a book in which if a tune appears I can save the trouble of quoting it here. If you have that book and my examples you will fare tolerably well; but there are sections of this book in which you will be just that little bit better off if you have also *Hymns Ancient and Modern* and/or the *Pilgrim Hymnal* within reach.

My main contention here is that hymn tunes are music. Everybody knows they are music of a special kind, but few musicians have any idea that they are, or anyhow can be, music, and great music at that. There is, for the church historian, no more illuminating commentary on the church's history than a study of its people's music— what they were offered, and what they accepted. We shall observe, as we follow the story through, tides ebbing and flowing in various ways: sometimes the musicians were content to provide what the unmusical wanted: sometimes they sought to share with them musical experiences they would otherwise never encounter. Ideas of taste and appropriateness varied with the currents of culture. What one age thought beautiful another despised; what one thought impossible, another rescued and honored. We are going to follow that track wherever it may lead.

Obviously this book has limitations—especially those imposed by the author's English background. Were it written, for example, by a German scholar its emphasis would be very different, and I am sure that an American one would have written it differently again, and in certain places much better. But you cannot write a story, no matter how objective you hope it will be, without a focus, and it will be obvious where my focus is. I should, anyhow, hate to think I had written a book which made it unnecessary for anyone else to contribute to the subject. This isn't the last word, even if only because the day after I send it off to the press a hymn tune may appear which makes me long to recall it. So far as I am concerned it's my third word—and very probably my last: but it may be a place from which others can start out.

I cannot begin to express my debt to others; as far as I can see, there is no original thought here, and it is all gratefully borrowed from somewhere, even if a failing memory conceals the fact from the writer. I have elsewhere listed the *Companions* to hymnals which have been my constant authorities (in, for example, the *Panorama*), and I here simply repeat my indebtedness to them. Many other friends have answered questions and corrected illusions. Once again I mention with honour Robert F. Newton and Andrew J. Hayden, whose *Check-*

List of dates of British writers and composers is so complete and exhaustive as to make me wish somebody had done the same for Americans. Detail after detail would here have been missed or misrepresented but for my constant correspondence with John Wilson. And I may add that when I was writing the later chapters I found great pleasure in mentioning so many people whom I knew personally, in both Britain and the USA, and whose friendship I am proud to celebrate.

Do not be offended if your favourite tune does not appear in the examples, or is not even mentioned in the text. Especially I trust that living composers who go without mention will not be offended at the omission, or over-envious of those who are mentioned. To all such I say: I may be wrong; so hope for a better judgment in another commentator.

I must add that while I have done my best to trace the copyright owners of tunes I have quoted which are not in public domain, I shall be glad to do what is possible to rectify any omissions. If there are any, they will be caused by the failure of correspondents to answer enquiries, or by their untraceability. We have done our best in this matter, and are very grateful indeed to all the people who have let us reprint their material; regrettably in a few instances I simply haven't been able to afford the fees asked, and so have had to delete the quotation from my final draft. But that happens rarely.

Te decet hymnus, Deus, in Sion!
et tibi reddatur votum, qui exaudis preces.

E.R.
Princeton, N.J.
1979

Abbreviations Used in the Text

Most references carry the prefix EH: this is the *English Hymnal,* full music edition, Oxford University Press 1933 and later.

AM, A & M or *Hymns A & M*	*Hymns Ancient and Modern,* edition date given or implied, Wm. Clowes Ltd. (AMS means Standard Edition, 1922 and later: where no date is given, the Revised edition 1950 is meant)
BBC	*BBC Hymn Book,* Oxford University Press 1951
BH	*Baptist Hymnal,* Baptist Convention, Nashville, Tenn., 1975
CH	*Church Hymnary,* Oxford University Press CH2, 1927 edition, CH3, 1973 edition
CP	*Congregational Praise,* Independent Press 1951 and later
EKG	*Evangelisch Kirchengesange* (Lutheran church in Germany)
Frost	M. Frost, *English and Scottish Psalm and Hymn Tunes, c. 1524-1677,* Oxford University Press, 1953
HCS	*Hymns for Church and School,* Novello 1964 (now Unwin Publications, Old Woking, England)
OBC	*Oxford Book of Carols,* Oxford University Press, 1928 and later
Panorama	*A Panorama of Christian Hymnody* (Routley), Liturgical Press, Collegeville, Minn., 1979
SHECM	*A Short History of English Church Music* (Routley), Mowbray, London, 1977
SP	*Songs of Praise,* Enlarged edition, Oxford University Press, 1931 and later
SPD	*Songs of Praise Discussed,* Oxford University Press, 1935
WH	*Westminster Hymnal,* Search Press, London, 1940
WP	*Westminster Praise,* Hinshaw, Chapel Hill NC, 1976
Y	*Hymnal for Colleges and Schools,* Yale University Press, 1956

Other references are spelled out in the text.

Contents

Plainsong Hymnody

Plainsong is the generic name for the church music of the earlier Middle Ages. Its appearance, now familiar to many, written on a four-line staff in a notation that bears little resemblance to that of modern notation, is the result of the formalization of writing developed long after the music first came into use, and its original notation used neither staff nor noteheads.

Professor Egon Wellesz in his classic treatises, *Byzantine Music and Hymnography* and *Eastern Elements in Western Chant* has shown that we may trace the origins of plainsong to the cantillations current in the Synagogue in our Lord's time. And the earliest forms of notation seem to have been based on the tiny accent-marks used in the Hebrew Bible to guide the cantor in his singing of the Psalms. Nothing is more probable than that the first Christians, singing their first hymns, used melodies familiar from that synagogue worship in which they had been brought up, nor is it improbable that the development of church music in the first days of the church's liberation (313 A.D. onwards) was a modest and steady development from those origins.

But if this is true, it establishes at once a very important fact about plainsong, which is that it was a musical vehicle for prose, Greek originally, then Latin; and that that prose was the prose of the Bible. It is prose not as opposed to 'poetry' but as opposed to 'metered.' The genius of plainsong, then, is entirely associated with its purpose which was to support the words of the Jewish, and later the Christian, liturgy.

All the special attributes of plainsong are really traceable to that fundamental proposition, except only its musical modality. We may begin by mentioning some of the most evident differences between plainsong and what most normal churchgoers to-day encounter as church music.

(1) It is entirely subservient to the natural rhythm of words, and that rhythm, originally, has nothing to do with artificial metre.

(2) This means that where a brief melody is used for successive units of text, in strophic style, the music must be flexible in order to accommodate different numbers of syllables. This is what casts plainsong into the form we usually call 'chant', in which the beginning and ending of the brief melody are invariable, but a central portion can be extended or abridged according to the need of the particular strophe.

(3) Whatever may have been the singing customs of Christians in the church's first three centuries—of which we know virtually nothing for certain—once the church became an established public institution, congregational singing was unknown in it, and it remained unknown until a very late stage in the Middle Ages. The music appropriate to the Mass and to the monastic offices was sung always by a cantor with a choir and only overheard by the lay worshiper. If then plainsong music 'sounds uncongregational' to the modern ear, that is what it was meant to be. No music can resist the pressures of development, and plainsong certainly developed quite dramatically during the Middle Ages; but that development was always appropriate to music professionally sung by people set aside to do it and people who were doing it daily. So plainsong is 'community music', or one might well say, 'chamber music'. Where it was sung by the members of a closed community, it was precisely chamber music, not designed to be listened to, and dependent for its effect on the simple fact that those who sang it knew each other well and did it very frequently. And even in the Mass, where many people were present who were not singing, it was still a vehicle for the sacred texts and nothing more than that. The texts were, until, a late stage, psalms sung either in course of the Offices or as 'anthems' at the Mass, the lections from Scripture, and the prayers of the Canon.

(4) The association of plainsong with *metrical* texts is then a later development which might be expected to have profound effects on the very nature of the music. The most obvious difference produced by a metrical text is where plainsong abandons the nature of chant and becomes 'through composed' musical structure. But another difference is connected with the way in which plainsong hymnody was first used, since until we arrive at the Sequences we encounter no hymnody used at the Mass itself. For its first five hundred years at least, hymnody was confined to the monastic Offices, those daily services which for a religious community supported the devotion of the Mass, and whose discipline provided for the thorough and regular reading of Scripture and singing of psalms. The metrical plainsong hymns—first found only in two metres, the octosyllabic and the Sapphic—developed most especially the characteristics of ecclesiastical chamber music for this reason.

It is hymnody that especially concerns us here, but the musical structure of plainsong is best illustrated by a short reference to the psalmody which is usually known as Gregorian chant.

Structure

'Gregorian chant' is so called because its organization into the forms still in use to-day is attributed to Pope Gregory I (d. 604). Under the system thus named, whether or not Gregory himself did it or whether it was codified by others during his pontificate, eight modes or forms of scale are recognized, and a number of variations of chant (in one case, only one) are assigned to each. The mode is the scale-framework, determined from two directions, (a) the actual notes of the 'white note' scale used, and (b) the relative positions of the final and dominant notes.

The 'final' of the tune is its last note; the 'dominant' is the note around which the melody hinges. Whereas in modern music the 'dominant' is always the fifth of the scale, in plainsong it may be the third, fourth, fifth or sixth. Example 1, which we give for other reasons than this, shows the *Nunc Dimittis* with its traditional

Antiphon for Compline. The 'chant' is where the words of the Canticle begin, and it will be seen that there is a 'reciting note'—the part of the chant which is flexible and accommodates varied numbers of syllables. This note is always the dominant, and in this case as written it is C. (The sign at the beginning of the staff indicates the line attributed to the note C and can be on any of the four lines: the other sign so used is for the note F and an example of it is at Ex. 5).

The 'final' of this melody is not reached in the course of the chant; it is achieved in the Antiphon, which is sung before and after the chant, and it will be seen that it is E—so that in this mode the dominant is the sixth of a white-note scale based on E. This mode is known as the Third Mode, and the full table of the eight modes is this:

I	D - D	Final D,	dominant A
II	A - A	D	F
III	E - E	E	C
IV	B - B	E	A
V	F - F	F	C
VI	C - C	F	A
VII	G - G	G	D
VIII	D - D	G	C

It is understood that only the notes of these scales are used in any melody once the mode has been chosen, with the exception of the note B which is occasionally flattened to avoid a too close juxtaposition of the notes B and F which form the unmanageable 'tritone'. (See our note later, p. 15 for a striking and familiar example of this).

It has also to be understood that there was no notion of absolute pitch in the plainsong era. In practice the dominant, the note most often heard, would be pitched where it was most convenient for singing. If we suppose a D-D register for all modes, the table comes out like this, the mode using the notes of the scale indicated to modern eyes by the key-signature:

A pattern emerges: Modes I, III, V and VII all have their final at the bottom of the scale, while the others have it in the middle. The first group is called 'Authentic' and the second 'Plagal'. A parallel to this in modern music is easily recognized in the tendency of singable melodies to fall into two similar groups—the 'D major' tune whose final is its lowest note (or more or less so), and the 'G major' tune whose final is about half way between the highest and the lowest. (In modern tunes which often use a compass wider than an octave it is not precisely 'highest' or 'lowest' that matter: we are concerned only with the difference between a tune like the OLD 100th and one like 'Praise, my Soul.')

Sometimes the Greek names of the modes, taken from Plato, are applied to these; in that case Modes I, III, V and VII are named Dorian, Phrygian, Lydian and Mixolydian; and their counterparts have the same names with the Greek prefix Hypo- applied to each. But it is better, in dealing with plainsong, to use the mode numbers, partly because the later use of Plato's Greek names does not correspond to his, and partly because there are other Greek names, such as Aeolian and Ionian, which do not appear in the Gregorian scheme; and in any case the Greek names apply only to the scale, and have no implications concerning the relative positions of final and dominant, a concern which for reasons we have already noticed applies only to plainsong.

Any plainsong melody, then, pivots on its dominant and moves towards its final. The musical function of the antiphons attached to plainsong chants was to complete the journey which some (not all) of the chants left unfinished. Their liturgical and intellectual function was, of course, to provide a comment on the canticle or psalm appropriate to the occasion on which it was sung.

The Gregorian system of psalm-chants provided an 'intonation' and a 'recitation' for each of the eight modes, together with a 'mediation': these served the first half of a psalm-verse; the second half had one of the several alternative 'endings' after the second recitation. The whole system of forty chants (in the Sarum system: more in that of Solesmes) was like a tool-kit with adaptable tools: one 'handle' could be fitted with several different tools; the First Mode (in the Sarum system) had eight such alternatives, the second, two, the seventh, eight, and so on, only the sixth being inalienably paired with its ending. The chant in our Example I (English) is, then, analysed thus, it being the Third Tone, Fourth Ending:

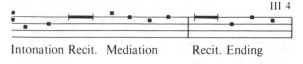

III 4

Intonation   Recit.   Mediation   Recit.   Ending

Notation

The most primitive form of plainsong notation is no more than a series of signs not unlike those of modern shorthand; indeed, that is very much what they were—reminders to the singer of what he had learnt by ear. For choirs these signs corresponded with the movements of a conductor's arm,—a conductor being, of course, of no use for providing a 'beat', which was irrelevant to this kind of music, and being there only to remind people how a tune went. The plainsong notation now familiar was developed in the monasteries where the scribes, writing with quill pens, devised a notation which could easily be written with those instruments and easily read by singers. To a modern eye unused to it, it presents no difficulties if it is remembered (a) that the presence or absence of a tail has nothing to do with note-value, (b) that two ascending notes are written on one stem while descending notes are written slantwise, and (c) that the sign indicates a three-note group beginning where the first stem has its top, descending to where the thick line has its lower edge, and returning to the note indicated by the square head (the above example indicates B - G - A). All notes have the same value, the only variations being in a slight lengthening of the last note, or the last two, of a phrase. More subtle variations and more complex neums will not here concern us and can be studied in books on the subject. Examples 2 and 9 provide a good variety of these signs, and Ex. 2 can be used as an exercize in translation by referring to the modern notation given/with it.

The hymn tune

Plainsong hymnody attached to Latin texts is originally a monastic technique. The expression 'Office hymn' regularly found with many plainsong hymns in the *English Hymnal* refers to the daily Offices, the 'routine' services, of the religious community which, based on the regular reading of Scripture and singing of the Psalms, supported the central observance of the Mass. One would naturally expect that the plainsong hymn tune would grow out of the psalm-chant. In all that follows we have to presuppose that there is no way of dating individual tunes, in the way familiar with modern ours, and also that most plainsong tunes do not have inalienable associations with

particular texts. But we can trace a very clear stylistic development.

What one would expect also, then, is that the primitive plainsong tune would be largely syllabic, as the psalm chants were, and would indulge in melismatic ornament only to the extent that it is found in those chants. What looks like a very primitive example is the tune associated in older English use with *Iam lucis orto sidere* (Ex. 3); although this does not appear in written form before Guidetti's *Directorium Chori*, 1582 (see later, pp. 18-19) it really consists of an intonation, recitation and cadence in each line, very much like the psalm-chant. A similar example is the tune often found with *Te lucis ante terminum* (Ex. 4). Singing these is (like singing the psalms) reading the text to very simple inflected music.

One supposes—again, it is a deduction from internal evidence, not an historical judgment—that the 'through-composed' tune followed later; it seems to have been found that a true melody, closing up the 'recitation' and replacing it with a regularly-moving tune, was an agreeable advance on the chant style. Our (Ex. 5) is a very modest effort in that direction—a two-line phrase repeated, with merely a different final inflection to bring the tune back home. *Conditor alme*, now very closely associated with Advent, (Ex. 6) is more ambitious—using wider melodic intervals and gaining a touch of eloquence. *O pater sancte* (Ex. 7), the only Sapphic tune in common use that is entirely syllabic, has a broader manner appropriate to its three long phrases, which imparts an intimation of that 'surging' quality so familiar in more developed plainsong.

Thus a 'tune' grew out of a 'chant'. The simplicity of these tunes ensured that they were all well known in the medieval church, and have survived (often grievously disfigured) in modern use.

But a touch of *melisma* was not unknown in the psalm chants, and it naturally was thought appropriate to hymn tunes. The distinction between 'ferial' and 'festal' customs ('routine' as opposed to 'festive') was reflected sometimes in the substitution of a slightly more decorative melody on High Days for that which was sung on ordinary days. So, when *Te lucis* was sung at Compline on a Sunday or a Saint's Day, the tune at (Ex. 8) came to be used. It looks like a development on the simpler tune, being in the same mode and sharing all but one of the four cadences.

Most plainsong tunes are melismatic, and many examples of such tunes can be found in the *English Hymnal* and the *Plainsong Hymn Book. O lux beata* (Ex. 9) is a typical example, and this introduces another development—that of simple melodic form. Any melody of any length becomes easier to remember if it has a repeated phrase. This one is unusual in plainsong in being on the a.a.b.a. form, the link back to the last line including a tiny modification of the melody. (It is exactly the same form as that of the Welsh tune ST.

DENIO, EH 407: H 301). Rather commoner is the form which uses the same phrase for the first and last lines, taking the two central lines for development material. Examples of this are our Exx. 10 and 11, and Ex. 11, anciently associated with Christmastide, but appropriated for so many other hymns in the later Middle Ages that it must have been a great favourite, is surely one of the delectable melodies in the whole plainsong repertory. (Our Ex. 3 and *Aeterna Christi*, EH 175: H 132 use the same melodic form). Most plainsong tunes, none the less, are 'through-composed', and such concessions as these to short memories are unusual—which, when we remember that this is essentially professional, not congregational, music, is understandable.

Rhythm and Metre

But we have here, in these last two examples, stumbled on a new and very important matter, which is nothing less that the medieval notion of the moral implications of metre. The best way to approach this is to look at Ex. 12, and then back to 10 and 11 in the light of it. Ex. 12 is the tune originally associated with the early hymn *Hic est verus dies dei* but appropriated for *Veni Creator* as soon as that later text became known. Many readers will be familiar with this tune in a triple rhythm, as transcribed from the Mechlin *Graduale* of 1848 (EH 154 ii), and the secret here exposed is that tunes containing a number of two-note *melismata*, especially when they are fairly regularly spaced, tend to fall into a triple rhythm. Our Ex. 10, heard by an unprofessional singer in the Middle Ages, would stay in his mind in the following form:

Now notice how the accentuation of the words is deliberately contradicted by the notation of the music at the points marked *. Notice also how in the *Veni Creator* tune the two-note phrases are carefully given to unaccented syllables when there is any danger of lapsing into a triple rhythm, and how the same thing happens in the third phrase of Ex. 11.

The principle behind this is the whole ethos of medieval worship. It is the ethos of separation from the secular world. This is supported by the professional nature of all the music used: it was the kind that only dedicated singers could sing correctly and that everybody else, living in the climate of secular dance music, would get wrong. For music outside the church was, as popular music always is, rooted in bodily movement. And the *body* was, in medieval moral theology, a principle from which the believer must

pray to be delivered. It is not necessary to attribute to medieval Christians a mournful denial of the world: on the contrary, such a view is quite unhistorical. But the body was, in those days, the source not only of all manner of mysterious and intractable temptations, but the source also of a great deal of incurable pain; the church's insistence on supernatural realities and metaphysical truths was not so much censorious as pastoral. Saints, we remember, were not only people who resisted the temptations of the flesh but were not infrequently people who achieved a supernatural mastery over the weaknesses and pains of the flesh.

So church music had to be in this sense *different*. Whatever people sang outside church (and they sang plenty), what was sung in the Liturgy must transcend the physical. Now hymnody imported difficulties here. In singing Gregorian chant to the psalms there was no problem because there was no regular 'beat'. But the texts of hymns had a regular 'beat', and this had to be counteracted. A little later on we shall find that after the Reformation this severe rejection of the physical was withdrawn, and plainsong tunes appeared in a new metrical form. But it is thought by many authorities to-day that in plain fact the system never proved to be watertight, and that plenty of plainsong music was in fact sung in a manner approximating to metrical rhythm. It cannot be proved, but on the face of it it is not improbable that the strictly unmetrical delivery of plainsong tunes, which modern musicians follow only because it was studied so closely and brought to such a high pitch of virtuosity at Solesmes in the 19th century was an ideal which perhaps only the best medieval choirs achieved. No doubt in the Middle Ages there were levels of musical purity and propriety as diverse as those of King's, Cambridge and the local parish church to-day.

The Sequences

But if the medieval church was sensitive about physical associations in music, it was no less sensitive about emotional associations. Many attempts were made by the early Fathers of the church to construct a system by which music could be criticized, selected and where necessary banned from church use. Much is said in those sources (for which see my book *The Church and Music* or Oliver Strunk's *Source-Readings in Music History*) about the unsuitability of certain instruments for use in church, and, following the lines suggested in Plato's *Meno,* the moral associations of certain modes. (This, by the way, is one of the areas in which the confusion between what Plato thought was the Dorian mode and what the church Fathers thought it was bedevilled a good deal of discussion). None of this really led very far because the attachment of moral categories to musical modes is a slippery business anyhow, and because all that the Fathers wanted to say about instruments in church was really governed by their overarching principle that things that brought secular association into the Liturgy were undesirable.

But in one area the authorities were on firmer ground, and that is the emotional associations of the *melisma* itself. We have already noticed that the ferial was distinguished from the festal by a modest elaboration of melody, which means that there is something 'festive' about that elaboration. Perhaps the association of certain elaborate tunes with penitential seasons, especially Lent, indicated a feeling that depth of devotion could be reflected in music of heightened expressiveness. There is, in any case, no need to prove that elaborate melody, especially melody with figurations emphasizing certain syllables, has a high emotional content because everybody has always known it.

Music history abounds in examples of the church's attempts to control the music of the liturgy. In the Middle Ages the two most famous of these are Pope Gregory I's direction that liturgical music should be as far as possible syllabic, and Pope John XXII's *Motu Proprio* of 1325 which sought to forbid what he thought of as the excesses generated by the new polyphonic styles. But from Aelred of Rivaulx to John Wesley we have regular protests against music's becoming too clever, against its elaborations which obscured the words of the text, and against the always present temptation to 'music-sprawl' which the enthusiasm of musicians is seldom ready to allow for. And again, a good deal of this was beating the air in as much as authorities whose field is moral theology do not necessarily understand the real nature of music, and are attempting to control what they imperfectly grasp. But the one creative moment that came out of all this was the invention of the Sequence.

Musically the origin of the Sequence is locked up in the obscurity of the Dark Ages, and the Sequences now most familiar are a later development of what seems to have first appeared in the ninth century. The affair began with the encounter between musicians and authorities over the festal eleborations of the liturgical *Alleluia* at such high seasons as Easter. The *Alleluia* is a celebratory musical response to the reading of Scripture. Where normally it would have been sung to a simple phrase, on very festive days a custom grew up of singing it to a highly elaborate melody. A fragment of one such act of celebration is reproduced in our Ex. 13, and a quick glance at it will indicate what sumptuous extravagance such melodies could achieve.

There were two ways around this problem, which church authorities regarded as critical because of the emotional associations of such elaborate vocalization. One was to introduce 'tropes', which are comments from other Scriptural passages on the subject dealt with by the Gospel, set to more restrained music; another was the composition of separate lyrics to 'follow' the lections (called for that reason sequences). Example 13, in the fragment quoted, contains a 'trope'; the words 'Christ our Passover...' are not in the appointed lectionary for Easter but they are a suitable eucharistic gloss. The 'Sequence', however, is a free-standing composition, and the earliest of these in print to-day is *Cantemus cuncti*, translated by J. M. Neale as 'The strain upraise of joy and praise'. It appeared in hymnals until recently (EH 494) but it seems to have dropped out of use because of the 19th century custom of setting it to an uninspiring chant, and it did not in fact gain wide liturgical acceptance in the Middle Ages. It is usually attributed to Balbulus Notker (c. 840-912) although Neale ascribed it to Gotteschalk (c. 805-868). It went with a through-composed plainsong tune called *Puella turbata,* whose origin is very obscure. What its initial words mean is a matter which scholars have been able only to guess at. If it is a religious association, they are thought to mean 'The troubled Virgin' (St. Matthew 2.3), and to be applied typologically to the shock produced in Israel by the Incarnation, which chimes with the original inscription over the song, which marked it for the Octave of the Epiphany. Some also ascribe it liturgically to the last Sunday of the Epiphany season in which traditionally the word 'Alleluia' is especially celebrated because it will not be heard throughout the ensuing season of Lent. The tune *Puella turbata* can be found in Frere's *Historical Edition of Hymns Ancient and Modern* (1909), p. 449.

But in some ways this is a false start, since this Sequence never became central to the Liturgy. It is, however, syllabic, devised to set words to an existing tune, and to 'rescue' the Alleluia from undesirable vocalization. It is the oldest free-standing composition of the sort known to us at present, and it is in rhythmical prose.

Much more important for our purposes is the Easter Sequence, *Victimae Paschali* (Ex. 14), written by the Burgundian priest Wipo (d. c. 1050). Notice first how the text develops into drama after the first few stanzas, reflecting the high dramatic sense which medieval liturgists developed from about that time onwards. The stanzas are in pairs, the two in each pair (after the opening line of salutation) being of identical rhythm, but the next pair always introducing a new pattern.

The opening of the music is the authentic medieval 'Easter sound'—found in the semi-secular melody 'Christ ist erstanden' (EH 134 i: AM 601: Y 103), in Luther's *(Christ lag in Todesbanden,* and in the plainsong tune associated with the Office of the Ninth Hour whose text has its climax in the word 'immortality' (EH 261).

The melody is almost entirely syllabic, following closely the rhythm of the Latin text; but the reader will at once note its wide compass, covering an octave and a fourth. This is common in Sequence melodies, and suggests the use of at least two choirs in their performance.

Other Sequences can be found in accessible sources, and most of these are metrical, some of the later ones strophic. The *English Hymnal* has a complete set—for

Advent (10), Christmas (22), Pentecost (155), Dedications (172), the Holy Name (238), All Saints (253), Corpus Christi (317) and Funerals (351). Of these the Advent and Christmas Sequences are early, metrical but not strophic, like the Easter one already mentioned. Then follow, in historical order, the three from the Golden Age of Sequences, *Jerusalem et Sion Filiae* by Adam of St. Victor (12th century), *Veni sancte Spiritus,* probably by Stephen Langton, Archbishop of Canterbury (d. 1228) and St. Thomas Aquinas's monumentally theological *Lauda Sion,* probably written in 1263. These three are metrical, the last using an expanding metre in its last two stanzas. The 'Rosy Sequence', a setting of the devotional poem *Dulcis Jesu memoria* (238) first appears in a Sarum manuscript dated 1527, and Sponsa Christi (253) was written in the 17th century by J. B. de Contes; the former has a beautifully fresh and serene melody, which seems, from its frequent appearance in music books near the date of its first writing, to have become immediately popular; *Sponsa Christi* has a tune which seems to have been pieced together from fragments of older tunes, beginning indeed with the opening phrase of *Victimae Paschali.* The remarkable individuality of all the classic Sequence tunes, not least their commanding opening phrases, makes it obvious that they were specially composed for their texts, and they always combine memorable melody with genuine simplicity of diction; but except for the Advent Sequence and *Veni sancte Spiritus* they all use a compass of an octave and a fourth (*Lauda Sion,* indeed, goes one note beyond even that).

The mightiest of them all, and that whose music has most frequently caught the imagination of later composers, is *Dies Irae,* (EH 351: H 468). This began as a devotional poem in 17 three-line rhyming stanzas, and when it was taken into liturgical use the last six lines, beginning *Lachrymosa dies illa* were added. The original was by Thomas of Celano, a contemporary of St. Thomas Aquinas (d. 1260). Nowhere is plainsong more controlled and yet more dramatic than here. The fragment quoted at Ex. 15 reminds us of one great and terrifying moment, at *Tuba mirum spargens sonum;* and the phrase set to those words comes again right at the end, at *Lacrimosa.* Notice also the use of the famous opening phrase as phrase 2 of the *Tuba* stanza. This tune is more florid and intense than any of the others, and clothes the august text in an almost cosmic melody—softening the asperities of the words and heightening their final promise.

Besides the Office Hymns and the Sequences there were many Latin lyrics which found their way into liturgical use long after they were first written, and histories of hymn texts inevitably comment on these. Among the most magnificent of these—which are more imaginative and less domestic than the Office hymns—are Venantius Fortunatus's *Pange lingua* and *Vexilla Regis,* written towards the end of the 6th cen-

tury. There is no means of telling when their celebrated tunes were composed. That of *Vexilla* (EH 94: H 63) is a noble example of the florid style, with a quite sophisticated relation between the second and last phrases, while that of *Pange lingua* (EH 95: H 66) is more restrained but musically so interesting that it requires a separate consideration at the end of this chapter.

The metre of *Pange lingua*—six line stanzas in eights and sevens—was especially loved by early Christian Latin poets. The original of *Corde natus* (for which see later, p. 19) was in this metre, and so was the massive *Urbs beata* ('Blessed city, heavenly Salem', (EH 169-70: H 383-4). The melody of *Urbs beata* is quite unusual in beginning on its highest note, returning to it only in the last phrase, but doing so at exactly the right structural point.

Much later we have St. Thomas Aquinas's trio of hymns specially written at the request of the reigning Pope for the Feast of Corpus Christi, and usually dated about 1263. One of these is the Sequence already referred to; the other two use the opening words, and presumably were written for the tunes, of *Verbum supernum* and *Pange lingua* (EH 330, 326: cf 95 and 2, but the tune of 2 need not be that which St. Thomas had before him). This again illustrates the fact that tunes were as readily transferred from one text to another then as they are to-day.

Versions and borrowings

The genius of plainsong could be said to be flexibility in all planes. We have noticed the rhythmic flexibility of the psalm chants, and have just referred to the way tunes were moved about from one text to another. But another implication of this is the way in which tunes turn up in different traditions in different versions. Nowadays we are especially conscious of this because the ecumenical movement has brought so much Catholic music within reach of non-Catholics, and caused encounters for the first time between traditions that formerly were quite separate. The 'Vatican' version of Pange lingua (Ex. 16A) in the *Liber Usualis* is different at several important points from the Sarum version we quote in our example; the same is true of *Vexilla* and many other widely used plainsong tunes. It is important to remember that no version can be certainly claimed as the 'right' one; that kind of judgment can only be made when manuscripts can be dated, or of course when a printed source can be consulted.

Again, one finds as plainsong tunes develop that one borrows phrases from another quite cheerfully. The very late Sequence, *Sponsa Christi,* was an example; but there are plenty of others; *Urbs beata,* for example, turns up again in the tune set in EH to an Office Hymn for St. Mary Magdalen (231); of its six phrases, the second tune uses most of phrases 3 and 4 of *Urbs beata* and copies the fifth and sixth note for note. The beautiful tune, clearly coined during the liturgical ferment of the late 17th century, for *Sol praeceps rapitur*

(Ex. 281) is a close paraphrase of *Pange lingua*.

But a third consequence seems as inevitable to us as it may appear controversial to others. This is that plainsong comes as near as music has ever come to coining a timeless, nationless language, and that therefore its adaptation to languages other than Latin is entirely defensible. We may go back for a moment to our Ex. 1, which we have deliberately given in both Latin and English. It will be seen (a) that very slight adjustments to the melody of the Antiphon are made for the English rite, which do not in the least damage its symmetry or alter its character, and (b) that the chant for the canticle becomes, for English use, III 4 rather than III 5, whose heavier ending is more appropriate to the Latin cadences. But why not? Provided that the translation is sensitive to the Latin rhythm, and its English is impeccable, plainsong sits as gracefully on English as on Latin, and never needs more than the most minute adjustments, or than the sensible choosing of a psalm tone, to make its effect. If it is well with English, it is equally well with other tongues.

A note on Pange Lingua (Ex. 16A, B, C)

It might fairly be said that no hymn tune to be mentioned in this book is more fascinating in its musical implications than PANGE LINGUA; for in it we see the beginnings of that restlessness which in the end exploded into the sophistications of the music we know. For this tune, alone of all the familiar plainsong tunes, breaks through the decorous restraints of modality.

What the story turns on is the tradition known as *musica ficta*, which in purely melodic plainsong music means the flattening of the B under certain circumstances and the introduction of the only 'accidental' that appears in plainsong. As we have already said, the custom arose when the ear protested at the juxtaposition of the notes B and F, which produced the 'tritone' —as awkward an interval melodically as it is harmonically. In harmonized music, with the advent of *organum,* the need for *musica ficta* becomes quite clear if one attempts to harmonize the melody of our Ex. 6 in fifths. Write a fifth under each note of the first phrase, and what can appear under the seventh note (F)? A B flat is the answer; if there were a B natural in the melody the contradiction would be regarded as piquant, not as anomalous. But B flat does the same work melodically—as for example in the middle note of the second melisma of the final phrase of VENI CREATOR (Ex. 12), on the middle syllable of *'creasti',* which is often read and sung as B flat, to avoid making a tritone with the F at the end of the previous melisma (on *'tu'*).

The three versions of PANGE LINGUA at Ex. 16 are not the only three in existence, but they are sufficiently diverse to make our point. Non-Catholics will be most familiar with version C, which is the Sarum Version as given in the *English Hymnal* and elsewhere. While it is customarily sung on Final E, giving it the superficial appearance of a Third Mode (or 'Phrygian') tune, it is written on final A. This is because of the lie of the melody in phrase 4, and specifically because of its fourth note (marked with a star). This fourth note is contradicted in phrase 6 at the same point by the flat sign: so this variable note must be B, and therefore the final has to be A. The Dominant is, as in the orthodox Mode III, the sixth of the scale (in this score, F). So the Dominant and the Final are where we would expect them in Mode III, but the B is the second, not the fifth, of the scale.

Turn now to version A. Apart from other variations of detail, we see here that the intrusive ambiguous note is omitted from phrase 4, where the melody has (in this score) two Gs and an E instead of G-F-E. So the melody can be scored as Third Mode, with C on the top line.

Then consider version B, the form given for the Procession at Corpus Christi in the *Liber Usualis* (Form A is provided for Second Vespers on the same Feast). Here we have the C on the top line, but the whole melody taken down one step so that its final is D instead of E. The result of this is that the ambiguous note in phrase 4 can now be an unmodified note: but this is achieved at considerable cost, because (a) the Dominant of the tune is now very dubious: either it is the fifth of the scale (the last note of phrase 1, importantly altered from the other version), or it is the flattened B, the modified sixth of the scale, which is impossible (the B flat is never a final or a Dominant). The fifth note of phrase 6 avoids contradicting the fourth of phrase 4 simply through being replaced by the note below (which is the tonic or Final).

The result of all that is a tune which, to be candid, cannot be written in any notation that keeps all the rules of orthodox plainsong at once. Version A may be the most primitive—avoiding those ambiguous notes altogether; but once that F, or 'F#' appears in the fourth phrase, the fat is in the fire. It naturally becomes an 'F#' to avoid making a tritone with the upper B—and it looks as if nobody had ever come upon the need to modify a note in order to avoid a tritone *from above* until now: flatten your B and you make peace with a tritonal F below—but now we are sharpening if to accommodate a B above. Version B is a confused and obviously desperate attempt to preserve orthodoxy. Version C boldly uses both the F# and the F natural but presents them, through transposition, as B and B flat, and all we lose in that version is the melodic framework proper to the Mode.

This is not mere pedantry. We are seeing for the first time—and shall we see it again in hymns before Henry Lawes—even before William Albright?*—a situation in which a singer is saying, 'I cannot say what must be said while I am confined to this language.' It is a commonplace in secular music, and in larger-scale church music: in hymnody it is so unusual that we have had to turn aside and look at it.

---

* I may as well say here that the remarkable tune by Albright to 'Father we thank thee who hast planted' is among those which copyright difficulties have prevented my including in the Examples. It can be found at # 1 in *Ecumenical Praise*, or # 77 in *More Hymns and Spiritual Songs*.

2

Sacred and Secular
In the Late Middle Ages

Much theological debate has gone on in the later 20th century concerning the relation between the sacred and the secular. In the Middle Ages it was not a matter of debate. From one point of view, it could be said that everything was sacred and everything was also secular. The distinction was made (and it was never made in the terms we use now) only when some particular activity was in question, and the question really was, 'Are we talking about the sacred or the secular aspects of this?' If the system of theology constructed by St. Thomas Aquinas can be judged the most monumental and also the most characteristic product of medieval Christian thought, one sees there everything brought under the rule of theology. St. Thomas applies his sacred logic to questions about the existence of God, and to the question whether if one is feeling depressed it is or is not 'a good idea to take a bath. Modern culture has re-peopled the universe with a multitude of deities superstitiously worshiped, but the medieval thought-structure held that there is one God in three Persons, and that this fact is irrelevant to nothing that a human mind, at its simplest or its most sophisticated, can conceive.

The important consequence of this for our purposes is that when we speak of sacred and secular styles in church music, we are speaking of just one of the many fields in which the Church followed specific customs, and where needful laid down specific regulations without implying that activities that fell outside those guidelines were in all circumstances forbidden or wrong. Medieval thought is always governed by the vital word 'distinguo'—'I distinguish'. The church distinguished between what was appropriate for worship and what was not, without making a judgment about secular music. It is a little like saying, as we should, that certain forms of behavior that are not improper in one's own sitting room are improper if one is travelling in an aircraft. The regulations governing air-travel are confined to air-travel. Should any modern person think of the medieval Church as being grossly oppressive and indecently omnipotent, he is urged to alter that view, and to understand instead that in expressing (however ineptly it did so in practice) views about the suitability of one kind of music for liturgy and the unsuitability of another kind, the Church was admitting its own limitations, not legislating for the whole of life. Or, to take another very obvious example, in insisting on celibacy for its clergy the church did not, *eo ipso,* imply that marriage for the laity was a dishonourable state, however extravagant the praises of celibacy and the implied devaluing of marriage we may find in the works of individual Christian saints from St. Paul onwards.

It is necessary at once to make that point after our brief survey of plainsong hymnody. Congregational singing, or community singing, was not an activity opposed to the church's teaching and customs: it was simply a different activity from that which went on in church. It is not even true that the laity had to choose between hearing sacred songs in church and singing secular songs outside it. Religion made a constant impact on life outside the liturgy; religion could not be confined to Sunday worship when Saints' Days could fall on any day of the week. Sacred signs and symbols were to be found elsewhere as well as inside the Sanctuary.

Hence, as I endeavoured to show in my book, *The English Carol,* the rich European culture of carol and sacred dance. Hence the appearance in the later Middle Ages of vernacular sacred songs, or songs in which the church language of Latin and the vernacular were mixed—known as *macaronic* songs, of which the most familiar to-day is *In dulci jubilo.* There was no thought that God could be worshiped only in Latin; that the Church should have a universal language for its public acts of devotion was a reasonable demand, especially when Europe was thought of as a Holy Roman Empire; but nobody seriously thought that a layman could address God only in Latin. The real difference between the life of the layman and that of the clergy was that it was lived through images rather than concepts, through pictures rather than words. So the medieval carols are full of legend where the Liturgy is full of dogma; so the porch plays and mystery plays and dramatic Cycles conveyed the Gospel more certainly than a sermon, and the stained glass windows more immediately than a Bible which none but the clergy could read.

By the same token, out-of-church religious song was essentially dance music, and indeed symbolic processional dance was an accepted form of popular devotion. Therefore the Renaissance-demand, which expressed itself in every form of art, and indeed in all important parts of life, tended to question the ecclesiastical assumption that the sacred and the secular must be separated by a conventional barrier, and caused church musicians to think again about the form their music should take.

The consequences of this inner debate form two streams, one more conservative and one more radical. Both are represented in books published in the same year—1582—but before we come to them we must mention a venerable and beautiful tune, BEATA NOBIS GAUDIA (Ex. 17A), which points the way towards the development of the conservative-modern style. BEATA

NOBIS appears in an undated book published at Constance in or just after 1500. It replaces a plainsong tune for the Whitsuntide office hymn beginning with those Latin words (for the tune and a translated text see EH 151). Although the 'new' BEATA NOBIS sounds nowadays attractively archaic, it is a gesture against the plainsong conventions. It is that especially in its use of the Eighth Mode, which is virtually the modern major scale, with the dominant a fifth above the final as we know it. It is still flexible and leisurely in its diction, but its accented syllables are the ones which have the *melismata* or note-groups, not the accented ones. This is a 'renaissance-ecclesiastical' tune, and easily the best known of its kind.

The tune of which this will remind many readers is AETERNA CHRISTI MUNERA, which is known in England and America, outside the Catholic church, in the version produced by Guidetti in 1582 in his *Directorium Chori*. We reproduce it as Ex. 17C. Now Guidetti was a pupil and friend of Palestrina, and assisted him, and later succeeded him, in revising the liturgical chant of the Catholic Church as a consequence of the findings of the Council of Trent (1545-63) and on an invitation from Pope Gregory XIII. Palestrina was the most distinguished musician of his age and was the natural person to invite to undertake this work, especially after the acclaim awarded to his Mass performed in the last days of the Council, in June 1563 in the Sistine Chapel. But (as Robert Hayburn shows in his indispensable book *Papal Legislation on Sacred Music,* Liturgical Press, 1979) Palestrina was in one important respect the very last person to be entrusted with the work, because he was a developed renaissance musician. In his revision of the chants, therefore, he approached the music in a Renaissance way, making a special point of eliminating that rhythmical character which is the very essence of medieval plainsong—the *melisma* on the unaccented syllable. Protests were made against the way he was revising the chants, and his work on them was suspended; but part of it was carried on later by his son, and part by his pupil Guidetti.

Now in Guidetti's AETERNA CHRISTI, we have what remains a splendid tune, evocative in its archaic flexibility as BEATA NOBIS is, but a strange debasement of the original, if we place it alongside our Ex. 17B (one of several versions of what was in those days as well known a tune as ST. ANNE is now). Notice how he eliminates some note-clusters and expands others, but especially how he alters the cadence of the third phrase so that the tune, now having three cadences out of four returning to the tonic, is removed at once from the plainsong family and placed firmly in the territory of 'modern' music. Indeed, it was probably the fact that the tune was so very familiar that caused Guidetti to take these liberties, and to bring it more safely within the area of contemporary musical consciousness. A lit-

tle later we shall see how the practice of producing new tunes, not in the plainsong style, developed especially in Germany. Those who want to explore the story of AETERNA CHRISTI in more depth can chase it through the pages of Frere's Historical Edition of Hymns Ancient and Modern, page xxxi and entries 96, 192 and 202. Almost certainly the use of the same phrase in the first and last lines did not originate with Guidetti, but was taken from one of the current versions; but the long pause on the fourth note is certainly Guidetti's addition.

Most of Guidetti's material is a good deal less interesting than this; another example is the tune we quoted at Ex. 3, which corresponds to nothing in earlier sources and may be his own invention.

Piae Cantiones (1582) is a very different matter. Though its texts are almost entirely in Latin, it is a Protestant publication. Its full title is, in translation, this:

> Sacred Songs of Church and Cloister of the clergy of past ages, in common use in the Renowned Realm of Sweden; newly and accurately revised and corrected by the labour of the same most reverend and honorable member of the Church of God and of the School of Abo in Finland, THEODORIC PETER of Nyland, now committed to print, 1582.

This vitally important source might have lain unnoticed to this day had not a very rare copy of it been brought back to England about 1850 or 1851 by G. J. R. Gordon, Her Majesty's Envoy and Minister at Stockholm.* This copy was passed to the renowned liturgist and translator, J. M. Neale, who, immediately noticing the fresh and attractive quality of some of its music, wrote several carols to bring that music into use, including 'Good King Wenceslas' to carry a tune there set to a spring carol, TEMPUS ADEST FLORIDUM, and 'Good Christian men rejoice', a paraphrase of *In dulci jubilo*. Neale passed it to his collaborator, the Rev. Thomas Helmore, as they were working on *The Hymnal Noted* (for which see later, pp 89-90), and later on it passed into the hands of the great musical antiquarian, G. R. Woodward, who published an edition of it through the Plainsong and Medieval Music Society in 1910, and who wrote a large number of new texts or translations to bring its tunes into currency in his *Cambridge* and *Cowley* Carol books.

The book contained 73 pieces, words and music, noted in a quasi-plainsong style, but presupposing rhythmical units. Its texts were those of medieval written carols (not popular ballads: hence the reference to the 'clergy' in its title), much altered to avoid references to the Blessed Virgin which would offend protestants—on which subject Woodward has some hilarious comments in his preface. The way the texts were treated reminds us of the way late 20th century

---

* G. R. Woodward says 'not later than the beginning of 1853'; but a *Piae Cantiones* tune, as we are about to see, appeared in *The Hymnal Noted,* 1852.

editors, especially in the USA, have altered classic texts in order to satisfy the demands of political pressure groups or liturgical innovators. It is a learned book—a 'campus book' as we might now say—and the 'revision and correction' of the music consisted largely in so noting the music that it could be sung in secular rhythms.

This brings us to the tune DIVINUM MYSTERIUM, first introduced to England by Neale and Helmore in 1852 in an unsingable version, corrected by the Editors of Hymns Ancient and Modern in 1904 (who got it right) and by Vaughan Williams in the *English Hymnal* (who in 1906 got it slightly wrong, but capitulated in the 1933 revision), but only achieving the status of a really well known hymn in the late 20th century.

It has to be noted at once that its association with the Christmas hymn *Corde natus* is due to Neale and Helmore in 1852. In *Piae Cantiones* and earlier it is associated with a Eucharistic hymn in a different metre (7.6.7.6.7.6 trochaic, like six lines of 'Good King Wenceslas').

At Ex. 18 we show an early version of the tune followed by a transcription of the *Piae Cantiones* version; the triple-time version now so well known in England is taken, of course, from *Piae Cantiones;* the free-rhythm version universally followed in the USA is a speculative reconstruction made by Winfred Douglas, and first given in the *Episcopal Hymnal* of 1916. No known manuscript of the tune corresponds to the Douglas version, and as we have said the plainsong tune was never used for this text in the Middle Ages. (One that was so used is in the *Plainsong Hymn Book,* 22).

Many other *Piae Cantiones* tunes are now in currency, as a result of the good work of Neale and Woodward, among which are PUER NOBIS (the four-time version: OBC 92: H 34) and RESONET IN LAUDIBUS (EH 612: H 45), and most of those now used are associated with Christmas carols and hymns (though not O MENTES PERFIDAS, a specially good example, at SP 272). At Ex. 19 we give another tune from this source, CONGAUDEAT, with its plainsong original. The modern transcription is again Woodward's, and the best single source for such transcriptions is his *Cowley Carol Book* (1902, 1919).

Piae Cantiones represents a true incursion into church music of the secular manner; but of course it was probably never used as a church hymnal, and has remained, as it began by being, a scholar's anthology.

Once measured music had captured the imaginations not only of the simple but also of the learned, the expected inception of the next stage after Guidetti took place. Two or three generations after the Council of Trent we begin to see Catholic hymn books containing dance-like and carol-like tunes, and even tunes which are reminiscent of the early 17th century German chorales. The Andernach *Gesangbuch* of 1608 *(Catholische Geistliche Gesange)* has a number of measured tunes newly composed as alternatives to plainsong, including that now called ANDERNACH (EH 50 ii) and REX GLORIOSE (EH 183 ii). ANDERNACH was provided as a simple alternative to the plainsong tune VEXILLA REGIS. Both these are stately Germanic tunes, but on the whole the Catholics were most successful when their tunes looked most like popular carols. The *Geistliche Kirchengesange* of Cologne (1623) provides the original of LASST UNS ERFREUEN (see Ex. 85B). much less formal than Vaughan Williams's version at EH 519, together with HILARITER (EH 164) and JESU DULCIS MEMORIA (EH 238 ii), and these all have an agreeable informality which suggests that their proper place is in a carol book. The great Benedictine editor, D. G. Corner (1587-1648) in his *Gross Catolisch Gesangbuch* (1631) has OMNI DIE (EH 382) and STABAT MATER (EH 115 i), both in the more reserved style—the second again replacing a venerable plainsong tune—and in his *Geistliche Nachtigall* (Vienna, 1648), IN DER WIEGEN (EH 578) and SOLL'S SEIN (EH 288), in the more secular manner.

The contents of Baeumker's great compendious work on Catholic hymnody, *Das Katholsche Deutsche Kirchenlied in seinen Singweisen* (Freiburg 1881-1911) show a steady and continuous development in Catholic hymnody up to the turn of the present century, and while he assumes that these are 'Church songs' one must not suppose that they had official sanction for use at Mass, whatever other occasions there may have been for singing them. Perhaps one of the very best 'carol like' Catholic tunes is AVE VIRGO VIRGINUM (Ex. 53), which goes right back to the *Geistlichen Lieder und Psalmen* of 1567; and it is clear as the story develops that music of every kind influenced these songs. PADERBORN, for example (EH 251), from Beuttner's *Catholisches Gesangbuch* (Gratz, 1602) suggests a folk song or ballad: MARIA JUNG UND ZART (EH 443), from *Psalteriolum Harmonicum* (1642: altered from a 1623 source) has all the true innocence of a nursery song. On the other hand the Genevan psalms were not unknown to Catholics, as the heavily disguised version of Genevan Psalm 98 at Ex. 20 indicates.

If Guidetti manhandled plainsong, it was because of renaissance pressure; so the devising of new tunes in the new style was obviously the sensible course to take; there could be no more composing of plainsong—any that was to be composed was imitative or tonally bogus. But plainsong was now and again reduced to a shamelessly metrical form—Ex. 21 shows how a new tune for '*Lucis Creator*' was made out of the proper plainsong tune for '*Iam Christus astra ascenderat*' (EH 51 ii, cf 150 i). Ex. 22 is slightly more speculative— AUCTORITATE SECULI (EH 176) is supposed to be a degenerate version of a plainsong tune now known as JESU DULCEDO CORDIUM (AM 387), but no ancient manuscript of the plainsong version has actually been found. Ex. 23 shows a Sapphic tune made out of phrases from the traditional UT QUEANT LAXIS tune (EH 191 ii).

These last two examples anticipate the account we shall later give (chapter 12) of the French Diocesan tunes, but we can say already that in those we shall find some pleasant echoes of the carol vocabulary. Pietism tended to substitute, in Catholic hymnody as in Protestant, the bourgeois ballad for the old carol, and 18th century Catholic hymnody outside France lapsed quickly into sentimentality—as chapter 12 will have to show. But as an example of the difference between the tune which aped the stately style and that which was content to be secular, the reader may care to compare two tunes which in modern books are both called ST. GALL. One is a LM tune, #54 in the Standard *Hymns A & M,* an arrangement of a late German chorale which stands a good chance in any competition for the dullest hymn tune in currency; the other is the rousing and bucolic melody at EH 292. The first is from the 1845 *Gesangbuch* of the monstery of St. Gall, the second from the 1863 edition of the same collection. This is the historical background against which the last section of our chapter 25 should be read.

Carols and Laudi

As we have said, full accounts of carols must be read elsewhere. It will be sufficient here to remind the reader that carols in the Middle Ages followed two streams—the popular, designed for those who could not read or write, with their 'burden-stanza' form, and often associated with processional dances, and the learned, fashioned for singing as an adornment of liturgy by trained choirs. The second form is that which survives in medieval manuscripts, and *Musica Britannica IV* contains many of them. The learned carols—which are often boisterous and entertaining in their music—used a form of measured rhythm, with the ingenuity of polyphony replacing the excitement of the dance; but in the nature of the case we have hardly any contemporary record of popular extra-liturgical carols from the days of their inception. What we have has been reconstructed by scholars from the oral traditions of those regions where carol singing was not suppressed by puritan opinion and theology. But occasionally something of that kind got into a manuscript, and one of these is the 'Prose of the Ass', noted in a manuscript at Beauvais dated before 1222, the date of the death of Pierre de Corbeil, its editor. It was written down (see Ex. 24) in the only notation known to writers, and so it looks like plainsong; but the tune, if sung in procession, would not have been sung in the contemplative rhythm of plainsong, but with some kind of beat—either a march or, more probably, a triple dancing rhythm. The procession itself was a dramatization, associated with Sens, Beauvais and other French religious centres, of the flight of the Holy Family into Egypt, in which the procession was led by a young woman sitting on a donkey with a young man walking by her side. (But another association of the tune is noted in Frost's *Historical Companion to*

Hymns A & M, 1961, pp 407-8). The melody as we have noted it is that of the third stanza in the Beauvais manuscript where it is given to the bass voices: at earlier stages it is slightly different. In modern use the tune was revived by Redhead (see later pp 91-A) in march rhythm (AM 524: H 324) and also appears in triple rhythm as ORIENTIS PARTIBUS, EH 129.

The *Laudi Spirituali,* sacred songs in the vernacular invented by the Franciscans of Florence in the 13th century, became a well known out-of-church vehicle of devotion in the late Middle Ages; they were given much prominence through their use in processions (we would probably call them demonstrations) organized by certain dissenting sects who, just before 1260, wished to warn the people of the imminent end of the world. This form of Millennarianism held that the year 1260 would be the year of the catastrophe, taking their cue from Rev. 11.3, 12.6 and 13.5. But *Laudi* were composed for less dramatic devotional purposes also, and they have given us the text of 'Come down, O love divine' (EH 152: H 376) as well as one dubious tune shown at Ex. 25. This tune, ALTA TRINITA BEATA, appears in modern books in the arrangement of Charles Burney, who quotes it in his *History of Music,* completed in 1789. But if EH 184 or H 135 be compared with Ex. 25, which is transcribed from an early manuscript, Burney will be seen to have made some fairly bold conjectures about the tune. In fairness to him it has to be said that if the tune was sung out of doors it probably sounded like the kind of march-tune he contrived rather than as the plainsong notation makes it appear: the original is anyhow difficult to determine, and at least one note in Ex. 25 is highly suspicious. Moreover, the version in plainsong notation given both in Frere and in Frost's revision does not credibly allocate neums to syllables. The metre of the original stanza was six lines of trochaic octo-syllables, and that of Burney's version is 8.7.8.7 D trochaic: so when all is said one needs to use a certain amount of imagination about this tune. The only other contribution of the *Laudi* to modern hymnody is LANGA (EH App. 60), but that has come so far from whatever its original was that it need not detain us.

A much more plausible and satisfactory tune from the same kind of source, but from Germany, is LAUS TIBI, CHRISTE (Ex. 26). The original text here seems to have been a 14th century German *Leyse,* which is a popular hymn using the words *Kyrie Eleison* as a refrain—a form which Luther found very useful as we are about to see. This tune in its modern version at EH 534 is treated somewhat as Bach treated early German tunes and becomes a very stately processional; apart from the omission of the refrain-phrase it has been altered only in detail, but that phrase establishes the mode and the final, which are of course obscured when it is cut off. (A new modern version could very well accommodate it, and the result might be magnificent).

3

The Age of Luther

If Luther was the liberator of congregational hymnody, as he certainly was, it is perhaps surprising that six or seven years passed after the inception of his Reformation before he gave his thought to hymns. The first few years, however, were occupied with high theological controversy, and saw the publication of his foundation-documents in Reformed doctrine. It was not until 1523 that he found time to put into order, for public use, his thoughts about worship. The documents on this subject are the pamphlet *Concerning the Order of Public Worship* (1523), *An Order of Mass and Communion for the Church at Wittenberg* (1523: it was first used in full at Wittenberg 29 October 1525), *A Christian Exhortation to the Livonians Concerning Public Worship and Concord* (1525) and the *German Mass* (1526). Only the *Order of Mass* specifically mentions hymns. (See *Luther's Works,* Vol. 53, pp 5-90).

It is very clear, however, from these documents that Luther wished to refine the worship of the Church by excluding what he thought were needless complications while retaining, through the use of music, the essential spirit of Christian devotion as enshrined in the church's tradition. He regarded medieval music not as something to be swept away but as something to be used with more restraint and discrimination than the prevailing customs of the church called for. He wrote out in full certain sections of the Rite which were traditionally sung to plainsong music, retaining the music but using its primitive and simple forms: he included a complete Epistle and Gospel in the Mass, fully noted, as an exercise in chanting, together with formulae for chanting to be adapted to any text. Theological alterations in the Rite, to accommodate the revived art of preaching and to exclude an over-emphasis on sacrifice and on transubstantiation came as a matter of course and have no musical significance.

One of the most characteristically 'protestant' changes Luther made in the ethos of worship (it still remains so) was to abolish daily Mass, and to make the Mass a celebration enjoyed and participated in by the whole Christian community. (Protestant worship-ethos still basically assumes that 'everybody will be there', while Catholic tradition says that the worship goes on constantly whether people are there or not). The sense of corporateness engendered by substituting congregational songs for some of the material traditionally performed only by monastic choirs naturally occurred to him as soon as his thoughts about worship became clear, and the implementation of this demand was the next step. The one clue to this project in the 1523 *Order of Mass and Communion* is the sentence (*Works* 53 p. 39):

The hymns and the *Te Deum Laudamus* at least confirm the same thing as the *Deo gracias,* namely, that after the exposition and homilies they used to praise God and give thanks for the revealed truth of his words. That is the kind of songs, but in the vernacular, that I should like us to have.

Luther's first inspiration seems to have come from the Anabaptists, who were already developing congregational songs of their own; for his first hymn, *Ein' Neues Lied,* which appeared on a separate leaflet in 1524, is a polemical song about the burning, on 1 July 1523, of Heinrich Voss and Johann Esch, the first two martyrs of the Lutheran Reformation. Hymns of this kind were part of the Anabaptist heritage and many of them still remain in the Mennonite *Ausbund* (1583, revised 1622). This turns out to be off the main line of Luther's hymnody, which was liturgical, but there could be no better introduction to the style of the Lutheran chorale than its tune (Ex. 27).

Notice first the musical form of the tune, which announces a long phrase, and then repeats it before going on to the new material, and then in the second half (phrases 4-8) uses two phrases which are repeated at different pitches. As Gustav Reese has pointed out, this was the favourite form of the songs of the Minnesinger, the German troubadours, who provided high-level entertainment for the German aristocracy (see his pp 250ff). In some of the other Luther chorales we shall notice a further aid to memory: the repetition of part of the opening phrase, often of its whole second half, as the final phrase of the tune. This again develops on the Minnesinger style, though it was usual with them (and Luther sometimes does it) only to refer to a short phrase of the opening material at the end.

Secondly, notice the rhythm. The 'beat' is a steady four-time unit, but it is diversified in phrases 6 and 8 with a syncopation at the marked point. There is no example in Luther's own collections of triple time tunes, although in other collections produced within his lifetime they are not unknown.

Now this is important. Luther has not, in fact, abandoned all the principles of musical discipline, any more than he has abandoned the principles of liturgy. It is clear from the beginning that he expects his congregations to sing music which, while it is essentially melodic, makes use of the highest developments of vocal music achieved up to his time. The very last thing Luther was, or could have been, was what we now call an adapter of popular styles. He had no use for the 'popular' in the sense of the careless, or the standards of ignorance. His melodies are the kind of melody which would appear in a pre-Reformation polyphonic motet, their mixture of basic measure with syncopation being what that style generated. The Minnesinger songs were of the same kind; and it is far removed from the popular music, the carol-music, which we mentioned in the last chapter. *Quem pastores* is not, and could not have been, a Luther tune.

The year 1524 saw the first official Luther hymnals. The oldest is the *Achtliederbuch* (January 1524), containing nothing by Luther himself; the first prepared directly by Luther's direction is *Geistliche Gesangbuchlein* (late summer, 1524), edited by Johann Walter: and this is a collection of short polyphonic motets founded on chorales: it is though that it was prepared in order that through being sung by the choir in simple arrangements the hymns might become familiar to the congregation before the congregation actually had its own book.* The first of a series of *Enchiridia* (Worship manuals) and the collection *Etlich Christliche Lieder* were also published in 1524, and in these sources we find 24 hymns by Luther, which indicate that he produced a whole series at considerable speed.

Ein neues Lied was included in Walter's book, which had all the 24 Luther texts in it, along with 14 others. The other Luther texts from 1524 are these:

2. *Nun freut euch* ('Dear Christians let us now rejoice'), described as 'The Believer's Justification', a kind of semi-autobiographical account of the operation of grace, exactly parallel to the original of Charles Wesley's 'O for a thouand tongues' (*Panorama* 60).
3. *Aus tiefer Noth* (Psalm 130 in verse)
4. *Ach Gott, vom Himmel sieh darein* (Psalm 12 in verse)
5. *Es spricht der unweysen* (Psalm 14 in verse)
6. *Es wolle Gott uns gnadig sein* (Psalm 67 in verse)
7. *Nun komm der Heyden Heiland* (Advent: from *Veni Redemptor Gentium*)
8. *Christum wyr sollen loben schon* (Christmas: from *A solis ortus cardine*)
9. *Gelobet seystu Jhesu Christ* (Christmas, from a vernacular hymn c. 1370)
10. *Wol dem der ynn Gottes furcht steht* (Marriage: Psalm 128 in verse)
11. *Wer Gott nicht mit uns diese zeyt* (Psalm 124 in verse)
12. *Myt frid und freud ich far do hyn* (Nunc Dimittis)
13. *Jhesus Christus under Heyland* (Eucharist: based on John Hus, 1366-1415)
14. *Gott sey gelobet* (Eucharist: emphasizing Communion in Both Kinds)
15. *Christ lag ynn Todess Banden* (Easter: based on *Victimae Paschali*)
16. *Jhesus Christus unser Heyland* (Easter)
17. *Kom Gott Schopfer heyliger geyst* (Pentecost, based on *Veni Creator*)
18. *Nun bitten wyr den heyligen Geist* (Pentecost)
19. *Kom heyliger Geist herre Gott* (Pentecost: based on *Veni sancte Spiritus*)

20. *Gott der Vater won uns bey* (Trinity)
21. *Wyr glauben all an eynen Gott* (Trinity: based on vernacular hymn, 1417)
22. *Mitten wyr im leben sind* (Death: based on *Media vita in morte sumus*)
23. *Dies sind der heylgen zehn Gebott* (The Ten Commandments)
24. *Mensch wiltu leben seliglich* (The Ten Commandments)

No. 2 is, as it were, a preface to the series: all the rest are strictly liturgical pieces, including the psalm-versions, in respect of which we recall that psalmody was in the Middle Ages the only permitted form of praise at Mass except on the festive occasions we referred to.

That series, all published by the end of 1524, represents Luther's 'first round', and it is largely occupied with hymns associated with the Catechism, and with psalm-versions which reflect Luther's respect for the medieval tradition in which psalmody played so large a part in Eucharistic praise. The series on the Catechism required two to complete it, and these appear as ## 32 and 33 in the following list, which includes the 13 texts that Luther wrote between 1524 and the end of his life.

25. *Jesaja dem Propheten das geschah:* Liturgical; through-composed version of the *Sanctus* in the *German Mass,* 1526
26. *Ein' feste Burg ist unser Gott,* probably written 1527, believed to have been in Hans Weiss's Wittenberg Hymnal, 1528, now lost; earliest surviving source, Klug, 1533 (Ex. 38)
27. *Verleyh uns frieden gnediglich,* based on the Latin Antiphon *Da pacem Domine in diebus nostris,* with new tune grafted on to the first phrase of the original plainsong; possibly written 1528/29; Klug 1533
28. *Vom Himmel hoch,* written 1534/5 probably for his own family; originally for an existing Christmas tune, but set to a new tune, possibly his own, Schumann, 1539 (Ex. 42)
29. *Te Deum Laudamus:* metrical version, with music adapted from traditional medieval setting, Klug 1535
30. *Sie ist mir lieb die werde Magd:* eschatological song based on a secular love song, text typologized into the imagery of the Church in the Book of Revelation; Klug 1535; new tune Babst 1545
31. *Gloria in excelsis:* for an order of worship at Naumburg, 1537: octosyllabic metre. Note that this is not the familiar metrical Gloria whose music is at Ex. 45.
32. *Vater Unser in Himmelreich:* The Lord's Prayer. Original tune by Luther (Ex. 39) as well as that well-known tune (Ex. 40) in Schumann, 1539

---

* A very recent parallel, with the same sort of purpose in mind, is John Wilson's *Sixteen Hymns Arranged as Simple Anthems* (RSCM, 1978); it is not easy, actually, to think of any other.

33. *Christ unser Herr zum Jordan kam:* Baptism; written 1541 (thus dated in a later book), probably printed on a broadsheet. Included in Klug 1543. In most books shared a tune with # 6 (Ex. 41) but tune in Magdeburg 1524 later kept for # 6, leaving this one in possession of melody at Ex. 41.

34. *Was furchtu, Feind Herodes, seer:* Holy Innocents; translation of *Hostis Herodes impie* (see EH 34), written 1541, associated with version of proper plainsong tune from 1545.

35. *Erhalt'uns, Herr, bei deinem Wort:* Occasional. With its tune, in Klug, 1543 (Ex. 43)

36. *Vom Himmel kam der Engel schar:* Christmas. Ms in Luther's handwriting exists. Noted by Luther to be sung in church to *Vom Himmel hoch* (as #28) or *A solis ortus* (as #8). In later hymnals sometimes set to the older tune of *Vom Himmel hoch* (see Luther's Works Vol. 53 p. 307), which was first in Klug 1535. Text 1543.

37. *Der du bist drey in Einigkeit:* Trinity; translation of *O lux beata Trinitas* with adaptation of plainsong tune (for which see Ex. 9)

Although all these are metrical hymns, the music of ## 25, 28 and 31 is through-composed; it need not concern us here except that it is worth observing that the familiar Lutheran hymn-paraphrase of the *Gloria, Allein Gott in der Hoh' sei Ehr,* is always associated with a tune (Ex. 45) whose first phrase occurs more than once in the setting given with Luther's version. But a few comments on some of the tunes that went with these hymns will expose most of the characteristics of the classic chorale of the 16th century.

We have already mentioned Ex. 27. There are several tunes in this series that use this pattern of an octave-span from the high initial note and since one of them is certainly Luther's, and another is very strongly suspected of being his, it is at least possible that this was a pattern he particularly favoured and tended to fall into. He was, after all, a musician, but surely not a composer who gave himself much time to develop a wide vocabulary. Ex. 39, VATER UNSER, is certainly his, and very probably EIN' FESTE BURG and VOM HIMMEL HOCH are also; quite probably EIN' NEUES LIED (Ex. 27) was by way of being a 'pattern tune' to show what kind of hymnody he hoped for; a distinct similarity of idiom in all four suggests that whatever we may say about the others, these are Luther's own tunes.

The simplest of all the tunes to Luther's hymns is NUN KOMM (Ex. 28). This seems to be derived from the plainsong tune known nowadays as JESU DULCEDO CORDIUM (Ex. 22)—and if that is right, the existence of NUN KOMM happens to be the best evidence we have that JESU DULCEDO was known in the Middle Ages. Some authorities have derived ERHALT'UNS, HERR (Ex. 43) from this same plainsong tune, but, if we are not

put off by the unusual and charming cadence of the second phrase, NON KOMM is a more plausible descendant.

By contrast, Ex. 29 is the most complex of the strophic tunes in this group. It goes back to 1524, although the now accepted version is that of Klug, as in the Example. We recall how J. S. Bach, faced with the need to use this tune in his great series of catechetical preludes (the Klavierubüng Part III, S. 669-89) was obliged to abandon his principle of working the whole tune out, and to write an ingenious piece based on its first four notes (S. 680). It stands half way between the regular chorales and the through-composed liturgical pieces; notice how it runs mostly in a gravely syllabic style, breaking out into a melodic flourish near the end. It is a very solemn musical utterance, as is appropriate to this climactic moment in the Mass.

Ex. 30 is a *Leyse*—comparable to Ex. 26 mentioned at the end of the last chapter. The origins of the tune are buried in the Middle Ages; it is vitually unique in Lutheran hymnody in its pentatonic diction—only one note almost at the end is outside that scale. We must resist the temptation (failing further evidence) to pursue the implications of that—the pentatonic scale is not in the Plainsong tradition, or indeed in that of continental Europe. Perhaps it is no accident that a deformed version of this in LM has for a long time had a special appeal in Scotland (the tune PAVIA, or SOLDAU, CH³ 295). In its Lutheran form it has a mysterious and restrained beauty.

Ex. 31 is another Leyse of a very different character; its opening suggests a march, and that is what it originally was—a pre-Reformation pilgrims' hymn, *In Gottes Namen fahren wir.*

Ex. 32 and 33 are alternative tunes for # 2 in the foregoing list, Ex. 33 also being associated with *Es ist das Heil,* another hymn of the Lutheran era. Both are in the 'Minnesinger' form, without the back-reference in the final line, but with the initial repeat; both use many wide-stepping intervals, and both suggest the energy of the Reformation.

Ex. 34 is one of Luther's most profound inspirations, if it is his. The hymn it sets to music (# 3) is a superb Christianization of Psalm 130, and if Luther did not mean the opening phrase of the tune to suggest 'Out of the deep', then there is no more felicitous accident in hymnody. This too is in the 'Minnesinger' form, with a touch of back-reference at the end. It is in the Third, or Phrygian, Mode, which always had especially sombre associations for Luther. The tune is best appreciated if one has at hand the original text or a translation (*Panorama* 3).

Ex. 35 is from the song-book of John Hus († 1415), and was clearly a very well known tune from his time onwards. It is in the First or Dorian Mode, with a massively eloquent climax, and for a tune of such relatively short compass it presents an unusually purposeful structure.

In Ex. 36 it might be said that Lutheran music is not seen at its best; this is the Lutheran version of VENI CREATOR (Ex. 12). It is a not untypical example of the way plainsong tunes were 'squared up' in Lutheran practice. The reason is obvious: it was to transform the essentially uncongregational idiom of the plainsong melodies into one which ordinary singers could pick up; the unwillingness to sever altogether the connection between a translated text and the tune of its Latin original reflects Luther's love of the aesthetic aspects of that liturgy which he so zealously reformed. But it will be interesting to compare the way plainsong was treated in Germany with that in which it was treated in Geneva when we come to that part of our story (Exx. 65-83). The version in Klug, 1533, is the one which still survives in Lutheran circles.

Ex. 37 is also based on plainsong: but this time it is a medieval antiphon—that is, a fragment of plainsong worked into a new chorale tune; the text is Luther's version, not in its original metre, of *Veni sancte Spiritus,* but the antiphon has nothing to do with the melody of that Sequence. The tune as we have it is very carefully constructed, so that it ambles purposefully through its very long journey, holding the singer's attention by its subtle use of repeated phrases.

Nothing could be a greater contrast than the celebrated *Ein Feste Burg,* Ex. 38. For one thing, the text here is a polemical one—more like that of *Ein' Neues Lied* (Ex. 27) than anything between them. For another, we have a full 'Minnesinger' form—the last phrase being a direct repeat of the second, which is also the fourth. For a third, we have short bursts of music rather than the long connected argument of Ex. 37, the energy of the syncopations contributing to its general atmosphere of belligerence. One notices the unusualness of the form of Ex. 35, with its isolated 'keystone' melodic note when comparing it with these long and rambling chorale tunes, which, by their tendency to run up and down the scale, give an impression either of exuberance, as here, or of remote contemplativeness. It is the rambling character in the 'big' chorales which has kept them from popularity in Britain—where even *Ein feste Burg* could not until the present generation have been called a popular hymn. (In the USA it is much more widely sung because, of course, there is a very large German-derived population there).

Exx. 39 and 40 are the two tunes set to *Vater Unser* in Luther's lifetime, and we have already commented on Luther's own tune, which never found its way into currency. The other one immediately 'caught on'. It was welcomed in Geneva and in Britain because of its very steady and symmetrical pattern, using notes only of two values throughout. But it has an interesting tonal ambiguity in being a tune which to the ear (without the words) appears to fall into two halves each ending on a tonic—the first on the high tonic, the second on the low one. All texts set to it, including the

original, are in the normal pattern of three couplets. The importance of a major alto third in the chord at the end of the line 3, when the tune is harmonized, is decisive in that it both makes that chord a resounding finish for the first half and also provides a leading note towards the one that immediately follows—a point which of course J. S. Bach was aware of. This is the most regular and symmetrical tune of more than four phrases in the whole chorale literature.

Ex. 41, the Baptism tune, is another 'Minnesinger' tune, as jerky and muscular as any in the Lutheran repertory; its modal ambiguity is very typical of the period—the ear places the final on D all the way to the last line which almost comes as an afterthought, and which in true modal music would end the tune on the dominant (since the note A has shown no sign of being anything but that in the rest of the tune).

What becomes very clear from this quick glance at the tunes used for Luther's own hymns is that their origins are either ecclesiastical or what we may call semi-secular. That is, a plainsong tune would be adapted for a translation from Latin, while for new hymns new tunes were composed on the model of the best non-ecclesiastical music of the time, and for hymns based on older German sources the German original tunes would be similarly adapted. There is no question here of using secular tunes, still less popular tunes, for hymnody. The nearest these editors get to using 'popular' melodies is in the adaptation of *Leysen,* which might be called popular hymns, but could not be called secular music.

Luther's reputation for 'using secular tunes' rests mostly on the tunes we show at Examples 46 and 47. INNSBRUCK, as we now call it, was the tune composed by Heirich Isaak (c. 1460 - c. 1527) for a song, 'Innsbruck, I now must leave thee', which seems to refer to his retirement in 1515 from the position of chapelmaster to the Emperor Maximilian I at Innsbruck. But Isaak was actually a church musician who composed 23 masses as well as some motets; and in 1539 his tune appeared with an adaption of his song to the sacred subject, *O Welt, ich muss dich lassen* ('O world, I now must leave thee'). Bach picked up the tune and arranged it in the *St. Matthew Passion,* but Brahms, in what is thought to be the very last of his compositions, no. 11 of his Chorale-Preludes, op. 122, uses the tune as Isaak wrote it. The tune became a favourite, and many other texts were written for it, including Gerhardt's famous *'Nun ruhen alle Walder'* (the original of 'The duteous day', EH 278: H 181).

WAS GOTT THUT, Ex. 47, has a similar origin, being a 1572 recension of a melody 'Il me souffit de touts mes maulx' published by P. Attaignant in 1530. This again became a very well known tune, and like the other has its place in the *St. Matthew Passion.* But neither of these goes to a Luther text, and 1572 was a long time after Luther's death.

After Luther

What we do see as the classic tradition of hymn singing develops is a fairly natural tendency in editors to observe what 'works' and what 'doesn't'. This will have been subject to the heavy dogmatic and liturgical demands of the Lutheran liturgy, but there was not now, once printing had come to stay, the same monopoly of culture in the church, or the same chance for the church to proscribe non-ecclesiastical styles, that had prevailed in the Middle Ages. Now, provided local regulations were observed, anybody could print, and what was printed was not necessarily offered for liturgical use.

During Luther's lifetime some publishers and editors seem to have noticed a need for something simpler and more accessible than the high style clearly advocated by Luther himself, and the most famous product of this is the tune to the metrical *Gloria* (not Luther's version) which as soon as it appeared took a place in Lutheran affections it has never since lost. This is ALLEIN GOTT IN DER HOH' SEI EHR, Ex. 45. Its unbroken triple rhythm, which reflects of course the carol style of the later Middle Ages, is unique in Lutheran liturgical music. Whether the fact that its famous opening phrase is the same as the third and fifth phrases of Luther's own 1524 hymn implies a derivation it would be hazardous to judge: but this was a 'winner'. It is not, in fact, a particularly interesting melody from the musical point of view—it is restricted to the compass of a fifth apart from one cadence-note and any harmonization of it has to sound very key-tied; but that is what, even in 1539 when it first appeared in Schumann's book, was beginning to happen.

It happened again, surely, with the NUN FREUT EUCH tune at Ex. 44—in a modified version very well known in the English tradition. This was written as a simpler alternative for Luther's # 2, and it is a 'full Minnesinger' form tune, phrases 2, 4 and 7 being the same, wholly syllabic and undoubtedly easy to learn; but it is one of the first tunes in post-Reformation style that show the fatal tendency of composers to let the construction sag after the half-way point—a disease against which few are wholly immune. In 1586 the tune was given a new text about the Final Judgment, and an imitation of this in English caused the tune to be imported to England in 1768; in the process it achieved a new fifth phrase and a modification of the sixth, and it is now better known among the English speaking churches than among the German.

Ex. 48, ICH DANK DIR, is a very good 'Minnesinger' example from the repertory of hymns that Luther inspired but did not write; this tune has often appeared later with most or all of its flourishes removed; a glance at AM 625 (where it is called ERFURT) shows how much it loses from the cutting of the corner in the last phrase—that return to the high dominant is melodically vital.

Ex. 49, HERZLICH THUT MICH ERFREUEN, is parallel to Ex. 46 in being a secular tune adapted to a hymn beginning with the opening words of its original secular partner. This is from a slightly more informal book of Walther's, published in 1552, *Eine schone gelstlicher und Christlicher newer Berkreyen*. Its rhythmic ambiguity is very characteristic of the period: it appears to be in ambiguous triple time, but the time-signature is C which means that every 'triple' unit is a syncopation.

Ex. 50, WIR LOBEN DICH, is one of the longest and most complicated tunes of the whole century—Minnesinger form, but obviously more of a solo than a congregational song, with an unusual relation between the cadence of the opening repeated phrases and the final cadence. This was 'learned music', and the Christmas association of its text suggests that it was something of a seasonal luxury. This extended style is not yet, as we shall see, quite extinct, but it is by the mid-century being attacked from the popular side.

Our Examples 51-3 show response to the need for easier and more singable tunes. Nicolaus Herrmann, in the two well known and well contrasted tunes at 51 and 52, produced a couple of 'winners' which have never receded from their original popularity. Ex. 51 is firmly in triple time and the key signature admits it; Ex. 52 is a merry Christmas piece with a repeated last line of words, and is the earliest example on the continent of Europe of that 'Common metre' which became the almost exclusive metre in early English hymnody. In Ex. 51 the starred note is written as given in the earliest source: but of course the reversing of the rhythm in that two-note phrase with its sudden syncopation came in fairly early and nobody wanted to go back to the original once this had become fashionable.

A non-Lutheran source of popular melodies is found in three hymnals of the Bohemian Brethren, 1531, 1544 and 1566. Our Ex. 53 is pure religious folk song, having all the qualities of late medieval 'outdoor music'—very easily learnt, and rhythmically entertaining (see above, p. 20). That was in the 1544 book. The earlier one of 1531, edited by Michael Weisse, gives us the beautiful melody MENSCHENKIND, Ex. 54 from which the deplorable 19th century tune RAVENSHAW (EH 436: H 399) was made by ruthless amputation. The high standard of melody in that community is further attested by the great tune MIT FREUDEN ZART, now very well known in an arrangement made by Riemann, 1895, and Vaughan Williams (EH 604: H 522) but originally a tune of more characteristic rhythmic waywardness; we reproduce this, in another connection, later at Ex. 85. NUN SEHT UND MERKET (EH 202), also from 1566, is another good illustration of the agreeably simple style of melody cultivated by the Brethren. (We shall be obliged later to notice how this was corrupted when this community reappeared in the 18th century as the Moravian Church).

As the century progressed, the same streams of development continued to run. On the one hand, there was the stream where simplicity was cultivated at the expense, quite often, of melodic distinction. Ex. 55, NUN LASST UNS GOTT DEM HERREN, first appears in Nikolaus Selnecker's *Christliche Psalmen,* 1587, and although J. S. Bach used it in a Cantata, one sees that it was he who rescued it by re-composing its final phrase and inserting an all-important climactic note (this version with simplified harmony is at EH 126). In its original form it could hardly be less enterprising: note once again that the time-signature is C, and the apparent triple units are syncopations.

But the large-scale chorale tune was by no means dead. in P. Reinigius's HERZLICH LIEB HAB ICH DICH, Ex. 61, we see it returning: this is the original of the final chorale in Bach's St. John Passion, and its great length is made tolerable by the impetus given to it by the repeated opening phrase (which unusually has three units). Everybody agrees, however, that the chorale makes its last and greatest gestures in the two immortal melodies of Philipp Nicolai, WIE SCHON LEUCHTET and WACHET AUF (Exx. 56, 57).

This pair, written under great personal stress in 1597, form not so much a peak as a watershed or Continental Divide: for the text of WIE SCHON is intimately personal and foreshadows the pietist tradition, while that of WACHET AUF is heraldic and visionary, far more imaginatively and evangelically scriptural than the Luther texts. The book in which they first appeared, *Frewden-Spiegel,* 1598, is a personal testimony by Nicolai. But the musical form of both tunes is thoroughly and triumphantly traditional.

It is impossible to dismiss the idea that WIE SCHON, whose text begins with a reference to the Epiphany before going on to become, in seven immense stanzas, a 'spiritual love songs' owes some inspiration to RESONET IN LAUDIBUS, (Ex. 56B) which had been picked up by *Piae Cantiones* in 1582 but which Nicolai could have known from another source. WACHET AUF is, however, a new composition, and as it has turned out, a seminal one. Its genius is in its use of thoroughly commonplace phrases which other composers have made use of memorably. It has often been pointed out, for example, that Dykes's tune NICAEA ('Holy, Holy Holy') shares many of its leading phrases with this tune, and that the passage 'The kingdoms of this world...' in Handel's *Hallelujah Chorus* from Messiah appears to quote the central and last phrases of this tune. But we are about to say (pp 33-A) that coincidences like these may be purely musical and not historical: during the 16th century a common coinage was being built up in hymnody upon which composers freely drew, whether or not they knew that they would later appear to have been directly borrowing from each other.

The melodic quality of the two tunes is, however, strikingly different. It cannot be denied that there is a melodic recession in WIE SCHON, just before the final phrase, of a kind which we do not find in WACHET AUF, whose phrases are all commanding, and all well balanced. Once again, when we come to consider J. S. Bach, we shall see how much we owe to him for making these tunes universal in their appeal and rescuing them from their original private context.

We must here pause to make two general points. The first is that what makes the 16th century chorales so fascinating to musicians and often so daunting to the uncultivated is their variety of metre. In the Luther *corpus* of 37, seventeen different metres are used; the only ones repeated with any frequency are the Latin octosyllables (Long Metre) and 8.7.8.7.88.7, the simplest form of "Minnesinger" metre. One sees in the originality of Nicolai's two metres, and in the great length of Exx. 50 and 61, what lyric freedom the Lutheran writers allowed themselves; they only very rarely exceed a ten-syllable line, and are usually happiest with eight syllables or fewer, but the arrangements of lines in a stanza show a freedom which they inherited from the cultivated *Minnesinger* and *Meistersinger.* In this they contrast to some extent with the French writers, and totally with the English, of the same period; for we shall see that the French writers loved long lines but, normally, shortish stanzas, while the English showed an overpowering preference for the ballad, or Common, metre.

Secondly, we must observe, what must have become obvious enough, that Lutheran chorales were designed for unison singing, whatever accompaniment they may have had, There was never a Lutheran prohibition on accompanying instruments as there was in Calvin's Geneva: but we do not find choral techniques appearing until the 16th century is well into its eighties. From this, however, two subsidiary points emerge which our Examples 58-62 illustrate.

It is instructive, for example, to see (Ex. 58) the first known four-part harmonization of EIN FESTE BURG, made in 1586 by Lukas Osiander. It is homophonic throughout, and every chord but one is in the root position (the one marked (a) being the only exception). Comparing this with Bach's version shows how flexible was the later vocabulary. This four-part version looks, on the face of it, as if it were thought of more as instrumental (especially brass) than vocal. Praetorius's version of WACHET AUF, (this is not the Michael Praetorius whom we shall later meet, and was apparently not related to him) shows a little more polyphonic flexibility—much more use of the 6/3 chord helps the vocal lines to run smoothly—but a remarkably static quality of tonality in that every phrase except the first (and third) ends on the tonic chord. This looks like a vocal arrangement, and once again will be worth comparing with Bach (see pp 66-68, Ex. 233).

Another offshoot of interest in part-singing is the appearance of descants, or fa-burdens, which become melodies in their own right. In Ex. 60 we have a very simple tune from Seth Calvisius's *Geistliche Lieder,* 1589, ACH BLEIB BEI UNS, alongside the four-part version in his *Hymni Sacri,* 1594, where the original tune is in the alto part—the kind of fa-burden technique we usually associate with arrangements where the melody is in the tenor. In Ex. 61 we have the great Reinigius tune, showing how once again it appeared when harmonized in an inner part. But in Ex. 62 we have something more remarkable—about which there has been some perverse comment.

Here we go back to a plainsong Office Hymn, which appeared in Lossius's *Psalmodia,* 1553 in triple time. This is the tune found in various places, including EH 44 and *Oxford Book of Carols,* 85, the original plainsong being at EH 61. But Klug's *Gesangbuch* of 1543 gives the tune as the upper line in the second section of example 62C (the lower line being Lossius). Obviously that upper line is a descant: the comment in *Songs of Praise,* taken over into the *Oxford Book of Carols,* that Lossius is a descant to Klug gets the information the wrong way up. But nowadays (and in *Piae Cantiones,* 1582) the 'descant' sounds a much pleasanter and more flexible tune and has taken the place of the original. One should regard EH 44 as a metrical version of EH 61, and the descant as an appropriate illumination of that tune owed to Klug.

Calvin's Psalters: 1539-62

We now turn to the other main stream of Protestantism, that which is based in Geneva. It is a different world from that of Luther; no two characters could be more different than those of Luther and Calvin, and each left his stamp on the culture which he founded. Many books have been written about Luther's personal life—more than one film has been made about it; his character was powerful enough to make him many friends and many enemies, and while his friends call him vivid, courageous and creative his enemies prefer to call him vulgar, opportunist and conceited. These of course are the qualities that are 'interr'd within their bones', and make no difference to historical judgments. But Calvin remains withdrawn, shadowy, a man whose life was in his writings. Luther never wrote a connected and definitive 'system of theology'; Calvin did—in the *Institutes,* first written in 1539, several times revised, the final edition coming in 1559: had he lived longer he would no doubt have revised it yet again. Calvin saw theology more as St. Thomas Aquinas saw it—all things brought under the imperial discipline of theology; Luther's theology was no less convinced or passionate than Calvin's but it is a little more like the British Constitution—a driving principle in the background, never systematically written down, but controlling all his decisions and arguments as the occasion called for them: so we have the essence of Luther in three quite brief and occasional pamphlets written in 1520: the rest of his massive output (far greater than Calvin's) is in Commentaries on Scripture and Directories for the reconstruction of the liturgy.

This is exactly what lies behind the different attitudes of the two men to public praise. For Luther the provision of hymns for use in the Liturgy was a proper answer to a legitimate demand; but the Liturgy itself was for him as conservative a reconstruction of the medieval Mass as could be achieved within the framework of his theology. Luther could not forget the beauty and integrity of the Mass, which he thought of as a supremely excellent thing spoiled; Calvin's intellectual approach to the Faith made him vulnerable, in the administration of his new society, to the pressures of a group of Elders who had political axes to grind and enjoyed a new kind of ecclesiastical power —with the consequence that many aspects of the church order as it was worked out in Geneva are the results not of Calvin's convictions but of the overbearing insistence of his Elders, of which the most conspicuous is their vetoing of Calvin's wish to celebrate the Lord's Supper every Lord's Day.

What immediately concerns us is that Calvin's own profound reverence for Scripture—to which his attitude was quite different from that of Luther—caused him to insist that public praise in church should be confined to the language of the Bible, adapted to the minimum extent required for congregational singing. He also was quite clear that there should be no other music in the Liturgy, and that psalmody should be accompanied neither by choir nor by instruments. It was this that built up the tradition of metrical psalmody. Note first of all that Luther's fashion of unison singing was practically based while Calvin's was theologically based. (No theological justification for unison singing appeared in Luther's tradition until that famous statement of Bonhoeffer in his *Letters from Prison* which later Lutherans have treated with such misplaced and regrettable literalness).

John Calvin, then, born 1509, died 1564, was the architect of the tradition of metrical psalmody. Geneva was always his home-base, but he was for three years, 1538-41, Minister of the Reformed Church in Strasbourg before returning for the last 23 years of his life to the Church at Geneva. Three other characters appear in the story we are about to tell.

Clement Marot (c. 1497-1544) was a court poet who had begun setting psalms in metrical versions before Calvin met him. A version of Psalm 6, with metrical versions of the Lord's Prayer, the *Ave Maria* and the Creed, appeared in his *Le Miroir de tres Chestienne Princesse Marguerite de France* (1533), and by 1536 he had completed thirty psalms, for which he was well rewarded by The Emperor Charles V of France (one of Luther's principal enemies). Marot's psalms were drawn on for the first Strasbourg Psalter, and when Calvin returned to Geneva on 1541 he followed him, and contributed new work to the Genevan Psalter of 1542. Marot remained a Catholic, and followed a lifestyle which Calvin could not approve. In the end Calvin withheld his payments and allowed him to die in poverty.

Theodore de Beze (or Beza), 1519-1605, was the versifier of all the Psalms in the complete psalter which were not by Marot. He arrived in Geneva in 1548, became Professor of Greek at Lausanne 1549, Rector of the Academy of Geneva 1559, and Calvin's successor in the Reformed Church at Geneva, 1564. He was a notable theologian and historian, and was responsible for the discovery at Lyon of the important *Codex Bezae* (1582), a biblical manuscript much valued by later scholars.

Louis Bourgeois, c. 1510 - c. 1561, was probably the ablest professional musician who worked under Calvin, and was responsible for the music in the 1551 edition of the Genevan Psalter. He was cantor at Geneva 1545-53. His relations with the Council of Geneva deteriorated after the publication of the 1551 Psalter, he being accused by them of having tampered with the melodies and thereby misled the faithful; this probably referred to his publishing, outside Geneva, a harmonized edition of the psalm tunes (Lyon, 1547). The last that is heard of him is that he had a child baptized in 1560: after that he disappears.

Claude Goudimel, c. 1525-72, did not hold a cantor's position in Geneva, being at the time based in Metz; but he was responsible for the music in the final edition of the Psalter and after Calvin's death published the first authorised four-part edition of the tunes, 1565. He was killed in the Massacre of the Huguenots on St. Bartholomew's Day, 1572.

The books we shall refer to—only the most important of the many books of psalms and tunes published during the period—are these: (1) *Kirchenammt,* Strasbourg, 1525, a book of hymns and psalms with their tunes, and also a Directory of Worship; (2) *Aulcuns pseaulmes et cantiques mys en chant,* Strasbourg 1539, being the first Strasbourg Psalter (ST 39); this contained the words and music of 18 Palms, the Commandments, the *Nunc Dimittis* and the Creed: six psalms were versified by Calvin, the rest by Marot; (3) *La forme des Prieres et Chantz Ecclesiastiques,* Geneva, 1542, being the first Genevan Psalter (G-42): six Psalms by Calvin, thirty, plus the *Nunc Dimittis* and the Commandments, by Marot; (4) *Pseaumes octante-trois de David, mis en rime Francoise,* Geneva 1551 (G-51); 49 and the two canticles by Marot, 34 by Beza, and (5) *Les Pseaumes de David mis en rime Francoise,* Caen, 1562 (G-62), the first (probably) complete Psalter, with the Marot Psalms as in 1551, the rest all by Beza. It also has Marot's two canticles and the 'Summary of the Law' by M. Cordier. (In the same year, 1562, Goudimel produced a four-part edition of the 83 Psalms in the 1551 Psalter—hence the ascription of certain harmonized tunes to 'Goudimel, 1562').

We begin, then, with the Strasbourg *Kirchenammt.* Strasbourg is some 440 km south west of Leipsig and some 280 km north-north east of Geneva; it is a frontier-town of symbolic importance in this as in many other strands of history, for metrical psalmody was really born there rather than in Geneva. We offer here three examples of tunes appearing in that book, Ex. 63, which was the tune for Psalm 130, Ex. 64, which was the tune for Psalm 137, and Ex. 65, which was that for the hymn, *'O Mensch, bewein' dein Sunde Gross.'*

Those three tunes show where the frontier runs. The first (63) is a simple, rather unenterprising tune, in the irregular rhythm of the Lutheran chorale style (it was quite soon reduced to a regular rhythm so that all its lines followed the style of the opening phrases). It seems to be the work of somebody who thought Luther's own choice of tune for his version of Psalm 130 too difficult or too esoteric. But it is still sung in Lutheran churches and it is stylistically rather like the simpler NUN FREUT EUCH tune at Ex. 44.

The tune for *An Wasserflussen Babylon* (Ps. 137) is rather different. Like Ex. 63 it has a repeated opening phrase, but it has a flowing serenity, partly generated by its use of only two note-values, and a touch of drama and poignancy induced by the very important phrase we have marked (2) in the example. It is longer than the AUS DER TIEFE tune because it has four 'development' phrases instead of the normal two. It is, of course, the basis of one of Bach's most sublime organ pieces, the chorale prelude *'An Wasserflussen',* S 653.

Now turn to Ex. 65, and you have something totally unlike the Lutheran chorale. This is believed to have been the work of Matthaus Greiter, c. 1500-52, who was a singing brother in Strasbourg Minster (it was at that time in Germany), joined the Lutherans in 1524, became a pastor, and founded a choir school in 1548. We have here what we may call the fully developed Genevan style, although we have not yet got to Geneva. Observe the following points in it:

(1) It uses the Lutheran repeated first phrase, though it makes no reference to it at any later point.

(2) It uses only two note-values, has no syncopations, and uses the same rhythmic pattern for every line of words.

(3) It is symmetrical; the stanza consists of four groups of three lines 8.8.7.

(4) It combines great length (the stanza has more syllables than that of WACHET AUF) with great simplicity of construction; note especially the repetitions, not only of the first long phrase, but of the first phrase after the double bar (with a notable point of development in the alteration of just one significant note), and in the construction of the last long phrase out of one line repeated at two different pitches from its original statement.

(5) —a consequence of 4—the tune actually uses very long phrases, not a succession of emphatic short ones as the longer Lutheran tunes often do.

(6) A great deal of tune moves by step. In 92 notes there are only fourteen movements by leap, and except at phrase-joins they are all of a third: but there is an octave leap upwards at the half way point, where it is most needed.

(7) It completes all this within the compass of an octave. It will at once be clear that this tune has only point (1) in common with the Lutheran chorales. In all other respects it is much more close-knit and disciplined and reserved in style than the Luther tunes were. And it foreshadows the Genevan style in the phrase marked *, which along with the phrase so marked in Ex. 64 should be carefully noted.

If we want to put all this untechnically, we should say that this is a wholly 'congregational' tune: it may be one of the longest hymn tunes ever written, but it at once captures a universal quality of singableness which the Lutheran tunes very rarely have. Few Lutheran tunes were ever 'exported' until very much later. This one began to travel at once.

It is, in fact, set to Psalm 36 in Strasbourg-1539, with only one note of the melody different from our example. Now the full story of how this small collection came to be made has not yet been told, and probably never will be. It is alleged that Marot was astonished to find that his psalms had been used in it, and did not know it until he arrived in Geneva. What is even more obscure is the source of the tunes. The normal theory is that they owe something at least to the music that was sung to them in their original context—the court of Charles V. That assumes that they were sung, and that Calvin approved the use of music that had that kind of origin, and about the second of those conjectures there are certain problems. Calvin's views on music are unascertainable: he refers to it now and again in a formal way as being, on Scriptural authority, appropriate to the praise of God—but one could say that and be tone-deaf. It may be, of course, that Calvin regarded music as morally neutral—and if he did he was well in advance of his time.

The only comments we can make on the music arise from the music itself: and this, we can certainly say, is interesting enough. We may now compare Examples 66 and 67 with 65. Ex. 66 is the tune for Psalm 51*. It did not survive into the Genevan psalters, but it is a stirring tune. Like Ps. 36 (Ex. 65) it is all in notes of two values only; but its lines are longer; the metre is 10.11.11.10 D. (The 21 pieces in this collection have twenty metres, only one being repeated). It has, as does Ps. 36, an eye to effects that assist memory. Uniquely in either this work or the Genevan Psalters it repeats its first long phrase as the third. Its balancing of cadences is subtle: the tonal tension between what we should call C major and A minor is dramatic. Its opening phrase is unusually commanding.

Turn to Ex. 67: this is Psalm 46, 'God is our refuge and strength', and if ever one is tempted to think of a primitive psalm tune in terms of 'word painting'—a dangerous and delusive process which moderns should avoid at all costs—we are so tempted here: square, solid, belligerent it sounds—eight syllables in each of eight lines, with a mountainous succession of intervals at the beginning—falling fifth, rising sixth. No—we must not be imaginative in that sense, because in 1542 the editors seem to have said, 'Not that tune for Psalm 46!' From the purely musical point of view the significant thing about Ex. 67 is its very emphatic use of the phrase we might well call the 'Strasbourg sign'—which we noticed in two of the 1525 tunes, and see here now in the most emphatic position. Indeed, the phrase of four notes ending with a falling fifth is found here, in Ps. 32, and in the Commandments tune: with a falling second it appears nine times in six other tunes, and with a rising second once.

The mysterious question is, of course, what tunes 'became winners' and what tunes did not—that is, what appealed both to editorial principles and to popular taste (in so far as any Genevan taste could be called popular). We shall see in a moment that what we

nowadays call 'congregational sense' seems to have been more or less invented in Strasbourg and Geneva. We mean by 'congregational sense' the capacity for composing what people who are unmusical without being tone-deaf can sing readily. This means making one's point in language which does not itself give trouble to the singer—language he is more or less used to. The piece may be composed by a person who has a very large vocabulary at his command, but in writing what people 'catch on to' he is obliged to use that part of the vocabulary which is common to him and them: just as a preacher whose sermons tend to contain words like *communicatio idiomatum* and *hypostasis,* no matter how excellent his arguments, is unlikely to hold the attention of a parish congregation.

The fact that of these 21 tunes only seven survived into the later Genevan psalters without radical alteration is some indication of what people found easy to sing—but even so its evidential value is limited, because these were editors with a strong hortatory sense, and these were congregations of an obedient kind who paid less attention than ours do to 'what they like'. We have to add the obvious fact that when a text was suppressed, the tune was likely to die with it; it was bound to, if the metre was changed. It is a curious fact that all the six psalms that Calvin put into verse in the 1539 Psalter were replaced in the 1551 edition by versions of the (by that time dead) court poet Marot (the Calvin psalms were 25, 36, 46, 91, 113 and 138); this accounted for the dropping of the Ps. 46 tune in 1551 (though not for the very different quality of the tune that was then used for Marot's new metre).

The best indications of this 'congregational sense' which is so remarkable in the Genevan tunes is to be found in certain tunes which appeared in 1539 and were used again in G-42, to the same texts, but were slightly and significantly altered. It would be tempting to assign these alterations to Bourgeois, but we cannot be sure that Calvin knew him as early as this. Whoever did it, however, had a very alert sense of what people would find easier to sing.

Attend then to Ex. 68, which shows Psalm 1 as it is set in 1539 and in 1542. Here is one of the greatest of all Genevan tunes—setting the pattern of psalmody as clearly and as early as O MENSCH BEWEIN' did for the Strasbourg style. It has six very long phrases in meter 10 10. 11 11. 10 10. Long phrases need more effort than short ones, and more acute memory: so the singer needs more help. Note then the four places at which small alterations are made in 1542 (and retained throughout the Genevan period). Point (1) is a matter of assisting the memory: 1542 aligns the first phrase with the last: 1539 makes the final phrase an eloquent

---

* In the original, Psalm 51 is mis-numbered 50, and Psalm 91, 90: no doubt there was some confusion about the then quite new Protestant numbering of the Psalms, since Calvin will have thought of the *Miserere* as Psalm 51, and Marot will have thought of it as Ps. 50. *In exitu* is numbered '113 or 114'—which Terry not implausibly suggests represents Calvin's despair at ever getting the numbers right.

development on the first phrase—a slight extension of rhythm and a repeat of the fourth degree of the scale make for a strong final cadence. But 1542 says—let the first phrase be the same, and then the singer will feel he is coming home when he gets to the end of the long journey. Points (2) to (4) all have to do with tonality —emphasizing the notes of the triad where the original emphasizes other notes of the scale. Point (2) alters only one note—the dominant placed where an anticipatory sixth originally was. In point (3) we have an altered treatment of those two very eloquent middle phrases; in both tunes the musical thought here moves from a concept based on an interval of a third

() to one based on a fifth

( ).

1539, by starting phrase 4 on the second of the scale shifts the emphasis at once: 1542, by starting it on the third, eases the singer into the new pattern. At point (4) the singer is returned to his triad more firmly than he was in the perhaps more expressive phrase

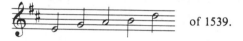 of 1539.

These tiny adjustments are all in one direction—that of making the unmusical singer happy with a difficult task. Considered as an expressive solo, the 1539 tune is far above any criticism: considered as a congregational tune, 1542 improves on it even if it has ironed out some of the subtle irregularities. This is not the first time we have seen editors doing this—and of course it is usually a hazardous thing for editors to attempt. In a moment we shall see composers doing it, and then hymnody is really on the road.

Ex. 69 is just as interesting in another way. Here the 1542 editor has done very little to the tune, and yet he has made it far more singable that it was in 1539. The 1539 Psalm 130 had a compass of an octave and a fourth, and such a compass is unknown in the Genevan style. The simple answer, which it took genius to see, was to raise the second phrase by a fourth. The result is what we can safely call a better tune—more compact and vocally more accessible. It is still a tune in a metre well known in English hymnody which ought to be more widely known. The other slight alteration, which the reader can pick out for himself, is again with a view to emphasizing the framework of the triad. This device of raising one phrase to narrow the compass and make the tune more compact was applied again in the case of Psalm 3.

It will be noticed that the Genevan and Strasbourg styles insisted almost always on syllabic diction; ligatures were very rare—but as we saw in Ex. 67, not

entirely unknown. Ex. 70 is a particularly beautiful example, with a quite unique three-note ligature, which was new in G-42. It is the tune for Marot's Psalm 6 (reputedly the first he wrote), and its lines are, for Geneva, unusually short. The falling intervals at the cadences of phrases 4 and 5 are particularly attractive, and the whole tune has that inevitability and purposefulness that all the best Genevan tunes have, but on an intimate and restrained scale.

The 1551 Psalter, under Bourgeois' direction, contains most of the Genevan tunes which have travelled furthest and become most popular, including Ps. 134 (we call it the OLD HUNDREDTH: Ex. 71B) and Ps. 124 (the OLD 124th: Ex. 72). There could not be a better example of simple melodic construction than Ex. 71B— which takes its opening phrase from the expansive German chorale given here with it. It was a tune which the English Psalters had to take into their repertory, although it meant that a psalm had to be versified for it in a special metre. (One cannot but feel that Kethe, when he wrote his psalm, had the tune before him as he wrote. What else can the placing of the word 'Come' in the first stanza mean—and the trochaic opening?) Watch, in Ex. 71B, how the tune grows out of the 'plagal' triad, and how it establishes the conventions of congregational melody and tonality by always going one step beyond the point regarded at each stage as the point to be emphasized.

In the first place, the melodic dominant of the tune (in G major) is the third, B: the harmonic dominant is, of course, D, but where no harmony is sung that is a secondary matter. The tune is in the 'plagal' position, with its final half way up the scale that is being used. So the plagal triad is established in the first line, which leads, via the lowest note of the scale, to the emphatic melodic dominant. This position is established in the second line by emphasizing the melodic note above the Dominant—that is, the fourth (C). Meanwhile the tune has accepted the harmonic implications of the melody, falling to the second (the fifth of the harmonic dominant scale) at the end of the phrase. The third phrase—always the point where a second-rate composer collapses—devotes itself to reminding us where the final is, and doing so from a new angle by momentarily establishing a narrower triad—the one we call E minor; again going past the note to be emphasized and back to it. That was a small diversion; attention is then commanded by the sounding, the only time in the tune, of the high fifth. That is a well placed rhetorical point, but the melodic significance of that high D is that it is one note past the melodic dominant on the triad. The triad is immediately sounded, now going downwards: the three notes that follow do the same thing melodically—again sounding the B with the note, this time, melodically one above it (the C); all that is then needed is the two-note cadence to bring the tune home.

The connection between this tune and the carol-like chorale NUN LOBT, MEIN HERZ, (Ex. 71A) is confined to the opening phrase, of course—but to see them along-side each other gives a vivid impression of the difference between the lyric waywardness of the Lutheran style and the intellectual tightness of the Genevan. We may add that the tune for Psalm 100 in the 1551 Genevan Psalter is a melody of far less significance, but that the association of the Bourgeois tune (if we ascribe all we have been talking about to him) with Psalm 100 is an English convention which is now everywhere accepted.

We need not apply the above kind of melodic analysis to the tune of Ps. 124 (OLD 124th: Ex. 72) but may encourage the reader to do so. Here is another inspired commonplace which has built itself into universal hymnody. In English use only one tiny rhythmic irregularity has been smoothed: otherwise it is now sung (or should be) as it was written in 1551. But a good clue to the importance of melodic analysis is the existence of the disreputable abridgment known as TOULON, which reduces the melody to four phrases by omitting the important third phrase—leaving it like a ship without a keel—and by hammering the rhythm of the last line back into the shape of all the other lines.

We differ only with the greatest nervousness from the great French authority Pierre Pidoux, whose book, Le Psautier Huguenot (Basel, 2 volumes, 1962) is the definitive work on this subject, but we are not prepared to accept his derivation of this tune from the plainsong JESU CORONA (Ex. 10)—the first six notes are the same but the mode is different, and we feel that any resemblance is accidental.

There are, however, some examples in the Genevan Psalter of 1551 of tunes directly derived from plainsong. Remembering the theology of Geneva it is surprising that there are any, and the six tunes from plainsong sources are often heavily disguised. Ex. 73, Psalm 141 in the 1562 Psalter, is a fairly close transcription, allowing for the needs of a slightly ampler metre. Ex. 74 is an entertaining revision of the very florid tune A SOLIS ORTUS CARDINE (EH 18) which softens the blow by preceding the plainsong part with a newly composed opening phrase, and of course prunes all the melismatic excrescences.

Ex. 75A shows the tune for Ps. 104 in the enlarged Strasbourg Psalter of 1542, and it is a fairly close reproduction in their language of LUCIS CREATOR, Ex. 21. In 1542 at Geneva the same tune appears extended to twice the length (it is a long psalm!) and Ex. 75B is the version, altered in details of rhythm but not in notes, in the 1551 Psalter. Here then is the Genevan style (with, we notice, the 'Strasbourg motif' making its appearance) grafted on to the plainsong style, and in Geneva the plainsong tune is a little less recognizable in the first half. We shall come back to this tune later (p. 43).

But naturally enough, most of the material in G-51 is new, and Ex. 76 is a very good example of the developed 'Bourgeois' style. It is the tune for Psalm 3, and is the final replacement of the S-39 tune, to go

with a new text. It is twice the length of the S-39 tune, and has the same fine compactness of construction we saw in Ex. 65. This was another tune that made an immediate appeal to the English editors, and appeared in their psalters as OLD 122nd, disfigured only by the adding of a syllable to the longer lines to produce an 'English' cadence. It will have been the tune Isaac Watts had in mind when he wrote 'How pleased and blest was I' even though that famous version of Psalm 122 has an odd number of stanzas. (But in his day people were probably singing only the first half of the tune).

Ex. 77 is even more famous: that is the G-51 substitute for the S-39 tune to the Commandments, and first appeared in the 1545 Strasbourg Psalter. No detail is altered in 1551 except for the insertion of rests, which the Strasbourg psalters never used but which no doubt they assumed. The simplicity of this melody ensured its popularity, and it appears uninterruptedly in the English tradition, very often deformed in order to give it a regular beat and a shape appropriate to Long Metre.

Yet another magnificent example is Ex. 78, the tune for Psalm 107 in G-51, taken in from Bourgeois' private edition, Cinquante Pseaumes de David, 1547—the one in which he harmonized the tunes homophonically in four parts. The commanding opening and austere demeanour of this great tune commended it to the Scots when they were compiling the Scottish Psalter, 1564/5, and it is there adapted to Double Common Metre without losing any of its essential character (EH 493). Once again, it is difficult to resist the notion that the composer of this tune had in mind the classic combination of triumph and remembrance of adversity that is at the heart of Psalm 107. (The one place in a modern book where this appears in its original form with an English text is Songs of Syon, 300).

Psalm 86 in the 1551 Psalter was another success: this well known tune was collapsed into Long Metre by the Scottish Psalter, and in that form pleased nobody, but the original became the basis of Holst's setting of this Psalm, with English words from c. 1620 clearly written with the tune in mind, for chorus and orchestra. This tune (see EH 640) uses repetitions most skillfully and naturally became popular at once.

Psalm 101, on the other hand, had a rougher passage at the hands of the English. Ex. 79 shows the miserable journey it traced on its way to being entombed in the regrettable S.M. tune, ST. MICHAEL (which in the form we know was piously and scandalously arranged by William Crotch). Its original form is again preserved at Songs of Syon 358 and was rescued for Sapphic metre at Y 199. In its original form it is a beautifully reflective melody in the same mood as COMMANDMENTS (Ex. 77).

Several 1551 tunes made their way quickly to Germany, where psalms or hymns were written to fit them. Exx. 80 and 81 show two examples. Ex. 80 is the famous 42nd Psalm which soon found companion texts in Germany, and like COMMANDMENTS, has constantly appeared in corrupt versions where texts in the proper metre were not available, both in Germany and in Britain. Ex. 81, the tune for Psalm 23, came from the Bourgeois collection of 1547, and is very clearly the original from which came the famous German tune HERZLIEBSTER JESU. Note that in order to see the comparison clearly the German tune should not be read as it appears in most English books (e.g., EH 70) but as it is always sung in the USA (H 71).

The complete edition of 1562, though a monument to the editor's industry, is musically less interesting than that of 1551, and fewer of the tunes that have travelled originate in it. The agreeable short tune for Ps. 136 (Ex. 82) is one of these, and it is a happy coincidence—probably nothing more—that Milton's famous paraphrase of that psalm is written in its seven-syllable metre (or is easily adaptable to it), so that the English hymn 'Let us with a gladsome mind' can be sung to it (Y 124). Another tune with regular seven-syllable lines, this time in sixes, is that of Psalm 135 (Ex. 83)—a tune so simple that it is time it became better known in English-speaking circles.

But it is from 1551 that the 'great' tunes tend to come: see for example DONNE SECOURS (Psalm 12: EH 564: Y 303) MON DIEU, PRETE-MOI L'OREILLE (Ps. 86, EH 640: Y 74), RENDEZ A DIEU (Ps. 118: EH 305: Y 14) and Psalm 138 (SP 661: Y 119). And this last one (Ex. 84) leads to the most important general point we have to make about the Genevan psalms.

We have noticed that internally they are a close-knit family. The 110 metres of the Psalter generated 125 tunes, and their style is unmistakeable. Not that they are tiresomely similar, but their diction is grave and lucid, their handling of long phrases is always skillful, and they are bound together by one or two motifs which often reappear (our 'Strasbourg sign' comes more than forty times) and by their syllabic style and their use of only two note values.

Now Terry, in his book, *Calvin's First Psalter* (Benn, London, 1931) has preserved for us a facsimile edition of the Strasbourg Psalter together with two versions of each tune in modern notation—one unison, one harmonized. Sir Richard Terry was a Roman Catholic, who, when he came on the Genevan Psalm tunes, embraced them with all the fervour of a mature convert, and the introduction to his book contains some extremely interesting judgments which, nearly fifty years after, are still worth pondering. True, his supporting authorities are all Catholic or nearly so, and he shows no knowledge of any Genevan musician but Goudimel, so he ascribes to Goudimel a good deal that Bourgeois could rightly claim. At the end of his introductory essay he has this paragraph:

The Lutheran chorale may be likened to a fertile spreading tree, shedding abundantly the seeds from which other trees were to spring. The Genevan psalm tune remains in its primi-

tive aloofness, like a marble statue; incapable as a statue of propagating its species; pathetic in its frozen grandeur. (p. xii).

One can admire the passion and conviction of that, coming from Terry—of whom we can fairly say that he injected into English Catholic music during his time at Westminster Cathedral a vitality comparable with that with which Vaughan Williams renewed that of the Anglicans, and that it was partly his study of these tunes that gave him the necessary enthusiasm for what was ancient and excellent; but that statement will not do. What he may have meant by it was that there has been no end to the Lutheran hymnals, and a steady development in Lutheranism of new material from age to age directly derived in the end from Luther, whereas once the Genevan Psalter was completed in 1562 nothing was added to it, and nothing altered, and the only contemporary Christian group that uses it without abridgement or alteration is the Reformed Church of the Netherlands. That is true. But the larger truth is that whereas the Lutheran tunes have a numerous progeny in Lutheranism, the Genevan psalm tunes have their offspring outside their own country and language. They are, as we shall see in the next chapter, the fountain-head of the whole tradition of English and Scottish hymnody. The German tunes used in Britain have always been immigrants, welcomed aliens, while the Genevan tunes, themselves until recently almost forgotten (except two or three that we have noted), live on in the more rugged and amateur customs of English psalmody.

But before we get to that, we may recapitulate a point which has been emerging for some time. We have noticed that the definitive 1551 versions of older tunes differ from their originals only in details, but that this difference tends often towards the establishing of a tonality that will make the tunes easier for ordinary people to sing. The assumption there is that if one tune had a better chance of popularity among the laity of the mid 16th century than another it would be in the Eighth or Ionian mode—that is, to all intents and purposes, in C major. All the tunes which travelled fastest were of that kind. The ecclesiastical modes were still the normal vocabulary of choral music—but choral music was Catholic at this time, not Protestant: it was professional, not lay music. What we noted about the 1542 version of Psalm 1, (Ex. 68), is the Genevan version of a process which was going on everywhere; and the best illustration of this is in Psalm 138 (Ex. 84) and MIT FREUDEN ZART (Ex. 85). To all general purposes these two are versions of the same tune. But that is not all. They are like a charter for ecclesiastical amateur music, because they use as their principal subjects the most elementary musical units that can be found in the 'major' key.

The simple diagram appended to Ex. 85 shows this. The tune's dominant is the fifth of the scale: it is entirely based on the triad, with the upper octave completing the frame. Then if the major third becomes a melody, the notes are (in our key) Eb, F, G: if the perfect fifth is made into melody, the notes are Eb, F, G, A, Bb; and if the triad is made into a melody it is natural to write the major third out the first time (Eb, F, G), and the second time to skip the third and write out the superimposed minor third (G, Ab, Bb). Having done that, you have the opening phrase of Ex. 65 and the penultimate phrases of both Ex. 84 and Ex. 85 (the introductory note altered in 85). If then the frame is completed by the addition of the upper octave, you can either go stepwise up to the top note (as well known tunes TRURO and DUKE STREET do—EH 420, 167) or, in order to give special prominence to the dominant, you can leap to the high note and come down from it. Then you have the opening phrase of Exx. 84 and 85. What is more, if you devise a tune which says no more than what we have set out so far, you have LASST UNS ERFREUEN (EH 519: H599, 'Ye watchers and ye holy ones').

Ex. 85 is a compression into a slightly shorter space of Ex. 84: and of course if you are an ingenious Scotsman and want to compress the essence of this into Common Metre, what you produce is DUNDEE (EH 43: Ex. 104) which for that reason is always known in Scotland as FRENCH tune. An alternative way of building a tune on these elements produces INNOCENTS (EH 37: H 235). And so on. Many more tunes could be mentioned which simply vary on this theme. The historic point is that it seems to have originated, anyhow for church use, in Geneva, and for this purpose Geneva drew on this archetypal hymn tune, O MENSCH BEWEIN' (Ex. 65).

The Beginnings of
English and Scottish Psalmody, 1549-64

Sternhold and Hopkins: The Old Version

The fact that the first English Protestant hymnody was metrical psalmody, as was the Genevan, begins in a coincidence and continues through a felicitous historical accident. The English Church had become a separate body from that of Rome through the act of Henry VIII in 1532 which replied to the Pope's censure of Henry's divorce of his first wife by constituting the British Sovereign the 'Supreme Head' of the Church of England. The next nearly forty yers were spent in constituting that Church and fashioning it into what is now known as the Church of England. The Bible was officially translated into English during Henry VIII's reign by Coverdale—and it is a typical example of Henry's capricious autocracy that he had connived at the execution of Tyndale for doing the same thing barely ten years earlier. The Coverdale Bible appeared in 1538. The first English Prayer Book, which consisted largely of Cranmer's inspired translations of Latin prayers fitted into a liturgical system which would express the ideas of the Reformation, appeared after Henry's death, in 1549. The Prayer Book of that date was regarded as a trial book—very much as the first modern liturgies of the Anglicans in Britain and America were, and it was revised in 1552 to become the official book of worship for the English Church. Further revisions were made in 1559 and 1604 before the final revision of 1662 produced the prayer book which was in universal anglican use until the revision of 1928.

The question, however, of the role of public praise in the services, which were adaptations of the medieval Mass and Offices, remained open. The attitude of the English liturgists to worship was more like that of Luther than of Calvin, although the Articles of Religion reflected Calvinistic theology. So the psalmody and canticles written into the services were medieval in precedent; but no provision whatever was made for hymnody. Indeed, until the radical revisions of the Prayer Book in the later 20th century the only exceptions to this throughout the Anglican liturgies were the *Te Deum* at Morning Prayer and the *Veni Creator* at Ordinations.

The inception of that English metrical psalmody which was the only legal vehicle of public prasie until hymns were formally authorized in 1821 (though by that time the law was almost a dead letter—see later pp 83-84) we owe to Thomas Sternhold, and the circumstances were curiously parallel to those in which Marot became the first poet of Geneva. Sternhold, Groom of the Royal Wardrobe at the end of Henry VIII's reign and through that of Edward VI, began metricizing psalms for the edification of the young new king (ten years old when he came to the throne in 1547: sixteen

when he died in 1553) and for the improvement of the Court. The strong puritan strain in him which sought to replace with sacred songs the trivial secular music that was the Court's normal entertainment led him to versify certain Psalms in the ballad metre that would enable them to be sung to tunes already known. Here, however, there is a tantalizing gap in our knowledge because we do not know to what tunes they in fact were sung, and we have no knowledge of their being sung in church in Sternhold's lifetime. The only conjecture we can rise to is that they may have been sung in the Court or by the young King to the kind of ballad tune which 350 years later Vaughan Williams brought back into English hymnody—such a tune, for example, as FOREST GREEN (EH 15: H 21), or perhaps to the kind of ballad tune we now find in the *Oxford Book of Carols;* but this is mere speculation, and our ground for it is the metre itself—fourteen syllable iambic lines —which Sternhold used very nearly without variation. What we do know, however, is that in 1549, the year of his death, a little book without music containing 44 psalms was published, of which 36 were by Sternhold and eight by his collaborator John Hopkins (d. 1570). This was definitely published in order to share with others the ideal of replacing trivial songs of amusement by easily-sung metrical psalms.

Sternhold's final total was 37: his 18th Psalm (which happens to be the source of the only Sternhold hymn now in currency, 'O God, my strength and fortitude', *Westminster Praise* 43) was evidently not completed when the 1549 book went to press, and first appeared in the final edition of 1562: one can understand its great length daunting him, for Psalms 1-21, all his, are in the 1549 book with that one omission.

We must suppose, then, that if metrical psalmody as a form of public praise was by this time in the mind of the English church authorities, they were at a stand when it came to deciding what music to use for it. The only music yet available specifically written for the new church was that of John Merbecke, who in 1544 had produced syllabic settings for the sung parts of the Office and the Eucharist which until very recently remained the basis of anglican liturgical song. When Queen Elizabeth I in her Injunctions of 1559 commended to the church 'a modest and distinct song' it was probably this kind of material that she had in mind rather than the new psalm music which was by then, but not in Sternhold's time, known.

It took forty years from its inception (at Henry VIII's repudiation of the Pope in 1532) for the Church of England to find its final shape in the Elizabethan Settlement of 1570, and this was partly because the process was brought to a standstill at the accession of

Queen Mary in 1553. She was a convinced Roman
Catholic and sought at once to reverse all that had
been achieved up to then by the new Protestants. During the five years of her reign, many English church
leaders went to the Continent of Europe while the rest,
if they were in sympathy with the new Church, went into retirement or hiding. Some of these emigrants went
to Holland, from which in due time they brought back
to Britain the ideas and principles which produced the
radical puritan churches, but many found their way to
Geneva. There they found Calvin's church structure
fully developed—with which they disagreed—and the
1551 Genevan Psalter in use, which they clearly loved.
They no doubt had a sight of John Knox, who after a
brief sojourn in Geneva and Frankfurt was to return in
1555 to oversee the inception of the new Protestant
Church of Scotland.

The result of their first discovery was the very deep
conflicts of conscience which ensued between those
who wanted the new Church of England to be Episcopal and those who hoped it might be Presbyterian. The
other discovery, however, was more creative and
peaceable. For those who felt that metrical psalmody
was the answer to the people's demand to be allowed
to sing in church found metrical psalmody in regular
use in Geneva and elsewhere in France and Switzer-
land. It was this that inspired them to complete the
Psalter. Probably John Hopkins had already added a
number of psalms to Sternhold's nucleus, but among
the Genevan exiles were one or two capable writers, the
best of whom was William Whittingham, and while
they were in Geneva the work began.

Naturally enough the question was, how the
Genevan style of music could be adapted to the ballad
metre which was still the uniform metre of psalmody,
and this seems to have been the first problem to which
the exiles addressed themselves. By 1556 they had produced the first *Anglo-Genevan Psalter,* which contained 51 metrical psalms plus a metrical version of the
Commandments, all in ballad metre (what we later
came to call Common Metre), and a number of tunes.
No doubt what they hoped for was a tune for every
psalm, with as few duplications as the Genevan Psalter
showed (which, we remember, in 1562 marked only 25
psalms to share tunes set to others). Equally naturally,
they wondered whether any of the inspiring tunes they
heard could be adapted to fit the English metre; but
the answer to this, when they took into account the
differences between the two languages as well as the
prevalence in Geneva of long and ample stanzas, they
eventually found to be in an attempt to write at least
some psalms in the Genevan metres, or something approaching them.

At this point we can look at Ex. 86, Psalm 137 in the
1556 Anglo-Genevan Psalter. We know this as the OLD
137th, and that form of naming indicates that the tune
is the 'proper tune', composed for a certain psalm or
adapted from a Genevan original for it. (Thus the

Genevan Psalm 134 becomes in English use the OLD
100th, and Psalm 107 as adapted in Scotland in 1564
becomes the OLD 107th).

Before examining it we will make a general point.
The rhythm of the earliest English psalm tunes is
always irregular, as so often that of the Genevan tunes
was. Moreover, in successive printings of these tunes
we constantly find inconsistencies between the new
version and the one it was copied from; a syncopation
will be here, not there: rests will be provided in different places. Apart from straight misprints, which
abounded in old printed scores (and of course were impossible to correct without making a complete new
printing-master), we constantly find rhythmic variations, and occasionally melodic variations too. Now it
is pedantic to insist that the earliest is necessarily the
'authentic' version, and it served only the needs of
specialist historians to prefer the earliest to a later version for practical use. What is needed in editing these
ancient tunes is to have a proper grasp of the principles
that governed their composition, and of the kind of
music their composers wanted them to be: this is a
technique not unlike that which governs the use of ornaments and melodic glosses in the modern interpretation of baroque music. And the principle that governed the composition of these primitive psalm tunes, inherited from Geneva, was the construction of a good
melody which would, by its avoidance of the 'beat' of
either the march or the galliard, carry an external
'sacred' quality. These people inherited a medieval
conviction that the church was set apart from the
world, and the one distinction they made between
sacred and secular was to avoid a regular beat in the
rhythm. This was assisted by their preference (also
Genevan) for unaccompanied unison singing. A
melody standing by itself and unimpeded by part
writing could have a plainsong-like freedom of flow,
and although the tunes are written in a notation that
provides, broadly, for two note-units one of which is
twice the length of the other, we need not be certain
that even this distinction was rigidly kept to. If non-
musicians are singing together the best way to keep
them together is to be clear about the relative value of
a semibreve and a minim; but in the composer's mind a
melody would form itself guided by the need to strike a
delicate balance between the need for emphatic notes
to coincide with emphatic syllables and the contrary
need to avoid a regular 'beat'.

OLD 137th (Ex. 86) is a first-rate example of this. Its
movement and manner are Genevan—two note-values
used to form four long phrases of fourteen syllables
each. The fact that it doesn't 'sound' Genevan is attributable solely to the metre, which is a metre Geneva
never used, and whose rugged symmetry prevents the
composer from using the melodic gifts that give the
Genevan tunes so much distinction. (To be candid, if
any Genevan tunes are second-rate, they are almost
always the tunes in square English-type metres—the

OLD 100th being an almost unique exception). There is only one point at which the inhibition of the metre shows: this is where the tune returns to its tonic at the half way point—a quality often found in these early psalm tunes, to which we are about to return. But the tune compensates for that in its rousing climax in the last long phrase, which is again slightly un-Genevan, and seems to be the result of the high pressure generated by the restricted thump of the metre.

Virtually all the early English psalm tunes were in Double Common Metre, the metrical psalms always being thought of in stanzas of four lines of fourteen syllables, and indeed being printed so when they went into print. A rare exception to this is the 1556 tune for Psalm 23 (Ex. 87), possibly the oldest strictly 'Common Metre' tune in the English repertory. The reason for this is clear: Psalm 23 was in two and a half four-line stanzas, and very short. A half-length tune was therefore appropriate. It is, actually, a pleasant enough tune to deserve a better fate than it has encountered (but the astute editor of Y did not miss it: (see Y 229).

In 1558 a new and expanded edition of the Anglo-Genevan Psalter was prepared and brought back to England when on the death of Queen Mary the exiles returned. This added nine new psalm versions and a metrical *Nunc Dimittis* by William Whittingham and two psalms by J. Pullein (which last were later dropped); this brought the total number to 62. Whittingham was clearly hoping that at least some Genevan tunes could be brought to England in a more or less unaltered form, and translated a few psalms in their metres; when the Psalter was completed twelve of the Psalms were retained in their Genevan metres (or adaptations of them to fit the English cadence): of these Psalms 50, 121, 124, 126 and 127 were by Whittingham: the others were by Kethe (100, 104, 112, 113, 122, 125) and Norton (111). The Genevan tune for Psalm 36 (Ex. 65), for example, came into England in four units of 88.8, adapting every third cadence, and that of Psalm 3 (Ex. 76) became 66.8.66.8D, with the same kind of adaptation. These new metres provided a most welcome relief from the monotony of the ballad metre, but except for Psalm 124 (Ex. 72) they tended to fall out of common use since they required tunes strange to the somewhat lazy English ear. But the 1558 psalter did introduce one new English metre which later in other hands proved to be very fertile: 6.6.6.6.4.44.4 (to be distinguished from 6.6.6.6.88 which comes much later), as in our Ex. 88. This is the tune for Psalm 148, later also used for a version of Psalm 136 written to fit it in 1562, (so it is called OLD either). Before 1700 it was the only tune available in this metre, apart from a private tune by Henry Lawes (see later, pp 52-3), and it is a fine and remarkable tune, being on final C with dominant F, and conveying a toothsome ambiguity of mode. One can regard the 1592 revision of its rhythm as definitive.

In Ex. 89 we have a tune made out of Genevan Psalm 134 whose opening coincides with that of the OLD 100th. (The Old 100th itself did not appear in England until the English Psalter of 1560/1 since its text had not yet been written). Here we have a DCM psalm tune, mostly full of what later became psalm-tune cliches, grafted on to a Genevan tune, and it was not the most successful of these operations. But Ex. 90 is a 'vintage' piece, freshly composed and then revised: it appeared in 1556 as the tune for Psalm 30, in twelve lines, but with its central section removed in 1558 it became a taut and satisfying melody with a very well-placed climax. In this form it is known as OLD 30th, and a beautiful edition for modern singing is John Farmer's harmonization of it in Este's Psalter, 1592, will be found at *Songs of Praise* 693: another version is at Y 273.

Once the exiles were back, and Queen Elizabeth had put in hand the final operations to establish the Church of England, the Psalter was fairly rapidly completed. Two streams seem to have been running: one based on Sternhold's 1549 collection, the other continuing the Anglo-Genevan tradition. Two psalters appeared quickly in the Sternhold line: the English Psalter of 1560 and a second usually dated 1561 but now thought to be later 1560. The first of these is chiefly interesting in attempting a few versions of psalms to carry German tunes, which did not commend themselves (the only German tunes to find a place in the English psalm-repertory were VATER UNSER, 40 for the Lord's Prayer and ERHALT'UNS, HERR, Ex. 43, for a translation of its own text). The 1560/1 Psalter is chiefly notable for the first appearance of the OLD 100th in its English form—with the second and third long notes of the Genevan last line reduced to half length, so that all the phrases are uniform.

The last Anglo-Genevan Psalter, 1560, contained 87 Psalms, and a number of new tunes including the English forms of Genevan Psalms 86 (which became OLD 70th), 36 (OLD 113th), 3 (OLD 122nd) and 104 (see Ex. 75). This was heavily drawn on by the Scottish Psalter, 1564.

Our Exx. 91 and 92 are from the 1560 Psalter. Ex. 91 is not now in use: if it were it would have to be called OLD FIRST, being the tune for Psalm 1, and it is a splendidly constructed tune, in this but in nothing else resembling the first Genevan Psalm (Ex. 68). Its placing of movements by leap in the melody is especially successful. OLD 18th (Ex. 92) is nearly as good, though it has that return to the tonic which we noticed in Exx. 86 and 89. As given in the source it has a regular rhythm, the long notes being confined to the beginnings and ends of lines—unusual at this period.

So the project marched on until the publication of *The Whole Booke of Psalmes* in 1562—the same year that saw the completion of the Genevan Psalter—brought it to its conclusion. But in a sense it was only a beginning, for unlike the Genevan psalter, the musical repertory underwent constant changes. In the 1562 psalter (our table gives the provenances of each psalm) there are, besides the Psalms, a *Venite, Te Deum, Benedictus, Magnificat, Nunc Dimittis, Benedicite,* Creed and Lord's Prayer all in metre, as well as a few other pieces which break the rule of unchanging psalmody—two *Lamentations,* a prayer for the Queen, a penitential prayer, a prayer before Sermon, and a Thanksgiving after Communion. All these except the *Venite* have their own tunes, but if the compilers ever dreamed of emulating Geneva in assigning a 'proper' tune to all, or even most, of the Psalms, that never came to pass. In fact forty-seven of the psalms have tunes of their own, and the other 103 are marked to share those tunes. This is not a miracle of editorial astuteness, because most of the time it is the psalms in the gap before the next appointed tune that are assigned to the tune just passed. The indications are that had the musicians attempted to provide anything like the generous allowance of 125 tunes for the 150 psalms that we found in Geneva they would not have been up to the job. Already psalm-tune clichés are found repeated from one tune to the text, and not all the 47 tunes for the Psalms have the quality of those we select for comment. A fairly average specimen is Ex. 93, the OLD 132nd, which readers will recognize as the ancestor of the tune ST. FLAVIAN (EH 161: H 59). This is the classic example of how a tune that fails in continuity could fall apart in use; as early as Barley's Psalter of 1599 it appears in CM, using only the first half. It is a worse case than OLD 137th (Ex. 86) because the second half adds nothing to what was said in the first, and the tune is quite satisfactory without it.

But Ex. 94 is interesting in a quite different way. This must have been a tune which the editors thought would immediately 'catch on' because they use it for three different psalms, printing it out in full each time —Psalms 77, 81 and 87. But each time its rhythm is different. At Psalm 81 it appears as a triple-time tune—one of only two at that time in existence. At Psalms 77 and 87 it appears in the more normal syncopated duple time. But the fact that the editors cunningly left the time-signature ₵ with all three versions strongly suggests that it was the triple time version that was original; it may easily have been a ballad tune already known, and if it is, it is the best clue we have to the sort of tune Sternhold could have had in mind when he started the project of metricizing the psalms. It is in any case one of the archetypal psalm tunes from which others developed—or one might better say the 'head' of another family like that we mentioned at Ex. 85. The opening phrase is found in the carol, THIS EN-DRYS NIGHT (EH 20) and in TALLIS'S ORDINAL (EH 453: H 298), and its last two phrases are identical with those of WINCHESTER OLD (EH 30: H 13). One tends to feel that the editors thought they could slip it in if they printed it three times, flanking the daring original with two more demure versions.

It is at this point important to remember that all these versions of the Psalter, up to and including 1562, were published for private use. The title pages always say that in so many words or imply it. There was not, by 1562, strictly a 'Church of England' that could authorize the use of it in church. It was, like all the greatest and most influential hymnals of England, a private venture, essentially the devoted work of a circle of friends who built on Sternhold's foundation. More psalms were written than were eventually included; successive editions occasionally show the discarding of a version in favour of another. Very rarely (Psalm 23 is an example) two versions are given side by side. But this fact, that it was, and could only have been, offered for domestic use explains the immediate appearance of the four-part edition, published in 1563 by John Day. Four-part singing was as normal a recreation for the educated at home as a game of bridge is to-day. It was certainly in the homes that the Psalter stood its best chance of becoming known; for when it was authorized for church use, all that was allowed was the singing of a psalm in metre at the end of the Office.

Day's was the first of many harmonized versions. Mostly he uses the material of the 1562 melody book, but now and again he introduces a new tune, or indeed a new setting which looks more like a miniature motet since its tenor voice does not sing what is recognizable as a psalm tune. Our Ex. 95 (OLD 51st) is a simple example: a more complex one is at Frost 160, which has a touch of 'fuguing' half way through and in which the underlay of the words is a great puzzle. But we shall find later that most harmonized psalters kept the psalm tune in the tenor, however complicated the elaboration in the other voices.

The Scots followed with their complete Psalter in 1564. This was a prayer book and Psalter 'appointed and received by the Church of Scotland'—from the first, therefore, an ecclesiastical book, not a domestic publication. It reprints everything from the Anglo-Genevan Psalter of 1560, filling the gaps either from the English edition of 1562 or by providing alternative translations of its own. The chief difference between it and the English Psalter is its much wider variety of metre, indicating a closer sympathy with Geneva and a higher hope (which turned out to be a good deal too high) of congregational competence. We find that in the Old Version of 1562 there are 137 psalms in (Double) Common Metre, four in SM, 2 in LM, and 12 in peculiar metres carrying versions of Genevan tunes (there are five places where two versions are given). In the Scottish Psalter there are 99 in DCM, 11 in LM, five in SM, and 35 in peculiar metres (allowing for duplications, there are 27 peculiar metres). Neil Livingston's Table, reprinted here on pp 45-46, indicates just how the Scottish version differed from the English, and it mentions two authors who were peculiarly Scottish, indicating also how much use they made of the existing work of William Kethe. Kethe, author of Psalm 100 in the English version, known to us as 'All people that on earth do dwell', was particularly interested in the Genevan tunes, and made his versions as close translations of the Genevan parallels (so that in the case of Psalm 100, Beza ought to have as much credit as Kethe in hymnal indexes).*

In this Psalter there were many reallocations of tunes, and some first appearances of tunes still familiar. We noticed at Ex. 78 the Scottish adaptation of Genevan Psalm 107 (the adaptation in DCM being known as OLD 107th, EH 493: Y 251); and at Ex. 35 the similar adaptation of a German chorale to become OLD 80th. The total number of 'proper tunes' in 1564 was 102—considerably higher than that of the English Psalter. But for all that, the first Scottish Psalter and the first English one had a great deal in common, and it was only after 1635 that a long and searching reappraisal of Scottish psalmody produced the 1650 version (still in use in Scotland) whose only contents in common with the English Psalter are Kethe's Psalm 100 and Whittingham's Psalm 124, both in Genevan metres. But the first strictly Common Metre tune in Scotland is found in the 1564 Psalter—this is OLD COMMON (Ex. 96)—a strange chant-like tune, evoking memories of medieval litanies.

Just as John Day produced a harmonized English Psalter in 1563, so in 1566 came the St. Andrew's Psalter, in which one David Peebles, a canon of the Priory of St. Andrews, was instructed by his Prior to prepare four-part settings, note for note, of the tunes in the 1564 collection. This Psalter is lovingly described in Dr. Millar Patrick's *Four Centuries of Scottish Psalmody* (1949) pp. 56-62, where he speculates, with becoming hesitations, on the role of four-part singing in Scottish psalmody. Peebles's versions seem to have been commissioned as soon as the melody-edition was available, and they were probably asked for so that under the new Scottish dispensation the

choral tradition of St. Andrews Priory might not altogether wither. A glance at the two Peebles settings preserved at 321 and 370 in the *Church Hymnary III* (1973) of the Church of Scotland indicates that they are choral, not congregational settings. It can also be remembered that there were in Scotland several well known and capable Song Schools. One Andro Kemp, who was Master of such schools successively at St. Andrews, Dundee and (1570-3) Aberdeen, left in manuscript forty settings of psalm tunes in parts. Dr. Patrick mentions a famous occasion when at the return of an exiled minister to Edinburgh (John Durie) a long procession sang Psalm 124, which the recorder of the incident, Calderwood in his diary, says was sung in four parts as the procession moved up the street: and Dr. Patrick's suggestion is that the procession contained some trained singers from some of these schools; in any case, Psalm 124 was already almost a Scottish National Anthem, and improvized part singing is a perfectly plausible guess. The point is that it might be too much to say, as Dr. Patrick does, that the Church of Scotland 'did not follow Calvin's example of forbidding such singing' (p. 60); it seems never to have gone on record on the point, but the complete absence, before 1625, of any harmonized psalters in general circulation seems to indicate that there was no demand for them comparable to that in England during that period; we are tempted to conclude that part-singing was neither so conspicuous a part of domestic life as it was in England, nor encouraged in the churches, although in both cases we can also say that in some places this might have proved an unenforceable rule, for not even the Kirk of Scotland could make people sing in unison, or even in tune, by law.

From 1564 the two traditions of psalmody ran parallel, each learning from the other, and the priceless legacy of the great Common Tunes is what will occupy most of our attention in the next section.

---

* Reference is often made in books on this subject to the *Anglo-Genevan Psalter* of 1561 (e.g. in Frost, *English and Scottish Psalm and Hymn Tunes,* p. 8. Recently a copy of the Anglo-Genevan Psalter dated 1560 has been found in the Library of Manchester College, Oxford, and collation of this with the 1561 edition is a reprint of it; therefore all tunes attributed to the 1561 *Anglo-Genevan Psalter* can now be dated 1560. This is particularly important because the English form of the OLD HUNDREDTH is one of them.

6

The Developed Psalm Tunes

The repertory was, then, established in England and Scotland by 1564. Before we go further, we must say a little more about the rhythm of the psalm tunes as found in the sources we have already examined, and as it develops. Broadly speaking, three forces seem to have worked on the composers of these tunes, not always in the same direction.

(1) The overriding force, in the composition of the melodies, must have been that wish to avoid secular 'beat' which is common to the music of plainsong and to that of the Strasbourg-Genevan style. But the movement of culture, especially in those strata where the Reformation made its strongest impact, was beginning to produce a shift of the axis from the sacred/secular dimension of the Middle Ages to the educated/popular dimension of the Renaissance. Both Luther's and Calvin's music were educated music: and the difference between educated music and popular music was beginning to be that the educated enjoyed subtlety. Polyphonic music had induced a new kind of rhythmic subtlety to melodic lines, nowhere perhaps more clearly visible than in the Masses of Taverner and Dunstable. The pressure of one voice-line on another produced those entertaining syncopations and subunits of rhythm, sitting with engaging awkwardness on the fundamental pulse-pattern, which were already giving polyphony such attractiveness (and alarming the authorities who hoped that Palestrina wouldn't do too much of it). One sees it again, in the period we are now in, in a piece like Byrd's *Haec Dies*.

So a melodic line, even when no harmony was permitted, tended to take on something of the rhythmic shape of a voice in a polyphonic composition, and just as in the Masses and motets of the time one might occasionally tolerate a false accent for the sake of a point of rhythmic wit, so one finds in some of the psalm tunes (like the original rhythm of Ex. 72) the occasional metrical bump.

But of course syncopation can produce a delightful effect of felicitous emphasis, especially when it comes in the form of a lengthened second note in the iambic metre of the psalm tunes. Our example 106 shows that happening, and any age which is not brainwashed by crude 'beat' can appreciate it.

(2) The second force was the first working the other way: the effect on a melody of being incorporated in a harmonized composition. We shall in a moment examine several examples of harmonized psalm tunes, and shall find that the harmonizer did not hesitate to alter one or two relative note-values in order to get his counterpoint running smoothly; Exx. 97-101 will provide evidences of this.

(3) The third force was the simple practical matter of getting a congregation going on a unison and unaccompanied tune, which produced the conventional 'gathering note', now so familiar. It must be noted that the 'gathering note' is, in congregational use, the merest practical device. Precentors did not conduct, and they had no organist to set the tempo and pitch in an introduction. We hear the same effect in an English cathedral, where at the beginning of a psalm the opening chord is held by the organist for an appreciable space of time—until the choir has heard the pitch of its opening chord. If some psalm tunes nowadays seem to 'sound better' with their gathering notes, this is largely because we to-day are sated with the waltzes and marches of the 18th and 19th centuries and enjoy the rhythmic irregularity that puts ten beats into an eight syllable line. It is, actually, far more musical to mix the 'gathering note' with, in the short lines of C.M., the lengthened second note which has its origin usually under category (2) above.

But the general point must be added, that in the course of their careers the psalm tunes were usually rhythmically altered in details by editors, and modern editors are entitled to do the same. If, for example, the tune DUNFERMLINE (Ex. 103) can never actually be found anywhere printed as it is in the *BBC Hymn Book,* 1951, with long initials for the long lines and long second notes for the short ones, that does not mean that there is anything inauthentic about singing it so: the same can be said about GLENLUCE as it appears in *Westminster Praise* (# 4). Undoubtedly in singing, whatever the score said (and only one person in any congregation had a score—the Precentor, if indeed even he had one) a congregation would tend to dwell on a second note approached by leap, as we have in DUNFERMLINE,

But in the period after 1562 the psalm tune was under another pressure in Britain. To be plain about it, the 'proper tunes' provided in DCM by the Anglo-Genevan editors proved to be too 'educated' for most people, and towards the end of the 16th century we enter the era of the Common Tune.

The expression 'Common Tune' was invented by the Scottish editor, Andro Hart, who in his 1615 edition of the Psalter introduced for the first time a group of tunes, all of half length, which he called Common Tunes, since he explained that they could be sung to any psalm. Hence our expression 'Common Metre'. But this was not the first time such tunes had appeared. For the era of the Common Tune is also the era of the domestic harmonized psalter, and it is in the series of harmonized editions, used by people at home, normally published as part books, that the real secret of the English psalm tune is hidden. These were not church books: so there was no pressure from the direction of church authority on the decision which tune was correct for which psalm. What the publishers of these books were concerned with was what people would enjoy at home: and it turned out that they enjoyed these harmonized psalms very much, perhaps most of all the harmonized versions of the new short tunes.

But for our first example of harmonized domestic sacred music we have to look at something which is not set to a psalm at all. This is that extraordinary little collection of domestic motets composed about 1553 by Christopher Tye for a ballad-metre version of the Acts of the Apostles. The text is some of the most delectable doggerel to be found even in the sacred verse of the time. The industrious poet persevered as far as chapter 14 of The Acts, and Tye composed a setting for each chapter, in principle in D.C.M., but having the sort of rudimentary contrapuntal interest that would please untrained singers. Some of these pieces have been resurrected in modern anthems to make short motets (with other words, one need hardly say), but our Ex. 97 is the setting for chapter 8, whose first stanza runs thus:

> The death of Steuen dyd Saule cofort
>   who dyd agre with them
> that wold haue slayne the godlye sort,
>   then at Jerusalem
> scattred they were both far and nye,
>   and through the regions crept,
> of Jurye and of Samarye
>   the twelve onely except.

Exactly what the connection between its second half and WINCHESTER OLD is (cf. Ex. 100) is beyond speculation, or between its last phrase and that of OLD 81st (Ex. 94), but it is very clear that the typical Common tune in English psalmody owes a good deal to Tye's style. (Chapter 3's tune turns out to be an ancestor of WINDSOR—see Frost 297).

It is sixteen years after Day's Psalter when we come across the next harmonized Psalm book (although there are other four-part sacred songs we shall take account of later). This book is Daman's Psalter of 1579, and it contains our Ex. 98, which is the tune now called SOUTHWELL. It is in Short Metre (6.6.8.6), the metre used for Psalms 25, 45, and 67 in the Old Version, and it is set in Daman to Psalm 45. Notice that in this version it is strictly 'Dorian' (no E flat); the flattening of the sixth appeared after the psalm-tune period. The harmonization makes the most of the 'Dorian' flavour in its emphatic opening chord.

That 1579 book of Daman was printed by John Day, and its full title was 'The Psalmes of David in English meter, with Notes of foure partes set vnto them, by Gulielmo Daman, for Iohn Bull, to the vse of the godly Christians for recreatyng themseluse, in stede of fond and vnseemly Ballades.' In 1591 he produced, through the printer 'T. Este, the assigne of W, Byrd' (we remember that at this date Byrd, the legatee of Tallis, had sole rights for music printing) a more ambitious project—two volumes, one with the melody in the tenor, the other with it in the soprano (most unusual). Their title pages are identical except for notice of that difference, and read, in part: 'The former (/second/) Booke of the Musicke of M. William Damon, late one of her maiesties Musitions: conteining all the tunes of Dauids Psalmes, as they are ordinarily soung in the Church: most excellently by him comosed into 4. parts....Published for the recreation of such as delight in Musicke.'

This happens to be the first time the Church is mentioned on a surviving title page, but of course this is not a church book. Our Ex. 99, the tune now called in Scotland DUNDEE and in England WINDSOR, is from the second volume. It is written like a solemn madrigal, with elegant imitations, and with music overrunning the words and requiring discreet repetitions. We are to understand from his title page that this and any other tunes he prints for the first time were well known already in church use—and we have already said, in respect of this one, that it clearly owes something to Tye. It is difficult to know what to think about the first appearances of tunes like this; we do not know whether there are tune-books which have perished—which is quite likely—or whether they were invented by inspired precentors and simply sung by dictation ('lining out') by their congregations. The question then arises, how they became 'ordinarily sung' in Church, that is, we suppose, well known. We must suppose that a good deal of creative work went on in those 'hidden years' 1562-1591 in fashioning these new Common Tunes, so many of which are inspired musical epigrams with a tightness of melodic argument which Bourgeois would have respected and which the Anglo-Genevan editors should have envied. But perhaps this one was originated by the precentor of whichever church Daman went to. What we can be sure of, however, is that it was publications like his that gave currency to many of these great tunes which may have begun as purely local compositions.

Conjectures of that kind are reinforced by the appearance the next year, 1592, of Este's Psalter. The distinguishing thing about this volume was that one needed not four part-books but one large book with the parts so printed that four people could sit at a table and sing them (two parts upside-down to the two others). Part of the long title runs, '...wherein the Church tunes are carefully corrected, and thereunto added other short tunes vsually song in London, and other places of this Relme.' (Just as Daman allows his name to appear Damon in 1591, so Este is so spelt by Daman, though his title page carries the spelling Est: in any case it is pronounced 'East'). In this book there are no fewer than 32 tunes that have not appeared before—all 'short tunes' as distinguished from the 'Church tunes' which is what he calls the official tunes in the 1562 Psalter. One of these is our Ex. 100A, which is later known as WINCHESTER (and later still as WINCHESTER OLD); his harmonization is placed alongside the later one of Ravenscroft, to which we shall return shortly. Here is another wholly admirable melody, the end-product, obviously, of a series of improvisations on that melody of Tye's we quoted as Ex. 97. Este was not a musician but a printer and publisher, and he commissioned settings, almost always in this simple form, from the best musicians of his day, among whom the name of Dowland often appears.

Ex. 101 is CHESHIRE, a tune of very different cast, but employing the device of a rising fourth in an otherwise mostly stepwise tune very differently, but no less eloquently, than Ex. 100. By this time melodies are being pitched at the level at which they were expected to be sung—more or less where we find them now: the very high pitch of this one's tenor is unusual, and gives us perhaps a clue to the change of musical taste and association between that day and this. At that pitch it was considered appropriate to the cheerful Psalm 146; nowadays we sing it a fourth lower and always to contemplative or penitential texts.

We can at this point omit reference to several psalters which appeared in the intervening years and move to the important Edinburgh Psalter of Andro Hart, 1615. Hardly any new tunes appear in the English harmonized psalters of Allison and Barley (Alison has infact one)—both dated 1599. Scottish psalters had been appearing fairly regularly, but Hart's of 1615 is, as we have said, the first to separate 'Common tunes' from the rest, and the first therefore to give them, or any tunes, arbitrary names. This was also a manual of worship, with prayers, a Calendar, a copy of the Church Discipline, and a new versification of the Song of Moses.

The most striking thing about it is in fact these twelve common tunes, of which six have retained their currency to this day, and deserve to retain it as long as hymns are sung. These are:

FRENCH TUNE (in England, DUNDEE)—Ex. 104
    (EH 43: H 396)
THE STILT (in England, YORK)—Ex. 102
    (EH 472: H 312)
DUNFERMLING—Ex. 103 (EH 64)
DUNDIE (WINDSOR—first time as a straight
    psalm tune) Ex. 99 (EH 332: H 284)
ABBEY—SP 492
MARTYRS—Ex. 115 (EH 449: H 547)

All these tunes are to be found in many standard hymnals now. The others lack distinction and have quietly perished, but fifty per cent is a handsome score in one innings. Our Exx. 102 and 103 show a contrasting style, and Ex. 115 (MARTYRS) carries the contrast much further. Eight of these tunes are new in Hart's Psalter, and five of the surviving six are new. The very unusual melodic line, with so many see-saw leaps, of YORK (Ex. 102) made it a great favourite for playing on church bells later on: but what its origin can be remains a mystery. We select DUNFERMLINE (Ex. 103) because of its perfect symmetry of melodic line (and we remind our reader of our note on rhythm at the beginning of this section). The ferocious MARTYRS was a favourite tune, almost a national anthem, during the turbulent Covenanting days. All Hart's tunes are printed uniformly with long initials and all other notes half length, but modifications of this appear in later Scot-

tish psalters; and all are printed, of course, with melody alone.

History then takes us back to England to the greatest of all the harmonized Psalters, that of Ravenscroft, 1621. Ravenscroft was both an editor and also a musician, and his collection of tunes is described in his title as, 'such severall Tunes as have beene, and are vsually sing in England, Scotland, Wales, Germany, Italy, Franch and the Netherlands: never as yet before in one volume published.' For this project he collected ninety tunes; 37 of them are 'proper psalm tunes', eight are 'Spiritual Songs', and the remaining 45 are 'Common tunes', many of which had not been printed before. He drew on the work of Allison (1599) for five of the 'proper' tunes, and on the work of twenty other composers, almost all of whom were alive and no doubt the recipients of commissions, for many others. Six of these had been contributors to *The Triumphs of Oriana,* the collection of madrigals celebrating Queen Elizabeth's seventieth birthday in what was to be the last year of her reign (1603),—namely, J. Bennet, William Cobbold, George Kirby, M. Cavendish, Thomas Morley and Thomas Tomkins. Other names distinguished in the wider field of music included John Dowland, Giles Farnaby (d. c. 1600), and John Tomkins. Three harmonizations (two of them for the tune YORK) were contributed by John Milton (c. 1563-1647), father of the poet (for one of these see EH 472 i, and for another by the otherwise unknown Simon Stubbs, EH 472 ii). Ravenscroft himself harmonized sixteen of the 'proper' tunes (collaborating with John Farmer in two others), five of the 'Spiritual songs' and 23 of the Common Tunes; one of the 'proper' tunes may be his own composition. The only tune through-composed by its original maker is Tallis's CANON, which appears among the 'Spiritual Songs' in an abbreviated form.

Ravenscroft followed the lead of Andro Hart in naming all his Common tunes; sometimes he changed Hart's names—it is he who called Hart's DUNDEE, WINDSOR, and Hart's STILT, YORK, and Hart's FRENCH, DUNDEE. He took the names of English cathedral cities for tunes he suspected of being English, of Scottish places for Scots tunes (except YORK which evidently he hoped to annex as English) and of places in or near Wales for the Welsh tunes—of which more in a moment.

The whole thing is thoroughly workmanlike, and once it was published very little was added to the English repertory for some fifty years. We have in Exx. 100B and 104 two examples of Ravenscroft's own harmonizations. In 100B, notice how his special delight in subdominant harmony caused him to smooth out the dotted rhythm in the famous third line—he did it to avoid roughness at the temporary modulation: this was pedantically perpetuated (without his harmony) in the first version at EH 30, to square up with the reproduction of his original at the second version: but few singers omit that dotted note in practice when the melody is in its usual place. Comparing this with 100A we can see that normal modern practice owes more to Kirby than to Ravenscroft. But his version of DUNDEE (Ex. 104) is now regarded in most of England (though not yet in the USA) as indispensable—the tune gains much from that flattened bass note in the sixth chord.

Example 105 could of course have appeared earlier because its original is from A-G 1556; but it is Ravenscroft's version which unashamedly sets the exquisite NUNC DIMITTIS tune in triple time, and gives it the appropriate time-signature, thus producing one of the most beautiful melodies in the whole repertory. Twenty-three of his Common Tunes are printed for the first time. They include at least ten which remain in currency, one of the most brilliant being BRISTOL, which is closely associated in Britain with 'Hark, the glad sound' (EH 6). We quote here two of the most unusual of the English tunes. Ex. 106, LINCOLN, is a throw-back to the modal system (which is now really disappearing), in being in (as it were) G major with melodic dominant C; its strong thrust downwards into subdominant harmony, contradicted by the harmony under the last chord of the third phrase (with a C sharp), produces a tension and drive that we saw paralleled in OLD 148th (Ex. 89). CHRIST'S HOSPITAL (Ex. 107) is quite unique in ending its second phrase on the sharpened third, and very unusual in its melodic texture (F - F with final D, which makes in modern use the unusual key of B minor appropriate).

Ravenscroft was obviously looking out for unusual tunes, and he seems to have found a few of these in Wales. The very fine tune ST. MARY, (Ex. 108) which appeared in the same year, 1621, in Archbishop Prys's Psalter for use in Wales, is fairly widely known still, though probably sung less often than it deserves; its outstanding quality is its unusual melodic leaps—but that is nothing to what Ravenscroft found elsewhere. What the origin of this music really is remains unknown: nothing could be less like the smooth flow of the great Welsh evangelical tunes of two centuries later. ST. DAVID's, Ex. 109 has an unusual compass and a remarkable number of almost unmanageable leaps; in a sobered-down version it is found in modern books (EH 166), and we owe that to the later editor Playford. The only 20th century hymn book that dared to print the original was the *Oxford Hymn Book* of 1908. BANGOR is in some ways even odder (Ex. 110) and has long since perished. We may suppose that tunes like this were sung to the metrical psalms in Welsh in the archdiocese of William Prys; the remarkable thing is that Ravenscroft knew these tunes at all.

This brings us to the one tune (Ex. 111) which may be Ravenscroft's own composition. This is a tune designed to replace the Genevan tune for Psalm 104 (Ex. 75B) which was taken almost unaltered into the 1562 English Psalter and remained the only tune available for that Psalm. Unhappily, when Kethe made his often very good version of the Psalm, he used an anapaestic metre, which required a triple time tune, not the iambic metre of the French: so that tune sat so awkwardly on the text that, quite apart from its enormous length, it was found impracticable. But Psalm 104 is a good psalm, and Ravenscroft sought to rescue it. The tune he composed (if he did) is so majestic and satisfying that everybody has wanted to use it (until quite recently) but every editor (except only he of the Yale hymn book—see Y 139 which transcribes the tune exactly) has felt obliged to re-write the rhythm of the final phrase, which fits Kethe's first stanza but none of the others (Kethe showing himself a wayward metrist at that point). Kethe's last line of st. 1 reads, 'Honour and majesty in thee shine most clear'—which Ravenscroft's tune fits; but the essential metre is that which is familiar to us in 'O worship the King', and one has only to try to sing Ravenscroft's last phrase to 'Pavilioned in splendour and girded with praise' to see what the problem is. However, in whatever practicable form it appears, it is a fresh and inspiriting tune, and it still appears as an alternative to HANOVER for 'O worship the King' in *Hymns Ancient and Modern*.

The rest of this story takes us back to Scotland. There were, before Andro Hart's of 1615, three psalters (1602, 1611, c. 1612) which are bibliographically important but do not affect our story since they offer no new tunes. But the granting of, as it were, official status to the 'Common Tunes' in 1615 seems to have produced a new resurgence of energy that lasted twenty years. The next important Psalter after Hart's of 1615 is the Aberdeen Psalter printed by Edward Raban in 1625. Only two copies survive and both have lost their title page which is tantalizing because it might have contained some cue to the purpose of the first 'tune in Reports' to appear in Scotland, which is in this book and is our Ex. 112. Here is the first four-part harmony since 1566, so far as we know, and it seems to have been, not an arrangement, Daman-wise, of an already existing tune but a through-composed miniature anthem. It is the first example of a form which was developed in the folowing few years, and it is still in Scotland associated with Psalm 95 (the *'Venite'*). It has little musical interest, and it is somewhat crudely set up—disdaining any avoidance of parallel fifths.

This 1625 Psalter is in four parts throughout, and the other new tune it provides is the very eloquent tune ELGIN (Ex. 113); here again the harmony would perhaps not escape the professor's criticism, but the part-writing contains more points of interest than we expect to find in Common Tunes. It looks as if the madrigal culture was paying a brief visit to ecclesiastical premises.

Raban printed another psalter in Aberdeen, dated 1633 which pursues the practice of playing patience with texts and tunes but adds nothing new. But the heirs of Andro Hart in Edinburgh brought one out in 1634 which introduces CHESHIRE (Ex. 101) for the first time to Scotland, and prints for the first time CULROSS (Ex. 114—that name is pronounced Kew-ross). Four part harmony is used throughout this book, and the harmonizer must have been entertained to discover that he could harmonize this tune by using line 3 (tenor) as line 1 (soprano) and vice versa. There is also a tune, new in this book, called GALLOWAY, which persisted for a while and then was deservedly forgotten.

This brings us to the climax of the whole series, the richest Psalter produced in the whole period—the Scottish Psalter of 1635, brought out in Edinburgh by the heirs of Hart. This is a new piece of work, upon which its editor, Edward Millar, had certainly been working for some ten years. Millar Patrick in his chapter 7 tells us that Millar graduated in 1624, and that a manuscript book of his was discovered bearing the date of 1626 in his handwriting and containing already 75 Proper Tunes and 16 Common Tunes harmonized by him as they appear in the 1635 Psalter— that being almost exactly two thirds of the tunes he edited. The book has 105 Proper Tunes, 31 Common Tunes, and eight Tunes in Reports—a total repertory of 144. Its texts are still based on the Anglo-Genevan and English Psalters, and its tunes are taken from the whole repertory thus far assembled (except Ravenscroft). They are harmonized sometimes in four parts, sometimes in five. Happily this book has been lovingly reproduced twice; first by Neil Livingston, who in a massive volume with 13″ x 8½″ pages printed everything in the Psalter together with many pages of essays and notes, and several pages of facsimiles, in 1864. Sir Richard Terry re-edited Livingston in a more modest but still valuable book in 1935, omitting the Essays.

This book shows how ample the Scottish repertory was; it was of course much wider than the English, at least so far as the book was concerned. Since it relies heavily on the established tradition, (and uses the harmonies provided in earlier books for such tunes as are not new) its contribution of new tunes does not need to be great. None the less for that, it is significant. Our Ex. 115 shows the 1615 tune MARTYRS as here harmonized (harmony actually from 1625). Exx. 116-8 are new in the book. WIGTON, Ex. 116, is demurely arranged but its melody shows that the vocabulary had by no means been exhausted by Hart and Ravenscroft —it is one of the most haunting of them all and during the 20th century has made its way in England and elsewhere (EH 474 revises the harmony very acceptably, and BBC 347, altering a detail of rhythm with complete justification, makes it even more delightful). The name WIGTON is very slightly puzzling: it may be a corruption of the Scottish WIGTOWN (the furthest southwest County of Scotland) or it may mean WIGTON, which is a village just across the bay, but in the English Cumbria, in which case it is the only English name given to a Scottish Common Tune. Ex. 117 is GLENLUCE, also new in 1635, and here the part-writing really does suggest a madrigal, at least at the beginning. It may be the needs of this delightful soprano flourish that give the opening line of melody a

Genevan kind of syncopation. But since it sprang into existence full fledged with harmony, the subdominant chord in the last line has been, from the beginning, the element that gave the harmony a special distinction. From this Psalter come also MELROSE (EH 451) and CAITHNESS (EH 445: H 353)—the former of which has an oddly irregular line, like one or two others in the Collection. Finally there is a tune which is ascribed to Millar the editor much on the same ground that we give OLD 104th to Ravenscroft. It is, of all things, a 'new' tune for Psalm 124—and how even Millar could have thought it would stand a chance against the popular and appropriate Genevan tune that by then everybody knew one cannot imagine. But if, as seems likely, he was a youthful enthusiast for psalmody, it may be an early work which he regretted. It can be read, by those interested, in the *Revised Church Hymnary* (1927), 645, only slightly adapted. But his 'Tunes in Reports' all of which except two he probably arranged himself, have some interest. Our Ex. 118 is the last of them, being a sort of vocal chorale-prelude on the Old 137th (Ex. 86), and it shows more than adequate musicianship. We know no more of Millar's career except that he may have been the minister of a parish in Ettrick Forest, near St. Mary's Loch in the Scottish Border country.

After 1635 the Scottish psalmody story goes downhill so rapidly that we are obliged to believe that the slide had already started when Millar was at work, and that he hoped—vainly as it turned out—to halt it. So far as church use goes the 1635 Psalter remains a monument—no more. For it was only fifteen years later that the 1650 Psalter, still in currency, appeared, and the contents of this make it very clear what had happened. Every Psalm in the 1650 book is in Common Metre, even if in a few cases an alternative in another metre is provided. The Common Tune had taken over. Dr. Patrick tells us that not long after 1650 the repertory of most congregations did not exceed a dozen Common Tunes, even though so many more were available. And as the 1650 Psalter went into subsequent editions (the last was 1929) the musical editors had to attend to the need to provide new Common Tunes from the expanding repertory, most of which turn out to be English and not a few of which are very far below the standard aimed at in the early 17th century. The 1929 Psalter shows 22 tunes in Long Metre (far more than the LM Psalms need), one in DLM, 123 in CM, 13 in DCM, 17 in SM, one in DSM, two in 6.6.6.6., four in 6.6.6.6.4.44.4, one frantic deformation of Genevan 42 in 8.7.8.7 D Iambic (usable as DLM), one in the metre of Psalm 124 and four 'reporting' tunes for CM: those are the only metres used in the Psalter now. There are no 'Spiritual Songs', the place of these being to some extent taken by the Paraphrases of 1781. It was, no doubt, the collapse of psalmody which allowed hymnody at last to find its way into the Church of Scotland in the mid-19th century, and one supposes that its final relegation is to be seen in the abandonment in 1973 of a separate Psalter, the Psalms now being included as hymns in *Church Hymnary* III.

It was much the same in England, although the turbulent church history of England in the 17th century, culminating in the final restoration of the Church of England to its Established place and the influence of the tastes of the restored Charles II, gives our story a very different turn. But after Ravenscroft even the diligent Frost can find only one new Psalter in fifty years—a little publication by William Slatyer, 1643, containing the first 22 Psalms and a fresh version of Psalm 1, adding no new tunes. But right at the end of the period we have two psalters by John Playford. The first is dated 1671, published in London by W. Godbid, and contains a collection of tunes, all harmonized in four parts with melody in the tenor. These are divided in three sections—Common Tunes, Long Metre Tunes and tunes longer than that. Of these last there are only 16, taken from the English and Anglo-Genevan Psalters, but there are 19 Common tunes. There are also a number of hymns designed to be sung after certain psalms and to their tunes—a curious revival, one might say, of the medieval Antiphons; to this extent the puritan horror of unbiblical material was relaxed. There is one new tune in the book, of no importance, and one which is altered in the book from the version in the 1635 Scottish Psalter into what has now become a very celebrated tune—LONDON NEW (Ex. 119). (Cf EH 394: H 310). A second Psalter from John Playford appeared in 1677 '. . . in a more Plain and Useful Method than hath been formely published'; it is harmonized in three parts with the melody in the treble—thus falling into line with the new style of the Restoration music. The one new tune in this book, our Ex. 120 (BRISTOL) shows how the new style of scoring was combined with the old style of composition. John Playford (1623-86) had a virtual publishing monopoly under the Commonwealth and during the Restoration, and to some extent anticipated the eclipse of puritan austerity by publishing English folk songs as early as 1650. His son Henry (1657-1720) took over the business in 1684, and was Purcell's first publisher.

That then is a sketch of the progress of the 'Old Version', and of how it generated a whole dynasty of tunes. Looking back over it, and of course its details can be amplified by a study of Maurice Frost's indispensable book and others in our bibliography, we see a development 'on paper' which cannot have been matched by a similar development in practice. The Reformation was a learned movement in the hands of Luther and Calvin and Knox, and the editors of the Psalters pitched their expectations high. One could say that the leaders of the learned stream of the Reformation had about as much idea of what ordinary people would be willing to sing in church as religious bureaucrats of to-day have about what ordinary people want to do in worship. But one could equally say

that without vision the people perish. Both have their bearing on Reformation psalmody. But whereas nowadays people have a hymnal of which they use hardly more than half (in the USA the fraction is usually much smaller), in the story of the Psalters we have a direct encounter between the Proper Tune and the Common Tune, and the Common Tune won. Congregations of Elizabethan times were not better singers than they are to-day, and it is fair to say that they would find, say, the Genevan 104th Psalm (Ex. 75) as difficult as any modern congregation would—for this may have been the church idiom of the time, but it was not the idiom of the people's secular music.

Yet if their hopes were disappointed, the editors of these Psalters did not live in vain; for later ages, especially our own century, have brought an appreciation of the quality of the best of these tunes, and even if they are not usually among the most popular, they are at least appearing in hymnals. And when all is said, there is the OLD HUNDREDTH among the six most universally sung tunes in all ages since it was first published in that obscure corner of the Genevan psalter, with its second-shortest psalm.

TABLE SHOWING THE DEVELOPMENT OF THE METRICAL PSALTER

This and the appended information are taken from Neil Livingston's edition (1864) of the Scottish Psalter of 1635, pp 28-9. The authors, represented by their initials, are Craig, Hopkins, Kethe, Marckant, Norton, Pont, Pullain, Sternhold, Whittingham and Wisdom.

Psalm	1549 (44)	1556 (51)	1560 (65)	1560-1 (87)	1562 (150 Eng)	1564 (150 Scot)
1-17	S	S	S	S	S	S
18					S	S
19-21	S	S	S	S	S	S
22					S	S
23		Wh	Wh	Wh	S	Wh
24					G	C
25	S	S	S	S	S	S
26					H	H
27				K	H	K
28	S	S	S	S	S	S
29	S	S	S	S	S	S
30	H	H	H	H	H	H
31					H	H
32	S	S	S	S	S	S
33	H	H	H	H	H	H
34	S	S	S	S	S	S
35					H	H
36				K	H	K
37			Wh	Wh	Wh	Wh
38-40					H	H
41	S	S	S	S	S	S
42	H	H	H	H	H	H
43-4	S	S	S	S	S	S
45-6					H	H
47				K	H	K
48					H	H
49	S	S	S	S	S	S
50			Wh	Wh	H	Wh

Psalm	1549 (44)	1556 (51)	1560 (65)	1560-1 (87)	1562 (150 Eng)	1564 (150 Scot)
51		Wh	Wh	Wh	Wh	Wh
52	H	H	H	H	H	H
53					N	N
54				K	H	K
55					H	H
56					H	C
57					H	Po
58				K	H	K
59					H	Po
60-1					H	H
62				K	H	K
63	S	S	S	S	S	S
64-6					H	H
67			Wi & Wh	Wh	H	Wh
68	S	S	S	S	S	S
69					H	H
70				K	H	K
71			Wh	Wh	H	Wh
72					H	H
73	S	S	S	S	S	S
74					H	H
75					N	C
76					H	Po
77					H	H
78	S	S	S	S	S	S
79	H	H	H	H	H	H
80-1					H	Po
82	H	H	H	H	H	H
83					H	Po
84					H	H
85				K	H	K
86-7					H	H
88				K	H	K
89					H	H
90-1				K	H	K
92-3					H	H
94				K	H	K
95			?H		H	H
96-9					H	H
100				K	?	K
101				K	N	K
102					N	C
103	S	S	S	S	S	S
104				K	K	K
105					N	C
106					N	N
107				K	K	K
108					N	C
109					N	N
110					N	C
111-3				K	K	K
114		Wh	Wh	Wh	Wh	Wh
115		Wh	Wh	Wh	N	Wh
116					N	N
117					N	C
118					M	C
119			Wh	Wh	Wh	Wh
120	S	S	S	S	S	S
121			Wh	Wh	Wh	Wh
122				K	K	K
123	S	S	S	S	S	S
124			Wh	Wh	Wh	Wh
125			Wi	K	K	K
126				K	K	K
127			Wh	Wh	Wh	Wh
128	S	S	S	S	S	S
129			Wh	Wh	N	Wh

Psalm	1549 (44)	1556 (51)	1560 (65)	1560-1 (87)	1562 (150 Eng)	1564 (150 Scot)
130		Wh	Wh	Wh	Wh	Wh
131					M	M
132					M	C
133		Wh	Wh	Wh	Wh	Wh
134			K	K	K	K
135					M	M
136					N	C
137		Wh	Wh	Wh	Wh	Wh
138			K	K	N	K
139					N	N
140-1					N	C
142			K	K	N	K
143					N	C
144					N	N
145					N	C
146	H	H	H	H	H	H
147					N	N
148		Pu	Pu	Pu	Pu	Pu
149		Pu	Pu	Pu	N	Pu
150					N	N

The difference between the English and Scottish Psalters in regard to the renderings of entire Psalms, if viewed in the order of time, are as follows: (1) Both retained the 44 psalms by Sternhold and Hopkins of 1549 & c. (2) Of the 43 added by the Genevan exiles the English retained 20 and the Scottish the whole. (3) The English added 87, including one second version, in 1562; and these 42 were transferred to the Scottish. (4) In 1564 the Scottish was completed by the addition of 21 from new sources. (5) In 1563 and '65, 4 second versions were added to the English. The versions thus came to differ in 41 instances, besides which the English contained 5 duplicates not in the Scottish.

Arranged according to authors the case stands thus:

	English	Scottish
Sternhold	40	39
Hopkins	60	37
Whittingham	12	16
Kethe	10	25
Pullain	1	2
Norton	26	8
Marckant	4	2
Craig	—	15
Pont	—	6
Wisdom	1	—
Anonymous	1	—
Totals	155	150

In versification the Scottish exhibits the following varieties:

99 Psalms in Common Metre
11 Psalms in Long Metre
5 Psalms in Short Metre

Besides these there are 27 varieties of metre including 35 psalms, as follows:

4 lines of 6 syllables each	Ps.143
6 lines of 6 syllables each	111,120
5 lines of 8 syllables each	36, 132
6 lines of 8 syllables each	112, 113, 117, 127
7 lines of 8 syllables each	76
4 lines of 10 syllables each	110
5 lines of 10 syllables each	124
7 lines of 10 syllables each	83
7.6.7.6 (D)	130
9.8.9.8 (D)	118
10.11.10.11	129
6.6.6.6.8.8 (should be 6.6.6.6.4.44.4)	136, 148
6.6.8.6.6.8	122
8.8.6.8.8.6	85
8.8.8.8.6.6	125
9.8.9.9.8.6	142
10.10.10.10.11.11	50
11.11.10.11.11.10	62

10.11.10.11.11.11	138
12.12.12.12.10.10	126
4 lines of 10 syllables anapaestic	67, 75
6 lines of 5 syllables anapaestic	149
6 lines of 10 syllables anapaestic	47
11.11.10.10 anapaestic	80
10.10.11.11 anapaestic	104, 105
9.8.9.8 iambic and 6.6.5.6.6.5 anapaestic	81
8.6.6.8 iambic and 7.7 trochaic	121

The English Psalter has 4 in SM, 2 in LM, 12 in peculiar metres (50, 104, 111, 112, 113, 124, 125, 126, 127, 130, 136, 148, of which all but 136 use the same metres in both English and Scottish)

The first in SM and the first in peculiar metre (120) are in Sternhold's original 19. The first appears in 1556 (Ps. 51); the first anapaestic in 1560 (67)

7

Unofficial Psalters and Hymn Books

We must now turn to a small group of psalters and songbooks which used texts other than that of the Old Version of 1562. We shall attend only to those which have provided us with tunes currently available, and first we will deal with those that contain anonymous music, then with those that use the work of named composers. The *Acts of the Apostles* (1553) with music by Christopher Tye we have mentioned already, anticipating its logical place in this section for reasons which were obvious. But in the period before Sternhold went to work there was the book of hymns and psalms which for the first time brought German tunes to Britain. This was *Goostly Psalmes and Spirituall Songes*, which is always ascribed, though not on its title-page, to Coverdale. The date of this book has to be guessed at, but Frost has narrowed it down to 1543-46, since there is evidence of its being edited by somebody who saw publications up to 1542 or so, and it was mentioned in a list of books ordered to be burnt by Bishop Bonner in 1546. It has 23 hymns and spiritual songs, all taken from the early Lutheran collections with very respectable versions of their appropriate tunes, followed by fifteen versions of psalms written with three exceptions to carry the appropriate German tunes, or German tunes otherwise used by Luther's editors. These are not in the order of the biblical Psalter, and their numbering shows the same confusion between Protestant and Catholic customs that we encountered in Strasbourg. Of our 'Luther' examples, nos. 14a, 29, 30, 31, 32, 33, 34, 37, 38 are all in this book: so are 45 and 64, and many other classics which were in c. 1544 fresh from the German presses. One tune which this book introduced to Britain is CHRIST IST ERSTANDEN (Ex. 121), probably the best known Easter song in Germany since a century before the Reformation, and maybe for much longer than that. We reproduce the rather puzzling quasi-plainsong manuscript of the 15th century which is probably its first written appearance, and it can be seen that Coverdale follows this very faithfully. (This is, of course, of the same family as Exx. 14 and 14a.) when one considers this book, and alongside it the book of *Gude and Godlie Ballatis* (Ballads) published in Scotland about 1540 by the Wedderburn brothers (which first brought *In dulci Jubilo* to Scotland, as well as many other German carols and hymns) one wonders how it would have been had that exile, consequent on Queen Mary's opposition to Protestantism, never taken place. Perhaps British hymnody would have followed the Lutheran style and the Genevan psalms would have been left in Geneva and Holland, and their English progeny might never have been born. But Coverdale's collection is a hymnal, not a psalter, and it pre-dates the Psalter fashion by several years.

Then there is that remarkable psalter of Henry Ainsworth, printed in Amsterdam in 1612 for the English congregations in that country whose descendants later returned to make such a fuss in the Westminster Assembly by commending Congregationalism just when the Presbyterians thought they would persuade England into their way of thought. Ainsworth's psalter is geared to the Genevan psalm tunes and has English versions of psalms which carry them. Our Ex. 122 shows the Genevan Psalm 23 (Ex. 81) discreetly adapted to an English translation of Psalm 18 (which in the 1562 Psalter was of course in C.M. and set to our Ex. 92). It was, however, Ainsworth's Psalter that was carried to America on the *Mayflower* in 1620: the origin of that ship's journey was, of course, in Amsterdam. It was distinctly a 'learned Psalter', however, and the very first book printed on American soil was the *Bay Psalm Book* of 1640, which restored the Old Version to the British exiles.

Robert Tailour's *Fifti Select Psalms...Paraphrastically turned into English* (1615) we must leave aside, because the music of these psalms is all in a fairly complicated motet form—clearly intended for very musical households: these can be looked up in Frost, ## 411-422, which take 39 pages to print. But we have to stop a moment to admire what is without question the worst-edited psalm book in the whole literature of the period. This is called either Simmons's Psalter, after its printer, or Barton's Psalter, after its author, 1644. Misprints abound, as we have noticed, in these old psalm-books: in this one there are nothing else. Every tune is misprinted, since consistently the alto clef is used where the tenor ought to be used. Oddly enough, in a later edition of 1706 reprinting Barton's work, a new lunacy is introduced in that every bar-line (and bar lines occur with every other note) is misplaced. The most hilarious entry in this comic collection is where it prints a tune it calls DUTCH BASS TUNE (Ex. 123) with the rubric: 'used commonly in Cambridge, and of late in Aldermanbury, it agrees in consort with the tune following, so that it is all one whether you take, for they may be sung both together.' In Ex. 123 we show this tune at the pitch it occupied in this book, with in the treble line the 'following tune' which was the OLD DUTCH TUNE from Daman 1579—a tune, one might say, which needs something to keep it alive. (And they have misprinted two notes anyhow in the BASS TUNE).

That would hardly be worth mentioning were it not a clue to the origin of the much more significant tune COLESHILL (EH 492)—called in 1644 LONDON LONG TUNE 'proper for solemn ditties'. Anyone can see that it bears some relation to WINDSOR (Ex. 99)—Daman again—but the fact is that this is another case of 'it doesn't matter which you sing'. It is perfectly possible to sing it and WINDSOR at the same pitch. Here in Ex. 124 we give it with COLESHILL as a bass to WINDSOR. It makes an indifferent bass, since so many parallel octaves are involved. But it sounds very much like a sort of amateur bass—putting in the obvious harmony notes without attempting to harmonize everything in the melody. After all this evidence of learned music there is perhaps something refreshing about this unassailable evidence of the antics congregations actually got up to.

When we come to the Psalters to which named composers contributed music we are in a different world again. One of the almost inseparable characteristics of the main-line psalm tunes is their anonymity: the only composer's name we have mentioned with anything like confidence (apart from harmonizing), is that of Bourgeois, and we have not mentioned any name, even tentatively, that is known in the wider field of music making. But now we are about to meet Thomas Tallis, c. 1505-85, the greatest musician of his time in England. Tallis's nine tunes are all to be found in Matthew Parker's Psalter, now believed to be dated 1557, and they are the work of a composer who is a complete stranger to the psalm-tune tradition.

The psalter itself is a complete version of all 150 Psalms made by Archbishop Matthew Parker (1504-75) during the reign of Queen Mary: for those five years he retired into private life, having been in 1553 Dean of Lincoln, but deprived of all his duties by Queen Mary. He became Archbishop of Canterbury in 1559, was the leader of the team which produced the 'Bishops Bible' (1568), and pursued his official activities to such energetic purpose as to be labeled by his enemies 'Nosey Parker.' He was an eminent theological writer—but no poet.

Tallis, a Gentleman of the Chapel Royal at the time, enjoyed that immunity from the asperities of church conflicts which seems to have been the lot of many Tudor musicians, and when the Parker Psalter was published by John Day, it contained eight tunes by him, one in each of the eight ecclesiastical modes, plus one written for another purpose.

The Preface to the book contains a rhyme, presumably Tallis's own, in which he describes the tunes; we reproduce it here with a reference to the psalm for which each was composed:

The first is meeke: deuout to see	Ps. 1
The second sad: in maiesty	Ps. 68
The third doth rage: and roughly brayth	Ps. 2
The fourth doth fawne: and flattry playeth	Ps. 95
The fifth delyght: and laugheth the more	Ps. 42
The sixt bewayleth: it weepeth full sore	Ps. 5
The seuenth tredeth stoute: in froward race	Ps. 52
The eyghte goeth milde: in modest pace	Ps. 67

These tunes are the work of a musician who is accustomed to writing modal polyphony, not to writing tunes for people to sing in unison, and they depend on their harmonies as much as on the tenor melody for their effect. It must have been an unusual experiment for Tallis, and the situation will have been like that of an eminent symphonist of the 20th century who is invited to write a hymn. As often as not, such a composer does not write a melody and harmonize it, but rather writes a vocal composition which sings better as a choral piece than as a congregational hymn. If he is also an accomplished song writer, that helps him (that was the case with John Ireland in the tune LOVE UNKNOWN, or with Vaughan Williams's early hymn tunes, at the time of writing which he was a song writer and had not yet become a symphonist). Tallis makes it quite clear that he hoped congregations would sing these tunes, for he says in the Preface, 'The Tenor of these partes be for the people when they will syng also, the other parts, put for greater queers, or so suche as will syng or play them priuatelye.' (We hasten to say that that is Tallis's original spelling). So the tunes contain a simple melody for ordinary people in the Tenor, and three other parts for choral singing.

When Tallis's tunes are performed to-day—and it is only since Vaughan Williams introduced them (the Eighth apart) to hymnody in 1906 that they have been attempted—they are sung with the melody in the treble, and they often give a curious effect of brooding monotony: this is because the composer was aware of that immobility in amateur singers which composers for them have to live with. They like repeated notes and stepwise movement—which they get in many popular tunes to-day, like PRAISE, MY SOUL, and 'The church's one foundation' (AURELIA). The widest interval he allows himself is the fifth—always placed where it is easily negotiated.

But he also has a clear conception of the idea of the Psalm he is setting—a quality which he expresses in his tune—and this gives each tune a personality of its own. The second part of each line in his rhyme always refers to the actual text of the psalm the tune is set to. Apart from the Eighth tune, which is the famous CANON (and acknowledged to be one of the most cunning canons ever composed) the most famous Tallis tune now is the Third, which 'doth rage, and roughly brayth'. We reproduce at Ex. 125 what seems to be the best interpretation of the printed book (which is very obscure in places), and we owe this version to Mr. John Wilson, who at #8 in *Sixteen Hymns of To-day for Use as Simple Anthems* (RSCM 1978) has an important note on it. The first stanza of the text for which this was composed runs thus:

> Why fum'th in sight the Gentiles spyght
> in fury raging stout:
> why tak'th in hand the people fond
> vayne things to bring about?
> The kynges aryse, the lords deuyse
> in counsayles met thereto
> Agaynst the Lord; wyth false accord
> agaynst his Christ they go.

The longer lines have an internal rhyme which the tune reflects in its rhythm. What appeals at once to the modern ear is the dramatic explosion of melody after the first two long phrases, and the way in which the fourth answers the third; in this version, which we believe interprets Tallis's mind more exactly than that which Vaughan Williams made popular, the absence of the long note between the two halves of the fourth phrase, causing that phrase to be crushed together in the middle, suggests energy and tension such as the Psalm expresses. This tune has been made more famous outside church than inside it by Vaughan Williams's *Fantasia on a Theme of Tallis* (1910) for double string orchestra and string quartet, which of course offers loving comment on every detail of this amazing tune: but perhaps it is necessary to remember that its original mood is *angry* rather than penitential or contemplative.

Ex. 126, the SEVENTH tune, is quite different. It is not now inarticulately angry but militant: see the trumpet-like opening. It sounds like a march. Psalm 52 was one which always received the attention of musicians in the main-line versions: its popularity (clearly much greater than that of 139, for example, which never had its own tune) throws an interesting light on the change in public taste concerning the psalms that four centuries have brought. This tune was set in the English Hymnal (496) to 'There is a blessed home': but the more obvious modern text for it is Lynch's 'Lift up your heads, rejoice.' (Panorama 216). Note that EH needlessly extends the value of the last note of the opening line, and correspondingly throughout.

Ex. 125 shows Tallis 'meeting' the ordinary singer with stepwise phrases carefully relieved with wider intervals; Ex. 126 shows him doing it with repetitions of phrases. He uses both devices in the SECOND melody (Ex. 127) which is a single stepwise phrase repeated three times at different pitches, with very little variation. (He calls it 'sad': Psalm 68 is hardly that if we used the word in its modern sense: but 'sad' means, in the 16th century, 'sodden'—what in describing an emotion we might call 'tense'—just as 'fond' in the quotation above means 'mad').

Another which has found very limited currency is the FIFTH (Ex. 128). This he calls 'laughing'—a tune for the wistful but in the end comforting 42nd Psalm. Robert Bridges's elegant new text for it, 'Enter thy courts' in 8.4.8.6 D obscures the fact that the tune was written for ordinary short metre (as at Y 347 and *Westminster Praise* 34). Its cheerful fifth mode and unbroken triple rhythm make it the happiest of the tunes in the series, with a captivating lack of symmetry caused by the setting of pairs of lines in continuous phrases.

Ex. 129 shows the melody of the FIRST tune; this has had an odd history in our century, since in 1899 Bridges in the *Yattendon Hymnal* printed it exactly as Tallis scored it, but neglected to tell us that the melody was in the tenor: so when it appeared in *Hymns Ancient and Modern,* 1904 and at EH 78, the people naturally sang the soprano melody. It is edited with the tenor melody at the top at Y 177; inauthentic though the EH version is, it makes as good music as the original, the secret being that Tallis was a master of part writing anyhow.

The FOURTH and SIXTH melodies, Exx. 130-1, are not now, or not yet, in currency. The FOURTH is designed for the *Venite*: in Tallis's verses the words 'fawn' and 'flattery' are both words that have degenerated in meaning since that day—they mean something more like simple praise. This melody is the only one whose *bass* does not sound the final of the mode: the final is the last note of the tune, but the harmony is built up, as is that of the opening chord, on A. (In Mode IV, A is the dominant, E the final). Tallis did this clearly to give the tune as wide a difference in mood from that of the THIRD mode as he could.

The SIXTH is the most plaintive of them all. Notice the very low *tessitura* of all the parts, and the eloquent 'sighing' effect of the rests in the middle of certain lines; the downward drag of subdominant harmony adds to the dark effect.

Four of these eight tunes are in triple rhythm—sometimes simple, like V, sometimes ambiguous, like I, III and VI, all three of which reflect in their rhythm an internal rhyme in the text. All this—the subtlety of detail, the original approach of a great choral composer to the demands of congregational use, and the very unusual emotional descriptions of the tunes provided by him, makes this series unique in the literature—and easily the most successful and at the same time profound contribution of a large scale composer to hymnody.

The EIGHTH tune, the Canon, was originally scored with each line being repeated (words and music) before the next was sung. The effect of this was to give each voice the chance to sing the whole melody through with its phrases in the right order, and to enable all voices to sing all the time: the dominant is sounded four times in the soprano part before the melody begins (to accommodate those sections of the tune which the other three are singing). It is too well known to need any more comment (EH 267: H 165, and in almost every other hymnal in existence).

The NINTH TUNE (Ex. 132) is commonly called TALLIS'S ORDINAL because it was written for the CM version of *Veni Creator* which all editions of the Book of Common Prayer from 1549 to 1662 carried. Here, uniquely, the melody is in the soprano part and its harmony, apart from the closing open fifth, is faithfully preserved at EH 453 and H 298. Percy Scholes in his *Oxford Companion to Music* called it a primitive example of sonata form—and, if 'development' is overlooked, that is what it is: subject A, followed first by subject B in the dominant, then later by subject B in the tonic. It is so unlike the other Tallis tunes, and so much more like certain psalm tunes (see above, p. 38) that there might be a case for saying that Tallis knew it and printed it along with his own tunes, without himself being the composer. (We have a parallel case coming up in the matter of SONG 67, wrongly attributed to Gibbons: see (p. 52). But whoever wrote it, it is among the simplest and greatest of tunes.

Two other tunes are attributed to Tallis in some books, but certainly are not to be found in any of his works. One is TALLIS'S LAMENTATION (EH 235) which is in Day's Psalter, 1563. On grounds of style alone it has many of the qualities we find in his tunes, and could plausibly be attributed to him, but its absence from definitive editions of his works casts doubt. The other is VENI CREATOR (EH 153), upon which commentaries are evasive and living authorities apparently silent. With the best will in the world we cannot now trace it or even date it, but what is immediately obvious is that, being in six phrases, it cannot be a setting of any translation of VENI CREATOR that we know unless it was composed for Cosin's famous version, 'Come, Holy Ghost, our souls inspire'—as set in EH—in which case it must be after 1627, the date when that version first appeared.

We now come to a tiny book produced in 1583 by a composer of whom, judging by its contents, we should like to know more. Hunnys, who died in 1597, was a Gentleman of the Chapel Royal, a younger contemporary of Tallis, and his small book is really three pamphlets bound together, whose titles are toothsome:

(a) Seuen Sobs of a Sorrowfull soule for Sinne...
    whereunto are added
(g) A Handfull of Honisuckles and
(c) Comfortable Dialogs between CHRIST and a
    SINNER.

The only available copy is dated 1583—the title page gives that date to all three entries—but the book was entered in the print-register in November 1581, which suggests that what we have is a later edition. What is more, in that book, although the title of the first section suggests that the 'Seuen Sobs' are the seven penitential Psalms, we have only three of them here (6, 38, 51), and the book contains only one 'Dialog',—in all twelve pieces.

Two of the 'Honisuckles' found their way into the English Hymnal, where no. 79 is the first of them—a lilting, wistful CM tune which sounds much better as a solo than as a congregational piece. The other, no. 403 (Ex. 133) is slightly adapted from a song called 'The Poor Widowes Mite', in principle in CM, and using the same simple tune for the refrain as for the stanzas, allowing for rhythmic adjustments. The effect of the major third in its second line is almost Byrd-like.

We cannot resist quoting the only 'Dialog' that appears in this edition—the only dramatic sacred song from this period or in this simple style known to us (Ex. 134). It is something of a luxury here because it may be beyond the strict boundaries of hymnody: but the whole of this little collection shows the way in which religious recreation was virtually equated with penitence. Nowadays this continuous meditation on sin would be regarded as oppressive—and we are almost certainly the losers for cultivating that attitude: but read the works of the Counter-Reformation saints

and one sees that this was perfectly cheerfully accepted as a means of renewing faith and refreshing the soul.

Hunnys provides, in this edition, no harmonies. Possibly he is waiting for a good editor.

Next we take a forty-year leap, and introduce the celebrated name of Orlando Gibbons. His lyric-writer was George Wither (1588-1667), a 'character' even by the standards of those salty days. Wither published in 1621 a book of *Songs of the Old Testament* containing fourteen tunes by an anonymous composer of commonplace achievements. He followed this in 1623 with *Hymns and Songs of the Church,* which has an appendix of music composed by Orlando Gibbons. Since Wither was very free with his metres, he needed tunes from outside the Psalm repertory, and the consequence is that in the Gibbons tunes, sixteen in all, we have the first examples of metres which have since come into favour for hymns.

The tunes, all scored in two parts, are at the end of the book, each marked with the number of the Song for which it is composed: hence our habit still of referring to them by such names as SONG 1. The first of them, indeed, is probably the masterpiece of the series (Ex. 135). Gibbons was right at the end of the long procession of great madrigalists who had adorned the Elizabethan age, and although he learnt much from his seniors in that craft he had equally the gift of making melody which was especially the distinction of the lute-composers, such as Ford and Campian and Dowland. He cannot have had congregations in mind when writing these tunes—for of course it would have been illegal to sing Wither's hymns in church: the surprising thing is, therefore, how very well many of his tunes serve the needs of modern congregations. The classic poise and purposefulness of SONG 1, with its very long stanza, has more than a little of the Genevan quality in it, without the wayward Genevan rhythm. It certainly deserves to stand alongside the First Genevan Psalm (Ex. 68).

All these tunes are shapely and well-defined, and many can be found in accessible sources:

Tune	Metre	EH	H	Y
SONG 1	6 x 10 (orig. 8 x 10)	384	470	23
SONG 4	4 (6) x 10	113		192
SONG 5	LM	483		154
SONG 13	4 (6) x 7	413	451*	342
SONG 18	8.8.6 D	357		
SONG 20	SM	442		306
SONG 22	4 x 10	438	433*	232
SONG 24	4 (6) x 10	325		202
SONG 34	LM	259	573	313
SONG 47 (46)	10.10 (part)	98	69	

* - melody altered

That accounts for ten (in the light of what we are about to say, twelve) of the sixteen tunes Gibbons contributed to Wither. It will be noticed that one or two of them, like SONG 1, appear sometimes with their first long phrase repeated (in the case of SONG 4, the second long phrase); in all cases the version with the repeat is the original, though none loses much by the omission of the repeat which is usual in modern use.

Two comments can be made—the first general, the second editorial. The general comment is that this series of tunes gives every appearance of having been written by a fine composer in a hurry. Our Ex. 136 shows that there is a kind of 'signature motif' that constantly appears in them—a rising phrase of four notes from the third to the sixth—when they are in the major key. In no case does this do any harm to a tune taken individually, and the tunes in minor keys (3, 4, 18, 20, 31, 41) have no corresponding sign; but in Gibbons's major tunes it is unmistakeable. And we notice, if we refer to Ex. 136H, that Gibbons made three tunes out of one—Songs 9, 34 and 44.

The other comment, which is in three parts, concerns certain individual tunes and their interpretation. The most important thing to say is that two of them are still appearing in hymnals in triple time, which is a mistake so far as the composer is concerned. All his tunes except SONG 18 are in duple time. The most conspicuous example is SONG 34 (ANGELS' SONG), which was noted in the *English Hymnal* in 1906 in a form much nearer to the original, having been in the two previous centuries, like many popular tunes, deformed beyond recognition. But the tune there appears with its first line in duple time and the other three in triple. It should be noted as in *Hymns A & M,* without bar-lines and assuming a syncopated duple time. (see again Ex. 136H). The other tune that thus appears is Ex. 137—SONG 5, which again is not in triple time. Naturally the swing of LM against these tunes gives them a 'triple' feeling: but this sort of rhythmic tension is stock-in-trade for madrigalists. If SONG 5, however, be read with the words which Bridges set to it in the *Yattendon Hymnal* (given at the example) the rhythmic error will be painlessly corrected.

SONG 46, the charming two-phrase tune introduced by *E.H.* is really SONG 47—that being the Wither poem which it fits, and the original SONG 47 is a long tune handling a particularly complicated stanza. The confusion (which is will now be difficult to correct) arose because of a misprint in Edward Farr's reprint of Wither, with the tunes, in 1859: it was this book which also caused the confusion about SONG 34.

SONG 67, still so-called, was discovered by Maurice Frost to be in Archdeacon Prys's Psalter of 1621, so there is no ground for attributing more than the bass to Gibbons. His inclusion of it in his series—the only C.M. tune he contributes—was presumably because he had encountered it and found it too good to miss. It is

now very well known, and should be ascribed to Prys, and its alternative name ST. MATTHIAS (from the Song for which it marked) is more appropriate.

Our last collection is very like that one: it is Sandys's *Psalms*, 1637/8. The ambiguity of date is explained by the book's having two title pages: one is for the Psalms, and gives 1637, the other for the whole book giving 1638; so we may assume that the tunes set to these psalms by Henry Lawes were added in the later year.

Henry Lawes stands the other side of the 'great divide' of 17th century music from Gibbons. He (1596-1662) was one of the very first practitioners in England of the new music styles which had been developing in Europe since the beginning of the century; he was greatly admired by John Milton and wrote the music for *Comus*. His psalm tunes, of which there are 24 in Sandys's book and none anywhere else, are some of the most remarkable compositions in this form to be found in any age. Whereas at least one of Gibbons's tunes survived through all the lean years as a very well known tune, none of Lawes's has ever achieved the first or even the second rank of mere popularity; but we are about to suggest that Lawes, if he has just complaint at being neglected, had an influence which he certainly did not count on.

It looks as if one of our comments about the Gibbons series could apply equally to Lawes's, for about some of these tunes there is a remarkable 'family resemblance', with unusual phrases turning up in first one, then another. Probably they were, like Gibbons, all written in a short space of time. But it also happens that many of them have an unusually salty character because of the unusual intervals they use. They really must have sounded to conservative ears in 1638 as the melodies of Britten sounded when he was first recognized.

Consider Ex. 138 first. This is Psalm 72 in his set, called in many hymnals FARLEY CASTLE, (EH 217: Y 79). In what sense is that tune a 'first' in English psalmody, and almost a 'first' in all hymnody? In that it finishes on the high tonic. The only other example known to me happens to be one of our examples here—Ex. 26, Luther's first tune (which, we recall, did not always appear with its ending in that form). Now for a reason we are about to mention, a high-tonic ending for a hymn tune happens not to surprise anybody in the English hymn singing tradition: but what it signals is the break with the tradition of pure melody. As long as music in principle presupposes an unaccompanied and unharmonized melody, the old plainsong tradition of returning to the final, and of the final being at the bottom end of the scale, is instinctively obeyed. A tune *comes down* in the end. But if the 'coming down' can be taken care of by a separate bass part, the ear is not dissatisfied with the high ending of a melody, or indeed, as later composers found, with the melody ending elsewhere than on the tonic. But search the length and breadth of the Genevan and English psalms, and, excepting only EIN NEUES LIED, the Lutheran chorales, and there are no tunes there that do what Lawes does here. It is precisely this separation of the functions of melody and bass, by which process the melody becomes the rhetorical principle and the bass the rational principle, that was being established in Europe ever since the first rudimentary operas were performed in 1600. It was, we shall later see, this music which entered England like a flood after Charles II was restored to the throne, but a musician as cultivated as Lawes would not have been unaware of it.

Psalm 72 is then a new experiment in melody. But so is Psalm 8 (Ex. 139—EH 234: Y 28). This is one of the most fascinating of all hymn tunes simply because of the unexpected turns the melody takes; the long stepwise passage in the third phrase is admirably judged, to balance the unusual leaps elsewhere in the tune. This is one of those great tunes which have even to-day never had a chance because of being paired usually with rarely used hymns (but *Yale* made a noble effort). This again is experimenting, as befitted a great song-writer, with the possibilities of melody, especially accompanied melody. Even the tiny Psalm 32 (EH 505: Westminster Praise 37) has a character all its own, packing a surprising amount of music into the most restricted of metres. And even PSALM 12 (BATTLE—EH 432: Y 285), an unusually restrained melody, has Lawes's characteristic 'saw-edge' profile in its second phrase.

But now consider Ex. 139 again, alongside PSALM 9 (Ex. 141), and then let the eye travel over the fragments, and one complete tune, in Ex. 141-2. The constant recurrence of signature phrases in the fragments will at once be obvious, but what will especially catch the eye is the opening of Ex. 141A, and the opening and closing of Ex. 142/8F (PSALM 136, which again has a high tonic finish). Can there, after that, be any doubt where the most celebrated of all English tunes, ST. ANNE, came from? This, we hasten to say, has nothing to do with Bach's E flat Fugue or the Handel Chandos Anthem that uses that four-note opening phrase. But when we consider ST. ANNE'S opening phrase, its finish on the high tonic, and the 'saw-edge' movement of its third line, the temptation to say that it was inspired by Lawes need be resisted no longer. Not that we withdraw the credit of the composition of ST. ANNE from Croft (about whom more in his due place); but the tune is not directly claimed as his in the original source (which does claim some others for him), and it is at least conceivable that Croft said, 'This is only partly my work'. The most famous of English tunes is, when all is said, a very odd melody indeed, and we here suggest that it owes its inspiration to one of the great eccentrics of hymnody, which Lawes certainly was.

It will be no surprise to be told that the Lawes tunes appear, as did the Gibbons tunes, with melody and bass; but the difference is that most of the Gibbons tunes could be sung quite effectively in unison without accompaniment—the Lawes tunes, never.

Psalmody After the Restoration, 1677-1738

If the Genevan period could be called the springtime of metrical psalmody, and the years 1615-35 the high summer, the period after Playford, say between 1677 and the Conversion of John Wesley in 1738, is its autumn—not precisely, though admissibly in some senses, its Fall.

During this period of sixty years two things happen: the introduction into England of the new Continental style of music at the Restoration, and the beginnings of hymnody, and both these are signs of a new age which, being more permissive about what is performed in church, allows powerful competition to arise against the exclusive rights of psalmody. In this period we shall be concerned solely with England, for the publication of the 1650 Psalter with its provision for the singing of all psalms to a few Common Tunes (or, logically, to one) plus the OLD 100th and the OLD 124th, meant that very little creative effort was called for in Scotland.

But the Restoration was a Great Divide in English music. The enforced exile on the Continent of a King (Charles II) who happened to have a high degree of artistic adventurousness, meant that after the puritan Interregnum of 1649-60 the new Court practised, encouraged, and shared the music they had learnt from the inventive composers of France, and Italy. The Chapel Royal, which although its foundation went back to the time of the Crusades, had fallen on evil days, was reconstituted, the office of Master of the King's Musick was instituted, and in church a new kind of ceremonious and celebrative music was at once heard, composed by musicians whom Charles II encouraged to learn from Couperin and Lully.

No doubt plenty can be said about the licentiousness of the Restoration Court, and indeed of the Restored Monarch: but the real difference in ethos between the new music and the old in England was that music for the puritans was a private activity, for the children of the Restoration, a public one. Puritans believed that the only public activities, and the only legitimate crowded gatherings, were the worship of the Lord's Day; anything else public or sociable was foreign to their natures. By contrast, under Charles II the giving of public concerts, the encouraging of personal musical virtuosi, and the performance in church of full-scale choral music with orchestras, was an accepted part of the scenery, promoted by the people at the very top of society.

Hence the great musical renaissance whose central figure was Henry Purcell (1658-95). Purcell contributed nothing to hymnody otherwise than indirectly —in, for example, writing an anthem the last page of which provides the modern tune WESTMINSTER ABBEY, AM 620, and in writing a melody, 'Fairest Isle', which with its secular lyric inspired Charles Wesley's 'Love divine, all loves excelling'. But other members of his circle contributed much, as we shall see, notably his gifted young contemporary, Jeremiah Clarke (1670-1707).

Psalmody, indeed, took its time to assimilate the new idiom in which the dance, not the ecclesiastical chant, set the style, and very little comes into hymnody of the 'new music' before 1700. But two tunes of Benjamin Rogers (1614-98) of Magdalen College, Oxford, point in the new direction—the famous MAGDALEN TOWER HYMN (Ex. 143), set to a metrical version of the TE DEUM, and O GOD OF LOVE (Ex. 144), first published after his death, seem to point the way. The Magdalen hymn (still sung on May 1st every year from the top of Magdalen Tower in a brief ceremony at dawn which had a good deal more pagan association than any puritan regime would have tolerated) is a free-flowing triple time tune making much out of a very restricted compass; the other one (if it is his: it is ascribed simply to 'B.R.' in its first printed source) has a restrained elegance and a shapely contour which foreshadow the style which is about to become fashionable in psalm tunes. With these we can mention Courteville's modest Psalm tune, ST. JAMES (Ex. 145), now very well known, which was included in a private book made for St. James's, Piccadilly (then called St. James's, Westminster) and dated 1697. This shows perhaps a less certain melodic gift, its constantly repeated upper third giving it a touch of tentativeness. But there we have a tune for the Te Deum, a psalm tune, and— what is most significant—a hymn tune.

Now we always say that Isaac Watts was the liberator of English hymnody, and so he was, for it was he who first successfully introduced hymns (of his own composition) into congregational worship. But he was not the only hymn writer operating when his first important collection appeared in 1707. It is a curious thing that anonymity is now disappearing from the Psalm tunes—we often know who wrote which—while the new hymns are virtually always anonymous before Watts's time. But a surreptitious kind of hymn writing really came in with Playford, who began very gently to develop on the tradition that allowed 'sacred songs' to be appended to the official Psalter. His 1671 book included a number of hymns, each placed after a Psalm and to be sung to its tune, and the 1677 book contained a new hymn, 'On the divine Use of Musick', with its own tune (Ex. 146), which is a pleasing example of the new style, as the last of a group of 17 hymns placed *before* the Psalms. (For its text see *Panorama* 21). We have, further, during the brief period when Catholicism was openly permitted, the hymns in John Austin's *Devotions* of 1668, and Thomas Ken's famous trio written in 1695 for the boys of Winchester School, not to mention Benjamin Keach's Eucharistic hymns, the only hymns from the puritan side, written in 1673, though now forgotten.

This not inconsiderable body of hymnody produced mostly during the period just before Watts, was clearly meant for domestic use, though a general relaxing of the prohibitions of the puritan culture probably made it possible for them occasionally to be used in church.

The new custom of adding hymns to the books published chiefly for private devotion liberated after 1700 a good deal of new music, and correspondingly the appearance of a revised metrical Psalter, always known as the New Version and written by Tate and Brady, in 1696, gave a new if brief impetus to the writing of psalm tunes of a traditional kind.

By far the most important source for the new hymnody is *The Divine Companion,* 1701, edited and published by Henry Playford, son of John. This was expanded and issued in a definitive edition in 1707, and the copy I am here working from is of the 1709 edition, exactly the same as that of 1707 (only one copy of which is known to exist and that in the Library of Congress); mine was owned by one of the composers (Thomas Clarke) who contributed to it.

This is a substantial little book of 180 pages, part of whose title reads: *'The Divine Companion, or David's Harp new Tun'd. Being a Choice Collection of New and Easy Psalms, Hymns and Anthems. The Words of the Psalms being Collected from the Newest Versions. Compos'd by the best Masters. To be used in Churches or Private Families, for their greater Advancement of Divine Music.'* There is a ceremonious series of introductory fanfares, including a Dedication, a Preface, two poems presumably by Playford, one celebrating the publication and another to the composers who have contributed, and a third anonymous poem 'to Mr. Henry Playford on the Publication of his Second Edition....' A sentence or two of the Preface are worth quoting, referring to the anthems in the book:

> We have, 'tis true, had Anthems long since sung, and continued in our Cathedrals and Cappels, which have rendered our Divine Music not inferior to that of Italy, and made it honourably receiv'd among those that have been Enemies to the design of it, whilst the Vatican has distinguish'd our English composures with Golden Letters, and Rome show'd a particular veneration for Te Deums, that were sung in places which had shook off her Idolatrous Worship. But our Parochial Churches, which are equally dedicated to God's glory, and innumerable, in respect of those before mention'd, have been altogether destitute of such necessary assistances to Praise their Maker by; and when they have the same claim as Christians to the *Hallelujahs* above after this life, have not been made partakers of the *Hosannahs* below in it.

The publisher then refers to the good work done by his father in promoting the practice of music and assisting in its teaching, and concludes that there is now no reason why the church's worship should not be adorned with music of a more complex and adventurous kind than it had enjoyed before.

So he produces a book in which are provided new tunes for metrical psalms, texts and tunes of new hymns, and a considerable number of short anthems. The only one of the anthems which is heard at all now is Weldon's setting of Psalm 150, 'O praise God in his holiness', but in their day many of these pieces were sung, and got into later collections.

The composers mentioned in the book, whose work is found in all the three forms, are Samuel Akeroyde, John Blow (1649-1708), John Church, Jeremiah Clarke (1670-1707), Thomas Clarke, William Croft (1678-1727: always referred to as 'Mr. Crofts'), Robert King, Benjamin Rogers (1614-98), William Turner (presumably he, 1650-1740, but always called simply 'Dr. Turner'), and John Weldon (1676-1736). Some of these are well enough known to have their dates recorded in reference books: one or two are known only here.

The 'Restoration' style means that tunes always here appear with a bass: sometimes this is conceived as an instrumental or continuo bass, often with figures; sometimes it looks more like a vocal bass. But the prevailing style of the two-part tunes is that of the solo song. Psalm tunes appear sometimes in three parts, and anthems of course in four.

The 'Restoration' idiom is beautifully illustrated in Exx. 147 and 148, both in the song style. Ex. 147 is now called DAVID'S HARP (from the title of its source) and its modern form is at EH 378: note the marked phrase in the melody, and also the third phrase of Ex. 148 (TUNBRIDGE)—both are typical 'Restoration' motifs, as is the imitative passage in the accompaniment of Ex. 147. Ex. 148 introduces Jeremiah Clarke, one of the supreme melodists of that school, and a fervent disciple of Purcell—Purcell's interpreter, indeed, when it comes to hymns. UFFINGHAM (Ex. 149) is now well known—at least it appears often in hymnals; composed originally for an evening hymn, it combines a constant downward movement by step with periodic lifts by wide leap, and is one of the finest of all tunes in the intimate and contemplative manner. (Its frequent pairing with the very extrovert 'Lord of all bring' is a capital error). But if one wants to see the fulness of the Purcellian style, KING'S NORTON (Ex. 150), composed for an eight-stanza hymn for Good Friday, is the most characteristic of all. Most certainly a solo—congregationally, one would have thought, quite impracticable, —its melody line has all the disciplined freedom of the best Restoration music. We must not pass over the wholly charming tune BISHOPTHORPE, (Ex. 151) which is usually ascribed to Clarke but is not in the *Divine Companion*—indeed it had not been found in print before 1786, and its ascription to him there must be seen against the background of the rather romantic ascriptions which are in those 18th century books. It may be by a later 'J. Clarke', but it is a good example of the Purcellian influence with its engaging melody and its use of dotted rhythms. Other tunes by Clarke include HERMON (beautifully realized at no. 8 in *Sixteen Hymns,* 1978, but often found as a C.M. tune with the penultimate phrase omitted) and a family of tunes with similar openings which includes BROCKHAM (EH 220) and ST. MAGNUS (EH 147: H 106)—that last one being ascribed to Clarke not because it is claimed for him in the 1707 book but because no fewer than three tunes very like it are so claimed. All these are in the more conservative psalm-tune style and were indeed composed for Psalms in the New Version (ST. MAGNUS for Ps. 117).

The other important composer here represented is William Croft, organist of St. Anne's, Soho. His style is the most conservative that we find in the book (except in the anthems, of which several are his). It is best seen in the tune he wrote for Psalm 136, New Version (Ex. 152), which we call CROFT'S 136th. This has a touch of Genevan majesty, plus the new energy of rhythm given by the 'New Music'; but its change of rhythm in the last two long phrases is unusual for this period, and it very eloquently brings out the effect of the metre, which gives great emphasis always to the four short lines that end the stanza. Those lines are always rhymed a.bb.a, and this is reflected in the harmonic implications of this melody. (It will be seen that EH 566 preserves most of the original bass). Croft also contributed the pleasant tune BINCHESTER (EH 398); its unusual rhythm in the first phrase—reflected only in the hymn Bridges wrote for it 'Happy are they: they that love God' arises from the fact that it is set to a version of Psalm 96 which begins with the phrase 'Sing to the Lord' in its first two stanzas, and has 'Give to the Lord' at the beginnings of stanzas 7 and 8: but the fifth syllable is never an emphatic one, and the tune's rhythm deforms all the other stanza-openings. Such matters did not irritate singers of those days as much as they would singers of our own. EATINGTON (EH 639) also appears in this source—another sound and unpretentious tune.

Dr. John Blow's tune for Psalm 100 (Ex. 153) is an adventurous and enterprising piece, starting with some precipitous leaps. It was written in three parts, and the *Medius* (which is often a tenor part) seems here to be designed for an alto voice (since if it were written an octave lower it would several times interfere with the bass). But our Ex. 154, which is anonymous, shows how the anthem-style began to infiltrate the hymn style even as early as this. The tune is set to stanzas in SM; but it is affected by the four-bar form, so that in its second phrase it has to spread a syllable over a long series of notes, while in the last it requires the repetition of two syllables. We associate this most with the later evangelicals, who could hardly ever manage without repeated words, but it appears at this early stage as a consequence of music's new freedom and confidence. It is becoming less a mere servant of the text, more as it were an adult person having conversation on equal terms with the text (and later on overbearing creature positively drowning the words).

John Church, who often appears in this book, was a special addict of this style; several times he writes for a CM text a tune in LM and directs that two syllables in the short lines be repeated. He was a composer of much more modest gifts than Clarke or Croft; his best tune was probably what we may call NEW 149th (Ex. 155)—a fresh tune in the 104th metre which was used in the New Version for Ps. 149 as well. Among other anonymous tunes in the *Divine Companion* are two especially worth recording—the very spirited new tune for Psalm 50 (Ex. 156) and the even more remarkable tune for the metrical Creed (Ex. 157), in which there is less stepwise movement than in almost any DCM tune in the literature, and whose disposition of intervals is yet so skilful as to make it at once singable. Notice how in these tunes especially, but in all the others we have so far considered in this section, the 'modern' sense of key is now highly developed. We have turned our back on the Modes for good, so composers are restricted in their vocabulary, and have to compensate for that by other melodic skills. (We shall see the zenith of this process when we come to J. S. Bach).

Of modern hymnals the *English Hymnal* deals most generously with the *Divine Companion*; it has eleven tunes from this source, of which we have mentioned all but Samuel Akeroyd's tune now called LAMBETH or CRUCIFIXION (EH 340)—a very grave tune which is believed to have been sung by the two Wesleys on the day of their conversion in 1738. But perhaps there is no book in early hymnody which so conspicuously combines historic importance with fascinating grace of content as does the *Divine Companion*.

The next source, however, deserves a good deal of respect. This is the *Supplement to the New Version* (1708), a music book designed to provide new music for Tate & Brady's Psalms. Its chief claim to honour is in that we find in it the tune ST. ANNE (Ex. 158), to which we have already attended (above, p. 53 and Ex. 142). It is not ascribed to Croft in that book, and it appears as in our example: a comparison with the bass there given with that which is now in common use reveals some interesting points. Here and there the modern bass is an improvement perhaps, but the elimination of the A minor harmony at the sixth chord of the third phrase, due to *Hymns Ancient and Modern,* was a mistake (rectified at EH 450). Parallel fifth and all, the original bass has a very solid and substantial character. Note, by the way, to which text it was originally set. It is also marked as the tune to be sung to a new metrical version of the Easter Anthems, 'Christ our Passover....'

The style of the *Supplement* is a good deal more

conservative and 'public' than that of the *Divine Companion,* since it is designed to carry the new official Psalter. It contains no hymns apart from those authorized for use along with the Psalms, but one of these happens to be 'While shepherds watched', which is marked to be sung to ST. JAMES (Ex. 145)—written out earlier with Psalm 19. It contains many of the Anglo-Genevan tunes, and plenty of material from Ravenscroft, but at one point it makes a strange departure from the text of Tate and Brady which we think had historic consequences. It is where it tries to set the Tate and Brady text of Psalm 130 to the Genevan tune (our Ex. 69B). Tate and Brady's new version has this psalm in SM, but that will not go with the tune. Another version appears in the *Supplement* in sevens and sixes, thus:

> From the lowest depths of woe
>   to God I sent my cry;
> Herken, Lord, to my complaint
>   and graciously reply....

The metre is quite consistent, and it is not the metre of Genevan Psalm 130. The Genevan metre is consistently iambic, (the same as 'The church's one foundation'); in the new version the longer lines are trochaic, so that it would really be necessary to sing the Psalm tune to it like this (though that is not how it is barred in the *Supplement*):

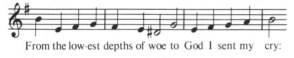

From the low-est depths of woe to God I sent my cry:

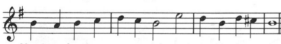

Heark-en, Lord, to my com-plaint and gra-cious-ly re-ply.

This would hardly be worth mentioning were it not that this metre became a great favourite with Charles Wesley, and is not found anywhere else before him. Since Psalm 130 has very special associations with him and his brother, they will have known this version—and Charles must have got this strange and urgent metre from the *Supplement.*

But it is not for oddities, rather for classics, that we go to the *Supplement.* Among its new tunes are Croft's HANOVER ('O worship the King', EH 466: H 288) and ST. MATTHEW (EH 526: H 517); the first in B flat, otherwise as we know it, the second in the more angular syllabic version which was later smoothed out to the form we know. The NEW 50th (Ex. 156) is included, and three new psalm versions provided for it. THE CREED (Ex. 157) with its abundance of melodic leaps, appears to have a common ancestry. And there also appears, with the metrical Lord's Prayer, the fine tune FOLKINGHAM (Ex. 159: EH 558), another tune, like ST. ANNE, with a high finish. All the older psalm tunes are given with melody only, the newer ones in two parts, and versions are as faithfully preserved as metre permits. The collection is clearly an attempt to ally the old psalm style with the new music, and we do not find here the flourishes and flights of imagination we found in the *Divine Companion.*

John Bishop (1665-1737) is another composer whose work has lasted. He was organist of Winchester College 1695-1737, and of the Cathedral from 1729; his epitaph, translated from the Latin, reads, 'A man of singular probity, of most honourable life, in his manners blameless, in the knowledge of music most learned, who, having served this college diligently for 42 years, peacefully took his place in the celestial choir, 19 December, A.D. 1737, aged 72 years'. His psalm tunes appear in a collection of original work, 'A Sett of New Psalm Tunes....', which Frost dated 1711. Ex. 160 is ILLSLEY, as it is now known, his tune for the Hundredth Psalm (Old Version), written in the old style with melody in the tenor. It has had continued use in England since his day (EH 61), and is a most satisfying melody, with particularly good part-writing. CHICHESTER (Ex. 161) deserves wider currency; it was written for Psalm 122 in the English metre as a simpler alternative to the great Genevan tune (Ex. 76). Ex. 162, BATH, is another very good example of his distinguished craft—a setting of Ps. 148 with a boisterous melodic fanfare at the end. There is also LEICESTER (or BEDFORD—EH 322, *Worshipbook* p. 631), equally sound in the graver style appropriate to Psalm 112. These are, like the tune of the *New Version,* church tunes as much as private tunes, and they all have a very sound sense of congregational capacity.

From this point a subtle change comes over the character of psalm books; many were published to go with either the New or the Old Version—for the New Version had a rough passage in England, being always more favoured in the new Colonies of America—and these begin to show a thrust towards the future with a corresponding waning of interest in the past. That tide ebbs and flows in all streams of history, and its effect is to generate books which may contain interesting new material but which show impatience with old idioms and a tendency to assimilate them to the new styles. As these words are being written Britain and America are passing through such a period. James Green's Psalter of 1715 shows some early examples of vandalistic treatment of old tunes, of which our Exx. 163 and 164 give a sufficient intimation. Green seems to have believed that if an old tune had a compass of more than a sixth it would be improved by pruning: so he lopped off the offending extremities of these tunes ST. DAVID and the OLD 104th; and when adapting an old tune to a new metre he did not scruple to alter the melody to make it sound more like a post-1660 piece—as in Ex. 164. Since there is no original work in Green worth pausing on, his counts as one of the earliest examples of a book that majors in mediocrity. There is better news in the psalter of Chetham (1718), which gives us BURFORD (EH 447: H 410), and better still in Anchors' Psalter,

1721, which produced the really distinguished melody WALSALL (Ex. 165: EH 13: H 501). There we have a return of the authentic Purcellian style.

William Tans'ur, who spelt his name thus fancifully but whom an earthbound parish registrar entered in his baptismal records as Tanzer, was an energetic music teacher in the region of St. Neots in England, and in one of several music books he produced, *A Compleat Melody, or The Harmony of Zion,* 1734, left us the very fine and expressive tune, BANGOR (Ex. 166: EH 300: H 68). This book reminds us to mention a third purpose of many books of tunes that appear about this time: we add to church worship and domestic singing the activity of music-teaching. John Playford was the first great publisher of books of musical instruction. Since his time we not infrequently find psalters and tune-books furnishing an introduction which teaches the singer how to read music. The *Supplement* of 1708 had one of these, and many of these later Psalters have them too. Music teachers were among the most energetic promoters of new psalmody, since hymn and psalm tunes furnish a very convenient source for simple melodies that can be used as examples in manuals of sight singing and part singing.

Another such manual was John Church's *Introduction to Psalmody*, 1723. We may suppose this editor to be the John Church who appears in the *Divine Companion.* After an instructive introduction he prints a number of known psalm tunes, and adds, right at the end, a tune of Henry Carey (the well known song writer) written for Joseph Addison's new hymn, 'The Lord my pasture shall prepare' (1712). This charming melody, Ex. 167, is now very well known in England in the form with grace-notes (which reflect perfectly properly the practice of singing in those days) as at EH

491, or more simply elsewhere with a plain repetition of the first long phrase: the original, as in our example, is the melody at H 295; but the score shows that it was designed as a solo with continuo accompaniment. This is surely another tune which Purcell would have loved.

Addison's remarkable short series of hymns in the *Spectator* (see the *Hymnal Guide* for details) generated another classic tune, variously called LONDON or ADDISON'S, Ex. 168, which appeared in John Sheeles's *The Skylark.* The book is undated and has often been placed about 1720; Frost says it is more probably c. 1740. But the tune is a monumental piece of architecture, a continuous and unresting melody with an imitative accompaniment (so imitative that it starts on a very unexpected note) that is one of the best examples in the literature of the 18th century 'urbanity' of style. Tunes of this time at their best resemble the genius of 18th century urban architecture in combining individual distinction with the modesty that makes it possible to repeat the design without becoming weary of it—just like an 18th century street in Bath or Edinburgh. The only concession to rhetoric is the need to repeat the final line of words, and since this brings a great tune to a resounding conclusion it is in this case entirely forgiveable.

With that we come to the end of the psalm-tune period, properly so-called, which had lasted virtually 200 years. Hereafter, though psalm tunes continue to be written, the emphasis is on hymnody. Such psalm tunes as did appear after this date, in England and later in a brief revival in Scotland, are thought of as hymn tunes, having at once been appropriated for that purpose. It is therefore a convenient point to break the thread of our story and return to the point in German hymnody, where we left it so many chapters ago.

German Hymnody, 1600-1850

When we left the Lutheran scene at 1600, the situation was that the high style of the classic Lutheran chorale was being challenged by a simpler, more ballad-like style whose popularity was beginning to gain ground. As the new century opened it was already clear that congregational song was going to be permanently affected by the demand of the people for reasonably simple music and by the fading into the past of the lofty rhetorical style that had characterized the larger-scale compositions that appeared during Luther's lifetime. Geneva had something to do with this; the restrained manner of the Genevan psalm tune attracted attention not only in Britain. We have already seen that just as one or two Lutheran tunes found their way into the Genevan repertory, so a few tunes from 1542 and 1551 fairly soon became common curreny with German texts (especially Psalm 42).

Our first few examples show the shape which German hymnody might have continued to take if the Thirty Years' War had not engulfed their culture. They are, as a group, an instructive study.

With Ex. 169 we begin a few years before the turn of the century with the tune made so famous by J. S. Bach, WIR CHRISTENLEUT. We shall constantly be referring to Bach, and in the next chapter we shall have to attend to him personally. The fact that a tune was taken up by Bach either in his cantatas, or in his organ works, or elsewhere may be taken as a reasonable indication that it was known to people in Germany in the mid-18th century. This one, with a place of honour in the Christmas Oratorio, obviously was such a tune, and indeed it is associated with a Christmas hymn; the first four words of each stanza make a detachable phrase in every case, and the tune causes that phrase to be repeated. Its popularity must be mainly due to its extreme simplicity. Not many tunes move only within the compass of a fifth, without a single note outside that range, but this one does, and it could not be easier to memorize. In all other respects it is limited and unenterprising, but congregations will put up with a great deal of that if it brings with it the premium of demanding very little effort on their part. (Musicians constantly wonder why congregations in church tolerate so much dull and tedious music; this is a different matter from tolerating positively vulgar stuff; but musicians have to live with a certain amount of this because not eveybody is like them: they are like good tennis players having to play with rabbits).

But when we get to Exx. 170-2 we get light from a quite new direction. Ex. 170 is 'Sellinger's Round', found in the keyboard works of Byrd, and very probably his. The resemblance between this and the famous tune associated in the English-speaking world with 'All glory, laud and honour', cannot go unremarked. 'All glory, laud and honour', which we call ST. THEODULPH (this being an unofficial canonization

by hymnologists of the author of the Latin original of that hymn) is in German VALET WILL ICH DIR GEBEN, a hymn for the dying, and this tune appeared with it in 1615, devised by Melchior Teschner. It takes its own line about tonality, being built on final C where the dance tune is built on final G, but obviously it was inspired by the dance tune. In Germany at that time (and one suspects, always) there was no very dogmatic attitude towards the separation of secular and sacred music, and a little later we shall see how the absence of a Calvinist inhibition about such things enriched the German hymn-vocabulary. The Byrd dance was probably known to musicians, less known to ordinary church folk. So this grand tune came of it, which remained a favourite from 1615 onwards.

Ex. 171 is a variation on that situation. Here we have a tune from Queen Elizabeth's Virginal Book (mis-titled: it is from the early 17th century) turning up in the Augsburg *Gesangbuch* of 1609 as IST GOTT FUR MICH, and again it makes a first-rate simple hymn tune. It sounds, in the original, like a transcription of a typical English ballad. One can hardly say that the British influence on German hymnody has been extensive—indeed, if pressed, we should have to admit that there are probably no other instances than these and conceivably Ex. 172.

Ex. 172 is one of only three Common Metre tunes which have come into common currency from Germany. The first we noticed at Ex. 52 and another is coming at Ex. 189. The metre is strictly English, and hardly ever favoured by German text writers. This tune, called in English books PRAETORIUS, looks in many respects like an English psalm tune, or a Scottish one, though it is never found in British books of the period. As rearranged at EH 549 it has a strictly Germanic grandeur, and its shape, with the high notes in the first half of the tune, is also typically German. But its existence may have been inspired by the fact that the metre was, by 1599, becoming settled in Britain as the standard metre for congregational songs.

Michael Praetorius, 1571-1621, who included this in his *Musae Zionae,* was an enterprising researcher who published a long series of popular tunes harmonized in four parts. Another example in EH is ACH GOTT VON HIMMELREICHE, 179. These were, like the Elizabethan psalm and song books, for the use of musical families or for church choirs, and contain many good tunes, some of which (we cannot be sure which) are his own composition. Praetorius, by the way, is a Latinization of the German name *Schulz* (which means a Guard, and corresponds therefore to the English patronymic *Ward*). Another famous Latinized name is that of Vulpius (presumably *Wolf*), who in the same year, 1609, produced a book of very good simple tunes, often of a ballad-like character. Ex. 173, CHRISTUS DER IST MEIN LEBEN, is one of the most famous, and here, perhaps even more than in Ex. 172, we see what looks like the influence of the CM Psalm tune. Its last phrase in the original (altered by Bach, Ex. 234) is the psalm-tune cadence-cliché. If it were written in CM (which would be a pity) it would look very like an English psalm tune,—sounding quite suspiciously like DUN-FERMLINE (Ex. 103) in its beginning.

Vulpius was clearly something of a genius at collect-ing or composing attractive melodies. Our Ex. 174 is now very popular outside Germany, and Ex. 175 is also making its way, deservedly. An important rhyth-mical point is introduced by these two tunes, which in modern scores should be barred as we show them. It obscures the characteristic baroque ambiguity of 3/2 when they are barred in 3-4 time. When GELOBT SEI GOTT first became known in Britain the 'Alleluias' were sometimes rhythmically misinterpreted (as in SP and CP); one has to think of them with the Germanic accent on the second syllable of 'Alleluia'. The same is true of DAS NEUGEBORNE KINDELEIN (Ex. 175)—only the learned Lutherans of America (in *Worship Supple-ment* 1969) restored the true rhythm in these tunes. But both are, in different ways, distinguished, the first ex-uberant, the second contemplative, and they are good examples of the new melodic style which began to humanize the German scene at the beginning of the 17th century.

That, of course, brings us to the immortal PASSION CHORALE (Ex. 176). This, as is now well known, started in 1601, as a secular love song, but by 1613 was appearing, without harmony but in exactly the rhythm of the example, as a hymn tune. We shall return to it when we discuss J. S. Bach. It has been associated with many texts in Germany: the first was HERZLICH THUT MICH VERLANGEN, but by the mid-century it had become associated with two famous hymns by Gerhardt, 'O Haupt voll blut und wunden' (our 'O sacred head') and 'Befiehl du deine Wege' (which we know as 'Commit thou all thy griefs').

We have here the syncopated common time, using two note-values, which became quite normal in Ger-man hymnody of this period. The archaic flourishes are beginning to disapper, syllabic melody is becoming accepted, and the interest of the melody is in its shape and rhythm.

Ex. 177 is a much less enterprising tune—in the 3-time popular style with many repeated notes. It lies behind the tune we call BRESLAU (EH 484: H 340), which is a reconstruction by Mendelssohn. Mendels-sohn had as keen an interest in hymn tunes as Bach, but a less sure touch in editing them. We have this and two other cases to notice in this section (Exx. 186 and 206), and in all three we see Mendelssohn altering the melody at important points. In this one alone we can judge that he improved the original. His architectural addition adds a soaring final phrase which arouses more interest than the rather limp ending of Ex. 177, and makes a fine tune of it. We cannot speak so kindly about the other two.

J. H. Schein, a distinguished composer of his time, left several chorales, including the admirable Ex. 178, MACH'S MIT MIR, GOTT, which lies behind the tune we call EISENACH (sometimes LEIPZIG: EH 138: H 93). This is in the original a very nicely-poised tune, with a pleasant Germanic rhythm. We owe the 'regular' form to J. S. Bach, but the reduction to LM to English editors, who often omit both Schein's rhythm and Bach's harmony and leave us with a rather undis-tinguished tune.

Then we have the quite remarkable psalm tunes of Heinrich Schutz, which take us for a moment off the main track of hymnody, since very few of them have found any sort of modern currency. But they repay any amount of close study (for example in Walter Blankenberg's edition, Barenreiter # 984, 1936). Schutz was undeniably the greatest German composer before Bach, and in his long lifetime (1585-1672) went through several distinct stylistic phases. The Psalms (1628, revised 1661), come from his middle period, before the period of self-imposed austerity during which he wrote the Passions (1662-6) which are pro-bably his most often performed works. We see in every one of them a touch of sparkling originality and a pro-found sense of the meaning of the words he was set-ting. Many are in fact quite simple tunes, though their intervals and compass have made editors of hymnals shy of using them. Ex. 179, Psalm 24, combines unusual intervals with essential simplicity. One looks at the first four notes of the second phrase and at once asks who else would have varied the rising triad in just that way, and how better the sober exultation of Psalm 24 could have been expressed. Ex. 180, Psalm 100, is very typical of the German love for putting all the high notes early in a tune (which one needs a really good composer to bring off without giving a sense of an-ticlimax). But if the psalm begins, 'O be joyful....' and descends to more contemplative expressions as it goes on (as reflected in Britten's famous C major *Jubilate*), how could this be better expressed than in that opening fanfare leading to a conclusion near the lower tonic? Psalm 121 (Ex. 181) is athletic in its climb from low D to high F: but then you sang Psalm 121 while you were making 3,000 feet of height in twelve miles between Jericho and Jerusalem. This is Schutz's 'humanistic' period in which every note expresses something elementary and, in this case, almost physical. Contrast that with the intimation of 'My soul longeth, yea fainteth' in Psalm 84 (Ex. 182).

Ex. 183 is one of his more ambitious and demand-ing settings, of which there are a few. We shall meet again the device of altering the rhythm in the course of a tune—a dramatic, one might almost say, operatic form of expression which tends to turn chorales into short motets. But then again—Psalm 45 is the one secular song in the Psalter, and that precisely is reflected in this setting. We would linger on these astonishing set-tings—Schutz used traditional tunes (with his 4-part harmony) to only 12 of the psalms, those being the ones with special associations with Luther. The only one of his tunes which appears in more than a very few modern books is his Psalm 19 (Y 24), but the Yale book has four others (## 75, 157, 239, 297) which include our Ex. 181.

Ex. 184 is a famous tune by Johann Schop, a very fine example of the new style, not without the surging and expansive gestures of the old. Schop is most famous for writing the tune behind 'Jesu, joy of man's desiring', which we shall meet at Ex. 235.

Ex. 185, Lowenstern's sombre tune CHRISTE DU BEIS-TAND, reminds us that we are now in the period of the Thirty Years' War, which was to bring such decisive changes into the German religious scene. Lowenstern wrote the text as well as the words of this hymn, which is paraphrased into a very different context in the English hymn 'Lord of our life and God of our salvation' (EH 435: H 395). In the original it is a hymn reflecting the suffering which Europe underwent as the War progressed, bringing stage after stage of confusion, plague and bereavement to Germany. The outcome of the War was a religious re-orientation whose most significant product was pietism (the German form of evangelicalism that had much to do with the inspiration of British Methodism). Now pietism—which takes its name from the *Collegium Pietatis* founded by Jakob Spener in 1670—is simply an attitude to religion, not a denomination. It exalts personal religion, prayer, charitable works and spiritual fervor at the expense of structure and doctrine: and structure and doctrine are the first casualties in a continental calamity of the scale of the Thirty Years' War. This is exactly what is reflected in the great explosion of hymnody that pietism produced (before it was officially so called), that gathered itself round the great text-writer Paulus Gerhardt (1607-76) and whose basic hymnal was *Praxis Pietatis Melica*, first edited by Johann Cruger (1598-1662).

Praxis Pietatis is said to have appeared in its first edition in 1636, in the darkest period of the War, but no copy of that edition has survived. Successive editions continued to appear, one in 1647/8 and another, the most important, in 1653. After Cruger's death the project was continued by Peter Sohren (sometimes called Sohr), who published an important edition in 1668. But the existence of this central collection inspired many other composers to write in a new style of free melody; and a similar spiritual change of direction among Catholics produced a new hymnody in that region also, largely associated with the Polish-born aristocrat and Catholic convert, Johann Scheffler (1624-77).

We are about to observe the musical response in hymnody to the pietist emphasis on the family and the individual in religion, and the best fruit of this was in the development of the gift of melody. The hymns of the pietists were sometimes extravagant in their expressiveness, but at their best they exhibit the art of the song writer, best performed by a solo voice rather than by a congregation. We shall encounter a new delicacy of melodic construction which enjoys its freedom from the rugged disciplines of congregational singing, but which also, where it is congregationally practicable, generates a broad stream of attractive and captivating tunes. In plain fact almost all the German hymns enjoyed by non-Lutheran congregations to-day are pietist hymns. Their words are almost always in the first person singular, and often, where the words have proved too intense for comfortable use by later cultures, the tunes have been transferred to others and kept alive.

Cruger's own style was conservative, certainly not uninfluenced by Geneva. Our first example of his, if it is his, is NUN DANKET ALLE GOTT (Ex. 186), one of the world's most famous tunes. In the first place, we must say that the ascription to him is not certain; if the hymn was written by Pastor Rinkart as a family grace at table, it is not impossible that he wrote a tune for the family to sing, or that the tune was this one. Only the arrangement for hymnal use may be Cruger's. But it is, obviously, one of the greatest melodies in the world. This is another tune which we often use in an arrangement by Mendelssohn—which of course transfers it at once to the context of the big congregation by harmonizing it expansively and slowing it down into a regular rhythm. But Mendelssohn deformed it by obscuring the imitation of the first phrase in the fifth: his raising of the fifth note of the fifth phrase to D (in G major) where the original has B was, one supposes, dictated by the new context he gave it in the *Hymn of Praise*, but it treated the composer's sense of structure rather cavalierly.

Ex. 189 is Cruger's charming CM tune—his only one in that metre—NUN DANKET ALL' UND BRINGET EHR, set to a long hymn of praise with many stanzas, and in English use paired with several different texts. This is real melody-making, rhythm and shape combining to make one of the most attractive tunes in this metre ever written, especially valuable for stanzas that use many trochaic openings. Ex. 187 is even more distinguished, and shows Cruger's debt to Geneva—it is, as we have said, derived from Genevan Psalm 23 (Ex. 81 and 122). The same quality is seen in the solid construction, and the use, except for one cadential phrase, of only two note values, in SCHMUCKE DICH, Ex. 188.

Ex. 190 is based on a Cruger tune, JESU MEINE ZUVERSICHT (EH 282: LUISE, H 190), but it shows a typical way in which a tune develops, or degenerates, in passing from one environment to another. The Cruger melody (B) starts out from a Lutheran melody (A) which appeared in 1539 to a kind of nursery-rhyme hymn in which the variations of words in the three stanzas are minimal. That tune in turn was simplified into a tune to a simpler metrical version of the Creed in six-line stanzas (replacing the text of our Ex. 29)—the date of the text being 1609 and of the revised tune, 1699. Cruger's new tune appeared in 1653 with the pietist text JESU MEINE ZUVERSICHT, but in the same

year in Runge's Gesangbuch a simpler version, with
the first long phrase repeated, appeared and this is the
version often erroneously ascribed to Cruger (B). J. S.
Bach picked up the Runge tune and arranged the
melody as at (D). Neander, in 1680, coined a popular-
style tune in triple rhythm using the opening phrase
(E), and the English tune RATISBON (AM 7: H 153) is a
conflation of the old 1539 opening, Neander's third
strain (after the double bar) and a new cadential phrase
(F). This was put together by Werner in 1815.
Sometimes authorities write disparagingly of RATISBON
as the perversion of the work of Cruger, but there is
not a note originally composed by Cruger in it.

Among other Cruger tunes in modern hymnals are
JESU, MEINE FREUDE (H 453: usually known in Bach's
version), HEIL'GER GEIST (EH 76: H 57), a very good
example of a great deal of musical argument condens-
ed into a very restricted space (21 notes only); HERR·
DEINEN ZORN, or LOBET DEN HERREN (EH 223: OBLA-
TION, H 205), a foursquare Sapphic tune predating by
a short interval the great series in this metre produced
by the French Catholics (later, pp 78-80) and the
tune we now call CRUGER (EH 45: Y 111), which is an
English adaptation of one of the composer's less successful inspirations.

Cruger was a musician and a theologian, lived his
last forty years in the service of St. Nicolas Cathedral,
Berlin, and undoubtedly was the Louis Bourgeois of
German pietist hymnody. His style is usually fairly
grave, but he was capable of producing AUF AUF, MEIN
HERZ (Ex. 191), which shows another side of the new
melodic inventiveness that was to serve pietism so well.
His successor, Peter Sohren, wrote in a similar style;
one tune of his is at EH 72: H 556, GUTE BAUMEN
BRINGEN—very much in the sturdy Cruger style but
originally breaking into triple rhythm, or syncopated
duple, in its final phrase. Ex. 196, another of his tunes
(original of EH 138 ii) has a similar rhythmic 'break'
for the last phrase—which indeed is difficult to inter-
pret, for without that intrusive Common Time sign the
tune would be in straight triple time. But the old
custom of ambiguous rhythm died hard—but it really
was, by 1668, nearly dead altogether.

Christoph Peter and J. G. Ebeling, contemporaries
of Cruger and no doubt friendly competitors, both
have a lighter and more overtly cheerful approach to
things. Peter's tune for JESU MEINE FREUDE (Ex. 192)
makes an interesting comparison with Cruger's, which
was published only two years before it; and DAS HERR-
LICH (Ex. 193) is another merry tune, with a very
satisfactory rhythmic 'break' in the slightly elongated
last phrase. Ebeling's amusing tune DU MEINE SEELE
SINGEN (Ex. 195) can be read at *Pilgrim* 189 and
deserves wider recognition. His WARUM SOLLT ICH
(sometimes called BONN: Y 57: EBELING, H 32), at Ex.
194, competes with a tune half the length by Cruger,
and in the end has won.

All these make fine congregational tunes—simple,

direct and melodious. But they are examples of the
song-writer's art in the new age: tunes which go best
when accompanied, and use the kind of melody that is
essentially the top part of a two-part musical structure,
more and more firmly framed in the common chord.
Modality is passing away: rhythmic subtlety will not
last much longer: what we now see is what anybody
calls simply a good tune. However, if one turns to the
later pages of Zahn—who arranges his monumental
catalogue of 8,806 tunes in expanding order of metre—
one sees the other side of pietist hymnody, which is an
extravagant exploitation of the solo, occasionally even
the virtuoso, manner. Of this we give just two examples out of the dozens we could have found.

Ex. 197, GEH AUF, is one of 107 tunes composed by
Georg Joseph for a publication in which he collaborated with Scheffler, the Catholic convert, called
Heilige Seelenlust (1657). One of his tunes lies behind
that which we now call ANGELUS (EH 266: H 168), and
in its original version is very clearly, like all his tunes, a
soprano solo. This one is—and far from unusually—in
the 'overture and first movement' style which Italian
composers were beginning to use in secular music. It is
almost unique, one guesses, in using in the same tune a
breve and a quaver (eighth note), the one being sixteen
times the value of the other. That is one way in which
secular music which one could hardly unfairly call
'show business' music invades Christian devotion. In
another style is Ex. 198, WIE SCHNECKT ES SO LIEBLICH,
a hilarious example of operatic coloratura. Its composer is a certain Hasse, of whom virtually nothing is
known, but whom we may suspect of being a senior
member of the family which produced that famous (in
his day) contemporary of Handel, Johann Adolph
Hasse, who was married to Faustina, a celebrated
operatic singer. This composer and singer were among
the foremost interpreters of the new Italianate music in
the 18th century.

That, we may say, is taking pietist individualism
quite far enough. But when the same personal fervour
is disciplined into public communication, when, we
might say, all this new energy is put through a narrower channel, then intensity increases, and we get
such masterpieces as the two tunes of Ahle, LIEBSTER
JESU (Ex. 199) and ES IST GENUG (Ex. 200). Glance at
the ruminative beauty of the famous baptismal hymn
tune in its original version (beautifully captured, even
with so much rhythmic alteration, in Bach's organ
preludes on the tune); taken very slowly as a solo,
LIEBSTER JESU makes a profound impact. But so do
those three rising major seconds in ES IST GENUG (Ex.
200), which so captured the imagination of Bartok that
he used the tune as the peroration of his Violin Con-
certo.

Similarly Georg Neumark, in the famous WER NUR
DEN LIEBEN GOTT (Ex. 201), written for his own text
which has so poignant a history, achieves a melody of
perfect balance and powerful rhetoric. (Notice that as

he wrote it the sixth is not flattened, as it is in most books to-day). The simplicity of that tune disguises its origin as a solo piece; UM DEN LIEBEN FRIEDEN (Ex. 202) is more obviously a solo—it may begin like a chorale, but its personal nature is given away by that chromatic passage after the double bar.

From the same period comes the world-famous tune LOBE DEN HERREN (Ex. 203), originally styled HAST DU DENN, JESU, because it first appeared with that text in 1665. We give here the 1665 form and that which appeared in the 1668 *Praxis Pietatis*, and it will be seen how both differ from what we are now accustomed to, which is an English arrangement of the tune made in 1863 by Sterndale Bennett for the first English translation of the words, 'Praise to the Lord, the Almighty'. That arrangement, made by just about the best musical mind in the business at the time, is an admirable translation into the congregational medium of a tune which once again was originally designed as a solo—and a Passiontide hymn at that.

From the next decade come several tunes now well known; one is the simple and sturdy tune we call HEINLEIN and usually set to 'Forty days and forty nights' (EH 73: H 55); this is now known to be not by the composer whose name it bears (for one of his, see EH 655) but by the short-lived Martin Herbst (1654-81), and appeared in the Nuremberg *Gesangbuch* of 1676/7. Of the same date is the tender tune SCHONSTER HERR JESU (EH 323: H 356 ii), composed for the original of 'Fairest Lord Jesus', and later swept off the map by the vulgar tune now inseparable from that text. That is from the Munster Gesangbuch, 1677. Another straightforward tune which immediately makes a good congregational impact is ALLE MENSCHEN MUSSEN STERBEN, now often called SALZBURG (EH 128: H 53) and sung almost exactly as it first appeared (allowing only for the adaptation of 8.7.8.7.88.77 to eight sevens) and not altered by so much as one melody note in Bach's arrangement. That is by Jacob Hinze, 1622-1702 and appeared first in 1678.

The romantic and tragic young schoolmaster Joachim Neander, whose pietism was so intense that he was dismissed by the governors of the school in Bremen where he taught, and who died of phthisis after living in a cave (in the valley still known as Neanderthal) in 1680, at the age of 30, was a musician and a text writer. Besides giving us the original of 'Praise to the Lord, the Almighty', he gave us both text and tune of 'All my hope on God is founded' (for the tune see CP 417, SP 442), and another most useful tune UNSER HERRSCHER or NEANDER (EH 380: H 90). These and others of his appeared in his posthumous collection of 1680. Johann Franck, a physician in Hamburg, composed many tunes for hymns by Heinrich Elmhorst (a now forgotten author) including the excellent tune KOMM SEELE (Ex. 204); only very slightly altered at EH 486 this too makes a fine congregational song, though its open-hearted candour and cheerful-

ness disguises the fact that originally it was set to a hymn on that favourite subject of pietism, the Passion.

The multiplicity of new texts produced by pietist authors was matched by a new freedom in the talent of composers, who frequently now were writing new tunes for texts which already had their tunes. Although the norm of all German hymnody was still, and indeed remained, the 'proper' tune which could be identified simply by the opening words of the text it was married to, we here have situations like that in Ex. 205-7, where in less than fifteen years 'O Gott, du Frommer Gott' gets three tunes—all so good that in one form or another they survive in use to-day. Ex. 205, originally appearing in 1646, was appropriated for the text in 1690 and altered—perhaps improved—in the process. Ex. 206 was written for the text in 1693, and lies behind the tune we call MUNICH (EH 195: H 402), which was adapted from Mendelssohn's arrangement of the older tune in *St. Paul*: this is the third time we meet a Mendelssohn arrangement, and once again he has added a modern extension to an old building, moving the focal point back one phrase. In this case we do not judge it an improvement, since the real force of phrase 7 is wholly lost in the new pattern. In Ex. 207 we have a tune which, though intended as a solo in pietist style, proved to have the makings of a superbly dignified chorale in the hands of Bach. All three are in their different ways great melodies, and show how the gift for almost instinctive construction of fine tunes was developing.

Yet another result of the population-explosion in hymns is provided in Ex. 208, which is the original of what we call WINCHESTER NEW (EH 9: H 10). In 1690 this appears as a tune to 'Wer nur den Lieben Gott' (cf Ex. 201) in 9.8.9.8.88: within a few years it appears expanded to take the longer lines of DIR, DIR, JEHOVA in 9.10.9.10.10.10. It is so solidly constructed that it can tolerate this process without fundamental disturbance, and indeed in its English form (Havergal, 1847) it still remains a wholly satisfying LM tune.

The 1704 version of that tune brings in the name of Johann Anastasius Freylinghausen (1670-1739). One might call Freylinghausen the further end of the historical arch of which the hither end is Cruger, for if Cruger brought the chorale to its highest point of congregational practicability and urbane attractiveness, Freylinghausen is the greatest pure song-writer of them all. He was admired by Bach, and no wonder. Between 1704 and 1714 he produced a series of editions and collections, the most celebrated being *Geistreiches Gesangbuch*, which are great storehouses of pure melody; the tunes are mostly his compositions or arrangements. We can here quote only a few, but consider Ex. 209, and its artful setting of a regular stanza in a beautiful and subtle metre. Here we have pairs of lines falling into two halves: first, two four-syllable phrases in the Form — u u —: then a long iambic eleven-syllable line. Our editorial barring is designed to show with what innocent artistry the composer balances two emphatic 3-4 phrases with a long phrase in 3-4/3-2, thus introducing good debate between the regular style of the music and the charming asymmetry of the text.

Ex. 210, surviving in *Songs of Syon* (# 354) shows a great melodist packing much energy and drama into the very restricted space of 27 syllables. It is like, but more significant than, the two tunes he wrote for 'Gott sei dank': both that which we know as LUBECK (EH 552: firmly domesticated at H 253) and that still called GOTT SEI DANK (e.g. *Presbyterian Hymnbook*, 6) are found much as we know them (the first exactly as EH 552) in Freylinghausen's work, and they are variants of the same tune.

Ex. 211 is another beautiful and restrained song-style tune, only in currency at EH 97 but rightly loved by those to whom it is available. Here again is the melodist's 'art concealing art'. FAHRE FORT (Ex. 212) is now known as the tune behind our MONKLAND (EH 532: H 308)—having passed into English use through its use by a Moravian community in England and its arrangement for a hymn, 'Praise, O praise our God and King' written by Henry Baker in 1861. But the real origin of this tune lies further back—as will be seen if FAHRE FORT is compared with the *Piae Cantiones* tune O QUAM MUNDUM at Ex. 212B. This explains the unusually irregular and episodic character of the tune as Freylinghausen gives it.

After Freylinghausen there is a fairly steady drift downhill. Eighteenth century German hymnody is very little used now by Germans, and survives usually in adaptations made in the 19th century by enthusiastic English editors.

It looks indeed as if the popular aspect of evangelical pietism is beginning to take over. There is a tendency in new hymns to write in shorter stanzas, and in the new tunes for everything to be on a much smaller scale both of construction and of imagination.

Ex. 213, SOLLT ES GLEICH, BISWEILEN SCHEINEN, first appeared in C. F. Witt's *Psalmodia Sacra*, 1715, in that form. It survives as STUTTGART (EH 40: H 1) in English-speaking use, and the version made of it by *Hymns Ancient and Modern* the one mostly now used, has a little more strength than the original. In any form it shows that strange German tendency to allow the melodic interest to fall off after the first half of a tune (we shall meet it again in a very different environment when we come to J. B. Dykes).

Ex. 215, WAS IST, DAS MICH BETRUBT, is a graceful and quiet tune which lies behind the well known English tune FRANCONIA (EH 370: H 418), and in this case we cannot claim that the English form is an improvement. The source is Konig's *Harmonischer Lieder-Schatz*, which contains other tunes of the same pleasant quality. Another short tune not without merit in the original is Ex. 216, RINGE RECHT, which becomes in English use, BATTY (EH 105: H 72)—the English version again being firmly domesticated. In the same

metre we have GOTT WILLS MACHEN, (Ex. 214: EH 253), by the Swiss composer J. L. Steiner (1688-1761) who was State Trumpeter at Zurich—and it looks like a real bandmaster's tune. In English use it always appears with rather hearty lightweight hymns which its march-like manner (the opening phrase reflects an internal rhyme in the German) seems to suggest. (The best arrangement of it is, we think, Walford Davies's extension of it with the entertaining hymn 'Angels holy'—see CP 39).

Ex. 217 is from Reimann's *Neuer Melodien Evangel. Leider* (1747)—the source which also gives us O JESU (EH 406). This may be the first time a tune appears with the maximum key-signature, and its rhythm is one which seems to have been very popular about this time. It appears again in the two versions of a tune at Ex. 218 (EH 42: AM 77, but compare AMS 746). The appearance of the tune in both 'authentic' and 'plagal' versions is unique in the literature; it is in a manuscript collection which belonged to Dr. Zahn and was the work of a certain Johann Heinrich Reinhardt, dated 21 June - 22 July, 1754. This tune shares a line with our Ex. 242, and it looks very like a popular tune brought into sacred use. In the manuscript the version we know in D is written in F: and one can imagine the composer wondering whether the very high final was really negotiable, and producing another version for that reason: it must have been that way round. As WAS LEBET, WAS SCHWEBET, the version with the high final has become quite well known in English-speaking books.

So things drifted on. Both the 'public' and the 'private' streams of sacred song seem to have been in spate. Easy tunes were being written for congregations which did not feel up to the demands of the classics, and alongside them, solo songs for the further diversion of listeners. To this latter group C. P. E. Bach made his contribution in a considerable collection published serially up to 1788, and Ex. 219 is one example from this—with very free use of baroque ornaments (like those we find in some English evangelical songs of the period). SO JEMAND SPRICHT hardly has the inspiration of the Schemelli book but it is a fair example of what seems to have been called for at that time. JESUS UNSER TROST (Ex. 220) is a more solid specimen in the public manner—much more like an average 'good tune' of the coming century, and well paired in Hymns A & M (609) with an Easter hymn. Of similar quality and attractiveness is GROSSE PROPHETE, which we know as QUEDLINBURG (Ex. 221)—yet another dactylic tune in elevens, from a manuscript chorale book of J. C. Kittel, preserved again by Zahn.

The composer J. A. P. Schulz (1747-1800) is best known now for his secular tune WIR PFLUGEN (EH 293: H 138) which goes with 'We plough the fields and scatter'—not in Zahn because of its secular origin. Schulz was at home in both the orthodox and the popular styles. Our Ex. 222 shows him writing a very simple tune in the metre of INNSBRUCK—two long phrases repeated, differing only at the cadences. His nursery-rhyme tune, Ex. 223, became very popular in Germany during the romantic period, and it is entertaining to find, in the celebrated EKG *(Evangelisch Kirchen-Gesangbuch),* of the present century—which is packed with classic German pre-1715 tunes—a concession to popular taste in the inclusion both of this and also of an arrangement of 'Home, sweet Home' beginning with the same first line but marked 'Irische Melodie' and set to a text (1834) which is clearly an ecclesiastical version of the old song, (Ex. 224).

Another 'popular' composer of the 1790s was J. H. Knecht, who in a series of publications produced a number of eyebrow-raising tunes. The soundest of his which is in modern currency is OHNE RAST, which we usually call VIENNA (EH 500: H 239)—and which we sing without the flattened note in the third phrase (Ex. 225); in England we also use DER NIEDEN MENSCHHEIT HILLE, which we call KNECHT (EH 452) as a pleasant setting of 'O happy band of pilgrims'; in America this tune is known in a new version twice the length, usual-ly called ST. HILDA (H 407). But Knecht and his col-league Christmann (they jointly produced the 1799 source of the foregoing tune) were clearly much in-fluenced not only by popular music but by the operatic music of the time, and perhaps in Ex. 226, SCHMAL IST DER PFAD, we have one of the earliest full-blown operatic-aria tunes of the kind which became so very popular in both Germany and England in the 19th cen-tury. The stanza-shape is exactly the same as that of Bonar's hymn, 'Light of the world', which has at-tracted a number of notable examples of the operatic style in English non-anglican hymnals (CP 177, for ex-ample: and CH² 189). To this matter we shall return in our Victorian section.

Ex. 227 is irresistible for anybody's collection of Stuffed Owl church music. The reader will first suspect that Mendelssohn must have known it—we remember what he did with that opening phrase. But as the tune goes on it breathes exactly the spirit, though it uses none of the phrases, of the *Marseillaise*—that in-imitable collection of unrelated phrases building up to a masterpiece of more or less meaningless rhetoric. And the date is right too.

The study of German hymn tunes at this period, which of course can be pursued in Zahn, is a project demanding the staying power of a really tough social worker. During the period 1825-1925 the most popular tunes in Europe certainly included GROSSER GOTT (H 273), whose English form is HURSLEY (EH Ap. 39) and Bortniansky's ICH BETE AN DIE MACHT DER LIEBE (H 499), which is sometimes called ST. PETERSBURG. It is the period of SICILIAN MARINERS (H 247), ST. ELIZABETH (H 236) and STILLE NACHT (H 33). Un-dulating thirds and sixths become almost an obsession with composers and congregations.

There was occasional relief from imposed sentimen-tality. J. G. Schicht (1753-1823), a late successor of Bach's at St. Thomas's, Leipzig, produced a number of sturdy and shapely tunes, of which Ex. 228 (EH 119) is one, and others are those we call MANNA (AM 389) and ASCENSION (CP 427). The original of our tune to 'As with gladness men of old', TREUER HEILAND (Ex. 229) has good qualities which the English revision ruthlessly removes, and the same could be said of AUF, AUF WEIL (Ex. 231) which Lowell Mason fashioned in-to our MANNHEIM (EH 426: H 524). Filitz's excursions into blamelessness—MORGENGLANTZ (Ex. 230: com-pare CAPETOWN, EH 501) for example, provide some relief from the prevailing diet of rich platitude, and perhaps the most agreeable thing that came out of this period was the same composer's WEM IN LEIDEN-STAGEN, which we call CASWALL or BEMERTON (EH 315 i: H 335), whose complete modesty and lack of pretension gives it an affinity with such English tunes as TALLIS'S ORDINAL.

In this age there was very little scholarly archaism, or attempt to recover the quality of the classic past; what archaism there was was tainted with the hyster-ical sentimentality of the Cecilian Societies. But it is pleasant to end this section with a tune by that renown-ed scholar to whose majestic compendium of German tunes we have so constantly made reference—Johan-nes Zahn, 1817-95. His *Die Melodien der Deutsche Evangelisches Kirchen-Leider* occupied him in publica-tion for almost forty years, 1854-93; but he was a gifted composer and allowed himself to include a few of his own compositions among the nearly 9,000 tunes he included in his six volumes. Our last Example, 232, is one of these, and although he prints it with a bar-line at every fourth beat, if we honor him by omitting those it has, in most of its phrass, an almost Genevan reticence, quite unlike anything being written at the time.

We have now reached the mid-19th century, and German hymnody has almost run away into the sand. The earlier 20th-century German hymnals indicate in their contents what the German congregations and pastors thought of all this; as we have indicated, they confine themselves almost entirely to the pre-1715 classics: there is hardly anything else in the 342 stan-dard hymns to which local editions of EKG add their own supplements, and in the later sections of this book there are occasional sudden slides into a style which equals the contemporary English in triviality. It was not until the days of Hitler's persecution that serious attempts were made to produce new music that honored the ancient styles, and we shall be able to mention this at a later stage—and also the revolu-tionary material which, hoping to sweep away the romantic sentimentality, has in part succeeded in sweeping away the classics as well. But all that must wait for a while.

10
J. S. Bach and Hymnody

It is always said of J. S. Bach that he never invented a musical form, but that whatever he touched, he illuminated. It cannot be said for certain that he ever composed a hymn or chorale tune, yet there was never, in the whole history of the subject, a more devoted hymn-lover than he. During that large part of his life that he spent in Leipzig (1723-50) hymns were constantly in his mind. That pietist culture into which he was born brought hymns right into the centre of Christian worship; but it was typical of Bach that he should be never merely content with playing them as an organist was obliged to do, but that he should ask every question about them and explore the furthest reaches of their musical content and associations.

In his organ works, one hundred and thirty-four compositions are devoted to the celebration of hymns which were in his people's repertory—The *Orgelbuchlein* (S 599-644), the Schubler Preludes (645-50), the 'Leipzig Eighteen' (651-668), the *Klavierubung* Part III (669-689) the Miscellaneous chorale-preludes (690-740) and the four Partitas (766-9). All the Cantatas use hymns and some take the subject matter of all their movements from the tunes associated with the texts they use. Most famously, the climaxes of the dramatic movement in the Passions are marked with hymns chosen with masterly sensitiveness.

It is the Cantatas and the Passions which give us what we call loosely the 'Bach chorales'—by which we always mean chorales arranged by Bach. In the surviving Cantatas, so far as we can ascertain, the oldest tunes he uses are those of the 1523/4 Luther books, while the newest was the 1679 tune we have at Ex. 207; it is as if a modern composer doing the same thing used the whole English repertory from the OLD HUNDREDTH to ABBOT'S LEIGH.

What we say here must take account of this prodigious output, and then deal briefly with that other great collection of sacred songs, quite different in purpose and musical texture, the Schemelli *Gesangbuch* of 1736.

We can distinguish the two kinds of music by calling the first kind the chorales, and the other kind the songs. Now the chorales which come from Cantatas and Passions we can trace to their sources, though in the dating of them we have to rely on the astute researches of William H. Scheide, the only scholar to put out a systematic method of dating the Cantatas; but many of the tunes we know are found only in the *371 Vierstimmige Chorale,* available for modern use in the classic edition of Albert Riemenschneider. The intricate history of the way this collection developed is recounted in that edition. The important point here is that no Bach manuscript of many of them has survived. Almost exactly half of them are not found in any extant work of Bach's (the number is 185), and we can only speculate on whether they belong to Cantatas

which have never been found, or whether they were written out by Bach in preparation for the part of the project he never lived to complete. The editions, however, on which Riemenscheider and his predecessors relied are the 200 Chorales published in 1764, edited by J. Agricola, Bach's son-in-law, and the ampler edition of 1784-7 published under the oversight of C. P. E. Bach, son of Johann Sebastian, who had protested in 1769 against the incompleteness, inaccuracy and general ineptitude of Agricola's work. We may now feel that in Riemenschneider we have the best attempt that can be made to reconstruct the entire collection, but he points out in certain places that the earlier copyists changed the keys of the chorales from time to time (our Ex. 236, for example, appears in D, not in C as in the St. Matthew Passion).

But so massive a collection provides all the evidence for a lifetime's study of this aspect alone of Bach's work, and all we need do here is indicate the general principles on which Bach made these arrangements of tunes so well known to his people.

The first thing to say is that this is public music, whereas the songs in the Schemelli Collection, as we shall see, are private music. They are conceived on a large scale, orchestrated for whatever instruments are called for in the work that contains each, and translated from the idiom of the original into that in which Bach wrote the rest of his work.

This means that in the very large majority of cases, the original tune undergoes considerable alteration. The provision of four-part harmony, often of a sophisticated contrapuntal kind, is one such major change. Another however is in the recasting of certain phrases in the melodies themselves.

Ex. 233, WACHET AUF, is a good place to begin in this brief visit to Bach's workshop. Ex. 57 is, of course, the original of this tune. Observe what, in arranging it for the final chorale in Cantata 140, Bach has done.

(a) In the first place, so far as the rhythm of so irregular a stanza can be reduced to regularity, it is so reduced. Compensating for the removal of rhythmic interest, the bass and the other four parts introduce harmonic interest.

(b) In the second half of the second phrase, the voices are not required to remain on or near the very high note, but are brought down smoothly to the cadence on the diatonic scale.

(c) When the climax comes with the return of that high note, it is made easier for the voice by being transferred to a strong beat. (Notice exactly the same process in the third phrase of a much simpler tune, at Ex. 234—cf. Ex. 173).

(d) In fitting the tune into the new orthodox harmonic system, note how the composer varies the cadences as much as he can (contrast this with the cadences of Ex. 59).

(e) The much slower movement demanded by the idiom of the choral writing and the introduction of the counterpoint causes Bach frequently to fill in leaps in the melody with passing notes.

All these are elementary devices to be found throughout Bach's choral-arrangements, and corresponding modifications of melody take place when he is weaving a chorale into the counterpoint of an organ prelude.

Ex. 235B is actually a composite edition from three of Bach's different arrangements of the tune WERDE MUNTER, of which he was clearly very fond. The original here is by Schop (for whom cf. Ex. 184), and it is in a spirited but rather monotonous rhythm probably more appropriate to a solo than to a choral piece; Bach smooths out the rhythm into a regular pattern of 4-bar phrases, in the process reducing the tune to a simple a-a-b-a form, and then introduces the counterpoint to put back the expressiveness of which the rhythmic reduction had deprived it. In Riemenschneider 95, 121 and 233, from which this version is taken (it is at *Westminster Praise* 31), there are subtle variations in the melody between the three versions as well as different harmonies. This tune appears also, much more famously, in regular triple time in 'Jesu, joy of man's desiring' (Cantata 147).

Ex. 236 is one of the six versions of the PASSION CHORALE to be found in the *371,* and one of the four in the St. Matthew Passion. EH 102 gives this as the second version (Riemenschneider 89) and an earlier version in the Passion (R. 98) as the first. Other hymnals that contain this tune use either R. 98 or the very similar version at R. 74 (the one which opens, in C major, with an A minor chord).

This is a familiar and splendid example of Bach's use of chormatic harmony to express deep emotion and stress, being the last of the versiⲓns in the *St. Matthew Passion,* at a point where the drama is at its height of tragedy. Enough has been made of this point in celebrated commentaries on Bach to make it necessary for us merely to refer to it here. But notice how at every point, from the sixth chord onwards, Bach takes the opportunity to introduce restlessness into the texture by the substitution of a chromatic for a diatonic bass.

Now Bach is introducing a whole new vocabulary into hymnody by using harmonic resources as rich as these. Chromatic melody has already appeared as an expression of stress implied in the associated text—we see it in Exx. 182, 199, 201 above. But the essence of Bach's technique is to use rich chromatic counterpoint once only, to express the special meaning of a particular stanza, and no tune thus harmonized by him is designed to be sung several times over to succeeding stanzas.

Moreover—the release into the vocabulary of all this harmonic colour caused later composers to use incautiously resources of a similar kind and to produce compositions which were merely sensational. The secret of the difference is what we expose in Ex. 236B. In the fifth phrase of the chorale there is a dramatic clash of tonalities—to which attention is drawn by the appearance of D sharp and E flat in the bass part of a single measure. What is really happening is that C major and C minor are being brought abruptly together. The two scales in contrary motion, one in one key and one in the other, contain notes every one of which is represented in the full harmony of that passage—the two starred notes appear in the same chord, and the dashed notes represent the actual sung melody. Bach's astonishing effects of harmony are always (and lesser composers' never) produced by the juxtaposition of perfectly commonplace musical ideas—by purposeful scales and (as we are about to see) simple unadorned cadential phrases.

Not infrequently, of course, a chromatic passage is introduced in one part—a simple section of a chromatic scale. Ex. 237 is Bach's version of MACH'S MIT MIR, GOTT (Ex. 178) in the *St. John Passion.* Notice two points of special interest—the harsh progression in phrase 2, and the steady chromatic bass, making necessary a series of remarkable discords, in the last phrase. (At EH 138 i we have a composite version, using mostly the plainer version, with no known source, at R. 44, but taking measures 3-4 from R. 310, which is in our Example.) Observe also the expressive 'sobbing' motif in the alto part of the fifth phrase—the repeated notes being tied over in the string accompaniment. Here again, the smoothing out of the rhythm is more than repaid by the dramatic harmonies—which, as we say, in any other composer would have been merely sensational.

For similar effects, and especially for the very expressive distribution of parts (occasional large gaps between tenor and alto, for example) see HERZLIEBSTER JESU at EH 70 ii, or in its later appearances in the St. Matthew Passion. (Note: EH 70 i is not Bach, but a plausible reconstruction of his idiom for congregational use).

One more example of this gift of Bach's for sound-painting is Ex. 238E, ACH GOTT UND HERR. In this example everything that can possibly happen does happen. In the first place Bach takes over a tune which on its first appearance in 1625 (same source as Ex. 177) is in the minor mode, beginning on D with no key signature (we have transposed this in our example into the key Bach uses). Later the tune began to appear in the major, which is the mode Bach uses. Once again, two versions of this are in currency, the plainer and more diatonic one at EH 329, and the one we give. This appearing in Cantata 48 (R. 279) plunges at once into chromatic harmony, introduces a most unexpected and moving cadence at the end of the third phrase, and reaches a climax so harmonically involved that it requires an extra two measures to unravel itself, one resolution after another. But the four chords in the second half of the first phrase can be analysed as in our appended diagram into what is essentially a five-part conception involving the simplest musical phrases. In four part writing the alto moves from F natural to F sharp after rising from C: but what we really have is a tiny splash of B flat minor in the bass fighting with a general colour of G minor in the other phrases, and the movement of every part is not in itself sensational but purely rational.

The effect of these chorales on hymnody in general was decisive in putting a professional seal, as it were, on what up to that time others had been exploring, charting and wrestling with. As elsewhere, nothing here was positively invented by Bach, but what others had done he took immeasurably further than any of his predecessors took it; and the three most important aspects of the modern hymn tune which, after Bach, remained accepted for two centuries, were first, the regular-measure rhythm, second, expressiveness, and third, four-part harmony. All these emerged from either the pietist culture or the development of music. Just as in the English scene we found that the 'new music' of the Italian 17th century gradually found its way into the vocabulary of all Europe, so we find, in pietist hymnody, a settling down of hymns into a song style which is quite unlike the primitive monodic style. Public four-part harmony was by no means unknown —we saw examples of it as early as Exx. 57-8. But after Bach it became more and more the accepted way of scoring a tune. And pietism, the religion primarily of experience and immediacy rather than of historic dogma, was an environment in which expressiveness in melody and harmony could develop freely. Since we cannot tell which, if any, melodies Bach composed (and those which he did will be among those we are about to discuss, not the chorale-arrangements) what we observe in Bach is the use of harmonic and contrapuntal devices to bring out the emotional content, not only of a whole hymn, but of a particular stanza in it. These are all devices which later composers felt free to use, and which many such composers used with an unsure touch. That is also why many German tunes in English-speaking use have appeard in versions which owe their rhythm, of not also their harmony, to Bach's versions. It is as if, once Bach had translated them into a universal language, they became available to cultures very different from those in which they had originally been born.

Bach's other contribution to hymnody is in his editions of melodies in the *Musicalisches Gesangbuch* of George Christian Schemelli (1676-?) which was published in 1736. Schemelli had been in the choir at St. Thomas's, Leipzig when at school—before Bach arrived there—and was cantor at Zeitz. He commissioned Bach to edit the melodies in this book (of which in the Bach Gesellschaft edition there are 75, in Riemenschneider, 68). These are all scored for melody and figured bass; when they appear in modern editions in four parts the inner parts usually follow the edition made by George Wüllner (1832-1902).

Some of these tunes are from older sources, including Freylinghausen; others, which are untraceable elsewhere, are thought to be Bach's own, but none can be positively so identified. Many are certainly good enough to be the work of the finest melodist in the world, and our Ex. 239 might well be one of them. If any internal evidence can be adduced, it would be the continuity of the melody and the regularity of the relation between melody and measure. Another which it is very tempting to call Bach's would be KOMMT SEELEN, DIESER TAG (R 67: BG 43: S 479: see SP 60).

Possibly Ex. 240, DIR DIR JEHOVA, is also his. It is a new tune for the hymn first set by the longer form of our Ex. 208, in a very different rhythmic pattern, with subtle ambiguities in the triple rhythm.

Ex. 241, EINS IST NOTH, has not been found elsewhere but its two-movement form suggests a possible earlier pietistic source, and the phrase immediately following the double bar appears again in Ex. 218 which looks rather like a secular song tune.

Ex. 242, SALVE CORDIS GAUDIUM, becoming in translation, JESU MEINES HERTZENS FREUD, has an interesting history which parallels that of Ex. 238. It begins with a tune in Ahle's *Choralbuch* of c. 1664, which is not by Ahle but, according to Zahn, by a 'good friend' of his; and this is Ex. 242A. In the Schemelli book, Bach decorates it as at Ex. 242C, but using the original minor tonality. In the *371* it also appears (Ex. 242B) recast by Bach in the major key, with its opening phrase aligned with the third phrase by being taken a third higher. (There is no other surviving source for 242B.)

Among other well known melodies in this collection are SEELENBRAUTIGAM, by Adam Drese, 1668, nowadays found both in its original rhythm (EH 272: AM 35) and with its rhythm reduced as in Bach's version, and AUF, AUF! MEIN SEEL' (Ex. 191). One of Freylinghausen's most stately tunes taken into the Schemelli book is JESU, MEINES GLAUBENS ZIER (EH 118: H 78). The following Table indicates how many of these tunes have found their way into modern use.

TABLE FOR J. S. BACH

Example in this book	Riemenschneider Number	Organ works Schmiede (BWV) #
		K: Klavierubung III
		L: Leipzig Eighteen
		M: Miscellaneous
		P: Partita
		OB: Orgelbuchlein
		Sc: Schubler
6		OB 602
28	28, 170	L 659-61: M 699: OB 599
29	133	K 680-1
30	36, 84, 97	
31	127	K 678-9: OB 635
32	183	
33	4, 290, 335	OB 638
34	10	K 686-7
35	30	K 688-9, L 665-6
36	187	L 667, OB 631

Example in this book	Riemenschneider Number	Organ works
37	69	L 651-2
38	20, 250, 273	M 720
40	47, 110, 267	K 682-3, M 737, OB 636
41	66, 119	K 684-5
42	46, 344	M 700-1, 738: OB 606
43	72	
44	260, 362	M 734
45	125, 249, 313, 326	K 675-7: L 662-4: M 711, 715-7
46	63, 103, 117, 289, 355	
47	41, 115, 120, 265	
48	2, 272, 341	
51	17	OB 629
52	54, 276, 342	M 732: OB 609
54	18	M 703, 724: OB 600
55	257	
56	86, 195, 278, 305, 323	M 739
57	179	Sc 645
60	177, 148	Sc 649
61	58, 107, 277	
62		OB 603, 607 (different versions of tune)
64	5, 309	L 653
65	201, 306	OB 622
71A	7, 116, 268, 296	
77	68, 247	L 668: OB 641

Example in this book	Riemenschneider Number	Organ works
80	29, 64, 76, 282	
121	197	OB 627
169	55, 321, 360	M 710: OB 612
(170)	24, 168	M 735-6
173	6, 316	
175	53, 178	
176 (217)	21, 74, 80, 89, 98, 270, 288, 345, 367	M 727
177		
178	44, 310	
185	50	
186	32, 330	L 657
187	59, 7, 105, 111	
188	22	L 654
190	175, 338	M 728
191	Schemelli 27	
199	131, 328	M 706, 730-1: OB 633-4
200	216	
201	62, 104, 112, 146, 339	M 690-1: OB 642: Sc 647
203	90	Sc 650
205	Schemelli 13	P 767
206	315, 337	
207	85, 312	
219	40, 279	M 692, 693 (minor) 714

11

English Evangelicalism, 1738-1800

The church history of the English eighteenth century hinges on the Evangelical Revival associated with the Wesleys. The effect of this on the course of English hymnody was far more decisive than that of pietism on German hymnody; one reason for this is the simple one that whereas hymnody in Germany is a tradition as old as Luther, in England it had hardly begun before the Evangelical Revival was upon it. This is a period in which it is easy to lose one's way, and the best way to treat it is to see the development of hymnody following two separate lines, one of which has its roots in the mainline psalmody of the previous 150 years, the other of which can trace its ancestry no further back than the music of the Restoration and is transformed by Evangelicalism into a quite new and original, but a very influential, style.

In order to make this point we will indulge in a slight overlap with chapter 8 and go back near the beginning of the century. Our Examples 243 and 244 will be the starting point. Ex. 243 is the tune HANOVER, ascribed, but not certainly, to Croft, and first appearing in the *Supplement to the New Version,* 1708 exactly as given here. Ex. 244 is the original form of the EASTER HYMN, which appeared in the same year in a different book, *Lyra Davidica.* HANOVER is a psalm tune in a psalm metre—designed for Ps. 67 in the *New Version* which used the same metre as Ps. 104 in the Old. It is a child of its time in enjoying the new melodic freedom given to music by the Restoration, and at the same time it has all the discipline and reticence of the psalm tunes. It has all the great qualities of eighteenth century architecture—that urbanity we have already drawn attention to—which gives it a most satisfying shape, a resounding climax, and a particularly unusual and well-designed finish. It is, one can easily say, one of the great tunes in the English tradition. EASTER HYMN is something quite as good but very different. It too has a beautiful shape and a measured stride: but this is a hymn tune—written for a translation of a Latin carol for Easter which has little more than its opening stanza in common with the hymn 'Jesus Christ is risen to-day' which we sing now. But this is a hymn—almost a carol—and what is more it depends for its effect on the repeated *Alleluia.* Moreover, in the form which we now know as one of the most celebrated of hymn tunes, this was touched by the heady breezes of the early Evangelical Revival, and what amounts to a descant over the final Alleluia has become the melodic line we know: that happened in Arnold's Psalter of 1741, where it is the tune for one of the hymns appended to the Psalter. Where HANOVER is reserved and stately, this becomes, quite naturally, exuberant, warm-hearted and expressive. We might say then that HANOVER stands at the head of one stream and EASTER HYMN of the other. Both are classics, but one is in the old tradition and the other foreshadows a new one.

It is something of an artificial distinction that we are making, because the Evangelical Revival left no part of the church or of society untouched, and its music is a force which nobody could ignore, whatever the tradition he stood in. But we have to find our way through a jungle of new publications, and this is the best way to find the paths we are looking for. If then we follow first the track of the more or less 'plain' tunes, and then that of the 'decorated' tunes we shall constantly see how one style affected the other. It will not be an absolute rule, but broadly we shall find the 'plain' tunes setting texts without repetitions of words, while in the other kind we shall very frequently find repetitions.

The psalm-tune tradition continued, as we saw at the end of chapter 6, inspired by the appearance of the New Version. Among the good tunes in a hymn-explosion that produced much indifferent material was STROUDWATER (Ex. 245), an English tune now much better known in Scotland, whose originality lies in its artful balancing of alternate lines using wide leaps and the other lines moving by step. By the standards which were by 1725 oppressing English psalmody it is fairly athletic, and it has been popular in Scotland only during the past century, and still waits to find its proper place in English hymnody. More conventional, but no less admirable, tunes are BEDFORD (EH 83), c. 1720 and EPSOM (EH 506), from Tans'ur's collection of 1734.

Exx. 246 and 247 can be considered together because they are by the same composer, but here we see the two streams diverging quite firmly. William Knapp was a precentor in the region of Blandford Forum in Dorset, and compiled *A Sett of New Psalm Tunes* in 1738, the year of John Wesley's conversion. From this both our examples come. WAREHAM (Ex. 246) has proved to be one of the most popular tunes in the English Long Metre repertory—understandably and deservedly. Its movement is very regular, using only once a movement by leap, but having a very engaging shapeliness. It is popular because it is supremely easy to sing. Later (1754) Knapp brought out another collection in which he included this in duple time, but this was not, by general consent, judged an improvement.

SPETISBURY (Ex. 247: he spelt it and the place of its origin with two t's) is a quite different kind of score, in distributing the melody over the tenor, alto and treble parts in its first half. When the melody is sorted out it becomes a very well-wrought piece, and rightly finds a place as an orthodox hymn tune in some modern books (AM 566). But this kind of part-singing was what made a special appeal to the Evangelicals, and as we shall see it is a technique they used frequently. In later books the orthodox triple time version of WAREHAM appears in the same metre as SPETISBURY— a metre of which Charles Wesley was fond, and which

WAREHAM accommodates very easily by de-slurring its passing notes. It is, indeed, found with the same text— 'All ye that pass by.'

The next tune to stop and admire is that which ought to be called STOCKPORT, or its original name, MOT-TRAM (mis-spelt 'Mortram') and should never be called YORKSHIRE—Ex. 248, the tune to 'Christians, awake'. The history of this hymn and tune are related else-where, but what we notice here is its magnificent ar-chitectural engineering. It was composed and first sung in 1750 (first printed, 1766), and nothing could evoke the classical poise of the mid-18th century better than this tune. Modern editions preserve its original bass ex-cept for the fourth phrase (for which one has to go to the now forgotten *Worship Song,* 1905). Eighteenth century singers quite often repeated the last two phrases of words and music, but this was not, it seems, the intention of the composer, who simply wrote the tune in two parts until the last phrase, which is scored in four parts and marked 'Chorus'. The composer was John Wainwright, a Manchester musician (Byrom lived in Manchester too, hence the hideous inap-propriateness of the name YORKSHIRE); his two sons, Robert and Richard, are both known in hymnody, Robert (1748-82) giving us the fine Psalm-tune MAN-CHESTER (EH 168) and Richard (1758-1825) the equally good LM tune WAINWRIGHT (SP 355). It was Robert, the elder, who was defeated in his application for the post of organist at Doncaster parish church by Sir William Herschel, the astronomer, and the story of how Herschel defeated him, pleasing the organ builder Snetzler by an extraordinary trick, is told on p. 129 of the Supplement to the *Handbook to the Church Hym-nary* (1936).

For some other good psalm tunes of the fifties, see ST. NICHOLAS (EH 265) from Israel Holroyd's *A Spiritual Man's Companion*, and LYNE (EH 296) and PLAISTOW (EH 69 ii) from the *Magdalen Hymns*, a book associated with one of the great charity-institu-tions we shall be mentioning in a moment. The sixties are chiefly notable for two very fine examples from Riley's *Parochial Harmony*, 1762: ST. BRIDE (Ex. 249) and ST. BARTHOLOMEW (Ex. 250), both named after famous City of London churches where their respec-tive composers, Samuel Howard (1710-81) and Henry Duncalf (dates unknown) were organists. ST. BRIDE (EH 74: H 417) is one of the best SM tunes available— like so many really good tunes of this century deriving its quality from its balance of leap-movement and step-movement. Notice especially the girder-like effect of the long downward scale contrasting with the arch-like shape of the other three phrases. ST. BARTHOLOMEW (EH 81) has waited a long time to become known, but since 1919 it has been associated with Watts's 'My God, my King, thy various praise' in the *Public School Hymn Book* series (see later, ch. 22) and it is now mak-ing its way. Exactly the same technique is used here— big leaps supported by strong stepwise melody.

One of the best known composers in a rather lean period in England was William Boyce (1710-79), song writer, symphonist and church musician, who proves to be a very capable writer of hymn tunes. His HALTON HOLGATE (AM 186) is just about recognizable in the very domestic version at EH 201, and is also known elsewhere as SHARON. It was originally composed in seven-syllable phrases with tied final notes in all lines but the last. CHAPEL ROYAL (AM 262) is another sound tune, and PORTSEA (Ex. 251: AM 124 ii) is another ex-ample of his solid no-nonsense style. All three were published about 1765 in Boyce's *Collection of Tunes* designed to be sung to the psalm-versions of Christo-pher Smart, that gifted poet who, like Cowper and John Clare, died insane, but whose work is now being reassessed by those who value imaginative literature on sacred subjects. (He wrote the poems which Benjamin Britten set in 'Rejoice in the Lamb'). Among other good tunes that belong to this decade are ISLEWORTH (EH 557), from the same collection as the Boyce tunes and also written for a Smart text, by the composer of ST. BRIDE, MOUNT EPHRAIM (EH 196), a highly decorative S.M. tune by Benjamin Milgrove whom we shall see again at Ex. 268, and CARLISLE (EH 190) from the Lock Hospital Collection, which again we shall be describing later.

The seventies bring us some vintage material, in-cluding the first appearance of DARWALL's 148th (Ex. 252). The manuscript of this has been preserved, and it furnishes a good example of how discreet editorial assistance can liberate qualities slightly obscured in an original. Darwall (1731-89) was Vicar of Walsall, and a decent amateur musician whose other compositions have long since perished; he wrote a tune for each of the 150 Psalms; two others—respectable tunes enough, appear in the *Church of England Hymnal*, edited by A. H. Mann (1895). But the substitution of the tonic for the fifth at the beginning and the provision of a more contrapuntal bass have made this one of the best loved of all tunes. It first appeared in Aaron Williams's *Universal Psalmodist,* 1770, as did the SM tune ST. THOMAS (EH 11: H 388)—which there ap-peared as the second quarter of a sixteen-phrase tune.

James Merrick's *Poems* (1763) which included a complete set of Metrical Psalms, attracted the atten-tion of several musicians, of whom the most distin-guished was William Hayes (1706-77), organist of Magdalen College, Oxford for 43 years up to his death, when he was succeeded by his son Philip. Hayes was, on the evidence of his *Sixteen Metrical Psalms* (c. 1774) made for Magdalen College, a very able tunesmith. NEW 112th (EH 298) is one of his tunes, and two others are at Exx. 253 and 254. Their names, like those of many psalm tunes of this period, are later than their compositions; MAGDALEN COLLEGE (Ex. 253: EH 457: H 314) is a most spirited and cheerful tune, for Merrick's version of Psalm 122 ('I was glad...': the version can still be read at CP 607), and

the graceful DCM tune we now call HAYES (Ex. 254) is
in much the same style as the earlier SURREY (Ex. 167),
very soundly constructed and easy to sing.

OXFORD (Ex. 255: AM 196 ii) is another well-built
tune, nowadays usually pruned of some of its ornaments, but with what we may call 'good bones'. That
appeared in *Twenty Psalms in Three Parts*, published
in Bristol about 1775; its composer is said to be one J.
Coombs—but there is plenty of doubt which of several
people thus named it is, or whether it was any of them.
Avowedly anonymous, but much more celebrated, is
the beautiful tune ABRIDGE (Ex. 256: EH 369), from
Isaac Smith's *Collection of Psalm Tunes in Three parts*
(usually dated 1770 but Frost puts it c. 1780); it is
known in Scotland as ST. STEPHEN.

Thomas Jackson (d. 1781) of Newark on Trent, to
be distinguished, desperately, from William Jackson
of Exeter, G. K. Jackson who emigrated to the U.S.A.
about 1795, Robert Jackson of Oldham (1842-1914),
William Jackson of Bradford (1815-66—he of the
famous *Jackson in F*) not to mention our distinguished
contemporary Francis Jackson of York—every one of
whom appears in the story of hymnody even if he is
not mentioned in these pages—published in 1780 the
tune we call JACKSON, but sometimes, and probably
better, BYZANTIUM (EH 210). This fine tune has been
taken into Scottish use as well as English and deserves
its continued popularity. We may as well mention also
that rumbustious tune EXETER, by Jackson of Exeter
(EH 528), sound and hearty if somewhat graceless, in
the unusual metre 888.888.

Another famous tune WARRINGTON (EH 263) comes
from Ralph Harrison's massive work, *Sacred Harmony* (2 vols, 1784, 1791)—being in the first we date it
1784; and from the same source comes BLACKBOURNE
(EH 456), a more sombre tune which reminds us that
in this very cheerful period we do not often come
across a minor-key tune.

Even more celebrated in England—one of the best
known of all tunes—is ROCKINGHAM (originally, CA-
TON), which grew out of TUNBRIDGE, Ex. 257. The
form we give appeared in Aaron Williams *Psalmody in
Miniature* about 1785, in the anapaestic metre of 'All
ye that pass by'; the form we know is due to Edward
Miller (1731-1807) who was for 41 years organist of
Doncaster parish church (taking over when Herschel,
whom we mentioned above, demitted office after a few
months). He had a copy of the Williams book, which
has been preserved, and agains TUNBRIDGE he wrote
'would make a good LM'. The excellent and almost
Mozartian LM which he fashioned is our ROCK-
INGHAM, and it appeared in his *The Psalms of David
for the Use of Parish Churches,* 1790. Its association
with 'When I survey' is somewhat later. Those who
have the *English Hymnal* at hand will see at no. 107 the
harmonies given to the tune later by Samuel Webbe,
Jr. (1770-1843) and, in the footnote, a reproduction of
his version of the third phrase, without the sharpened

fourth—a most delectable variation, but nowadays
usable only if the choir is singing a stanza on its own.

William Jones of Nayland (1726-1800), so called
because he was a very well known theological writer as
well as an accomplished musician, contributes another
excellent psalm tune in what the English call ST.
STEPHEN and the Scots, NEWINGTON (EH 337: H 11); it
is one of the fairly small number of CM tunes which
return to the tonic half way through without giving an
impression of weakness—this because of the strength
and good sense of the individual phrases. That is in his
Ten Church Pieces for Organ, with four Anthems...
(1789), printed at the end and marked for Psalm 23.
He called it 'St. Stephen's tune'. Another celebrated
tune, very much in the Handelian idiom, was TRURO
(EH 420: H 484) which is now so well known on both
sides of the Atlantic, in England with 'Jesus shall
reign' (following EH), in America with 'Lift up your
heads.' The American version follows a corrupt text
which was in currency in England in the 19th century.
In the same collection the well known writer of glees
and sociable songs Henry Harington (1727-1816) contributed the graceful tune we call HARINGTON or
RETIREMENT (EH 85)—whose part-writing suggests the
accomplished part-song writer; he did in fact arrange it
from a glee, but it makes a very acceptable hymn tune.

In the closing years of the century we come across
DUKE STREET (EH 167: H 542), the inevitable tune for
'Jesus shall reign' in America, and often sung in
England to 'Fight the good fight'—perhaps slightly
unimaginative in its rather monotonous rhythm and its
searching out the high tonic in three phrases out of
four—but rather better if the original slurring in
phrase 3 is followed, which it never now is: the fourth
syllable in that line should have three notes, not two.
This, though always thought of as English, was first
published in Scotland, in *A Select Collection of Psalm
and Hymn Tunes* (Glasgow, 1793). It is marked for
Addison's hymn, 'The spacious firmament' (which it
fits very badly), and is anonymous: in 1805 it is attributed to one John Hatton; this may be the John
Hatton who lived at St. Helens and died in 1793, in
which case we are not far wrong in calling it an English
tune. DUKE STREET was the name of the church where
this Hatton was organist.

About the same time an undated collection of tunes
in two, three, four and in one case five parts for Isaac
Watts's *Divine Songs for Children* was published by
G. K. Jackson—the one who almost at once emigrated
to the USA: this contains the tune called DUBDIN, (EH
433), there set in four parts to 'And now another day is
gone'. There is good music in this tune, but the rest of
the contents of the book are fairly naive.

Finally there is UNIVERSITY (Ex. 258), composed
probably by John Collignon, Professor of Anatomy at
Cambridge, who died in 1785; the tune first appeared
in Peter Hellendaal's *Collection of Psalms*, published

in Cambridge, 1780, and later in Randall's *Collection* published also in Cambridge in 1794, from which it is often attributed to Randall. Its generous melodic line and flexible tunefulness make it a good tune to end this section with, for it has all the warmth of the evangelical style added to the discipline of the psalm tradition.

It will have been observed by American readers how infrequently we can give an American reference for the tunes of this period. The reason for this will be quite obvious when we come to discuss American hymnody. The older Psalm tunes were part of the American heritage: these were not. At the time of the Declaration of Independence the American hymn repertory was very limited, and there was very little demand for new tunes. When the demand came, much later, there was a plentiful supply of American psalm-style tunes to be used.

But it will be equally obvious how many of the tunes we have mentioned in this quick survey are in English currency, and how many are very well known indeed. They represent the best musicianship to be found in 18th century hymnody, and they form the backbone of the modern repertory very much as the German pietist tunes form the centre of the German repertory. But what we are about to see is that an English version of pietism took a very different line.

This difference of direction was the product of a musical cause—the new freedom of vocabulary we have mentioned—and also of religious and social forces. The religious force that kept early psalmody under strict discipline was that basic Calvinism, which affected all parts of the church in England, not least the High Churchmen of the Establishment, which laid much emphasis on the need for total regeneration accompanied by a discipline expressed in the church's authority and in the close regulation of all aspects of civic and personal behaviour. Perhaps it ought to be said once again that Calvinism is caricatured if it is represented as a religion of total inhibition; but then it happens to be a religious system which it is alarmingly easy to caricature. Moreover it is a system which requires a high degree of intelligence and mental balance if it is not to become a system of legalistic pessimism. That is the weakness that goes along with the visionary power which in the right hands—in Calvin's, of course —it develops. The quality of the psalm tunes of Geneva and Britain shows Calvinism at its best: as we said, the high pressure resulting from the narrowness of the channel.

Those tunes we have just been looking at continue that tradition: new musical possibilities and richness, when intellectually disciplined, generate new melodies as good as the old ones. There is no musical form of expression which intellect cannot redeem and regenerate. But suppose that the discovery of new experiences and new possibilities is accompanied by a positive reaction against discipline: the result in modern political life is, we all know, inflation. In the church's history it

is exactly parallel. The coinage of communication begins to lose its value; quality of output becomes related to a fall in true living standards—in aesthetic quality if we are talking of church music. It was so in the early 18th century. The evangelical theology was a positive reaction against certain aspects of Calvinism which had come uppermost because Calvinism had become distorted; it was too fragile a structure to stand the mauling of popular thinking, too finely balanced not to be bent here and there by the gales of politics. Therefore the Evangelicals under Wesley proclaimed that a salvation which had been denied to all who were not 'elect' was available for all who would repent and be converted, and they encountered powerful opposition from a Calvinist Establishment which represented Wesley as an apostle of spiritual permissiveness. Neither the popular idea of Calvinism nor the Establishment idea of Wesley were anything but caricatures—but that is how things go. And what Wesley found himself left with was an evangelical permissiveness which seemed to him as grotesque a parody of what he meant by 'Methodism' (which after all means basically a highly disciplined personal 'rule of life') as the image of grey repressiveness is of true Calvinsim. Hence, of course, his often stated opposition to just the kind of music we are about to encounter.

But there is also a social force at work, which is that more people are enjoying more music than they had ever done before. Music is now coming down through the social strata; it is no longer produced for and conditioned by the standards of the highly educated. Moreover, the notion of 'listening to music' well performed by increasingly gifted musicians, rather than making music, however ineptly, produced the change in the meaning of the old word 'consort' into that of the new word 'concert.' The real progenitor of all popular music in England, in the sense in which that expression is now used, of course, Handel; *The Beggar's Opera* also had a good deal to do with the way music began to slip through several floors of the social skyscraper.

There is a close parallel, then, between the development of music and the growth of evangelical religion. The virtuoso on the concert platform had his counterpart in the virtuoso of the pulpit. Communication from a distance to a crowd replaced, as the norm of religious custom, the essential 'chamber music' in which the Mass and the 17th century puritan meeting were nearer together than either was to the new evangelical preaching-service.

History had been waiting, by Handel's time, many centuries for this development. After all—in the medieval plainsong we have sacred chamber music overheard: in Reformation psalmody we have domestic music made by amateurs: but in Evangelical music we have a third kind—the concert. (It is an ignorant philistinism, of course, that confuses the highly wrought music of the English cathedral Evensong with a 'concert'). Music is now developing the faculty of affecting large numbers of people who are listening but not participating; and music is now strong enough and resourceful enough to do this without much help from words. It is, of course, a great mercy that the first evangelical text writer was as good a poet as Charles Wesley; but broadly speaking even in his day hymn singing tended to be a musical occasion in which even if you could not distinguish the words, or even if the music distorted them ruthlessly, you knew perfectly well what the words were because they all conveyed the same message. That is much more true of later 'Gospel Song' worship than it was of 18th century Evangelical worship, but the nature of the music makes it obvious that the emphasis had shifted from words to music, so that music did not now reinforce and serve the words, but often drowned them altogether. This had happened in German pietism, as we saw: but whereas the extravagances of pietism were fairly quickly forgotten by German churchgoers, and only its simple and well constructed melodies remained (our Ex. 198 is not the sort of thing that appealed to Bach), the style coined by the more highly decorated forms of Evangelical music has remained in English hymnody, and in American, to this day.

Evangelical religion depended largely on the solo evangelist, and the hymnody of the Wesleys depended largely on the solo singer. (If you are evangelizing a crowd of thousands in the open air, where would you, in those days, get hymn books for them to sing from?) And even where a hymn tune looks like a reasonable congregational proposition, the inner dramatic force of it is derived from the solo song. Ex. 259, ISLINGTON, is a fairly demure tune by the standards we are here going to examine, but notice how it introduces a rhetorical repetition of four syllables in the last line, and how the words of the text, a Charles Wesley hymn welcoming new members to a Methodist meeting, sound like one person speaking to another, not like a community speaking to God. This is from the first Wesley tune book, the *Foundery Collection* of 1742, and its charming melodic shape is typical of the Handelian gift for melody which the early evangelical composers rejoiced in.

So, in all conscience, is Ex. 260, called INVITATION (elsewhere DEVONSHIRE or KENT: EH 347). The composer here is J. F. Lampe probably—a bassoon player in the Covent Garden orchestra who edited a fine collection for Wesley, *Hymns for the Great Festivals*, 1746. (See SHECM p. 45 for another fine tune of his in this collection). As it originally appeared the tune is straight LM, but copiously decorated; the ornaments are almost certainly for the instruments accompanying rather than for the voice. But stripped of these, as we find it in some modern books, it is a distinguished piece of melodic engineering: if one regards the significant high notes in each phrase as C - D - E flat and F, one observes not only that they appear in a continuous

rising scale but that they are placed in a symmetrical pattern—nine beats between the C and the D, nine between the E flat and the F. Just as in Charles Wesley the evangelicals had a great hymn writer, so in the first generations they found some fine musicians to make their new music for them. The very good tune IRISH (EH 504: H 444) comes from another collection edited by Lampe, *A Collection of Hymns and Sacred Poems* (Dublin, 1749: hence its name).

None of this is particularly extravagant, though it is already showing traces of the solo-ethos. If one wants to know what kind of simple tune Wesley himself approved, one turns to SAVANNAH (EH 135: H 427), a tune Wesley picked up from the Moravian settlement in Herrnhut and brought back to England with him. Nothing could well be simpler than that; but even his genius for discipline could not stem the tide of solo music once it had started running.

Ex. 261, HOTHAM, the first tune printed with 'Jesus, lover of my soul', from the most important Methodist tune collection *Harmonia Sacra*, begins to open up new possibilities. It has nothing like the melodic sureness of touch that we find in Lampe: its phrases are much more disjointed and its melody less continuous. But it makes up for that in the rhetoric of its last two phrases, where words are repeated and the tune gathers strength. Here is an undoubted solo, with a touch of the repetitive song-song of the evangelical preacher about it—reassuring, delivering a simple message, and rhetorically forceful in the hands of a good singer.

Harmonia Sacra, later reprinted as *Sacred Harmony*, is fascinating in providing the first 'official' tunes for many still familiar Charles Wesley hymns. Our Ex. 262 here is a typical example of the more elaborate tunes found in that book. They are always scored for solo voice and figured bass, (though this one at one point puts in a little extra harmony); usually they are set in keys appropriate to a tenor or a soprano. Always they have discreet dynamic indications (invariably on the same pattern: start mezzo, reduce to *piano,* finish *forte*). This superbly Handelian tune—a much better construction than we often find in this book—provides for an anthem-like repetition of words in the last line: the preacher's peroration.

Ex. 263, BRENTWOOD, introduces another side of Evangelicalism; the tendency of crowd-religion to impose conformity. It is the famous revision of TALLIS'S CANON found first in the *Divine Musical Miscellany*, 1754 and then becoming very popular indeed throughout the English churches for about a century. The eighteenth century evangelical lived very much in the present; his interest in history was minimal. It therefore did not occur to him, as it would have done to an early 20th century musician, that Tallis's music ought to be left alone and not revised. He was less interested in the purity of a canon than in an amusing melody: and some of the later versions of this revision are very entertaining indeed. (In SHECM pp. 46-8 the reader will find another tune thus, as we should say, vandalized: the PASSION CHORALE appearing as BRIGHTHELM-STONE). All music must now sound like mid-18th century English music. A tune of Hassler's made famous by Bach must now be translated into Handel's language. Handel, Pepusch, Arne and Boyce were the arbiters of the vocabulary of religious amusement. This sort of imposed stylistic conformism always takes place when there is a surge of 'popular' taste, as in our own age we know only too well. Of course, much of the Evangelicals' energy was directed to reclaiming the lost and reassuring the underprivileged, and in such conditions the delicacies of musical experience are sacrificed to a musical style which by its familiarity, and its association with secular styles, restores people's faith in a world which God loves. It is wholly understandable, and persons of sensitive taste have to remember it. Naturally, we are beginning here to uncover a problem and a tension which never disappears from hymnody once it has escaped in this mid-eighteenth century scene, and we shall have to return to it. It is the problem of the counterpoint of reassurance and judgment, of freedom and authority.

Ex. 264, SCARBOROUGH, should be compared with Ex. 147. It is indeed DAVID'S HARP, as it were, 'new tun'd'. Where Ex. 263 was a total revision of an old tune in the new style, this one is a new tune with its end part reconstructed. It will be noticed that the peculiarly 'Restoration' turns of phrase (redolent of the courtly music of Charles II's time—not an association precious to Evangelicals) have been removed, and that the new ending has a change of time-signature, a small repetition of four syllables, and a return in the final phrase to something like the original. Evangelical music was quite happy about such adaptations; indeed, the composers often lifted melodies out of Handel's works—such as the aria, 'He shall feed his flock', which became well known as a setting for 'When I survey the wondrous cross'—which, with needful word-repetition, it fits without difficulty. 'Drink to me only with thine eyes' became an accepted tune for 'There is a land of pure delight.' 'I know that my Redeemer liveth' was naturally adapted for Samuel Medley's hymn, 'I know that my Redeemer lives.' Never mind the source—if it was a good tune that would catch the listener's ear, it was pressed into service, and if it was an old tune in an old idiom, why, they were as happy to adapt it as modern editors are to translate texts into 'you', and modern liturgists to invite congregations to say 'And also with you. . . .'

This example introduces the *Lock Hospital Collection* of 1769, one of the most important sources for the new style of Evangelical music. The Lock was one of that network of large charity-institutions—for orphans, prostitutes, the insane and the sick—established under the auspices of the Evangelical Movement about that time. It was presided over by Martin Madan, an able musician as well as an obviously excellent administrator, who later on had to retire from his ministry because he published a pamphlet arguing that bigamy was better than prostitution. The importance of these institutions was that they became vigorous music centres.

The no doubt drab life of the inmates was largely diversified by musical activities and they could easily provide 'captive' choirs. The Lock seems to have been a leading force in this movement, and some of the hymns in that collection are really anthems—with different music for each stanza. (One such is reproduced in SHECM, pp. 47-8). We may remark in passing that another such institution, the Foundling Hospital, gave us two of the best hymns in the language, 'Spirit of mercy, truth and love' and 'Praise the Lord, ye heavens, adore him.'

Exx. 265 and 266 are from the *Lock Hospital Collection*. Ex. 265, MANSFIELD, is a very merry setting of one of Watts's most inspiriting texts, in four parts, thoroughly choral, making the words repeat themselves until the music has finished. One supposes that it was a great favourite at the Lock. Ex. 266, RONDEAU, is an ingenious idea; this was in three parts, and it sets the opening line of a CM stanza to a phrase which is repeated twice in each stanza with that line—almost a kind of 18th century 'antiphon', since that line remains unchanged throughout the hymn.

Benjamin Milgrove was a musician in the employment of the Countess of Huntingdon's chapel at Bath, and he clearly had an enterprising choir and congregation to work for. His tune HARTS (EH 177), now a demure 77.77, was originally a long tune with a rousing chorus (see SPD at # 520); his HARWICH (Ex. 267) follows the old style of putting the melody in the tenor, but one must suppose that if the congregation sang it, it probably stopped singing after phrase 3 while the choir conversed on the words 'come, see', and came in again with the last line: this entertaining mixture of choral and congregational techniques often proved successful where evangelical congregations were singing in ordinary worship.

Isaac Smith's Collection of c. 1780, which produced our Ex. 256, has also some cheerful 'decorated' tunes such as SILVER STREET, our Ex. 268. This like Milgrove's HARTS, simply provides a straight SM tune and attaches to it a fanfare of Hallelujahs which lengthens the hymn by about 200 per cent and encourages heartiness in the congregation.

It will be seen that we are by now moving away from the solo style and finding a choral-congregational style. This is what the Charity foundations encouraged; their congregations were of the kind that could be formed, as it were, into a choir supporting the select choir; and this kind of antiphony became very popular in ordinary churches such as those for which Isaac Smith edited his book. Our Ex. 269, MILES LANE, is, of course, the most famous of all examples of this. This was written by William Shrubsole when he was 19 years old for the Congregational church in Canterbury, and its form is just like that of Milgrove's HARWICH: the initial 'crown him', sung three times, is given to sections of the choir, the congregation singing the tenor line where the harmony is in full four parts. The score looks very much as if it was designed for male voices, but there is no evidence about that and it would be an unusual way to score a tune in this period. The melody of this tune was famously written of by Vaughan Williams, who called it one of the finest melodies ever written and drew attention to the fact that not a note of music apart from this seems to have come from this composer.

Ex. 270, CHESTERFIELD, is the original of another tune now well known (EH 375: H 319). Although it now goes with fairly confident texts, its original association is with 'O Thou from whom all goodness flows' (EH 85), text and tune coming from the same hand. Haweis was an evangelical anglican clergyman (1734-1820) who had been on Madan's staff at the Lock Hospital and had also been chaplain to Lady Huntingdon. His tune in the original form is a very tender piece, probably designed as a solo, and there is deep pathos in that repeated phrase which now, of course, has disappeared from hymnals.

Another very important collection of tunes was John Rippon's *Collection* of c. 1796; this was a private commercial venture, gathering up all the tunes which were most sung together with some which he hoped to introduce, and was much drawn on by the Baptists. Our Ex. 271, confusingly called EXETER and equally confusingly being by Thomas Jackson not of Exeter but of Newark (see above p. 72) is a pleasant piece in trio form, with a special bassoon part in its second half. In the example the bass notes with downward tails are those of the separate bassoon part provided in the original open score. Although the other bass part looks instrumental it is marked as 'vocal bass', and the texture of the upper parts suggests that they are for two sopranos, not soprano and tenor (or of course two tenors). Here again we have the Handel aria-style: music for listening rather than for congregational use; it is a straight DCM without word-repetition, charming in its way.

With that we see how the two styles came together; we see the same composer producing an orthodox psalm tune and an aria, and the same collection containing tunes in both forms. The question now is going to be whether one or the other will finally win, for they represent two different activites. But the overriding historical truth (as pointed out in SHECM chapter 7) is that during a period in which Anglican music-making in the Cathedrals and non-evangelical parishes was in a deep slump, and in which Reformed Christians were content with a handful of psalm tunes, the most energetic music making was being carried on in the meetings, chapels and institutions of the Evangelicals.

Here, as everywhere else, they left an indelible mark on English religious culture.

There remain to be discussed some tunes which fall within this century but which are quite outside the main streams we have mentioned. These include the the three tunes of Handel and the one tune of Haydn which represent the offering of two supreme composers to hymnody. Hymn tunes by composers of the first rank are almost as rare as hymns by great poets.

Handel's three seem to have been written when he was on a visit to Gopsall House, the residence of Charles Jennens, who had compiled the libretto of *Messiah* and other Handel oratorios—though at this date he had been superseded by other librettists. The date must have been after 1746, which is the date when all three of the Charles Wesley texts for which the tunes were composed were first published. It may be assumed that Jennens showed Handel two of the latest Wesley collections, and that Handel decided, or was persuaded, to set them to music.

GOPSAL (Ex. 272) has been described by John Wilson as 'the only familiar tune written by a very great composer for an English hymn.' That cuts Vaughan Williams down to size, and unhappily it will not pass in the USA, where the tune has, so far as we know, not appeared in a hymnal before 1976. But it is virtually universal in England (not in Scotland). It was, like the other two tunes of Handel's, written for solo voice and figured bass, and with the others it shared a curious history in that all three were lost to sight until they were discovered in the Fizwilliam Museum, Cambridge, in 1826 by Samuel Wesley. He published them on a leaflet—absent-mindedly saying in a note that he had found six tunes by Handel (the other three can safely be assumed not to exist). GOPSAL was gradually brought into use in hymnals, first in an arrangement by Havergal (see p. 90) who disfigured it considerably in his transcription. Something nearer to the original, but in four parts, eventually appeared in *Hymns Ancient and Modern* and the *English Hymnal* but a true realization of the music had to wait until 1964 when in *Hymns for Church and School* (# 117) John Wilson made a version with accompaniment from the figured bass and a unison melody line. This, for congregational purposes, had to be in C. This version was slightly altered in John Wilson's *Short Companion to Hymns and Songs* (1970) and that version appears in *Ecumenical Praise* (1977). An adaptation of it with part of the stanza in four parts, retaining Handel's D major, was made for *Westminster Praise*, 1976. Apart from the imaginative yet authentic organ part, the distinction of John Wilson's arrangement is that it includes, for the first time, the postlude which was implied by an extra line of figured bass (without any melody) in Handel's manuscript—as given in our Example. This postlude starts out from a bass phrase which is the same as the opening phrase of the melody.

The most interesting thing about these three tunes is

that they are in three quite distinct Handelian styles, just as the three texts are in three different Wesleyan styles. The trumpet-like manner of GOPSAL, and its D major key, suggest the triumph of the Resurrection and the Ascension; CANNONS (Ex. 273) is set to an invitatory hymn, 'Sinners, obey the Gospel word'—which has a frown in it but also a bracing strength exactly reflected in Handel's forthright G minor and his fierce rhythm. This tune appears at EH 66. The third (Ex. 274), sometimes called FITZWILLIAM, sometimes DESIRING TO LOVE, which is the title of Charles Wesley's 'O Love divine, how sweet thou art', is in a pastoral F major, tender and lilting. If Handel wrote the three more or less at a sitting, he showed a great composer's flexibility and sympathy with texts which is, in the 18th century, quite unusual in hymnody. This tune has appeared only in the *Methodist School Hymn Book* (1950). All three then are solo songs, and perhaps the third uses one or two intervals which even in a lower key a congregation would find difficult to sing cleanly, but there is certainly nothing uncongregational about CANNONS, and GOPSAL, despite one very high note, has become a firm favourite in England.

The other tune is, of course, a melody which is German in origin but which as a hymn is strictly English. Apparently the words of 'Praise the Lord; ye heavens, adore him' were written with it in mind (they appeared on an undated leaflet about 1800, one copy of which mentions Haydn's name). Although AUSTRIA was originally written in 1797 for the Emperor's birthday, and later that year incorporated in Haydn's String Quartet op. 76 no. 3, and although later it was associated in Germany with a patriotic jingle, 'Deutschland, Deutschland uber alles' it was at the time recognized in England as one of the great melodies of all ages. Its use was discouraged during World War I, but never in World War II. It is a text-book study of melodic structure, and one of many examples (MILES LANE, Ex. 269, is another) which could be brought in evidence to prove that a wide compass is no barrier to the popularity of a great tune. For the original string quartet score, see Ex. 275.

Two other well known tunes which come from unusual sources can be mentioned here. One is the tune we call MOSCOW, or sometimes ITALIAN HYMN (EH 553: H 271). This appeared in the *Lock Collection,* 1769, and the composer was Felice Giardini, an Italian-born violinist (1716-96) who came to England in 1750 and became leader (Concertmaster) at the Italian Opera and was at one time famous and successful. In his later years he died in poverty—in Moscow. In England the tune appears in a later form, but something much nearer the original, usually called ITALIAN HYMN, is widely used in the U.S.A. (Ex. 276).

The other is the well known tune MORNING HYMN, written for Ken's 'Awake, my soul, and with the sun' by Francois Hippolyte Barthélémon (1741-1808). He was born in Bordeaux of a French father and an Irish mother, came to England in 1765 and like Giardini became a very well known violinist. His tune first appeared in another book associated with one of the charity foundations, *The Hymns and Psalms used at the Asylum or House of Refuge for Female Orphans,* which is undated but is placed between 1783 and 1788. It looks like, and is, a children's tune—see EH 257: H 151.

12
Roman Catholic Hymnody, 1680-1850

The French Diocesan Tunes

Here we take up a tale which we laid down long ago (ch. 2), and follow the story of Roman Catholic hymnody through the eighteenth century. The essential book for study in this connection is Dr. C. E. Pocknee's *The French Diocesan Hymns and their Tunes* (Faith Press, 1954), and if here we venture to differ from one or two details in his interpretation of this very important section of hymn music, this presupposes our gratitude to him for making available a good deal of material which formerly was hidden in the libraries of the learned.

The tunes we are referring to in this section are those which, brought into English knowledge by J. B. Croft about 1880 and made part of general currency by the *English Hymnal* in 1906 were referred to in *E.H.* simply as 'French Church Melody', or as 'Church Melody' with the name of a diocese but no date. Nearly all of them are in the metres of the Office hymns—Long Metre or Sapphic, and those which have come into modern use are among the best hymn tunes of any age.

Their emergence is associated with reforms of the Breviary and Missal, and to get this picture clear we must for a moment go much further back into history.

The mental restlessness of the Renaissance was in no sense the monopoly of Protestants. Perhaps the violence of Protestant dispute made the Cahtolics more cautious in responding to that spirit than in other circumstances they might have been: but in Martin Luther's lifetime a critical eye was being turned on the traditional liturgies. Cardinal Francis Quignonez in 1535 issued a revised Breviary which in its very gentle amendments of liturgy and hymn texts expressed the first stirrings of criticism. While this met with no overt papal disapproval at the time, we hear Pope Paul IV announcing in 1558 that no local revisions should be made until the Council of Trent, then in session, had moved on the matter—from which we may conclude that some such activities were appearing in the dioceses. In 1568, under the general influence of the Council of Trent (which closed in 1563) the Reformed Roman Breviary appeared, and like the rest of the reforms following that Council it sought to restore simplicity and intelligibility to the texts without in any way deforming the Offices.

But there was nothing final about this: once you have permitted revision, there is no knowing where it will stop, and people will ask why, if you revise this, you do not revise that also. In due time another Reformed Roman Breviary appeared, under the authority of Pope Urban VIII in 1632, which altered the texts of the hymns much more radically.

That might have been enough, but the middle of the sixteenth century found Catholic France deeply divided on theological issues. The network of theological thought called Jansenism and the particular disciplinary issues associated with Port Royal showed a deep, and to many alarming, infiltration into the Catholic church not only of Renaissance principles, but (what was much more sinister) of Reformation principles. Indeed, we find both the attitude of puritanism—intellectual criticism brought to bear on all written texts including the Bible, and that of evangelicalism—the valuing of experinece as highly as authority, very emphatically stated in the process of these controversies. This is an atmosphere in which of all things hymnody thrives. And it is a very important factor in the generation of that long series of locally revised Breviaries and Missals—all French—which produced the music we are here concerned with.

The point is, of course, that people now began asking why, if revision of ancient texts was permitted, they should not write some new texts to replace many which, in that restless and enquiring climate, were thought outdated. This began with the Paris Breviary of 1680 and its associated music book, the *Paris Antiphoner* of 1681.

Ex. 277, CHRISTE SANCTORUM, is a transcription of what is now a very well known tune (EH 165: H 157) from the *Paris Antiphoner*. It is not here exactly, but it is almost, as we now sing it (the important difference is the elongated notes just before the end which have now come to stay but are no part of the original). And before we look at any others we have to digress on the matter of the interpretation of these tunes.

We said earlier that the hymnody of Catholicism before 1680 was devotional or carol-like—much associated with Christmas, or with certain locally composed devotional hymns. It developed as a popular reaction to the learnedness of plainsong much as the pietist hymns of Germany developed as a reaction against the learned Luther style. But there was nothing liturgical about this music—it had nothing to do with the official Breviaries. The real question is, what style was now being developed at a higher and more public level?

It is, we think, something like an attempt to reproduce a psalm-tune style, with its compromise between plainsong and ballad. Reflect on what the makers of the Anglo-Genevan psalms had in mind, and you have the picture. What the compilers of the new brevaries seem to have wanted is something which has a touch of plainsong about it—and reflects at least some of the ancient anti-secular values of plainsong, but none the less responds in some way to the development of music. Now what happened was exactly what happened when the classic psalm tunes were overtaken —at exactly this period—by the measured music and operatic styles which King Charles II had brought back to England from—France.

In Ex. 277 we therefore have what is to all intents

and purposes a new-style measured melody in uncompromising F major—written on the four line staff because that was the only notation allowed for church music, and with a notation resembling that of plainsong. It is a fine march-like tune, very shapely, businesslike and uncluttered, but it is the new music.

Now for a moment we can look back at Exx. 22 and 23, where we compared a plainsong melody with its later measured equivalent. There we transcribed the measured form as we know it now. This, however, sometimes means an interpretation of the Diocesan Breviary scores which does not agree with Dr. Pocknee's explanation; for his conclusion is that the forms of these tunes we now use are, being measured, degenerate.

This conclusion depends on an interpretation of the neums as carrying certain durational meanings—which of course by now they certainly did, and which is, probably, something of a new idea in 1681. But whereas his interpretation insists that there are four kinds of neum each with invariable value, thus: ■ ■ = 2 ■ = 1½ ■ = 1   = ½, what we believe is that there was no consistency about this at all. In Ex. 277, on the Pocknee system, the opening note of each line—an oblong with a tail—is the note representing 1½ units, which is surely improbable. In that system our Ex. 23B would look, in transcription, like our Ex. 278.

It really seems that the new style of music writing did not settle down to any consistent compromise between the system which causes different neum-shapes to represent weight or emphasis, and that which causes them to express, as the notation of secular music does, duration. Eventually it became obvious that you cannot have both at once.

But it is clear that a few of the tunes in these sources were indeed based on plainsong melodies, as Exx. 22 and 23 show. Ex. 22 comes out in the *Poitiers Vesperale*, 1746, as our Ex. 279. One can see how easily it would have skipped into the dance-like triple rhythm we know; and the typical 'reversed triplet' of plainsong is, according to the notation, allowed to become a normal triplet in line 3—the two-syllable slur coming on a strong beat, not a weak one.

The plainsong-based tunes are, however, a minority. Most of them are new—and very fine examples of the new style they are. A late one, Ex. 280, from the *Chartres Antiphoner,* 1784 (EH 188) shows an interesting attempt to preserve an old rhythm which is not so much plainsong as that of Reformed music. On our interpretation of the notation (and we must always remember that there was no sign for a 'rest' in the notation these sources used) we have exactly the rhythm of Ex. 185, a much earlier Sapphic tune from a Reformed source.

But in actual performance, we cannot believe that in that age very much attention was paid to guarding against secular rhythms. It was not an age of obedience but one of criticism. The four-line staff was a gesture: the ambiguous notation was gesture. But if we now

think of the Sapphics in four time and the LM tunes in three we are doing no violence at all to the spirit of the age, and if we attempted to sing Ex. 278 as here transcribed we should almost certainly be doing what was never done at the time of its Catholic currency, and producing what is no more than a moment of historical pedantry. So from here onwards we can with a good conscience think of these tunes in their modern form.

If we do that we can distinguish between the new tunes and the occasional genuine neo-plainsong tunes. Now and again a new plainsong tune was coined. Just before the year we have arrived at, SPONSA CHRISTI (EH 253 i) appeared in the *Paris Gradual*, 1666, and the RORATE (EH 735) in the *Officia Propria* (Paris) 1673. The quasi-plainsong ADORO TE (EH 331: H 204) is found in a Paris *Processionale*, 1697, and apparently the ATTENDE (EH 736) did not appear until a later Paris *Processionale* of 1824. While the prose plainsong no doubt retained something of the character of classic plainsong, everybody who knows ADORO TE in congregational use knows how inevitably it slips into a regular 6.5.6.5 D rhythm in performance, no matter how stubborn the organist.

The *Paris Antiphoner* (1681) itself gives us what looks like a new plainsong tune but what is clearly a reduction of PANGE LINGUA (Ex. 281, cf. Ex. 16: AM 37), now used as a delightful setting for the new translation of SOL PRAECEPS RAPITUR. But otherwise the tunes are clearly of the kind that falls into regular measure. Two of them we now know in different forms. One is REGNATOR ORBIS (Ex. 282), originally in the unusual Alcaic metre, a metre of classical Latin lyric (11.11.9.10, mixed dactylic and trochaic). The form we know was coined by Helmore in 1852 (see below pp. 89-90), and it has no ancient association with Abelard's 'O quanta qualia'. (Notice by the way the marked note in the last phrase: there is no reason why this should not have been preserved in the alteration). The other is THURE FUMANTES (Ex. 283: cf. EH 174 for one modern form, AM 505 for another). In this one we have preserved what the original notation *may* mean, but tend to guess that in performance the first half of the two opening lines did not actually travel at half speed. We shall mention this again in a moment, but it may here be commented that in modern use the allocation of this tune to texts in 6.6.6.6 D (as AM 505) does violence to the original shape of the tune, which, as a Sapphic, divided the long phrase 5.7, not 6.6. (So we defend EH 174 and CP 564 against all the other hymnals that use it in the *A & M* form).

The same 1681 source gives us also the delightfully carol-like ST. VENANTIUS (EH 38) and that beautifully contemplative Sapphic, CHRISTE FONS IUGIS (originally MATRIS INTACTAE: EH 335). This tune, by the way, is the only one in this series whose composer is identifiable—he is Philippe Goibaud Dubois, 1626-94, but nothing else is known of him.

There seems to have been little more composing activity until the last and most dramatic wave of revision. Local amendments to the Breviary were indeed made constantly during the generation following 1680, and one tune familiar in modern use comes from a Paris *Processionale* of 1689: this is SOLLENNIS HAEC FESTIVITAS (EH 123). It oftens appears as a simple LM tune but actually it is one of a series of tunes set to a long processional—all of which are transcribed in EH. But it is around the year 1730 that we find a new burst of musical activity. The major influence in the most radical of the revisions of the Breviary was a paper published in Paris in 1720, written by Frederic Maurice Foinard, whose title in translation is revealing: *'Project for a new Breviary, in which the Divine Office, without changing its customary form, may be especially conformable with Scripture, instructive, edifying, in a natural style, without repetition or circumlocution,'* —than which what could be more puritan? It was to be a return to ancient simplicity, and as Dr. Pocknee says, to 'sustain the attention, nourish piety, and rekindle the desire to use the Offices'. In this work Foinard particularly calls for the writing of new hymns, and the wider use of the new ones already existing. He wishes for the true and vivid colours of doctrine and Scripture to be restored to worship.

One cannot attribute any canonical status to this document but it represents the kind of thinking which conservatism could not at the time resist, and the end-product of that thinking was the *Paris Breviary* of 1736, authorized by Archbishop Vintmille, and edited by the Rector of the University of Paris, Charles Coffin (1676-1749). In this book there were only 25 hymns by authors of pre-Reformation date; there were 89 by Claude and Jean-Baptiste de Santeuil, whose work had already appeared in the Paris Breviary of 1680, and 97 by other French contemporary writers. The 1680 Breviary had kept seventy medieval texts, so this was indeed a radical updating, and a number of Coffin's texts are known in English translation (such as 'On Jordan's bank').

This impetus to new creative work produced some fine new tunes, of which we may briefly mention a few. In the *Rouen Antiphoner*, 1728 we have COELITES PLAUDANT (EH 242: H 123)—one of the most spirited of them all, and newly adventurous in going well outside the octave span of melody; the same can be said of JESU CORONA (EH 65). Another which has found plenty of currency beyond the *English Hymnal* tradition is REX GLORIOSE (Ex. 284); in EH it appears in its 1728 form at 125, and with three notes altered (the last three of phrase 2 being lowered a third) at 215, and in that form it is now known as O AMOR QUAM ECSTATICUS, having been found (in the Oxford Hymn Book, 1908) to be an excellent setting for 'O Love, how deep, how broad, how high' by its editor Basil Harwood, who seems to be responsible for that alteration. There is also in this book a new tune in the metre of the sequence VENI SANCTE SPIRITUS for an Epiphany hymn

beginning PROMPTO GENTES ANIMO, which can be read at EH 653. (See also EH 18 and 151).

The *Lyons Breviary*, 1738, provides our Ex. 21B—a plainsong adaptation, as we saw. The *Bayeux Antiphoner*, 1739, contains DIVA SERVATRIX (EH 208), yet another delicious Sapphic. The *Poitiers Vesperale,* besides containing Ex. 279, has the sturdy tune ISTE CONFESSOR (EH 435: H 228), often now sung to 'Lord of our life and God of our salvation'. Then in the *Grenoble Antiphoner* of 1753 we have the admirable tune DEUS TUORUM MILITUM (EH 181: H 344)—more widely known in the USA than in Britain—whose very existence shows how the 'new music' had taken hold. Its opening phrase with its celebration of the notes of the common chord is as far from plainsong, and as near to Handel, as even the radical French allowed themselves to go. The *Chartres Antiphoner* of 1784, which we mentioned concerning Ex. 280, has also ADESTO SANCTA TRINITAS (EH 159), an innocent carol-like melody which gives us the occasion to say that while the *English Hymnal* form of these melodies seems entirely justifiable, the very austere and over-ecclesiastical harmonies sometimes provided there are not necessarily the way to adorn them. The harmonic vocabulary of 1680 will do very well, and since the tunes are designed for unison singing, a pedantic note-for-note bass is not by any means essential. In that particular example, we venture to challenge even R. V. W., who harmonized it, by saying that he seems to have missed its real quality.

That seems to mark the end of musical creativeness in the diocesan Breviaries, though it is by no means the end of the Catholic story we are telling. Further confirmation of our theory that these are basically 18th century tunes and should be so treated is given by the fact that in the 19th century the new antiquarian interest of the Cecilian Societies caused them to drop from favour. The Cecilian Societies were full of the kind of people who call all development degeneration, and they reacted strongly against the musical spirit that had produced the Diocesan tunes. A corresponding, and typical 19th-century, movement in the church to discourage local variations in custom and promote universal unity caused the diocesan Breviaries gradually to be given up. The first to renounce its local book was the diocese of Langres (1839); Paris followed in 1856; the last was abandoned in 1875, in Orleans.

A tune which may or may not fall within this general category but whose origins remain obscure is O SALUTARIS (EH 330 ii), attributed doubtfully to the Abbe Duguet, and found with that hymn in Breviaries of this period. In style and provenance it is, however, an odd one out, and although it was possibly composed during this period, it was not composed for a new or old office hymn but for one of the hymns which form an integral part of the Mass for Corpus Christi.

English Catholic tunes

In England the situation was, of course, profoundly different. The toleration extended to nonconformists in 1689 did not embrace Roman Catholics, and the only Roman Catholic worship which was not illegal was either that of the private chapels of Roman Catholic landowners or the London embassies of foreign Catholic countries. Two of these have their place in our story.

The worship of these Embassies was public worship, and was the only environment in which Catholic music of any quality could be heard. Mostly that did not amount to much, but the Sardinian Embassy some time before 1780 appointed an Englishman, who was probably a Protestant, Samuel Webbe (1740-1816) to be its organist (his son, Samuel Webbe Junior was an organist in various Protestant churches and is responsible for the plain CM version of RICHMOND, Ex. 270). Webbe was (almost certainly) the compiler of the first two parts of a large work entitled *An Essay on the Church Plain Chant,* 1782, and in 1792 he published *A Collection of Motetts and Antiphons.* In both these works we find three hymn tunes that have become well known. They are MELCOMBE ('New every morning', EH 260: H 155), VENI SANCTE SPIRITUS ('Come, thou holy Paraclete', EH 155 ii: H 109 ii) and TANTUM ERGO ('Alleluia, song of sweetness', EH 63: H 54). These, like all the other music in the earlier source, are written in two parts on a five-line stave but with plainsong-type neums. They are all credibly ascribed to Webbe himself: they certainly must all come from the same hand, because their insistence on stepwise movement suggests a very cautious composer walking with very small strides in insecure country. The most successful of these is surely VENI SANCTE SPIRITUS, written to provide an easy tune for the great medieval Sequence (cf PROMPTO GENTES, EH 653, in France), and this owes as much to the captivating metre of the original as to any ingenuity of musicianship. MELCOMBE is too well known to stand any comment but that its alliance with a familiar morning hymn was perhaps not one of Hymns A & M's most felicitous moments; nothing suggests morning less than the persistent downward movement of this tune—which was originally designed for *O Salutaris Hostia.* TANTUM ERGO, as its name suggests, was written for the other Benediction hymn which begins with those words. It later appeared with a repetition of its opening phrase under the name COR-INTH (CP 159).

Webbe was a composer of modest gifts but admirable intentions; he should not be libelled with the ascription of a lunatic tune called BENEVENTO, whose presence in the *English Hymnal* (469) is a mystery—that is a patchwork of phrases from a motet of his (1792 source) beginning *Tibi omnes angeli* (a phrase from the *Te Deum*). But Webbe is responsible for the ornate version of O FILII ET FILIAE ('O sons and daughters'), EH 626 ii, which is now going out of

fashion and being replaced by something nearer the original late plainsong tune.

The Portuguese Embassy, however, did something much more important for us in bringing to England the tune ADESTE FIDELES ('O come, all ye faithful': EH 28: H 12). The English history of this tune is quite remarkable. For many generations—we shall in a moment see why—it was ascribed to all sorts of composers or marked 'Anonymous', until in 1947 in a celebrated pamphlet, *Adeste Fideles,* Dom John Stephan proved its true origin. It was first written down, and is usually thought to have been composed, by J. F. Wade (1711-86), an Englishman who was at the time a music copyist at the great monastery of Douay, in France. The text has not been found earlier either. Both appeared together; in a manuscript plausibly dated 1744 the tune appears in plainsong notation on a four-line staff, and the notation suggests triple time. But another manuscript clearly written very soon afterwards alters the notation into indisputable four-time. This gives us the melody as we know it except for the fifth note from the end, which is the second, not the fourth of the scale.

The familiar repetition at 'O come let us adore him' is quite remarkable as early as 1744. It suggests, of course, the style of the evangelical hymns, so often written in the metre 8.7.8.7.4.7 which was coined for this very purpose, to provide a repeatable short line near the stanza's end. It is much less likely that Wade knew many tunes of this kind in 1744 than that he knew the music of the light operas which became fashionable in the years around 1730; folk-opera has always taken pleasure in this sort of textual expansion at the end of a 'number', and folk-opera is really the common source for this gesture in Wade's tune and for the cliche of repetition on evangelical tunes, especially in Wales. (See below, chapter 18).

But when it was brought to the Portuguese Embassy (where the church music was some of the best in London—Samuel Wesley frequented the place when he was young and wrote music for it) it had only the Latin words. No English translation was available before 1845, and the one we know dates from 1860. None the less, the tune was overheard by Protestants and was deemed too good to miss. So when it first appeared in English tune books, Ex. 285 is what it looked like. That version is from Rippon's famous *Collection* of c. 1795, and Rippon provides one form of it to take 'Begone, unbelief' in the metre of the 104th Psalm, and another alongside that to take Long Metre—as indicated in the example. Notice how much of the bass there given is retained in the version now so well known—but that fifth note from the end is still the second, not the fourth. The important and eloquent leap up to the fourth at that point may have been introduced by Vincent Novello in *The Psalmist,* Part II, 1836. The intrusive passing-note at the cadence just before the 'refrain' was introduced to accommodate the single syllable that the English metres placed over that cadence. But notice—and why later editors never followed this one cannot conceive—how in the repeated phrase, the bass imitates exactly the melody the treble voices announced.

That is, obviously, a masterpiece—it can be called the greatest and most universal Catholic tune, or the greatest evangelical tune, as one pleases. In America it is only now, in the late 20th century, that people are beginning to sing 'How firm a foundation' to any tune but this, and it is at least plausible that that text, with its particularly careful construction of the last line in each stanza, was written to carry it. The date (1787) would be just right.

Wade is also now credited with ST. THOMAS (EH 623: H 5 i), originally written for the *Tantum ergo* text—a strong and reticent tune often associated with 'Lo, he comes' (though not really in the same class as the tune HELMSLEY).

Catholic Hymnody from other sources

Germany provides from this period only three tunes of Catholic origin that are in the general repertory. A Catholic book of devotion—unofficial, of course—called *Tochter Zion* contained the original of ST. BERNARD (EH 71: H 413) which was made into a CM English tune by the Catholic musician John Richardson—who belongs in the next section we shall devote to English Catholic hymnody. The very entertaining and slightly ribald tune ELLACOMBE (EH 137: H 187) was a popular Catholic tune in the late 18th century but its English form is due to *Hymns Ancient and Modern* which altered it at many important points. For the originals of both these see the *Companions*.

Then there is the tune often now called ORIEL (EH 507: H 326), originally written for *Pange lingua* and first appearing in Caspar Ett's *Cantica Sacra* (Munich, 1840); blameless, undistinguished and worthy, it has a good deal more solidity than most music from 19th century Catholic sources.

Indeed, the passing of the 'Diocesan hymnal' age left Catholics with nothing much to pursue but popular hymnody of an extra-liturgical kind. We must assume that the only Italian post-Reformation tunes to appear in modern books, LUGANO (EH 529) and MONTE CASSINO (EH 150 ii) come from this stream, though their true sources have passed into obscurity. When we return to Catholic hymnody after the Re-establishment of the Hierarchy in England in 1850 we shall encounter more examples of these popular styles, but there is an attractive though embarrassing Catholic tune, PADERBORN (AM 226) which reappears in a popular—one might almost say 'jazzed up'—form at EH 568, which still has a considerable following. It is embarrassing because of its opening, which by a mere coincidence is exactly the same as that of HANOVER (Ex. 243). As a hymn it is given first in the *Catholisches Gesangbuch* of Paderborn, 1765, but it was clearly also a folk-song, being included in one of Brahms's collections.

But finally—and this brings us back to the French-speaking musical culture—there is the plainsong revival associated with the Belgian city of Mechlin (Malines) to be accounted for. This was a product of that Cecilian movement which discouraged the modernism of the Diocesan tunes. Three melodies in the form presented in the Mechlin Gradual and *Vesperale* (1848) are in the *English Hymnal*: VERBUM SUPERNUM (2), VENI CREATOR (154 ii) and PANGE LINGUA (326 ii). The second of these is still very well known; the original of the first has been lost; the PANGE LINGUA is now almost always given in one of the authentic versions (Ex. 16). But a moment's consideration of the Mechlin form of PANGE LINGUA (Ex. 286) or that of VENI CREATOR (Ex. 287) will convince a reader that plainsong had been wholly forgotten in the Catholic church at large by the mid-19th century; for it is clear that the editors of these tunes take the line that while nobody will want to sing plainsong in its original form, it is better to sing it in an easier version than not at all.

In both tunes at least the modality is kept; but one notices at once how the phrases of PANGE LINGUA are smoothed out—especially the one that gave us so much trouble when we were discussing Ex. 16. VENI CREATOR has fallen into as uncompromising a triple rhythm as any Diocesan tune did, and all the 'reversed triplets' are turned round to make singing easy. The people who were to sing these were soaked in the operatic and instrumental music of the time, and had no ear for the characteristic plainsong style. But this was typical of the years around 1850: an attempt, about which we shall say more when we get back to England, was being made to recover the ancient heritage of the church. If the first attempt was a rather inept one, it was this that inspired the research that brought plainsong back in its authentic glory.

The English Nineteenth Century - I
Evangelical and Activist

English Psalmody

At the opening of the 19th century, English hymnody was enjoying all the fruits of evangelical enthusiasm, and in the main stream of hymnody we see a steady development of those styles which evangelicals had made popular, with a very mild reaction on the part of a few who wished the more reticent psalm-tune style to be perpetuated.

Metrical psalmody was still far from dead in the parishes, but the last years of the 18th century had seen the establishment of larger and larger nonconformist foundations which encouraged and popularized hymn singing. So a good deal of that kind of music which had been born in the great charity foundations escaped, through collections like that of Rippon (c. 1795) into the repertory of a far wider public.

We can still not intelligibly speak of an anglican style and a nonconformist style: what we have is an evangelical style, welcomed wherever evangelicalism was embraced, and quiet reaction against it. Moreover in 1800, hymn singing outside the charity foundations was fairly shabbily served by the local musicians. Organs were still very primitive. Barrel-organs were much in use by 1800—a product of new technology which made it possible to dispense with an organ player and not to regret too much the passing of the gallery-band, by installing a machine which would produce sounds by the turning of a handle, and supply a repertory of a dozen or two dozen tunes by the manipulation of a dial. The late Noel Boston's *Church Barrel Organs* (1967) provides a unique account of the barrel-organ culture, and the lists of hymn tune repertories it contains (largely overseen by John Wilson) indicates what tunes were known in the parishes in the years around 1800. It is also shown by Mr. Wilson that the speed at which one needs to turn the handle to get a *tempo* acceptable in modern days indicates how very slowly the tunes must have been sung. On the whole hymn singing was a dreary business in the parishes, but broadly speaking one had to choose between that and an alarming heartiness in the new, large, well-appointed and crowded nonconformist tabernacles which were the product of the new virtuoso-style evangelical preaching. You were more likely to find an organ with full pedalboard in one of these than in a cathedral, let alone a parish church.

These, no doubt, provided the market for a good deal of what was composed in the first half of the century. One of the most successful nonconformist composers was Samuel Stanley (1767-1822), who was song-leader at Carr's Lane Chapel, Birmingham. Carr's Lane became a very famous Congregational Church which by 1900 was second only to the City Temple in

London in promoting that curious combination of evangelical fervour and intellectual demand for which that denomination, in its best days, was celebrated. Stanley—an innkeeper from a nearby street in the city (who of course lived in the days before the Nonconformist Conscience would have found his leadership in a large chapel quite incongruous) published in 1802 a collection called *Twenty-Four Original Tunes* of which four are still in currency: they are SIMEON (EH 320), CALVARY (EH 530), and our Examples 288 and 289. All these have an inextinguishable cheerfulness—even CALVARY, which was composed for a very solemn Passiontide hymn, 'Hark the voice of love and mercy' (CP 133) and must be thought of as his nearest thing to a plaintive or contemplative tune. Ex. 288, WILTON is perhaps his most characteristic, with plenty of movement in the harmony, but a sturdy demeanour which renounces word repetition: and WARWICK (Ex. 289)—though perhaps a little over-athletic for modern taste —is equally sound as music. This kind of tune, hopeful and amiable, is what the early 19th century constantly produces from all directions in the English church.

A procession of quietly competent CM psalm tunes graces this period, of which WILTSHIRE (EH 502: H 441) is one of the best; this (usually associated with 'Through all the changing scenes') is a youthful composition, c. 1795, by George Smart (1776-1867) and has a pleasantly Haydnesque turn of phrase. The same evocation of the courtly 18th century slow movement is in BELGRAVE (Ex. 290), by William Horsley from *National Psalmody* (1817); Horsley is better known for a less distinguished tune, HORSLEY, which we now associate with 'There is a green hill', but which appeared first in his *Twenty-Four Psalm Tunes and eight chants* (1844) without name or text-association. BELGRAVE appears to have been authorized by its composer with both versions of the opening note. About the same period must be the sound tune STOCKTON (EH 82); this is by a Stockton organist, Thomas Wright, (1763-1829), but remained in manuscript until it was discovered and edited by Dykes for *Hymns Ancient and Modern*—in which process Dykes spoilt its last phrase by dropping the last note but three to the lower octave.

ST. PETER (EH 405: H 455), now so well known for 'How sweet the name of Jesus sounds', was composed for Psalm 118 by A. R. Reinagle, organist of St. Peter in the East, Oxford, and included in his *'Psalm tunes for the Voice and Pianoforte'*, 1830; as a setting for that fierce and festive psalm it seems to be remarkably tame and unenterprising, with its consistent stepwise downward movement. One would not say that of the very unusual tune WESTMINSTER, by James Turle

(1802-82) which appeared in the second volume of *The Psalmist*, c. 1837, as given at Ex. 291. It is the first English example we have quoted to use that ending on the third of the scale which a generation later was to become so popular, and in the wrong hands so vexatious. Its association with 'My God, how wonderful thou art' dates from *Hymns A & M*, but the very generous sweep of its first half makes it a good setting for those words.

The agreeable tune HIC BREVE VIVITUR, Ex. 292, seen in *Hymns A & M* (569) with 'O heavenly Jerusalem' was originally a CM Psalm tune, as shown, in Alfred Pettet's *Original Sacred Music*, 1826, set to Psalm 42, 'As pants the hart'. Its present name is derived from its association in the *Oxford Hymn Book* and the Standard *A & M* with 'Brief life is here our portion.' We see here a trace of that melodic freedom which we found in the evangelical 'solo' style. Ex. 293, BIRMINGHAM, originally a no-nonsense LM much in the style of DUKE STREET but now used as a 4 x 10 tune (EH 429), must be an English tune, although its first appearance is in an American source (Wyeth's Repository II, 1813: see below p. 130). Its diction is not at all like that of the 'shape note' tunes in that source which come from the American folk-hymn stream, and since there are plenty of English evangelical tunes there and elsewhere in hymnals of that kind, we can assign BIRMINGHAM confidently to an English origin though it has not been so far found. Anyhow it is at least a generation older than 'Cunningham 1834' to which it is usually assigned.

The cheerful evangelical manner of Samuel Stanley is seen again in WARSAW (Ex. 294: EH 386), from Holdsworth's reprint and extension (1832) of Chetham's Psalmody. It is there ascribed to 'Clark', which is unhelpful because there are as many Clarks as Jacksons in our story; but this may well be Thomas Clark, who certainly composed the psalm tune CREDITON (EH 206, 1810). AFFECTION (EH343), in the same mood, comes from Yorkshire, appearing first in Greenwood's *Psalmody*, published in Halifax in 1838.

Nonconformity, within which after 1800 one has to include Methodism, did not really sustain the promise of Stanley during this period. It tended to produce florid tunes which lived on, and to a large extent dissipated, the capital built up by the 18th century evangelicals. One must include among such tunes the very famous SAGINA (M 371), still widely sung to 'And can it be'. Here there is little inspiration in melody or harmony, and what there is has to be beaten out very thin in order to accommodate a word-repetition, which, associated with a text so monumentally intense, comes near profanity. This is from Thomas Campbell's *Bouquet*, 1823, a collection of 23 tunes all original and all named after unusual flowers. Much the same has to be said of the equally famous DIADEM, used for All hail the power of Jesus' name', especially in the USA; by an odd coincidence it was composed,

like its more distinguished elder brother MILES LANE (Ex. 269) by a man of 19 years old, James Ellor, 1819-99. It appeared in the north of England in 1838, from which fairly soon the composer emigrated to the USA. Here the repetitions on 'Crown him' are so hectic as to turn the whole thing into a short anthem, and divert the singers' attention far away from the import of the text. (See Appendix 6 in the British Methodist Hymnal, or 73 in the Methodist Hymnal of the USA). Less flamboyant, but not much more inspired, is W. L. Viner's DISMISSAL (EH 523: H 489 ii), which first appeared in 1845. This was another English composer who emigrated to the USA.

Scottish Psalmody since 1749

In Scotland the Psalter was still the national manual of praise, and to it in 1781 the Paraphrases were added. Undoubtedly the Paraphrases introduced quite new standards of English text writing, but no attempt was ever made to revise the Psalter to the same literary level; and the presence of the Paraphrases with five authorized hymns in the Psalter made no difference to the progress of music because they introduced no new metres.

Our Ex. 295, ST. PAUL, provides an agreeable link with the older psalm tune style; it is attributed to Tait of Aberdeen in a book whose only surviving copy lacks a title page but whose date is deduced from other data to be 1749, and it is a very dignified and serene melody, still very popular in Scotland. But this reserved style did not last much longer. Ex. 296, GLASGOW, so named from its place of publication (Moore's *Psalm-Singer's Pocket-Companion*, 1756) has all the swinging cheerfulness of the post-Purcellian style— one wonders how it resisted any word-repetition, being much in the style of English tunes which used repetition shamelessly. MONTROSE (Ex. 297) is remarkable in a quite different way. It seems to throw back to one or two of the more eccentric tunes in *Ravenscroft* in its use of the widest possible skips in its melody, but it used them with all the assured touch of Playford's LONDON NEW (Ex. 119) and although its use in Scotland has been local and limited, it has more recently come to the attention of the English, especially since being used in a Coronation fanfare devised by Walford Davies in 1937. It has a background in one of the many turbulent periods of Scottish Church history and is credibly dated about 1746, but its first printing was in Gilmour's *Psalm-Singer's Assistant,* 1793. Another tune in the same mood—whose phrases are almost mirror-images of those of MONTROSE, is BALFOUR (EH 186: H 312), by G. J. Knowles, 1750-89.

Perhaps the most important early 19th century Scottish collection was that produced for St. George's Parish Church, Edinburgh (now no longer in use as a church but still a landmark in Charlotte Square) by R. A. Smith, who was soon to become its precentor, in collaboration with the minister, A. M. Thomson, in

1820. The title of this was *Sacred Harmony* and it became a standard source of psalm music for Scots, being a kind of Scottish Ravenscroft in gathering together all the best psalm tunes, but also adding some important new compositions. Easily the best known of these new tunes is MARTYRDOM (EH 367: H 450), widely associated in England with 'As pants the hart'. The tune is known in Scotland in both the triple time form in which it appeared, arranged by R. A. Smith, in *Sacred Harmony*, and in duple time, in which form it was claimed by one Hugh Wilson as his own prior composition (though no earlier source for this form seems to be known). Some have said that it comes from an old Scottish ballad, and its near-pentatonic flavour makes that possible. It is always regarded in Scotland as a very melancholy tune, and its association in some English sources with upstanding hymns like 'I'm not ashamed to own my Lord' is as much a misinterpretation of the tune's original intention as the setting of RICHMOND (Ex. 270) to 'City of God.'

But perhaps even more famous in Scotland, though still little known outside that country, is ST. GEORGE'S, EDINBURGH, the florid tune for the last four verses of Psalm 24 by Thomson (Ex. 298). One remembers that the older Psalters had, at the end of the early period, delighted in 'Tunes in Reports', psalm tunes which were really brief motets: and this is clearly a development of that tradition, fertilized by that of the English evangelicals. There are surely few tunes which have combined such measureless lack of distinction with the achievement of such devoted national affection. No later psalter dared to omit it, and the return in Scotland to a churchmanship which honours the Sacraments in the mid-20th century gave this venerable tune a new lease of life. It is pure early-19th century 'religious folk' music and takes its place with the OLD 124th as one of the national songs of the Church of Scotland. Smith in the second edition of 1825 contributed an 'opposite number' to this in the tune INVOCATION for the other Eucharistic Psalm (Ps. 43 verses 3-6), which stood until recently in the Scottish Psalter (1929 edn., no. 189), but was severely relegated by the editors of 1973; this again is an anthem-style composition which many congregations have loved, but it has not quite the staying power of Thomson's tune.

Smith plundered the evangelical books of England for some of the new material in his book, and our Ex. 299, TRIUMPH, is a fair example of what he felt would enrich the music of the Kirk at that time: originally published in England in 1802, by Zerubbabel Wyvill, this is a DCM tune requiring repetition of the last couplet of each double verse and giving a little choral variety during its long journey.

That tune may look rather extravagant and trivial; but Scottish parish Psalmody during the 18th century had sunk as low as had the English in terms of repertory and performance, and there was no cathedral tra-

dition in Scotland to fertilize music from the professional direction. The composers were all parish ministers or precentors, and there can have been few choirs apart from that at St. George's capable of making much of any new repertory that was offered. But clearly after 1820 things began to stir a little. The new music from south of the Border made its impact. Two really noble tunes followed closely on the *Sacred Harmony* tradition—or, being both from Glasgow we might well say they answered it. One is Ex. 300, KILMARNOCK, by Neil Dougal, the blind musician of Greenock—a pentatonic tune of great strength and eloquence, and the other, Ex. 301, is the more tender STRACATHRO, which exploits evangelical expressiveness but disciplines it within the true psalm-tune style. Both have in different ways the authentic Scottish character; but they are the last examples of it. ORLINGTON (Ex. 302), appearing first in 1854 in Thomas Campbell's *Sacred Psaltery*, returns to the operetta-style of Ex. 298, which was proving irresistible even in the country of John Knox. And what is perhaps the most famous of all Scottish psalm tunes outside Scotland is virtually also the last—Jessie Seymour Irvine's CRIMOND, which was first printed in 1872. It now has to be stated—for many readers of this will be young enough not to remember it!—that no English hymn book carried it before 1947, and that in the last edition of the Scottish Psalter (1929) it is not among the tunes recommended for 'The Lord's my Shepherd': indeed in the table of recommended tunes it is not recommended for anything, Psalm or Paraphrase. It was catapulted into popularity by two mid-twentieth century events—a series of Sunday broadcasts by the Glasgow Orpheus Choir under the late Sir Hugh Roberton, which constantly featured it, and its inclusion in the music at the wedding of the present Queen of England. It is the only Scottish psalm tune known to have been written by a woman, and did not see print until it had been harmonized (indifferently) by an Aberdeen tobacconist named David Grant who was also a precentor. One way and another this now exceedingly popular tune is the most anomalous and unusual of all Scottish tunes: and it is musically unusual in being the only one in the repertory to make use of 'sequence'—which it does in its third line.

Just 101 years after the appearance of the last Scottish psalm tune, the Psalter was officially abandoned by the Kirk as a separate book of praise. Hymns, by 1872, had come to stay, and it is in that field that Scottish composing talent functioned from that point onwards.

Music Making for Everybody

In a sense the developments we have just observed in early 19th century hymnody went on against the background of the old style worship and the old style British society. The counterpoint was between the culture of the Psalters and that of the Evangelical hymns. The one important new social development in the church was the rise of the cult of virtuoso preaching and the establishment of those large preaching houses which became the centres of prosperous and convinced nonconformity.

But in the country at large a good deal more than that had been happening, and the Industrial Revolution, the first population explosion, and the growth of the new cities was already producing a society of consumers, which in music means a society of listeners. (The preaching-houses were in their way a response to this). More particularly, the idea of the *concert*, no longer a *consort* of chamber-musicians but a large event patronized by many listeners, had now become firmly rooted, and the corresponding cult of the conductor and the virtuoso player, creating a market for music of a dramatically advanced kind, was part of the ordinary cultural scenery.

This had two effects on our story, one of which was private and cultivated in its origin, the other in a quite new sense popular and public. The first of these streams of influence was a development on what the charity-foundations had begun when they used airs from Handel and occasionally secular tunes for their hymns (see above pp. 73-74). The central figure in this movement was a Leicester stocking-manufacturer called William Gardiner (1770-1853), who in his six volumes of *Sacred Melodies*, 1812-15, collected tunes from the works of what he called the 'great masters' and adapted them to sacred words, with the avowed intention of displacing Stenhold and Hopkins and substituting these cultivated tunes and texts. Scraps of Gardiner's work still are to be found in current hymnals, and the best known are probably a LM tune called WALTON or FULDA (or in the USA, GERMANY: HT 95: Pm 423, its normal USA association is 'Where cross the crowded ways of life'), and LYONS, so often sung to 'O worship the King' in America (H 564). The first of these is a tune beginning with a phrase from 'O Isis und Osiris' in Mozart's *Magic Flute*, the second is from a tune in one of Michael Haydn's masses. The point here was not that the tunes were of sacred origin —usually they were not—but that they were by the 'great masters'—'good music' in the meaning that that phrase was gathering in the new consumer-society.

Although Gardiner is mostly forgotten—and indeed the sooner his work passes into history, the better—the idea of using as hymn tunes the kind of music which people were now hearing at concerts was taken up by other editors and arrangers. In particular that very influential collection, *The Psalmist* (4 volumes, 1835-43), edited by Vincent Novello and published from his publishing house whose foundation in 1811 revolutionalized the techniques of cheap music printing, contained many of these.

Now the morality of this sort of thing is in our time very properly questioned, and such adaptations from great classics as we are left with have proved mostly to be an embarrassment which popular taste will not allow us to get rid of. But the appearance of so many tunes thus adapted in the second quarter of the 19th century is historically understandable. Our three examples, Exx. 303-5, show how widely the net was cast —an aria from Mozart's *Don Giovanni*, a snatch from Beethoven's early A flat piano sonata, and Handel's Dead March in *Saul*, all from *The Psalmist*.

The difficulty about this is that usually a tune has to be radically altered—abridged, with extra rhythmic points ironed out into a 4-measure pattern, cadences which joined a melody to the next subject replaced by full closes, and so forth. And in this respect some, of course, were worse than others, and broadly speaking tunes taken from vocal works stood a better chance of making tolerable hymn material than those taken from instrumental ones.

Indeed, among those in *The Psalmist* we find the tune then called BELLEVILLE, but now called WESTMINSTER ABBEY (AM 620: WP 9), which is the last page of an anthem by Purcell and needs no more transcription to make a hymn tune than did Haydn's AUSTRIA. Since its revival in 1939 by Sir Sydney Nicholson in *Hymns Ancient and Modern* it has proved a very acceptable setting for 'Blessed city, heavenly Salem': as BELLEVILLE it was in the fourth volume of *The Psalmist* (1843).

Handel, we have already seen, was fair game for the editors. The use of BRUNSWICK (EH 555) as a hymn tune in 8.6.8.6.8.6 (originally CM with a repeated couplet) goes back probably to 1760. SOLOMON (EH 80), quite close to the original melody in 'What though I trace' (*Solomon*, 1748) is a 19th century adaptation. SAMSON (CP 489) is a much less satisfactory tune (though for several generations inseparable from Watts's splendid text 'Awake, our souls, away, our fears') because it is compiled from phrases scattered about in the aria 'Then round about the starry throne' (*Samson*), and it seems to have appeared first in the *Bristol Tune Book*, 1863.

The most famous of all such adaptations is the tune now always associated with 'Hark, the herald angels sing.' This, originally called ST. VINCENT, now known as MENDELSSOHN or BETHLEHEM, was lifted from an oratorio written by Mendelssohn, *Festgesang*, in 1840: it was written to celebrate the invention of printing, and the phrase now sung to 'Joyful all ye nations rise' was set to the words 'Gutenberg, der deutscher Mann.' The adapter was W. H. Cummings, of Waltham Abbey, who had it sung there from 1856 and contributed it to the *Congregational Hymn and Tune Book,* 1857. Another Mendelssohn air used as a hymn tune is *Song without Words* # 9, which, as FELIX, is sometimes set to 'O perfect love' (AM 463).

Schumann's *Nachtstucke* in F generated in America the tune CANONBURY (Pm 406), which seems to have been in wide use ever since the days of Lowell Mason, and is still, obstinately surviving. This is a particularly bad example of a poor tune being made out of a beautiful original, since the four phrases in the hymn tune are only the *exordium* of a much longer melody, and by themselves they are a shapeless torso, with no climax at all. Another tune which is still surviving in Scotland is SPOHR, from Ludwig Spohr's *Calvary* (1835), known in England as adapted in an anthem 'As pants the hart'.

Beethoven is best known in church for the tune HYMN TO JOY, which was coined out of the famous theme in the last movement of his Ninth Symphony (Pm 8), and is now exceedingly popular in the U.S.A. because words were written for it by Henry van Dyke beginning 'Joyful, joyful we adore thee.' Although on the surface this looks like a fairly painless adaptation, since the original is indeed in 8.7.8.7 D and does not actually need any distortion of the melody, in practice the use of it is an act of bad taste because (a) the characteristic syncopation of the beginning of the final phrase is always omitted (except in one or two conscientious modern books) and (b) Beethoven could never have dreamed of the tune's being sung in four part harmony without variation four times to successive stanzas. The adapter of this was Edward Hodges, who published his arrangement in the American book, *Trinity Collection of Church Music,* 1864. Hodges had been an organist in Bristol before emigrating to the USA and becoming organist of Trinity Church, New York. An arrangement of the Ode to Joy, however, was already in American currency, having appeared in *The Mozart Collection*, New York, 1846. Hodges's American sojourn lasted from 1839 to 1863, and he died in 1867 aged 71. But before leaving England he seems to have made an arrangement of the tune now called FARRANT (EH 339), made out of the simple motet 'Lord, for thy tender mercies' sake' much as the old psalm tunes were made out of Tye's *Acts*. This is not used in America but did appear, with acknowledgment, in Havergal's *Old Church Psalmody*, 1847. The original anthem is now known not to be by Richard Farrant, and is usually thought of as 'anonymous, school of Tye', since it is in form so very like Tye's settings of *The Acts* (see above, p. 41).

These are only a few examples from a wide repertory of classics-based hymn tunes, and it will be seen that the results varied from the inoffensive via the dull to the outrageous. The genesis of it all was the new kind of interest in classical concert-music, and if the adaptations were usually insensitive, that at least indicates the spirit in which classical music was listened to by all but a very few.

Compositions in imitation of the classics were, of course, more plentiful than compositions parodying them, and from this point onwards there is an increasing tendency in hymn composers to allow themselves to be influenced by operatic styles, usually filtered down through the parlour-ballads. Our Ex. 306, PORTLAND, shows what Vincent Novello, the founder of the great publishing house and editor of *The Psalmist*, thought appropriate in the way of 'modern hymnody'. The composer is the otherwise obscure T. Cooke, and he has caught exactly the atmosphere of the Rossini school of opera in the flexible melody, the romantic submediant modulation, and the 'virtuoso quartet' manner of this tune.

The Singing Mania

The other important factor in changing the shape of England's musical culture was what Percy Scholes, following certain contemporary writers, called 'The Singing Mania'. This was the sudden uprush of interest in amateur choral singing directly inspired by three people: Joseph Mainzer, who was born in Treves into a German family in 1801 and died in Manchester in 1851, John Pyke Hullah (1812-84) and John Curwen (1816-80). Mainzer and Hullah are known to hymnology for one tune each—MAINZER (CP 14) and BENTLEY (CP 398), neither of which makes much showing among anglicans.

The epochal year of the movement was 1841. In February of that year Hullah opened classes in Exeter Hall, London, for school teachers of both sexes, in music teaching. These were soon opened to the general public and in July 1842 Hullah claimed that he had fifty thousand students. His teaching was based on *Wilhelm's Method of Teaching Studies, Adapted to English use*, which appeared in early 1841, and the network of singing classes whose centre was at Exeter hall had within a few years spread all over the country. His own *Grammar of Vocal Music* appeared in 1843. The movement was recognized by the Educational Committee of Her Majesty's Privy Council (now the Board of Education), and although inevitably there was surrise and opposition, and a good deal of satirical comment on this provision of music for the masses (which generated the predictable neologism 'Hullah-baloo') the movement penetrated even to the University of Oxford: indeed, it was Cox's *Recollections of Oxford* (1844) which first coined the phrase 'Music Mania'.

Only two months after the inception of Hullah's classes, Mainzer appeared in England. He was then forty, an ex-priest of great musical enthusiasm, and in the eleven years left to him he promoted singing classes on a massive scale. He started a journal, *The National Singing Circular,* which shortly became *Mainzer's Musical Times and Singing Circular* and is the lineal ancestor of the present *Musical Times,* and he issued a textbook with the eye-catching title *Singing for the Million.* He held enormous singing festivals, and was especially well received in Edinburgh and the north of England. Some learned critics accused him of being a charlatan, and undoubtedly he was a superb showman. The wave of new interest in everything German which followed the marriage of Queen Victoria in 1841 to a distinguished German came at just the right moment for this remarkable foreigner who reached a pinnacle of show-business success which many have achieved since but which before had been undreamed of.

The third event of 1841 concerns a Congregationalist minister, John Curwen, who in that year took part in a discussion about Sunday School music in a conference at Hull, and was inspired to discover what the best way of teaching music in Sunday schools (which at that date were still not confined to children) might be. He sought out a pious and distinguished lady, Sarah Glover of Norwich (one of the two founders of Spring Hill College, Birmingham which now exists as Mansfield College, Oxford*) who had perfected a system of teaching sight singing by the use not of a music staff but of letters—that known as sol-fa (in America, solfeg). Sarah Glover's system was based on the medieval system of Guido of Arezzo, whose note-names she partly used. During the next generation sol-fa became the accepted method of class teaching in schools and many amateur singers were able to join choral societies through having learnt this method. Music using it was printed in quantity. Percy Scholes vigorously defended it in his *A Mirror of Music* (1944), from which these facts have been taken. The method persisted in Wales and Scotland right into the present generation.

The confluence of these three streams of enthusiasm changed the whole scenery of English music-making. It is significant that one critic of Mainzer wrote firmly, 'Singing cannot be taught in classes'—with which one can compare certain reactions to the Suzuki method of class teaching in our own time. What that writer meant was that music, as the puritans always held, is not a crowd-activity, and that mass-production would vulgarize it. But such critics could not stop the formation of choral societies in every English town of any size, some of which still survive and do excellent work.

All this is in a field wider than hymnody, but hymn singing was affected by it chiefly in the new fashion of singing classes in the churches—almost always in the nonconformist churches. Henry J. Gauntlett (1805-76), of whom we are about to hear a good deal more, was the director of such a class at the Islington Congregational Church, and similar classes were held at Carr's Lane, Birmingham. These were as it were open choir practices which anybody in the congregation could attend, on paying a subscription, and learn not only the hymns but also the anthems for next Sunday, as well as larger works. Gauntlett was, indeed, active in the early stages of preparing the first Congregationalist hymnal with tunes alongside the words, *The Congregational Psalmist*, although he did not live to see its

final publication. But much earlier Gauntlett had been associated with Novello in the production of *The Psalmist* (4 volumes, 1835-43), a very successful series of books designed to promote part singing in church.

Hullah's contribution to hymnody was in editing his *Psalter* (1843), which is a very well-contrived collection of tunes for the metrical psalms and for a few additional hymns such as the old Psalters authorized. This contains no new material and hardly any contemporary material, and suggests that Hullah thought of the church in a very conservationist way. In his preface he has much to say about the need for improving church singing, and especially for improving church taste, and his book rigorously excludes the Handelian material and operatic fancies which even *The Psalmist* was content to carry.

But if there is an illustration of the truth that the primary cause of inflation is crowds and crowd-anxieties, it is to be found in early 19th century English music-making. A huge demand for new currency caused the debasing of that currency. The people asked for it and the new presses supplied it and the composers were only too glad to compose it. So the situation arose which I have sketched in chapter 7 of *A Short History of English Church Music* (1977). Much of the music was platitudinous, bombastic and grotesquely over-stated, but what went with it was a new availability of music of the most lofty quality—Beethoven, Schubert, Brahms—to a public of whom Mozart and Haydn had never dreamed, and a constituency wider, if also more careless of taste, than Handel ever foresaw.

This movement, and behind it the influence of the charity-choirs of the later 18th century, established the tradition of part-singing in church, and created a demand for hymnals with printed tune and words alongside each other. The first of these was W. J. Blew's *Congregational Hymn and Tune Book,* 1852 (another book in which Gauntlett had considerable interest), but we shall soon be celebrating a far more famous example—*Hymns Ancient and Modern*, 1861. But right down to 1852 the hymnal of any church consisted of a words-book for the congregation and a separate tune book, with or without even one stanza of words, for the precentor or choir if there was one. After 1852 tune-books begin to disappear, except in the practice of small denominations, and the last of them was the *Bristol Tune Book* (three parts, 1863-81), used by Baptists and Congregationalists until the arrival of their full music books (respectively in 1900 and 1887).

---

* Three descendants of Curwen have had close association with the Reformed interest in Oxford; Nathaniel Micklem (1888-1976), Principal of Mansfield College 1932-53, Romilly Micklem his brother (1892-1960), Chaplain of that College 1922-38, and in the following generation the Reverend Caryl Micklem, at the time of writing Minister of St. Columba's United Reformed Church in that city. See *John Curwen*, by Bernarr Rainbow, Novello, 1980.

The English Nineteenth Century - II
Liturgical Seriousness and
A New Popular Taste

The Oxford Movement

The most pervasive adjective in the thinking and preaching of the Tractarians was 'Ancient'. The thrust of the Oxford Movement was towards the recovery of those pre-Reformation customs and attitudes which its promoters believed to have been mistakenly set aside at the Reformation, and after its inception in 1833 some of the best minds in the Church of England set themselves to reconstruct theology, liturgy, scholarship and ecclesiastical art. Turning their backs resolutely on all the aesthetic developments, especially in music, which had accompanied the Evangelical Revival, they gave themselves to the exploration of all things 'Ancient'.

It is not surprising, and it is much more forgiveable than some 20th century critics have allowed, that there was more than a dash of romanticism about all this. Here and there the historical foundations of what the Tractarians promoted were like those upon which Sir Walter Scott wrote his novels. Everything that the first generation of Tractarians did had to be done twice in the end. The 'romantic' aspect of their reforms was centered in the attachment of a certain moral significance to what was 'Ancient'. In hymnody, for example, Percy Dearmer (the archpriest of the second Tractarian movement) poked quiet fun at the early translators of Latin hymns for believing certain Latin originals to be ancient which were in fact written some years after the hymns of Isaac Watts,—these being the texts of Charles Coffin which we recently mentioned (ch. 12). And by the same token it is possible to be slightly ribald about what Thomas Helmore thought plainsong was.

What it is wise gently to recognize is that there was a tendency to think that if it was Latin it was ancient, and that if it was ancient it was restrained and unemotional and the best possible antidote to that evangelical 'enthusiasm' which offended the Tractarian temperament.

The architects of the new tractarian hymnody were J. M. Neale (1818-66) and Thomas Helmore (1811-90). Of Neale much has been written elsewhere; he was the first person to apply scholarly standards to the research into liturgy and hymnody, and to distinguish between what was truly ancient and what had come of fairly recent Catholic revivals. (There are no Neale translations of Charles Coffin: those are from Chandler and Williams, who were at work fifteen years before Neale). Neale's enthusiasm ran in many directions— towards Latin hymnody, Greek hymnody and English or foreign carols. But his work emerged from the libraries of scholars and took its place in the pew-racks of the parishes when he joined with Helmore in the *Hymnal Noted* (1851-8).

Neale was a priest of the Church of England who spent most of his life as Warden of Sackville College, East Grinstead, a small refuge for elderly men, which occupation gave him plenty of leisure to pursue his liturgical and hymnic studies. Helmore, also a priest, became Master of the Choristers at the Chapel Royal in 1846, and a priest-in-ordinary there in 1847. He edited the first English edition of the plainsong psalter —*A Manual of Plainsong,* which was later revised by Frere and later still by J. H. Arnold, and in these forms has been the norm of English plainsong chanting for more than a century. He also published a carol book for Christmas and another for Easter, textbooks on music, and, for us most importantly, the *Hymnal Noted.*

This collection of Latin hymns with (mostly) Neale's translations first appeared as a melody book, and then (Pt 1, 1852: Pt 2, 1858) as a fully harmonized collection of Latin hymns with their plainsong melodies. There are, in the complete edition, 105 pieces, with over 200 tunes.

Almost all these are taken from the Sarum Breviaries, though occasionally there are excursions in other directions, including *O quanta qualia,* set for the first time to REGNATOR ORBIS (Ex. 282), *Adeste fideles,* not yet in the English version we know, and *Veni Immanuel* (Ex. 307). This tune has been the subject of a good deal of discussion—and among those who have followed wrong tracks is your present author in the earlier version of this work. Helmore noted it as a tune from a source in the Lisbon Library, and after many people had sought in that library for it Mother Thomas More discovered it in the National Library of Paris, and reproduced it as at Ex. 307A. But it is in fact almost certainly a late medieval tune. It will be noticed that Helmore has taken his own line with it (307B), to make a setting for Neale's 'Draw nigh, draw nigh, Emmanuel'; but it will also be noticed that in his interpretations of the plainsong rhythm he has followed a system which no modern editor follows, and that his harmonies, though restrained by contemporary standards, use a strictly 19th century vocabulary. This hymn, now the most popular of Advent hymns, has become part of the people's music through the work of a succession of editors; and having lodged itself firmly in the congregational mind, it resists all attempts of modern pedants to re-work it in the style of Solesmes. Those eloquent shouts at 'Rejoice! Rejoice!' have nothing to do with the plainsong tradition, but are first-rate hymnody. Just as the text was smoothed out for congregational use by *Hymns Ancient and Modern* in 1861 (and Neale does not seem to have minded), so the tune was 'congregationalized' by being adapted to a rather more regular rhythm, by the introduction of three-beat pauses at the ends of all the lines. Nowadays the accepted compromise with plainsong is to abolish that pause at the ends of phrases 1 and 5. It may be noted also, however, that Helmore quite clearly states in his preface that all his workings are in four parts and can be sung so by any who wish.

Ex. 308 shows his working of a true plainsong office hymn tune (cf. Ex. 9), again in four parts and not disdaining certain 19th century harmonic devices. Ex. 309 shows how he interpreted the text of DIVINUM MYSTERIUM (cf. Ex. 18). All this was romantic antiquarianism if one wants to see it that way, but it did represent the introduction of plainsong-styles to a culture which had totally forgotten them. It was quite uncompromising in its resistance to operatic evangelical hymnody, and that was where its true significance lay.

All this plainsong was later re-worked for parish use, and now and again plainsong tunes, thanks to Helmore, have found their way very far from the high-church parish into the non-anglican books of England and America. What we may judge a great pity is that no such work has yet been done on the music of the Greek Orthodox church.

Neale was as interested in Eastern Christianity as in Western, and having completed his cycle of Latin translations he turned to Greek sources, from which he translated many pieces, some of which are well known hymns. The only attempt to provide a musical edition of his *Hymns of the Greek Church* (1862) was made in 1882 by the Archpriest S. G. Hatherly, an English music graduate and a highly placed dignitary in the Orthodox Church who had known Neale very well. His musical edition is described in his prefce as a gesture towards healing certain unhappy conditions in the relations between the Orthodox Church and the Anglicans in the mid-19th century, and indeed that Preface is an interesting sidelight on the ecumenical history of that period. But the difficulty he faced was twofold: Neale had not attempted to reproduce the Greek metres in his translations, so any attempt to set versions of the Greek tunes to the translations was bound to produce impracticable incongruities: and where Hatherly turned to contemporary composers to provide new tunes for Neale's versions the results were uniformly unhappy. For the new antiquarians were, in general, indifferent musicians, and in 1882 you had the choice of good musicians who wrote bad music, or pale scholarly musicians whose music was too limp even to bear the weight of the paper they were written on. The only solution, if Greek Orthodox music of the medieval period is to be revived (a process in which the Orthodox Church itself is on the whole not interested) is to make new translations which will carry the quasi-

plainsong music of the originals, and then pass those originals through a process comparable to that which has re-established western plainsong.

There were other aspects of antiquarianism, however, than the revival of old Catholic music, and the central figure in what one might call protestant antiquarianism was W. H. Havergal (1793-1870). Havergal's *Old Church Psalmody* (1847) was designed to be a 19th century Ravenscroft, and indeed he was inspired to its compilation by having become interested in Ravenscroft and having in 1845 produced an edition of the complete 1621 psalm-tune book. Havergal was an evangelical rather than a Tractarian: indeed, his daughter Frances Ridley Havergal was one of the most formidable private evangelists of her generation (many of her hymns are still much sung). Frances brought out an enlarged edition of *Old Church Psalmody* in 1870 as a memorial to her father, and this included many compositions by both father and daughter, as well as numerous interesting notes on the tunes.

For Havergal, more or less anything he did not write himself was 'Old Church Psalmody'; but what he did was to make available not only the treasures of old English Psalmody but also many German tunes which, for want both of interest in Germany and of English translations in the right metres, were unknown to English parishes. It was still true in 1847 that there were no appropriate translations, so the tunes had to be adapted to English metres, usually with musically unhappy results. Among those which we now know are FRANCONIA (EH 370: H 418), for 'Blest are the pure in heart' (cf. Ex. 225) NARENZA (EH 518), now sung to 'Ye servants of the Lord' and adapted from a 16th century Catholic carol (which can be read at SP 223). Another famous 'Havergalized' tune is WINCHESTER NEW (EH 9: H 10), 'On Jordan's bank'; an English version of this (cf. Ex. 208) had been known in the 18th century, but Havergal re-worked it with gathering-notes at the beginning of each phrase (never now used).

Havergal was a collector rather than a scholar, as Ex. 310 indicates. Any modern reader will recognize this as a desperately domesticated version of Ex. 56a; but Havergal, after explaining why he did not include a 'bogus' Tallis tune for VENI CREATOR, says, 'In the absence of any authentic tune suited to the words, the editor has inserted one which has been deemed likely to meet with approval; though of German origin it accords with the style of Tallis.' But what is interesting about Havergal is his 'conversion' to the old style of psalmody. His daughter preserved in the 1870 edition one tune he had written (as she says) about 1830—that is, before she was born. This is our Ex. 311, and it is, of course, an attempt at the Samuel Stanley evangelical style. The 'spirit of the age' possessed Havergal when he came upon Ravenscroft and thereafter he is an apostle of austerity and restraint. Unhappily, he had virtually no musical imagination, and so his compositions, which increased in number towards the end of his life, turn out to be uniformly dull. The tune ZOAN (AMS 307: H 545 ii) is quite typical and, though formerly popular, quite unmeritable. But Havergal, both in the Preface to his *Ravenscroft* and in the notes in *Old Church Psalmody*, writes with all the zeal of a convert about the iniquity of cadences which use the 6/4 emphatic chord, which he calls 'feeble and secular', and about the incongruity of modern operatic styles.

A footnote to Havergal—he wrote a number of anglican chants, but three of these were designed to be sung to hymns. Our Ex. 312, one of the best known of English chants, is marked with the surprising association that the Example shows, and carries the note 'Double Counterpoint', drawing attention to a good deal of imitation in the four parts. Another of these three used also to be well known—it is the chant in D, marked *Per Recte et Retro* in which Part III directly reverses Part I, and Part IV, Part II. Crotch, whom Havergal admired, had already done this with his Chant in G.

Havergal had his limitations, but he was a considerable influence and, so far as music theory went, a good workman. Another self-styled antiquarian was Richard Redhead (1820-91), who produced three collections, *Church Hymn Tunes*, 1853, a revised edition of this in 1859, and *Ancient Hymn Melodies*, 1859. From *Ancient Hymn Melodies* the only tune in currency now is that called REDHEAD 66, METZLER'S REDHEAD, or WAVENEY (EH Ap. 29: AM 146); this is an agreeable CM tune whose character comes from its early upward octave leap and its modulation to the relative minor; but nothing 'Ancient' about it is discoverable. From his 1853 book we have the famous English tune for 'Rock of Ages' called REDHEAD 76, AJALON or PETRA (EH 477: H 471 i), REDHEAD 47 or ST. PRISCA (EH 513: H 79) and REDHEAD 46 or LAUS DEO, for 'Bright the vision' (EH 372: AM 161). Of these the last is easily the best; the other two have an inhibited quality which suggests strongly that for Redhead the 'ancient' emphasis meant, as for others, anti-enthusiastic and decorous demeanour. But Redhead was in the centre of the Tractarian musical movement. He was organist at (what is now called) All Saints', Margaret Street from 1839 to 1864, and his rector for a while was Frederick Oakeley who gave us the first English translation of *Adeste Fideles*; together they edited a plainsong psalter, *Laudes Diurnae*. Like Havergal, Redhead did better work when he was not composing.

The other great antiquarian of this generation was Sir Frederick Ouseley (1825-89), an aristocratic cleric best remembered for his foundation of St. Michael's Tenbury, in 1856. As soon as he had graduated he became a formidable force in the deepening of scholarship and devotion in the Church of England. As a composer he was totally undistinguished, yet no professor could ever have faulted a single progression in his work. He left a good deal of cathedral music, and was called on by the editors of *Hymns Ancient and Modern* constantly for new tunes, of which he contributed a considerable number to its first four editions. Every one of these is blameless, and, very few are in use now (although two or three survive in the current *A & M*). Yet just once he seems to have thrown off the inhibitions of decorous anglicanism and to have produced a truly beautiful melody—CONTEMPLATION (Ex. 313: AM 177).

This was the age, then, when the Anglican Church was pulling ecclesiastical rank on society: the watchword was, one might say, 'Let the church be the church and not pretend to be anything else', and the Tractarians without doubt saved the Church of England from becoming a bourgeois adjunct of Methodism. The age when Samuel Sebastian Wesley was crusading for proper organs and decent conditions of work for choirs, when Ouseley was setting up St. Michael's, and when the new Puginesque churches were springing up in the downtown areas of industrial cities was not an age of artistic creativeness but rather one of artistic derivativness. But it started something, as we are about to see.

The Great Victorians

This has brought us to the era, the second half of the 19th century, which was dominated by the new anglican hymnody, influenced by the Tractarian Movement, and presided over by the most famous hymnal dynasty in all history, that of *Hymns Ancient and Modern*.

We recall that hymnody in the Church of England was technically legalized by a decision of 1821, although it had been in use in evangelical circles long before then, and that the Tractarians had opened up a new field by treating hymns not as an adornment of the Prayer Book but as a Companion to it. The first generation, as we saw, was mostly a generation of translations, either from Latin and Greek, to service the new liturgical consciousness in the Church of England, or from German, to respond to the new relations between the English and German cultures fostered by the presence of the Prince Consort. A little more will be said about that in its place.

The inevitable outcome of this new liturgical sense was the new notion (in England) that a hymn went with its 'proper' tune. Researches into medieval hymnody had tought the English editors this; for although plainsong tunes did sometimes move about from one text to another, the hymns most emphatically promoted by the new liturgists were promoted with their 'proper' tunes, so far as these were ascertainable, and in the *Hymnal Noted*, for example, hymns that had no plainsong tune were provided with tunes that became at once inalienable, like *'Veni Immanuel'* and *'O quanta qualia'*.

The result was a new kind of hymnal: that in which the tune of each hymn was given with its text, and the first of these to appear was W. J. Blew's *Church Hymn and Tune Book* of 1852. There shortly followed William Mercer's *Church Psalter and Hymn Book*, 1854 (enlarged, 1856, and several times reprinted thereafter), which showed a tune on every page opening but grouped several texts with it; and then came R. R. Chope's *Congregational Hymn and Tune Book* of 1857 (enlarged 1862) which printed a tune with every text and never repeated a tune.

The new enthusiasm for choral singing engendered by the song schools ensured that the tunes would be printed in four parts for all those who wanted to sing them. But Mercer in 1857 produced an edition of his book with texts only, and this fashion of having two editions, one with texts and one with the full score, persisted for at least three generations. The modern English practice of adding a third edition, with melody only, for the congregation, and phasing out the text-only edition, began much later—well into the 20th century.

All three of the books we have here mentioned were successful and influential, but although in the next three decades there was an enormous output of new hymnals with words and tunes, the advent of *Hymns Ancient and Modern* was to the new movement what Luther was to the Reformation: Mercer, Blew and Chope take their place with Wyclif and Hus. This production of hymnals with tunes for each hymn remained for a while an anglican gesture: the nonconformists continued for a while to issue word-books and separate tune-books, the most widely sold of which tune books was the *Bristol Tune Book*, 1863 (final expanded edition, 1881). But by the end of the century all the major denominations had books following the new style (The *Congregational Psalmist,* 1886, the *Congregational Church Hymnal,* 1887, *Church Praise,* 1885, *The Baptist Church Hymnal,* 1900, and the music-edition of the *Methodist Hymn Book,* 1876).

Hymns Ancient and Modern, whose first official edition appeared in 1861, gathered up the discoveries of the previous editors, and proved to be the most successful of them all. We shall have to mention the complex reasons for this, but basically the thing that gave it such immense power was the skill with which it translated into parish practice the principles of the Tractarians. It was, and has always remained, a work of private enterprise: indeed, the Church of England has never had an official hymn book. Its moving spirit was the Reverend Sir Henry Baker (1821-77), Vicar of Monkland in Herefordshire, and its first presiding musician was W. H. Monk (1823-89), a professor of voice in London. With a few friends, these two set to work in the late 1850s to make a hymnal which would express and propagate the principles of the new-style Church of England. Here are their principles.

(1) The arrangement of the book corresponds very closely to that of the Book of Common Prayer, 1662, as the following table shows.

BCP	Hymns A & M
Morning and Evening Prayer with the Litany and Occasional prayers	Morning, Evening, Sunday, the days of the week: 1-30
The Collects, Epistles and Gospels for the Church's Year	The Church's Year, Advent to Trinity: 31-134
The Psalms	'General Hymns', Sundays after Trinity: 135-202
The Holy Communion and Baptism	The Holy Communion and Baptism 203-210
A Catechism	Confirmation, 211 (in later editions: Children's hymns here)
Marriage, and other Rites Marriage: (Visitation of the Sick:) Burial: (Churching of woman) Prayers at Sea: Ordination (Accession)	Marriage 212-3, Ember Days 214-6 Missions (associated with Ordination) 217-20: Burial 221: 'Eternal Father strong to save', 222.
	Special occasions: 223-46 Saints' Days and Celebrations: 247-73

The correspondence is exactly right down to the final section, and we may note that although it seems to have been *Hymns A & M* that coined the tiresome expression 'General Hymns', that section—68 hymns in the first edition, 182 in the 1950 edition—is arranged in broadly theological sections leading from the Being of God at the beginning to Christian experience at the end. Chope and Mercer had adopted an arrangement more like that of the present *English Hymnal,* beginning with Advent, thus laying stress on the centrality in liturgy, if not on its place in the Prayer Book, of the Eucharist. *Hymns A & M* has continuously kept close to its original scheme throughout its revisions.

(2) The second *A & M* principle was the incorporation into parish worship of the hymns of the ancient Offices, translated from Latin. Of the first 134 hymns, which deal with the Offices and the Church's Year, eighty are translations of Latin office hymns (one more is translated from Latin via Spanish, and another from Italian). That is almost exactly sixty per cent: and many of these are from the new Latin hymnody of Charles Coffin (see above, ch. 12). *The Hymnal Noted* was drawn on to some extent, but there was a distinct preference for the older CM translations of Latin hymns, which could be sung to easy English tunes.

(3) The third principle was the principle of restraint, which kept the allotment of hymns down to 273. Hymnals outside the Church of England had been getting larger and larger: the 1855 *Congregational Hymn Book* with its 1874 supplement ran to 1,281 texts, and that was nothing unusual. Such books, of course, were still being used with separate tune-books, and one simple economic fact which abruptly reduced the size of hymnals was the formidable project of producing a book that size with a tune for every hymn. But this was not the only consideration. The *Hymns A & M* company originally saw a hymnal as an essentially modest companion to the Prayer Book, in which the principal

acts of praise were the Psalms, the Gospel Canticles and the Te Deum. It soon became clear that there would be a demand for a more ample hymnal, and 113 hymns were added in a Supplement of 1868, a revision of 1875 brought the total to 473, and a supplement of 1889 added 165 more to those; the biggest book ever produced by this company was the 1875 edition with First and Second Supplements, first bound in one volume in 1922, which ran to the comfortable figure of 779, nearly three times the length of the original edition.

But this principle of restraint at the editorial level repeated itself in the choice of contents—and so, later, did its relaxation. In this early book the music is firmly anti-enthusiastic. 'O come, all ye faithful' is the only hymn in it which calls for repeated words, and the only tune which is even remotely touched by revivalism. All those Latin translations have either plainsong tunes recast in the *Hymnal Noted* style, or psalm tune, or very modest new ones, and the style of new tune accepted by the editors—the example being set by Monk himself—is almost entirely quiet, syllabic, and diatonic. There is very little sign in 1861 of the special technique for the release of emotion which later editions substituted for revivalist enthusiasm. The whole thing is serious, decorous and demure.

What then were the qualities in the book that made it such an immediate success, and enabled its editors to enter at once upon projects for its expansion? The outstanding quality was what we now recognize as editorial judgment. If a great deal of the book now looks rather dull, and if the hymnological scholarship would now be thought defective at many points, what these editors (one must attribute much credit to Monk here) gave people was a book which made decisions about what tunes should be sung to what texts, and those decisions turned out to be surprisingly shrewd. We will now give a list of these tune-decisions, and the reader can judge how far these decisions were accepted by later editors and congregations, especially those of non-anglican communions and those who were American. In this table we will include only those hymns which, so far as we can see, people generally associate with tunes set to them by the editors of 1861 and 1868; we will indicate where they provided a new tune that was widely accepted; and we admit that there will be some blurred boundaries in the framework of our choice. But so far as can be ascertained these collocations, not before indicated, were the decisions of Monk and his team, and it is interesting to notice that not a single decision of Mercer in 1853-8 coincides with those of the *A & M* team, and only three from Chope's *Congregational Church Hymnal* of 1857 ('Now that the daylight fills the skies', JAM LUCIS: 'Alleluia, song of sweetness', TANTUM ERGO, and 'Brief life is here our portion', ST. ALPHEGE).

A & M 1861	Text	Tune (*New †arrangement)	USA?
2	New every morning	MELCOMBE	Yes
5	Christ whose glory	RATISBON	sometimes
6	Forth in thy name	ANGELS' SONG†	
17	Sun of my soul	HURSLEY†	yes
18	As now the sun's declining rays	ST. PETER	
14	Abide with me	EVENTIDE*	yes
15	The sun is sinking fast	ST. COLUMBA*	
16	Through the day thy love	DRETZEL†	
17	Sweet Saviour, bless us	ST. MATTHIAS*	
21	On this day the first of days	LUBECK	
33	Hark a thrilling voice is	MERTON*	yes
35	On Jordan's bank	WINCHESTER NEW	yes
40	Hark the glad sound	BRISTOL	
44	While shepherds watched their flocks	WINCHESTER OLD	occasionally
59	Earth has many a noble city	STUTTGART	yes
60	The people that in darkness	DUNDEE	
64	As with gladness men of old	DIX†	yes
66	Hail to the Lord's Anointed	CRUGER†	
71	There is a book	ST. FLAVIAN	
78	Forty days and forty nights	HEINLEIN	yes
85	We sing the praise of him	BRESLAU	
86	All glory laud and honour	ST. THEODULPH†	yes
87	Ride on! Ride on in majesty	WINCHESTER NEW†	
92	Glory be to Jesus	CASWALL	
100	O come and mourn with me	ST CROSS*	yes
112	Christ the Lord is risen again	WURTEMBERG	
113	At the Lamb's high feast we sing	SALZBURG	yes
114	The strife is o'er	VICTORY	yes
121	Hail the day that sees him	ASCENSION*	
135	Holy, Holy, Holy	NICAEA*	yes
139	Our blest Redeemer	ST. CUTHBERT	yes
141	Blest are the pure in heart	FRANCONIA	yes
142	Jerusalem the golden	EWING*	yes
143	O love, how deep, how broad	EISENACH†	occasionally
146	Conquering kings	INNOCENTS	
148	O Holy Spirit Lord of grace	TALLIS IX	
149	My God, how wonderful	WESTMINSTER	
150	Rock of ages	PETRA (REDHEAD 76)	
157	Jesus the very thought of thee	METZLER'S REDHEAD (66)	
158	Songs of praise the angels sing	CULBACH	
159	Thou art the Way	ST. JAMES	yes
168	To the name of our salvation	ORIEL	
169	Let saints on earth in concert	DUNDEE	
177	Jesu, grant me this	SONG 13	
179	Jesus, Lover of my soul	HOLLINGSIDE*	occasionally
180	Soldiers of Christ arise	ST. ETHELWALD (§)	
184	Ye servants of the Lord	NARENZA	
185	How sweet the name of Jesus	ST. PETER	often
189	Jesus, meek and gentle	ST. CONSTANTINE*	
192	God moves in a mysterious way	LONDON NEW	rarely
197	O God our help in ages past	ST ANNE	yes

A & M 1861	Text	Tune (*New †arrangement)	USA?
200	Nearer my God to thee	HORBURY*	
212	The voice that breathed o'er Eden	ST. ALPHEGE (§)	
222	Eternal Father strong to save	MELITA	yes
223	Come ye thankful people come	ST. GEORGE'S	yes
224	Praise O praise our God	MONKLAND† (¶)	
255	Who are these like stars	ALL SAINTS	
283	The Son of God goes forth	OLD 81st	

1868

274	The radiant morn	ST. GABRIEL	
275	The day is past and over	ST. ANATOLIUS (Brown)*	
276	At even when the sun was set	ANGELUS†	yes
285	Christian dost thou see them?	ST. ANDREW OF CRETE*	yes
297	O happy band of pilgrims	KNECHT†	
298	The world is very evil	PEARSALL	
300	The head that once was crowned	ST. MAGNUS	yes
303	Bright the vision	LAUS DEO (REDHEAD 46)	
304	Come ye faithful, raise the anthem	NEANDER	
305	Praise to the Holiest	GERONTIUS*	yes
310	As pants the hart	MARTYRDOM	
311	Thy kingdom come, O God	ST. CECILIA	
314	When morning gilds	LAUDES DOMINI	yes
317	I heard the voice of Jesus	VOX DILECTI (§)	occasionally
318	Crown him with many crowns	DIADEMATA	yes
319	The church's one foundation	AURELIA	yes
320	Light's abode, celestial Salem	REGENT SQUARE	
321	Jerusalem on high	CHRIST CHURCH	
326	Christian, seek not yet repose	VIGILATE*	
329	Lord of our life	CLOISTERS	yes
330	The King of love	DOMINUS REGIT ME*	yes
334	Be thou my guardian	ABRIDGE	
342	Lead, kindly light	LUX BENIGNA	yes
348	Once, only once	ALBANO	
362	There is a green hill	HORSLEY	
368	Now the day is over	EUDOXIA (¶¶)	
373	Thine arm, O Lord, in days	ST. MATTHEW	

Notes: (§) - now being superseded: (¶) - transferred now to 'Let us with a gladsome mind', of which the A & M hymn is an imitation: (¶¶) - first time in a hymnal, though associated with the text by its author.

Broadly speaking, if a reader without looking at a hymnal associates a tune with the text in the second column, that tune will be the one which the *A & M* editors chose for it (and which nobody chose for it before in a hymnal), or which they wrote or commissioned. It is an impressive list of on-target shots, the more so when one allows for all the ancient hymns whose tunes were predetermined. It contains 85 hymns of the 386 in the 1868 edition, and omits all mention of texts that have not travelled far beyond their original collection.

This was an achievement: but a greater one was in the kind of new tune which these editors 'spotted'. It became clear at once that here they had struck a rich seam. Mercer has been content with one tune for anything from one to seven texts at a page-opening; Chope had been more scholarly and careful with his music-editing. But these editors' setting of 'Our God, our help' to ST. ANNE was matched by their discovery of Dykes's NICAEA for 'Holy, Holy, Holy'.

Victorian Composers - I

John Bacchus Dykes, 1823-76

This has brought us to the most famous hymn tune composer in English history. If we consider the work of Dykes in some detail we shall expose all the influences at work in the music of the great Victorians, and shall see that it was Dykes who settled the course of the English hymn tune on the track which ever since his time it has followed.

We are obliged to say that in his inspired commonplaceness Dykes was quite unique; he captured the secret for which congregations were waiting as surely as Luther captured the secret of the Reformation. Earlier in the 20th century we spoke and wrote of Dykes as a composer who had been decisively reacted against, and of his style as one which had passed into history; but we deceived ourselves. The further we get from him in time, the more impressive his place in history becomes.

The first thing to say about him is that he was a northern Englishman—a Yorkshireman born in Hull, educated at Wakefield, graduating at Cambridge, curate at Malton near York, minor canon of Durham Cathedral, and from 1862 to his death Vicar of St. Oswald's, Durham. This is important. It was an avowedly tractarian hymn book that made him famous, and whose resounding success his contributions ensured, but the North was not tractarian country. The old satirical description of the Anglo-Catholic style as the 'London, Brighton and South Coast Religion' (the title taken from that of a railway company famous before 1923) had plenty of demographic truth in it, and Dr. Dykes of Durham does not in his own person represent any of the pugnacious reforming zeal of the followers of Keble. He is an avowed provincial, living about as far from London as it is possible to live in England, and spending most of his working life in a huddled mining town that scrambles up the sides of a great ravine brooded over by England's most impressively-sited cathedral: a place where coal-black energy rubbed shoulders with the most refined ecclesiastical aesthetic.

So Dykes, in his association with *Hymns A & M,* represents the modern and forward-looking life-style. His contributions to that book in its 1861 edition balanced neatly the demure office-hymn principle, and in their own blend of decorousness with tuneful appeal threw a bright light of friendliness over a collection which otherwise might have been forbiddingly dark-toned. Later editions, as we shall see, capitulated completely to the music-style that centered on Dykes; it was not the conscientious but bogus plainsong that sold the book, or the translations from the Latin, but texts like 'Abide with me' and 'The King of love' and the tunes of Monk and Dykes.

Although, as we shall see, *Hymns A & M* was Dykes's most enthusiastic customer, it is not that book which prints his first tunes. That honour seems to go to the 1857 edition of the *Hymns for Use in the English Church,* edited by J. Grey, Incumbent of the parish of Houghton-le-Spring, another mining village near Durham, who took Dykes into consultation in preparing his book. Three tunes of Dykes are there: ST. OSWALD (see Ex. 315C), ST. WINIFRED (see the Table further on) and LINDISFARNE. Before moving on to his famous tunes in *Hymns A & M* we may pause on LINDISFARNE (Ex. 314), which was still a well known tune for 'Jesus lives!' in 1900, though now it has been more or less forgotten.

Certain points in that tune anticipate points of style for which later Dykes became famous. Let us note them. First—the strong points are the commanding start and the good part-writing. Dykes rarely falls into the tune-writer's trap of writing dreary and monotonous parts for the alto and tenor, even when the harmonies they generate cause raised eyebrows. In more detail—notice the unison opening (a); Dykes, a good part-writer, knew how to gain a special effect by suspending part-writing altogether, and he used this effect oftener than most of his contemporaries. We see it again in the opening of 'Ride on' (ST. DROSTANE: Ex. 315A), in the middle of the carol 'From far away we come to you' (a most excellent piece throughout), at the end of ST. CROSS (mentioned later), and throughout the arrangement of WIR PFLUGEN ('We plough the fields': EH 293: H 138) which he made for *Hymns A & M,* and which is still almost universally in use. Unison effects with organ harmony appear in some of his other tunes—such as VOX DILECTI (AM 351: H 424) and COME UNTO ME (AM 350).

But there are other points of style which tend towards weakness; accented discords such as that at (b) are usually thought of as faults in Dykes; but quite often they are produced by the composer's desire to avoid monotonous inner parts, as this one is. More serious is what happens at point (c), where the strong modulation to the dominant of G minor at the end of phrase 3 is abruptly contradicted by the F natural in the alto two chords later. This is the result of the lie of the melody, which at that point drops to the F natural where what the ear hopes for is some working out of the possibilities in the minor tonality. Dykes's tunes rather often have this key-tied quality, which, since it often emerges from the melody itself, defy all attempts to reharmonize the tune or re-work its bass. A much more famous example is the junction of phrases 3-4 of ST. OSWALD (Ex. 315B), where once again a promising excursion to the minor is frustrated by the melody's premature return to tonic-harmony implications. Oddly enough, the third tune of his that survived from the 1857 book into other collections, ST. WINIFRED (see Table) does exactly the same thing at its half way point, and it is just possible that this weakness had something to do with the fact that the 1861 *Hymns A & M* did not actually use any of the three.

We can, however, see what Dykes was doing. LINDISFARNE was not the first in the field for 'Jesus lives!' Gauntlett's ST. ALBINUS, which later proved to be the winner (EH 134: H 88) had appeared in 1852. But that tune, splendid though it is, needs a big congregation to carry its high melody notes, and Dykes may well have thought that something gentler was needed at Houghton-le-Spring. His tunes are always parish tunes, never cathedral tunes.

But the central point about Dykes's music is, of course, that it is shamelessly and delightfully romantic. The 'romantic' is, among other things, attentive to detail and attentive to distance. Romantic art always deals in long perspectives, and at the same time with minutely-executed decorations, celebrations of natural sentiments and objects; so in the hands of any but very strong practitioners it side-slips into overstatement and bombastic bathos. What is remarkable about Dykes, when one investigates the church music by which he was surrounded, is not his extravagance but his restraint. If sometimes he does side-slip, surprisingly often what he celebrates is the more lovable qualities of romanticism.

Another glance at LINDISFARNE introduces what we have to say about this. Dykes obviously read the text very carefully before setting it, and said, 'What notes, if we are not to use Dr. Gauntlett's triad, best express those first three syllables?' The answer is—a trumpet-like rising fourth in unison. And what appropriately sets the concluding 'Alleluia'? Why, an ecclesiastical flattened seventh in the harmony and an augmentation of the rhythm. Now Dykes usually had a very keen eye for the total image of a text, and especially for the phrase that would bring its opening verse to life. This is at the same time a faculty for seeing a text from a distance and for seeing it in detail.

' A famous example is his tune for 'Praise to the Holiest'—GERONTIUS (Ex. 315A, AM 185: H 343). We have in its opening line 'the height' and in its second, 'the depth', exactly as that first verse demands. If the rest of the tune does not really take the responsibilities that go with such a superb opening statement, that is where Dykes shows his limitations.

Almost the same comment—but not quite—applies to the equally famous tune ST. DROSTANE for 'Ride on!' (Ex. 315C: AM 99: H 64). Once again the opening phrase suggests the invariable opening line; but the plodding melody of the second half is specifically designed to portray the 'humble beast' of Palm Sunday. Here, however, the author of that incomparable text allows himself the legitimate license of varying the emotional shape of his stanzas, so that what portrays the 'humble beast' does not prove adequate for the climactic 'then take, O God, thy power and reign.'

Word-painting abounds in Dykes's tunes. The use of a tentative melody and snatches of energetic harmony is famously exemplified in MELITA ('Eternal Father', AM 487: H 512) and ST. AELRED ('Fierce raged the tempest', AM 313, see Ex. 319). Indeed, a restless bass is as sure a sign in Dykes of emotional struggle as is chromaticism in Bach. Our Ex. 316D, O SALUTARIS HOSTIA, a tune which remained in manuscript until it was printed in his *Collected Hymn Tunes*, looks somewhat extravagant until one realizes, from what the words of the third line say, why he wrote all those quick-moving thirds in the bass and tenor of the corresponding phrase. Another celebrated word-painting example is ST. ANDREW OF CRETE ('Christian, dost thou see them': AM 91: H 556), where the monotonous melody is supported by the 'prowling' under parts.

Yet none of these points of style are anything but episodes in the total body of Dykes's remarkable output. What is common to almost all the tunes he wrote is another aspect of romanticism. They are influenced, as those of everybody else after him for a generation were, by the fact that the prevailing musical culture of the time dealt in listener's music rather than performer's music.

In his skilful part writing Dykes is often a madrigalist or a chamber-music writer: but the 'listener's music' culture prompted composers to write for effect, and this, as we have just seen, is very much what Dykes did. One effect which this had on his work was to lead him into an area of music which is much better performed by a choral group than by a congregation. A glance at Ex. 317 gives two well known examples of this. LUX BENIGNA, his very well known tune for 'Lead, kindly light', in congregational performance tends to come out as in the example: and so does the end of ALMSGIVING ('O Lord of heaven and earth and seas'). The subtlety of the rhythm at the opening of LUX BENIGNA is too intricate for the rugged handling that a congregation gives it, and so is that of the end of the other tune.

The other consequence of writing 'listener's music' is the tendency to preface tunes with musical 'stage directions', which, where Dykes used them, we have included in our examples, and the abundance of expression marks, especially of arrowhead accents. This is the kind of thing that properly belongs to the performing copy in the hands of a choir.

But then we get a strong impression from the tunes of Dykes and of some of his imitators that hymn singing in the Victorian parish (as distinct from the large nonconformist church) was largely a choral activity. It is not easy to think of congregations joining heartily in the singing of tunes which (not in Dykes, but elsewhere) were often pitched to high F sharp; and the delicacies of Dykes's harmonic touches would be largely lost on a congregation, though they would catch the ear if the congregation listened to the choir. Congregational singing was supposed to be a very important part of non-anglican worship, but such singing, as we now think of it, was not really promoted in the parishes until the early 20th century reformers, Walford Davies, Martin Shaw, and the other disciples of the *English Hymnal* School made their determined efforts to get parishes to enjoy it. Indeed, since when one writes a hymn tune one always has in mind some particular kind of singing body, the texture ot Dykes's tunes is itself evidence of the singing habits of the congregations he wrote for.

Other points of effect, in the dramatic settings of words, are devices like changing from minor to major tonality in the setting of a diologue-text like 'I heard the voice of Jesus say', which we find in VOX DILECTI (AM 351: H 424). Several other tunes use this. Once or twice Dykes wrote what amounts to an anthem-setting, and the most remarkable of these is his setting of DIES IRAE (AMS 398), one of two he wrote, which is pure Gothic-romanticism—enough, surely, to terrify anyone who attended a funeral at which it was sung.

Modern ears appreciate Dykes most, therefore, when he is trying least hard for effect, and when he writes a melody which stands up to repetition without the kind of overstatement that becomes embarrassing. NICAEA, 'Holy, Holy, Holy', is obviously his finest tune, and the one which has a thoroughly romantic text for which it has by no means the earliest setting. If that opening triad is a tone-picture of the Trinity, so be it. (Schubert in his E flat Mass uses the same device at the *Sanctus,* though with startling harmony). It is the only tune of Dykes which in any sense reaches back into history. Its affinity with WACHET AUF has often been commented on, and Dykes probably knew WACHET AUF from Mendelssohn's arrangement: but in the process of composition the derivation was probably unconscious. He was here drawing on the common coin of hymnody, which elsewhere he hardly ever does. So he was not often as 'inevitable' as he is there: but the solemn and beautiful ST. CROSS ('O come and mourn'), diatonic throughout, with those open octaves at the end making exactly the right point, has a chaste authoritativeness which ensures that it is the only possible choice for Faber's words. The same gentle unaffectedness is in DOMINUS REGIT ME ('The King of love', AM 197: H 345)—which only in the lingering dominant sevenths of the final line makes any concession to sentimentality. The tune LUX VERA (Ex. 318), almost unknown because there are few useful texts in its metre, deserves mention in the same company; had Dykes had a 20th century congregational sense he would have provided some kind of pause at the end of the long lines—but as a melody it is unexceptional, and the harmony that goes with it is appropriate and unemphatic. GETHSEMANE (Ex. 319), for 'Rock of Ages', never printed in his lifetime, has a good deal more grace and vitality than the tunes well known for that text either in Britain or in America.

When one looks through the 276 tunes in his *Col-lected Hymn Tunes,* which were published by his widow and whose very appropriate dedication to 'the Late Great Queen' puts the date at 1901, one is struck by the rarity of really alarming tunes like SANCTUARY (Ex. 320). Here we have what Martin Shaw pardonably called 'hysterical sensationalism' and what perhaps more modern ecclesiastical speech would call triumphalism. It is supposed to be a processional march, but although the repeated notes have some structural significance, they come at all the wrong places, and the composer is driven to paper over the resulting cracks with harmonic distractions. This is a tune which one would be happy to attribute to a much less able composer, of whom that age produced legions.

But those 276 tunes are something of a monument to Victorian parish music. They include, as no. 275, a setting of The Reproaches, which was clearly intended to be the last thing in the book. No. 276 was slipped in after the indexes were completed, and is a curiosity in being a setting for a Welsh text (translated into English by its author but given in both languages in the Collection). It is our Ex. 321, and is quite the most uncharacteristic of all his tunes; its first half is in the style of the early 18th century psalm tune, and perhaps the marked falling off of interest in its second is the one typical Dykes feature. It suggests that Dykes was persuaded to set the Welsh text, and, not knowing Welsh, had no word-images to inspire him, so went out, as it were, on what would be for him a 'blind date'. Hence, perhaps, the reversion here to an older hymn-tune style, such as those composers used who wrote psalm-tunes without much thought about the minutiae of the text they were setting.

Of these 276 tunes, just over 200 were published in Dykes's lifetime in various books. The richest sources for 'vintage' Dykes are the 1861 and 1868 editions of *Hymns A & M* and the second (1862) edition of Chope's *Congregational Hymn and Tune Book,* both of which, of course, followed the new style of attaching a tune to each hymn and printing tune and text alongside each oher. We will here give a table which shows how Dykes 'took over' the musical style of *Hymns A & M* in the three editions produced in his lifetime, and it will be seen at once that most of the tunes of his which have survived the change in English hymn singing habits come from the early period. A reader who glances down the second column and who immediately associates a tune with the title there given will find that it is a Dykes tune more often in 1861 and 1868 than in the later stages. But the reader will also see that, when we add the editions of *A & M* after 1875, there is no edition which did not pick up something of Dykes that earlier ones had missed—right down to 1950.

Where a date is mentioned, that is the date of the tune's first appearance in another hymnal; otherwise the tune was composed for *Hymns A & M.*

1861		Hymns A & M Standard	Revised
ST. CROSS	O come, and mourn with me	114	113
NICAEA	Holy, Holy, Holy	160	160
HOLLINGSIDE	Jesus, Lover of my soul	193	193
ST. CUTHBERT	Our blest Redeemer	207	230
HORBURY	Nearer, my God, to thee	277	352
MELITA	Eternal Father, strong to save	370	487
DIES IRAE	Day of Wrath	398	

1868			
ST. ANATOLIUS (1862)	The day is past and over	21	
PAX DEI	Saviour, again to thy dear name	31	31
ST. ANDREW OF CRETE	Christian dost thou see them?	91	91
ST. DROSTANE (1862)	Ride on, ride on in majesty	99	99
RIVAULX	Father of heaven, whose love	164	164
GERONTIUS	Praise to the Holiest	172	185
ST. AGNES (1857)	Jesu, the very thought	178	515
DOMINUS REGIT ME	The King of love	197	197
VENI CITO	O quickly come	204	
VOX ANGELICA	Hark, hark, my soul	223	
O PARADISE	O Paradise	234	
VOX DILECTI	I heard the voice of Jesus say	257	351
ST. BEES (1862)	Hark, hark, my soul (1)	260	344
ST. SYLVESTER (1862)	Days and moments	289	
ECCE PANIS	Lo, the angels' food	310	
ALMSGIVING	O Lord of heaven and earth	365	480
CHARITAS	Lord of glory who hast bought us	367	

1875			
STRENGTH AND STAY	O Strength and Stay	12	17
KEBLE	Sun of my soul (2)	24	83
IN TENEBRIS LUMEN	Sweet Saviour, bless us	28	
SALVETE FLORES	Sweet flowerets of the martyr band	68	
STABAT MATER	At the cross	117	
COMMENDATIO	And now, beloved Lord	121	
EASTER CHANT	Light's glittering morn	126	
LINDISFARNE (1857)	Jesus lives!	140	
OLIVET (1870)	Thou art gone up on high	149	
GLEBE FIELD	Joy because the circling year	153	
VENI CREATOR	Come, Holy Ghost (3)	157	152
ECCE AGNUS (1872)	Behold the Lamb	187	
ALFORD	Ten thousand times	222	284
COME UNTO ME	Come unto me, ye weary	256	350
ST. OSWALD (1857)	Through the night of doubt (4)	274	292
ESCA VIATORUM	O food that weary pilgrims love	314	
SANCTI VENITE	Draw nigh and take the body	313	
DIES DOMINICA	We pray thee, heavenly Father	321	401
HOSANNA WE SING	Hosanna we sing	340	
FIAT LUX	Thou whose almighty word	360	
FIRST FRUITS	God the Father whose creation	385	
REQUIESCAT	Now the labourer's task	401	467
DERRY	Forsaken once (5)	416	323
SANCTUARY	Hark the sound of holy voices	436	
BEATITUDO	How bright those glorious	438	528
LITANIES 1, 2, 3		464, 467, 473	

Notes: (1) Originally for 'Jesus, name of wondrous love'
(2) Transferred to another text in 1950
(3) Transferred to another translation in 1950
(4) Originally called ST. AMBROSE and set to 'Praise the Lord, ye heavens, adore him'
(5) Originally for 'Just as I am', but apparently not published with those words. (Probably then not specifically 'written for' *Hymns A & M* 1875 as Frost claims)

Thus between 1861 and 1875 Dykes's contribution to Hymns A & M rose from seven to 57 tunes; that is, an eightfold multiplication while the hymnal itself ex-

panded by 75 per cent, from 273 to 473 hymns.

In later editions the following were picked up:

1889

THANKSGIVING, originally for 'The Lord of harvest' as set in the Collected Tunes, but from the 1866 supplement to Gray's Hymnal, where it has no words; later called TRINITY COLLEGE. Set in 1889 to Hymns 483 and 486.

ETIAM ET MIHI, from the first (1870) *Hymnal Companion,* for 'Lord, I hear of showers of blessing' (629).

1904

ST. WINIFRED, from Grey, 1857, for 'Christ of the holy angels' (Copeland's translation of *Christe Sanctorum*); set in 1904 to 'O Son of God, our Captain of salvation' (233) (in 1950, 123).

1916

LUX VERA, *Parish Church Hymnal,* 1872 for 'O Brightness of the immortal Father's face' (Eddis's translation of *Phos Hilaron);* set in 1916 to 'Still throned in heaven' (687) (Ex. 318).

1950

JERUSALEM, from Chope, 1862, first picked up in the *Shortened Edition,* 1939, and set in 1950 to 'Good Joseph had a garden' (438).

Since these tunes are still in print in existing editions of *Hymns A & M,* they can be regarded as current, though not all are now in common use. Others that are still used though not in *Hymns A & M* include HOSANNA ('Hosanna to the living Lord', H 316) and ILKLEY (CP 291 and elsewhere), originally one of five tunes he wrote for 'Sun of my soul' but now set to other texts. Dykes thus is shown to have a fertility and staying power which has over a hundred years defeated the most puristic editors.

William Henry Monk, 1823-89

The presiding musical genius of *Hymns A & M* was William Henry Monk, who saw the book through its first four editions, dying just as the fourth, of 1889, was published. He must take some of the credit for recognizing the talent of Dykes, but as a composer he was much less adventurous. His one 'universal' tune is EVENTIDE ('Abide with me', AM 27: H 467), and perhaps, for all its modesty, it is his most characteristic tune. That is not a word one finds applicable to much of his work, for the 56 tunes he contributed to these four editions mostly give the impression of having been written 'to order'. It is usually Monk who provides a tune for any hymn (there were not yet many) in an awkward metre, and he is a master of the simple, ordinary, serviceable tune that does its work and then quietly fades out. The best known of his other surviving tunes (in the 1950 edition only 16 were left) are ASCENSION ('Hail the day', AM 147: H 104), EVELYNS ('At the name of Jesus', AM 225: H 356), ST. ETHELWALD ('Soldiers of Christ, arise', AM 303) and ALL THINGS BRIGHT AND BEAUTIFUL (AM 442), with ST. MATTHIAS ('Sweet Saviour', AM 28: H 182) and UNDE ET MEMORES (AM 397: H 189) still showing some appeal.

Our examples show the quality of his work in various forms. Ex. 322, CEPHAS, is a sound enough tune, typically one which has now been superannuated with its text (than which many worse texts, we may say, are still in use); Ex. 323, ST. CONSTANTINE, is a charming miniature, and probably the first tune to delay its final cadence to the end of the final stanza—a device more used by much later composers. Ex. 324 (1889) may well be the tune which caused him most trouble and gave him the greatest challenge, being written for a dialogue-text which one feels would have delighted Dykes, had he been alive to tackle it. It is the only example in which Monk attempts anything like a dramatic style, and he reduces the demands of the tune to the simplest that can be consistent with setting those very unusual stanzas by Henry Twells (the most original writer of hymns in the Victorian era).

Monk is never vulgar, never extravagant, often distractingly dull. If we may believe what his widow said, his tune for 'Abide with me' was the most intensely personal utterance he ever contributed to hymnody, and perhaps it is its piercing sincerity which has elevated it so far above all his others in the affections of world-wide hymn singers. Though it seems to break all the rules now regarded as binding on melody-makers—having, at first sight, no climax to speak of and a notably drooping manner—it struck home at once, and only the coldest pedant can deny the quality of greatness to it which it is matched with Lyte's wistful and beautiful words. But on the whole Monk's greatest asset was the kind of modesty which made no claims beyond making a text singable. He is hardly ever 'expressive', hardly ever in any positive sense 'romantic', and hardly ever adventurous. Perhaps the tune of his that one would choose if one was looking for the strongest and most unusual flavour is his LM tune ST. BERNARD (Ex. 325).

Nearly all Monk's strongest survivors were written for the 1861 edition, although ALL THINGS BRIGHT was first in that of 1889. To that 1861 edition he contributed 19 compositions, of which five were withdrawn within his lifetime; to the 1868 edition, six; to the 1875 edition, 13; to the 1889 edition, 18—a total of 56. But he was also responsible for the general musical editing, which involved many arrangements and recastings, and we must certainly say deformations, of older tunes, to some of which we have already drawn attention.

Henry John Gauntlett, 1805-76

Gauntlett is the most flexible and strenuous of all the Victorian tunesmiths, and the composer of some of the best known 19th century tunes outside the Dykes canon. These include what must be one of the very best of all 19th century tunes, ST. ALBINUS ('Jesus lives!' AM 140: H 88), which first appeared without its soaring final 'Alleluia', and also ST. ALPHEGE (Ex. 328), ST. FULBERT (AM 128: H 456), ST. GEORGE ('To Christ the Prince of peace; AM 198: H 118), HAWKHURST (AM 232), UNIVERSITY COLLEGE ('Oft in danger', AM 291: H 558) and IRBY ('Once in royal David's city', AM 432: H 236). All these well deserved their fame. They are obviously the best work of a very gifted tune-writer, and even within that small circle we see a musicianship which adapts itself to congregational needs in more than one way. IRBY, written in 1849 for Mrs. Alexander's hymn on the Incarnation (which is, by the way, a hymn about the youth of Christ, not exclusively about his birth) sums up in itself Gauntlett's unusual flexibility of style, for, written originally as an informal piece with simple piano accompaniment, it has become, in the now world-famous arrangement of A. H. Mann, a stately processional of chorale-like dignity. It succeeds in doing this, despite a return to the tonic chord in every line, and does so because of the inspired placing of the short notes.

Gauntlett's musical career, which began at professional level in 1844 when he was nearly forty, took him into all the main centres of church music life; and the small chain of tunes we provide in Exx. 326-330 shows how far he travelled. It is said that he wrote ten thousand tunes; it certainly looks as if he was a compulsive tune-writer. But uniquely among the great Victorians he really does begin in the early 19th century psalm-tune style. Ex. 326, called WELLINGTON from his birthplace in Shropshire, appeared in the second series of *The Psalmist,* about 1837. It does not seem to have been written for any specific text, and its melody is in the melismatic style of so many tunes in that collection. He was, indeed, involved in it from its inception, and besides two or three original tunes it contains a very large number whose harmonies are attributed to him, and as the series progresses through its four volumes his name appears more frequently. This was the early song-school style, as we saw, and his sympathies were at this time with the florid late psalm tune tradition.

Most of Gauntlett's best known tunes were contributed to Blew's *Church Hymn and Tune Book,* of 1852, a book designed to do more or less what *Hymns A & M* did so successfully—to provide a hymnal companion to the Prayer Book. Gauntlett's style here is always firm and restrained, and produces tunes which turn out to have real staying power. ST. ALBINUS (Ex. 327), ST. ALPHEGE and ST. FULBERT are all there, ST. ALPHEGE with its appended Alleluia as at Ex. 328.

A little later, Gauntlett, having served two London parishes as organist, is found at the very strong Congregationalist church, Union Chapel, Islington, where he promoted a famous and well-attended congregational singing class, and joined with the minister, Dr. Henry Allon, in the first stages of the *Congregational Psalmist*. Its first stage was a tune-book, published in 1865, of which he was music editor. His contributions to this were many, and they are somewhat less austere than his 1852 work. The most enterprising of them is our Ex. 329, MALDON, which is obviously composed for a situation where the congregation is a choir and joins in the anthems—notice the high pitch, the anthem-like work-repetition, and the general air of festive drama.

There was no area of church music in which Gauntlett was not interested, and he made useful contributions to the new Gregorian scholarship; but towards the end of his life he was drawn into the *Hymns A & M* circle. He does not seem to have directly contributed anything to the first two editions, though Monk picked up some of the best things from the 1852 source; but he wrote several tunes for the 1875 edition, of which one was the very pleasant LM tune HAWKHURST (AM 232), and another the astonishing composition we show at Ex. 330. Here we are back with the florid style of nearly forty years before, but now we have an authentic piece of Dykes-like listener's music. Indeed the tune looks more like the basis of a romantic piano piece than anything else—notice the *staccato* marks in the second line, and the extraordinary leap upwards in the third. This is a remarkable composition from the hand of the composer of ST. ALBINUS and ST. ALPHEGE.

So Gauntlett ran in and out of the musical provinces then available—from the psalm tradition via Tractarianism and the new nonconformist zeal to the parish-choral style, and he seems to have been equally at home with them all. In modern books a dozen or so of his tunes are still gratefully used, and two or three are among the immortals.

Henry Smart, 1813-79

Smart's contribution to the literature is, on the whole, reliably sound. In larger styles he was conventional and rather dull, and we do not hear his anthems or service music now. But when he was organist at St. Pancras Church in London he was a near neighbour of the central church and central offices of the Presbyterian Church of England, then newly erected, and his best and most famous tune, REGENT SQUARE ('Light's abode' in Britain, 'Angels from the realms of glory' in the USA) was named after that church. This (written for 'Glory be to God the Father',) and several other tunes he contributed to the first new-style hymnal of the Presbyterian Church of England, *Psalms and Hymns,* 1867; among the others are BETHANY (AMS 677), HEATHLANDS (AM 264), ST. LEONARD (AM 443) and EVERTON (AM 207); the last is rather cautious, but

the other three are excellent fast-moving compositions. *Hymns A & M* in 1868 commissioned REX GLORIAE (AM 148: H 103), TRISAGION (AM 288: H 121), and PILGRIMS (Ex. 331). This last tune is associated with a hymn which has achieved a good deal of later notoriety as one of the most disreputable productions of an over-enthusiastic author, but the tune is in its way quite admirable, and worth quoting. It has a very typical firmness of tread, and handles the ungainly stanza with a sure touch and the sentimental words with becoming reticence. MISERICORDIA ('Just as I am', AM 349) is one of the better of a large number of mostly dreadful tunes that those words inspired. But Smart was a good congregational writer, and REGENT SQUARE will be with us as long as we are singing hymns.

Edward John Hopkins, 1818-1901

Hopkins, whose lifetime coincided almost exactly with that of Queen Victoria, was organist of the Temple Church in London for 55 years—1843-98. His hymn tunes were collected after his death by his pupil, W. H. Stocks, and number 155. The most widely used of these is ELLERS (AM 31: H 487), which he wrote in two versions; the first was a version for unison singing with through-composed organ accompaniment in G, which he called BENEDICTION, the other in 4-part harmony in A flat, called ELLERS (both versions appear in *Church Praise,* 1885, but its first appearance, in the varied versions, was in the *Supplemental Hymn and Tune Book,* 1869).

Apart from one early tune published in 1844, Hopkins began his hymn writing career with his contributions to Chope's *Congregational Hymn and Tune Book,* 1862 (2nd edition), which has his well known CM tune ST. HUGH (Ex. 332)—a graceful composition originally written for Cowper's 'There is a fountain'. He contributed one or two to *Hymns A & M* in 1875, but a good deal of his hymn composition was done late in life. He was appointed musical overseer of two important non-anglican hymn books, *Church Praise,* 1885 and the *Congregational Church Hymnal,* 1887, and wrote several tunes for these books. In the Preface to his Collected Hymns—a task he left unfinished at his death—he devotes most of the space to explaining a new technique of tune writing which he had developed —and this seems to have been an interest he embraced at the end of his life. It is based on a revival of the medieval idea of the Hexachord and the Octochord, and the principle is that one selects a scale upon which the melody is written, and uses only the diatonic notes of that scale. The principle is illustrated in our Ex. 333, WRAYSBURY, to which he prefixes the notes of the scale he is using. This he does with the first 35 of the Collected tunes, and also nos. 38-40, 51 and 108. One tune is written on a six-note scale, the next thirteen on a seven-note scale, the rest on the full octave. In practice this means that if, for example, the fourth of the scale is sharpened (as in Ex. 333), the natural fourth is not used.

In singing, one scarcely notices anything but that the tunes are very easy to pick up, being always composed within the octave. Of course, the self-imposed limitation is not observed in the under parts, which use the full romantic vocabulary, and few of Hopkins's tunes are of the kind which can dispense with harmony. But most of those which use this principle are new compositions for the 1885 and 1887 books mentioned above; two of them are still sung in non-anglican circles, ARTAVIA (CP 109) and SUNNYSIDE (CP 275). The archaism of the principle has little to do with the Tractarian interest in ancient music, and nothing could well sound more firmly Victorian than the typical Hopkins tune. (Oddly enough, ELLERS, which some people have tried to ascribe to one of the ancient modes, is not in the 'octochord' group: it uses both D flat and D natural). Probably his interest in the possibilities of tune-writing on a limited compass had as much to do with his long association with an elderly masculine congregation at the Temple as with any very fervent interest in the principles of ancient music. It is not possible to ascribe true greatness to any of his tunes—whether or not they follow the limiting pattern they are usually lyrical, sometimes rather limp. ST. BRANNOCK, for 'For the beauty of the earth' (CP37, not on the octochord) is one of his more successful and sensible tunes.

Joseph Barnby, 1838-96

Barnby is perhaps the most notorious 'Victorian' of them all; he was one of a small group of very influential musicians whose lives fell wholly within the reign of Queen Victoria, and who were as well known in secular music as in sacred. His two most important posts were at St. James's, Piccadilly (1871-6) and the precentorship of Eton College (1876-95), and his *Collected Hymn Tunes,* published in 1897, contains 246 pieces.

Few Victorian hymn tune writers wrote so much that perished so quickly. Probably the only Barnby tune that is now very widely known is LAUDES DOMINI ('When morning gilds the skies': AM 223: H 367). That one was soundly castigated by the renaissance school—for example, in *Songs of Praise Discussed,*—but it has survived all that. The fact that its harmonic structure is so close to that of the once famous part song, 'Sweet and low', by the same composer, indicates that Barnby used the same style for his hymn tunes that he used for his sociable and elegant secular songs.

He knew exactly what he was doing. Two quotations from his own words provide a most interesting historical sidelight on that movement from the Helmore style to the Dykes style which we mentioned recently. In the preface to the 1869 edition (vol. I) of his *Original Tunes to Popular Hymns for Church and Home,* he says this:

> If the outward form into which these tunes have been thrown be likely to be censured, much more so I fancy is the modern feeling in which they were conceived. The terms effeminate and maudlin, with others, are freely used now a days to stigmatize such new tunes as are not direct imitations of old ones. And yet it has always appeared strange to me that musicians should be found who—whilst admitting that seventeenth century tunes were very properly written in what we may call the natural idiom of that period—will not allow nineteenth century ones to be written in the idiom of their own day. You may imitate and plagarize the old tunes to any extent, and in all probability you will be spoken of as one who is 'thoroughly imbued with the truly devotional spirit of the old ecclesiastical writers', but you are not permitted upon any account to give your natural feelings free play; or, in short, to write spontaneously. . . . For my part, I have elected to imitate the old writers in their independent method of working, rather than their works.

That is about the most outspoken defence of the new romantic style to be found anywhere in the field of hymnody, and it is as convinced as the arguments advanced by the Twentieth Century Church Light Music Group in the 1950s in defence of a new popular hymnody. It indicates that there was a good deal of resistance to the style Barnby espoused in the generation which was just getting to know *Hymns Ancient and Modern. (A & M* in 1868 had commissioned LAUDES DOMINI, CLOISTERS—'Lord of our life', AM 253: H 395 and ST. JOSEPH OF THE STUDIUM, AMS 441).

But in Volume II of the same work, 1881, all is sweetness and light. He there writes:

> Happily, no excuse is needed now for composing Hymn Tunes in the natural style and idiom, so to speak, of our own time. The Modern Hymn Tune has long ago been accepted by all shades of religious opinion as a valuable aid to devotion. Nor has it been found less useful as a means of driving out the arrangement of secular airs which, from time to time, have threatened to make their way 'within the borders of His sanctuary.'

Whether by that last sentence Barnby meant those arrangements of Beethoven and other masters of secular music, or whether he meant secular folk songs of the popular kind, he does not tell us. The present writer vividly remembers witnessing a sharp encounter between the music director of his school chapel and the head master's mother-in-law, who was affronted by the musician's refusal to have 'Come unto me, ye weary' sung in chapel to the tune of 'Home, sweet home'. That suggests more, one suspects, of what

Barnby might have been thinking of. He was looking for hymn tunes which were hymn tunes and nothing else, but did not disdain the idiom of the music which people admired outside church.

Barnby was, then, accepted by *Hymns A & M* before he was thirty, and was the youngest composer represented in the 1868 edition. In 1872 he had 'his own' hymn book in *The Hymnary,* published by Novello, which proved successful enough to run into a second edition two years later. He shows himself here in other ways an interested dissenter from current opinion. He declines to name any tune, describing it in the index, chant-wise, as 'S. S. Wesley in E flat'; he does not print double bar lines to indicate the ends of phrases; and he insists on a crotchet (quarter-note) unit in defiance of the custom of using what they called 'open notes' (minims)—thus anticipating a custom which only returned in the mid-20th century in hymnal editing.

The most typical 'Barnby' tune is perhaps ST. CHRYSOSTOM (AM 202: H 460), still fairly well known, and here given at our Ex. 334. He valued it enough to use it in a 'flyer' for *The Hymnary* in the *Musical Times,* 1871. It is essentially in the idiom of his, and everybody else's, popular bourgeois secular music, full of highly charged emotion such as befitted the English Catholic text 'Jesus, my Lord, my God, my All,' mostly imparted by accented sevenths but reaching its climax in the refrain-phrase. Perhaps his strongest

melody is LONGWOOD (Ex. 335)—which elsewhere (*Church Music and the Christian Faith*) we have suggested could be rehabilitated by the use of stronger harmonies and a brisker pace (with which compare what *Hymns for Church and School,* 1964, does with LAUDES DOMINI at no. 230).

A few of his tunes are through-composed pieces, which have a certain dramatic sense; one of these, THE FOE (Ex. 336) was contributed to the 1889 *Hymns A & M* (which took nine other tunes of his, all clustered between nos. 497 and 555). Its first strain is strong enough to be worth quoting, having a touch of the French Diocesan tune about it: a closer look at the tune (AMS 498) will, however, reveal that Barnby's staying power was limited: the thing gets much worse as it goes on. But normally he is shamelessly sentimental. At one time his tune ETON COLLEGE, for the 'end of term hymn', 'Lord, dismiss us', was known wherever there were boarding schools, and aroused fond memories in hundreds and thousands of *alumni* (AMS 577): but the 1950 editors, cautious though they were about such things, dropped it in favour of Hopkins's ST. RAPHAEL (AM 458). His tune for 'For all the saints' (variously called ST. PHILIP, SARUM and PRO OMNIBUS SANCTIS and still printed at AM 527) is as good an example as could be found of a tune which kills its text stone dead. And yet—Barnby is to be reckoned with. He shows that the Victorians were not always careless or trivial in their aims.

Victorian Composers - II

Sir John Stainer, 1840-1901

England produced no better example of a good min-
iaturist who was without the equipment to handle large
forms than John Stainer. His two outstanding musical
qualities were a high degree of craftsmanship in details
—he wrote a textbook of harmony and practised what
he preached—and a pressure of emotional sincerity
unusual in composers of that time. He wrote 156 hymn
tunes (there are 157 in his *Collected Hymn Tunes,*
1900, but one is printed twice in different keys), and
what he says about them in his preface is disarming. 'I
am afraid that some of those into whose hands this collection of tunes may fall will call me to task for having
composed such a large number of them'. He goes on to
pay tribute to the *Hymns Ancient and Modern* group
who, in co-opting him as a composer for their 1875
revision, drew from him his first essays in the form,
and especially to Dykes, whom he most generously admired. Stainer was, indeed, a musician of great influence, especially in his years at Magdalen College,
Oxford, and St. Paul's Cathedral, who, whatever any
may say about his music, was known as a good friend
and teacher by all those who sat under him.

In his hymn tunes he had a certain respect for what
he called the older style, the 'severe character', though
he was at his best when he was composing in what he
called, in the same preface, the 'ultra-modern'
fashion. He contributed 22 tunes to the 1875 *Hymns A
& M,* and in the 1889 edition there are several more of
his. After this he was in great demand, and his hymnological career found its climax when the Church of
Scotland invited him to edit the music of the 1898
Church Hymnary.

Many of his tunes are still easily accessible. One of
his most characteristic—now beginning to lose favour
—is VENI SPIRITUS, Ex. 337. The most important quality to notice in this is the way in which he composes
almost the whole of the tune in the relative minor of
the key in which it begins and ends. This is so common
in his compositions as to be the one thing that makes a
tune immediately recognizable as his; the same quality
is present in his famous choral setting of 'God so loved
the world' in *The Crucifixion,* and it is seen strikingly
in another hymn tune, WOODLYNN (AMS 494), a very
highly-charged Passiontide tune he contributed to the
1889 *A & M.*

One of his very best tunes in the unaffected style
(what for him was 'severe') is the final chorale in *The
Crucifixion* (Ex. 338). This justly maligned work is far
more objectionable for its theology than its music; the
music is often much better than the unspeakable libretto deserves. At least two of the seven hymns in it are
excellent material—this one and CROSS OF JESUS (AM
54). LOVE DIVINE (AM 205) is still innocently enjoyed
—the only tune that successfully sets that great text in
four-line stanzas.

But if one were to choose a tune which has all
Stainer's qualities, strong and weak, it must be REST
(Ex. 339), one of those he wrote for the 1875 *Hymns A
& M,* and the only one of any real quality. Here we
have an unusual sense of continuity in the join of
phrases 2 and 3, and an expressive setting in the unison
phrase 5 of a quasi-refrain phrase, 'O happy saints.'
Perhaps it is that phrase which has caused the tune to
be disapproved by the stern critics of the 20th century
(one may notice that its 'alto' part is the same phrase
as phrase 5 of the melody of 'Eternal Father strong to
save'); but taken as a whole it is an unexceptionable
melody, with a good deal less of that dwelling on
chromatic discords that Stainer often allowed himself.

Among his well-known and approvable contributions to *Hymns A & H* are also (from 1875) SEBASTE
('Hail gladdening light'), VESPER ('Holy Father, cheer
our way'), ST. PAUL'S ('Lord Jesus, think on me'),
CHARITY ('Gracious Spirit, Holy Ghost')—the last of
which is especially graceful.

Exx. 340 and 341 are curiosities but not merely so.
Ex. 340, PER RECTE ET RETRO, is the only hymn tune in
existence which can be read backwards without the
change of a note in melody or harmony; he included it
in the 1898 *Church Hymnary,* though no doubt he had
devised it before—in the spirit in which one might
devise a mathematical crossword. Probably of no use
as a hymn tune, it nevertheless reminds us that as a
musical engineer Stainer was unsurpassed in his day:
and this becomes evident in another way in which he
used his uncommon ingenuity, which is exemplified at
Ex. 341, COELESTIS CURIA. Those who really know
their 1950 *Hymns A & M* will have observed the
remarkable processional hymn (604), 'Daystar on
high'. This is in a special ceremonial form, using a
melody three times for each stanza, first sung by men's
voices in unison and unaccompanied (or accompanied
by brass), then sung by all voices in four-part harmony, and the third time being used as the bass of a
new melody set to repeated Alleluias. The words of A
& M 604 were written by his son, J. F. R. Stainer (b.
1866); but he wrote three other tunes in the same manner for processionals (nos. 8, 9 and 13 in the *Collected
Tunes,* 'Daystar' being no. 10). In each case the main
melody is devised so as to make a good bass, with a V-I
ending. Ex. 341 and A & M 604 are the best in that one
really does not suspect when one starts out that the
melody was supposed to do duty as a bass. None of
these was published, though one supposes that they
may have been used at St. Paul's (where they would
sound to full advantage), but the 1950 editors, more
than fifty years after their first composition, boldly
revived SCIENTIA SALUTIS, and all honour to them for
doing so.

Stainer's reputation has been so heavily blackened
by later critics that it was necessary, with these two last

examples, to emphasize the point that he was a matchless part-writer, contrapuntist and handler of the musical language. What he lacked was the fertility and depth of imagination which could stand up to the endless demands his friends and admirers made of him for compositions. The shorter the piece, however, the more likely he was to write it well, and in the field of anglican chant there are few more exquisite specimens than his chant in E minor, written for Psalm 13 in the *Cathedral Psalter*.

Sir Arthur Sullivan, 1841-1900

There could not be two more different characters, two more differently endowed musicians, than Stainer and his contemporary, Sullivan. Stainer was essentially a church musician, modest about his own work, admiring others more than himself. Sullivan was a man born, temperamentally as well as by the working out of history, for show business—England's greatest show-business musician since Handel, and perhaps her most gifted native composer since Purcell.

The secret of Sullivan is mostly in that association with Sir George Grove which took him to Vienna in 1867 and made him a witness to the rescuing from the garbage-pile of Schubert's *Rosamunde*. What on earth would have happened if what they had rescued was the G major String Quartet or *Die Winterreise* baffles the imagination, but the answer might well be—nothing much. Sullivan was 26 by that time, operating as a church organist in two London churches and already well known as an energetic and popular composer in the secular fields. The set of his mind was already established, and the discovery of Rosamunde (as well as a different kind of 'discovery' of Schumann) was what he was waiting for. Rosamunde is Schubert's light music at its most attractive, and it really would be possible to attribute the opening paragraph of the Rosamunde Overture to Sullivan if one met it new and untitled. (See Ex. 342). Sullivan was ready to develop a talent for melody, a light touch with details of libretto, an ingenuity of scoring, which Schubert would have admired. And of course in 1877 with the opening of the series of Savoy operas, he found the ideal *metier* for that.

Nearly all his hymn tunes were written well before the Savoy period. He started early, with one of the many hymnals called *Psalms and Hymns*—this one being that published for the Presbyterians by Nisbet in 1867—but in 1872 he became well known in hymnody through *The Hymnary*, whose music he edited, and to which he contributed plenty of his own work.

When one remembers that he was an energetic choir-master in his London churches, and built up a choir from almost nothing by recruiting men from the local police force, one then says, what is ST. GERTRUDE, the famous tune to 'Onward Christian soldiers' (EH 643: AM 629) but a first-rate march for a choir of local Lestrades? All the tunes of any character which he

wrote (his collected tunes number 58 plus eight arrangements) seem to have been born for the Savoy stage before their time. Is not that one a good possibility for, say RUDDIGORE? Is not ANGEL VOICES (Ex. 345) a trio for female voices for THE MIKADO that has lost its way?

The tragic thing about Sullivan's church music—of which he wrote a great deal throughout his life—is its staggering incongruity and lack of taste. For he was caught in a trap which was devised by his own temperament. What he wrote naturally was strictly show-business music, and this he wrote superbly. But a nature as extrovert as his was always vulnerable to delusions of grandeur. Most of his celebrated quarrels with W. S. Gilbert were based in his hankering after 'Grand Opera'; he fairly early lost any sense of humour he may have had. And if Grand Opera could not come his way, the church provided a tolerable outlet for these aspirations, and the result is a great deal of pretentious and sentimental material fit now only for a ribald concert of bad music, 'The Lost Chord' and the last two pages of 'O gladsome light' from the *Golden Legend* show what he thought a holy atmosphere was—endless repeated notes from the most gifted melodist of his time.

So poor Sullivan produced in hymnody almost nothing that is not either incongruously flippant or owlishly pompous. HUSHED WAS THE EVENING HYMN (Ex. 344) is perhaps the only really innocent tune he wrote; its part-writing is indifferent (the *Bristol Tune Book* published it in unison, and very sensibly), but at least it has a well-constructed melody and a sense of the picturesque text it was written for. But too often he was merely dreary. More lamentable than his effusive sentimentality, perhaps, is the miserable hesitancy of a tune like FALFIELD (Ex. 343). It is hard to conceive how a good composer could have thought this quite dreadful melody an adequate setting for 'Love divine, all loves excelling'. But then when one looks at the tunes he arranged, or harmonized, or otherwise brought into currency from other sources, and finds that he thought NEARER HOME (or MONTGOMERY: EH Ap. 51: AM 352) and LEOMINSTER (EH 361) tunes fit to perpetuate, one realizes that what he thought the church wanted was a very different conception from those of Dykes or Stainer. We are still singing LUX EOI (AM 137)—originally set to 'Hark a thrilling voice is calling'—and GOLDEN SHEAVES (EH Ap. 17: AM 484), and they both have a touch of character which soon wears thin. One of his better tunes was written at the end of his life for a hymn celebrating the Golden Jubilee of Queen Victoria—BISHOPGARTH (Ex. 346); but taken as a group his tunes are by far the worst, the least sincere, the most pretentious and misconceived, of any written by a major Victorian composer. What they do tell us, more eloquently than any of the rest of his music, is that in some ways this was a frustrated composer—one who had been tempted by his influential friends (not excluding the Queen herself) to cultivate talents which he simply did not possess, and therefore becoming more and more discontented with those for which posterity has so gratefully and justly honoured him. It is a misfortune of the church that the Easter season brings his unmeritable work into so much prominence: for in Britain besides LUX EOI, for 'Alleluia Alleluia: hearts to heaven and voices raise' we can still hear on Easter Day 'Christ is risen' to RESUR-REXIT (AMS 138) and 'Welcome happy morning' to FORTUNATUS: and the Americans are still addicted to ST. KEVIN (H 94) for 'Come, ye faithful, raise the strain'.

It is something of a shock to recall that one of Sullavan's teachers in church music was Helmore. But let this sorry stuff rest in peace. 'Iolanthe' is still doing good business.

Samuel Sebastian Wesley, 1810-76

S. S. Wesley, grandson of Charles and son of Samuel, stands well apart from all the other church musicians of the 19th century, and this by his own purpose. In the first place, he was the ablest and the most learned musician serving the English church in the mid-19th century; his musical world was a very different one, a far less specialized one, than that of the other comosers who contributed to hymnody. He inherited from his father a deep interest in European music, which was much more than that kind of approval of it as good entertainment which was the normal British attitude. At the same time, he stood in the high English tradition of composing, and to a large extent revived it and transformed it. Unlike such composers as Dykes and Gauntlett, he is now better known for his works in the larger forms than for his hymn tunes; unlike Sullivan, he made no contribution to secular music. But he wrote very substantially for the church, reviving and re-clothing the tradition of the verse-anthem on the grand scale.

Most church musicians in the humbler forms are amiable creatures enough. Wesley was from the first a truculent dissenter, and it needed somebody as articulate and as careless of popular opinion as he to achieve those reforms in organ building and in the working conditions of cathedral musicians which, with very little outside support, he did achieve. He was content to stand right outside the popular tradition of church music which was being built up by the *Hymns A & M* group of composers; he was essentially a lonely figure, and less sociable and less popular as his life advanced.

Most hymnals contain only a few of his tunes, of which the one which is popular world-wide is AURELIA ('The church's one foundation'). There is a case for saying that this is his most uncharacteristic tune, since it is the only one which has that rugged congregational quality which ensured success in an age in which congregational demands were being taken seriously.

Hymns A & M in its current edition (1950) shows twelve of his tunes; no other current book has as many as that, though researchers will find a good deal of his work in the *Oxford Hymn Book,* 1908, which prints his name seventy times over compositions and arrangements, and in *Moravian Liturgy and Hymns* 1914, which uses thirty of his tunes and arrangements.

His actual output was a good deal greater than this, and its source is a remarkable publication called *The European Psalmist,* which was published by private subscription in 1872. This is a sort of scrap-book of hymn tunes, into which he wrote anything he discovered from other sources or composed himself. It contains 618 hymn and psalm tunes, followed by a few anthems and a large collection of anglican chants. Broadly speaking it is arranged with the psalm-tunes at the beginning (SM, LM and CM tunes are grouped together); but as it goes on it contains more and more tunes of his own. His own compositions are distinguished by bearing his full name, and of these there are 136: 109 of these appear after no. 400. Harmonizations and editions carry his initials, and the majority of the rest of the collection contains tunes so marked. It is not really possible to date most of the compositions he himself contributed, except by referring to the hymnal he quotes, as almost always he does, as the source of the text he is setting, or, of course, to the first hymnal known to have contained the tune.

But he was clearly a great collector. Having more or less combed the older English books in the first part of his scrapbook, he then turns to German sources, inspired no doubt by his father's passion for Bach; and as a new English book appears he seems to go through it to find which hymns are unsatisfactorily set, and provide new tunes for those. He pays much attention to his distinguished grandfather's work, and many of his father's tunes (and one or two from his uncle Charles, Jr.) are included, as also are the three Handel tunes which his father discovered.

It is entertaining to observe what happens when *Hymns A & M* makes its appearance. He writes new tunes for a few hymns in the 1861 edition, but many more for hymns in the 1868 Supplement, which clearly exasperated him a good deal. There are many hymns which to this day are associated with the 1868 *A & M* tune for which Wesley provides an alternative, and in no case did he actually win. Among these are 'Jesu, lover of my soul', 'Abide with me', 'The King of love my shepherd is', 'Rock of ages', and 'Jesus lives'.

The only hymnal with which he seems to have had any official association was Kemble's *Hymns,* of 1864 (the first source of AURELIA). But it is very unlikely that he ever heard most of his tunes sung in his lifetime if they were not in that book. ALLELUIA (AM 399) will have been an exception—this was in the 1868 Supplement of *Hymns A & M*; and HAREWOOD (AM 243) must have been another, since it was the earliest of his tunes to be published anywhere, going right back to

Hackett's *National Psalmist* of 1839; a few of his compositions are also in Novello's *Psalmist,* in its later editions up to 1843. But nobody took any notice of the delectable HEREFORD (AM 329) until *Hymns A & M* took it in 1904; in the later 20th century it could be regarded in Britain as his second most popular tune.

A composer as lonely as Wesley naturally finds it difficult to establish a style, for style comes from creative reaction to a community rather than from individual isolation. His church music in larger forms moves about in a large area which ranges from esoteric 'musician's music' at one end to something close to vulgarity at the other; and it is the same with his hymnody. Many of his tunes which still appear in hymnals are strangely undistinguished; in his most creative moments he often gropes and flounders. But now and again he shows a talent whch none of his contemporaries could match. Our Ex. 347, WIGAN, is a melody which one feels would have fascinated Bach, and which certainly must have been inspired by his familiarity with the high German style; it is the more impressive because Wesley is not an inspired tune-smith, and most of his hymn tunes depend rather heavily on harmonic ingenuity. This could be said to be his greatest tune: it is one of those he wrote for texts in the 1861 *A & M* and probably dates from soon after that year; but *Hymns A & M* did not take it until 1950, and its first appearance in a hymnal seems to have been in the *Oxford Hymn Book,* 1908.

Ex. 348, CORNWALL, is another captivating yet elusive tune; he wrote it for one of his grandfather's most numinous and majestic texts, 'Thou God of glorious majesty', although it is now associated with a quieter though no less beautiful one, 'O Love divine, how sweet thou art,' (AM 195). Nobody took any notice of it until *Hymns A & M* used it in 1916. It is a most musicianly composition, very well worth learning, but its intervals, especially in phrase 3 with the movement to the mediant minor, prove to be slightly forbidding to congregations, and seem to disqualify it from widespread popularity. This was his trouble: he was either esoteric or commonplace, and rarely managed to combine real inspiration with congregational accessibility. Ex. 349, BRECKNOCK, for a translation by his great-uncle John, 'Thou hidden love of God' has great passion and a good deal of the spaciousness that one finds in the best pages of his choral work: that great stride over the 6/4 common chord in the third phrase of melody is very characteristic. But again, it is hard work for a congregation.

Ex. 350 is one of the many tunes he wrote as an answer to the new popular style of the 1868 *Hymns A & M.* It is pleasant to see the name of *A & M's* presiding genius, Sir Henry Baker, in the list of subscribers who made the *European Psalmist* possible, but the difference between this tune and Dykes's ST. AELRED for the same text (AM 313) shows from what a distance Wesley approached congregational hymnody.

This is musician's music again—all the tension of the 'Fierce raged the tempest' text, which in Dykes is on the surface where congregations cannot miss it, is in the Wesley tune in the tonality, heaving all the time against subdominant harmony.

In Ex. 351 we get a more intimate impression of Wesley's work. The text of 'Abide with me' seems to have fascinated him; for he arranged for it a tune from an obscure 18th century source, and composed two others. This one appears in both forms at consecutive numbers, 539-40, in *The European Psalmist,* and it will be seen that the second version is more than an SATB version of the first. The first is the only tune he wrote in a unison texture, and he clearly thought of it as a solo: it is contemplative and intimate, almost of the texture of a string quartet slow movement, gaining in intensity as it moves towards its very evocative final phrase: the second version has a less striking climax, but keeps the very static form of melody, depending for its effect on a wrestling between the melody and the harmony below. Even in a collection do diverse as this, it is quite unique. But this was not the only tune he rethought as time went on. Ex. 352, WINSCOTT, originated in the first form as a tune for 'Sun of my soul' (a text which as we saw earlier evoked many tunes from composers of this period—five from Dykes alone), and very harmless it is. But it looks as if, when the second edition of *A & M* appeared, the composer went back to the tune, and recast its second half to remove that most dramatic climax, particularly appropriate to the last line of the hymn, 'We lose ourselves in heaven above'; the first version is 370 in his collection, the second comes late, at 589. ST. MICHAEL'S NEW (EH 244) is another tune he wrote twice: the EH version is the second, and marginally better, version (*E. Ps.* 492, 493a).

Auden's phrase 'awkward and alive' describes Wesley adequately. He was full of tensions and contradictions, but most certainly 'alive'. His regard for history, very unusual at that date except among the liturgical specialists, for whom he had no use at all, caused him to cast about for good tunes from the past that should be revived: and it is only now beginning to be realized that one of his greatest gifts to hymnody was his inspired arrangement of ELTHAM (Ex. 353). Here was a thoroughly 'awkward' tune from *Harmonia Perfecta* (1730), a collection which consisted mainly of older tunes rearranged but which showed this as one of its few original contributions: it really is unsingable except in Wesley's version, which so brilliantly overcomes the harmonic hurdle in the third phrase; as he has arranged it it becomes one of hymnody's great miracles. With its architecture, based on its first four notes and its ruthlessly consistent cadence, it now appears in all its structural magnificence. Apart from an appearance in the 1904 *Hymns A & M* this tune, in this version has had to wait for the 1970s to appear in hymnals in Wesley's version. (It was, of course, celebrated by Parry in one of his most exquisite organ preludes, but Parry's harmonization is not Wesley's).

The tunes in *E. Ps.* are all transcribed (except only that remarkable ORISONS) in an archaic form—the accompaniment, furnishing treble and bass parts with full harmony, is on the two lower staves, and the alto and tenor parts have staves to themselves above. This is archaism: yet the composer is groping for, and just occasionally reaching, musical expression far more 'contemporary' and demanding than was within the grasp of the other hymn writers of his time. So he remains a quarry for modern editors, and the best of his material he probably never heard.

The Victorians in General

What has just been said about Wesley is enough to make any reader cautious about echoing the usual snap-judgments about Victorian hymnody. It is less homogeneous than one often is told; certainly the dreary repetition of the judgment that it is a procession of mournful dirges* is the kind of sentimental half-truth in which our age delights, and against which we should be glad in these pages to fire a volley or two. What is nearer the truth is to say that the coinage was undoubtedly debased and inflated through the bourgeois enthusiasm for churchgoing at intellectual cut rates, and that therefore there was a great deal of amateurish and unprofitable stuff printed in the hymnals and on octavo sheets for easy-going choirs. But the Victorians were at their best when they were sincere, and that normally meant when they were not ashamed of celebrating the positive aspects of their culture. Most of the best 19th century tunes are open-hearted and friendly and confident: one can name dozens—like REGENT SQUARE (see Smart above) and CONTEMPLATION (see Ouseley) and NICAEA (see Dykes). Affectation and posturing were their great temptations. But often a composer who wrote almost nothing else comes up with a tune which captures the imagination—like EWING ('Jerusalem the golden', EH 412: H 597), or one most of the rest of whose work is unmeritable strikes the authentic vein, as did Steggall with CHRIST CHURCH (Ex. 354), and the composers of Exx. 355-8, every one of which is a thoroughly sincere and well-crafted tune, still to be admired after the tide has come in and submerged what is better forgotten. Ex. 357, very little known (and sharing a line with Dykes's DOMINUS REGIT ME) is a particularly well-constructed and satisfying melody of the chorale-type, the work of a distinguished obstetrician who wrote several tunes for the 1889 *A & M* but who never again touched this height. Who can deny the inspired simplicity and effectiveness of PRAISE, MY SOUL (EH 470: H 282), the only tune of Sir John Goss that has re-

mained in currency? What a masterpiece of inspired obviousness! That will last as long as hymnody lasts. (It is horrifying to have to report that some American editors recently have shortened its seventh and eighth notes—a stroke of vandalism hardly believable even in this age). And need anyone try to resist the innocent simplicity of our last example (358), THE INDWELLING SPIRIT? That is by C. C. Scholefield (1839-1904), who in 1874 had composed ST. CLEMENT, another obstinately immortal tune, for 'The Day thou gavest', and who wrote this for *Worship Song,* which was published the year after his death.

In music as in literature there are treasures buried in the Victorian jungle which are waiting for rediscovery, and if that is true, the Victorians did not labour in vain.

Non-Anglican Hymnody

The English Catholic Revival

English Catholic hymnody, as we explained earlier, was confined to the foreign Embassies in the eighteenth century; and although Catholic legal Emancipation came in 1833, it was not until the re-establishment of the Hierarchy in 1850 that anything so public as hymnody was needed or practicable. But around the year 1850 there was a great deal of activity. A number of Tractarian anglicans had by then embraced the Catholic Faith (such as Edward Caswall, one of the first generation of translators from Latin), and the very popular hymns of F. W. Faber, published from 1854 onwards, made hymn singing from the 'forties an acceptable part of Catholic worship.

But hymnody was still—and until 1964 remained—absent from the central celebration of the Mass, and new-founded monasteries had the Latin Office Hymns. Hymnody was, for Catholics, associated with the much-loved evening service of Benediction and, above all, with mission work directed at the Conversion of England; for Roman Catholics did not propose to be content with the toleration newly extended to them. This was to be the beginning of a mass movement for conversions. One of the central hymns in this movement, the 'Ein Feste Burg' of the Catholic mission, was 'Faith of our fathers'—a hymn now lustily sung by American protestants who are less conscious of its original intention than of the picturesqueness of its language.

Therefore there is nothing in the new Catholic hymnody to correspond to the learned and authoritative gestures of the Tractarians. It is avowedly evangelical, and designed to appeal to the unchurched and to the very large numbers of humbly-situated people who formed the new Catholic congregations in the new cities.

---

* Repeated for example in just one more flashy journalistic article in the *Manchester Guardian Weekly* for 24 March 1979 and noted on the very day this page was written.

With the almost unique exception of that towering genius, John Henry Newman, the Catholics of the Victorian era were short of creative and contemplative talent, so they fell headlong into the trap that awaits those who seek to minister to the underprivileged and uneducated. The music they gave them was music that imitated the idioms of popular secular music, but lacked the genius of folk song at its best. If the key-word of the Tractarians was 'Ancient', that of the new Catholics was 'Easy.' *Easy Hymn Tunes for Catholic Schools,* 1851; *A Collection of Easy Litanies,* 1852; *Easy Music for Church Choirs,* 1853—those are the sources of many tunes that made headway at once. Our Ex. 359, called INTERCESSION or ST. LUKE by later editors (Catholics then and now have been unwilling to adopt the protestant custom of naming their tunes) may qualify as one of the most malignantly undistinguished melodies ever composed: that was in the 1852 *Easy Litanies,* and also in *Easy Music for Church Choirs* (to which source, 1853, Frost assigns it, a year too late).

Tyneside turns out to be a fertile spot for new Catholic hymnody through the work of Henri Frederick Hemy (1818-88), born in Newcastle of German parents, who edited *Easy Tunes...*, 1851 and *Easy Music...*, 1853. The well known tune STELLA (named from a Tyneside village: EH Ap. 54: AM 202) is from this source; and from a later work by the same editor, *Crown of Jesus Music* (1864), ST. CATHERINE or TYNEMOUTH (H 185). James Richardson (1816-80), one of the composers often met with in Hemy's book, arranged ST. BERNARD (EH 71: H 413) from a tune in the Catholic German book, *Tochter Zion,* 1740; LUGANO (EH 529) first appeared in Britain in Cape's *Catholic Hymn Tunes and Litanies;* and ST. ALBAN (EH 216), from the *St. Alban's Tune Book,* 1865 is perhaps one of the more tolerable tunes from this group of sources. But nobody can claim that any of these are masterpieces, and perhaps a less kind comment than that is appropriate to Schulthes's REQUIEM (Ex. 360), in earlier days a great favourite far beyond the Catholic circle. These tunes are mostly, as they claim to be, 'Easy'—diatonic, of small compass, very manageable. But where they are not like that, they degenerate into a sensational chromaticism like that of REQUIEM, which has the same quality as most of the ecclesiastical ornaments that went with the Victorian Catholic culture.

Through the rest of the 19th century this kind of composition flourished, and very little attempt was made to raise the quality of Catholic hymnody. One of the central tunes of the whole movement, ANIMA CHRISTI, ('Soul of my Saviour') by W. J. Mather, 1823-77 (an almost exact contemporary of J. B. Dykes) sums up the whole vocabulary of Benediction, and plenty of rather unwholesome tunes were generated by the two office-hymns of that service, *O Salutaris* and *Tantum ergo.* An effort was made in the various editions of the *Arundel Hymns,* produced 1898-1904 for the famous Catholic church at Arundel just outside the Duke of Norfolk's estate, to widen the vocabulary; but this sumptuously-produced book (originally in seven volumes) contains a good deal of material that expands the vocabulary of sensationalism in the direction from which the operatic stage was beckoning. Our Ex. 361 shows the transcription in that book of the passage in J. M. Haydn which produced the psalm-tune SALZBURG (already known since 1885 to the Presbyterians in England, who had it in their *Church Praise,* and later to become one of Scotland's favourite tunes). The only sign of a movement towards simplicity and unpretentious strength came later when Sir Richard Terry (1865-1938) applied to the 1940 edition of the *Westminster Hymn Book* the fruits of his long researches into French and English Psalmody; and this, for the Catholics, turned out to be a very short-lived fashion.

Nonconformity in England

The Victorian scene is very largely dominated by the anglicans; after the evangelical explosion up to 1860, the nonconformists do not produce anything significant; they were as captivated as the anglicans were by the new lyrical style, and were content with it. Gauntlett himself spent some very strenuous years with the Congregationalists at Union Chapel, Islington, and must have been largely responsible for setting the fashion which prevailed in the Reformed Churches until well after the renaissance which began about 1900 in the Church of England. One of the most significant nonconformist composers of that age was Josiah Booth, who was based in London and had a great influence on nonconformist taste in his day: but his dates were 1852-1929 and that makes him a contemporary of Stanford, though his style was certainly that of E. J. Hopkins. The most active musical developments in nonconformity were associated with the north of England, where in the Victorian age churches were very large and well-filled and where aesthetic taste was shamelessly pretentious. The kind of tune which induced primitive emotions in very large congregations was much in demand, and probably the most influential and popular tunes among these congregations were a handful of tunes all of which began life printed on leaflets, but not all of which were by nonconformist composers.

The group of tunes at Exx. 362-5 represents the most typical hymnody of English nonconformity at the turn of the century. All of them appear rarely in hymnals because they were published in leaflets which sold in hundreds of thousands and carried heavy copyright fees; but in the industrial north of England (which means Lancashire and Yorkshire, even though there are three counties north of those) they were in the early 20th century probably the four best-known tunes. DEEP HARMONY (362) first appeared in a hymnal as late as 1962—the *Baptist Hymn Book,* but every Baptist had known it for fifty years. Its composer, Handel Parker (his parents had firm convictions about music: two of his brothers were named Jubal and Haydn) came from a Baptist background and was organist of the Oxenhope (Lancs) Baptist Church when he was ten, and at fourteen of the parish church in the same town. RIMINGTON (363) is from a Methodist background—Francis Duckworth was well known as a musician in Ribblesdale and Colne (Yorks). ARIZONA (364) was by an anglican composer who was organist at the parish churches of Todmorden, Preston, Morecambe and Southport, all in the same part of Lancashire; the tune was originally written for a travellers' hymn and its leaflet was much used on transatlantic liners (and also, at one time, for a sung grace in Rotary clubs). LLOYD (365) was the work of a Baptist organist who at one time played in the church in Sale where Carey Bonner was minister.

All these musicians were contemporaries of Stanford and Harwood, using a new-found popular idiom suitable for the sol-fa reading choir in the industrial north, whose members demanded music that was easy to sing. The choral movement started by Mainzer and Hullah was now in its heyday in this region: every town had its choral society, and every choral society performed with enthusiasm music written in firmly restricted idiom. This is why all these chart-hitting tunes turn out to be variations on a single basic musical idea. There is a very slow and primitive harmonic movement—outwards to the dominant, home (usually) via a reference to the subdominant emphatically stated by the tenors. It was music which any congregation could learn by ear in a minute or two, and it went with the northern nonconformist culture. Indeed, this group of tunes exposes the nature of the kind of hearty and fervent hymn singing which English nonconformity, especially in the north, most enjoyed. That secret is the welcome offered by a certain kind of religious mind to music which large numbers of people can sing very easily. The northern chapels, whether large or small, were fully populated: a congregation was always a crowd. The content of religion was not necessarily what is called 'evangelical'. It might be anything from hell-fire fundamentalism to modernist liberalism: but whichever it was, the crowd was there and the presentation in the preaching was dramatic and usually simple. This was the reverse of contemplative, and the personal discipline required of its adherents was moral and physical rather than intellectual. Teetotalism, for example, was almost universal in those circles, and other prohibitions on those indulgences which most threatened the enthronement of hard work and industrial obedience were imposed and accepted. What was not accepted was deviation from the cultural norm. Questions were not asked if they gave the answerer the least difficulty.

That is exactly what the popular hymnody suggests. What strikes one about it now is its monotony. Two or three subjects alone are dealt with, in the hymnody as by the preachers. People in England still talk of 'old Methodist tunes', meaning certainly not the tunes which John Wesley knew and approved, but tunes of a certain style; the canon of 'Old Methodist tunes' certainly included the Roman Catholic STELLA (EH Ap. 54) and LYDIA (MHB 1), a tune of dubious provenance shared at one time with the Anglicans, and many others which are neither particularly old nor Methodist, but are in E flat major and have a harmonic system as naive as that of the American Gospelsongs—to which in many ways they corresponded in form and function. Reams of hymn tunes appeared in the books which confine themselves to the most basic of musical subjects: one is the triple-time repeated-chord opening, of which we give a random sample of a dozen in Ex. 366; another is the chromatic embellishment of a static harmonic statement, as in Ex. 367. A third is the rising melodic sixth from dominant to mediant as in the openings of CRIMOND and BELMONT. It was attractive not because it was sensational so much as because it was familiar. What you sang over and over again had the familiarity of one's home, the coziness of what, in those tough times and regions, was no doubt a fairly drab dwelling. 'It's not much but it's *mine.*' The rapid dissolution of this whole social structure in the years after World War I was a traumatic experience for the seniors who had enjoyed it; but the plain fact is that if you are saying only two or three things and the new generation doesn't care for any of them, they go elsewhere. What is most to be criticized, or pitied, or censured (according to one's mood) about Victorian religious aesthetic is not really its sensationalism but its narrowness and its intolerance of deviation. A hundred years later, especially in America, this religious attitude is still the church's greatest threat.

This is the kind of criticism we are bound to apply to the anglican hymnody of the same period; but things were much worse with nonconformity because in those days it was so bereft of true religious discipline, and especially of intellectual discipline. It was never the intellectual faithful who drew the largest congregations: it was the preachers whose talents came nearest to those which a generation later were monopolized by Hollywood. And there was no liturgy, as there was in the Church of England, to fortify the faithful by gently dropping into the people's mind the church's teaching through the familiar and hallowed words of the Prayer Book and the Psalter. The industrial North lived on results and quick profits, obtained never mind at whose expense, and it was impossible for this not to be betrayed in the forms of religion which were most popular. So in later days we have that long string of autobiographies in which their authors complain of the narrowness of the religion in which they were raised.

The other form of hymnody which nonconformity rejoiced in was the imported American 'Gospel Song' and its English imitations. This properly belongs in a later chapter and we shall deal with it there. In England this became the religious diet of the new industrial poor, provided by missioners who won their allegiance with these catchy, simple, fervent songs. At a later stage anglican industrial missioners took them over—hence that section in the English Hymnal, nos. 567-585, which is in the later editions headed in very small type 'not for ordinary use'—that cautionary heading being thought necessary in 1933 but certainly not in 1906. But the implications of class-structure in the use of this kind of music must be left to our American chapter.

It has to be said that nonconformity produced nothing in hymnody to compare with the best of the anglican material (such as Exx. 357-61). There was no really influential nonconformist composer before Eric Thiman, who was born in 1900. The Baptists were fortunate in their eminent editor and composer, Cary Bonner (1859-1938), who compensated by editorial skill for the slightness of his composing talent; but the Congregationalists 'borrowed' E. J. Hopkins for their hymn book of 1887, as did the Presbyterians in 1885, and the Methodist Hymn Book of 1904 was similarly edited by the organist of Westminster Abbey, Sir Frederick Bridge.

One other author and composer at one time exceedingly active in producing material for nonconformists must be mentioned, we fear without affection: H. Ernest Nichol (1862-1926). He wrote a very large number of tunes, providing his own lyrics under the near-anagram 'Colin Sterne' which were chiefly aimed at the children, especially at the very lively market in Sunday School Festivals. Up to 1950 this material was in very wide circulation, and it bears all the marks of mass-production. It corresponds closely to the later American material associated with the name of J. W. Peterson; and here again its popularity was ensured by the vigour with which it said the same thing over and over again, with no attempt at deviation from a restricted regime of march-like choruses. A good deal of this can be found in the *Sunday School Hymnal* (1905), edited by Carey Bonner, which was easily the most successful book in British circulation among children's classes, and unhappily one of the most influential.

The Edwardians, c. 1890-1920

Aesthetic progress is usually the consequence of dissent and tension, and the turn of the 20th century was the scene of much of this in church music. Broadly speaking there were two possible answers to the questions posed by the condition into which English church music had fallen in about 1890; in both choral music and hymnody these questions received successful answers, and the result of that was the vitality of 20th century church music in all forms. The first of these answers was to provide new and more substantial music in the vocabulary which the degenerate musicians had used, and this was provided by the small group we here call the Edwardians. The other answer, to reconstruct the vocabulary, was offered by the musicians we shall consider in the next chapter but one.

As we have just indicated, the great Edwardians were contemporaries of the more successful degenerates. They were, broadly speaking, born in the 25 years following 1848, the date of birth of Charles Hubert Hastings Parry.

C. H. H. Parry, 1848-1918

In one respect Parry is the legitimate successor of S. S. Wesley—that is, in being a musician who moved in a larger field than that of small-scale church music. But there the resemblance ends. However, the common quality of the greater Edwardians, especially of Parry, Stanford and Wood, is that they are men of very wide musical learning and culture, thoroughly at home in secular music, and aware of the developments in the whole field. Especially we find in Parry and Stanford an awareness of the idiom of Brahms, at that time the leading contemporary symphonist and song-writer.

Parry is a thoroughly contemporary composer in his day; Wesley was something of an archaist, influenced in his style more by Haydn than by Mendelssohn; and although he composed very little secular music, his church music was well outside the normal field of discourse, in consequence of which, he found himself more and more relegated to the outer edge of musical conversation. Parry, by contrast, brought to church music a talent not only nourished by Brahms but capable of communicating the real essence of the developed 19th century musical message. He wrote a great deal of music not much of which is now remembered; he lacked self-criticism, which Brahms found so necessary in the fulfilment of his own destiny. But Parry was, like Brahms, a master tunesmith, and this is what made his contribution to hymnody, though modest, so impressive.

It still surprises people to learn that Parry was never an orthodox Christian believer: he was certainly not a churchman. This is because he is most widely remembered now for his settings of religious words. Two comments are in order: in the first place, his sensitiveness to poetry, especially of a mystical kind, was a new development in English church music and set a fashion which others ably followed. He enjoyed the poetry of the Faith even if he rejected its dogma. In the second place, as Stainton de B. Taylor pointed out in his *The Music of Parry and Stanford,* towards the end of his life he was clearly very much occupied with mystical literature, especially that of those 17th century poets whose chief subject of meditation was death. The *Songs of Farewell* (1916-18), his last important work, now most unhappily in eclipse and certainly due for revival, are the profoundest things he ever wrote, and a supreme example of applied Christian aesthetic. The same could be said of that Choral-Fantasia for Organ on the tune ELTHAM, which we alluded to in passing at the end of our section on S. S. Wesley.

Hymnody, one might have thought, would be the kind of church music to which he would be least drawn, because hymnody is the music of the visible and institutional church. But it looks as if he discovered in himself a gift for hymn writing in the course of composing his anthem, 'Hear my words' (1894). Here again he celebrates a debt to Wesley, for this is the last of those English verse-anthems (anthems in several movements featuring prominent solos) which enjoyed a steady development all the way from the Tudors. But here instead of ending with a conventional fugal chorus, he ends with a setting of a hymn, Baker's 'O praise ye the Lord', using one tune for stanzas 1 and 3 and another, in the dominant, for stanza 2. A good deal later (1916), the leading tune was printed by itself as LAUDATE DOMINUM (AM 376), and was at once recognized as a first-class congregational tune.

In 1904 he was drafted in by the editors of that years' *Hymns Ancient and Modern*, and wrote a number of tunes on commission, some of which are conventional and blameless, but one or two of which, like RUSTINGTON (AM 292), GAUDIUM CAELESTE (AMS 779) and supremely INTERCESSOR (AM 115) show a quite new kind of melodic genius. Our Ex. 368, FRESHWATER, was one of those he contributed to the 1904 book: this is more of an anthem than a hymn, and had been composed shortly after Tennyson's death. (It was not the first musical setting of 'Crossing the Bar', Tennyson's last poem: that was composed for the poet's funeral by Sir Frederick Bridge and can be found at 640 in the English *Methodist Hymn Book*). Its exquisite reticence and expressiveness are vintage Parry, and show his characteristic sensitiveness in handling poetry.

But Parry's supreme congregational achievement was, obviously, JERUSALEM (Ex. 369)—again written for a poem which is not in any sense a hymn. This is one of the half dozen tunes which every Englishman knows and, in a ruggedly sentimental fashion, loves. It has been referred to as the English national anthem (there is no other), and if it is to be included in the ranks of national songs then it is the finest piece of music, by a long way, to have that honour. (The runner-up would be the National Anthem of the Netherlands, which goes back to 1626—see Ex. 568). But looked at simply as a piece of melodic engineering, it is flawless in its judgment of what ordinary people are glad to sing. It breaks most of the rules which lesser composers feel obliged to follow when writing long tunes: for we tell ourselves that a long tune must contain plenty of repetition, goes best when the phrases are of unequal length, and had better stay as near to a compass of an octave as possible. Parry's tune is constructed not by repetition but by intellectual development—see the relation between the marked phrases; it is in Double Long Metre, which hardly any other composer has managed to handle successfully: and it has a compass of an eleventh, yet nobody has ever been heard to complain that it goes too high for him to reach. It is, we might say, the last great vulgar tune (in the most exalted sense) in musical history, and it comes from that period when Parry was writing his greatest music. See the hymn-book Companions for the story of how it came to be written—by one who never dreamed that it would become what it has become. The other quality which lifts JERUSALEM right out of the common rut of community song is its subtle use of minor tonality: it is emphatically in B minor for much of its first half, and rises in the second triumphantly out of an E minor start. It even calls for slight and eloquent modifications in the rhythm when the second stanza comes round without tripping anybody up. All the way it enables people to make great music as if that were the most natural thing in the world.

This is where Parry is significant, and for the creation of a tune like this we can forgive the reams of learned Professor's music that he wrote in other forms. If a hymn tune is primarily a tune, then Parry set a new standard, modest though, in point of quantity, his contribution was, and unlikely as he was ever to be found singing a hymn in a church pew.

Charles Villiers Stanford, 1852-1924

Parry's great colleague Stanford is an even slighter figure in the literature of hymnody, and an even more influential one in church music generally. If Parry's ancestral background was Welsh, Stanford was a full blooded Irishman; when Parry was Professor of Music at Oxford, Stanford held the corresponding Chair at Cambridge. Parry was an agnostic, Stanford a fairly contented Christian. Stanford is best remembered now for his series of settings of the Prayer Book Canticles, in which certainly we find his best-contrived church music. And like Parry, his influence on hymnody was less in what he contributed than in what he stood for. For in those canticle settings he set a fashion of writing not episodically but coherently, with purposeful use of

prominent motifs and modulations which are really modulations and not just tiresome accidents. Like Parry he saw no reason why church music should not be music.

His excursions into hymnody were, it turned out, hardly ever successful. What we can thank him for is introducing us to ST. PATRICK'S BREASTPLATE (EH 212: H 268: AM 162) and ST. COLUMBA (EH 490: AM 29), the results of his researches into Irish folk song. At the present time his most widely used original tune is no doubt ENGELBERG (AM 527: H 366). This is a through-composed setting for 'For all the saints', contributed to the 1904 *Hymns A & M*, which was an enormous improvement on the horrendous Barnby tune at that time in currency, but which was swept off the scene two years later by Vaughan Williams's SINE NOMINE. Determined attempts to revive it with new texts, begun by the *Hymnal-1940* and continued through the recent composition of Frederick Pratt Green's 'When in our music' (*Westminster Praise* 12) are at last having success. It is a tune which, probably considered rather athletic in 1904, now proves both manageable and attractive.

But most of the time Stanford, it might be said, packed too much music into his compositions to make them congregationally acceptable. There's a touch of Irish perverseness in them which is exceedingly attractive to the musical but which leaves ordinary singers gasping. AIREDALE (AM 205) is a fascinating piece of music: but a comparison of it with Parry's JERUSALEM is an object-lesson in the question of what ordinary people will and will not rise to. Our Ex. 370, ALVERSTONE, for 'Praise to the holiest' (like AIREDALE, from the 1904 *Hymns A & M*) is another example of music which a musician cannot ignore, but which would have a better chance of performance if it were published as a choral anthem.

Stanford was always interested in hymns—he wrote many through-composed alternative versions of hymn tunes which were published, with other composers' work, in a book of alternative accompaniments associated with the 1904 *Hymns A & M*, now very difficult to come by but most interesting. (He manages to incorporate a good deal of the figuration of Bach's 'St. Anne' fugue in his last verse of 'Our God, our help.')

Charles Wood, 1866-1926

Charles Wood, also an academic musician (Music Director at Gonville and Caius, Cambridge), makes a third in this distinguished trio, and again influencing hymnody by example rather than writing many hymn tunes. Wood was modest and retiring where the other two were extrovert and famous. His craftsmanship in the writing of anthems, often, like Parry's choral pieces, founded on unusual and evocative poems, has been celebrated in the histories of church music, and his secular music, as well as his church music, has been very amply dealt with in Ian Copley's *Charles Wood* (Thames Publishing Co., 1978). For his hymn tunes, see Leonard Blake's very perceptive article in the *Bulletin of the Hymn Society* # 124; it is there pointed out that Wood wrote a number of hymn tunes which were never published, of which our Ex. 371 is a particularly graceful example. Wood, like Stanford, was an Irishman, and contributed several tunes to the 1919 Irish Church Hymnal; at an earlier stage he was much involved in the 1904 *Hymns A & M*, to which he contributed three tunes, clearly commissioned by a committee who needed them for unique metres; of these RANGOON (AM 270) is still alive, though it has a military manner which is most uncharacteristic of this gentle composer. By far his most beautiful tune must be CAMBRIDGE (Ex. 372)—written at a late stage for *Songs of Praise,* 1925. Allowing for the absolutely polar difference between their temperaments, it is, one could say, what corresponds in Wood's output to JERUSALEM in Parry's, and it goes with a text in that contemplative manner which Wood so much enjoyed. This admirable musician is now receiving as much exposure as Stanford and Parry in cathedral lists, and contributed much to the raising of the standrads of hymn writing.

B. Luard Selby, 1853-1919

We now come to a quartet of composers who were much more confined to church music than the three we have just mentioned. Selby was a hymnologist who after the death of Steggall was put in charge of the music of the 1904 *Hymns A & M*, and who wrote 25 tunes for that book. Four of these survived in 1950, and of those two have real merit, ECCLES (89) and IVYHATCH (175). On the whole, though, Selby comes out as a composer who sees the need to react against late 19th century conventionality and shallowness, but cannot quite see how this is to be practically done. That turned out to be the chief weakness in the 1904 book, which was a brave attempt to do what the *English Hymnal* two years later did with such resounding success. He sometimes attempted an archaic idiom, sometimes a contemporary one, and, as always, he was most successful when he was least self-conscious. Perhaps our Ex. 373, GUNDULF, is as good an example as any of his place in the story. This is a tune designed to put a new dress on 'Lead kindly light'. At least twenty composers attempted this after Dykes led the way with his inextinguishable LUX BENIGNA (EH 425: AM 298). Selby's tune (Dykes's was relegated to an Appendix) has a 16th-century manner—there is a strong echo of Genevan Psalm 23, or HERZLIEBSTER JESU (Exx. 81, 187) towards its end. But it was romantic to think that a tune of such austere demeanour could displace LUX BENIGNA: the editorial rule, 'If you want to change a tune, ask whether people who want to sing those words would ever sing your substitute, no matter how much better it is' was unknown to the 1904 editors. A study of the work of the well-intioned Selby throws strong light on the achievement of Parry, and,

of course, on the composers of that other school which we shall be examining shortly. It was a good thing to try to do but these editors did not do it rightly.

Alan Gray, 1855-1935

Gray was an honest composer almost all of whose work has been forgotten, except a number of very popular, and very elementary, descants that he wrote for well known hymns. For 20 years to 1912 he was organist at Trinity College, Cambridge, and was active in the promotion of university music. He wrote a few hymn tunes, most of which are now to be found only in the obscurer sources (e.g. two at 110 and 111 in the 1916 *Congregational Hymnary*), which is where they belong. But in Ex. 374, BATTLE CRY, we have a strong and well-made tune which foreshadows the 'big unison style' later to become very popular in public schools (see below, pp 148-150).

Basil Harwood, 1859-1949

Yet another contributor to the Edwardian circle is Harwood, who was organist at Christ Church, Oxford, and edited the very important and interesting collection, the *Oxford Hymn Book,* 1908. Harwood is most famous now for LUCKINGTON (AM 375), a wide-ranging, bell-like tune for 'Let all the world in very corner sing', and for THORNBURY (EH 545: AM 256) for 'Thy hand, O God, has guided'. The first of these was in the *Oxford Hymn book*; the second was actually composed earlier (1898) but not included in the Oxford book, possibly because Bishop Strong, who had much to do with the choice of texts there, did not authorize the text for which the tune was composed. Both these are tunes for large occasions, going best where there is a massive singing body; and it is certainly true of Parry and Stanford that they are at their most characteristic when they are 'thinking big'. This is emphatically not the case with Wood, but on the whole the Edwardians seem to have envisaged situations where there were large settled congregations, or where a special festival called for a big tune (which was the case with THORNBURY). But Harwood is interesting in that he has two quite distinct styles, of which the more characteristic is a wistful, contemplative one. He contributed a large number of tunes to the *Oxford Hymn Book,* whose other point of interest is the very generous exposure given to S. S. Wesley; and indeed, Wesley was very much Harwood's master in this field, especially the Wesley of ORISONS (Ex. 351). Harwood's tunes are often quiet and reserved and ruminative, like CUMNOR (Ex. 375) and RAGLETH HILL (376), which is the second of two tunes he provided for 'Lord it belongs not to my care', directing a change of tune at stanza 3. LUCKINGTON is perhaps the only Harwood tune that can be sung fast. Many of them have such complex inner parts as to insist on a very slow tempo; and we see his delight in very stately singing in his introducing to the repertory of the now well known tune

GRAFTON (EH 33: AM 383 ii), which when it first appeared in the *Oxford Hymn Book* was in D flat major, marked to be sung very slowly, and on which he made his own musical comment in his exquisite organ-prelude on the tune. In his other compositions Harwood occasionally experiments with free rhythms, foreshadowing Walford Davies, and his special delight in plainsong tunes is made clear in the way he uses BEATA NOBIS (EH 185) in his famous C sharp minor Organ Sonata. As in Wesley, there is a great deal of chamber music in Harwood's work.

Edward C. Bairstow, 1874-1946

Sir Edward Bairstow was one of the leading figures in English church music during the first half of the 20th century, but he was an out-and-out Edwardian, a disciple of Brahms and Parry, uninfluenced by the Vaughan Williams school, and did his best work as organist of York Minster. In his choral works he invested the romantic idiom with a strength which would have pleased Parry, and he combined a genius for tender miniaturs with a capacity for rising to large occasions which did not wholly prevent his writing a good deal of English *Kapellmeistermusik*. His tendency to think in fairly substantial musical paragraphs made him impatient of the discipline which hymn tune writing requires, and he wrote very few tunes. He contributed one to *Hymns A & M* in 1904, and another to the 1916 *Supplement* (no. 506). The earlier of these is CLAMAVI, our Ex. 377—and it shows that quality of Roman *gravitas* which in his person and work he so often showed; it is the kind of tune which Stanford would have written—and for exactly the same reasons —stately and musical and dramatic, but perhaps lacking that last ounce of congregational sense which gives a hymn tune the promise of long life. Neither of these tunes survived beyond the books in which they were printed; both are well worth attention.

Henry Walford Davies, 1869-1941

From the point of view of hymnology, Sir Walford Davies brings this group to a climax, for more than any of the others he was a committed hymnodist. All the others wrote hymn tunes as a side-interest, but Davies became the leading English educationist in hymnody in the 1920s, becoming famous through his use of the then new technique of broadcasting, and nothing could have been more historically appropriate. Stylistically Davies forms a bridge between the Edwardian and the Renaissance styles, making emphatic statements in both kinds, but although in the larger forms he was not a great composer, he made up for this by insisting on living with the congregational idiom of ordinary singers, and giving much of his life to the encouragement of music-making in others. As a teacher, and he was a magnetic teacher, he lived in a

different world from those of Parry, Stanford and Wood (to all of whom he owed something). Outwardly his musical environment was much like those of the other Edwardians, for after twenty memorable years as Director of Music at the Temple Church in London he became Professor of Music at the University of Wales and later organist of St. George's, Windsor, and his immense public reputation was recognized in his appointment as Master of the King's Musick. His effect on the young was nation-wide, and his broadcasts were relayed into many school classrooms, being among the first to be so treated. These broadcasts as often as not dealt with hymnody.

His name does not appear in the 1904 *Hymns A & M* but it is in Garrett Horder's *Worship Song* (1905) which contains the first printing of his CHRISTMAS CAROL ('O little town of Bethlehem': SP 79); this already shows most of the qualities which he made his own. He edited *In hoc Signo,* a booklet of 52 hymns 'In War and Peace', in 1915, and this contains, besides some interesting compositions of his own, several collocations of words and tunes which turned out to be inspired, including that of 'The Lord will come' with the Genevan OLD 107th, and 'Judge eternal' with PICARDY. He appears several times in the 1916 Supplement to *Hymns A & M,* and while at the University of Wales he edited *A Student's Hymnal* (1923), a book of hymns in English and Welsh, in which he put into practice three principles—his special interest in part-writing, his delight in new and irregular rhythms, and his capacity for evoking melodies from other people: for in that book are a number of tunes marked 'University of Wales' which were composed, as it were, in committee, his students collaborating with himself in devising new tunes. (Of these, CHILDHOOD, EH 227, has travelled a long way).

In 1927, with Sir Henry Hadow and David Lloyd George, he edited *Hymns of Western Europe,* a fascinating anthology in which the guiding influence was his, and which has still plenty to teach later editors.*

Davies's style of composition was too idiosyncratic to allow him to make a success of larger forms. More than any other Edwardian he is a composer who leaves his thumbprint on every bar he writes. Our Ex. 378 is very characteristic. HAMPSTEAD was composed for 'O love that will not let me go' in *In hoc Signo,* and there printed as we give it—with the melody in an unbarred separate stave. This detail leads back to two of his principles: to make new tunes easily acceptable by printing the melody separately, and to relieve the monotonous congregational 'thump' of regular rhythm by making the singers think in phrases rather than in bars, or measures. But we also see in this tune Davies's very emotional approach to hymnody; the text is, of course, one of the most highly charged texts

---

* For example—the setting of 'See the conqueror mounts in triumph' in *Festival Praise,* 1979, to the tune EBENEZER was clearly unconsciously owed to *Hymns of Western Europe,* which has that collocation and exactly the same selection of stanzas.

in all hymnody, and its original tune, ST. MARGARET (by A. L. Peace, one of the first outstanding contributions of Scotland to hymn music) has actually turned out to be inseparable from the text, no matter how good the intentions of later composers were. Davies opens with a very characteristic phrase—based on a rising major sixth, and closes with an unusual cadence (altered by him when it went into the 1916 *A & M Supplement*) involving the dividing of parts to enrich the harmony.

TEMPLE (Ex. 379) is an earlier tune, his one contribution to the *English Hymnal* (454): it introduces at once that rhythmic freedom which he exploited in many other tunes (of AUCTOR VITAE, AM 394), and foreshadows again his special sensitiveness to harmonic effects, from its unison opening to its unusual and quietly sonorous close.

When we recall that Parry's JERUSALEM (369) came into existence as the result of a suggestion made by Robert Bridges to Walford Davies, we are not surprised to see that Davies himself could write a 'big tune' when required: in this mood he was perhaps not usually successful, but VISION (Ex. 380) from *In hoc Signo* has proved to be a 'winner'. Note again how much it owes for its effect to a rising major sixth. This was written to bring into English use the American 'Battle hymn of the Republic' without associating it with the American tune, which unhappily had acquired ribald associations in Britain. An even more fulsome use of the rising sixth, plus a harmonic enrichment, which between them become rather extravagant, is in RESURRECTION (Ex. 381), from the Welsh *A Students' Hymnal,* 1923. Davies was capable of overstatement when his enthusiasm ran away with him. And his tendency to become obsessive about that rising sixth is indicated in the series of phrases in Ex. 382, which mentions some tunes that have survived and some which have sunk under their own emotional weight.

Davies was a Victorian in his free-ranging emotion, a Renaissance composer in his use of rhythm and in very occasional tentative excursions into modality; he was a true Edwardian in wanting to write strong new music in the old vocabulary and in being thoroughly well-read in all the great classical composrs. He was a teacher of the old fashioned kind, very much *de haut en bas* in an age which found that approach acceptable and, in his hands, captivating. Dignity and consequence were part of his nature and his musical environment, in which respect he differed totally from that other figure of the Renaissance whom we shall shortly have to mention as working on parallel lines, Martin Shaw. It is rumoured that these two geniuses could not bear one another, and we shall shortly see why that may have been so. But in the closing years of the 20th century Walford Davies is turning out to be less of a back-number than the Renaissance school seems to have thought him.

18

Welsh Hymn Tunes

A note on the pronunciation of Welsh names

Welsh tunes are almost always named after places, and the appearance of these names is sometimes puzzling, especially to Americans. The Welsh language is wholly consistent (unlike the English) in the values it gives to consonants and vowels, these values being governed by very simple rules. When pronouncing these names, follow these basic rules:

A — always *ah,* never ay as in hay

C — always K, never S

DD — vocalized th as in *th*at

E — always ay, never ee

F — normally V: ff is as English f.

G — always hard, as in get

I — always ee, except in a diphthong: IA is a short 'yah'

LL — untransliterable, a breathy 'L': to pronounce LLAN, say CLAN, then remove the 'K' sound but keep the breath you used for the K

O — very long, with a touch of 'aw'

RH — a breathy R, allowing the tongue to vibrate

U — eee

W — a vowel - oo

Y — except in a final syllable, short U as in cut: in a final syllable, or a monosyllable, or a monosyllable regarded as a separate unit in a compound word   ee.

AE — long English I as in light

AU — as AE

AO — ow

EI — as AE

AW, OW — very long ow

IW — 'you'

R — note that consonantal R does not modify a preceding vowel. A Welshman saying 'Glory' says not 'glawry' but glohry.
Arglwydd (Lord) is a-r-glooeedh, the r always being rolled.
LLEF is approximately HLAVE.
HYDRYDOL is approximately Hu-vru-dol.

The English habit of de-emphasizing weak syllables is foreign to Wales: all syllables receive a much more even accent and all vowels and consonants are pronounced with much greater distinctness than is normal in English.

Welsh hymnody has become part of the total English-speaking scene only during the twentieth century; and even to-day it is an island in the geography of hymnody. The position of Wales is totally different from that of Scotland in this story for reasons which are partly political but even more importantly religious. Scottish hymnody, as we have seen, was set in its pattern from the Reformation until the late 19th century by the existence of a powerful and pervasive Presbyterian Establishment, which not only confined hymnody to psalm singing for a long time, but provided a dogmatic spine for the whole body of Scottish life. Though the population of Scotland is small and scattered compared with that of England, that population is to-day very largely concentrated in the Lowlands (which means strictly the southern region rather than the lowest in altitude). But the lowland towns are ancient towns, and in other days when the population was more evenly distributed, even where communications were difficult the existence of the historic Presbyterian tradition in much of Scotland, and of the Gaelic speaking, often Catholic, tradition elsewhere, formed a principle of continuity which largely overcame the difficulties which the rugged northern terrain presented.

Wales, by contrast, has always been a country based on the village. It is more obstinately mountainous than Scotland—it does not really have a 'Lowland' area— the nearest approach being, of course, Glamorganshire. In the early Middle Ages, when invasions of Saxons and Norsemen threatened to erase the ancient British Christian culture, Wales, and to some extent Ireland, was the reception area for refugees of the old British religion who set up tiny communities in the inaccessible regions and brought to Wales that always highly individualistic religious style which has ever since been so typical of that country. Place names beginning with the familiar 'Llan' are derived from the establishment of these religious communities. 'Llan' means, primarily, an enclosed space or 'lawn'; then it comes to mean the community buildings, or the most important of them, the Chapel. The name LLANTRISANT means 'a community of three saints' (that is, three members), LLANPUMPSANT, a community of five. Or the rest of the name may signify some local identifying feature, or some saint's name. Once west of Offa's Dyke, these communities reckoned they were safe from the marauding continentals, and, what is more, safe from the organizing genius of St. Augustine of Canterbury, whose brief from the Pope in 597 was to evangelize the new inhabitants of central and eastern Britain, now beginning to be called the English, and by whose influence the English diocesan system was originally set up. In Wales the only competition with the little bands of 'saints' was druidic paganism, and their inevitable attitude toward that was pacific and syncretistic—a good deal of druidic culture infiltrated into their religious style.

The secret of the special quality of Welsh hymnody lies somewhere in the simple fact that when cultural styles change, geography does not: and a small country with large tracts of forbidding and barren land will never grow rich, as England did later in the Middle Ages, on farming. It was only the industrial revolution with brought any sort of wealth to Wales, and in a similar way it was the Evangelical Revival which fashioned Welsh religion as we know it. For both of those forces found, as it were, fertile soil to work on: just as the coming of the mines brought employment to people whose living had been scanty (and of course took advantage in quite immoral ways of that fact), so the evangelists of Wesley's time found a welcome from a country where there was no sort of religious Establishment to oppose it.

What we have to say here is, then, entirely taken up with the results of the Evangelical Revival, whose beginning actually antedated Wesley's conversion by a few years, but which was given great impetus by Wesley's followers, especially Geroge Whitefield who, with Hywel Harris, fanned the evangelical flames to furnace-heat.

Hymnody was an essential to the Welsh revival as it was to the English. So what music was waiting for the evangelical song-leaders to use? The answer seems to be—very little that was ancient. The great tune BRAINT (Ex. 383) seems to stand almost alone as a genuinely primitive Welsh tune—modal and austere. Some of its intervals seem to throw back to the extraordinary Welsh psalm tunes of Prys's Psalter, 1621, of which we had two examples in ST. MARY and ST. DAVID (Exx. 108-9) and of which a few others got into *Ravenscroft*. But what we now think of as the typical 'Welsh sound' seems to originate in the secular ballads current before and after 1700. If we here confine ourselves to Welsh hymn tunes still current, we find several examples which suggest a ballad background for the Welsh Sound. We offer three in Exx. 384-6.

The ballads, as it happened, were finding a new role in the Ballad Operas which appeared in the 1720s as an English gesture against the Italianate operas of Handel. The most famous of these was the *Beggar's Opera*, 1728, which was very largely composed of well-known song tunes; along with that, during the short period 1728-50, appeared many others, including the *Cobbler's Opera* (1729) and *Flora, or Hob in the Well* (1729) which, originating in England, was the first ballad opera to be produced in America, getting a performance at Charleston, S. C., in 1735. The origin of the ballad tunes found in these and similar works is, of course, obscure: they cannot be dated or assigned to authors and composers (except in a few cases); and any attempt to produce an 'authentic' version is as futile as any such attempt with other kinds of folk music.

But what the ballads certainly gave to the Welsh evangelical hymn tune was its very characteristic form. In our examples we have included modest formal indications, which show that where the tunes are written for symmetrical ballad-type stanzas, they very often fall into the form A-A-B-A (simple ternary) or A-A-B-a (similar to the Lutheran chorales, the last line referring to the opening but approached through a bridge-phrase from the 'development' line).

Ex. 384B, CYFAMOD, is a good example of the transformation of a ballad tune, and it shows in what modes that transformation tended to take place. CYFAMOD as here transcribed (*Llyfr a Thonau*, 1929) is a very solemn tune, in a rhythm which corresponds to the typical Welsh elongation of emphatic syllables under high emotional stress. (No other Welsh tune is transcribed in 5/4: but a similar rhythm with strong

anapaestic stride is often found in 4/4, as in CRUGYBAR, Ex. 391). It seems to have been derived, however, from the ballad we show with it, 'Can love be controlled by advice?', which was in the *Beggar's Opera*, and in two Welsh folk song collections, Parry's *Collection of Welsh, English and Scotch Airs*, 1761, and Jane Williams's *Collection of Glamorgan Folk Tunes*, 1844. The ballad may be of Welsh origin, but it certainly was given plenty of popular exposure in England. Note what has happened to it: its rhythm has been elongated: it has been transferred from a solo or unison song to typical Welsh SATB: and its melodic form has become more subtle, being now not A-A-B-A but A-A-B-a, with a quite new section substituted at B, and a dramatic point made at the return to (a). We gather that when tunes of this sort were baptized into Church use, the pressure of the religious atmosphere bore very heavily on them. What may have begun as light secular music becomes exceedingly fervent and solemn music when it is received into the evangelical circles, and it is, of course, in the new solemn form that the Welsh hymn tune takes on all those qualities we now associate with it.

There seems to be a similar story about the tune FFIGYSBREN (Ex. 385: more anciently known as BETHESDA or CLOD), which may be associated with a tune that was in the *Cobbler's Opera* under the title 'The Fashionable Lady', and in Henry Carey's Musical Century (1738) as 'Death and the Lady'. Its transformation into a hymn tune (*Caniadau y Cyssegr*, 1839) seems to have caused certain simplifications in the melody. CAERLLEON (EH 334: SP 193) is derived from a tune 'Come, open the door, sweet Betty', which was in *Flora* and *Cobbler's*.

Certain Welsh hymn melodies were available to the evangelical editors. These include GWALIA (Ex. 386) and what looks like its first cousin, MORIAH (EH 437: SP 573), both tunes on the simple A-A-B-A form. GWALIA was in Madan's *Lock Hospital Collection* (1769) (cf. Exx. 264-6) and MORIAH was in his *Collection of Psalm and Hymn Tunes* of the same year. The remarkable tune RHYDDID (Ex. 387: EH 222: SP 643) though not found in any existing English collection, is attributed to John Jones, who was organist at the Middle Temple in 1749, at Charterhouse, 1753, and at St. Paul's, London, 1755. And the equally unusual LLAN-GOEDMOR (Ex. 388: EH 539: SP 242). which first appeared in the periodical *Y Gwyliedydd* in 1826, is there attributed to John Jeffries of Llanynys (1718-89) and described as 'Jeffreys 113th Psalm'; its unusual metre (obscured by its being mis-set to a text 8.8.8.8.88 in *E.H.*) is that of the 113th Psalm in the Old and New Versions.

This indicates that in the 18th century there was some coming and going between Welsh and English in the matter of hymnody. Evangelists sent from England to Wales could have brought back tunes like GWALIA and MORIAH; they could equally have taken tunes from England and rearranged them for sacred words. But what must be remembered is that what we know as the Welsh tradition was the result of the pressure of evangelical emotion upon whatever music was in the beginning adapted for their hymnody, and that the tunes thus formed were the pattern from which new hymn tunes were minted.

It goes without saying that the Welsh were always natural folk singers. If religion before the evangelicals was at a low ebb, it was secular subjects they sang about, including legendary and historical matters concerning their own nationhood. But once the fervour had taken hold, the hymnody was in a very powerful sense folk hymnody, and this means that if we supply dates for the first printing of tunes, quite often, anyhow in the first half of the 19th century, we may assume that the tunes were in currency long before those dates. The chapels will have been strenuously creative: a precentor will have devised a new tune on the familiar pattern, and the harmony will at once have been provided by the native genius of the Welsh for singing in harmony. The printed versions will be, if not definitive, at least approximations to what custom had already set up.

The Welsh tune, as it developed, had certain very clear patterns. It must be remembered that plenty of tunes were composed by Welshmen which might just as well have been composed by Englishmen, and Welsh hymnals abound in them. But what we know as the characteristic Welsh style involves one or more of the following qualities:

(1) A clear musical form based on the ballads, to which we have already referred. We must now add to what we have said the special hymn-form, which has no ballad-ancestry, of 8.7.8.7.4.7, in which the '4', a short line, is always repeated once or twice, and the final line may also be repeated. This is the metrical form of 'Guide me, O thou great Jehovah' which, first printed in Welsh in 1745, may well be the first appearance of the metre; in his later work Charles Wesley made use of it (e.g. in 'Lo, he comes with clouds descending') and it is very probable that 'Guide me', with whatever Welsh tune went with it, became known in England at an early stage, possibly even before its familiar composite translation was made in 1772. Welsh tunes for this metre are always characterized by a repeated first phrase, and by a climactic development in the repetitions of the short line: and the massive BRYN CALFARIA (EH 319: SP 274) first printed in 1852, is one of the finest developed examples of this form.

(2) Melodically, Welsh tunes in the major key not infrequently make emphatic use of the major triad—as the examples set out in Ex. 389 remind us; RHYDDID and LLANGOEDMOR, already referred to, provide two more such examples, and yet another is in CRUGYBAR, Ex. 391. A very unusual tonal effect is found in the very well known tune JOANNA, or ST. DENIO, for 'Immortal, invisible' (EH 407: SP 535: H 301), which begins by going down the notes of the subdominant triad.

(3) In the minor mode, however, the typical Welsh tune has a grave stepwise movement, and, in its developed form, a rich harmonic support. Perhaps the finest example of this is in a through-composed masterpiece, TREWEN (Ex. 394), but many of the tunes of Ieuan Gwyllt, 1822-77 (Wales's supreme master) have the same intense urgency, of which MOAB is usually agreed to be the finest (Ex. 393).

(4) But there are exceptions to both (2) and (3), for example the remarkable and widely contrasted tunes HYFRYDOL (EH 301: SP 260: H 479) and LLANGEITHO (Ex. 390). HYFRYDOL is reputed to have been composed by R. H. Prichard in 1830, when the composer was 19, though its publication date was 1844. This, after a repeated first phrase, builds up through deft use of sequences to a stunning climax, which is the more remarkable when one sees that it is all written within the compass of a fifth, and the sixth degree is used only once. Very probably it was first heard, in the evangelical manner, as a solo, and very soon taken up by congregations who found it blissfully easy to sing. LLANGEITHO does not even provide a repeated first line, and is even more probably a tune first heared as a solo; its ambitious compass probably debarred it from immediate popularity, although it first saw print in 1839.

Perhaps one of the reasons for the special power and eloquence of the best Welsh tunes is the good fortune of their composers in having the developed vocabulary of music available, but in being also under a kind of intense social discipline which ensured that they would not mishandle it. All well-known Welsh tunes are in conventional major and minor keys, not in modes; there is never any neo-archaism about them. They are, so far as the text-shape permits, in regular two-bar units and very rarely deviate from a regular rhythm. In fact, their composers use the same musical material that is used by their English contemporaries, yet how differently they use it!

It is perhaps no accident that the solemn, minor-key Welsh tune seems to come into currency later than the cheerful, major-triad tune. The first one we noticed was CYFAMOD, very definitely a sombre tune: but as a hymn tune it is relatively late. On the whole there are few of the great minor-key tunes in hymnals before 1850. An early example not based on any secular source is EIFIONYDD, by John Ambrose Lloyd (Ex. 392). This is dated 1848 (*Telyn Seion*), and is interesting because Lloyd, one of the best known Welsh composers of his age, was in fact a very unreliable composer. He was so well known that he was much influenced by the contemporary English style, and some of his anglicized tunes are full of Victorian inconclusiveness. A blameless one, which has nothing Welsh about it, is CROMER (EH 237: SP 531).

Ieuan Gwyllt, already mentioned, was the next really outstanding Welsh composer: apart from MOAB (Ex. 393), English books sometimes show ARDUDWY (SP 695) and LIVERPOOL (SP 586).

When we come to Joseph Parry (1841-1903) we are in a different world again, for Parry was a highly placed professional musician who, having spent much of his youth in Pennsylvania, returned to Britain to be musically trained and ended as Professor of Music in the University of Wales. All this could almost be deduced from his justly famous tune ABERYSTWYTH (EH 87: SP 542: H 415), which is Welsh to the backbone, and yet much more subtly contrived than the usual Welsh tune: the use of the first half of A as the final phrase of the tune is unique: but it is, following the great climax at the beginnng of phrase 7, exactly what is needed to make a completely satisfying tune. DIES IRAE (Ex. 395) is just as eloquent—the form here is a very satisfying A-A-B-A.

Many other Welsh tunes have found wide acceptance, and many more deserve it. The *English Hymnal* has a generous selection, most of which are worth study. RHUDDLAN (EH 423: SP 552) is an adaptation of an old patriotic song 'Come to battle'—firmly triadic in melody, better known at present outside Wales than in it. Another triadic tune is BRYNHYFRYD (SP 241), in a metre of which the Welsh are very fond, 8.7.8.7 iambic; that first appeared in 1817. RHOSYMEDRE (EH 303: SP 127: H 504) looks to English eyes like a meditative stepwise tune majoring in repeated notes, and it is a surprise to foreigners to learn that in Wales it has the festive association of Easter; it is a tune which yields up its secrets only after many hearings, and it treats the metre 6.6.6.6.88 in a typically Welsh way—requiring the repeat of one of the long lines (traditionally the fifth, not the sixth). Its printing date is 1838. Along with JOANNA and LLANGEITHO, *Caniadau y Cyssegr* (1839) provided the grand LM tune LLEDROD (EH 556: SP 448)—once again major key and tradic, but with an exuberant extension of the third phrase which gives it special character. It is in much the same melodic idiom as the earlier LLANGOEDMOR. MEIRIONYDD (EH 473: SP 629) is a very cheerful 7.6.7.6 D, more stepwise than triadic, and first came to print in 1840. *Ceinion Cerddoriaeth* (1852), and still the cheerful manner predominates. Darker tones appear with DOLGELLAU (EH 349: SP 263, 1855), ERFYNIAD (EH 430: SP 270, 1859) and LLANGLOFFAN (EH 207: SP 643: H 521, 1865).

The last generation of great Welsh tunes seems to have been the work of composers living between 1860 and 1900. There is, of course, the redoubtable EBENEZER (EH 108: SP 309: H 519), whose history is in a way an epitome of the uneasy relations between the Welsh and the English. This superb tune, which like HYFRYDOL is written entirely within the compass of a

sixth (but this time a minor sixth) is one of the Welsh tunes which caught the English imagination early. It was written by Thomas J. Williams, 1869-1944, when the composer was very young, and appeared first in *Llwalyfr Moliant,* 1890, being already part of an anthem of his, 'Light in the Valley': that, at least, is what most of the *Companions* say, although that excellent authority Huw Williams, on whose researches I have relied heavily in this chapter, dates it about 1896. But it does not always appear in Welsh hymnals, and is not included in *Llyfr a Thonau,* 1929. It was in the *English Hymnal,* 1906, and very soon became an indispensable tune for English books; but even more at present it is indispensable in the USA, since its association with an English adaptation of an American poem which is known as the hymn 'Once to every man and nation'.

The secret of the tune's attraction, apart from its extreme A-A-B-A simplicity, is its obsessive use of what amounts to a 12/8 rhythm. In one or two of our examples (LLANGEITHO, GWALIA) and often elsewhere we find a triplet-division of the basic units of rhythm introduced for a special effect: but here it is used throughout, since congregational singers cannot be expected to be pedantic about the distinction between triple rhythm in the body of the tune and dotted rhythm at the main cadences.

Some books still call it TON Y BOTEL (the tune in the bottle); this is the consequence of a newspaper article in 1902 which put about the romantic story that it was found on a scrap of paper in a bottle washed up on the Welsh coast. Legends of that sort sometimes circulate about ancient tunes, but it is unusual to find one in currency during the lifetime of a composer.

Many other tunes by composers living in the 20th century are to be found in *Ll. a. T.* One known only in Wales is the haunting miniature, CYMER (Ex. 396) and one of the very last must be MAELOR, by John Hughes, 1896-1968 (Ex. 397), which appeared first in *Ll. a. T,* 1929. In a later Welsh hymnal, *Y Llawlyfr Moliant Newydd* (1956) the youngest Welsh composer was born in 1900—more than fifty years before the book's compilation, and that tells its own tale.

The fact is, of course, that the steam went out of Welsh evangelicalism once 20th century secularization had taken hold in Wales, and that when the 'island' quality of Wales disappeared as the result of modern communications the Welsh creative genius was dissipated. While in the later 20th century we have seen a number of very good 'main line' composers who are natives of Wales (not, like Parry, Vaughan Williams and Walford Davies, ancestrally Welsh) we have seen an abrupt decline in the production of Welsh hymn tunes. We have also seen a pervasive anglicization. We saw before how, when a Welsh composer achieved a status higher than the strictly national and local, his style could be corrupted or at least diluted by English fashions: that happened to John Ambrose Lloyd, though Joseph Parry was strong enough to resist it. It happened even more to Caradog Roberts (1878-1935) in most of whose tunes there is a fatal weakness attributable to anglicizing forces which were first noticeable in the industrial south of the country. The case of David Evans (1874-1948) is somewhat similar. Evans, a great deal of whose work is in *Llyfr a Thonau* and in the 1927 edition of the Scottish *Church Hymnary,* was the successor, and a devoted disciple, of Walford Davies. (Many of his tunes are written pseudonymously under the name 'Edward Arthur'). His style is very warm, in the Davies manner, but, like that of Davies, not more than one tenth Welsh. His tune YN Y GLYN (EH 563), written for the memorial service for a famous Welshman, is no doubt inspired by EBENEZER, but it reads like a good imitation of a Welsh tune composed by an Englishman.

But probably the Welsh tune which has had greatest coverage in the English speaking world is CWM RHONDDA (AM 296). This first appeared in 1905 and is the work of John Hughes, a Welsh precentor in the old style. CWM RHONDDA has become a 'vogue tune' since about the 1930s. It does not appear often in Welsh hymnals; it was not considered necessary to print it in the *English Hymnal* or *Songs or Praise,* or the *Hymnal-1940,* and *Hymns A & M,* which has always been shy of Welsh tunes, included it only in 1950. It has been the influence of Methodism that has given it its impetus outside Wales, especially in Britain and America. It is a sound enough tune, in the 8.7.8.7.4.7 metre with repetitions of the last two lines, but with development, not repetition, of the opening section. The first phrase of the final repetition appears ambiguously, sometimes with the descending figure in the bass (this is the original), sometimes in the treble. It bears exactly the same relation to the high tradition of Welsh tunes that CRIMOND bears to the Scottish psalm-tune tradition, and is now heard much more often outside Wales than in its own country. The character and fate of BLAENWERN, very often heard in England with 'Love divine', is very similar: the *Baptist Hymn Book,* 1962, was the first English book to include it, but it was being sung very widely before that book printed it (its Welsh date is 1916) and was included in response to popular demand.

The vintage Welsh tune, then, is a folk song which is at home in the restricted chapel-centered life of the old Welsh village and in the fervour of Welsh evangelical religion. Its folk-song quality is preserved in the custom, in Welsh hymnals, of attributing all tunes to their composers, when they are known, by initials rather than full names; the spontaneous enthusiasm of the Welsh for singing makes hymns a quite different kind of activity in Welsh services from what it is in the English churches; hymns will be sung, seated, two or three at a time, often with the last verse of a hymn repeated. Welsh hymnody also goes closely with the Welsh language and the Welsh vocal style, with its abundance of rich tenor sound, and many of the finest Welsh tunes lose a good deal as soon as they are exported from their religious milieu and sung to translations. 'Guide me, O thou great Jehovah' sung in English, at English speed, to CWM RHONDDA in G major is a quite different experience from 'Arglwydd arwain' (the same hymn) sung to CWM RHONDDA in C major, with Welsh deliberation, by a Welsh male voice choir. It is only the more rugged of the Welsh tunes which have emigrated successfully.

Victorian English hymnals did not take any notice of Welsh hymn tunes. None appeared in *Hymns A & M* until 1904, and only in 1950 did that organization include any but ABERYSTWYTH. This is because the culture which produced the tunes was the Calvinist-Methodist Church, born of the evangelical revival, which exhibited an enthusiasm quite foreign to Tractarian anglicanism. It was the *English Hymnal* that in 1906 first took Welsh tunes seriously, and it is largely due to its influence that certain Welsh tunes are now common currency in England. The most widely used seem to be CWM RHONDDA, HYFRYDOL, EBENEZER, GWALCHMAI, JOANNA (ST. DENIO), ABERYSTWYTH, LLANFAIR and RHUDDLAN; in the USA the selection would probably be HYFRYDOL, JOANNA, ABERYSTWYTH, LLANFAIR, CWM RHONDDA, BRYN CALFARIA and LLANGLOFFAN, with EBENEZER more popular than in Britain. The difference between these choices reflects little beyond the fact that in the USA BRYN CALFARIA, LLANGLOFFAN and EBENEZER are set to hymns which are constantly sung.

American Hymnody to 1900 - I
New England and the Appalachians

The American tradition of hymnody falls into four clearly defined streams which before 1900 were culturally separate, and which during the 20th century began to influence each other.

Accepting for the moment the nomenclature at present fashionable, and tolerating for a moment its imprecision, we classify these streams as (1) the New England style (2) the Southern Folk Hymnody (3) the Black Spiritual and (4) the Gospel Song: and their cultural relations can be represented by the following diagram:

```
                  NE
    -------------------------
    SF                     BS

            GS
```

The visual implications of that pattern are that the New England style is associated with the north-eastern States in its origins, the other three with what is always called the 'South' but is geographically the South-East; while if the pattern is divided diagonally, the 'north-west' half represented hymnody presupposing literacy and musical education, while the other half presupposes its absence.

1. THE NEW ENGLAND STYLE

By this we mean the hymnody which developed directly from the singing customs prevailing in that part of the USA in which the original movement towards independence flourished, and in which the religious 'establishments' (to use that word in a non-legal sense') were directly derived from Anglicanism or from the English Reformed Churches (Presbyterian, Congregationalist and, in 1776 to a smaller extent, Baptist and Methodist).

The Anglican and Reformed traditions were, in 1776, still much concerned with psalm singing: for the Anglicans the book of praise tended to be Tate and Brady, for Congregationalists, Isaac Watts's psalms and hymns, for Presbyterians, the Scottish Psalter. What hymnody was generated before 1776 in America, and there was very little of it, was in the style dictated by the limitations of psalmody. Therefore, from the publication of the first book printed in America, the *Bay Psalm Book* (1640) to 1776 it was possible for American congregations to survive on a very limited repertory of imported psalm tunes. The evidence suggests that the situation was much like that in 18th century Scotland, where a quite small proportion of the psalm-tune treasury served the practical needs of most churches. The attempt, in Ainsworth's Psalter, to introduce a broader and more demanding Genevan style

(that being the Psalter the Pilgrim Fathers brought with them in 1620-1) was at once defeated by the fasion set by the *Bay Psalm Book*.

The 'Bay' in the title of the *Bay Psalm Book* is the bay on which Boston stands, and Boston, Massachusetts, is the source of this first stream of musical culture which begins to surface in original hymn tune writing just about the time when Independence was declared. The one activity which promised to produce some original writing was the establishment in that area of song schools for amateur singers, which took place about 1730-40. In 1698 an edition of the *Bay Psalm Book* with an 11-page supplement appeared, and that supplement set out the psalm tunes with a bass added, and a syllabic notation under the notes (derived from current English practice). John Tufts (1689-1750) produced in 1721 in Boston a book of 20 psalm tunes 'with directions how to sing them', and this was much in use by itinerant teachers who visited song schools in the area.

All this was pretty crude by the standards which were later to be set up, but its most significant fruit was *The New-England Psalm-Singer* (1770) 'composed' (which at that date includes 'edited' or 'arranged') by William Billings.

Billings (1746-1800) is regarded as the first native American composer, and the bicentennial of the Declaration of Independence has aroused a new wave of interest in his work. He began as a tanner with a passion for music, and participated enthusiastically in the Massachusetts song schools. His music is innocent —indeed naive in its idiom and vocabulary, but it proved to be just what was wanted to widen the horizons of amateur singers. Publishing that first book at 24, he enjoyed another thirty years of increasing influence and popularity, putting out new compositions and collections with tireless regularity all through the turbulent years of the Revolutionary War and the establishment of the United States. Ex. 398 shows one of his most famous and satisfactory tunes, PARIS, a tune in the psalm tune style of the English 18th century, which at once shows, as all his music does, that he sought the liberation of hymnody through the freer post-Handelian style which English evangelicals were espousing at the time. His equally well known 'When Jesus wept', a tune in the form of a round, is exactly the kind of music to appeal to song-schools (Ex. 399), and Ex. 400, BETHLEHEM, is his very appropriate answer to all the 'repeating' tunes for 'While shepherds watched' that were proliferating in England. It is all very easy-going music, with no harmonic enterprise, and indeed without that fastidiousness concerning parallel fifths and octaves which came naturally to the English post-Handelians. Most of Billings's work is like this—melodically florid, with some rudimentary entertainment for inner parts and plenty of word-repetition, but totally without any sort of affectation or sentimentality.

Much more famous now than any tune of Billings is CORONATION (Ex. 401), written for 'All hail the power of Jesus' name' by another Massachusetts man, Oliver Holden (1765-1844), a prosperous joiner and shop-keeper who gave the land on which the first Baptist church was erected in Charlestown, Massachusetts. He was another strenuous musical amateur who edited several collections of tunes in the new style, and this one was in his *Union Harmony,* 1793. Whether it was inspired in any way by MILES LANE, the English tune, nobody can say. It has the same general style, with a touch of jubilant repetition, but does not, of course, rise to the level of excitement generated by that remarkable tune (Ex. 269). It is scored in a way which suggests male voices, as was MILES LANE, and substitutes for the English imaginativeness a sort of stolid worthiness which became very characteristic of the American tunes we are about to consider. It is a good 'song school' tune, and has the touch of evangel-ical energy which Billings exploited and which the early New England Baptists would have welcomed in this addition to the repertory they had brought from England.

But the real 'explosion' came with Lowell Mason (1792-1872). Mason was born in Medfield, Massachu-setts, and from 1812 to 1827 lived in Savannah, Georgia. As a teenager he had taken a leading part in the song schools, and while pursuing his profession in Savannah he took music lessons in harmony from a local musician, F. L. Abel, and was organist of the First Presbyterian Church.

Returning to Boston, he became first President of the Boston Handel and Haydn Society, and gave him-self for the next 45 years to the promotion of singing and the raising of the standards of church music. His influence in the end went far beyond the borders of his home-state, and it is fair to say that he personally set the direction which for at least a century American hymn tune writing was to take. In his writings he has much to say about the triviality and dulness of the music of the churches—the influence of the song schools found the walls of the churches difficult to penetrate—and he inspired many other musicians to compose and enrich the repertory.

Now Mason makes, it has to be admitted, a poor showing among composers when he has to take his place in the rich repertory now at our disposal. But consider the facts. Consider, if you will, such a tune as OLIVET (EH Ap. 58: H 449), for 'My faith looks up to thee'—still, in Britain as in America, the inevitable tune for that text. It is, we have to say, key-tied and unenterprising, unimaginative and very tediously har-monized. But then think of Mason meeting a young theological graduate in the street, and saying that he

had just come across a hymn the young man (22 years old) had written and had dashed off a tune to it and was publishing it in his next book. The young graduate was Ray Palmer, later to become a leading American text writer, and this was the hymn. That was Mason: energetic, always in a hurry, enthusiastic, observant and always looking out for young people to encourage.

Of course he never gave himself time to become an imaginative composer even in this limited form. And consider the musical environment presupposed by 'The Boston Handel and Haydn Society': America was, like England, a land without Bach. Without Bach, Handel becomes a composer of attractive tunes whom anyone thinks he can imitate, and the Haydn is the Haydn of the big choral works rather than the Haydn of the late string quartets. Musical culture is, in the 1830s, choral-oriented: activist, never con-templative. And when Mason talks of raising the stan-dards of church music what he really means is widen-ing its vocabulary, making some sort of bridge be-tween church music and what is going on in music elsewhere, letting in some fresh air on the stuffy and restricted repertory of the few psalm tunes which peo-ple actually knew.

In this he was almost the Vaughan Williams—well, anyhow the Stanford—of his day, striving to get the church out of its deep ecclesiastical musical rut. But there was even a touch of the Tractarian about him, for he never espoused the style of evangelical music, and frowned on 'repeating' tunes. His style was demure in the way that that of *Hymns Ancient and Modern* was demure, but his enthusiasm for getting music into the church from secular sources was basically the same as that of the Dearmer school. Of course, the folk music of the American bourgeois was not country music but, precisely, Handel and Haydn, so Mason had no chance of making contact with those rich sources of beautiful melody which we see as the sources of American folk hymnody (see our next sec-tion); and the trouble, if your 'folk music' is Handel and Haydn, or any eminent symphonist or large-scale choral writer, is that the greater the composer, the smaller the musical themes he makes use of. They are precisely not the people one looks to for examples in the composition of continuous but finite melodies such as hymnody needs, and such as true folk songs pro-vide. That explains the hesitancy and tentativeness of Mason's composing style. (It equally explains the singular lack of success with which modern composers in larger forms handle the hymn tune).

The whole story of Mason is summed up in his earliest tune, Ex. 402, called HAMBURG or sometimes BOSTON, and now his most treasured tune in the USA for the hymn 'When I survey.' He was still in Savan-nah when he wrote it, and it is his attempt to bring the Gregorian style back into hymnody. As a hymn tune it has no merit whatever and claims none: the attempt to square up Gregorian chant into a regular 4/2 rhythm and to harmonize it with straight chords was fatal to the enterprise. But in an age whose best music historian was Charles Burney, what else could one expect?

That Mason was capable of writing decent, honest tunes, is attested by Exx. 403 and 404. UXBRIDGE is an anonymous kind of tune which could have been written by any competent composer; using the accepted formulae of the time, coming in, as it were, on the age-long conversation of hymn writing, it has the place in his repertory that NICAEA has in that of Dykes. ELTON, written nearly a quarter of a century later, is by far his best tune—worthy of a place alongside the good LM tunes of any generation, and here he shows real originality and real competence.

Notice one thing about the Mason tunes, especially his CM and LM examples: they may be short of melodic inspiration and harmonic suggestiveness, but they usually have a very strong rhythmic interest. This is the choral-director and promoter of song schools at work. He clearly had noticed the rhythmic possibilities of the psalm tunes, and he very rarely writes a tune in these metres in which all notes are of the same value. There is an endearing American strenuousness about this—the rhythms, sometimes so repetitive as to become rather tiresome, suggest energy and alertness, the qualities that were building up the American character in the early 19th century.

Mason arranged as much as he composed—any good tune from anywhere would do. Here, of course, he was vulnerable to the arranger's errors: either it wasn't a good tune or it didn't make a good hymn tune. PARK STREET (Ex. 405) is still very much used in the USA. Its origin is in a dance tune composed by Frederic Marc-Antoine Venua (1786-1872), a fashionable violinist and light music composer; Gardiner (see pp. 86-7) included a hymn-arrangement of this tune in his *Sacred Melodies,* 1812-15, and Mason picked it up from there and named it after a famous puritan meeting-house in Boston. Mason drew largely on Gardiner, and the tune LYONS, much used in the USA for 'O worship the King', (H 564) is another which he introduced to the repertory from Gardiner's books.

BOYLESTON (Ex. 406), named after a Boston street, Mason claims to be founded on a Gregorian tone. Much less of any possible Gregorian tone survives here than in HAMBURG (Ex. 402) but one supposes that he had in mind Tone VIII ending 1. This and AZMON (Ex. 407) share the typically insistent rhythmic pattern of which he was very fond, and which after many repetitions begins to make one long for MELCOMBE. AZMON did at first appear in straight 4/2 CM rhythm (1839), but Mason substituted 3/2 in its 1841 printing. The tune behind it is by a German violinist and singing teacher, Carl G. Glaser (1784-1829), but had no currency in German hymnody.

Both those are still widely sung in America: even more so is DENNIS (Ex. 408) with 'Blest be the tie that binds'. This is really Mason's composition; the initial idea comes, he says, from a tune by H. G. Nageli, a Swiss composer, publisher and editor who published some of the first editions of Bach's music. But the tune of Nageli's is hardly recognizable in DENNIS, which has the extraordinary quality of providing, in triple time SM, a note for every beat of the music, and of repeating hardly any notes in the process. It is a good deal more emotionally demonstrative than Mason's tunes normally are.

Much more of Mason is still in currency: and the best current source for tunes by him, or by composers he directly inspired, is the 1955 Presbyterian *Hymnbook* which, because of its unusually large allowance of metrical psalms and paraphrases which call for more CM and LM tunes that American books now usually show, draws heavily on the Boston early 19th century style.

The English were singing one of Lowell Masons's arrangements for a long time without knowing it. When 'Lead us, heavenly Father, lead us' became very popular after its inclusion in the 1875 *Hymns A & M* with the tune MANNHEIM, and thereafter became one of the most often used wedding hymns, it brought into wide use a tune which Thomas Binney had arranged in his *Congregational Church Music* in 1853. The original from which it was taken was Filitz's chorale shown at our Ex. 231. Binney said that he had received the arrangement from Lowell Mason, and in giving it its first printing in England he achieved something of a 'scoop'. It is a typical Mason arrangement—what character there was in the original has been punched out of it by the rather ruthless abridgment.

If Mason composed many, and arranged more, he inspired even more tunes from other composers. He set a fashion which others eagerly followed. Our Ex. 409, HUMMEL, is a typical example. One could not call it a wildly successful tune, but its composer, H. C. Zeuner (1795-1875) was a German immigrant who became organist of the Park Street church in Boston and accompanist for the Boston Handel and Haydn Society. Its odd rhythmic experiment is obviously inspired by Mason's example.

Thomas Hastings (1784-1872), a Connecticut man who worked much in New York, was another of Mason's circle, collaborating with him in many community singing enterprises (we should now call them workshops). His most famous tune, TOPLADY (Ex. 410) drove out all competitors for 'Rock of Ages', and will last in America as long as that text is sung. Hastings's gifts as a composer are imperceptible, but he was at work in the song schools before Mason returned to Boston, and his *Dissertation on Musical Taste* (1822) was very widely attended to. The tune TOPLADY does not strike a reader as a notable example of musical taste: but here is another example of what we said above—the environment dictated a very slow start in matters of musical education.

Then there is FEDERAL STREET (Ex. 411), another very famous American tune. Henry Kemble Oliver (1800-85) had an adventurous and varied life, so typical of the career of the 19th century American—a Harvard graduate, a prominent educationist, adjutant-general of the Massachusetts Militia, superintendent of a cotton mill, state-treasurer of Massachusetts, organizer of the Massachusetts Bureau of Statistics of Labor, mayor of Salem, Mass., 1877-80, and for thirty years a church organist. In a group run by Lowell Mason for the encouragement of composers, Oliver submitted this tune, which he had written in 1832, and Mason put it in his *Boston Academy Collection* of 1836.

Simeon B. Marsh, composer of MARTYN (Ex. 412) was influenced less by Mason than by Thomas Hastings; his working life was spent in New York State. MARTYN has been the American tune for 'Jesu, lover of my soul' and antedates HOLLINGSIDE by a generation and ABERYSTWYTH by nearly two. Only at the time of writing is ABERYSTWYTH beginning to provide serious competition in the USA. The style here is much more that of Hastings than of Mason, and to some extent pre-dates that of the 'Gospel songs' of the 1860s.

Both Mason and Hastings had a part in the musical training of Virgil C. Taylor (1817-91), a Connecticut-born musician whose activities as a singing-school leader ranged as far as the State of Iowa. In his tune MENDON (Ex. 413) we begin to see more serious weaknesses—harmonic ineptitude, and a lingering on the dominant seventh, with an absence of melodic architecture: if the Mason style was the level at which lesser composers aimed, there was always the chance that they would exploit its weaknesses, which chance many of them, naturally, took. The same kind of melodic stagnation is in RATHBUN, Ex. 414, still inseparable from 'In the cross of Christ I glory'. The composer, Ithamar Conkey, was organist of the central Baptist church in Norwich, Connecticut, and was clearly another influenced by Hastings.

The difficulty, as the century advanced, was that those standards for which Lowell Mason worked, though exalted in theory, were not musically at a high level. There is, search as one will, nothing in the second half of the century to compare with those rare but admirable examples of real music-making among the English Victorians. We do not quite yet encounter sensational chromaticism of the kind we encountered in the more alarming Victorians, but one feels that this was mostly because the American composers knew much less music anyway, and did not expose themselves to many temptations. so if there is weakness, it is in the direction of dulness and melodic inanity. The worst American tunes are malignantly blameless.

Perhaps one of the best from the later 19th century is the still widely used BEECHER (Ex. 415). Its composer was a German immigrant, John Zundel (1815-82) who was organist of several churches in the New York metropolitan area. Zundel was a typical disciple of Mason in being the first to promote real congregational singing in the most famous church he served

(Plymouth, Brooklyn, where Henry Ward Beecher was minister) and BEECHER is certainly a sound congregational tune. But it is, surely, ruined by its stagnant and sticky bass; it is indeed one of the few 19th century 'period pieces' which can be greatly improved, without losing any of its character, by radical rewriting of the bass counterpoint. This is 'Handel and Haydn' misinterpreted as writers of tunes whose bass doesn't matter.

ALL SAINTS NEW (Ex. 416) is a much less happy example of the style which corresponds to that of the English Victorians. It is by Henry Cutler, a Boston native (1824-1902) who was organist at Trinity Church, Wall Street (New York), and was one of the first Americans to promote the ideals of the English Tractarians in the matter of choir vestments. He was fired from his position for taking the choir on a concert tour without the Rector's permission and thereafter served other churches in New York State and Philadelphia. But if ever there was a broken-backed and paralytic melody line, we have it here. Unhappily the same could be said of the much venerated ST. LOUIS ('O little town of Bethlehem'), which originated in Philadelphia and was the first tune composed for those words, whose author was at the time Rector of the church where Lewis Redner, the composer, was organist (St. matthew's, Rittenhouse Square).

It is only towards the end of the century that we find the special temptations of chromaticism being yielded to by composers who could not write strong melodies. Ex. 417, CUSHMAN (Herbert B. Turner, a minister in Virginia) is the only example we have here from a southern state, but its composer was born in New England. This has all the attributes of the 'English Victorian' style, compensating a weak bass with chromatic distractions.

If one looks for a composer on the American scene who compares in influence and output with the English Parry, the answer is in Horatio Parker (1864-1919). We refer here only to his musical standing, for he was a dedicated church musician who had a distinguished career in New York and later in Boston. But his musical horizon was as much wider than that of his contemporaries and immediate predecessors as Parry's was than that of Dykes. He spent three years in study in the Munich Hochschule fur Musik, and there his teachers included Rheinberger and Abel. He wrote plenty of music for organ and orchestra, two operas, and a cantata *Hora Novissima* which is still performed. His contributions to hymnody were not extensive, but they show the effect of a wider musical culture. What they do not show is any resistance to current fashion. So his tendency is to write hymn tunes in which there is a good deal more music, but in which that higher pressure is not disciplined by much modesty of diction. His tune to *Vexilla regis* (H 64) is still in use, and by later standards it is not notably successful; his most characteristic tune, MOUNT SION (Ex. 418) has the diction of a 'big chorus' in a cantata, and a plumpness of style which does not compare favourably with that of Parry: but at least Horatio Parker, especially in the larger forms, liberated the music of the USA by making it more conscious of the possibilities of a wider vocabulary. He edited the 1892 edition of the Episcopal *Hymnal*, and his work there showed a soundness of judgment not to be found in any hymnal of that time, or indeed of thirty years after it.

This, then, is the 'New England' style, and we can see puritan New England gradually submitting to the lure of the bright lights of New York in these later compositions. It is a striking fact that the age which produced, in American hymnody, some of the most imaginative and distinguished texts of the 19th century should be musically so poverty-stricken. The weakness, increasing with the dilution of the Mason style and the multiplication of hymn books, is always in melodic structure and intellectual integrity. Drawing on a rather meagre reservoir of musical culture, concerned mostly for the promotion rather than the creation of music, the 'New Englanders' found their hymnody following much the same pattern of degeneration which the English were experiencing. Because their musical vocabulary was more restricted, and perhaps their capacity for listening narrower, they neither plumbed the depths nor achieved the heights that the English found within their reach. Moreover, being urban and puritan, and ignorant or contemptuous of the rustic music which was being sung in neighbouring states, and even in their own, they missed what their less educated contemporaries were enjoying, and in the end bequeathed less of importance to the hymn-tune treasury.

2. AMERICAN FOLK HYMNODY

What the New Englanders missed was the music being preserved and created in the villages and farmsteads of the Appalachians. This was a repertory which overlapped hardly at all with that of the urban north, and it is only during the past forty years or so that it has received serious study, and only during the last 25 years that it has contributed to the main-line hymnals. This is broadly called Folk Hymnody, but before examining it we must mention the special musical technique of reading which was so closely associated with it, and the culture which produced it.

Shape-notes

The story of what we propose to call 'country hymnody' (we shall see in a moment why) has a common origin with that of the New England hymnody in the singing classes of the earlier 18th century and the work of Billings. But it takes a sharp turn in a new direction with the introduction of the method of notation called 'shape notes' or 'character-notes'. This was invented in Philadelphia in 1801 with the introduction of *The Easy Instructor*, published there by William Little and William Smith. They called it 'a new method of teaching sacred harmony' (meaning, part singing), and

their eye was firmly on the music of the church. The tunes in the book are from the repertory of the Billings age and culture, many imported from Britain, but the notation, using the normal five-line staff, provided a different shape of note-head for each degree of the scale. It was a kind of visual sol-fa, and, as its inventors plausibly claimed, an improvement on the use of letters (called in America at this time 'solmization') to remind singers of the pitch. Once the invention had appeared, others took it up, and there is no consistency from one book to another, as the three following examples show. The earlier form provided four note-shapes, using three of them twice in the full scale; later editors experimented with seven shapes, as we see here:

Wyeth, 1813

Funk, 1816

New Harp of Columbia, 1867

Shapes correspond to degrees, not pitches

It will be seen that the system could become quite complex for the printer, but as an aid to sight-singing it became so popular that shape-note books appeared from many sources during the following fifty years.

Country Music

The first shape-note hymnals were produced in New England, the earliest (also 1801) being *New England Harmony*, edited by Timothy Swan (1758-1842), and were clearly designed to assist fairly uneducated people in part-singing. But another force bore on the shape-note culture with the introduction of what has been called 'folk hymnody' in Jeremiah Ingalls' *Christian Harmony*, produced from Newbury, Vermont, in 1805.

'Folk hymnody' was first isolated as a *genre* of hymnody by George Pullen Jackson in his three vitally important books, *Spiritual Folksongs of Early America* (1937), *Down East Spirituals and Others* (1943) and *Another Sheaf of White Spirituals* (1952), in the last of which he coined the expression 'White Spiritual' which is sometimes used to distinguish the kind of hymnody we are now approaching. If it is urged by more modern scholars that some of Jackson's judgments have to be modified, that should not diminish the respect in which his pioneer work should be held. Some of the best recent literature on the subject is in the introductions written by Dr. Irving Lowens to the facsimilie edition (1976) of the 1816 *Kentucky Harmony* and by Dorothy D. Horn, Ron Pedersen and Candra Phillips to the similar edition (1978) of the *New Harp of Columbia* (1867).

What Pullen Jackson called white spirituals, and others call folk hymnody, is hymnody based on the folk music of a certain kind of people; it is probably not simply folk tunes made into hymn tunes, but much more probably hymn tunes composed in the folk idiom. True, one does find in the collections we are about to refer to hymn tunes which are clearly folk songs made over: the *New Harp of Columbia*, for example, contains 'Auld Lang Syne', 'Home, sweet home', 'Scots wha hae wi' Wallace bled', 'O where and O where is my Highland Laddie gone' (or, 'The Bluebells of Scotland') and 'The Farmer in the Dell' made over as hymn tunes with scarcely any alteration; and the tune AMAZING GRACE (Ex. 428, formerly NEW BRITAIN) has been traced to a Scottish bagpipe tune. But the story is more interesting, and more complex, than a matter of identifying secular tunes behind the 'folk hymns'. It is primarily a matter of encountering a way of life which is the direct opposite of that which prevailed in New England.

This is, indeed, the truth which has been made clearer in America than anywhere else: that in the end almost everything in a culture depends on whether it is urban or rustic; whether its foundation is in the land or in ideas, commerce and abstractions. The two cultures need each other—the ambitious and the unambitious; indeed the matter is so basic to any understanding of human society that it is taken careful notice of in the Old Testament, where the whole question is paradigmatically worked out in the story of Jacob and Esau. The strange thing, perhaps the reader will already have been thinking, is that it has taken so long for us to reach the point where the relation between hymnody and folk song has to be discussed. But the shape of the story of hymnody has insisted on that. Far back in the Middle Ages, the great divide in religious song was between the liturgical plainsong and the earthy, rhythmical carols—the music of calculated abstraction and the music of the land and the body. From Luther onwards hymnody took its cue very largely either from cultivated music or from the ecclesiastical side of medieval music; for the Reformed churches were sensitive about their relation with the secular world, and were cast in a psychological mould which favoured the cerebral and the speculative rather than the world of images and tangibles. Hymnody, we have already seen, comes from the edges of protestantism, the most 'protesting' parts—the English puritans, the evangelicals, the less liturgical parts of the church. It has often flourished most luxuriantly in the most world-denying sections of the Christian culture, which in turn have divided themselves either into extreme separatist groups (such as the primitive Mennonites in America, or the modern Southern Baptist Convention) and the religious cultures most closely associated with industrial and scientific progress.

So that this shall not become too theoretical and too little in contact with history, let us recall what in fact happened in America about 1800.

The really new thing about the America of 1800 was the appearance of a new kind of immigrant. Basically people have come to America either because they were doing tolerably well in their own country but reckoned they could do better in the New World, or people for whom the New World was a possible refuge from intolerable conditions at home. The colonizers of New England were of the former kind: literate, devout, ambitious. The Pilgrim Fathers had their eye on a New Jerusalem which should be built around the Bay at Boston and came because there seemed little chance of realizing their ambitions, temporal as well as spiritual, in Holland and England. They were followed for the best part of two centuries by people who, in one way or another, came with a vision and an ambition.

But somewhat later another kind of immigrant appeared, very largely from Britain, and in Britain, from Scotland. This was the poor man whom conditions at home were making poorer and for whom life was becoming impossible, of whom the most pitiable was the crofter in Scotland who was turned out by the Highland Clearances. There in the Highlands large landowners, espousing new methods of administering their estates, found the crofters uneconomic and quite literally turned them out of their homes (often burning down the cottages of tenants who resisted the order to remove themselves). Famine and hard times in other parts of Britain produced the same kind of helpless immigrant who came to America in order to survive.

We are not here considering that forced immigration which was the slave trade—that belongs to the next section. We are considering the man who, getting to America somehow, places himself under indentures to a resident farmer. He, the immigrant, knew nothing but the land, and expected nothing but the bare means of survival. He had no ambition but to stay alive. Indentures were his answer; they meant that for a stated period he allowed himself to be the property of a farmer, and at the end, was on his own. This was a good bargain for an enterprising farmer who had not the wealth to buy slaves. He got the services of the immigrant for nothing more than maintenance, and at the expiration of the agreed term was happy to pay his indentured servant off with a gratuity out of the money the servant had helped him to earn. The American war of 1812 brought many such men, with their families, to the United States, where they served for a while as mercenaries, then entered into indentures, and finally became settlers in their own right.

The immigrant, once he was on his own, needed a piece of land in which to set up his small holding. The question was, where to find it. The answer came direct from the impressive geography of the eastern States. If our maps be consulted at this point it will be seen that Virginia, one of the chief centres to which these poor whites came, is divided in a north-east/south-west direction by a mountain range which is the Appalachians. But the Appalachians are part of a system of ranges which run in a series of wide concentric arcs

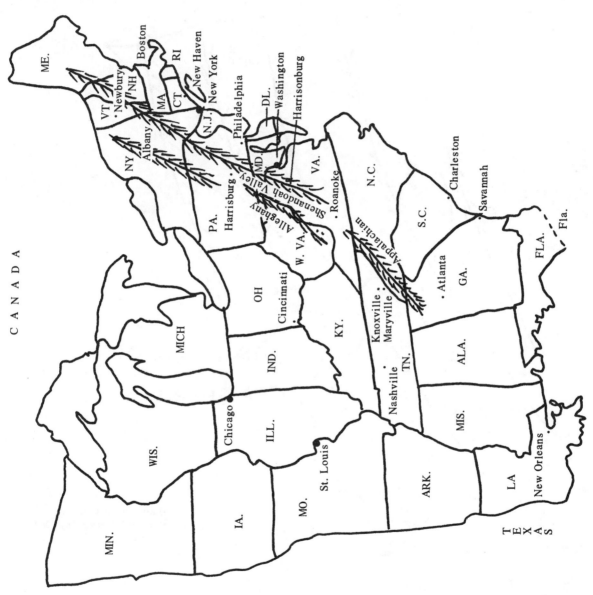

USA - East and Mid-West

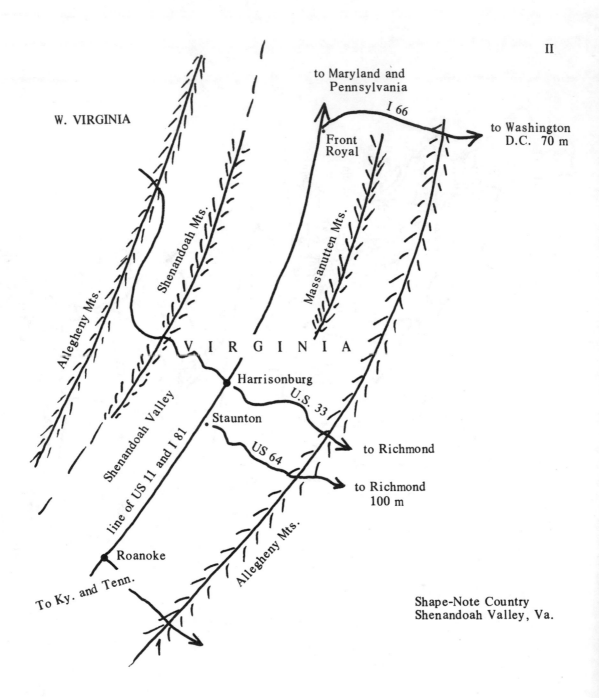

Shape-Note Country
Shenandoah Valley, Va.

III

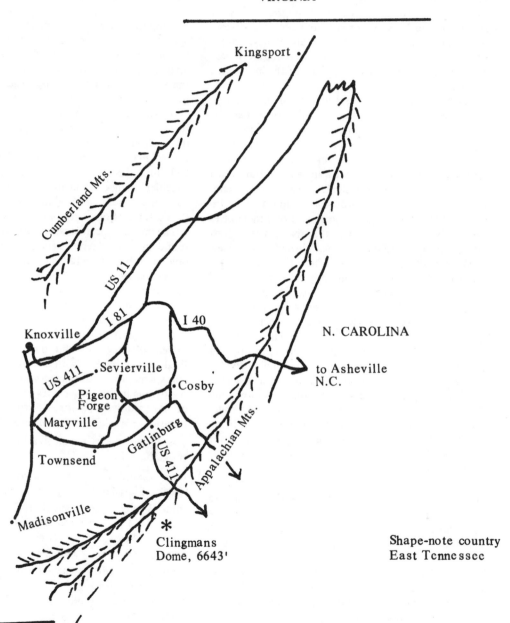

VIRGINIA

Kingsport .

Cumberland Mts.

US 11

I 81

I 40

Knoxville

N. CAROLINA

US 411

. Sevierville

. Cosby

to Asheville
N.C.

Pigeon
Forge

Maryville

Gatlinburg

US 411

Appalachian Mts.

Townsend .

Madisonville

Clingmans
Dome, 6643'

Shape-note country
East Tennessee

GEORGIA

through the Eastern States and divide them from the region now called the Mid-West. Virginia itself is cleanly divided: on the seaward side is a broad expanse of fertile land, with room for really large estates many of which were slave-owning. West of the first and longest range there is a broad glacial valley, some 60-70 miles from east to west, forked by the Masanutten range at the north end and bounded on the west by the Alleghenies in West Virginia (only later divided from Virginia). This is the Shenandoah Valley, which becomes the headquarters of the hymn-culture we are about to consider, and where many of the indentured servants found work.

But when they came to set up their small holdings, they needed something much smaller even than the modest estates of the indenture-holders, and this they only found in the largely unexplored valleys of the mountains themselves. Taking the line of least resistance they tended to follow the ancient trail which runs parallel to the Alleghenies, just west of them, which is now known as Route 11 (duplicated by Interstate 81). They might go north and find themselves eventually in the Alleghenies of New York, New Hampshire or Vermont, or the Adirondacks of New York State. But much more often they went south, following the mountains still, into the eastern parts of Kentucky and Tennessee. There was one alternative— to pass through the mountains at a point near Roanoke, where there always was an ancient track, and move south into North Carolina. Those who did this found a largely waste land, infertile, mostly flat except at its western end where the mountains divided it from Tennessee, with no navigable rivers—a land which nobody in a large way of business wanted, and therefore to hardly any extent a slave-owning state. But if they stayed west of the mountains they came on a series of small and remote valleys, either up in the hills themselves or just at their foot, where they made their homes.

To get an impression of what became of these people, it is useful to read *Neighbor and Kin*, by Elmora Matthews (Nashville University Press, 1971) or the editorials in Elliott Porter's *Appalachian Wilderness*. These and similar studies present these tiny communities to us as family-centered, chapel-centered, land-based social cells whose culture—and as we shall see, whose music—reminds the British of the villages of Wales or the Gaelic-speaking protestant ouposts in the Scottish Highlands. The emphasis is all against any forces from outside which would upset the equilibrium of this closed society. The chapels belong to no mainline denomination (they are commonly, though not invariably, called 'Baptist Mission'); education is suspected; seminary-trained pastors are not wanted; a high wall of defence is raised against the encroachments of progressive civilization.

These communities were, and to a large extent remain, as nearly pure 'Esau' communities, uncompetitive, unambitious, inward-looking, as any one can find in the English-speaking world. Even their manner of singing involves a kind of voice production unknown anywhere else. And music of a certain kind means everything to them, for it is just about the one communal activity, the one pursuit in which people of neighbouring communities meet, that they have.

This rugged and work-centered life has its innocence and also, naturally, its ugly side. The story of how the original inhabitants of the southern valleys, who were Indians, were treated by the invading settlers is harrowing; the political activities of some sections of the poor white community have written some of the more sinister pages in American history. But we have to take this as we find it, and it is at once clear why 'country people' in the south refer to themselves as 'hill people', and (just like the people of the far west, with their 'frontier' mentality) being 'hill people' is always the basis of any prejudice they may wish to express against the customs of other regions and cultures.*

The music associated with these communities is to be found in a long series of shape-note books, always oblong in shape with tunes set in four, three or (rarely) two parts, the melody in the tenor when there are three or four parts, the words of the hymns written between the staves of music, stanza 1 under the treble, stanza 2 under the alto, and so on, anything after stanza 4 (which is rare) appearing below the music. Quite often these books begin—as did so many of the 18th century English tune books—with instructions for singing and an explanation of the shape-note system. The texts of the hymns in the earlier ones are all from the English calvinist tradition (Watts, Newton, Doddridge and an occasional Wesley)—original texts begin only later.

A by no means exhaustive list of the shape-note books runs thus:

John Wyeth, *Repository of Sacred Music,* Harrisburg, Pa., 1810 (standard tunes in shape-notes)

John Wyeth, *Repository,* Part Second, Harrisburg, Pa., 1813 (includes folk hymn tunes): reprinted, Da Capo Press, New York, 1964, ed. Lowens

Ananias Davisson, *Kentucky Harmony,* Harrisonburg, Va., 1816, reprinted Augsburg Press, 1976, ed. Lowens (enlarged edition, 1820)

J. Funk, *Die Allgenmeine nutzliche Choral-Music,* Harrisonburg, Va., 1816

Alexander Johnson, *Tennessee Harmony,* Cincinnati, Ohio, 1818

Allen D. Camden, *Missouri Harmony,* St. Louis, Mo., 1820

James Carrell, *Songs of Zion,* Harrisonburg, Va., 1821

---

* The suspicion of education in these areas is beautifully epitomized in the sign which identifies a certain modern school building on a lane between Jones Creek and Cosby, Tennessee: ELEMENTRY SCHOOL. This was certainly visible in 1975.

William Moore, *Columbian Harmony,* Cincinnati, Ohio, 1825

J. Funk, *New Harmonia Sacra,* Harrisonburg, Va., 1832 (latest edition for use, 22nd ed. 1959)

William Walker, *Southern Harmony,* New Haven, Conn., 1835

William Caldwell, *Union Harmony,* Maryville, Tenn., 1837

John B. Jackson, *Knoxville Harmony of Music Made Easy,* Madisonville, Tenn., 1838

B. F. White and E. J. King, *Sacred Harp,* Philadelphia, 1844 (frequently revised: last revision, 1935: latest edition, 1960)

W. H. and M. L. Swan, *Harp of Columbia,* Knoxville, Tenn., 1848; *New Harp of Columbia,* Nashville, Tenn., 1867

(The *New Harp* republished by University of Tennessee Press, Knoxville, 1978, ed. Dorothy D. Horn and others)

But observe the places of publication. One book only, *Southern Harmony,* comes from New England. The publishers and editors of these books were in the first place businessmen who had an eye for a lively market, of whom Wyeth was a good example. A few tune-books aimed at local congregations had appeared in New England before his time, but his operation, centered on the State Capital of Pennsylvania, Harrisburg, was by far the most successful up to that time. Harrisburg is on the ancient road which follows the Appalachians to their west, and from it books could easily travel either north or south. Two books for use in Kentucky and Tennessee are published in Cincinnati, Ohio, but that city is just across the river from Kentucky and was already becoming an important metropolis. The *Missouri Harmony,* right out in the mid-west at St. Louis, suggests a pioneer who had found his way there from the Virginia region (following a trail celebrated in the famous Stephen Foster song, 'Shenandoah' with its nostalgic backward look, 'across the wide Missouri'). But the metropolis of the first folk-hymnody publications was Harrisonburg, in the centre of the Shenandoah Valley.

Harrisonburg is again on the southern route, and a good point from which to offer songbooks to departing travellers; it was also the centre of a Mennonite settlement (German speaking)—which explains the odd Germanic title of Funk's earlier collection. The primitive Mennonites enjoyed a life-style not unlike that which developed in the southern farm-communities, though severer and even more world-rejecting. Shape-note and folk hymnody flourished among them, and it is no accident that the best collection of folk hymn tunes in a standard hymnal is to be found in the 1969 *Mennonite Hymnal.*

In the second generation, Tennessee clearly feels strong enough to do its own publishing, and the area south-west and west of Knoxville proves to be a field from which many books come. The fact that nothing seems to come from North Carolina, the other side of the Appalachians, is a faithful reflection of the way in which terrain influences culture; in North Carolina you can see the next farm from your own, and the unique exclusiveness of the East Tennessee life-style passes away much more quickly.

So we now come to the contents of the shape-note books, and to the handful we provide in our examples. Wyeth's *Repository,* Part Second, 1813, is a good early example of the kind of anthology produced for these communities, and imitated and borrowed from by a long succession, of which the foregoing list gave some examples.

Ex. 419, KEDRON is the composition of Elkanah K. Dare, 1782-1826, a schoolmaster in Wilmington, Delaware who appears to have been the editorial overseer of the second part of the *Repository.* Its melody is in the tenor, as the melody always was when these tunes were set in three or four parts. The custom was for all those who wished to sing the melody, men or women, to sing this line, the other lines being for men who were disposed to sing them and could read them. Officially, of course, the direction was for ordinary SATB singing, and in the great communal hymn singings this was, and is, observed: but in practice what happened was that always does happen in church, the melody not in fact being confined to one singing part. The tune is modal, using all the notes of the octave, with a compass of a ninth, and there are no accidentals in any part. The harmonies are quite independent of conventional rules of part-writing; consecutive unisons, fifths and octaves are part of the vocabulary, and these represent the amateur part singing of communities who do it instinctively—producing not the sophisticated part-writing of the Welsh tunes, but reflecting something of the Welsh delight in part singing as it expresses itself in singers who do not wait for training before they begin to harmonize.

Observe also its rhythm. In modern notation the bar-lines would be in quite different places, indicating a slow swinging triple time (as our dotted slurs suggest). This is very much a folk-song rhythm, which comes naturally to a solo singer. There is no pressure on a solo singer to keep to a steady march time, and many well known folk songs—like 'Barbara Allen'—have this swinging, relaxed rhythm which comes often in these 'folk' hymn tunes.

Ex. 420 is anonymous, called CONSOLATION in these books, and in modern books, MORNING SONG. This does look like an adapted folk song: it strongly suggests the English 'Old King Cole' tune which comes up, for example, in the 'Bellman's Carol' (*Oxford Book of Carols,* 46). Observe that its second half is marked for repeat: this was very common practice. The singers, once started, tend to be unwilling to stop, and the repetition of the second half of a stanza, words as well as music, is very often marked in these books.

(Hence, in this case, the adaptation of this tune in modern books for hymns in 8.6.8.6.8.6).

Ex. 421, TWENTY-FOURTH, presumably originally designed as a psalm tune, is marked in Wyeth as by 'Chapin'. There were two Chapin brothers, Lucius (1760-1842) and Amzi (1768-1835) who were natives of the Shenandoah Valley, and whose names appear often in Wyeth and also in Davisson's *Kentucky Harmony* (1816, 1820). Accomplished musicians of their kind, they provide a clear link between the Pennsylvania provenance of Wyeth and the Harrisonburg books which quickly follow. Here again we have the 'Barbara Allen' rhythm, but this time with a very entertaining contraction of it in the second phrase, which suggests the free rhythms of folk song. One imagines the folk-singer, with a tune of this sort, hastening to complete the commanding second phrase and contracting the rhythm without scruple. What has appeared here is one of the finest CM tunes ever set down—whichever of the Chapins it was that wrote it.

Ex. 422, NEW MONMOUTH, is attributed (but very questionably) to Billings in Wyeth. Undoubtedly it is made of cloth first woven in South Wales: it has, both in form and in the lie of the melody, everything in common with what we supposed (p. 117) to be the folk-origin of a certain very characteristic kind of Welsh tune. it reminds us that there were plenty of Wesh immigrants to Pennsylvania in the early 19th century.

Ex. 423, ZION'S PILGRIM, from a later collection of 1831, is another tune with a very strong Welsh flavour, especially in its metre (which it shares with the Welsh carol tune, 'All poor men and humble', called OLWEN in Wales).

Ex. 424, BABYLONIAN CAPTIVITY, is unusual in its metre, and is another tune attributed to Dare. Dare comes out of this book, in which he has eleven tunes, as a very gifted melodist, always in the 'folk' idiom.

Ex. 425 is a great curiosity, being a tune composed well before the appearance of Wyeth; it appears first in a printed source in *The American Musical Miscellany*, a book of mostly secular songs printed at Northampton, Mass., in 1798, as the music for a ballad, 'The Indian Philosopher'. Later it was imported into England and in a simplified form became very popular with English nonconformists (see CP 607, M 531) under the name HULL. Its name in Wyeth suggests that it was thought to have reference to India, but its appearance in a minor-key form in the northern *Plymouth Collection*, 1855 (Ex. 425B) headed 'Western Melody' seems to indicate that the compilers of that book attributed it to American Indians. It is, however, not a folk song but a ballad, probably with no history before 1798.

Ex. 426 appears in Wyeth as we give it (HALLELUJAH), but it is a tune which came into common use earlier than most of these, and as NETTLETON (Ex. 426B) it is now very well known, having suffered a certain amount of alteration and some very necessary re-barring.

There is a good deal of variety of style in these tunes, as we are seeing. One of the saltiest is PISGAH (Ex. 427), now referred to as COVENANTERS. This is, in all parts, almost entirely pentatonic; the melody uses a leading note only at the cadence of each half, and the other notes outside the pentatonic scale are those marked. Observe the way in which the exuberance of the tune is reflected in the other voice parts: the two upper staves are scored for equal voices, not for soprano and alto, and the voices frequently cross each other. The repetition of the whole tune, with a refrain made out of the last two lines of the stanza, (and the repetition again of the whole of this) shows again how the singers, once launched on a good tune, were unwilling to leave it alone. This again is one of the finest examples of the style.

Later books, of course, take over these tunes from each other and add new discoveries. *Virginia Harmony* seems to be the first to carry the now artificially celebrated 'Amazing grace' tune, called NEW BRITAIN (Ex. 428) and now known to be derived from a Scottish bagpipe tune. *New Harmonia Sacra* (a descendant of the Funk books) gives us the again pentatonic PROTECTION (Ex. 429), and *Southern Harmony,* the one printed in New Haven (1835) provides the delectable RESIGNATION, now become widely known with Isaac Watts's 23rd Psalm, for which it was set from the beginning, (Ex. 430).

This brings us to the *Sacred Harp*, which, first published in 1844, is still in print, like Funk's *Harmonia Sacra,* as a book for congregational use. This is, by a long way, the largest and most comprehensive of these collections, and is still in use at the famous Sacred Harp Conventions near Nashville, Tenn., where in the summer a hymn-singing marathon continues for several days in the open air, attracting thousands of singers and observers. The first edition of 1844 was put together by B. F. White; a large revision and extension was undertaken by J. S. James and S. M. Denson in 1911, and a further revision by two sons of Denson, Paine and T. J. Denson in 1935, bringing the completed book to almost 600 pages. The book prints not only the whole text of most hymns but some details about their authors and composers; these are, of course, hardly in the tradition of careful scholarship, and where knowledge runs out conjecture takes over. At one point a Chapin tune is attributed to the distinguished French composer Chopin, and given his name. But the 1960 edition of the book, which has some additions even to the 1935 edition, contains some compositions dated as late as 1959, largely anthems rather than hymns.

From the contents of the *Sacred Harp* in its continuing editions it is obvious that the folk hymnody of earlier times developed very much in the direction of anthems, which themselves developed out of the fuguing and repeating tunes, in the Billings style ultimately derived from the English evangelical style. These compositions come from a stream that has nothing to do with what Pullen Jackson called folk hymnody, but are stricly in the ecclesiastical manner of the evangelical 18th century. But their presence in the books—some of them appear in the earliest collections—and their increasing popularity among the Sacred Harp Singers, brings us to the necessity of discussing what 'folk hymnody' really means.

Jackson, as we said, worked on the principle that the folk hymnody was mostly folk songs of a secular kind adapted as hymns: and in some cases it certainly was. But apart from a few isolated examples such as NEW BRITAIN and CONSOLATION, that is not, certainly in the earlier books, what it mostly was. These tunes—from KEDRON onwards—are the new compositions of musicians whose idiom was that of the folk singers. Even the attempt to align the incomparably beautiful melody WONDROUS LOVE (Ex. 431) with a secular song, 'Captain Kidd', has now been discredited (that first appears in the 1844 *Sacred Harp*), and the real clue to the composition of these tunes is, surely, in such a tune as WINDHAM (Ex. 432). WINDHAM, a nobly eloquent melody in the 'Barbara Allen' rhythm with a contraction near the end, goes clear back to *The American Singing Book,* 1785, a good generation older than Wyeth, and is the work of Daniel Read, 1757-1836, a Massachusetts shopkeeper. It is in the shape-note books from Davisson onwards, but its origin is not in the South.

The fact is that hymn music always is to some extent folk music, in that hymn tune writers, almost always people of limited composing gifts, are people who reach out for the music that is nearest to them. If folk music is the music that non-musical people whistle or sing in the shower, why then all successful hymn tunes are folk music. If your nearest music is Handel, you write Handelian tunes: if it is parlour-ballads, you write like them: and indeed if you know nothing but church music, and other hymn tunes, your compositions become second-hand folk music received by way of the church community. The number of 'hands' through which the idiom has passed before it gets to you probably conditions the degeneracy of your music. Almost certainly the best hymn music has been that which came as directly as possible from folksong, simply because folk song and ballad is itself the musical form which most easily adapts for hymn singing. Hymns are ballads, not symphonies; the temptation to take one's tunes, or one's style, from the high tradition of Viennese symphonic music led to disaster in the 19th century simply because the greater a composer is, and the more profound his music, the briefer are his themes or subjects. So the symphonist simply cannot write a folk ballad, nor the ballad singer a symphony.

What gives the country hymn tunes of America their captivating freshness and eloquence is not the fact that these tunes were once sung to secular words, but that the music 'within reach' of its composers was folk music innocently and sincerely contrived. Folk music deals with the subjects nearest to the people's experience—love, work (including war) and death. Hymns (at their best) deal with the subjects closest to the Christian's experience. The folk singer is primarily a soloist, so his rhythms are free and natural, not restricted by the demands of a congregation learning by ear; he and his hearers know no music but this, so it retains its style for long periods. The singer and his hearers are a community having little to do with the busy and complicated culture around them—and this of course is what the shape-note singing communities also were. But one can look from end to end of the massive collection of *English Folk Songs from the Appalachians* compiled in 1932 by Cecil Sharp, or of the mostly northern folk-carols collected later by Elizabeth Poston, without finding any tunes which are duplicated in country hymnody, which makes it quite clear that the country musicians were mostly inspired ballad-singers who simply took the style, not the tunes, into use for Christian communities, and did so wherever there were 'country communities' to welcome them.

But by the same token, the musically much less interesting fuguing and repeating tunes, which are English evangelical via Billings, are 'folk music'—but, because they are 'folk music' at several removes, lack inspiration and freshness. For such tunes one should go back to tunes like HELMSLEY (EH 7: H 5), and one or two of those in our earlier examples, to find the authenticity which has gradually dried out of them in the long journey. An *obiter dictum* in the very interesting introduction to the facsimile reprint of the *New Harp of Columbia* supports this. There Dorothy D. Horn writes:

> I once drove to a rural section of Indiana to hear a widely publicized yearly singing in which the descendants of the original pioneers met to recreate the singing school that had played an important part in the lives of their ancestors. What I heard was the most unmitigated musical trite: songs celebrating the beautiful spring, true love, or whatever, and tearjerkers relating the death of a loved one, all set to the tritest of tunes. On inquiry I found that the original singing school had used the wholly admirable *Missouri Harmony* but in the 1880s the younger members had demanded something more elegant.

The present writer can testify to an exactly similar experience. Being invited to conduct a hymn singing festival in Brecon in South Wales, about 1955, he found that in about fifteen hymns in the program, not one was in the Welsh language, and only one was set to a 'vintage' Welsh tune (LLANGLOFFAN); all the rest of the music was degenerate Victorian English music, or inferior 20th century music. In both cases the same thing happens: the dilution of a style which remains fresh only when it is confined to the intimate context of a small community, and which becomes corrupted when it is mixed with styles from the wider community which the local composers are not competent to handle. It is not that the style of the wider musical community is in itself necessarily degenerate (although the New England style, as we have seen, was degenerate in being second or third hand folk music), but that musicians and congregations trained in one style tend, when another enters their experience, to appropriate its least authentic elements.

Finally—it will be noticed that many of those tunes which in their use of the pentatonic scale suggest a Scottish 'racial memory' appear in the books of the later generations—1830 onwards; this reflects the increasing immigrations of Scots to the southern valleys, for reasons we have already mentioned. Scottish names and place-names abound in that region; *Neighbor and Kin* especially concentrates on places called Fraserburgh, Buckeyville (Buckie) and Applecross. But the racial origins of this country hymnody have their roots all over Britain. None the less for that, the tunes as they appear in the books have a local diction which is strictly American and original, and it is not surprising that now that they are becoming part of the general repertory they are among the most greatly loved by Americans for whom the New England Style had nothing new to offer.

The second part of the Introduction to the reprint of the *New Harp of Columbia* provides a most interesting account of one series of community singing events which still regularly takes place at Headrick's Chapel, on the road between Townsend and Pigeon's Hole, in East Tennessee, and that should be studied by those interested in this vitally important corner of hymnology. But these events, which abound wherever the country style is surviving, are really the end-product of the camp meeting. This, a product of the Kentucky Revivals of 1797 and the following years, was an open-air affair attracting large numbers of people at which singing and preaching were combined; and it was from these camp-meetings that the later tradition of using community singing as a 'warm-up'—for revivalist preaching seems to have emerged, as we are about to see in the 'Gospel song' tradition. Revival preaching was not a noticeable part of the life of the valleys, and

is not part of the Sacred Harp 'sings', although testimonies are occasionally interpolated in the hymn-singing festivals. It plays no part in the Headrick's Chapel program (or those in other places in the same network) where speech is limited to a minimum and continuous singing is the rule. But elsewhere singing did support fervent and vivid preaching 'for conversion', and when it did, the music tended to be of the most undemanding sort. Quite soon it took on a new manner which leaves behind the localized innocence of folk song, and emerges in the end in that mysterious product of American culture, the 'Gospel Song'. But the 'Gospel Song' has another venerable source, which is the Black Spiritual, and to which we must now turn.

Folk singing remains lively in the Appalachians, but now it has taken a new turn. The descendants of those who abruptly evicted the original Indians are now threatened by modern industry mostly in the shape of strip-mining (in Britain, opencast mining), and this and other subjects of protest have provided fuel for the modern singers. To study these, see *Voices from the Mountains* (New York, 1975) and other collections noted by Guy and Candie Carawan, or visit the cabin in the hills above Cosby, where records and books are sold by one of the leading folk-singers of the present generation.

Yet another aspect of contemporary Appalachian folk singing is in the now famous work of John Jacob Niles, whose records and arrangements, which he continued to make to the vary end of his long life, have helped to make 'country hymnody' famous throughout the English-speaking world.

(Note to previous section: The very charming tune LAND OF REST, H 585, though clearly of the 'country' tradition, is not found in any of the shape-note 'country' hymnals. It was noted first in Annabel Morris Buchanan's *Folk Hymns of America*, 1938 with a song 'O land of rest, for thee I sigh', which Mrs. Buchanan said she had heard from her grandmother, and first included as a hymn tune in the *Hymnal-1940*. According to her account the song was much sung in the Appalachian valleys, and she suggested a common origin between it and 'Swing low, sweet chariot'. It is certainly a tune with a strong Scottish 'racial memory' in it).

American Hymnody to 1900 - II
Black Spirituals and Gospel Songs

THE BLACK SPIRITUALS

Perhaps the most tragic social and economic misjudgment made jointly by the British and the Americans in the 18th century was the slave trade which forcibly transported many thousands of negro people from West Africa to the southern states. There is no need here to rehearse the details of that, but obviously it was the origin of what we now call the Black Spiritual.

This is the true folk music, sung long before it was written, and sung by people who were natural singers. One of the most conspicuous qualities of the African black people is their rich and magnificent voices, and another equally conspicuous quality is their invincible cheerfulness and capacity for joy. Never have such qualities been put to so stern a test, or produced such triumphant evidences of their inextinguishableness, as these were in the slave-conditions into which the black people were thrust on the farms of Virginia and South Carolina snd Georgia in the late 18th century. Exactly where the Spirituals came from, or who first sang one, is a question nobody will be able to answer. They learnt their Christianity from their masters and from Christian missionaries, and to them Christianity became a story of supernatural deliverance which they took to their hearts. It provided pictures of a heaven which kept them sane in their slave-conditions, and a story of deliverance which they projected into a promise for themselves.

The words of Black Spirituals, like the words of all true folk song, celebrated the matters closest to their experience and their longing. These were—liberation (especially in terms of the Exodus and the crossing of the Jordan), and the merciful gift of death as a passage to a better land for people whose identity and development had been rudely torn apart and refashioned by the slave system. Along with those two immediate concerns, the Spirituals became also teaching-songs for Sunday Schools, which re-lived the Gospel experiences and the Old Testament stories; the best known and most moving of these is 'Were you there?'—the first of the Spirituals to find a place in main-line American hymnals.

The story of how the Black Spirituals became known to the whole English-speaking world in a very brief period is told in *The Story of the Jubilee Singers,* by J. B. T. Marsh, 1892, which is a rewritten history based on two earlier accounts by G. D. Pike. The Jubilee Singers were a band of black singers formed from the students of Fisk University, the first Black college opened in America, which began its life at Nashville, Tenn., in January 1866. The singers formed themselves almost at once, and in 1871 began a series of journeys which took them to Britain and many other countries. The story of how these trips were financed—by a university which began with nothing and people who had no possessions—and how they encountered prejudice and discrimination of the most primitive sort, together with such episodes as their being honoured by Mr. Gladstone in Britain and by heads of state elsewhere, is eloquently told in this book. As soon as people heard the Spirituals, they were captivated not only by the astonishing sound made by the black singers but by the haunting beauty of the songs themselves.

This book adds to its account of the travels of the Jubilee Singers the texts and scores of 139 of their songs—presumably their whole repertory. Of these T. F. Seward in his 'Preface to the Music' writes:

> Their origin is unique. They are never 'composed' after the manner of ordinary music, but spring into life, ready made, from the white heat of religious fervor during some protracted meeting in church or camp. They come from no musical cultivation whatever, but are the simple, ecstatic utterances of wholly untutored minds.

Untutored indeed, but profoundly gifted: the music of these songs is unmistakeable and authoritative. The Reverend Alexander Sandilands, an English missionary who spent his working life in what is now Botswana, made in 1951 a collection called *120 Negro Spirituals* which was designed to return to the Africans these songs of their exile; and he notes that in his selection only seventeen do not use either the pentatonic scale or that scale with one occasional extra note (like our Ex. 427). The pentatonic scale is the nearest thing to universal music known to us; although we associated it with Scotland in our previous section, it is in fact found all over the world—especially in China and India. It certainly was the African vocabulary which these black people revived when religion took hold of them and demanded expression.

The rhythm of the Spiritual is also distinctive. In the 139 songs in the *Jubilee* collection only two are in genuine triple rhythm (one other in 6/8). All the rest use a very powerfully accented duple, and the reason for this is the 'beating of the foot and the swaying of the body' (Seward) which always accompany any Black singing. The black people are uninhibitedly physical—their speech is always accompanied by expansive gesture, and so, naturally was their singing. In procession, they almost dance rather than adopting the decorous shuffle which is normal in white ceremonial.

Within this limited range of rhythm and scale these musicians contrived a large repertory of songs, with a very wide spectrum of expresisiveness. They are, of course, designed for people who cannot read and therefore they take on the folk-song quality of 'solo and chorus'. A narrator, as in the medieval carols and in all music designed to be learned by rote, tells the story: the people join in an invariable chorus, or, very often in the Black Spirituals, litany-like responses in the course of the song. This is where they differ completely from the white 'country hymnody', which is designed for people who can read but don't read much. This quality, of course, gives Black Spirituals a dramatic force which their singers exploited to the full. And it is of the utmost importance to remind those white congregations which are now beginning to sing Black Spirituals from their hymnals that any attempt to treat them as normal community-sung hymns destroys their character at once. No Black Spiritual should ever be sung, at least in worship, from an open book, and it is preferable that they be unaccompanied. It is better even that their harmonies be improvised from the simplest vocabulary than that they be sung, as now so often they are, as 'art songs'.

These songs are now so well known and so eloquent in their reiteration of simple thoughts and phrases that we do not need to furnish many examples. One of the 'archetypal' Spirituals is clearly 'Swing low' (Ex. 433) —a song welcoming death as a passage to heaven, to a lilting pentatonic tune. The corresponding archetype of the liberation song is 'Go down, Moses' (Ex. 434); no scene in the Bible was easier for the Black slaves to identify themselves with than the Egyptian slavery and the epic deliverance contrived by Moses. In the *Jubilee* collection this has 25 stanzas, the last two of which are:

> I'll tell you what I likes de best,
>   (Let my people go!)
> It is the shouting Methodist,
>   (Let my people go!
>   Go down, Moses...)
>
> I do believe without a doubt
>   (Let my people go)
> that a Christian has the right to shout,
>   "Let my people go"
>   Go down, Moses...

There the native and invincible exuberance of the Black temperament defies the modern Pharaohs with glee.

'Roll, Jordan, roll' (Ex. 435), employs a kind of *musica ficta* in its alternation, according to melodic context, of the sharp and flat seventh. This is, of course, not an obedience to musical theory but the natural lie of a half-improvised melody. The whole thing is a chorus except the line marked 'Solo', which simply changes with each successive singing, and is one of those lines on which variations can be devised as long as people want to sing.

In THE GOSPEL TRAIN (Ex. 436) we have a touch of social comment: the most spectacular product of the industrial revolution to make itself evident in the South was the railway, and a good deal of black labour was used in its construction. Typically, the Black singer takes his inspiration from the primitive fascination that early steam trains exercised on everybody, and spiritualizes it into a liberation song.

Exx. 437 and 438 are unusual cases. 'I went to the hillside' is a two-stanza song with a chorus which repeats the music of the stanza, possibly of fairly late and developed style; it is written on a modal scale with flattened seventh, and is a more highly organized melody, with a much wider compass, than the primitive Spirituals were. It has been turned into a fine hymn tune, McKEE (H 263) in CM, with one or two of its corners judiciously cut. 'Gabriel's trumpet' is one of the two songs in triple time, a solo, a kind of lullaby perhaps, without a chorus. Gabriel in the Spirituals is always the announcer of the general Resurrection, not the angel of the Incarnation.

From the outset, the Jubilee Singers appropriated America's most celebrated song, the 'Battle Hymn of the Republic', with the original words, 'John Brown's body.' It is, of course, not a Spiritual but a new song based on a camp-meeting tune and at once adapted to the abolitionists' national anthem. (Julia Ward Howe's words, 'Mine eyes have seen...', were written within a year or two of the coining of the original). As a patriotic song, that tune—with either set of words —penetrated where 'The Star Spangled Banner' could not reach, and is still perhaps the most truly unifying song that America has. It is not a 'spiritual' of either kind, but it is a tune coined by a genius.

THE GOSPEL SONGS

With every possible respect to the vital and zealous culture of America, we must begin this section by remarking upon the singular American genius for appropriating general epithets to sectional interests. The most notorious of these appropriations is the designation of one rather exclusive Christian denomination as 'The Christian Church'. Another such appropriation is the use of the expression 'Gospel Songs' to describe a small, though very influential, section of hymnody. One would have thought that any Christian hymn was a Gospel Song, but the revivalist hymns we are about to describe have been called 'Gospel Songs' in America ever since a collection of them, made by one of their foremost composers Philipp Bliss, appeared with the title *Gospel Songs* in 1874. As soon as the distinguished song-leader Ira D. Sankey joined with Bliss in producing, from 1875 onwards, *Gospel Hymns and Sacred Songs,* the title became accepted, and we are now stuck with it.

Hymnody of this kind is especially associated now with the churches of the Southern Baptist Convention in America, and the Southern Baptists have in our time produced two excellent and judicious scholars of their own music, Dr. William J. Reynolds and Dr. Milburn Price. In what is said here I am content to rely on what these two have said about this matter, in Reynolds's *A Survey of Christian Hymnody* (1953) and in its updated version by Price, *A Joyful Sound* (1978). Three of our four examples are dictated by the choice they made in the exemplary appendix which those books provide.

The 'Gospel Song' is hymnody reduced to its simplest terms. It is cast in the form either of a solo song, or of a solo song with a refrain, and this it has in common with the Black Spiritual. It is interesting to recall the comments made on it when it was still a fairly new form, by the English church musician, John Spencer Curwen, in *Studies in Worship Music* (2nd series, 1885)—to which comments the valuable section in *A Joyful Sound* has drawn my attention.

> The American Gospel Hymn (he writes), is nothing if not emotional. It takes a simple phrase and repeats it over and over again. There is no reasoning, nor are the lines made heavy with introspection. 'Tell me the story simply, as to a little child'. The feelings are touched; the stuffest of us become children again.

Writing of its musical content, he says further:
> The old hymn tune, with fundamental harmony at each beat, moves with the strength and stride of a giant, while the attenuated effect of these American tunes is largely due to their changing the harmony but once in a bar.

This was a gentle and cautious judgment, made by a learned and cultivated Congregationalist minister who was also a musician, and a member of the family that had produced the sol-fa notation for the English song-schools. Now that these songs have been with us for a hundred years, the story becomes a little more complex and the judgment has to be widened. But at least Curwen has isolated for us the quality which distinguishes these songs: they are nursery rhymes.

They are the product of Revival. America underwent a series of waves of revival. There was that Kentucky Revival of about 1800 which we mentioned just now. But before that there had been the First Evangelical Awakening whose central figure was Jonathan Edwards, in the 1730s; and after it came the Second Evangelical Awakening, of about 1859, and it was this that produced the Gospel Songs which in the first instance were, just as the Black Spirituals had been, songs of testimony and songs of education. Adults were converted by testimony: children brought to the faith by simple educative songs. The special technique of the Second Awakening centered on the solo preacher and the solo singer, two men working together towards a single end; the typical revival service had (we have already noted it) a musical program to alert the sensibilities of the people, followed by a rousing address to capture their wills and affections.

The musical content of these songs is, in their primitive form, designedly slight. In our examples 439-442 the reader will at once see, not only that changes of harmony move from bar to bar rather than from chord to chord, as Curwen observed, but that

they are virtually confined to three chords, the tonic, the subdominant and the dominant. This means that all their interest has to be in a melody which implies this very rudimentary bass structure, and therefore that the melodies themselves all need to run to a prescribed pattern. They do not, in the earlier stages, run to much chromatic harmony: but as the Gospel Song developed, the possibilities of chromatic harmony, within the pattern of the 4-5-1 bass, for arousing emotion were not overlooked. The relation between George Bennard's THE OLD RUGGED CROSS (a solo, first printed 1913) and BLESSED ASSURANCE (Ex. 440) is exactly the same as that between CUSHMAN (Ex. 417) and the Lowell Mason style.

It is easier to find a description than a definition of the 'Gospel Song', but apart from this extreme musical simplicity, what is common to them all is that they are songs designed to produce an immediate effect on listeners or singers; as solos they are sung *to* a listening congregation, carrying their message of conversion and salvation direct to their emotions through their evocative music: as community songs they are usually solos providing for an immediate congregational response in the refrain. Balancing the preaching for which they are a preparation, they are themselves a form of preaching, with a minimal rational and maximal emotional content.

In *The Church and Music* (1950) a passage near the end comments on these songs as they affected English people under the missions of Dwight L. Moody and Ira D. Sankey (respectively evangelist and song-leader) in the 1870s. There I ventured to describe them as a kind of spiritual ambulance-operation, rescuing the faith of the depressed industrial peasantry of Britain whose lives had been so grievously distorted into ugliness in the new industrial cities. These songs, usually in Sankey's expanding collections which culminated in *Sacred Songs and Solos,* 1200 pieces, 1903, were very much used by the Salvation Army, whose mission was to penetrate to all those places where religion had been squeezed out of life by artificial ugliness and poverty. That opinion, so far as the British scene goes, I see no reason to modify because it seems to be history.

But in America there is another aspect of this. It must be noted that many of the 'Gospel Songs' first appeared in children's publications—ministering to immaturity in a simple way. But the communities which have mostly espoused them, especially in the 20th century (and they show no sign at all of receding from popular favour) are not necessarily underprivileged communities whose religion needs rescuing from ugliness. They may be very prosperous communities whose religion needs rescuing from infantilism (which is the disorder of wanting to remain a child when one should be growing up). The delusiveness of 'simplicity' and the misapplication of the passage about becoming as children in Matthew 18 escaped the generous eye of Curwen, but cannot be allowed to escape ours. Further moralization about the use of these songs is inappropriate here.

But they are without doubt the one contribution which America has made, without derivation from foreign styles, to hymnody. Mason depended on Handel and Haydn, the White Spirituals on Scottish and Welsh and English folk song patterns, the Black Spirituals on the African background of their singers. The 'Gospel Songs' are native to America, and the export trade in them remains buoyant.

In the first wave of composition there was what amounted to an industrial mass-production of these songs. Fanny Crosby, 1820-1915, the blind author and singer, is reputed to have written 8,000 such songs. William James Kirkpatrick (1838-1921), whose *Devotional Melodies* (1859) was one of the earliest collections of such songs, produced over 100 collections through at least twenty publishers. (See Ex. 439). Philipp Bliss, 1838-76, before his untimely death in a railway accident, was an energetic composer, for the last four years of his life abandoning music teaching for the life of a singing evangelist (see Ex. 441). Phoebe Palmer Knapp (1839-1908), composer of Ex. 440, who as a widow had an income of $50,000 a year and had a pipe-organ in her suite at New York's Hotel Savoy, composed over 500 songs. Ira D. Sankey (1840-1908) is perhaps better known and more widely sung in Britain than in America, but the international influence of his *Sacred Songs and Solos* was virtually boundless.

The peculiar English attitude to these songs is demonstrated in that section of the *English Hymnal* which alone contains much material from America. It is headed 'Mission Services' and contains 19 hymns, 567-585, which exemplify the 'Gospel Song' style partly in American imports and partly in British imitations. The vintage pieces here are Bliss's 'Hold the fort' (570), Fanny Crosby's 'Safe in the arms of Jesus' (580) and Lewis Hartsough's 'I hear thy welcome voice' (573); it also has Sankey's famous tune to 'There were ninety and nine' (text by the English Elizabeth Clephane), which is said to have been improvised as a solo in an evangelistic meeting, and which has much in common with the old carol 'The seven joys of Mary' (which, by the way, is on p. 141 of the *New Harp of Columbia* in shape-note form). 'Daily daily sing the praises' is what amounts to a Catholic imitation of the Gospel song style (no. 568), though 'Stand up, stand up for Jesus' with MORNING LIGHT (581) is more strictly in the New England manner. (But a much more emotive tune than MORNING LIGHT, STAND UP! by Adam Geibel, Baptist Hymnal 389, is the 'Gospel Song' replacement, dated 1901—see Ex. 485).

The words of Gospel Songs are usually new words, often written by the composers of the tunes. But when Gospel Singers used older texts they quite often wrote new tunes, and adapted the texts so that a refrain was

provided. A well known example is MARCHING TO ZION, by Robert Lowry, 1826-99, for 'Come, we that love the Lord' (BH 595) which adds a newly composed refrain to the text; Lowry was another extremely prolific composer of songs of this kind. The extension of old texts for the purposes of providing a good sing, in the manner we saw at Ex. 427, is seen again in CLEANSING FOUNTAIN (BH 107) for 'There is a fountain filled with blood'; this is a camp-meeting tune of unknown origin which appears more often in the Gospel Song collections than in the shape-note books, and may go back to the early 1800s; a shape-note book, *Wesleyan Sacred Harp*, 1854, does provide the equally well known tune for 'O happy day' (BH 457). Both these tunes abridge and distort the original texts (by Cowper and Doddridge respectively), and proved very popular in the revival meetings where textual distortion did not matter at all provided the music gave people a chance to relax into singing.

Gospel songs are still being written. The 1975 *Baptist Hymnal* contains a number dated up to 1969. The way in which new variations can be found on such very simple and restricted themes, both theological and musical, is quite astonishing. There is hardly any development in either direction; just that touch of chromatic seasoning is all we find by way of development on the primitive style. But just as the tradition of large-scale evangelism, associated with the assumption that nursery rhymes are the correct singing material for all present, adapts old texts to its purposes, distorting them in the process, so modern forms of the same technique gather in material from other sources and traditions if it will suit their purposes. Not many 'standard' hymns are known to, or sung by, churches in this tradition; but a hymn like 'How great thou art' (O STORE GUD, BH 35), though of Swedish origin, has been drafted into the Gospel Song program and promoted in celebrated large-scale evangelical crusades. It has turned out to be, in its use of the 4-5-1 Gospel Song bass, its very slow-moving harmony, and its melodic insistence on the rising sixth in 6/4 position, exactly what such movements needed.*

ETHNIC HYMNODY

A fifth stream in American hymnody during the 19th century can be generically called the Ethnic stream—hymnody brought to America by immigrants and supporting worship styles which had been current in their homelands. In the nature of the case this hymnody contributes nothing to the advance of hymnological history since its origin is in past history and it has its place in chapters we have already written. Where it does impinge on our story is at the point where hymnody in these groups begins to stop being ethnic and becomes American—but that development takes place in the 20th century, and will be referred to later (pp.

---

* The remarkable resemblance between this tune and that of Hitler's *Horst Wessel Song*, the theme-song of the Nazi Youth Movement, may be judged anything from curious to sinister.

176-7). The dividing line between truly ethnic hymnody and such hymnody as we have been considering in the last two chapters comes where we can distinguish what is brought across the Atlantic as an import from an older culture and what is composed in America by people drawing on ethnic memories. In this sense BIRMINGHAM (Ex. 293) is ethnic—an obviously imported English tune, while PISGAH (Ex. 427) is American. For further comment, see the later passage already referred to.

England: The 20th Century Renaissance

The turn of the 20th century was the time, in England, of that great reassessment of hymnody, and indeed of all church music, which is often referred to as the English Renaissance.

This has two main streams, the liturgical and the critical. Liturgically, it became clear to the leaders of the Anglican culture that the work of the Tractarians needed to be done over again. That which, in their operations, was historically romantic, and in which scholarship was sometimes distorted by enthusiasm, needed to be disciplined by the kind of research and reasoning which, once the initial polemics were a thing of the past, could be pursued.

The central figure in liturgical reassessment was Canon Percy Dearmer (1867-1936) whose talents and temperament contained many impulses which were never, in his life, finally persuaded to run in the same direction. He was in the earlier part of his life a liturgist; in the later part, he was an aesthetic critic with a decreasing interest in the liturgical and dogmatic values of the Tractarians.

The four hymnic enterprises in which he was involved reflect the course of his personal spiritual adventures, as we are about to see. These were the *English Hymnal* (1906), *Songs of Praise,* (1925 and 1931), the *Oxford Book of Carols* (1928) and the revised *English Hymnal* (1933) and they form a circular pattern of a most interesting kind. The first three of these books proved to be publications of enormous influence and lasting force in English hymnody and church music.

Most of the Dearmer story belongs elsewhere, and some of it is recounted in the *Panorama,* but the heart of it, so far as hymnody is concerned, is contained in the first words of the Preface to his *English Hymnal* (1906), 'The *English Hymnal* is a collection of the best hymns in the English language.' Such a broad claim had never been made before, nor has any Preface aspired to it since. What it indicates historically is that people had suddenly become interested in the difference between a 'good' hymn and its opposite. The study of hymnology had been made respectable by the appearance of Julian's *Dictionary of Hymnology* in 1892, and by the monumental researches of Frere which were to appear in his Historical Edition of *Hymns Ancient and Modern* in 1909. But the critical aspect of hymnology had also been instituted and sealed by no less a person than Robert Bridges (1844-1930), later to become Poet Laureate, who in his *Yattendon Hymnal* (1899) had produced for a country parish a supplemental hymn book which not only revived many forgotten ancient classics but also provided critical notes on every hymn; many of these were forcefully, even caustically, expressed. Bridges, who was a superb metrist and also a cultivated musician, called constantly, here and in other writings, for hym-

nody which an educated person could respect, and he was uniquely equipped to give a lead since, where a great old tune had been forgotten, or distorted, because no English text existed in its unusual metre, he could provide that text. So in one small book of 100 hymns he set a new standard of text writing and tune-choosing; his book contains only one or two newly composed tunes, being almost entirely constructed by the pairing of fine but forgotten tunes with appropriate words, new or old.

This was the new age of the collector and researcher. Another such genius of the time was George Ratcliff Woodward (1848-1934), who again was an accomplished writer and a good musician with no ambitions whatever as a composer. His special field was ancient carols, and in his *Carols for Eastertide,* 1894, he produced the first of a series of books (it was followed by the two *Cowley Carol Books* and the *Cambridge Carol Book*) which sought to enrich the carol repertory by reviving fine tunes from the remote past, and thus resisting the tendency, which had been begun in Bramley and Stainer's *Christmas Carols New and Old,* to overlay the true carol tradition with a boring detritus of parlour-music by Victorian church composers. His contribution to hymnody was hardly less substantial in his *Songs of Syon,* which was first issued in 1904 as a tune book with a separate words book, and later appeared, expanded and edited partly by Charles Wood, in 1910. That second edition remains one of the best sources for well-edited versions of chorales and Genevan Psalms. Not content with this, he produced a modern edition, including facsimile reproductions, of the tunes in *Piae Cantiones* (1582) in 1910.

But the project before the editors of the *English Hymnal* was a different one. What was obvious was that in this circle where new standards of taste and research were being established the parishes might be forgotten by the pedants. And the *English Hymnal* people had before them the warning of the 1904 *Hymns A & M,* which was a good effort at raising standards marred by pedantry. Just about the time when that book appeared, Percy Dearmer was calling on Ralph Vaughan Williams and suggesting the idea of a quite new kind of parish hymn book, to be edited by a small circle of friends presided over by those two, to be freer than any hymnal had ever been from the tyranny of popular tradition, and to share with the parishes the new values which the scholars had been celebrating.

But it was not only the matter of public taste that was in question. Upon this Vaughan Williams, in his part of that same Preface, memorably said that good taste is a moral concern, and depends on simplicity and not on pretentious ingenuity. The other problem was that the parishes were, in fact, singing very badly. It was not only that they must be persuaded to sing healthy music: they must be persuaded to sing at all. More and more the anglican books had been forming habits in congregations which more or less assumed that the singing would be done by the choir and listened to by the congregation. What else can we infer from the high pitches at which tunes were so often printed in *Hymns Ancient and Modern* and the books that imitated it? It was all very well for the nonconformists, who had a tradition of hearty singing and who had still plenty of association with song schools and choral societies and therefore were accustomed to singing in four vocal parts. The social structure and congregational temperament of the parish was not like that; it had been served well by the choral style we noticed in the Victorians.

So the *English Hymnal* editors made life as difficult as possible for themselves by at the same time urging good music, which meant a great deal of unfamiliar music, on congregations who were to be encouraged to sing it, mostly in unison, in accessible keys. (Vaughan Williams drew attention to this, saying very sensibly that a tune pitched low could always be transposed up, because where a good choir made that practicable one could expect an organist to be able to transpose, but where the congregation might need the most help it might not have an organist who could transpose down).

This leads at once to the judgment, which more than seventy years of use has confirmed, that Vaughan Williams rose to this occasion with distinction. At the time when he entered on the work he was 32 years old, and fairly obscure; but this was the only time in English history when a musician who achieved international standing edited a hymn book, and the secret of its success and influence was that he was not primarily a church musician; indeed he was not a church-goer. But he brought to the task all the musical equipment he had assembled during his youth, and a resolution to give English music back its nerve which he shared with a considerable circle of friends. He fell in at once with Dearmer's passionate crusade for sincerity and simplicity to replace the romantic pretentiousness of the late 19th century. He had studied the English musicians of the past and saw no reason why England should not again produce craftsmen of the integrity and independence of Dunstable, Byrd and Purcell.

So it became a truly *English* hymnal, and the heart of its contents was music of the English tradition: plainsong from the Sarum rite; the psalm tunes; Tallis, Gibbons and Lawes; Playford, Clarke and Croft. Around these he built a structure out of material from the Genevan psalter, the German tradition (principally but not exclusively that of Bach), the French Diocesan tunes and the more reticent of the English evangelical tunes. Most of the contents of the book come from the periods we have already examined, and many of the tunes in our examples before about ex. 300 were made available, or made famous again, by this book. The

Welsh tunes were introduced to Anglicans; EBENEZER, for example (108: H 519) was put before them for the first time, and HYFRYDOL, (301: H 479) was, by a cunning reharmonization, delivered from the sing-song effect that nonconformist books had given it, and shown in its full glory. Even a few American tunes—Mason's OLIVET, (439: H 449), that odd tune ADVENT (342: Ex. 426b), one shape-note tune, PLEADING SAVIOR (593: H 117) and two or three Gospel Songs were admitted. Nor were the Victorians entirely overlooked; while Vaughan Williams could never tolerate ST. CLEMENT ('The day thou gavest': H 179) he expressed his regret at being prevented by copyright difficulties from including Dykes's tune to 'The King of love', and did not attempt to interfere with the associations of his music with 'Lead, kindly light', 'Nearer, my God, to thee', or 'Eternal Father, strong to save'. True, those leading Victorians whom we mentioned in chapters 15-16 assemble only twenty tunes between them, and Stainer's name is not mentioned in the book; but Vaughan Williams did not allow his detestation of most Victorian church music to dictate all his choices. He was still close enough to the parish (or was kept close enough by Dearmer) to know at what points to make concessions; and where a tune of dubious merit was clearly going to be wanted, he provided for its use in an appendix of 23 tunes, most of which are 'bad' tunes printed under protest—ST. CLEMENT among them (about which we have already ventured to judge him wrong).

In one sense, almost everything in the book was new, since every tune was traced to its origins, so far as it could be, and re-edited in a form as near its original as was practicable. But in another sense, very little was new. The book provided a total of 608 tunes (Appendix excluded but including plainsong) for its 656 hymns, and of these thirty are contributed by new composers, or appear for the first time. Vaughan Williams's own contribution amounted to four masterpieces, all marked 'Anonymous' in the first printing. These are DOWN AMPNEY (152: H 376), RANDOLPH (524), SALVE FESTA DIES (624: H 86) and SINE NOMINE (641: H 126). Three of these would be regarded as the inevitable tunes to their associated texts by the great majority of singers now throughout the English-speaking world ('Come down, O love divine', 'Hail thee festival day', and 'For all the saints' respectively) and the only serious competitor for 'God be with you' to RANDOLPH is the original American tune.

These four tunes are worth a moment's pause. Every one of them exhibits that simplicity and subtlety, that commanding understatement, which Vaughan Williams was wanting to commend. Every one of them is strictly congregational music, though all four are in very different moods. The common origin of distinction is in rhythm. Observe how the ceremonious majesty of 'For all the saints' is lightened by the appearance of the 'Alleluia' two beats before one expects it; how in 'Come down, O love divine' the attractive but difficult metre is made entirely practicable by writing slow music for the short lines, faster music for the long ones; how the jubilation of SALVE FESTA is expressed in several entertaining syncopations, and how even the tiny tune for 'God be with you' wraps two inner phrases round with a repeated phrase in a distinctive rhythmic pattern. At a stroke, as it were, Vaughan Williams produced four new-minted folk songs.

The only other composer of distinction among the eighteen who contributed alongside Vaughan Williams was Gustav Holst. Holst was even less of a conventional church musician or churchgoer than Vaughan Williams; and Holst's three tunes represent one pure folk-song (CRANHAM: 25: H 44), one fine setting of a very expansive and difficult metre, SHEEN (310) and one unsuccessful nursery tune for a mission hymn (BOSSINNEY, 571). Holst, except in 'In the bleak midwinter', remained a musician's musician, but at a later stage he did a good deal more work in this form without which the literature would have been the poorer.

The youngest composer in the book was John Ireland, (1879-1962), whose tune EASTERGATE (520) to the then very popular hymn 'Holy Father in thy mercy' turned out to be a miscalculation: he achieved immortality a little later with his great tune LOVE UNKNOWN. Walford Davies contributed TEMPLE (Ex. 379); Sir Arthur Somervell had three tunes including KENDAL (566: H 496), worthy rather than remarkable. Clarence Bicknell's COME, FAITHFUL PEOPLE (619) had real imagination—he and Parratt (HUDDERSFIELD, 270) were the only contributors aged more than 46. Nicholas Gatty's TUGWOOD (146) is a tune of great strength and simplicity which ought to have had wider notice. But on the whole the new material by these others tends to be music written for hymns not often sung, or replacing well-known losers, and virtually none of them travelled any further than the covers of the *English Hymnal*. Indeed, one notices that in the section of 159 hymns called 'General', where all the best-known non-seasonal hymns appear, we have only five new tunes. The high mortality rate of most of the others is explained partly by the fact that a tune sung only once a year, or more seldom, stands no chance of becoming a favourite, especially if it competes with a well-known one. (See Ex. 443)

The four Vaughan Williams tunes stand out as exceptions to the obscurity of most of the other new tunes. What really symbolizes the true influence of *EH* much more closely is LASST UNS ERFREUEN (519: H 599). Here is a hymn tune from a Catholic collection of 1623 published in Cologne which was revised in its

1625 form by Vaughan Williams and presented for the first time with 'Ye watchers and ye holy ones' but now claims an almost embarrassing variety of partners.* It is as well known as 'For all the saints' and probably more often sung. Here is *EH* bringing into the present the treasures of the past. It was in the exercise of editorial skill, that special virtue of the good hymnologist, that the book got its message through. This is the skill which knows where to find a fresh tune in the existing repertory and knows to what text it should be set. At this point, every association made by *Hymns Ancient and Modern*— upon whose success in devising so many famous partnerships we have already commented—was clearly examined. We will examine that section of 159 'General' hymns and see what this editor in fact did. Of those 159 hymns, 64 were in the 1889 edition of *Hymns A & M,* and retain their tunes as there set (even if the tunes themselves are usually recast in a more primitive or authentic form). There are 45 more which were in *A & M* but whose tunes are changed.** In many of these cases the new association was ignored in the parishes by organists who kept an old *A & M* on the organ-desk, but in a respectable number of cases (considering the competition), *EH* scored 'hits' in the sense of suggesting new associations which many other editors have followed. These would include:

417, 'Jesus, my Lord, my God, my All' to ST. CHRYSOSTOM* (rejected by *A & M* but at that time a very popular association elsewhere)

420, 'Jesus shall reign', to TRURO*

435, 'Lord of our life and God of our salvation' to ISTE CONFESSOR*

445, 'O for a closer walk' to CAITHNESS*

466, 'O worship the King' to HANOVER (not so set in 1889 but so set in the 1904 *A & M*)

468, 'Peace, perfect peace' to SONG 46*

471, 'Praise to the Holiest' to RICHMOND (+)

490, 'The King of love' to ST. COLUMBA

Those marked * are set, as alternatives or as the sole association, in the 1950 *Hymns A & M; RICHMOND* (+) was an alternative in the 1916 Supplement but used elsewhere in 1950; ST. COLUMBA was, in CM, in the 1904 edition, and never appears with 'The King of love' in *A & M*—for obvious reasons.

Fifty texts in this section are not in *Hymns A & M;* eight of these are American hymns introduced for the first time to Anglicans. There were some notable suc-

---

* John Wilson has now (1980) conclusively shown that this tune, which in 1623 appeared in the form shown at Ex. 84, was by 1625 known in the shape which Vaughan Williams used for his revision. V-W harmonized it at EH 519, but the only alterations he made in the melody were to bar it in 3/2 time and to lengthen the last note from one to three beats. See the article on this by John Wilson in the *Bulletin* of the Hymn Society, January 1981, (no. 151).

** It must be understood that in these paragraphs we are referring to the 1906 edition of the *English Hymnal;* a number of these partnerships were upset in the 1933 musical revision, and in such cases the tunes dislodged were all transferred to a second Appendix.

cesses here in the part of the editors, such as these, every one of which was accepted by *Hymns A & M* in 1950:

375, 'City of God' to RICHMOND

388, 'Fierce was the wild billow' to ST. ISSEY

398, 'Happy are they' to BINCHESTER

407, 'Immortal, invisible', to ST. DENIO (JOANNA)

408, 'Immortal love, to BISHOPTHORPE

424, 'King of glory', to GWALCHMAI

438, 'Love of the Father', to SONG 22

464, 'O thou not made with hands' to OLD 120th

475, 'Rejoice, O land' to WAREHAM

492, 'The Lord will come' to ST. STEPHEN

504, 'Thy kingdom come! on bended knee' to IRISH

In all these cases when the text went into the 1950 *Hymns A & M* the tune went with it. (EH 398 and 438 took their tunes from the *Yattendon Hymnal*). Beyond these we should mention:

402, 'He who would valiant be' to MONKS GATE

423, 'Judge eternal' to RHUDDLAN

456, 'O Lord and Master' to WALSALL

474, 'Prayer is the soul's sincere desire' to WIGTON

Those lists are not statistics but spot-checks; a study of the whole book would amplify them; but the great majority of the tunes there mentioned have already appeared in these pages, or fall within categories we have dealt with. The one category which now fails to be mentioned is that of British folk song (Ex. 444).

This is where Vaughan Williams found his inspiration. It was a most happy accident that just at that time, round the turn of the century, English folk song was being so assiduously researched by Cecil Sharp, Lucy Broadwood and other members of the English Folk Dance and Song Society. We may refer back for a moment to what we said a few pages back about the refreshing effect of folk song on American hymnody. We there said that American folk hymnody seems to be mostly new tunes composed by people who were in touch with the folk song idiom. To some extent this is what one might say of Vaughan Williams's four early tunes. But much more than in America, folk songs were taken into the *English Hymnal* just as they stood. The difference in the situation is obvious. In the Appalachians, the folk-composers knew no music but the folk songs. In England, learned musicians collected the songs from rustic people just in time for them not to be forgotten for good. Had the Folk Song movement happened even in our time, seventy or eighty years later, the collectors would have found country life much more overlaid by the power of the media, and rustic songs much more difficult to come by. But what they did find, in great numbers, were songs with

secular or legendary words, mostly in the ballad metre, which could easily be revived as carol or hymn tunes because the original words were already known only to the locals. And a study even of the *English Hymnal*, let alone the *Oxford Book of Carols* or *Songs of Praise,* which are much richer sources for tunes of this kind, shows what a treasury there was of perfect melodies waiting to be opened up.

Perhaps the folk songs which Vaughan Williams and his friends adapted that have travelled furthest are FOREST GREEN (EH 15: H 21) and KINGSFOLD (EH 574: H 101). FOREST GREEN, which started out as 'The Ploughboy's Dream' can be credited with the impressive achievement of being taken seriously even in the USA as the tune for 'O little town of Bethlehem' despite the fact that the original tune for that text was composed, as the text was, in Philadelphia; it is much sung in the USA to other texts as well. KINGSFOLD seems to have been one of the most pervasive of all folk tunes in its day; the *Oxford Book of Carols* associates it both with the ballad of Job and with a carol on Dives and Lazarus; the *Cowley Carol Book* has it in a different form and attributes it originally to a ballad beginning 'We are poor frozen-out gardeners'; Benjamin Britten arranged it in one of his songcollections with the Irish words, 'The Star of County Down.' This tune, in its EH form, is also found in almost every English-speaking book.

But these are only two. The variety of style and form in these tunes is further attested by the innocent grace of CAPEL (EH 488: H 586) and RODMELL (EH 611) on the one hand, or the austerity of KINGS LYNN (EH 562: H 521) on the other.

Not all these tunes have been documented in the folk song repertory. Plenty of them do not appear in the Folk Song Society's Journal (for example, SHIPSTON, EH 390 and SUSSEX, EH 385). MONKS GATE (EH 402, H 362) does, but it has been fairly radically recomposed by Vaughan Williams to fit 'He who would valiant be'. RUSPER (EH 379) turns up unexpectedly as the tune behind the melody very well known in the USA, TERRA BEATA, for 'This is my Father's world' (*Pilgrim* 485). Altogether there are 44 different tunes listed in EH as traditional English ballad or carol melodies, of which four we now know to be misascribed (7, 213, Ap. 54, 591 ii). But forty represents a substantially larger contribution that that made by the new composers, and virtually without exception they make delightful congregational songs.

And that says nothing of the folk songs from Ireland, Wales and Scotland. The two Irish traditional tunes, ST. PATRICK'S BREASTPLATE (EH 212: H 268) and ST. COLUMBA (EH 490: H 345) are strictly hymn tunes—'folk hymns' no doubt; Irish folk song appears a little later in this story. One magnificent tune was taken from Scotland, the late 17th century lament, CAMERONIAN MIDNIGHT HYMN (EH 401): this, though marked as a Scottish Hymn Melody, is a ballad from an age long before Scots were singing hymns, to be dated shortly before 1700. Wales provided three, 'ALL THROUGH THE NIGHT' (268: H 169), RHUDDLAN, an ancient battle song (423) and the extremely impressive YMDAITH MWNGC, or MONKS' MARCH (203), which is not so ancient as some earlier authorities said, but does appear in Playford's *Dancing Master*, 1665. (It may have nothing to do with monks, but be named after General Monck (1608-70) the first Duke of Albemarle, who completed the conquest of Scotland in Cromwell's time, later became Lord Lieutenant of Ireland, and has a very long entry in the *Dictionary of National Biography*—which leaves Wales somewhat out in the cold as an origin for this tune).

One very celebrated English song which *EH* included, in an obscure place, as a hymn tune, has become far better known to hymn singers in the USA because of its association with several often-used texts: this is DEO GRACIAS, or the AGINCOURT SONG (249).

Songs of Praise

This crusade for the improvement of taste in hymnody became part of a larger operation designed to improve public taste in all things musical. At this point we encounter that remarkable apostle of English excellence, Martin Shaw (1875-1958) and his brother Geoffrey (1879-1943).

Martin and Geoffrey were two of the seven children born to James Shaw (1842-1907), a native of Leeds who spent all his life as a rather impecunious church musician*, first in Leeds, later in London. Vaughan Williams's generous faculty for the admiration of others extended to the Shaws, but the family background could not have been more different. Geoffrey found his place in school teaching, and later as an Inspector of music in schools, but Martin was, until the age of sixty, a free-lance who lived on a minimal and very unstable income and lived only for the propagation of music. Martin was at the Royal College of Music at the same time as Vaughan Williams, and both shared an impatience with the dependence of English music on German styles. Martin's early professional years were spent largely in the theatre—more than once he accompanied Isadora Duncan on continental tours as conductor of her orchestras, at least one of which he later described as 'solid, stolid and squalid'; with Gordon Craig he collaborated in the revival of Purcell's dramatic music. He was composing all his life and the list of his works in the *Centenary Appreciation* (see Bibliography) runs to 312 items, most of which were not church music. In 1908 he became Percy Dearmer's organist at St. Mary's Church, Primrose Hill (Hampstead), having already met him through being invited to spend much time in the British Museum copying tunes for the *English Hymnal*.

This can be read about in the essay just mentioned. Martin Shaw's contribution to hymnody was very largely put on record in the two editions of *Songs of Praise*, 1925 and 1931. These and the *Oxford Book of Carols* were edited by the new triumvirate, Percy Dearmer, Vaughan Williams and Martin Shaw; but the senior composer was by now internationally renowned and busy with large-scale creative work, so that while his interest in the new projects was as eager as ever, it tended to be Martin Shaw who did the musical donkey-work and took the detailed musical decisions.

Songs of Praise was the book that made the *English Hymnal's* influence known far beyond the confines of the Church of England, and far beyond the bounds of the parish. It was designed less for liturgical use than as a book for schools of which neither the senior English master nor the senior music teacher need be ashamed, and as a book for churches where intellect took precedence over liturgy. During the years of its gestation Percy Dearmer, who had undergone a profound change of temperament and become no longer primarily a liturgist but rather a seeker after aesthetic values in church art, had founded what he called the Guildhouse in London. This was a Sunday afternoon meeting for worship and intellectual stimulus, very much after the pattern of the high grade preaching houses of contemporary nonconformity, held, indeed, in a disused Congregational Church. It majored in stimulating preaching and in first-rate congregational music of which Martin Shaw was in charge and which he accompanied on a grand piano. *Songs of Praise,* with its generous offerings from the English non-hymnic poets and its profusion of new music, took over where the *English Hymnal* left off. The *English Hymnal* had celebrated George Herbert and John Donne: *Songs of Praise* included Shakespeare and Shelley, Wordsworth and Masefield. And instead of the rather pale offerings of tentative contemporaries we got from the *English Hymnal, Songs of Praise* challenged the mature and eminent composers of the new English Renaissance to write for congregations—which some of them did, and few with success.

The kind of respect for congregational tradition that *EH* so skilfully blended with its crusading zeal exerted much less pressure on *SP*. It did not attempt to be a book for traditionalists. And being so, the place where in the end it had its most resounding success was the schools of England. Martin Shaw and his brother Geoffrey had their eye on the young, and hoped to catch them before bad singing habits had taken hold.

The schools we here refer to were largely the state schools, in which religious observance was quite normal (and indeed, after 1944, obligatory), and part of the *Songs of Praise* project in the 1930s was the production of various 'graded' shorter editions specificial-

---

* James Shaw composed a number of hymn tunes: those who enjoy pursuing the curious byways of the hymn story can find many of them in *Worship Song*, 1905, and will probably judge that they are remarkably bad tunes.

ly for school use, which after 1944 were multipled by the production of school books for different local authorities, all founded on *Songs of Praise,* under the general editorship of Canon G. W. Briggs. In seeking to serve the schools, the Shaws produced a parent book which broadened the impact of those *English Hymnal* standards which its editors still espoused.

Songs of Praise appeared first in 1925 with 470 pieces. Its impact was sufficiently notable to warrant immediate work on an enlarged edition, which came in 1931. This provided 703 texts and 763 tunes. Its title was to an inspired degree precise: it contained all the great hymns the editors approved, but along with them many 'songs', often with rather romantic and pantheistic words, with music in the style which Martin Shaw had made especially his own—the big massed unison song. There are about 35 of these in the book, in various moods, of which Martin Shaw composed several. Those interested should consult, as particularly good examples, BERRY DOWN (590) by Ernest Bullock, CROSSINGS, (661) by Armstrong Gibbs, STEPNEY (325) by Holst, RING OUT (634) by Geoffrey Shaw, and HENHAM (616) by Martin Shaw. This was the first general hymnal to take Parry's REPTON (481: EH 383), which was actually first used in the Repton School Hymnal, and which has since become very popular as a tune to 'Dear Lord and Father of mankind.' The young of all ages, however, were catered for, and some of the first children's hymns of the modern kind appeared in this book, right down to nursery-rhymes in a special section for very young children. There is plenty of material which is suitable for meetings rather than services, whose words again strike a modern eye as somewhat star-gazing, but which generated a large number of valuable tunes.

On the whole this kind of music stayed with *Songs of Praise* and did not travel much further, having its special association with progressive schools and with the Guildhouse services. But many fine tunes of a different texture were contributed to the wider treasury by this astonishing book. Perhaps the most celebrated association of tune and text which it originated was that of EBENEZER with 'Once to every man and nation', which was at once exported to America and made that one of the USA's best loved hymns. *Songs of Praise* is also responsible for 'Morning has broken' —through an odd accident. The Hebridean tune BUNESSAN had appeared in 1927 in the *Revised Church Hymnary* with its traditional carol, translated from the Gaelic as 'Child in the Manger'; either the *SP* editors did not know this or they rejected it, and they commissioned the text which forty years later the media pillaged with such desolating results.

Pre-eminent among great 'first appearances' in *Songs of Praise* must be KING'S WESTON (392: H 356), the only tune written by Vaughan Wiliams in his mature years which has become famous. Its popularity at present is almost confined to the USA, where it is

now the only accepted setting for the great hymn 'At the name of Jesus'. But Vaughan Williams contributed a number of new tunes to this book, adding ten to the four he had put anonymously into the 1906 *English Hymnal*; or ten and a half if we take account of a very good and quite unknown tune which he and Martin Shaw wrote in collaboration—COBBOLD (*SP Appendix* 2). Most of these new tunes are fine stirring unison songs set to texts of transitory value, but the most remarkable of them is the contemplative and mysterious MANTEGNA (Ex. 445) written for an American poem, 'Into the woods my Master went'.

Holst has ten tunes, of which two were in *EH*. The most impressive is HILL CREST (86: Ex. 446), written as the closing song in the Nativity Play, *The Coming of Christ* (1928). This is a swinging melody in the seventh Gregorian mode, with a fascinating text. But the exquisite miniature BROOKEND (Ex. 447) shows how simply he could write and how much both of salty counterpoint and of real tenderness he could pack into a small compass. This is very typical of the idiom he constantly employs in some of his more ambitious tunes in *SP* and in his larger works. His one 'big tune', THAXTED (319: 'I vow to thee, my country'), arranged from a theme in *The Planets* by himself, shows the direct influence of Vaughan Williams, and indeed the interaction of these two geniuses is one of the most interesting studies in English 20th century music.

The two Shaws, Martin and Geoffrey, made the most substantial contribution both to the content and to the policy of the book. Apart from the unison songs just mentioned, Martin's two most famous tunes in the book are MARCHING (SP 678: EH 503) and LITTLE CORNARD (64: H 131). These were among a number he wrote for his supplemental tune book, *Additional Tunes for Use at St. Mary's, Primrose Hill* (1915). Many of these tunes, of which MARCHING is the only well-known one, were composed for hymns made famous by tunes of Dykes and the other eminent Victorians. Vaughan Williams could say a good word for Dykes now and again, Martin Shaw never. In one case he wrote a really beautiful tune whose writing was an act not so much of courage as of foolhardiness: for he dared to re-set 'Holy, Holy, Holy'. This was starting a war he had no chance of winning: but his tune BROMLEY COMMON (SP 187) is one of the best pieces of music he ever wrote and deserves a new text, if one in that metre is possible. It is most interesting to see what Shaw did to keep clear of the famous Dykes tune—including beginning out of key—and yet how his climactic note has to come where Dykes put his, and his last line has to be a paraphrase of Dykes's.

Despite his love of folk song, Martin Shaw's tunes do not often show its influence—his successful ones, never. Perhaps it comes through in the very fine tune PURPOSE ('God is working his purpose out': EH 548: H 538) which, like KING'S WESTON, is much better known in the USA than in Britain, and has been described to the author as a great favourite with Latin American protestants. It is the best canon in hymnody since that of Tallis. On the other hand, SAWYERS (Ex. 448), written for 'Dear Lord and Father of mankind', is so close to the classic Victorian idiom that in the present writer's hearing Martin Shaw was actually asked whether he wrote it seriously, or with his tongue in his cheek. The answer was an indignant defence of its sincerity. Many of his hymn tunes were written for children and in a very simple style, but one of the most remarkable is the last he wrote, CALDERON—contributed to the RSCM's Gift Book (1936) or 'O valiant hearts' and printed in a hymnal only in *Westminster Praise* (1976).

As composers of hymn tunes there is little to choose between Martin and his brother Geoffrey. Possibly Geoffrey has the edge on Martin as a composer of singable tunes, and this would be because he was temperamentally much less unorthodox and rebellious than his brother. Once again, what was perhaps his best tune is better known in the USA than in Britain; this is LANGHAM (SP 326: H 532) for Laurence Housman's fine poem, 'Father eternal, Ruler of Creation', which is in almost every up-to-date American hymnal now. But he wrote more tunes than Martin which deserve wider currency, among which we would certainly include GRESHAM (H 593), DYMCHURCH (SP 93) and FREEDOM (SP 322). His lifelong association with music in state schools gave him an assured touch in writing for young and alert singers. He can also be regarded as the discoverer for English congregations of several good tunes from earlier sources, among which are BALFOUR (EH 186: H 312), STRACATHRO (EH 445: H 325) and BIRLING (EH 274). All three of these were taken into Songs of Praise from the 1919 *Public School Hymn Book*.

Plenty of *Songs of Praise* material was 'music before its time' and during the heyday of that book failed to get off the ground; but here and there we find a fine tune which a later and more musically sophisticated age ought to revive. The youngest composer in the book was Patrick Hadley (1899-1974), perhaps the most undervalued good English composer of that generation. His PEMBROKE (Ex. 449) is a much simpler tune than it looks, and it might have stood a good chance even then had the editors adopted Sir Walford Davies's editorial technique of writing the melody on a separate line: it is athletic for the accompanist, but stately and simple for the singer. Of course it needs a text different from that provided in *SP,* but a later book sets it to the American hymn 'I look to thee in every need' very satisfactorily. And for a good example of the fact that there is still fine music to be written in CM, there is Harold Darke's CORNHILL (Ex. 450) but it lost ground through being set in *SP* to a little used text (and in 1933 EH to another).

Songs of Praise had two aims: one was to loosen up the style of hymnody by bringing it closer to the style of the choral song and making it appeal to the educated young, in pursuit of which purpose it gathered in plenty of thoroughly contemporary and demanding music. The other aim, which had a more lasting effect, was to spread the standards of *EH* through a wider constituency than *EH* could reach. For the *English Hymnal's* excellence would be exposed only to liturgically-oriented parishes, and there was no way of being sure that that old hymn book would not be kept in use for the tunes. But with the *EH* influence channeled into the schools, where singers were less hide-bound and where good music-making helped them quickly to assimilate new material, the message spread and took root. Moreover, when the time came for the revision of the nonconformist hymnals after 1931 (that is, of the Methodist and Baptist books in 1933 and the Congregationalist book in 1951) *Songs of Praise* was on the editorial desks; English nonconformists would not expect to consult *EH*, which they thought of as being for 'high churchmen', but the ecumenical flavour of *SP*—strong in every department except Gregorian plainsong—was such that not a few non-anglican churches actually adopted it for a while, pending the updating of their musically backward books.

It is a matter to which your present writer can testify that in the revision of Congregationalist hymnody, which had to wait until 1951, the editorial meetings were constantly hearing—'The children are all singing this in school and will demand it.' Three specific examples bring the point home. The *Congregational Hymnary* (1916) did not contain 'Praise to the Lord, the Almighty', 'Come down, O love divine', or 'King of glory'. All these were in the 1906 *EH*. But it was *Songs of Praise,* and its derivatives used in schools, that created the demand,—that, and the advent of broadcasting, to which we shall turn in a moment. The three hymns just mentioned are now in every English hymn book and are among the most popular (and two of them and the tune of the third are in most American hymnals by now).

The *English Hymnal* might be called conservationist, *Songs of Praise,* adventurous. But conservation is also an adventure: so the two complemented each other in the crusade—astonishingly successful— for new values in congregational music and for the encouragement of good congregational performance.

The final gesture of this team was the 1933 edition of the *English Hymnal,* in which the hymn texts remained unaltered (except for a few details) but many tunes were added from the store assembled by *Songs of Praise*; the result is a book of 656 hymns (as before) with 745 tunes (95 of them plainsong). Many hymns now have two, or even three tunes, if one counts the 49 tunes in the 1906 book relegated to the third Appendix, and no hymnal in ordinary use provides anything like so generous a musical supply. There are very few new tunes in EH 1933 that are not in *Songs of Praise*.

In this edition the book remains in print and in wide use. Two modified versions of it appeared after World War II—the *Hymnal for Scotland,* which is the 1933 edition plus a short appendix of 14 hymns especially called for by the Episcopal Church in Scotland; that appeared in 1951, and the *English Hymnal Service Book* (1962), a shortened edition containing 298 hymns from the 1933 edition, 37 hymns not in that edition (including a number of Christmas carols) and a pointed version of the Prayer Book Canticles and Psalter. By this date all three of the original triumvirate were dead, and we are in the second half of the 20th century, with which it is not yet time to deal.

Two Educational Forces in England

Education on the broadest scale was the aim of *Songs of Praise,* and its field of action was the state schools of England. But we must now mention two other peculiarly English institutions which assisted in the transformation of taste in hymnody: the Public Schools and the British Broadcasting Corporation.

THE PUBLIC SCHOOLS

Non-English readers will need to be reminded that in England the 'Public School', whose heyday of distinctive existence ran from about 1850 to 1950, was a single-sex residential school normally founded with a distinct religious emphasis. The name was not in any sense anomalous when the first ones were founded in the fifteenth century; they were very largely charitable institutions and provided a liberal education long before education became compulsory for all children up to (at the time) 12 years of age in 1870. With the coming of universal education in England (Scotland had had it for at least two centuries) the Public Schools took on a new character: that of quite unashamedly providing an education for those who were prepared to afford it, of a kind suited to the professional classes, and of a kind peculiarly available when its subjects were living together in a close-knit community. This form of education began at 13, ended at 18, and was designed to prepare its subjects for Oxford or Cambridge. It would be inappropriate to say more here about the character of these schools than that almost every modern autobiographical testimony gives the impression that they were crude, cruel, much given to sodomy, and purveyors of an education which fitted nobody for anything of importance. That is because people who write autobiographies are usually individualists whose memories retain only the disagreeable conformism of such schools, and their sometimes barbarous methods of enforcing discipline.

All we need say is that these institutions, accommodating anything from 200 to over 1,000 boys (or more rarely girls, in smaller numbers) were always distinguished by compulsory religious observance and were places where, since the children were removed from their homes and under the discipline not only of the school rules (which were sometimes as petty and irrational as the customs prevailing at that time in the Army and Navy) but of each others' presence, emotions ran at high pressure. They were exceedingly sentimental communities—which means that they could be cruel.

They were, in earlier days, philistine about music, but under the influence of Thomas Arnold of Rugby in the mid-19th century they became a good deal more humane, and their educational program, though very much biased in favour of letters rather than science, became broader. It was in the 20th century, however, that they became musically significant. Following the lead of the Church of England (which was, naturally, the allegiance of almost all of them) they improved the chapel music by installing decent organs and appointing able musicians.

And once you get an able musician with a captive congregation who (whatever they might have said) rather enjoy the relaxed discipline of Morning and Evening Prayer as a contrast to the artificialities and acerbities of the daily round, he tends to compose for them, and what we get is a quite distinct style of congregational music whose most obvious characteristic is that it goes well with 500 untutored voices singing in unison, and can make musical demands which it is easy, through congregational practice and the sheer weight of numbers in a constantly changing congregation, to 'sell to the troops'. Your first-year boy learns from the singing of the other 400, and a tradition builds up quickly. Moreover, if anybody doesn't like it, there is no way in which he can express that dislike. That, we hasten to say, was the condition of things until the Second World War began what has become its almost total disruption now.

A study of the development of the 'public school' style, one of the more interesting social aspects of our story (and, to anyone who is not English, one of the most intractable) can be carried out by looking at the hymnals used in these schools. They might, of course, use the hymnal of the church they were associated with —that is, *Hymns A & M* or the *English Hymnal* or, in the case of denominational schools like the Methodist Kingswood and Rydal or the Congregationalist Bishops Stortford or Caterham, or the Catholic Stonyhurst, the hymnal of their denomination. But not infrequently they used a hymnal of their own editing: one of the earliest of these was the Rugby School Hymnal (words only), and another early one was the Repton School Hymnal, again words only—such books using a standard book for the tunes. More than one enterprising publisher put out books which were designed for such schools, and contained texts only, with references to several hymnals for the tunes. But the high tradition of 'public school' singing centered mostly in the publication of the Headmasters' Conference (that is, the conference of headmasters of these schools) which was the *Public School Hymnal,* first printed in 1903. This was at first a fairly conventional book owing much to *Hymns A & M.* Its 1919 revision was much more outgoing—it contained a good deal of work by Geoffrey Shaw, it had the first appearance of John Ireland's superb tune LOVE UNKNOWN (SP 127), and it showed much closer knowledge of non-anglican hymnody. This was revised again in 1949, and that edition is the richest in tunes of the kind we are about to examine—some of which are almost caricatures of the style. The final end-product was the beautifully edited and extremely judicious collection, *Hymns for Church and School,* 1964, which belongs to a later chapter.

Turn to Ex. 451, WELLS, by Basil Johnson (1861-1950) of Christ's Hospital. This was in the 1903 *Public School Hymn Book* and in the revised *Church Hymns* of the same year, and is the precursor of the 'public school' tune. Note carefully the difference between it and both the *A & M* Victorian tune and the Parry-Stanford Edwardian manner. It uniquely combines an energetic and purposeful melody with very warm-hearted harmony. The harmonic vocabulary is indeed late 19th century, but the surge of the melody, which goes as high as a hymn tune dare go and uses a compass of an eleventh, is something new when it is superimposed on the harmony.

And that is what we are about to see developing. Not all the public schools had directors who could compose well, but there were few which did not have scraps of manuscript lying about in the organ lofts. Looking for a lead, they found it in W. H. Ferguson (1874-1950), who was both an anglican priest and also a school music director in his youth (at Lancing until 1911), later a well known headmaster (Radley). His WOLVERCOTE (Ex. 452) is the archetypal 'public school' tune and is now in England probably the most familiar. Written for 'O Jesus, I have promised' and appearing first in the 1919 *Public School Hymn Book* it is now the primary tune in England for that hymn. The qualities are all there: the warm-hearted harmony, with plenty of organ figuration, set for unison voices; chromaticism now moves further back in the structure to produce a thoroughly romantic modulation, and it is the first successful tune to move right out of the home key for a whole long phrase. It is easy to pick up because of its A-A'-B-A structure, and it sounds splendid with a big organ and congregation. Ferguson wrote a number of tunes in this style—the others are somewhat less successful, tending to slide over into sentimentality: but CUDDESDON is still often sung in Britain to 'At the name of Jesus' (Church Hymnary 300 ii) and LADYWELL (*A & M* 297) is still heard with 'All hail the power of Jesus' name'. LADYWELL certainly, and WOLVERCOTE probably, were composed for Lancing before 1911. He was capable of a more restrained style, as in FRILFORD (BBC 345) and AMATOR HOMINUM (EH 276), both of which are excellent.

This, of course, has nothing to do with the *English Hymnal* tradition, and is really an extension of the Edwardian. It is no accident, indeed, that Parry's tune REPTON (EH 383) was first sung at Repton school, and first printed as a hymn tune in the 1919 *Public School Hymn Book;* this is a typically Parry melody, with generous sweep and warm harmony, taken from an early cantata, *Judith,* and fitting the metre (though goodness knows, not the sense) of 'Dear Lord and Father of mankind', and this is what public schools loved and encouraged.

The next tune, Ex. 453, MIDIAN, is not a public school tune in origin because its composer, Sir Hugh Allen (1869-1946) was never a schoolmaster; but he was Oxford University's most eminent musical enabler —being not content as Professor of Music merely to lecture and instruct, but giving his life to extracting great music from others. It was he who proved that the Mass in D of Beethoven could be sung by the Oxford Bach choir (which was by no means entirely composed of academics or undergraduates) and it is probably he who invented the now popular activity of community hymn-singing in England. During World War I he organized meetings in Oxford's Sheldonian Theatre (not a theatre in the usual sense but the gathering place for academic ceremonies) simply for the purpose of enjoying hymn singing, and at one of these he produced MIDIAN. Oxford students were very largely public school products and their college chapels had a touch of this ethos about them. Allen, who wrote hardly any music, threw this tune at the students and it at once became famous. The modulation is as dramatic as anything in hymnody, and parish hymnals have remained shy of the tune, leaving it to the public school books to preserve it. But what it does illustrate is the originality and adventurousness that this life-style liberated in hymn tunes. One can imagine Allen betting a neighbouring organist that he could write a singable tune with a melodic leap of a minor ninth, and when winning it encountering the rueful response, 'Very well: but you don't have my parish'.

Most of the products of Oxford and Cambridge chapel organ lofts do not follow this pattern; we remember the contribution of Basil Harwood of Christ Church (above, pp. 113-4)—but his THORNBURY (EH 545) is very much in the 'Public School' style and dates from after his Oxford days; and there is E. W. Naylor of Emmanuel, Cambridge, with his now very popular FROM STRENGTH TO STRENGTH (CP 497) for 'Soldiers of Christ, arise', which dates from 1902: but Charles Wood of Gonville and Caius attempted it only once in RANGOON (AM 270)—compare what we said of him above, pp. 112-3. The most beautiful product of an Oxford chapel may well be ALBERTA (Ex. 458), composed by W. H. Harris (1883-1973) when he was Director of Music at New College: and this has much of the warmth and sweep of the school style about it. It remains the only really successful competitor with Dykes for 'Lead, kindly light'; but we shall come shortly to an even greater contribution of this composer.

Returning to the schools, we have in Ex. 454 the most hair-raising example of modulation—more alarming even than MIDIAN. This, SHERSTON, by W. K. Stanton (1891-1978) first appeared, in the key of our example, in the *Wellington College Hymn Book* (1937) which as Director of Music there he edited, and in which he has a large number of compositions, some pseudonymous, which all show a very powerful original talent, though very few of them have travelled off that campus. (This one was, with the alteration of one melody note, in the *BBC Hymn Book,* and is also in the *Canadian Hymn Book,* 1971, at no. 104).

Perhaps MIDIAN and SHERSTON are untypical in being such unusual feats of originality. But most of the other examples follow a fairly well defined track. At Lancing Ferguson's successor was Alexander Brent Smith (1889-1950), who wrote four very successful tunes during his tenure of office, 1911-34. Two were published privately in 1919, ANTIPHON and THE CALL, the second of which, for 'Come, my Way', has been used in a number of books: see HCS 261, for example, or Westminster Praise 36: the original key was B flat. Two others remained in manuscript and were lost when he left the school, to be revived in *Congregational Praise,* 1951. COTSWOLD (Ex. 455) is here given as sung at Lancing before 1934, not as it was re-cast by the composer later for SATB. Another excellent tune from the same period is WINTON, Ex. 456, composed for Winchester College by Sir George Dyson (1883-1964) when he was Director of Music there.

Harrow School's Director for many years was Sir Percy Buck, 1871-1947, and he contributed many tunes to the *Harrow School Hymn Book* which he edited in 1927. His style is much gentler—reminiscent usually of that of Harwood—and he was much given to writing in free rhythm. MELLIFONT (Ex. 457) is one of the tunes he wrote for that book. The *English Hymnal* has four more: RESURRECTION MORNING (136), DRAW NIGH (307), both written for it, MONT RICHARD (633), from the Harrow book, and GONFALON ROYAL (141), from the 1918 *Public School Book.* His most successful and best known tune is SEBASTIAN (AM 283) for 'Sing Alleluia forth in duteous praise'.

Eton's contribution is mostly in the work of Henry G. Ley (1887-1962), whose best known tune is RUSHFORD (HCS 308: H 560) a tune which admirably copes with the metrical difficulties of 'Fight the good fight'. But this first appeared in one of the very best of the local school books, the *Clarendon Hymn Book,* 1936, which was edited for Charterhouse. This book, which took the wise course of giving brief biographical identifications of all its authors and composers (for the enterprising boys to consult during the sermon), was edited by Thomas Feilden (1882-1974), Director of Music there until 1948, who turns out in his own modest contribution not to be a composer of any great consequence, but the book is perhaps more distinguished in introducing the name of John Wilson (HADLOW, Ex. 460), to whom a little later we shall be attending. For this book also Herbert Howells wrote the tune by which he is best known among hymn singers, MICHAEL (Ex. 459), which is both a very characteristic example of his highly individual style and also well within the accepted school tradition.

The *Public School Hymn Book's* revision in 1949, which brought its contents up from 426 to 553 hymns, was in the hand of C.S. Lang (1891-1971), Director of Music at Christ's Hospital, who contributed nineteen tunes, almost all of which are in a very rich style. PADSTOW (Ex. 461) is an example: fairly often the tunes end on the fifth of the scale, and sometimes have florid organ accompaniments. Our last example in this

category, MAJESTY, Ex. 462, comes after the close of the age in which this style flourished, but it is by Richard Llewellyn (b. 1925), Director of Music at Charterhouse since 1965, and makes a good epilogue; it has great simplicity, despite a daring modulation, and provides a useful alternative to the German chorale tune GOTT IST GEGENWARTIG ('God reveals his presence') which never was one of the most inspired of 17th century tunes.

Hymns for Church and School (1964) was the last book from the Headmasters' Conference; already it had been felt tactful to change the title, and under the musical editorship of John Wilson (Charterhouse) and Leonard Blake (Malvern), neither of whom is a composer in the style we have here been examining, became the most significant new hymnal of its date in England. The fastidious standards of the *Clarendon Hymn Book* were continued here, and although it contains some of the tunes mentioned in our examples it is not at all wedded to this kind of music. Its new contributions will be mentioned in our next section. This book, it might be noted, substituted for the biographical notes in *Clarendon* a fairly extensive introduction on the history of hymnody whose existence suggests that the standard of preaching was by this time earning even less confidence (see later pp. 162B).

Other composers more or less in this tradition whose work is worth studying and can be found in *HCS* are E. T. Sweeting (1863-1930: 219 WOLVESEY), H. A. Dyer (1878-1917: 187 BROMSGROVE), W. Greatorex (1877-1949: 311 WOODLANDS, also H 389), R. S. Thatcher (1888-1957: 190 NORTHBROOK, also WILDERNESS, H 574), Armstrong Gibbs (cf. p. 144 above: 317 LINGHAM), G. G. Stocks (1877-1960: several tunes in the 1962 *Winchester Hymn Book* and more in the supplement, *Hymns for use in Chapel,* made for Repton School) and Sydney Watson (b. 1903 STONOR, AM 404, and several valuable tunes in the *Winchester Hymn Book*).

The 'Public School Style' ran out of steam in the 1960s, although its contribution to hymnody of a certain spacious humanity had been made by then and remained important. The Winchester book just mentioned (1962) was one of the last private books of this kind to be published (and one of the best), and *Hymns for Church and School* (1964) provided a fitting summary of what this dynasty had achieved. The crisis of identity encountered by these schools, in which an important factor was the abolition of regular compulsory daily chapel, meant the end of the context in which these alert and inventive musicians did their work.

BROADCASTING

The other powerful and pervasive educational force at work in the earlier 20th century in England was broadcasting. The British Broadcasting Corporation, ever since it started in 1922 as the British Broadcasting Company, has been unique among broadcasting networks in providing a daily broadcast religious service, as well as a good deal of other serious religious broadcasting.

It is perhaps the greatest difference between Britain and the one other country whose hymnological history is in any sense comparable, that the religious emphasis in broadcasting in Britain was so close to that of the schools. American broadcasting is uniformly commercial, supported by the goodwill either of wealthy industrial or commercial sponsors, or of the conscience-money paid by listeners and viewers for the privilege of watching what are called in America 'Public service' networks. In Britain the BBC is not (as Americans often think) a government-controlled enterprise. It is answerable to Parliament, which is a very different matter. Every five years its 'charter' comes up for renewal, and is debated in Parliament, and it is then that any matters of broad policy are brought to the attention of its directors. In practice, despite the debate and despite a good deal of journalistic discussion at those times, what Parliament positively requires is, so far as detailed program-content goes, minimal. The one thing that the BBC has to undertake to produce (at present) is a 15-minute program summarizing the business transacted in Parliament on every day when the Houses are in session.

Its income is guaranteed during the period of the Charter, and comes from license-fees charged to every person owning a television set (formerly, a radio receiver). Its directors are naturally concerned that its programs shall entertain and educate their listeners and viewers, but they are not in any sense bound by the politics of any party (even the one in power) or the opinions of any wealthy sponsor. It is less paranoiac, then, than the USA networks about 'ratings'—though with the advent after World War II of an alternative commercially-sponsored broadcasting system these matters are more discussed than they used to be.

Historically, however—so far as we are here concerned—the important point is that the BBC was founded as a radio network long before the advent of television, and was designed to put on show what people thought in 1922 was Britain at its best. It was not unimportant that its first Chairman, Sir John (later Lord) Reith was a devout Scottish Presbyterian to whom it was unthinkable that religious observance should be excluded from such plans. So, although the BBC regularly broadcasts religious services from churches, and programs designed to instruct or to involve listeners in debate and serious thought, the heart of it all is the 15-minute service broadcast every weekday which is strictly a 'daily office' without preaching, structured from the first on a non-denominational pattern of prayer, Bible reading, and praise. Two hymns and a psalm always appear. In the beginning the service always came from a small studio and the singing was always done by an unaccompanied professional octet; that has changed only in so far as an organ is sometimes now used to accompany unison-texture tunes. The service was always, and still is, led by an anonymous member of the BBC's religious broadcasting staff.

The situation then is something like that in the state schools; the program in these services is set up not by any kind of popular demand but by people who are set aside to do it. This is what the firm provisions of the Constitution in the USA, which separates Church and State, could not permit either in school or in church. A basic religious observance is still regarded as part of the British scenery.

From the early days the music was directed by Sir Walford Davies, and his successor, who worked with him from the first, was George Thalben-Ball, who continued for about forty years to be the chief musical director for religious broadcasting. Happily for these planners, *Songs of Praise* was available by 1925; the first hymnal of standard form which had no denominational affiliation. So from 1925 to 1951 this was the hymnal for these services: and therefore those values for which it stood were quietly and unobtrusively passed into the homes of the listeners. Those listeners would get their familiar hymns, but also the new *'English Hymnal'* music (not normally the most inventive contributions of *Songs of Praise* because this was not the place for them.) So once again, 'Come down, O love divine' and 'Praise to the Lord, the Almighty' were becoming known to many people who were not yet able to sing them in church.

It is, indeed, the main reason why congregational taste in the USA has moved so much more slowly than it has done in England, that in these two departments of education Britain gave itself a head start. The quite remarkable gesture of the American Episcopal *Hymnal-1940* towards raising standards was backed by neither a school hymn singing tradition nor a broadcasting tradition. To that we shall attend a little later.

After a quarter of a century of *Songs of Praise*, the BBC published its own hymn book, the *BBC Hymn Book*, which appeared in October 1951. Work on this book had begun before World War I, and had been suspended, as had every other comparable activity. The *BBC Hymn Book* was designed to be interdenominational, and a careful eye will detect that the advice given to its compilers by the Methodists and the Church of Scotland was a good deal better than that which it was given by the Congregationalists of 1938. Musically, the book was adventurous and a shade idiosyncratic, but it was a genuine attempt to fuse the traditions of *Hymns Ancient and Modern* and of *Songs of Praise,* and its editing was in the hands of three enthusiasts all of whom were closely associated with the BBC.

The editor in chief was Walter K. Stanton (1891-1978) most of whose experience, before he joined the BBC music staff, was as a schoolmaster, and whom we have already mentioned as a leading 'public school' composer. He contributed 26 tunes to the new book. George Thalben-Ball (b. 1896) was naturally a second member of the team, and his experience had been gained from his assistantship to Sir Walford Davies and succession to him both at the Temple Church and at the BBC. The third member was Cyril V. Taylor (b. 1907), an anglican priest who was at the time on the religious broadcasting staff, and later became Warden of Addington (the Royal School of Church Music), later still a parish priest in Dorset and finally precentor of Salisbury. All three were active and creative musicians, and all three composed very little apart from hymn tunes. (Stanton's output of choral anthems was respectable but not extensive). Thalben-Ball contributed 23 tunes and Taylor 20 to the *BBC Hymn Book*.

The book is fascinating in its being, one might say, the final gesture of early 20th century English pedagogy. Knowing that their compositions would at once get a wide hearing, the editors, with 69 contributions between them, did not hesitate to make their message heard. It was a great mercy that their gifts were so diverse. We are at present able to say that few of their tunes travelled far, but one must give honour to the enthusiasm with which they preached their gospel, on what was to prove to be the eve of the new iconoclastic age.

Stanton's tunes tend to be somewhat impatient, the kind of tune which gives the learner no help, but which can be taught to a captive audience. He imported some of his material from his *Wellington College Hymn Book,* and composed a good deal more, of which the most distinguished, and probably the best tune he ever wrote, is HAMBLEDEN (Ex. 463). Thalben-Ball's idiom is gentler, as became a disciple of Walford Davies, and his tunes, though like Stanton's they are musician's music to a large extent, are always friendly. The best of them may be ARTHOG (Ex. 464); but notice the intellectual thrust of its phrases. It was actually the kind of tune which, placed before a non-musician, made no impression at all. (One observes, if one is an English organist who makes an introduction for congregational singing out of the first phrase or two of a hymn

tune, that there is no point at all at which one can stop in this tune before the end). One of his most attractive pieces is JESMIAN, written (like so many tunes) for 'Brightest and best' (*BBC* 63).

Neither of these composers made such an impact as the composers of two other tunes associated with this book. One of these is the sombre and magnificent CAROLYN (Ex. 465), by Herbert Murrill (1909-52) whose early death was such a loss to English music. This is a tune which later editors found it difficult to ignore, and it has been imported to America in *Ecumenical Praise* (1977). But even that pales before the quite incomparable ABBOTS LEIGH, by Cyril Taylor (Ex. 466).

ABBOTS LEIGH had actually appeared the year before, in the 1950 edition of *Hymns Ancient and Modern*, and its composer later became one of the Proprietors of that company. But it had appeared as early as 1941 on a leaflet, and is the archetypal example of a hymn tune taught to the whole of Britain through broadcasting. Its secret, which gives it a sort of timeless authority that makes one feel as soon as one has heard it that one knew it all one's life, comes from the fact that its composer remembered what it was like to be in a pew singing. It has exactly the kind of universal appeal that one attributes to Dykes's NICAEA, and for the same reason. No main-line hymnal from 1951 onwards dared omit it, and it came to America in the *Worshipbook* (1972) and it is now making brisk headway there.

Cyril Taylor is the only one of these three who has continued to compose after 1951 and has allowed his style to change. His influence in this book was most salutary in keeping many of the committee's decisions 'down to earth'. The book was not adopted in many parishes, though parishes of an ecumenical kind, like the Guild Churches of London or the churches associated with university campuses, looked on it with favour, and it was adopted very early at the University Church of Oxford.

Other English Hymn Books, 1900-60

Nobody thought it worth while trying to resist the tide which the English Hymnal, the school books, and the BBC book had generated, but hymnals of other traditions used the new ideas in their own way.

Hymns Ancient and Modern—what had become if it after the false-restart of 1904? Well, the 1904 book did at least set new standards of taste and scholarship, and the question was, how these were to be applied in a way that would not have the calamitous effect that had proved fatal to the 1904 edition. Losses were to some extent cut with the publication in the inauspicious year 1916 of the *Second Supplement,* whose musical editing was placed in the hands of Sydney Nicholson (1875-1947). After the first World War a new edition was produced in 1922, which incorporated all the additions and revisions of 1916. But as an interim measure the 1916 edition provided 141 new hymns, and new or revised tunes for 107 hymns already in use, mostly imported from the 1904 edition. There was an 'iron curtain' of copyright prohibition between the *Hymns A & M* company and the *English Hymnal,* and the 1916 supplement could not hope to do more than rescue the viable material from the 1904 edition and give it a second chance. Nicholson had to omit his very early contributions to the 1904 edition (which must have been composed well before he was 30), because their associated texts were vetoed by the editorial committee. The 1922 edition, being three hymn books in series (the 1875 edition plus the 1889 supplement plus the 1916 supplement) was cumbersome but serviceable, and thus it continued for another generation.

Hopes for reviving the book at the end of the thirties were dashed by the outbreak of war, but in 1939 a *Shortened Edition* appeared, which was the 1922 book re-set, with a large number of little-used hymns referred to only by the first lines (with suggested tunes); but Nicholson took the opportunity of including a few tunes which *A & M* congregations had not heard before—several by Gibbons and other early composers, and a few composed or arranged by himself, of which the finest—and the finest of all his tunes—is certainly FENITON (Ex. 467).

This tune has an almost symbolic significance: it expresses its composer's temperament and ideals, and marks a change in the direction of the *Hymns A & M* style—a slight change, as is appropriate to what had become by now such a majestic and ponderous vessel as the *A & M* tradition. But it is one of the few tunes from that tradition which really does presuppose a cathedral setting: it is marked *Slow,* it is extremely spacious, it needs a resounding organ and plenty of echo, and it expresses the joyful mystery of the Eucharist when celebrated in festive style in an English

cathedral on a fine morning about 10 a.m. A good deal of Nicholson's work in hymns was on this grand scale —his other famous tune is CRUCIFER for 'Lift high the cross,' a broad and cheerful processional.

The temptation to digress at length on this extra-ordinary man, one of the most elusive and unusual personalities in English church music since S. S. Wesley, is strong and must be resisted. He was the son of a Victorian adventurer in the high tradition, who was born in 1808, to whom Sydney, his eldest child, was born in 1875, and who lived to be 95 having among other things been the first Chancellor of the University of Sydney in Australia. The aristocratic tone which had been built up in the household into which Sydney was born discouraged any such menial and socially dubious career as the pursuit of music, but Sydney rebelled against that and became organist of Carlisle Cathedral, later of Westminster Abbey. As a musician he was not first-rate in any department* but this was compensated by Sydney's inheriting a good deal of his father's strenuous and enterprising temperament; for it was this keen eye for business and administrative flair which enabled Sydney to found the Royal School of Church Music in 1927†, which has become the only international centre of Church Music in Christendom.

Nicholson's hymn tunes are mostly to be found in the 1950 edition of *Hymns Ancient and Modern,* whose completion he did not live to see. But the new direction he gave to *Hymns A & M* was a broadening of its musical horizons to include more than that local 'parish sound' on which up to 1889 it had certainly placed its major emphasis. Inevitably, being of the same generation, he shared one or two of Vaughan Williams's insights—especially a wish to see music of greater dignity and depth in hymnody; but he had no interest in those folk-origins of hymnody which had appealed to V-W, and his appointment to the musical charge of *A & M* was wise because his policies of improvement tended to move at the slow and conservative pace which ensured that he would not upset the stately rhythm of *Hymns A & M's* progress.

The 1950 edition, called *Hymns Ancient and Modern Revised* and still (1979) the central publication of this company and the most widely used hymnal in England, was guided through its final stages musically by Nicholson's successor at the RSCM, Dr. Gerald Knight (1908-79) and the then organist of St. Paul's Cathedral, Dr. John Dykes-Bower. A later member of the Board of Proprietors was heard to say, about 1967, 'when this book was published it was already out of date' (which presages some more radical changes of direction such as we shall attend to shortly). The fact

---

* This is the opinion recorded in Dr. W. K. Lowther-Clarke's unpublished biography of S.H.N.
† A fascinating book waits to be written comparing the careers, ideals and achievements of Sydney Nicholson and of John Finley Williamson who founded Westminster Choir College in the USA in 1926.

was that towards the end of an age of great progress *Hymns A & M* refused to substitute an enthusiastic scramble for its customary dignified gait. It had now settled into the position it had built up of being a hymnal which should cautiously examine all that others were doing, pick out what the parishes and cathedral congregations would find most practicable, and ignore the rest. It made a virtue of the 'iron curtain' situation between itself and the *English Hymnal* by taking the line, 'let them keep it: we don't need it.' Nicholson never said, 'V-W found a lot of good folk songs, arranged them and copyrighted them: let us go and find some more he missed.' Knowing that in plain fact 'For all the saints' would be sung to the English Hymnal tune whatever he did about it (and what he did was to retain Stanford's ENGELBERG and write another tune of his own alongside it) he was sure that in 99 cases out of a hundred his judgment about what people would rise to was right. And the astounding thing about *A & M*, then and, as we shall see, in its later offshoots, was that this judgment is in fact 99 per cent right. You may go to the *English Hymnal* for learned and distinguished music, and to *Songs of Praise* for unusual and adventurous music, but if you want to know what English anglicans are actually singing, you go, as you went in 1875, to *Hymns A & M*.

Naturally therefore its contribution to the development of the hymn tune is modest. But it has its moments. Neither Dr. Knight* nor Dr. Dykes-Bower reckons to be an eminent composer (though in other ways their eminence is undisputed), but Dykes-Bower's small contribution to the 1950 *A & M* is quite first-class. His most ambitious tune is ELTON (Ex. 468), in the metre of 'Who would true valour see' but written for a fine hymn about St. Thomas. Compare with that his AMEN COURT (237) and STANDISH (407) and you have here a craftsman who knows what a parish can enjoy and can construct a beautiful and chaste melody.

One of the book's most beautiful contributions is REMISSION (Ex. 469). The composer of this, Leonard Blake, was mentioned in our 'Public School' section, since his working life was spent mostly at Worksop School (for which he edited a very good hymnal, the *Worksop College Hymn Book,* 1937) and later at Malvern College, for which again he edited a masterly Hymn-Supplement; and he was one of the two editors of *Hymns For Church and School* (1964). But in his small number of hymn tunes he does not espouse the 'Public School' style. REMISSION is his most characteristic piece, written for a very unusual and beautiful hymn.

A & M tunes are rarely elusive; they are direct and friendly and approachable—like Heathcote Statham's very fine ARNCLIFFE (381) and many of the good news tunes in the children's section. Our Ex. 471 MERNLE,

was written for 'I love to hear the story' by a composer who was about 15 years old when he wrote it, and is a tune of pure genius which makes one wish that the composer had done much more in this line. Another charming tune by a young composer is Roy Jesson's BARNET (223) for 'When morning gilds the skies', again written when the composer was a chorister in Barnet parish church and 'spotted' by Nicholson. (Jesson had a short life—1926-72—and again we wish more tunes had come from him).

Another composer featured in this book is Greville Cooke (b. 1894), a parish priest with a very sound sense of congregational taste. His GOLDEN GROVE (307) is a good hearty setting of 'Stand up, stand up for Jesus', but his EMMAUS (Ex. 470) is one of the very few tunes in the book that one could call elusive and demanding.

We print this tune a tone lower than it appears in *A & M* because this testifies to something that Dr. Gerald Knight once said to the present author: that, taken very slowly and in that key, the tune has a presence and emotional content which this author had up to then entirely failed to notice. (Taken fast its repetitive rhythm becomes a little irritating). It was written not for the text given it in *A & M* but for 'Come, O thou Traveller', and its name, EMMAUS, taken along with the biblical reference of that text, suggests that its composer was a preacher of classic imaginativeness.

But the greatest moment in this book is without question William Harris's tune NORTH PETHERTON (Ex. 472B). What could an editor do who knew that 'Come down, O love divine' must be in his book, but who was debarred from using DOWN AMPNEY? Anything less than a tune of genius would never be sung—the *English Hymnal* would be on the organ desk and the people would sing DOWN AMPNEY by ear. Observe what Harris did—being faced with so daunting a challenge. He chose a key as far as possible from that of the older tune, and then chose a rhythmic pattern which was exactly as ingenious as Vaughan Williams's and yet in no way a copy of it—triple time for the short lines, duple for the long ones; the result was the finest tune this gifted composer ever wrote.

This then is the place to say that the vitality and inventiveness of English hymnody owes a great deal to the fact that the Established Church in England has never had an official hymn book. It had three hymn traditions running in parallel (we have mentioned only two so far), and influencing each other very little. The two traditions we have mentioned ran in good counterpoint. *A & M* was always the majority book, always conservative and cautious: *EH* was the dissenting tradition that injected new life into English hymnody. The two tunes juxtaposed at Ex. 472 are the best argument for the law of copyright, and more, importantly, the best illustration of the often overlooked fact that

---

* Dr. Knight died in September 1979, shortly after this paragraph was written.

the Ecumenical Movement is nourished by counterpoint, not block-harmony: not by agreement but by lively and courteous debate.

The Revised Church Hymnary, 1927

Turning now to some other hymnals of the period, we mention first the Presbyterian tradition. Presbyterians in Britain had two streams of hymnody when the century opened; that of the Church of Scotland, served by the *Church Hymnary,* 1898, and that of the Presbyterian Church of England, served by *Church Praise,* 1885, revised 1908. The *Revised Church Hymnary* of 1927 was designed to be a pan-Presbyterian book, for all English-speaking Presbyterians in Britain and beyond. It contained 707 hymns, with an English supplement containing a selection of metrical psalms, but a separate complete psalter (revised 1929) for use in Scotland.

With magnificent impartiality the Church of Scotland (obviously the ruling influence in this book) appointed a Welsh editor, David Evans (1874-1948). He was a pupil of Walford Davies and his successor in the Chair of Music at the University of Wales. His musical heredity was therefore in the high tradition of anglicanism and he knew his *English Hymnal* thoroughly. Three of Vaughan Williams's four famous tunes and many of his folk song arrangements went into the *Church Hymnary* and its tune-versions were often those made current by *EH.* In the general area of taste, then, Scotland was abruptly aligned with the traditions of the English renaissance.

During its long reign of 46 years this book achieved in Scotland almost the status of a monopoly—the Episcopal Church apart. Churches outside the Church of Scotland tended more and more to use it as the national self-consciousness of Scotland developed, and it became the normal book of the Congregationalists and of the United Free Church and of the schools. Scotland was, then, fortunate in having a musical editor who knew his way about in the hymnody of 1900-1920. Texts, where they were new to Scotland, were normally anglican, and the great evangelical classics were used hardly less sparingly than they were in *Hymns A & M.*

The weakness of the book was in its paucity of interesting new music apart from the considerable contribution made by its editor; and we have to say that David Evans was no Vaughan Williams. Under his own name and that of 'Edward Arthur' he contributed twenty tunes, and it is fair to say that only one of them seems to be likely to travel far. This is our Ex. 473, LUCERNA LAUDONIAE, for 'For the beauty of the earth', a tune very much in the Walford Davies style with its opening rising sixth and its ingenious use of rhythmic change. YN Y GLYN (CH 529: EH 563) is one of his tunes in the 'high Welsh' style which did travel as far as *Songs of Praise* and EH. Apart from this, it is for one or two excellent collocations of text and tune that CH is especially honoured—pre-eminently in setting Percy Buck's GONFALON ROYAL (see EH 141) to a very attractive hymn of praise (at no. 23) and thus making Scotland the one country in which that first-rate tune is really familiar. One other very distinguished piece, 'Be thou my vision', is among the good things this book took from Ireland.

The Irish Church Hymnal, 1919, 1960

Irish Protestants have been well served. Presbyterians, largely in Northern Ireland, have of course shared the *Church Hymnary,* but the Episcopal Church in Ireland has developed an ecumenical tradition which deserves much honour. The *Church Hymnal* of 1919 was, for its date, a sound collection of 707 hymns and 20 carols, musically somewhat wedded to pre-*EH* values (the name of Vaughan Williams is not in its composers' Index). It is interesting in containing three tunes of Charles Wood (cf. pp. 112-3) not found elsewhere, but its chief contribution is in two or three Irish tunes which it introduced for the first time, edited by L. L. Dix and C. H. Kitson. The one which has now gone all over the world is SLANE, with 'Be thou my vision'. This was given a good deal of impetus by being included in the Scottish book (above), but the Irish book of 1919 must have the honour of having invented the hymn. There is also there the great tune MOVILLE (Ex. 474), associated with a text attributed to St. Columba.

It should also be said that the 1960 revision of this book, musically much better-educated, is one of the best all-round hymnals in existence; the evangelical nature of the Irish Episcopal Church ensured that in both editions there should be a good representation of the great English non-anglican classics, and this, allied with a wide and sensitive tune selection, made the 1960 *Hymnal* the envy of many denominations outside the anglican.

The Methodist Hymn Book, 1904, 1933

English Methodism has always prided itself on its hymn singing; but naturally enough its hymn-singing tradition is basically a 19th century regional development. Methodism, ever since the original missions of the Wesleys, has flourished in those parts of England which in the 18th century were less and less reached either by the indolent Establishment or the market-town culture of the Calvinist churches. There are still places where Methodism attracts the largest congregations, and there are many (in England, not in Scotland) where the voice of Dissent is virtually the voice of Methodism. After the death of John Wesley, in whose lifetime the formation of any kind of Methodist Church was a dissenting denomination was discouraged, Methodism followed several streams, and fell into a multi-denominational pattern in which basically the primitive evangelicals were on one side and the Wesleyans, who retained many of the customs of the Church of England, were on the other.

The 1904 *Methodist Hymn Book* was basically a

Wesleyan book, following the 1876 book which was the first Methodist Hymn Book to print words and tunes together. Its musical editor was Sir Frederick Bridge, organist of Westminster Abbey, who acted in a professional capacity without attempting to show any criticism of Methodist musical values. Those values were those of the 19th century singing school and choral society, and no attempt was here made to widen the limited range of nonconformist musical education.

But there is one name among the many new composers in this book—contributor of one tune—which identifies a point of development; this is the Rev. F. L. Wiseman (1858-1944). Dr. Wiseman lived to see his work appreciated much more widely—he has 11 tunes in the 1933 book, and they have a touch of originality about them which must, at the time of their first appearance, have been a strong taste for traditional Wesleyans, however modest they appear to be now. Our Ex. 475, GOD OF MY LIFE, is typical of his capacity for introducing just a single point of originality (in this case, as often in his work, rhythm) into a tune which otherwise is traditional enough to find favour among musical conservatives.

The 1933 book was a book designed to serve a United Methodist Church in which the major separated streams came together. It is an enormous book, by 20th century standards (as was the 1904 edition) containing 984 hymns, and the needs of the 'primitives' were served in the inclusion of a large number of 'Gospel songs'. Due notice was taken of the most important contributions of the *English Hymnal* school, and some attempt was made to widen the musical vocabulary. One of its more conspicuous names was that of George F. Brockless, organist of the Central Hall, Westminster, who made a number of interesting contributions; our Ex. 476, GRAINGER, is a very unusual and original CM tune with more than a touch of folk idiom about it.

Alfred Beer (1874-1963) also wrote some original tunes: as music director at the famous Methodist 'public school'. Kingswood, he was able to exploit some of the opportunities of a 'captive congregation' which we referred to above, pp. 148-9, and his tunes tend to have a generous sweep and warmth of manner which enable them to compete with well-established but disreputable favourites. Ex. 477, ANCHOR, faces the formidable competition of the very popular and certainly calamitous tune SAGINA for 'And can it be...' and is certainly about the best tune available for that majestic but intractable text.

One would not expect too much in the way of 'far-out' composition in circles where hymn singing is conservative and hearty; but it was the *Methodist Hymn Book* which ventured on NEARER, MY GOD, TO THEE (Ex. 478)—certainly the most remarkable essay in

polytonal melody up to that time, eclipsing in originality anything that *Songs of Praise* had achieved. Its composer, T. C. Gregory (b. 1901) was a pupil of Alfred Beer and the youngest contributor to the *Methodist Hymn Book*: he became a Roman Catholic in 1941.

The Congregational Hymnary, 1916 and Congregational Praise, 1951

English Congregationalists, after their first official hymn and tune book of 1887 (see p. 92A) made a thorough revision in the *Congregational Hymnary*, a book which never carried a date but which is known to have been published in 1916, in the worst days of World War II. Congregationalism was at the time suffering what could now be called a crisis of identity, in which the conservative values of Calvinist theology were under attack, and the liberal values of what was then known as the 'New Theology' (associated with such names as that of R. J. Campbell, who preached it in the first decade of the century) were enthroned. It was an unsatisfactory book both theologically and musically. The chairman of its editorial committee was Sir John Maclure, who was also associated with the *Public School Hymn Book* of 1919; but nothing could be more different than those two books, for most of the music in the *Hymnary* was either old tunes ineptly edited or new tunes very much in the style of our Exx. 362-5. There is no new tune in that book which has travelled beyond Congregationalism, and the singing habits it inculcated were quite unworthy of an intelligent Christian group.

The revision of this was projected before World War II, but, as in several other cases, suspended. A new committee was formed, however, before the War ended (1944) so once again a Congregationalist book was in preparation in war-time. The result was *Congregational Praise, 1951*. A proper account of this book would take more notice of theology than of music, since its contents (which to some extent were recovered from the 1887 book after being ejected in 1916) were compiled very much under the influence of such critics of the *Hymnary* as Bernard Manning (who had died before the new committee was formed). But musically it was not totally insignificant, largely because its musical chairman was Eric H. Thiman (1900-75).

Dr. Thiman could claim without too much overstatement to be the Martin Shaw of nonconformity, and he certainly was the first considerable church composer to come out of Congregationalism. His work in that church and in the wider circles of the Free Church Choir Union had great influence in the raising of taste in church music among people whom the entrenched anglicanism of Martin Shaw refused to acknowledge as existing.* Thiman had standards which were very much those of Martin Shaw. As a composer he was

---

* There is a good illustrative story about Martin Shaw; towards the end of his life he was told that his cantata *The Redeemer* was to be performed at Tackett Street Congregational Church, Ipswich—in the county where he lived. He was quite persuaded that his music was being attempted by a few untutored singers in a tiny tabernacle, and said as much: but when he was urged to go, he was astonished to see a large building with a very able choir under the distinguished direction (as it still is) of Mr. Gordon Hawkins.

almost militantly unoriginal, but what he composed could be sung by people who had not got further than Stainer, and did them good. He appears first as a hymn composer in *Congregational Praise,* where he has a number of tunes. Our Ex. 479, MILTON ABBAS, is one that has travelled, and deserved to; as a setting of 'Christ for the world we sing' it is rhythmically appropriate and, like all his work, entirely congregational. Though many of his tunes in *CP* are likely to remain there, his influence was decisive, and can be seen in the music of some of his colleagues who also contributed to that book.

A good example of a *CP* tune from another hand is EASTWOOD (Ex. 480)—by the Reverend Eric Shave (b. 1901),—this tune has actually become the most popular and widely known of all the original contributions to the book. The same friendly quality can be found in Vernon Lee's EASTVIEW (420) and J. H. Loring's ED-MONDSHAM (517); and perhaps the most interesting 'discovery' of the committee was the then young composer Jack P. B. Dobbs (b. 1922), whose tune TEILO SANT (Ex. 481) has proved to be a most welcome new tune for the great text 'Eternal Light!' (We give it in our example as he originally wrote it, in 1943, in his early twenties: the version at CP 21 is simplified to reduce the three-octave span of its score).

On the whole, CP was important within its denomination rather than outside it, although it did reintroduce some texts which other editors have considered, and certainly produced a choice handful of new hymns in an age when good new hymn texts were hard to find.

The Baptist Hymn Book, 1933 and 1962

English Baptists were very much in the same condition as the Congregationalists during the first half of this century. There was a massive *Baptist Church Hymnal* published in 1900 which was sound on texts and very provincial in music; its successor, the *Baptist Church Hymnal Revised,* 1933, corresponded very much with the 1916 *Congregational Hymnary,* substituting romanticism for theology at many points, and showing very little knowledge of musical developments since 1900. Only the few very popular offerings of the Vaughan William school were in it, and the Exx. 362-5 style was even more prominent than in the *Congregational Hymnary.* So the *Baptist Hymn Book* of 1962 had to make a similarly adverturous leap. This was in the hands of a new generation of musicians and text-critics, and was an enormous improvement. Our comments on CP apply, *mutatis mutandis,* to this book; it contains a selection of 'Gospel songs' which the Congregationalists abandoned after trying them in 1916, but its selection from mainline hymnody is sound and sane; musically it follows the same principles as CP—becoming a sort of nonconformist *Hymns Ancient and Modern*—cautious rather than innovative. The most significant composer in it is John Hughes (1896-1968), an example of whose work we had at Ex. 396, and whose distinguished talents were placed at the service of the Baptists, to their lasting benefit. The tune selection took full advantage of the production of the *BBC Hymn Book,* and, taking advantage of the interval which had elapsed since the 1950-1 'explosion' of hymn books, its editors produced what remains the finest all-round non-anglican selection of tunes available in Britain.

But this has taken us a little beyond the terminal date we set for this section (1955), and it is time to make a new start on the second half of the 20th century.

24

Confusion and Creativeness in Britain Since 1955

'Light', 'Pop' and 'Folk'

The revolution in church music, church behavior and theology which began in the mid-1950s had effects which I have ventured to summarize in Chapter 12 of *Twentieth Century Church Music;* that book was written in 1962/3, immediately in the context which produced the theological explosion of *Honest to God,* and although little more than 15 years later that seems a remote age, the opinions there expressed seem to me to be the opinions I should still offer, though I should (but this is not the place for it) portray the consequences of this revolution in darker tones.

Broadly speaking, this last period (upon which comment must necessarily be of a tentative kind) has been, in all church music, the most creative and at the same time the most intellectually disorganized of all periods. In every gesture made by the new musicians there have been points of strength and points of grave weakness, and many excellent intentions have been corrupted by the unscrupulous, who have in a permissive age made the most of their new freedom to spoil what was meant to be good.

The first gesture in hymnody in what was to become a radical revision of taste can be dated exactly: Sunday, 14 October 1956. The Sunday evening hymn singing program on BBC radio was then, had long been, and has remained the most popular of all religious broadcasts on that network, and listeners were alerted in a special note in the *Radio Times* to the fact that if they heard this program they would hear something quite new. On that day it came from the parish church of Martock in Somerset, and after three or four conventional hymns a piano was substituted for the organ and the congregation sang the tune CHESTERTON (Ex. 482). The composer of this was Geoffrey Beaumont (1903-70: later known as Father Gerard of the Community of the Resurrection). A few months later (early 1957) the Beaumont *Folk Mass* was published and became the talk of the country, and the Twentieth Century Church Light Music Group was formed, which proceeded to publish several series of hymn tunes and liturgical settings that became exceedingly popular.

That statement introduces the words 'Light' and 'Folk', and presupposes what came to be known in the early fifties as the 'pop' culture. On that culture the best brief statement is that of a well known painter in that style, who was quoted in *The Listener* by Lawrence Alloway as saying, 'I think of my purpose as a search for what is epic in everyday objects and everyday attitudes.'

Alongside that let us place again (both these quotations are mentioned in *Twentieth Century Church Music*) Geoffrey Beaumont's statement in the Preface to the *Folk Mass* that he was inspired to write that work by an East End of London Vicar who was 'deeply concerned that nothing had been written since the Elizabethans which could properly be called a Folk Mass.'

Now we have met 'Folk' before—twice; in the American story folk music as music composed for church use which used the vocabulary of the secular music that people knew best; in the English story it was mostly the revival for church use of folk melodies whose secular words were known, if at all, only in isolated localities. Beaumont's use of the word is more like the American use; he wished to produce music for the church in the idiom that most people knew best, which was, according to him, the idiom of modern light entertainment.

He was a very good composer of this kind of music, and had been since his undergradute days in the twenties. He had a keen appreciation of its best qualities, and saw no reason why these should not be 'baptized into the church'. And in Ex. 482 we have just that: a very pleasant, flexible, well-shaped melody, scored with a typical two-measure introduction and with an accompaniment which the instrumentalist is expected to improvize on rather than to play with fundamentalist accuracy, rhythmically interesting, using mild syncopation, and replacing a very dull tune associated with a not particularly inspired text.

The Twentieth Century Church Light Music Group then proceeded to multiply its resources and press its arguments. Three books of new hymn tunes were quickly published, the first of which was *Thirty 20th Century Hymn Tunes* (1960). Our Ex. 484, PORTICO, represents Beaumont's later style, which recalls a book of solos of his, *Rhythm in Religion* (1961), all written in this new informal style. Mostly the new tunes were written for familiar texts from *Hymns Ancient and Modern* and the *English Hymnal*, but one of the most famous and widely used of these new songs was LORD JESUS CHRIST (Ex. 483), by Patrick Appleford (b. 1925), who represented the younger generation of composers that Beaumont gathered round him, and who wrote his own text for this and five other pieces in that book.

Now Beaumont was a genial and concerned priest with a thoroughly serious pastoral conscience who was especially eager to recover for the church the interest of the young. Without intending a word of disrespect to his most laudable ambitions, we have to judge that at two points he miscalculated. One of these was that the music he wrote and inspired in others was not a kind of modern music which appealed to the secular young, and the other was that he recruited too many clergy into his circle of composers. The composers represented in *Thirty* are four clergy, one ordinand and two schoolmasters one of whom was a professional musician. The difficulty with zealous clergy is that they cannot always resist the temptation, in matters aesthetic, to confuse what the people want with what the people will be nourished by. So what we got was in effect a new round of 'Gospel songs', all written in one style, all purveying the same musical message, which had the effect in worship of destroying at a stroke that historic neighborliness which the use of many different authentic styles produces in the proper use of hymns. What began as a gesture of invention became almost at once an imposition of conformity. It was soon found that music of this sort appealed little to the unchurched young; the people who were enthusiastic about it were the pious young and the new high-church evangelicals among the clergy. The typical milieu for this kind of music was the modern kind of large-scale conference where high-powered contemporary aspirations were driven home with assiduous intensity. Late at night one would find groups of young lay people and clergy gathered round a piano having fun with this music in much the same way as one finds students in American church music departments 'letting their hair down' in off moments with Gospel Songs.

The style is very consistent, and designedly profane. Where there is any emotional content, this is achieved by the use of Stainer's vocabulary, as in the harmony of Ex. 483. Plenty of middle-aged pious were seduced by this music, and one or two of the tunes produced by the Group have found their way into standard hymnals, among them CAMBERWELL, for 'At the name of Jesus', by Michael Brierley (b. 1932), from *Thirty*. The almost malignant lack of subtlety in this music inevitably had its effect in inducing a crude conformism in attitudes to religion, and it is not too much to say that the English church became—and remains—deeply divided on the question of the legitimacy of these attributes.

Returning to our first quotation, then, we see here an attempt to detect 'the epic in the every-day'; but the question of the Gospel's attitude to the 'everyday' was not asked: it was assumed. The assumption was that the church, if it took this new line, would totally accept the 'everyday', and turn a blind eye to the aspects of 'the everyday' which were mean, tyrannical and careless. The thing that this music taught us was that there is a vast difference between forgiving sin and not noticing sin. There is, of course, no touch of penitence, no feeling of 'I may be wrong' and no discipline or chastity in this kind of music. It presupposes that the church's traditional line about discipline and chastity has been misconceived. Well: that is exactly what many theologians were saying.

The parallel with the 'Gospel Songs' is uncannily close: the conformity, the manufactured enthusiasm, the complete shutting out of any message but its own,

and the fatal ease of composing the music—they are all there. A glance at Ex. 485, STAND UP FOR JESUS, will prove the point historically. This is an American tune, first published 1901, composed by Adam Geibel, German-born, who came to the USA in infancy and formed later a publishing company whose lineal descendant is the Rodeheaver-Hall-Mack Company. Anyone coming on it for the first time might well be forgiven for thinking it was a product of the Light Music Group—and that is the point. It now circulates where Gospel Songs are most loved in America, though it is not exactly in their style. But it certainly is in a 'popular' style, if one uses that adjective sufficiently pejoratively.

But there is a difference—which the Geibel tune alerts us to; the Gospel Songs came from a culture in which there was hardly any music to be had, and were aimed in the first instance at people whose cultural resoures were minimal. But the Light Music Group was inviting the church to *choose* this as an alternative to all the other music it knew and could use. The Gospel Songs were not designed to displace great standard hymns, since the first people to sing them knew hardly any standard hymns. The Light Music Group was in open rebellion.

The permissiveness of this music celebrated not so much freedom as intolerance—which was the primary product of the permissive society. The fact that nothing could have been further from the temperament and pastoral purpose of Beaumont himself only shows how the deliberate destruction of a tradition invites corruption as soon as it is made explicit. Just as Sankey's imitators wrote far worse music than Sankey, so the imitators of Beaumont went deeper and deeper into the fantasies of pious delusion as time went on.

The one composer who sought to retrieve something positive from this situation was Malcom Williamson (b. 1931), an Australian who came when young to England and has later become one of England's most sought-after composers. He is impossible to categorize, for there seems to be no style in which he is not at home. But from the first he has been a thoroughgoing professional and a very facile tunesmith. So, in a series of hymn tunes written in the early 1960s, he showed that, while he could not be tied down to any single style, he could write 'pop' music as well as anybody, and indeed, by the exercise of his composing gifts, could produce, when required, more fiendishly vulgar sounds than the innocents of the Light Music Group could ever descend to. For an example, see, or better hear the recording of, his 'Jesu, lover of my soul'—a reminder, this, that this kind of music never delivers its effect when read from a score.

But Williamson is at his best when he is simple. His 'pop' tunes and Mass settings are imitative—very professional, but third hand music. They are, as I ventured to point out in *Twentieth Century Church Music,* like the product of a skilful novelist who writes a local vernacular or dialect very sensitively. What happens when Williamson is writing, as it were, 'straight', is what we see in Exx. 486-8. Exx. 486 and 487, CHRIST WHOSE GLORY and HAIL TO THE LORD WHO COMES (Williamson, coming from the pre-1964 Catholic Church, never names his tunes) both have informal piano-score acompaniments which need a good deal of editing for the organ: but their melodies are as simple and innocent as melodies can well be. (Compare, as settings of the same text, Ex. 487 with Ex. 484). Ex. 488, from *6 Carols for Children* (1963), shows his special facility in writing for children— which has later appeared in the delightful short chancel-operas, *Genesis* and *The Winter Star*. It also shows very well how much music he can make out of the most elementary musical subjects. This, indeed, is a very rare example of the symphonist turning to hymn tunes—in using such tiny fragments of music and building them up into a continuous piece he is doing what the symphonist does, and of course he is one.

As a Catholic, in his youth unusued to hymns, he later became fascinated by English hymnody, and confessed himself an unashamed admirer of the Victorians —especially Barnby, He certainly does not disdain harmonic colour such as the 19th century composers delighted in—there is a touch of it near the end of Ex. 487, and plenty of it in his later tunes. He also became interested in texts by Watts and Wesley, and set a number of these in his *16 Hymns and Processions* (Agape, 1975). His prodigious facility as a composer has perhaps led him to write too much, and to be insufficiently vigilant against the temptation to let the simple become the trivial, but what he seems to have taken from the Light Church Music composers is their protest against the one weak point in Vaughan Williams's argument—the insistence on *dignity,* which is, of course, not a Christian virtue. The opposite of dignity does not have to be malignant sloppiness, and when one finds in its place true simplicity one is returning to a value which might have been lost without the informal composers.

Compared with what we now have to mention, however, the Light Music offerings were innocent entertainment. For we now encounter the formidable frown of Sydney Carter. We dealt with him in the *Panorama*, for he is a folk-singer whose texts are more important than his music. Carter (b. 1915) emerged in the 1960s as a new kind of Christian folk-singer who successfully built a bridge between the 'folk underground' and that orthodox society with which it was at odds. 'Folk song' to him is disposable song, written, sung and thrown away, expressing the immediate feelings of a close-knit group. If we said earlier that folk-song is essentially about love, death and work, then the folk-song of the 'alternative society' was about society's mistakes in respect of all three. It is almost always protest: rancorous and often ingeniously pointed criticism of accepted attitudes. Carter saw

that, however corrosive that might become in a secular context, the Church could use it and perhaps sanctify it. So he wrote songs which at first remained obscure but later, through the promotion of an enterprising publisher, became known all over the world. The texts of three of these are in the *Panorama* (521-3); for a complete collection with fascinating comments by the author, see his *Green Print for Song* (Stainer & Bell, 1973).

His favourite key is E minor and his favourite attitude that of fierce and satirical protest. Even 'Lord of the dance', his most famous song and one of the few really cheerful ones, its tune taken from the old American Shaker melody, is a protest against the spiritual immobility of conventional Christianity. Most of his tunes are true folk music in that you feel they were there before he discovered them. They cannot be sung to any words but his own, so they are not true hymn tunes, but they have just that touch of innocent originality that makes some of them authentic folk music: perhaps the most gracious of them is EVERY STAR (Ex. 489). It ought be said, however, that the whole spirit of Carter is so much at odds with conventional commercialism, as much as with conventional religion, that the very widespread printing in hymnals of his words and music has distorted their function. Most hymnal editors do not trouble to indicate that these songs are, like Gospel songs, songs for solo voice and chorus, dramatic songs appropriate to unconventional liturgies: so their use as hymns has often caused people to object to Carter's style in a quite unfair way.

Carter's place in hymnody is not that of a composer; he is more of a prophet, and like Beaumont (only much more so) he turns out to be less imitable than we thought. He has many imitators, most of whom miss his genius completely. But if we here mention that talented composer and lyric writer David Goodall (b. 1922) we are not even mentioning an imitator, since this composer—who has the advantage of an articulate theology—was writing songs of this kind before he had heared of Carter. His music is not yet well known, but we produce at Ex. 490 the music he wrote for his own remarkable text, 'I want to go out', which is at #524 in the *Panorama,* and which remains one of the most penetrating products of this culture.

The distinguishing thing about this new folk style is that texts and tunes usually come from the same hand; in standard hymnody this hardly ever happens, and certainly hardly ever successfully. The other obvious quality is its informality. The Light Music Group's music needs a good deal of production, a good light pianist, some additional instruments, a capacity to improvise, and all the trappings of light entertainment-music. Not so folk, which can be done with a single guitar, and by a player who does not need to have a wide harmonic vocabulary. In this sense it is unpretentious.

But it has another side: it does not deny its association with a life-style which can become by turns unpleasantly weak or unpleasantly violent. That most perceptive of British theologians, Daniel Jenkins, used the phrase* 'the indignant self-righteousness that arises out of weakness' in a book on politics, which expresses exactly what we have here; and there is a violent and destructive side to all this 'protest', as we came to see, especially on academic campuses, at the end of the sixties, against which this kind of instant protest-music has little defence. Indeed, the weakness of post-Carter songs is that, like the Light Church Music, they tend to encourage immaturity and stop the springs of self-criticism, and do this a good deal more dangerously than standard hymnody does.

What we can call the post-Carter strain of religious song was developed in the later sixties by successive publications of Stainer & Bell, Ltd., especially the three widely-circulated books, *Faith, Folk and Clarity, Faith, Folk and Nativity, Faith, Folk and Festivity* (1969-71) and later, *One World Songs* (1979). These songs are often given with a melody line and guitar symbols, and major in rugged folk-poetry with a social 'bite.' They are indeed the late 20th century Gospel Songs—solos with choruses quite often, limited in musical style, unliturgical and informal, sometimes very impressive, but indigestible in large doses because of the low theological protein-content. These books have been extremely popular, along with successive selections from the Carter treasury, and have appealed clamorously to concerned Christians; but they are ephemeral comment rather than material designed to last—effective journalism rather than literature.

One of the healthiest and most promising of these song collections was what was called in England 'The Gospel Song Book' (1969); its title had to be altered in the USA to *Now Songs* (Abingdon, 1971). The new composer there is Malcolm Stewart (b. 1925), a theologically educated Roman Catholic, whose biblical songs are both theologically and musically literate and are mentioned in the *Panorama*. Another musician on the edge of this group, whose contribution to hymnody has been small but whose influence in the promotion of new and informal church music was important, is Donald Swann (b. 1923), who early in life achieved great fame as the musical partner in the Michael Flanders/Donald Swann entertainments, but who later wrote a good deal of church music. His compositions (for example, in *Singalive,* a collaboration, 1978, between him and Arthur Scholey) are usually solo songs, with or without choral embellishments, using a sophisticated and professional entertainment style and mixing 'Faith and Doubt' with simple celebration in a humane and captivating way.

We are getting a long way from orthodox hymnody, but that was what happened in the period 1955-70. 'Straight' hymnody in that period was recovering from the exertions of the immediate post-war years and had relatively little to say. This was abruptly changed in the years following 1969.

The Evangelicals

At this point, on our way back to orthodox hymnody, we have to pick up a strand of our story which we dropped several chapters ago—the progress in England of main-line evangelical hymnody. In the Church of England the scene was dominated by *Hymns A & M* and the *English Hymnal* in their great and fruitful competition; but both those books presupposed a fairly 'high' (which to be honest only means articulate) doctrine of the place of the Church of England in English society. Evangelicalism is, of course, not a denomination, but it does gather together people, whatever church they belong to, who share ideas about the nature and mission of the church which differ importantly from those of the 'high' churchmen. Evangelicalism is never denominationally fastidious, still less exclusive, and it has contributed greatly to the progress of the Ecumenical Movement.

Evangelical views produced many private hymnals, but they were catered for mostly, so far as widely-used books were concerned, by the *Hymnal Companion* (1890), *Church Hymns* (latest edition 1903) and the *Church Hymnal for the Christian Year* (1917). Less formal occasions were served very widely by *Golden Bells* (1926), revised 1964 as *Hymns of the Faith*. Tractarian Evangelicalism (there was such a thing; it expressed the social conscience of the Tractarians along with a 'high' doctrine of the anglican Church) was served by the *Church and School Hymnal* (1926)—a very unusual and original collection with some interesting folk tunes and some remarkable texts (see *Panorama* 484 for one of them), and by the *Mirfield Mission Hymnal* (last edition 1936).

Mostly these books have very little musical interest, and the furthering of musical taste was not among their editors' aims. True, the 1903 *Church Hymns* brought in Basil Harwood to edit its plainsong, and provided a very good over-all selection of texts, more charitable to the non-anglican tradition that its two massive competitors; but the music inod over-all selection of texts, more charitable to the non-anglican tradition that its two massive competitors; but the music in these books is derivative at best and at worst regressive. Gradually, as one edition succeeds another, we find a general tendency to become more aware of the development of the hymn vocabulary, and that is healthy, providing a more balanced selection: but there is not enough new material, or material in new styles, to offer serious comment.

In the last period two evangelical books appeared which have considerable character. One was *Christian Praise* (1957), edited by evangelical anglicans but designed for interdenominational use, which set quite

---

* The British: their Identity and their Religion, SCM Press 1975, p. 21.

new standards of music. The new source on which it drew most heavily was *Congregational Praise;* it was a typical evangelical book, with plenty of Charles Wesley, not much on the Sacraments, and a large section of carols. This has still great possibilities as a conference-book for inter-church use. But a larger gesture was made when Tyndale Press, one of the major organs of anglican evangelicalism, offered a book to serve all those parishes which did not use either *Hymns A & M* or the *English Hymnal.* This was the *Anglican Hymn Book,* 1965. Its major service to those circles was to offer a far more cultivated standard of music to 'low-church' congregations, much influenced by the fact that some useful school-musicians on the committee fed into it some of the best of the school music. The most original composer to appear here is William Llewellyn, whom we noticed earlier—our Ex. 462 was first in this book. But another composer much featured in the book is the first woman hymn composer we have mentioned in all these pages: Peggy Spencer-Palmer (b. 1900). Her first published hymn tunes appeared in *Congregational Praise,* of which our Ex. 491 is one; all her tunes have a broad melodic sweep, a sure harmonic grasp, and a warm-hearted manner which suggests the best tradition of school-hymnody (which in fact was her milieu). We must allow her a second example (Ex. 492), from the 1965 book, which shows with what a sure touch she could handle a very intractable metre.

'Conservative' would be the right word for the music of this book; apart from two of the three fine tunes which Llewellyn contributed (the others are 136 and 439, the second of which is half way between the gentle 136 and the very commanding Ex. 462) there are hardly any tunes which suggest a forward look; but the ablest conservatives are given a very good run. And one of these is one who by 1965 was quite a veteran, and who crops up fairly regularly in books of the early fifties, but nowhere so generously as in this book. This is Kenneth Finlay (1882-1974), the first significant Scottish composer of hymn tunes.

Finlay was a naval engineer who exactly half way through his life (age 46) took up music professionally and became a schools-inspector. He was a fastidious composer whose style has a neatness and precision that place him apart from his contemporaries. He has a Scottish reticence, yet at his best a real eloquence. He contributed twelve tunes to the *Anglican Hymn Book,* but his earliest tunes in a hymnal go back to the 1927 *Church Hymnary,* which included FINNART (491) and his most famous tune, GLENFINLAS (Ex. 493) which has been loved by two generations of children (who don't notice its close resemblance to the song 'Mighty like a rose'). In America he is hardly known, but the *Methodist Hymnal* (1966: #157) has his charming CM tune AYRSHIRE, which first appeared in the *Irish Hymn Book Supplement,* 1936, (Ex. 494). One of his most characteristic tunes is LYLE ROAD (CP 118: AHB 195),

and perhaps the most characteristic of his new compositions in *AHB* is CARRICK (Ex. 495), whose pentatonic flavour recalls the composer's Scottish background and is shared by several others of his tunes. Modest effectiveness is what he always produced, and he anticipated by a couple of generations the Scottish talent which has now so recently come to light.

Another tune from this book in a very gentle and winning style is JONATHAN (No. 439), by its musical editor, Robin Sheldon (b. 1932); this has more recently been rescued from the text for which he wrote it. It deserves to travel far and is beginning to do so.

More recently the Evangelicals have provided two more hymnals, both of massive size: *Christian Worship* (1976), published primarily for the Brethren Movement and *Grace Hymns* (1977) published by the Grace Publications Trust. Musically both are more conservative than the *Anglican Hymn Book,* and both are comprehensively stocked with sound evangelical texts, leaving the tunes to take their chance. Their standards, without being in any sense progressive, are thoroughly respectable and the later book is chiefly of interest in showing much new work by the good evangelical hymn writer Timothy Dudley-Smith (for some of whose earlier work, see *Panorama* 501-2).

One should include among 'evangelical books' the extremely successful *Youth Praise* (1966) and *Psalm Praise* (1974). Here the musical style is directly derived from that of the Light Music Group, and the new compositions tend to be, especially in the earlier book, confined to this style—of which we have already said enough to make clear our judgment on these books. They owe their effectiveness to the zeal of that energetic mission-composer the Reverend Michael Baughen, and have had a very wide circulation among the evangelically-convinced young of the Anglican Church. But they have not contributed anything to the movement of musical sensibility that had not already been offered by the Baumont school.

Hymns for Church and School, 1964

Hymns for Church and School, and the names of its two music editors, John Wilson and Leonard Blake, have dodged in and out of our story like secondary characters in a novel who, one begins to think, are going to assume unexpected importance. That is exactly how it was with this book which, we recall, is the last in the 'Public School' dynasty. Like the other three it was put together by a committee appointed by the Headmasters' Conference, but its external history was strange and, in our story, significant. Its editors felt it necessary to take the expression 'Public School' out of the title—and there is a signal of social change. Its publisher, Novello, extruded it from their list thirteen years after it appeared, and it is now distributed by another publisher (Unwin, of Old Woking). It was, to be sure, edited during those years when the vulgar reaction against orthodox hymnody was running in full spate, and looking back on it suggests a picture almost of an island of orthodoxy in a raging sea of confusion.

The interest in this book is very largely musical, because of the four executive editors, only the two musicians claim (and very justly) to be scholars in the field of hymnody. Their good fortune was to have in John Wilson one who within a few years was to be recognized as the leading textual scholar in hymn music, and to serve four more books in the capacity of editor or consultant. His personal contribution to the critical assessment of versions was as important in texts as in tunes, and these two music editors between them raised the craft of editing to a quite new professional level.

The book has 346 hymns, of which a dozen or so are new texts, and 386 tunes, of which some 25 had not appeared before. In length, then, it is the second-shortest of the four public school books, but its generous supply of tunes includes not a single tune which anyone could judge a clear failure. Many have great distinction. Leonard Blake contributes six tunes, Wilson five, three of which were in the *Clarendon Hymn Book,* 1936. Of the other composers of new tunes the most eminent and senior is Herbert Howells. From him the editors commissioned five tunes, of which two are surely outstanding. One is SANCTA CIVITAS (41), which introduces to England the distinguished American text 'O Holy city, seen of John', and the other is Ex. 496, SALISBURY, which we quote as being the most characteristic of all. Howells's contribution to hymnody is not large: we quoted an earlier tune at Ex. 459, and *Songs of Praise,* in 1925, had from him an early tune called ST. BRIAVELS which was replaced, for the same hymn, in 1931 with a somewhat more manageable tune, SEVERN SP 582). But in those he contributed, a whole generation later, to *HCS,* he was producing mature work closely related to the large quantity of church music he was producing at that time, and the two we mention are clear masterpieces.

Two composers of the next generation appear in hymnody for the first time in this book. John Gardner (b. 1917) has three tunes, all of which are remarkable and original; of these we choose HILLSBOROUGH (Ex. 497) for display here; it is the simplest of the three, but like the other two, it gives the clear impression that every note and every progression has been thought through with great care by the composer. Gardner was until 1977 Director of Music at St. Paul's School, where Holst had been before him: and Holst would have been proud of Gardner's tunes. John Joubert (b. 1926) appears once with a tune, MOSELEY, for 'For the beauty of the earth' (14) which is adventurous, almost defiant, in its insistence on a harmonic structure based on consecutive fifths between bass and treble. Joubert is a composer of wider interests and achievement, perhaps, than Gardner, but in hymnody a good deal more controversial. He will appear again in a moment. Among other composers who provide new material are Sydney Watson (p. 150), Norman Greenwood (1902-62), J. H. Alden (1900-76) and Sir William Harris.

New Adventures in Britain

The Cambridge Hymnal, 1967

Further back we observed a considerable difference of ethos between *Songs of Praise* and the *Public School Hymn Book* in their approach to schools. Now we have just the same kind of difference, but a much wider gap, between the *Cambridge Hymnal* and *Hymns for Church and School*.

The *Cambridge Hymnal* was designed to be a supplemental hymnal for School Assembly (since 1944, as we remarked before, built into the official curriculum of state schools). The policy of the Cambridge University Press, whose only important excursion into hymnody this is, was to provide a book of lyric and music of which the most demanding English and Music teachers need not be ashamed. Why, they asked, have a double standard in these things? Why tolerate in worship what the children would be encouraged in class to deride? To this end, after some consultation with hymnologists and school teachers, the project was placed in the hands of a distinguished man of letters, David Holbrook, and an equally distinguished musician, Elizabeth Poston, neither of whom had before ventured into the field of hymnal editing. Both were articulate people of strong opinions, famous in the secular aspects of their crafts, and they came to hymnody with minds as fresh and untainted by prejudice as even Vaughan Williams brought to the *English Hymnal*. What they produced has something in common with *Songs of Praise* in being heavily weighted in the direction of good literature and lively music, and light on theological tradition. What mattered to them was not whether a piece of music would run well congregationally in church but whether it would appeal to a decently-organized music department in a school. It was therefore open to them to commission music from as many composers eminent in other fields as *Songs of Praise* had drafted in, and the book abounds in sensitive and often highly original music which lies far out towards the edge of hymnody.

Among the composers of new material in the book are Sir Lennox Berkeley (b. 1903: WIVETON, Ex. 498), John Gardner (b. 1917: ST. OLAF'S, 113), Herbert Howells (ERWIN, 61), Gordon Jacob, John Joubert (b. 1927: BISHOPS, Ex. 499), William Mathias, Arthur Oldham, Alan Ridout, and William Wordsworth. Stravinsky and Britten also appear in the composers' index though neither here makes a contribution to hymnody. Elizabeth Poston herself made many arrangements and composed several tunes, of which 'Jesus Christ the Apple Tree' (111) deserves a place among the really great melodies of the 20th century. Another of her compositions, written later, appears at our Ex. 525.

Elizabeth Poston's special gift is for song writing, and her special interest has been in the discovery and editing of carols and sacred songs of a traditional kind,

especially American. The lead she gave is therefore in broadly the same direction as was that of Vaughan Williams sixty years earlier—professional music inspired by the freshness and integrity of true folk song. Quite often she scores a hymn tune as a song, not including the melody in the accompaniment (again see Ex. 525); and the score is always spare and uncluttered. Most of her colleagues, however, turn out to be essentially choral composers whose contributions require an alert body of well rehearsed singers.

The book has 139 hymns followed by a section of 58 carols and rounds, and it has been found most serviceable when used in addition to a more normal hymnal containing the traditional material these editors felt free to overlook. Certainly it was the most unusual collection bearing the word *Hymnal* in its title to appear since *Songs of Praise* and in originality and audacity is surpassed only by the American *Ecumenical Praise* (1977).

The Supplements

In effect the *Cambridge Hymnal* was a generously proportioned Supplement, and it was only two years after its appearance that the explosion of official denominational Supplements began. In the *Panorama* we have referred to this. The standard hymnals all needed revising in the light of the intense activity that had been taking place since 1951, and each editorial committee felt that the best thing to do was to keep the traditional book alive but supplement it with a collection of about a hundred new pieces. They did not need to commit themselves to the dangerous task of making room for new material by discarding large numbers of older classics. They were free, as the *Cambridge* editors had been, to concentrate on new material or the revival of older things which filled gaps left by the older generation's selection.

The *Hymns Ancient and Modern* Committee and the Methodist Conference led the way by publishing, almost at the same moment in 1969, *100 Hymns for To-day* and *Hymns and Songs* respectively. The first of these was the more successful and sold its millionth copy in 1978. The collection was directly in the *A & M* tradition of picking up what people would sing and take to themselves. It is an alphabetical anthology of new hymns, or of hymns overlooked in 1950, designed to serve the new theological needs which had become evident in the intervening years. Eye-catching novelties have never been on sale from *Hymns A & M,* and its actual contribution to the advance of hymn music was small. But fair dealing all round was very much its policy, so that we find Carter's 'Lord of the Dance', Appleford's 'Lord Jesus Christ' and Howells's SANCTA CIVITAS, not to mention Gibbons's SONG 1 set to 'Eternal Ruler of the ceaseless round'. It did so well exactly what its editors planned to do that at the time when this is being written a second supplemental series is about to appear, no doubt in the same style and directed with the same skill.*

Hymns and Songs was a different story. Methodism's hymnody had even in 1933 been atrophied by the genius of Charles Wesley, and no Methodist style of music had been achieved since the days of the early 19th century evangelicals. *Hymns and Songs*, a book of 74 hymns, 25 'songs' and five canticles, made gestures in both directions, by introducing Frederick Pratt Green as the first significant Methodist hymnographer since the Wesleys (and indeed, as it has proved, the leading English hymn writer of his generation) and by seeking out Methodist musicians who could compose in a modern evangelical style. Of these musicians the most significant are Francis Westbrook (1903-75), whose BENIFOLD (Ex. 502) has a sturdy 18th century integrity, and Ivor Jones (b. 1934); both these are minister-musicians whose influence in Methodism has been of great importance. This collection also brought forward John Wilson (see earlier p. 150) as a composer and editorial consultant, and the book owes to him that meticulous editorial care for which he has continued to become well known. Wilson's LAUDS (Ex. 500) appears here first, set to 'Songs of praise the angels sang' and he has four other tunes of which two are given for the first time. (John Wilson is denominationally unclassifiable but at the time when he was involved in this book he was a member of the Methodist church). Our Ex. 501, perhaps his most ambitious contribution to hymnody, illustrates a partnership between him and Pratt Green which has proved very fruitful. Many of Pratt Green's hymns were written at Mr. Wilson's suggestion, and four more of them, in addition to Ex. 501 and another which had appeared before, are in the very useful little book edited by Wilson, *Sixteen Hymns of To-day for use as simple Anthems* (1977). The existence of this book exemplifies Mr. Wilson's special concern with the promotion of fine hymnody, which in another way is illustrated in his annual series of hymn-singing festivals held in Westminster Abbey since 1970 under the title 'Come and Sing'.

Next came an undenominational supplement, *Hymns for Celebration* (1974), also edited by John Wilson. This was a short book of 28 hymns designed for use at the Eucharist and published by the Royal School of Church Music. It celebrates the ecumenical emphasis which during the years since 1968 that institution had been fostering, and besides some of the material from earlier books in the 'Wilson' dynasty, it shows some interesting new music in Michael Dawney's remarkable antiphonal tune BAY HALL (15), Melville Cook's fine CM tune METROPOLITAN (6) and an arrangement of the Dutch National Anthem (Ex.

576) based on a suggestion by Dr. Lionel Dakers, the Director of the RSCM.

The United Reformed Church, founded in 1972 by the Congregationalists and Prestyterians in England and Wales, produced in 1975 a Supplement for the combined church called *New Church Praise*. It is less of a gathering-in of recent good material, and more of an anthology of material published for the first time, than any of the other Supplements. Textually it is the best source for the developed hymnody of that gifted writer, Brian Wren (see *Panorama* 497-500), and musically it is significant for its large selection from the work of Peter Cutts (b. 1937).

Cutts could well be the most creative composer of hymnody to come out of English Congregationalism. He stands in the succession of Eric Thiman (p. 156) but his approach to music is very different. He derives a great versatility from a true sympathy both with music in popular styles and with learned church music. His first appearance in a hymnal was in 1966 when his tune WYLDE GREEN—composed about 1955—appeared in the American Methodist Hymnal, 1966 (# 62). This is rich in harmony and strong in melody, rather in the classic 'Public school' style. SHILLINGFORD (1962: Ex. 503) has a daring modulation that comes from the same tradition, BIRABUS (Ex. 504) a Howells-like richness and pathos, ASKERSWELL (Ex. 505) handles the most intractable of stanza-metres with urbane facility; SWITHEN (Ex. 506), written for a haunting text by David Goodall (see Ex. 490), has a surface quality of waywardness plus a very assured touch with harmonic construction (especially in the interludes); and SHRUB END (Ex. 507), one of the very few tunes of his in regular four-part texture, treats a searching text of Brian Wren with cool austerity. Even this considerable series of examples does not exhaust his versatility; his best known tune, BRIDEGROOM, composed in 1968 and first appearing in *100 Hymns for To-day,* has a lightness of touch which exactly matches the lyric quality of its text. Of all contemporary hymn tune composers Peter Cutts has the widest vocabulary and the keenest eye for the subtleties of a modern text.

The other composer well represented in *New Church Praise* is T. C. Micklem (b. 1925), a distinguished minister-musician who has eight texts and fourteen tunes in the book, all appearing for the first time. He, like Cutts, explores both orthodox and experimental idioms, and Ex. 508, RODEL, captures the restless fierceness of an impressionistic poem by Ian Fraser (*Panorama* 488) with great skill.

About the same time, in late 1974, appeared *Praise for To-day,* designed by the Baptists to supplement the *Baptist Hymn Book* of 1962. Here the parent book was both relatively recent and also exceedingly well edited, so there was less scope for the editors. The Baptists

---

* A second Supplemental book was published by Hymns *A & M* in 1980, after this paragraph went to press. This is *More Hymns for To-day*, containing a further 200 hymns; a review of it will be found in *English Church Music* (RSCM 1980) and another in the January 1981 issue of *Church Music* (RSCM).

had recovered in 1962 a good deal of ground lost in a rather ineptly-edited official book of 1933, and the need in *Praise for To-day* was to find an evangelical lightness of idiom which would adequately compensate the fairly learned character of the parent book without returning to those Gospel Songs of which the parent book anyhow contained an adequate ration. Musically the book is not much more inventive than *100 Hymns for To-day*, but it collects two new tunes by Herbert Howells from the *New Catholic Hymnal* (1971—see below p. 169) and introduces a thoughtful new composer in George Towers (b. 1914) who handles a popular rhythmic style with some discernment.

The latest, but we are assured not the last, of the official Supplements was *English Praise* (1976), which attempts the formidable task of supplementing the *English Hymnal*. Here we have met another situation: a parent book of commanding authority and excellence whose texts had not been revised for seventy years, its tunes for over forty. The editors certainly inherited and honoured Vaughan Williams's love of folk song, though they were less sure where to find it and how to adapt it; uniquely among new supplements it also contains a number of well known 19th century tunes which E.H. rejected but which its constituency insisted none the less on singing. It has no V-W or Holst on its editorial board, but it does feature one or two choice pieces by Professor Arthur Hutchings (b. 1906), including FUDGIE (Ex. 509) which had appeared in the *English Hymnal Service Book,* and a very good new tune by Christopher Dearnley (b. 1930), FINNIAN (Ex. 510). Since E.H. was edited in the days before hymnals contained corals, many carols appear in its pages, and perhaps the general ethos of the book is governed as much by the country-culture of the carols as by any other. It is a cheerful collection, shrewdly adjusting what some felt to be a tendancy in *E.H.* towards sombre dignity.

Undoubtedly the Supplements have given a much needed freedom to composers of new tunes: even to authors of new texts, who were supplying a more clamorous need. The economic and ecclesiastical necessities that produced them have proved on the whole to be liberating forces. (See note on p. 170)

The Church of Scotland

Among the large Christian groups in which the 20th century has seen swift and dramatic development in hymnody we must mention two with very diverse histories—the Church of Scotland and the Roman Catholics. They have this in common, that each was restricted up to the mid-19th century by an inhibition on hymnody, and each waited until the later 20th century to begin to make up the lost ground.

Scottish hymn composers, up to the time when we were last considering them (which was 1872) were preoccupied with psalmody, and the gradual easing of the customary restrictions on 'hymns of human com-

posure' did not at first produce a demand sufficient to require anything more enterprising than the borrowing of tunes from England and other established sources. The Scottish hymn singing tradition then became stronger in the Free Church of Scotland (which existed from 1843 to 1929) than in the 'Auld Kirk', and some examples of the text writing of that stream of devotion are provided in *Panorama* 340ff. When the two streams reunited in 1929 to form once again the Church of Scotland, their hymnal, the *Revised Church Hymnary* of 1927, was not noticeably a Scottish book, drawing largely on English text writers and musically edited by a distinguished Welshman. Certainly there is no discernible Scottish style in hymn music there—the one composer who showed signs of becoming a success in a Scottish idiom (later amply fulfilled) being Kenneth Finlay, whom we have just mentioned (p. 162).

The change in ethos when we come to the 1973 *Church Hymnary, Third Edition* is therefore dramatic. By that time Scotland's sense of separate identity nationally and ecclesiastically, had been nourished by theologians and politicians, and in hymnody we see for the first time a Scottish musical style asserting itself.

We are here, obviously, following fairly closely the story told in the *Panorama* about the hymnody of our contemporaries, and therefore must, before commenting on the new *Church Hymnary,* mention the Dunblane Workshops (for which cf. *Panorama* ch. 25).

The series of Dunblane Workshops—held at Scottish Churches' House, Dunblane, between 1963 and 1967 to explore new music for the Church—were ecumenically organized and designed to serve all the churches in Scotland (and any others who were interested). Their Convener was a Scot, and the most forward-looking of the younger Scottish musicians appeared at its sessions, including Reginald Barret-Ayres (b. 1920), George McPhee (b. 1937), Eric Reid (1936-70) Douglas Galbraith, and Peter Youngson. But non-Scottish musicians were involved in these activities too: at different times Peter Cutts, Cyril Taylor, Alan Luff and Sydney Carter were there, and the secretary of the series was also an Englishman. Contributions from outside the workshop team in music and texts included work first published in *Dunblane Praises* by John Ferguson and David S. Goodall. It was, however, the first attempt in history by the Scots to establish a Scottish tradition of modern church music and as such, historic.

Perhaps its musical contribution will turn out to be less enduring than that of its text writers. But plenty of material was submitted, a good deal informally published and then gathered up in *New Songs for the Church I and II* (1969). The words of our Ex. 508 were first printed in *Dunblane Praises I* (1964) and our Ex. 490 in *Dunblane Praises II* (1967). Dunblane explored informal hymnody in the hope of injecting into it a little professional musicianship, and the two contributions which have travelled furthest are Ex. 511, ABEL, by Reginald Barrett-Ayres ('Am I my brother's keeper?') and the hymn and tune for children, 'Trotting, trotting through Jerusalem' (Ex. 512) by Eric Reid who was so tragically killed in a motor accident in 1970. More work by these two, and by other members of the consultation, can be studied in *New Songs for the Church* (1969).

A good deal of the Dunblane work consisted in providing new antiphonal canticles in various styles, principally to adorn the new liturgies of the Church of England and the Scottish Episcopal Church: these have to be placed outside the terms of reference of the present work, but the same source (volume II) collects most of those which were written there.

When the first Dunblane Consultation was convened in 1963, work on *Church Hymnary III* had already begun, and it was thought possible at one point that the Dunblane findings would be taken into consideration by the editors of that book. With a single exception (our Ex. 587) if they were considered they were rejected, so the line of development represented in the new hymnal is a quite different one. *Church Hymnary III* is as Scottish as the earlier editions were English—and in itself that is historically both significant and welcome. There was a clear swing away from the informal style of the sixties in that book's music. (Our Ex. 486 is the nearest approach to informality permitted in the book). But the contribution of Scottish composers suddenly becomes substantial. Indeed it is eye-catching.

Kenneth Leighton (b. 1929) was an Englishman who had held an appointment on Edinburgh University's music faculty and then, after a short stay in Oxford, returned to be Reid Professor of Music. He counts, then, as a Scottish composer and is regarded as a leader in that field. His chief contribution to church music is in larger forms, and in organ works: but Ex. 513, HEADINGTON (clearly composed during the Oxford interlude) not only is characteristic of his style but proved to be a pace-setter for his colleagues. His music is always intellectually disciplined, exploring the outer reaches of the normal musical vocabulary, and eminently performable in what ever style and texture it affects. Most of his work in *CH III* is in the liturgical pieces, but here, as there, what looks to the eye like extravagant chromaticism is actually closely-written counterpoint, making adequate but not impossible demands on the ear.

There is about these new Scottish compositions a fierce and committed professionalism which sounds a quite new note in the story. Most of the new composers are younger than Leighton, and it is no accident that the most inventive Scottish musicians tended to find their way into academic positions; perhaps the academic life is not the most promising environment for the cultivation of that sanctified vulgarity which marks the work of the successful hymn tune writer—one believes that even Luther would now admit that—

and what we don't find in the new Scottish hymn book is any sign of an 'ABBOTS LEIGH'. The impression it gives, when one looks at its new music, is that it is backing the 21st century against the 20th, and inviting the congregational ear to welcome quite new experiences in melody. Ex. 514, by the distinguished composer Frederick Rimmer, one of the seniors, b. 1914, suggests exactly what Rimmer has been—an academic musician with a fertile mind who plays the organ in a university chapel with an able choir. Of the next generation, Martin Dalby (b. 1942), already established as a symphonist and large-scale composer, contributes a tune which shows more patience with the congregational demand for repetition, and also a tight sense of form comparable with Leighton's—see Ex. 515, SOUSTER.

Sebastian Forbes (b. 1941) is the opposite of Leighton—a composer of Scottish ancestry born and working in England; like Dalby he is well known in a field well beyond church music, and his KILVAREE (Ex. 515) is perhaps the most remote of all the remarkable new tunes in *CH III*; it has been pointed out that had its key signature been six sharps it could have been noted with six fewer accidentals; but whichever way you take it, it is a remarkable piece of 'musician's music', again beckoning a congregation towards formidable challenges.

These are only a few of the very unusual tunes to be found in this quite remarkable book—remarkable not least for its combination of conservatism in choice of texts and in selection of older tunes with adventurousness in new musical commissions. But this was a good time for Scotland's Presbyterian professionalism to assert itself; for its nearest neighbour, England, as we have seen, was flirting with malignant amateurism in the sixties, and it was clearly the view of the editors that the Dunblane Consultation was tainted with that. That Scottish composers were not incapable of writing modest diatonic tunes is indicated by Ex. 517, David Dorward's MONIKIE; Dorward (b. 1933) is yet another musician who has made a considerable impression in the secular music field.

What *CH III* celebrates is nothing less than a renaissance in Scottish music every bit as important and decisive as that which Vaughan Williams led in England sixty years earlier. Just as the English renaissance composers resisted England's dependence on German and Italian models, so the Scottish composers resisted Scotland's dependence on England and Wales: it is significant that the contribution of David Evans, so substantial in the 1927 book, is reduced almost to vanishing point in the 1973 one. We cannot leave this book—which is recommended to every serious student of the subject of hymn music—without mentioning its most delicious 'discovery', the setting of an English folk tune called SEARCHING FOR LAMBS to 'The Lord's my Shepherd' (Ex. 518). This tune belongs to a large family of English folk songs and carols (compare 'This is the truth sent from above') but has never appeared in this form before in carol book or hymnal.

The Roman Catholics in the 20th Century

Much more dramatic, of course, than the liberation of hymnody in the Church of Scotland (which at least did have a long tradition of psalm *tunes*) was the effect on the Roman Catholic church of the Second Vatican Council from 1963 onwards, and especially their becoming free to pursue the treasures, and no doubt to succumb to the blandishments, of vernacular hymnody. The position in England had been since 1850 that vernacular hymns were confined to popular extra-liturgical services, and their music (as we saw) presupposed a singing congregation upon which few intellectual demands could wisely be made.

Now since it will not be possible in this book to make any assessment of any discernible Catholic style in America, this is the place to emphasize the great difference between the Catholic cultures of these two English-speaking countries. The distinguishing thing about England in the 20th century is the educational transformation of the Catholic constituency, which means broadly the shift of emphasis from Irish immigrants to English converts. Since the days of G. K. Chesterton (1874-1936), Hilaire Belloc (1870-1950) and Ronald Knox (1888-1957) there has been in England an articulate Catholic elite who, mostly in writing fiction, theology, humor and devotion, created a mind among Catholics that would welcome educated hymnody. There is no parallel to this yet in the USA, where the Catholic Church is (as is its proper nature) inter-racial but on the whole strongest among groups which rejoice rather in a folk-culture than an academic tradition.

Another way of putting the point we are here making is that in England for a season Catholic hymnody lost its innocence. We have seen how Catholic hymnody showed a friendlier attitude to secular music than that of many Protestant groups; and the carol-like hymn, whether innocent or, as it could become, vulgar, persisted through all the changes of history. Whether one rejoices in the earthy vigour of tunes like ELLACOMBE (EH 137) and OFFERTORIUM (AM 176) or shakes one's head over the vulgarity of SAWSTON, and other tunes in the Appendix to the *New Catholic Hymnal,* one remains impressed with the welcome given in Catholic circles before 1963 to the popular music that people among the faithful liked best. We are about to see that for a while in England this 'earthy' quality in Catholic hymnody is replaced by a more Vaughan Williams-like approach—by offering to the new post-1963 congregations not what they heard immediately around them but what people of taste in this age, or people of innocence in a long past age, enjoyed.

An interesting source for study of Catholic hymnody in England is *Arundel Hymns.* This was part of an enormous project, becoming a seven-volume collection of hymns and liturgical music, and appearing in 1905 as a selective compendious hymnal. The background of this was the Cathedral Church which stands just outside the walls of Arundel Castle in Sussex. Arundel is the seat of the Howards, the ancient English Catholic family whose head it the hereditary Earl Marshal of England. Henry Fitzallan Howard, fifteenth Duke of Norfolk (1847-1917) commissioned the work on the Arundel books, whose content one might describe as innocently operatic. People whose 'folk' music was symphonic and operatic found the opulent music in these books very much what they wanted. Our Ex. 361 is transcribed from the Arundel book, and it is quite typical. By the Catholic standards of its day it was highbrow; but there is all the difference in the world between such music as this and the 'pure folk' of Vaughan Williams. *Arundel Hymns* might be called the last great gesture of the Cecilian tradition. The original tunes here have much in common with the lyric ballad of the Victorians, and the only one to commend itself far beyond the covers of this book was WELWYN (Ex. 519), by Alfred Scott-Gatty (1847-1918). This has found much greater popularity in the USA than in Britain.

The advancement of Catholic hymnody thereafter centered in Sir Richard Terry (1865-1938), whose long tenure as organist of the Metropolitan Cathedral at Westminster gave him a chance to be influential. Terry edited the 1914 *Westminster Hymnal* for cathedral and parish use, and while by present-day standards its music does not measure very high, it was more modest in its aims and demands than *Arundel.* Terry composed a number of tunes which tend to mark him as the Catholic Stainer, of which BILLING ('Praise to the Holiest') has had plenty of use outside Catholic circles, and HIGHWOOD (Ex. 520) is probably the most imaginative. HIGHWOOD needed to be separated from its original text ('O perfect love') before it gained acceptance beyond its parent book, and its first appearance as a hymn tune was actually in the *Methodist Hymn Book* (1933). In later life Terry became interested in the psalmody of the Genevan Reformation, and edited a facsimile edition of the 1539 Strasbourg Psalter and also the revision of Neil Livingston's monumental edition of the 1635 *Scottish Psalter.* This came too late to have any influence on his own composing style but he seems to have communicated this interest to his successors in the 1940 *Westminster Hymnal.*

The major musical influence in the new generation was Dom Gregory Murray (b. 1905), who has been the most beneficial and vigorous single influence in English Catholic hymnody during his lifetime. The *Westminster Hymnal* of 1940 contains a good deal of work both in the editing and composition of tunes (its over-all editor was Fr. W. S. Bainbridge), and not infrequently these tunes of his have a truly Genevan poise. Ex. 521, HOLCOMBE, seems to be derived both from Wittenberg and from Geneva, and it introduces to Catholic hymnody a new dignity. He is always an excellent tunesmith, and SURREXIT (Ex. 522) and UBI

CARITAS (WH 200 and now in many other places) show his gift for healthy and singable melody.

This new stateliness and restraint presupposes a market for educated hymnody; but the market for the popular style had not dried up, and the question was which way things would go when the dam burst in 1963. Up to that time hymnody was still limited. Original texts by non-Catholic authors were not permitted, and 250 English texts was deemed a sufficient allowance in the 1940 *Westminster*. Once vernacular hymnody was permitted at Mass, no matter what its denominational source, the demand for new style hymnals and hymn tunes was suddenly urgent.

The first mainstream hymnal to meet it was *Praise the Lord* (1966), edited by Wilfred Trotman, and this was closely followed by the *Parish Hymnal* (1968). These were both cautious. They mostly addressed themselves to the question, which were the best hymns the Protestant ought to share with the Catholics. The judgment of Trotman was on the whole towards the popular, and that of the *Parish Hymnal* was mostly that of *Westminster* brought up to date and adapted to the new situation.

The appearance of these books, which carried the *Imprimatur* but were in no sense official hymnals, roused certain enthusiasts to consider whether something more original and distinctive could not be offered, and the outcome of this was two widely different publications, the *New Catholic Hymnal* (1971) and the second edition of *Praise the Lord* (1972).

Both these set quite new professional standards, and the professionalism is strictly hymnological; it was a question, in the minds of the editors of both, what a good hymn was, and both groups came to that question with fresh minds, but approached it in quite different ways. The *New Catholic Hymnal* was a joint enterprise conducted by Anthony Petti, a Professor of English in Canada, and Geoffrey Laycock, Director of Music at a Teachers' Training college in Norwich. If anyone expects from those facts that there will be much in common between this book and the *Cambridge Hymnal* (1967), that reader will not be disappointed, for it is an original and demanding collection. It is conceived in a mood of violent opposition to the consenting standards of the *Parish Hymn Book* by two industrious and scholarly laymen who began with hardly any knowledge of hymnology, and learnt as they went. They were influenced almost equally by a desire to start Catholics out on a high road of hymnody and by certain practices which had recently been developed in America. As a result most of each text is printed within the music-staves, the book is arranged in a single alphabetical series (except for a short Appendix of material thus marked out, in the manner of the *English Hymnal,* as popular but inferior), and many older texts are rewritten to substitute 'you' for 'thou' in their diction. In this last matter we have here the first English hymn book to adopt a policy which we see variously applied in such well known American hymnals as the *Worshipbook* (1972) and the *Lutheran Book of Worship* (1978).

A line of composers hardly less distinguished than that of the *Cambridge Hymnal* was assembled, and the music editor set the pace in contributing 18 tunes. There is no evidence here of the folk idiom of the Vaughan Williams school. It is a new start. Laycock has many styles, from the hearty to the intimately contemplative. He feels that he took advantage of the opportunity of trying out his experiments on an intelligent and receptive constituency of young people. Many techniques of the song-writer are fearlessly adapted to hymnody in his compositons, of which our Ex. 523, VERBUM DEI, written for Kaan's 'God who spoke in the beginning' is a good example. His accompaniments are often, as was appropriate to his environment and training, pianistic rather than organistic; his rhythms and harmonies are free-ranging and closely adpated to the variety of texts he was required to set. His colleagues took much the same line. This is pedagogy of the most cheerful and exuberant sort, and is a direct gesture against the 'concenting' attitude of traditional Catholicism in hymnody.

The most impressive discovery of the book was one of its youngest composers, Michael Dawney (b. 1944). We met him above on p. 165, but this is where his name first appeared in hymnody, and his tune FELIN-FOEL (Ex. 524) has a firm and gentle tread which beautifully matches a new text based on Isaiah 53. It appears in a through-composed version, but its essence is in its diatonic simplicity. Elizabeth Poston contributes a most distinctive tune, PRAISE GOD (Ex. 525), with a typically spare score and folky manner, which like a true song-writer she adapts precisely to a light-hearted version of Psalm 148. These are two distinguished contributions among many, not all of which are as successful. But a Laycock tune which is travelling fairly fast is HARVEST (# 170), bouncy and rhythmical, which is arranged more elaborately in John Wilson's *Sixteen Hymns...*(1977).

The second edition of *Praise the Lord* has little in common with the 1966 version but the title and publisher. It was edited by three young men—two musicians and a priest-musician—and was aimed more at the parish and less at the schools than *NCH*. It takes from accepted non-Catholic sources much more than NCH does, is less impatient of the 'high' tradition of 1906-55, and sets out its contents in a more conventional English style. But although its new tunes are less numerous than those in *NCH* (it is a rather longer book), it has many moments of originality. TERRY (Ex. 526), by Paul Inwood, is the most original approach in the literature to Sapphic metre, well contrived and owing something to the harmonically adventurous 'school tunes' of the earlier generation. FRANCOIS (Ex. 527), by the same composer, is one of the few tunes in existence scored with a 3-stave organ accompaniment, and as a setting of an Easter hymn in the traditional 'Lyra Davidica' metre, shows a salty combination of baroque texture and modern enthusiasm. (Both these were entered pseudonymously in the original book).

Both books abound in unusual approaches to hymnody; *Praise the Lord* stays nearer to what protestants recognize as the middle of the road; it has ampler provision for plainsong than *NCH*, and a section of responsive psalms and canticles, a form which *NCH* does not attempt. The modernism of *NCH* is more aggressive, the total view of *PTL* probably wider. It is very clear that as represented by these two books, the English Catholics got away to a very promising start. And if one wants to gather how far these musical inventors hoped that community would travel, the best indication is the last dozen or so hymns in *NCH* which, being an appendix of material included only in response to demand and not as a matter of policy, corresponds to the famous 'dustbin' in the *English Hymnal* and is perhaps, though shorter, more alarming.

Something of a protest against the wholesale abandonment of plainsong hymnody which was the unintended result of the Vatican II promulgations was delivered by a group called The Panel of Monastic Musicians, in a small hymnal, *A Song in Season* (Collins, 1976), which though not confined to plainsong provides a liturgical supplement to the parish books now available. And some original experimental writing can be found also in *Sing a New Song to the Lord* (Mayhew MacCrimmon, 1970), compiled by yet another group of interested enthusiasts.

American Catholicism has not yet found anything like a central focus of hymn-culture, and probably will not for a long time. Catholic hymnals have abounded during the second half of the 20th century—and plenty were in use before that. On the whole the level of taste was until very recently complacently low, and the story is now complicated by the fact that very soon after Vatican II a lead was taken in hymn-publishing by certain groups who majored in a style involving guitars and informal singing which has proved, by its immense commercial success, to be inhibiting of anything more imaginative. The most educated Catholic hymnal up to the time of writing is *Worship-II*, published 1975 by the Gregorian Institute of America; and the most interesting new music there is entirely the work of Episcopals and Lutherans. In the 'folk' style the most famous offering is 'They'll know we are Christians by our love', a song now known all over the world, and originally published in a Lutheran booklet, 'Praise for To-day' (1966); as a protest-song especially associated with the student unrest of the late 1960s it has taken to itself a certain truculent emphasis which may in the end prove to be a principle of ephemerality. James Thiem's 'Sons of God' is one of the better things in a very large store of material whose chief quality is musical monotony. Undoubtedly the best work is being done at present by people who are seeking to provide simple liturgical settings for congregational use, and who are devising new ways of singing antiphonal psalms. Here the outlook is promising, and this is, of course, an area in which the Catholic tradition gives more support and guidance than it does in that of English-speaking hymnody.

Note for page 166:
While this book was in the press two further Supplemental hymnals have appeared in Britain: *Songs of Worship,* 1980, which has affiliations with the *Anglican Hymn Book* (p. 162) and *Broadcast Praise,* 1981, a supplement to the BBC Hymn Book (pp 151-2). They came too late for detailed review.

The Twentieth Century in The United States, Canada and Australia

The first quarter of the 20th century witnessed a condition of stagnation in American hymn music. The position developed up to 1900 was much the same in 1930; the developments were in quantity rather than in quality. The one great success story was the spread throughout the protestant denominations of the 'Gospel Song' style. Publishers who specialized in, or gave plenty of room to, collections of hymns perpetuating the style of our Exx. 439-442 and 485 prospered mightily, not least because there was very little to compete with it. The White Spirituals were still locked up in East Tennessee, the Black Spirituals were the preserve of a race not yet politically liberated; the Boston style proved capable of development only in the direction of deeper and deeper sentimentality and pretentiousness.

One of the first main-line hymnals to show any reaction against this rather mournful state of things was the Presbyterian *Hymnal* of 1933, which is still (1979) in use in many Presbyterian churches. Edited by a learned musician who was a parish organist and a professor of church music, Clarence Dickinson, it drew more heavily on British Presbyterian culture than its predecessors had done, and indeed provided a more English selection of hymns and tunes than its constituency was used to, its chief quarry being of course the 1927 *Revised Church Hymnary*. But by a curious turn of fate, all three Presbyterian books currently in use could have been said to have been published about five to ten years before they should have been, and therefore to have just missed certain developments at each stage which would have helped them towards the goals they were seeking, and this was certainly an example. It was an early example, in non-Baptist hymnals, of the now ineradicable custom of printing the whole of a hymn text between the music staves—its Preface says that its publishers did so in answer to urgent demand. This demand, acceptance of which has done more than anything else to make the modern American attitude to hymnody so profoundly different from the English, was created by the popularity of 'Gospel Song' books, which always used this style, and is further testimony to their enthronement as the popular hymnody of America at this time.

But one thing Clarence Dickinson did not miss was the work of two Episcopals, Tertius Noble and Winfred Douglas. Tertius Noble (1867-1953) was an Englishman who had been organist at Ely Cathedral and York Minster before moving to St. Thomas's Episcopal Church, New York, in 1913; he became one of New York's most influential musicians, and held a professorship at the Union Theological Seminary School of Sacred Music. He was a greatly loved teacher and an advocate of more fastidious musical standards, his conservative style of composition did neither him nor American music any harm, because nothing so like the style of Parry as his best tune, ORA LABORA (Ex. 528) had been heard yet in the USA. Another almost admirable tune of his, very popular in the USA but not used by the Episcopals, is ROCKPORT for 'Hail to the Lord's Anointed'. His style was spacious, and his tendency to arrange older hymn tunes in a cathedral manner showed where his sympathies lay. But as a gentle yet firm promoter of good standrds he paved the way for what was about to come.

Winfred Douglas, born in the same year as Noble, and Dearmer, (1867-1944) was an Episcopal clergyman with a special gift for music and especially hymnology. He devoted most of his life to hymnological study and raised it, in the USA, to professional standing. his excellent tune to 'He who would valiant be' (Americans never use the original Bunyan text), given at Ex. 529, shows an originality, combined with a simplicity of approach, which in those circles was something quite new. It is one of the first native American tunes—the first indeed of those now widely known—to explore the possibilities of rhythmic change in its course, and it has remained the inalienable tune for that text throughout the USA. But his influence as a composer was slight compared with the influence of his scholarship and example. In the Episcopal *Hymnal-1940,* his individual influence through musical composition was less than that of Vaughan Williams in the *English Hymnal,* but his influence through other channels equalled that of Vaughan Williams and Percy Dearmer combined, for he was equally at home as an editor of music or as a translator of texts. True, he did contribute the admirable and very unusual northern folktune LIGHT (Ex. 530), from Joshua Leavitt's *Christian Lyre,* 1832, which turns out to be a tune which looks as if it has escaped from the shape-note books to New England but is in fact a rare survival of the same kind of tune from the northern countryside. But Douglas assembled a quite remarkable band of composers who between them contributed nearly fifty new tunes to the book in a style which celebrated modesty and understatement in a manner which was in the USA quite new.

The *Hymnal-1940* was the last in a series of anglican hymnals which had been published at intervals of about a generation since 1826, but the revolution in musical taste which it assumed—we cannot quite say that it achieved it, since other editors were slow to get the message—was far greater than any such gesture made by its predecessors. Douglas did not wear his heart on his sleeve as Vaughan Williams did, so he did not write an eloquent preface. (That is perhaps the difference between making your great gesture at the age of 73 and making it at 34). But in its presentations of plainsong, its notation of classic tunes and its careful attention to texts the book set quite new standards, and it is quite clear, from the style of the new tunes, that its committee were looking for craftsmanship rather than impressiveness.

David McKay Williams (1887-1978) who was born in Wales three months before his parents emigrated to Colorado, sets the style in his six contributions. MALABAR (Ex. 531), a unison tune with very lightly scored accompaniment, is a model of simplicity and firmness, and GEORGETOWN (H 437) shows that interest in rhythmic eloquence which we saw, in a different way, in Douglas's ST. DUNSTAN. Another long-lived composer, Alfred Morton Smith (1879-1971) contributed three excellent tunes, of which SURSUM CORDA (Ex. 532) is the best known, both in the USA and Britain. It found its way first into the *BBC Hymn Book* and later into the *Church Hymnary* (3rd edition). Leo Sowerby (1895-1968) was a very influential teacher and a sensitive composer who wrote much for the church and contributed two tunes to the *Hymnal*. TAYLOR HALL (Ex. 533) has a modest manner and an original rhythmic treatment of DSM. ROSEDALE (*More Hymns,* 50) is a later tune which has found many friends—in a more expansive style. Harmonic adventurousness is not usually found in this book, but LYNCHBURG (526), by the Swedish immigrant composer Henry Hallstrom, (b. 1903: to the USA, 1913), the youngest composer in the book, is an unusual and graceful CM, which has not yet travelled further, but on its merits might have done.

The absence of sensationally original music in the *Hymnal-1940* is its greatest strength. The time had not come for that, any more than it had come in Britain when the *English Hymnal* first appeared. American hymnody had to be rescued from the posturing artificiality of the later 19th century composers, and the balance between this and the high standards of literary composition set during the previous century had to be redressed. Winfred Douglas showed his true genius in fostering a sense of style and occasion along with a new simplicity of diction.

Editors of other hymnals were, it seems, too preoccupied with other problems to take full advantage of the lead that Douglas gave. The other matters that engaged their attention were mainly political. There was a considerable movement in the 1950s to bring together the various ethnic strands which diversified the denominations. Presbyterians, Lutherans and Methodists were all groups which were regionally and culturally subdivided, and the years 1950-65 were marked by parallel efforts to unify these groups. Furthermore, there was a growing consciousness that the USA was approaching the second centennial of the Declaration of Independence, and this brought a real effort to look for historic American music instead of relying on English patterns. The *Hymnal-1940*, being associated with a group within the Anglican Communion, was therefore at a disadvantage when non-anglican editors were at work.

Before noticing the consequences of that we must mention the *Hymnal* (1941) of the Evangelical and Reformed Church. This was a group deriving its origns from non-Lutheran German protestantism, and it had already absorbed much more of the customs of American Presbyterianism and Congregationalism than the Lutheran bodies wished to take to themselves. The 1941 *Hymnal* is an undistinguished work musically, except in that it contains three new tunes by Tertius Noble (including ROCKPORT, for 'Hail to the Lord's Anointed') which was at once acclaimed as a 'winner' by succeeding editors, and for its inclusion of our Ex. 534.

This, a setting for 'O the bitter shame and sorrow', a strong evangelical text up to then wedded in Britain with many awkward tunes (including one with the, to the British, evocative name of O THE BITTER), was sent for setting to Pietro Yon (1886-1943), the organist of St. Patrick's Cathedral in New York. Here history was made in that in America a Roman Catholic organist had never before been asked to assist in the editing of a Protestant hymnal—let alone such a distinguished man as this. Yon, who is well known for some organ pieces and composed much church music for his own communion, was an Italian immigrant born in the Piedmont district of North Italy, and his tune suggests that, being naturally a stranger to congregational hymnody, he had picked up a 'congregational gift' from his protestant Waldensian neighbours. This is the only tune of any distinction newly found in that hymnal, and it does what it was designed to do, which was to rescue a text agreeable to the evangelicals from musical misfortune.

The *Presbyterian Hymnbook,* 1955, illustrates very well the principle we mentioned just above. Edited by an able and energetic musician, David Hugh Jones (b. 1900), it does not look at all like that other Presbyterian book edited by a Welshman, the 1927 *Church Hymnary*. On the contrary, it explores further than any hymnal the strictly American tradition of tune-writing. If it has a weakness here, this was not of the editor's choosing. It is simply that the American tradition open to his explorations was at that time mostly that of New England, and that tradition was both shallow and decadent. The folk hymnody of the South had not yet been excavated by northern editors, and 'Amazing Grace' is one of only a small handful of southern tunes used in that book. New compositions of merit are very few, but our Ex. 536, HINMAN, by the prolific and celebrated composer Austin Lovelace (b. 1919) is one of them. Lovelace has written few hymn tunes, but many hymn-anthems, and his style, in more than 300 choral compositions, is uncannily close to that of England's Eric Thiman (cf. Ex. 479). Indeed, Exx. 536 and 479 are useful for comparison because both are composed for the same metre and both handle it in a rhythmically original way.

Two hymn books of the fifties have special interest. One is *Hymns for Colleges and Schools* (1956), which emerged from Yale and proves to be a kind of American *Songs of Syon*. On a campus there is never any need to be bullied by tradition, and the Yale book, beautifully edited and presented, took full advantage of this privilege. Its editor was content to recall young and alert worshipers to the heritage of the past. It contains nothing new of importance, but a large number of ancient tunes edited and re-introduced, and judiciously set to usable texts. It remains the most attractive hymnal for the intellectuals, but pays for that in being short on great evangelical hymnody.

The other important hymnal is the *Pilgrim Hymnal*, 1958. This was produced by the Congregationalists on the very eve of their being merged with the Evangelical and Reformed Church (see just above) into the United Church of Christ. It was a parish hymn book in the sense in which the Yale book was not, but it was compiled by an editorial committee who had a wide knowledge of other cultures. If it has a weakness it is the same as that of the Yale book—a tendency to unitarian liberalism in its texts too little balanced by evangelical fervor; but musically its scholarly and enterprising style made it one of the best respected hymnals in the USA, especially for campus use. One of its most distinguished offerings is FINLAY (Ex. 535), by H. W. Friedell (1903-58). Friedell collaborated with the late Lee Hastings Bristol (1923-79) in a young people's hymnal which contained this and one or two other excellent tunes of his, for which see the *Hymnal for Christian Worship,* 1970. In its fairly modest offering of 496 hymns plus about 100 liturgical pieces, the *Pilgrim* included a few fine new tunes, such as RAMWOLD (Ex. 537), a typical example of unpretentious candour, and it was the first hymnal to include anything from Persichetti's *Hymns and Responses,* 1956—for which see later, Ex. 550.

The *Methodist Hymnal* of 1966, being the first hymnal of the United Methodist Church (corresponding therefore to the English 1933 *Methodist Hymn Book* just as the American 1935 book corresponded to the English one of 1904) was edited by a very large committee representing the various religious interests which were combining in the new body, and whose acute consciousness of the need to please many diverse cultural traditions inhibited their inventiveness. Among the new tunes in it we may certainly mention WALDE (238), by the well known composer and conductor, Lloyd Pfautch (b. 1920), and VICAR (Ex. 538) by V. Earle Copes (b. 1921); both these are further examples of the new 'clean-limbed' style which American composers were espousing. One wishes that this hymnal's editors had been a little less injudicious in their selection of English tunes—in which field they seem to have backed many losers—but this was the first hymn book to include a tune by Peter Cutts, and it also includes, uniquely in America, Kenneth Finlay's AYRSHIRE.

Hymns for Christian Worship (1970), a very thoughtful and well-edited collection, presents several excellent new things in its very limited spectrum of 381 hymns. Among these is Ronald Arnatt's SOUTH GORE (Ex. 539), written for Bishop Bell's 'Christ is the King', a fine text in the rather intractable metre 888.888. Arnatt (b. 1930) has in the later seventies written useful tunes for other texts, and this is another example of a tune offered by a musician who is primarily a conductor and concert organist. It has a touch of the spaciousness of the English public school tune. Lawrence Schreiber (b. 1933) contributed NATIONAL CITY (Ex. 540), another enterprising tune, for 'All praise to thee': and here at last we see a sign of harmonic experiment.

It would, of course, be unwise to expect much original music from the Southern Baptists of the present generation, since they have to swim against so vigorous a tide of specialized tradition. But the judgment that not all Baptists in the Southern Convention are employed in composing new 'Gospel Songs' is amply vindicated in the *Baptist Hymnal,* 1975; this, succeeding the 1956 edition of the same name (which was in Baptist terms a very cautious and conservative collection) has some very unusual and enticing new offerings. Donald Hustad (b. 1921), a leading musician and teacher in that communion, contributed only one tune, OREMUS, to that book (Ex. 541), but it is a little gem in its way: and the national leader of Baptist music, William Reynolds (b. 1920), one of the world's best hymnologists, catches the pentatonic spirit of 'country hymnody' in MORA PROCTOR (Ex. 542). These two musicians have done much to widen the visions of this very conservative group, but in the field of hymnody the going is still slow.

American Lutheranism has in the latest generation shown the most hopeful signs of strong indigenous hymnody, and a good deal of the best material comes from the powerful German-based Missouri Synod of the Lutheran Church, which remains at a distance from the rest of Lutheranism in the USA, and from the ecumenical movement. The Missouri Synod is as conservative as the Southern Baptist Convention, but it has its musical focus not in the Gospel Song but in the German chorale. The other large bodies within American Lutheranism are Scandinavian-based, rather more liberal in theology, and have a much less certain musical touch. Scandinavian folk-hymnody, of which there was a good deal in the 1958 Lutheran *Service Book and Hymnal,* turns out (to any whose only experience of it is the much travelled and magnificent KIRKEN, (Ex. 580) disappointing, with a tendency to fall towards the style of the sentimental 19th century ballad. The Lutheran Church in America—which now embraces most of the Scandinavian-based groups, is hospitable to many styles, including the English, and

oddly uncertain in his choice from them. One of the
few original composers from this culture is Leland B.
Sateren (b. 1916), whose MARLEE (Ex. 545) is very
much loved, and justly.

The German-based Lutherans relied heavily on classic and pietist chorales in translation in their 1941
Lutheran Hymnal, a book of very solid worth but
making no attempt to break new ground and looking
just like what it was, a book of praise for immigrants.
A new generation, however, produced the *Worship
Supplement,* 1969, a book of worship music and 93
very carefully chosen hymns, and this turned out to be
a most important gesture. Our Exx. 543, 544, 546 and
549 first appeared in it, and all of them show plenty of
imagination. Carl Schalk, b. 1929, in FORTUNATUS
NEW (Ex. 543), a new tune for *Pange Lingua,* shows
himself one of the most flexible of the new composers;
there is very little that is ethnically Germanic about its
striding modal manner. David N. Johnson (b. 1922) in
the very popular DEXTER (Ex. 544), written for a new
and amusing hymn about the sanctifying of modern
life and study that first appeared in *Contemporary
Worship* - I (1969) (a joint venture from the Missouri
and other Lutherans) uses a rhythmic ambiguity taken
straight from the 17th century pietist chorale: note that
although there is no change of time signature,
measures 6 and 14 are strictly in 3/2; the amiable and
open-hearted manner of this tune have ensured that it
began to travel immediately.

Jan Bender's WITTENBERG NEW (Ex. 546), for a sombre and magnificent text by the great Lutheran text
writer Martin Franzmann (1907-76) is much more
powerful and demanding material, and so skilfully
contrived as to be far more singable than it might appear on paper. Bender (b. 1909) is a native of Germany
who spent most of his working life in the USA but
returned to Germany to retire. Here we have a real
resurrection of the classic rhythmic energy of Luther's
time, together with a spare and austere 3-part harmonization, wholly contrapuntal, which celebrates the
high professional standards of this group of composers. In exactly the same way Paul Manz (b. 1919)
offers in BOULDER (Ex. 547) severe counterpoint, but
with the lower parts keeping up a steady beat against
the syncopations of the melody. This tune has at the
time of writing appeared only on a leaflet.

Daniel Moe (b. 1926) holds to the same high professional standards in his very salty tune CITY OF GOD (Ex.
548)—a melody of Genevan poise supported by counterpoint reminiscent of Hindemith in its ruthless
diatonic dissonances and decisive resolutions. Richard
Hillert (b. 1923) has a moment of deep thoughtfulness
in MISSION (Ex. 549), a tough tune very subtly harmonized: perhaps the absence of a key signature is
something of an affectation—the baroque 3-flat F
minor is its true tonality and all those accidentals look
a bit forbidding. But if these composers have a fault it
is that they are in fact as forbidding in their attitude to

non-German theology and churchmanship. The best
composers of this culture are a group who know each
other very well, and who are at present regarded as the
undisputed leaders in Missouri-Lutheran music; being
so gifted, they command a great respect far beyond
their own communion. They are at their best in the recent edition of Luther's Chorales produced in 1977
from Concordia College, River Forest, Illinois, by
Schalk, Hillert and Paul Bunjes (b. 1914); perhaps
their wholesale re-editions of non-German tunes in the
1978 *Lutheran Book of Worship* are less wise, because
they give that book a ferociously Germanic accent
which belies the statement in the preface that
Lutherans in America are no longer immigrants but
natives. The style they have developed, that of contrapuntal accompaniment to strong melodies, is one
which they practised in the organ edition of the
Worship-Supplement, in which all the tunes, whatever
their origin, have the kind of highly intellectual accompaniment that we see in Exx. 548-9, even when they are
by Vaughan Williams; and many of them are harmonized two or three times. But when that is said,
what has happened is the liberation of German-based
Lutheranism from a rather mournful combination of
unison singing and organ scores harmonized in 19th-
century block chords; and where the tradition of
unison singing is so firmly entrenched (Bonhoeffer
gave it a new kind of authority in his famous statement
that it represented the true unity of the church) there is
room for this kind of musicianship to prevent its
becoming needlessly stodgy. The best thing the tunes
of these composers—of which there are plenty more to
investigate—is their combination of modern imagination with rigid professional principles which includes
the ability to write what, however austere its manner,
congregations can sing. Their style takes off directly
from that which we shall encounter soon in the *'Wehr
und Waffen'* school of early 20th century hymn
writing, (p. 179).

A cheering aspect of American hymnology since
1940 has been the increased interest, in most quarters,
in scholarly and precise editing. The first-rate *Hymnal
Companion,* which followed the *Hymnal-1940* in 1949,
was not the first of the American 'Companions' but it
set a new standard, which was followed by other
editors, especially in the *Guide to the Pilgrm Hymnal*
(1968), the *Companion to Hymns for Christian Worship* (1970), the *Companion to the Methodist Hymnal*
(1970) and the *Baptist Hymnal Companion* (1975); the
Presbyterians are the only major group not to have
produced some form of hymnal companion since that
which went with their 1933 *Hymnal.* The existence of
such a book gives one confidence in the parent book
because it suggests that the editors are both alert and
knowledgable. Another hymnal which nobody who
studies American hymnody should ignore is the *Mennonite Hymnal* (1969), perhaps the finest example of
hymnal editing yet available; it is a pity it never achiev-

ed a Companion, but as the book of praise for one important section of the complex Mennonite network in the USA is is an exemplary piece of work.

The *Hymnal-1940* has had a very long life for an American book, and the attempts to provide it with updating supplements have been slightly confused. In 1971 the Standing Commission on Church Music of the communion produced *More Hymns and Spiritual Songs,* edited by Lee H. Bristol, and this book of 71 hymns—increased 1977 to 80—explores the folk hymnody of the USA and also includes a number of interesting new texts and tunes. Daniel Hathaway (b. 1945) contributes a very impressive tune, with his own text, JOB (33) which has a Germanic toughness and a superb melodic sweep; Ronald Arnatt (whom we met at Ex. 539) contributes some new ones, and a bold moment comes when Vincent Persichetti's tune VENERABLE (Ex. 550) appears with the text for which he wrote it. Persichetti (b. 1915) published his *Hymns and Responses for the Church Year* in 1956, and this is an eye-catching collection of tunes in modern musical language. VENERABLE is one of the few which have yet been included in hymnals, because the congregational ear still finds Persichetti's tonality a little daunting; but they are magnificent choral pieces, and written in many styles which show great alertness to the import of the very interesting texts he chooses to set.

The extent to which contemporary Americans have explored the further reaches of melody and harmony, thus baptizing into congregational use the musical idioms which have been familiar in secular music through two generations, is encouraging. One of the more unusual hymnals in recent USA production is the *Hymnal of the United Church of Christ* (1975)—the United Church of Christ being that larger body into which the Congregationalists entered just about the time when the *Pilgrim* was published. This is a short book of 300 hymns, very eclectic, with some omissions which must have surprised the users of the *Pilgrim* compensated by some very unusual and heartening new material. Persichetti's VENERABLE is there, so are Howells's SANCTA CIVITAS and Cutts's BRIDEGROOM: and among the unusual American tunes are our Exx. 551-3. Ex. 551, NEW SONG, by Lee Burswold (b. 1933) has a manner reminiscent of Persichetti, very salty and unexpectedly practicable. GROVE STREET (Ex. 552), by J. W. Jenkins (b. 1928) is less aggressively atonal and more like the broad mid-20th century English tune; and Ex. 553, PILGRIMAGE, by J. W. Neely (b. 1945) has the kind of gentle subtlety that seems to place it within the family we encounter in the English *New Catholic Hymnal.*

The *Worshipbook* (1972) of the Presbyterian Church is a wayward book bearing signs of hasty editing by a group whose main attention was on liturgy rather than hymns, and it contributes very little in hymn music that is new: but there is one moment of genius (Ex. 554) where one of its music editors, Richard D. Wetzel (b. 1935) rises to the challenge of

Auden's lines beginning 'He is the Way'. These have attracted the attention of several recent editors and have been set by several musicians; the way in which this tune, NEW DANCE, handles the irregular metre of the haunting lines, and provides the one available setting which can be called congregational, is impressive indeed.

The Roman Catholic hymnal, Worship-II (1975), published by the Gregorian Institute, is the most serious-minded of Catholic hymnals so far to have appeared in the USA, but while its judicious selection of classic hymns arouses admiration, it is not possible to find in it any sign yet of a creative Catholic style. What we do find, however, is a series of twelve tunes by the gifted anglican composer Calvin Hampton (b. 1938). One of them appears at Ex. 555. Hampton's scores are usually complex and contrapuntal. An organ accompaniment independent of the melody line gives many of them an appearance of being strophic songs in the manner of the classic *Lieder*-writers. Each tune is composed with a clear eye to the text, and the number of styles he explores is as great as the number of tunes he has written. PIKE (W-II 200) is a tour de force with its *ostinato* accompaniment; Ex. 555 is more lyric, with the melody incorporated in the organ part in the usual way. Often he composes an 'Amen' into his tune, which involves the congregation in the liturgical solecism of singing 'Amen' after the hymn, but the ingenuity with which he does it almost persuades us to forgive in this case that otherwise tiresome and obsolete custom. It is fair to say that nobody so far has achieved as completely as Hampton a liberated hymn-writing style while at the same time insisting on providing a truly congregational tune. Among English composers only Peter Cutts shows this sort of versatility.*

No account of modern main-line hymnody can omit mention of Richard Dirksen's VINEYARD HAVEN (Ex. 556). This is, without question, the American ABBOTS LEIGH. It was first published, like that other, on a leaflet in 1974, but within a year or two it was being sung all over the USA. It was composed as a processional for the installation of a Presiding Bishop (Archbishop) in Washington's National Cathedral, and within three years three hymnals had included it. The choice of text was unfortunate—rarely has so great a tune been composed for so pedestrian a text as 'Rejoice, ye pure in heart'. The great weakness of American hymn tune writing is the acceptance by composers of the universal habit of never reading hymn texts, and of relying on their opening line for the judgment whether they are worth setting. Distinguished exceptions to this deplorable set of mind are Persichetti and Calvin Hampton, who most certainly do read their texts. But we cannot have everything at once, and the masterly way in which VINEYARD HAVEN combines harmonic originality with a rousing pure-folk melody is a portent of continuing hopefulness. This tune also appears—and is thus reproduced in *Ecumenical Praise*—

in the octavo edition with through-composed organ part and three choral settings.

Two recent supplements, without denominational allegiance, recently appeared in the USA. One was *Westminster Praise* (1976), a small book of 60 hymns designed to serve the campus of Westminster Choir College, whose chief aim was to enlarge the repertory by reintroducing some ancient hymns and tunes but which contains a good deal of new material also, including work by the American composers David York, Alice Parker, Jane Marshall and Michael Pavone. A more ambitious project was *Ecumenical Praise* (1977), which could be described as the most forward-looking and unusual of all American collections. Perhaps there are more tunes here than anywhere else which cause a raising of eyebrows and a cocking of the connoisseur's ear. Many of these experiments are through-composed pieces too long to be quoted here, and a few of them are adventures in electronics. But William Albright's tune ALBRIGHT (# 1) is a beautiful example of impressionism disciplined by a simple melody; and two really distinguished pieces come from the eminent composer Ned Rorem (b. 1938), a specially gifted song-writer who had not before written hymns. Several tunes by Alec Wyton (b. 1920), one of the editors, show what can be achieved with very simple materials. Some tunes show that discomfort with which secular composers of distinction approach hymn tune writing: but the book is not a command, but an invitation towards the 21st century, and it will be interesting to see whether the new offerings here, or those in the *Church Hymnary, Third Edition* (or neither, or all) commend themselves to the 'generation yet unborn'.

Our Ex. 557 may be a 'scoop' in being printed here for the first time. Its composer, Ronald Neal, was born in 1953 and will be the youngest (in the sense of latest born) composer represented in this book; it was composed for his own church (Central Presbyterian Church, Lafayette, Indiana) to a text of his own, and shows a very sure touch with melody and harmony in a modern, though not forbidding, style.

And that tune—with so many on which we have just commented—suggests that there is a surge of creativeness in American hymnody, especially in music, which looks at present like overtaking and surpassing what the same generation saw in Britain. There is, of course, another stream of hymnody which takes a quite different line. The style which in Britain is associated with *Youth Praise,* emerging from the 'Light Music' culture, has been hospitably espoused by certain American publishers, including some who cater largely for contemporary Catholic hymnody. A good deal of the simply 'popular' music is trifling in content, and most of it is so expensive to reproduce that we are not here giving examples of it. It is doubtful whether it, any more than the 'protest-folk' of Britain, can really be called hymnody. The best of these songs are antiphonal and biblical: the worst are humanistic or, now and again, downright irreligious. But pro-

bably we should wait another generation before finally assessing it.

In the Preface to the *Lutheran Book of Worship* (1978), which is easily the most interesting preface to any current American hymnal, there is a revealing phrase which exposes the secret of contemporary developments in the United States. 'Most north-American Lutherans no longer regard themselves as transplanted Europeans.' That does not apply only to Lutherans. What the twentieth century has seen in hymnody and the other arts is the consequence of the fading of that ethnic consciousness which in contemporary politics is being artificially intensified. In Richard D. Wetzel's most interesting book, *Frontier Musicians on the Connoquenessing, Wabash and Ohio,* which is a history of George Rapp's Harmony Society from 1805 to 1906, we have a very good account of the persistence of a German ethnic tradition in the Mid-West; and that is how it was with all the immigrant traditions. One could not in those days speak of an 'American' style. It is fair enough to say that it took 150 years from the Declaration of Independence for ethnic consciousness to begin fading; but that— only five generations—is quick work. And after that there has been a half-century during which communications have been opened up, intermarrying has taken place, compuses have insisted on the mixing of cultures, and racial groups, politics apart, have been free to think of themselves as Americans. What we have noted in these last few pages indicates that a very energetic development in a positive American style has been the result—still salted with racial musical memories but no longer derivative. It is a very different story with hymn-texts, as we indicated in the *Panorama*; and of course the corruptions of language which have, at the time of writing, extinguished good text-composition can always enter into music, and to some extent have done. But the main stream is flowing strongly and hopefully.

Two recent hymnals of cultures which have strong ethnic roots may here be interestingly contrasted. The Mennonites in Canada and the USA are a very close-knit cultural group, containing many streams; some remain profoundly conservative and resist all attempts to become part of the American life style; others are liberal and observant. The *Mennonite Hymnal* of 1969 is one of the most educated and outward-looking of all American hymnals, containing what was at that date by far the best selection of those 'Country Tunes' which we mentioned in chapter 19, as well as a very judicious selection of material from all Christian sources.

On the other hand there are the Moravians, whose musical tradition is as vital as that of the Mennonites, but whose *Moravian Hymnal* (also 1969) preserves the 18th-century evangelical habit of adapting all older tunes to the style of the musicians of the third quarter of the 18th century, and which contributes nothing in any contemporary style at all. The Moravian musical tradition is, of course, instrumental where that of the Mennonites is vocal (and indeed until very recently unaccompanied).

There is the contrast: flexibility on the one hand among the morally and socially rigid Mennonites, and an obstinate allegiance to a single musical style among the very friendly and sociable Moravians. Thus the counterpoint continues.

CANADA AND AUSTRALIA

The story of Canadian hymn music is a much shorter one than that of the USA, for the obvious reason that Canada has no Declaration of Independence. Canada has therefore been less self-conscious about relying on English precedents for its hymnody. Its political structure is, of course, simpler than that of the USA, being basically an uneasy combination of the French Catholic and the British and Irish Protestant streams. The English-speaking Catholic culture is increasingly important, and so is the ancient Mennonite culture mostly centered round Winnipeg: but neither of these offers anything of importance in our particular field as yet. Nor, indeed, does the French Catholic body. But the Protestants have shown considerable energy within the last two decades.

Protestants in Canada basically relied on hymnals of two dynasties, the Presbyterian and the Anglican. Content for some generations with imported books, the Protestants issued their first significant hymnal, *The Hymnary,* in 1930, celebrating the formation a little earlier of the United Church of Canada out of the Methodist, Congregationalist and Presbyterian churches. The ethos of this book was chiefly Presbyterian—the Scottish Presbyterians were the backbone of the English-speaking immigrant culture, and there was always a tendency for the Governor-General to be a distinguished Scot. So the format and contents of the 1930 *Hymnary* followed the lead set by the *Revised Church Hymnary* of 1927. It was a substantial book, and for its date a judiciously edited one; the two great influences in hymn music whose imprint it bears were Ernest Macmillan and Healey Willan; its editor in chief was Dr. Alexander Macmillan. On the whole its new music is cautious and conservative, and its most distinguished contributor was Healey Willan (1880-1968), who is regarded as the father of Canada's independent church music style. His tune ST. BASIL (Ex. 558) is one of his best, one of several contributed to the book. It is conservative but sound, and nothing more original than this was expected at that date in Canadian protestantism.

The Anglican Church in Canada had already had a useful hymnal, *The Book of Common Praise* (1908); its music does not tell us anything we had not learnt from *Hymns Ancient and Modern* in the 19th century. It was revised in 1938 under the title *The Hymnal,* and, containaining 812 hymns, this was one of the most massive hymnals ever edited for an Anglican body. Here again we find cautious hopefulness rather than great originality. It found a link with the 1930 *Hymnary* in using some tunes by W. Wells Hewlett (1873-1940), who had been an adviser to the United Church book and had contributed five tunes to it; his STRATFORD ON AVON, new in the Anglican book, is almost exactly in the style of the later 18th century Psalm tunes, and shows how pervasive the Presbyterian influence was in Canada. The most unusual tune in the book was BELLWOODS (Ex. 559), by James Hopkirk (1908-72), an attractive exercise in free rhythm.

This was a quiet start. Oddly enough it was Winfred Douglas in the USA *Hymnal-1940* who collected two tunes from Canada which turned out to be resounding successes. One was ST. JOAN, by P. B. Coller (b. 1895), an Englishman who emigrated to Canada in the 1930s (Ex. 560)—which has never been used in Canada; the other was THE KING'S MAJESTY (Ex. 561), by the Canadian-born Graham George (b. 1912), easily the most original mind of his generation in Canadian church music. This found its way to England in the *BBC Hymn Book* (1951).

This cautious beginning gave way in 1971 to a very brisk gallop when the Canadians took the bold step of publishing a hymnal for the Anglican Church and the United Church to use together. This book, reducing the combined total of the two earlier books (1,503) to just over 500 hymns, pushed the business along at a speed which some Canadians have found healthily bracing and others a shade breathless. Most of the efforts of the imitators of Victorian styles were discarded, and room was made for a large number of newly composed tunes, all of which have character and some of which certainly achieve distinction. There is, for example, a later tune by Graham George for 'Fight the good fight', Methodist Hymnal 1966, #175, craggy and aggressive, on which one should read the composer's own note in Stanley Osborne's superb *Companion* to this hymnal, *If Such Holy Song . . .* The composer there shows himself broadminded enough to say that there is still a place for PENTECOST: but in his new tune he gave of his best. Dr. Osborne (b. 1907), the central hymnologist of this book, contributed one or two choice compositions of which the best and most-travelled so far is MASSON (Ex. 562), a beautiful miniature, eloquently simple. Derek Holman (b. 1931), who went to Canada in the late fifties from a lecturership at the Royal School of Church Music, composed a number of very sturdy and thoughtful tunes; CARN BREA (Ex. 563), written for a good modern text, has verve and energy which are typical of his work. Franklin R. C. Clarke (b. 1931) produced a most useful new tune in CAUSA DIVINA (Ex. 564) for a new hymn written in the metre of 'Praise to the Lord, the Almighty', with a gentle modulation very easily accessible to a congregation. His tune GOD OF CONCRETE (Can. 90), written for a steely modern text that has become very popular, has a very different mood, entirely appropriate to the words. Another 'craggy' tune is DOMINION-CHALMERS Ex.

565), by William France (b. 1912), again written for a modern text about urban life, and reflecting the asperities of the text in its precipitous harmonic plunges. More serene, beautifully adapted to a text attributed to St. Columba, is SOWBY (Ex. 566) by Godfrey Ridout (b. 1918): this sweeping melody deftly suggests the Celtic folk tunes. (This Ridout, by the way, is not related to the equally distinguished English composer Alan Ridout). And PIER PAUL (Ex. 567) by H. B. Cabena, (b. 1933) seems to be a rare combination of ingenuity and grace. The composer in Canada since 1957; the text for which the tune is written is beautiful, and in a most unusual metre, but being a hymn for infant baptism stands little chance of being often sung, which is a pity when both words and tune are so distinguished.

These are only a few of the new tunes in a hymnal whose editors were as courageous and forward looking as those of *Church Hymnary III*, and it is, from this point of view, well worth close study. It will for some time be a book whose music future editors dare not ignore.

The situation in Australia is promising, but as yet has not developed as far as it has done in Canada. Until very recently Australian hymnals were as derivatives as were the Canadian books, but a leap forward came with the publication as recently as 1977 of the *Australian Hymn Book*. This is, like the Canadian book, an ecumenical venture, designed for all those churches which care to use it, including (as the Canadian one does not) the Roman Catholics. Textually it leans away from the Tractarian form of anglicanism towards the evangelical, and it compensates for the lack of plainsong hymnody by a very generous selection from Watts, Wesley and the other evangelical classics. Its music shows great learning and alertness on the editors' part, but there is little new music that indicates that a native Australian style has established itself. It is, though profoundly different theologically, the *English Hymnal* of Australia in its revival of great things from the past, but unlike the *English Hymnal* it does not find the very recent past intolerable, so there is an excellent selection of music of all ages. The editors are wide awake enough to have picked up to unusual a treasure as our Ex. 587. Indeed, the most original music from Australia up to now has been in the popular style. James Minchin's *Jazz for the Church*, in several small volumes, has had good success, and one of the tunes from this was imported to the USA in the *Worshipbook* (see no. 490 there); Canon Laurence Bartlett (b. 1933) has also composed some successful music, mostly in this style, of which the tune ONE-FIFTY, for Fred Kaan's paraphrase of Psalm 150, has travelled to the USA (*Westminster Praise* 3) and to Britain (*New Church Praise*, 80).

The *Australian Hymn Book* was republished for use outside Australia, as an ecumenical hymn book, in 1979 under the title *With One Voice*.

Contemporary Hymnody in Non-English Speaking Regions

This final chapter must consist of a quick look at some developments in hymnody outside the English-speaking world. Your author is fully conscious that were this book being written in, say, Germany, all the rest of the book would probably be crushed into one chapter, and the material in this chapter, or even this section of it, might well fill the rest of the book. There is no hope of doing full justice to international hymnody here, especially that of the parts of the world farthest from Britain and America. But we can perhaps celebrate the fact that hymnody has, during the 20th century, just begun to be international at all. Hymnody is an intensely regional and sectional church activity; that is its nature and will always be so. No attempt to resist that should be taken seriously. But the contraction of the physical world during our century has very naturally promoted ideas of international hymnody, of sharing others' hymnody not in the way in which German hymnody was shared in Britain by Catherine Winkworth's translations, but as a much more radical revision of customary insularity.

The 'spine' of this chapter must be the hymnal *Cantate Domino*, and it will not be out of place to repeat here a little of its story, which we have also referred to in chapter 28 of the *Panorama*. Cantate Domino began in 1924 as a hymn book all of whose texts were printed in their original language and several others, sponsored by the World Student Christian Federation. This small trial book was immediately expanded in 1930 to 80 hymns, and in 1950 to 120, under the same sponsorship and edited on the same principles. A totally new edition was put in hand by the World Council of Churches in 1968, which was the first in which Roman Catholics and Eastern Orthodox hymnologists took part. Convening the editorial committees was, of course, a complicated project, and the work was completed in four intensive sessions of three or four days each, and by correspondence. The central committee had four members, Joseph Gelineau, SJ, the distinguished French priest-musician Dimitri Stefanovic, representing the Orthodox Churches of Greece and of his native Yugolsavia, Dieter Trautwein, a prominent minister in youth work in Germany who became Provost of Frankfurt in 1970 while the work on Cantate Domino was in progress, and your present writer. But editorial committees when they met were always expanded by the presence of members of the World Council Staff, observers, special advisers, and distinguished ecumenical figures who happened to be passing through Geneva at the time. The result was a book of 202 hymns, again in the original language plus any number of others from one to eight, representing a far wider constituency than the three earlier editions had done. This appeared as a melody-only edition in 1974,

but owing to a most unfortunate situation arising from the original publisher's losing interest in the project, the full score edition did not finally appear until 1980. I acknowledge at once that what I write here is based very largely on the information which came my way in the course of directing the publication of this book which is, of course, the best available compendium of international hymnody.

GERMANY

To begin with Germany, the situation of German hymnody in about 1930 was that while there was an enormous treasury of great classics available, in practice congregations had tended to succumb to the blandishments of the romantic style, and a movement among theologians and pastors resisting this tendency was by that time becoming noticeable. This had a good deal to do with the teachings of Karl Barth and his circle, who called for a return to objectivity and depth in theologial thought. When, therefore, Hitler came to power in 1933 and the Christians in Germany were at once divided between those who could and those who could not conform to the dictates of his tyranny, there was a tough theological circle waiting to dispute his claims on the Church. The Christians of all protestant denominations who took this view gathered together in the Confessional Church, and they produced in 1934 a tiny paper-covered book of hymns called *Wehr und Waffen* (a quotation from the opening stanza of *'Ein feste Burg'*). This contained a number of new hymns, as well as some classics, and some new tunes with them. Our Ex. 568, BRUDERSCHAFT, by the theologian Heinrich Vogel was composed a little earlier but included in the book, and Ex. 569, HIER IST GEDULD, by Otto Dibelius, a prominent Confessional pastor, was new in it.

Both these tunes have a folk-song style, a strenuous simplicity, which reflected the resolute cheerfulness with which these heroes resisted the demands of the tyrant, often suffering grievously, some indeed (like Dietrich Bonhoeffer) becoming martyrs. The whole set of the little book is against the sentimentality of current custom; and of course it is no accident that romanticism became anathema to people in this condition, for the cult of 'Blood and Soil' as propagated by Hitler's counsellors was the very nadir of romantic sentimentality.

Much of what came out of the Confessional resistance has, of course, been lost, but DIE NACHT IST VORGEDRUNGEN, (Ex. 570), one of the most moving tunes of all time, is one such tune which has retained its hold and which is now in all current German hymnals.

The pattern thereafter is very like that of England in the same period. If we regard the 'high church' return to the classic chorale as the norm of Christian praise as parallel to Vaughan Williams's revival of the psalm tunes and the diocesan melodies, then the reaction which followed is comparable to that which England suffered after 1955—but there is a very important difference. A new popular hymnody certainly appeared, in a style which owed nothing whatever to the chorales, but its quality was basically professional, not amateur.

We owe the new form of German hymnody to the *Kirchentag* movement, whose guiding spirit, in the years immediately after 1945, was Count von Thadden. This, which still exists, began as a grand-scale conference chiefly for young people from all countries, for the promotion of peace and of new Christian thinking. Its early rallies were on a scale comparable to the largest rallies organized by the Billy Graham company, but the difference was that they were a decisive gesture against pietism. There was a great deal of radical doctrine and social thinking in these conferences, and the new generation of Christians in Germany was permanently affected by it. The music associated with the movement was sociable, trenchant, and highly professional. Germany has been the only country successfully to attempt the composition of modern popular hymns to fully professional standards. One of the key-figures in this kind of composition has been Heinz Werner Zimmermann (b. 1930), whose contribution has been less in hymnody than in works of larger scale, but in whose music we find a quite new blending of what he describes (some say without true precision) as jazz idioms with strictly academic standards of composition. The hymnody which we find in such new collections as *Christen Lieder Heute* and *Schalom* (1971), is full of rhythm, adapted for guitar accompaniment, always in unison texture, and always lively; but unlike what corresponds to it in England and America, it avoids cliche and coins a new vocabulary. There is no sign here of a return to pietistic platitudes such as we encountered in the English Twentieth Century Light Music Group. Our Exx. 571-4 give some idea of the originality and sensitiveness of which this group of composers was capable, and a study of *Schalom* (some of whose contents are in *Contate Domino*) will provide some fascinating experinces in this new style. HERR DU BIST AN VIELEN TISCHEN (Ex. 571) is a communion hymn by Dieter Trautwein (b. 1928), one of the central figures in the new German hymnody; another key-figure is Rolf Schweizer, whose SINGET DEM HERRN (Ex. 572) is now travelling far outside Germany. The two examples of O. G. Blarr (Exx. 573-4) show perhaps an even more profound sensitiveness to the possibilities of new but eminently practicable music. (For some texts associated with this new music, see *Panorama* 574ff and several pieces in *Ecumenical Praise* and *Cantate Domino*).

The reaction against pietism has cut deep, and the attitude of the new German-speaking Christians to the pietist classics—still so much valued outside Germany—has undergone radical revision. The new songs are often fiercely political where the old ones are warmly evangelical. But even 'A mighty fortress', which is far from pietist, has gone under a cloud in these circles; the trauma of 1933-45 was as good a reason as any for a suspicion of history and a cult of creativeness.

We include Ex. 575 to illustrate that last point. The associated text is at *Panorama* 555, and I am allowed by Dr. Jan Bender, until recently Professor in the Music Faculty at Wittenberg University, USA, to quote what he wrote to me about it.

> You will certainly remember that Adolf Hitler invaded Austria in 1938 and united it with the 'Fatherland'. There were poets enough who lauded the annexation, and one of them (I forget his name) made a text of which the first stanza is still in my memory. Now the Nazis looked for a composer and found the young, gifted Distler. A setting was assigned to him by somebody (I donot know by whom) and after a few days he delivered the melody for a piano accompaniment. This was printed on a postcard and distributed for sale. (There is one single postcard left in the world after the composer, the poet, the Fuhrer and the Reich passed away....) The melody was so outstanding that it stuck in that old rotten memory of mine for 28 years. In 1966 I wrote *Six Variations on a Theme by Hugo Distler*....But as I was satisfied with the Variations only, I continued looking for a poet. (In 1970) I asked Martin Franzmann for a text and I gave him the rhythm of the melody....In 1971 he sent the text which was immediately accepted by the publisher of the 1966 Variations.

When one hears the tune sung to Franzmann's text it is impossible, unless one knowns this story, to believe that the text was not composed first. A more extreme example of the application of dedicated professional excellence to an originally trivial (indeed pernicious) assignment cannot be found in the annals of hymnody.

THE NETHERLANDS

Dutch Protestantism has always made the Genevan psalms the centre of its praise; indeed, it is the only surviving Christian group that does so. So until fairly recently its habits of praise corresponded to those of Scotland up to the mid-nineteenth century. There was always in Holland a rich tradition of carols and folk songs, and the celebrated *Nederlandtsch Gedenck-clanck*, 1626, a book of patriotic songs celebrating the release of the Dutch from Spanish rule, contains such rousing tunes as KREMSER ('We gather together...', H 315) and the present Dutch national anthem (Ex. 576)—surely the finest national anthem in existence so far as music goes—which recently has been adapted as a hymn tune (*Hymns for Celebration*, 1974, 26). The delightful harvest song VRUECHTEN, now widely known with 'The joyful Eastertide', (*English Praise* 37) comes from about the same period, as does the carol 'King Jesus hath a garden'. But the Dutch Reformed Church took lofty ground about such music as this, and one of the important protests against this repressiveness came from the Dutch Remonstrant Church in *Oude und Nieuwe Gesengen*, 1954; this contains many new hymn texts and some tunes in a fairly learned style. Its editor, A. C. Schuurmann, contributed several, of which our Ex. 577, in the metre of WACHET AUF, is a typical example.

The Reformed Church revised its translation of the Genevan psalms in *150 Psalmen* (1961), keeping the Genevan metres and tunes, and produced as a companion to it *102 Gesangen* (1965), a small collection of wide ecumenical scope. Much of the material here is from the historic treasury but some good new tunes in simple style appear, such as our Ex. 578 by T de M. Oyens. Ex. 579. ZIJT GIJ WAAROP, comes from the same source. In the post-1963 Dutch Catholic Church the collaboration of Huub Oosterhuis and Bernard Huijbers has produced some interesting and inventive new material, mostly in a somewhat more informal musical style.

SCANDINAVIA

It has already been remarked that the Scandinavian survivals in American Lutheran hymnody tend to have the character of somewhat debased folk song. A pioneer of folk-song collecting in Norway was Ludvig M. Lindeman, who composed many tunes; the one which has true greatness is that which is in the USA called KIRKEN (Ex. 580). But on the whole the Lutheran Church in Scandinavia lived on German capital until well into the twentieth century, and in music contributed nothing else of distinction. The solitary tune by the eminent composer Carl Nielsen (ALTAR, Ex. 581), has only come into prominence long after it was composed. It was not until the 1960s that a renaissance took place: but then it was dramatic. In 1960 was authorized *Andlig Visa* (1964), a supplemental hymnal of opulent dimensions, introducing many new hymns and tunes and providing them with descants, instrumental variations, historical notes and performance directions. Here we encounter for the first time the names of such text-writers ad Olov Hartmann and Anders Frostenson, who were soon to become more famous. This was followed by the even more remarkable *Psalmer och Visor* (trial edition 1971, full edition 1975). This contains 197 new hymns, numbered from 613 upwards so as to provide a substantial supplement to the existing hymnal, which continue to carry on the process begun in the earlier book. Here we see, not a development of the learned and florid style which we find in the 1964 book, but a quite new simplicity: an austere and spare acore, a modal melody, a free-ranging harmonic idiom which always keeps within a congregation's range. Exx. 582-4 are characteristic; Ex. 584 moves towards the more sophisticated diction of the most distinguished composer in the book, Sven-Erik Back, whom we meet in Exx. 585 and 586. Ex. 585 is a twelve-tone melody cunningly devised into a hymn tune, making use of the short lines which the modern Swedish writers tend to favour, and Ex. 586 is hardly less austere, and certainly equally original in its use of unexpected cadences. There is a most impressive correspondence between the mood and ethos of these new Swedish tunes and the new texts for which they are composed. The more consenting and 'popular' idiom is, of course, not dead in Sweden: GUDS KARLEK ('God's Care'), at *Ecumenical Praise* 104, shows what Sweden can produce when the popular evangelical mood prevails.

FRANCE

Catholic France had its great moments in hymn music during the early 18th century (see chapter 12); but broadly speaking little happened between the liturgical revival of 1681-1736 and the Second Vatican Council. Some tunes of French origin have found currency, and maybe wider use than in their original contexts, of which the most famous is no doubt GRAFTON (EH 33), which was first used as a hymn tune in 1881 but obviously is founded on a popular melody. It was always, as we have noted, the service of Benediction which gave scope for hymn tunes in pre-1963 Catholicism, and this is one of the newer tunes made available for the *Tantum Ergo*. But the stirrings which produced the liturgical changes of 1964 are certainly heard in the monumental Canticle of the Word (Ex. 587), whose text, by Didier Rimaud, and tune, by Jean Langlais (b. 1907), were written for a service of Vigils associated with the Conference on the Bible and the Liturgy held in Strasbourg in July, 1957. Langlais, perhaps the most celebrated and prolific of French liturgical composers, wrote only this hymn tune (and when consulted about it in 1963, when the English translation of the text was made, had forgotten he had composed it); but it is a masterpiece of eloquence on the most massive scale. It has now passed into *More Hymns and Spiritual Songs* (1971), *The Church Hymnary* (1973) and *New Church Praise* (1975) and will no doubt travel further.

Cantate Domino contains many examples of similar, though simpler, antiphonal canticles by members of the Centre Nationale de Pastorale Liturgique in Paris, of which the celebrated psalmodist Joseph Gelineau (b. 1920) is a member. These, through promotion in the French parishes and in the protestant community of Taize, have proved to be a most valuable vehicle for congregational participation in communities where congregational singing as protestants understand it had been quite unknown. See especially Gelineau's Canticle of the Passion (*Cantate Domino* 78) for a particularly moving example. The 'straight' hymn tune comes less easily to the French composers, but when they do attempt it the result is usually carol-like and innocent and charming; for examples of this see Ex. 588, an original composition by Claude Rozier, and the arrangement of VENI REDEMPTOR (Ex. 11) at Ex. 589. Ex. 590 is Gelineau's own setting for the Bonhoeffer text translated 'By gracious powers' (*Ecumenical Praise* 57: *Cantate Domino* 48) which was composed in 1970 at a meeting of the *Cantate Domino* editors. In the preparation of that book it became clear that many French composers, like Gelineau himself, had never before attempted a strophic hymn tune: but the results of their answers to requests for hymn tunes indicate that a quite fresh and creative approach can be expected of them.

European protestantism has not yet contributed much beyond what we have mentioned. One might have expected something of the Italian Waldensians, but their current hymnal, *Innario* (1949) uses music of a derivative evangelical kind, and religious folk song which has little contact with the real folk-origins of music. Catholic cultures outside France are beginning to produce canticles and semi-sacred songs: one would expect Spain to major in guitar-music, and a few offerings from the Hispanic culture in *Cantate Domino* do not disappoint that expectation. Finland is capable of producing things as dramatic as 'Jesus Christ came to Capernaum' (*Ecumenical Praise* 14: *Cantate Domino* 67). The Eastern Orthodox Communion remains wedded to liturgical music almost none of which is, in the accepted sense, congregational hymnody, and, as we have already said, no serious attempt has been made yet to relate Eastern chant to western hymnody in the way in whch medieval plainsong and modern Roman Catholic music has been enabled to contribute.

OUTSIDE EUROPE

Once we move away from Europe we are in what used in past days to be called the Mission Field. For the study of hymnody, it is only the indigenous productions of those regions which received Christianity from the hands of European or American missionaries that is of any interest. Inevitably in the first generations of modern missions, protestant hymnody in these regions was English or American hymnody translated, and set to English and American tunes. What hymns were taught in Africa, India and the Far East depended on the tastes, memories and attitudes of the teachers, and there are some hair-raising pages in the older missionary hymnals which indicate that evangelical zeal did not necessarily go hand in hand with good taste: but that we knew already.

It is an historic fact to which the present writer can testify that in 1945 a diligent search failed to produce anything practicable from the indigenous musical cultures of Africa, India or China apart from what had been included in the early editions of *Cantate Domino*, and certain Chinese tunes which had been zealously transcribed, but in the process translated into Western idiom, by that assiduous scholar in America, Bliss

Wiant. The situation is different now, but it is a familiar fact to Western Christians who serve Christian communities in those continents that the traditional Christians there are as conservative as any traditional Christians at home; the hymns they know and love are in Western idioms and set to Western tunes but this does not worry them at all. The strangeness and 'otherness' of the hymn tunes has the same effect that the language of the King James Bible has on many modern Christians. It has a reassuringly 'churchly' sound, and the idea of using indigenous tunes, often associated with secular or even heathen life-styles, is hardly less alarming to (say) an African Congregationalist than the singing of a hymn to the tune of a sea-shanty would be to at least some English Christians. None the less, the writing of Christian lyrics in the languages of their countries has been encouraged by missionaries, and the adaptation or composition of indigenous tunes has similarly been encouraged, and there are now many collections of such lyrics, especially from African countries, from which material like our Exx. 591-5 can be taken. The melody from Cameroun (Ex. 591) is a traditional funeral-dance, adapted now for an Easter hymn; the Malawi wedding song (Ex. 592) goes with a lyric based on Psalm 148. Ex. 593 first appeared in the American Methodist Hymnal (1966) and is a modern composition from Nigeria. JESU JESU AMEFUFUKA (Ex. 594) is one from a large collection issued in Tanzania. The Malagasy tune (Ex. 595) is less dance-like than the others, less suggestive of primitive drum-beats, and is also a fairly recent composition.

In India the propagation of indigenous music seems to have a mush longer history. As long ago as 1864 an English missionary, the Rev. John Parsons of Monghyr, published a *Hindustani Choral Book*, and this is referred to in the preface of the *North India Tune Book*, edited by Mrs. J. D. Bate of Allahabad in 1886. The tunes there collected mostly fall into two classes, the *Bhajans*, associated with Hindustani texts and presupposing a drum-beat, and the *Ghazals*, associated with Urdu texts, whose traditional accompaniment was the *sitara*, a form of guitar. It will be observed that the almost invariable form of these tunes is 'burden-stanza', and that, like most African tunes, they require a soloist to perform the verses and a congregation to join in the refrains (Ex. 596-8). Our Ex. 599 is a modern tune (part of a longer composition to be found at *Cantate Domino* 28: *Ecumenical Praise* 8); western notation approximates here to the Tamil-style melodic mode by writing it in the harmonic minor key, with invariable flattened sixth and shaprened seventh. A percussion instrument and a melodic instrument are called for in its accompaniment.

Native Chinese hymnody did not have long to develop before the Communist Revolution of 1948. One Chinese tune, our Ex. 600, has become fairly widely known in the West, though in a corrupt version. This tune, which originates in a Buddhist chant and is often sung in the West to 'Let us with gladsome mind' is really pentatonic, like almost all Far Eastern folk music, and our example gives a more primitive form of it. The hymnal *Hymns of Universal Praise,* whose final edition was dated 1948, just before the anti-Christian curtain was lowered, produced some fine lyrics (notably by T. T. Lew, see *Panorama* 586), and some excellent tunes, a few of which have broken through to the West, mostly to America. INDEPENDENCE (Ex. 601) is a particularly good example. One or two English hymnals have taken up SHENG-EN, composed by a Chinese musician Su Yin Lan, born 1912, killed in a Japanese air-raid in 1937.

In later years the tradition of Chinese Christianity has been publicly celebrated only in Taiwan—though nodoby should imagine that in mainland China it is extinguished. The leading Taiwanese musician is Loh I To, a professor at the University of Taiwan, and he has established himself as a major composer of what one might call 'learned' Chinese music. The remarkable tune LIGHT AND SALT (Ex. 603) is one of many hymns and carols he has composed; observe how all three parts in this remarkable 3-part Invention are in the pentatonic scale. It shows that counterpoint, not block harmony, is the true context of Chinese music.

The East Asia Christian Council, in its Hymn Book (1962), edited by the distinguished ecumenical Christian from Sri Lanka, D. T. Niles, collected a good number of hymns from Far Eastern sources, and should be consulted by anyone who is interested. The hymnal of the Thai Christians is also a fertile source of beautiful tunes (for one of which see *Westminster Praise* 35).

Latin America is beginning to produce a hymnody of its own; the most impressive example is our Ex. 604, a sombre and plaintive tune written for a text which breathes the spirit of socially revolutionary Christianity such as thrives in the regions which until so recently were regarded as oppressed and backward. The text is at *Panorama* 590. and the origin is in Brazil. There is a Spanish flavour about the melody which has a good deal in common with the ethos of the classic hymn tunes of Wales.

But we can here only offer a hasty sketch of what is going on in the Christian communities which now are developing their own sacred songs. The twenty-first century, not this one, is the time for assessing this music. We must be content simply to note that there are now few places in which a strong national and indigenous Christian music is not being produced. But we offer our last example (Ex. 605) just to remind the reader what we are being delivered from. It is not easy just now to imagine an Arabic Hymnal; but the obstinate and indomitable missionary spirit of about 1900 was prepared to attempt to 'sell' 'Eternal Father, strong to save' to an Arabic-speaking Christian company, and to print it in the only manner an Arab would find readable. The sight of this reminds us, however, that most of our western transcriptions of Indian or African tunes would look hardly less odd to Indians or Africans. The process of making a truly international and inter-racial hymnody has only just begun; when we recall what the 18th century evangelicals made of TALLIS'S CANON and DAVID'S HARP (Exx. 263-4) we see how cautiously we must walk in this almost uncharted region of hymnody.

CONCLUSION

Hymnody is the organic part of the Church's liturgy. Even those communions which traditionally regard the Creeds as unalterable, or the Scriptures as inerrant, regard, in our time, hymnody as the part of the church's worship which expresses the changing moods and needs of the generations. From this it has followed that while nobody tries to add anything to the Canon of the Bible, and while the rewriting of creeds and liturgies is almost always the work of expert liturgists (who may or may not accurately judge the people's demand for such revisions), hymns and hymn tunes are written by ordinary people, and editors of hymnals are always obliged to consider a mass of new material when they sit down to the work of producing a new collection.

Obviously, some of this material is useless from the start; and some of it is meritable but fails to engage the sympathies of congregations, so it lies 'dead' on the printed page. But the progress of hymnody, and the irrigation of the congregational vocabulary, depend on the continuing work both of those whose work never finds acceptance by editors and of those whose work, favoured by editors, either never or only very slowly receives a welcome in ongoing worship. If the obscure and unsuccessful stop their work, and if the learned who (we think) pitch the demand too high stop theirs, the production of 'winners' will be atrophied. Hymnody, then, is a peculiarly important aspect of the ongoing work of the church.

What we have seen in these pages is how hymnody emerged from the exclusive professionalism of the Middle Ages into the rough-and-tumble of the religious marketplace. If we have been unable to judge some popular hymnody to be great and beneficial hymnody, that is all part of the story; for here, as nowhere else in the building up of common devotion, we live dangerously, and publish our mistakes, and back losers, and reflect that part of the church's life which is at the far end from that dogma and preservation of traditional truth which generate the inspiration for ordinary Christian living.

Our story illustrates the paradox of hymnody: that it is at the same time ecumenical and divisive. On the one hand, for a long time now any congregation has sung hymns and tunes which were composed for traditions with which that congregation is in dissent. 'Praise to the Holiest' and 'Faith of our Fathers' were being sung by protestants long before there was any question of their entering into any kind of encounter with that Roman Catholic Church which had produced them.

On the other—hymns, and especially their music, can become addictive, and produce intolerance between cultures, so that there remain people who are unwilling to take into their tradition anything but American Gospel Songs or Lutheran chorales.

It is for this reason that we have tried to indicate at each stage what people of any culture thought they were doing when they sang hymns. For hymnody remains the folk song of the Christian folk, or *laos*, and the statements people make about their faith are most clearly made in the hymns they choose to sing. In practice we sing our hymns as chosen for us by clergy or musicians who hold places of authority in the churches: but alongside the vocabulary this builds up, there is the vocabulary each Christian builds up for himself or herself, the 'favourite list', the repertory of hymns to which each Christian goes back when the authoritarian pressure is off. It is that repertory which really speaks of the individual faith of the Christian.

All through the ages the skilled writers and composers have sought not only to increase and develop the repertory of the singing congregation but to increase and develop that of the individual Christian. They have done this, as we saw, sometimes by composing and writing new things, sometimes by reviving material long forgotten. So the Christian's faith is nourished by both new and old things, and perhaps especially by old things which appear new because they have been revived after long neglect. Some ages emphasize one side of that, some the other.

As we stare at a future which contains exactly as much assurance and uncertainty as any future holds, there is only one generalization which it is safe to make. That is that in one way or another Christians will always want to sing about what means most to them, and therefore there will always be hymnody. The nearest thing we can offer to a reliable speculation is this: that in the composition of new texts and tunes those who make them will have the best chance of success if they can judge exactly what proportion of originality and what proportion of accepted tradition their new composition contains. What is done for people who are neither literary connoisseurs nor cultivated musicians, and what is designed to become part of their religious lives, must contain something which is already theirs, and something which is newly given.

One might possibly use as an anology what we know as 'The Lord's Prayer'. This, the common liturgical heritage of all Christendom, the archetypal 'folk-prayer', is on the one hand a prayer cast in absolutely traditional Jewish style, and on the other, a prayer implying a totally new notion of what 'Our Father' means. It is, in exactly the right proportions, considered as a pattern offered to a group of people before the Resurrection, original and traditional. So, to compare less exalted things with what remains uniquely sacred, the tune SINE NOMINE for 'For all the saints', combined a large proportion of tradition with a small but vital leavening of originality—and it succeeded. The composer of tomorrow's hymnody must equally love the tradition and have his or her own comment to make on it—or, if they prefer the expression, rebel against it. But no—it is not the contempt and bitterness of rebellion that we want. It is the developing counterpoint of good conversation. It is a conversation which will continue for a long time yet.

1

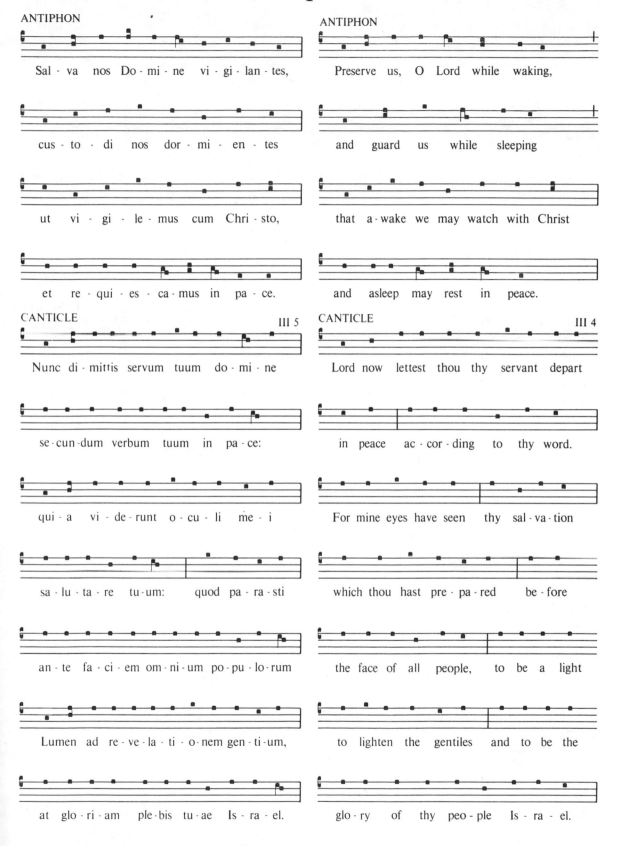

ANTIPHON

Sal - va nos Do - mi - ne vi - gi - lan - tes,

cus - to - di nos dor - mi - en - tes

ut vi - gi - le - mus cum Chri - sto,

et re - qui - es - ca - mus in pa - ce.

CANTICLE   III 5

Nunc di - mittis servum tuum do - mi - ne

se - cun - dum verbum tuum in pa - ce:

qui - a vi - de - runt o - cu - li me - i

sa - lu - ta - re tu - um: quod pa - ra - sti

an - te fa - ci - em om - ni - um po - pu - lo - rum

Lumen ad re - ve - la - ti - o - nem gen - ti - um,

at glo - ri - am ple - bis tu - ae Is - ra - el.

ANTIPHON

Preserve us, O Lord while waking,

and guard us while sleeping

that a - wake we may watch with Christ

and asleep may rest in peace.

CANTICLE   III 4

Lord now lettest thou thy servant depart

in peace ac - cor - ding to thy word.

For mine eyes have seen thy sal - va - tion

which thou hast pre - pa - red be - fore

the face of all people, to be a light

to lighten the gentiles and to be the

glo - ry of thy peo - ple Is - ra - el.

2

MODE I

An - nu - e Chri - ste sae - cu - lo - rum

Do - mi - ne no - bis per hu - ius

ti - bi ca - ri me - ri - ta ut qui te

co - ram gra - vi - ter de - li - qui - mus

hu - ius sol - va - mur

glo - ri - o - sis pre - ci - bus.

3

MODE V

PCH 139   H 164 II

4

MODE VIII

PCH 143

5

Immense Caeli Conditor   MODE II

EH 60

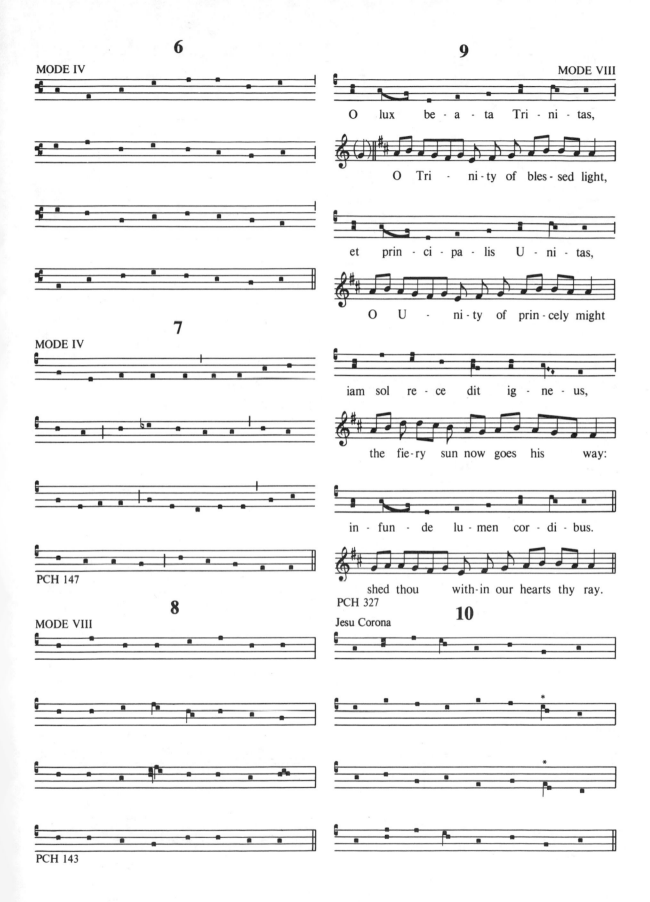

6

MODE IV

7

MODE IV

PCH 147

8

MODE VIII

PCH 143

9

MODE VIII

O lux be - a - ta Tri - ni - tas,

O Tri - ni - ty of bles - sed light,

et prin - ci - pa - lis U - ni - tas,

O U - ni - ty of prin - cely might

iam sol re - ce - dit ig - ne - us,

the fie - ry sun now goes his way:

in - fun - de lu - men cor - di - bus.

shed thou with - in our hearts thy ray.

PCH 327

Jesu Corona

10

11

Veni Redemptor

12

Ve - ni cre - a - tor Spi - ri - tus

men - tes tu - o - rum vi - si - ta

im - ple su - per - na gra - ti - a

quae tu cre - a - sti pe - cto - ra.

PCH 160

13

MODE II

Christ

our Pass -

- o - ver

is sa-cri-ficed.

CLERKS

Christ

our Pass -

- o -

CHORUS

- ver is sa-cri-ficed.

to - res   4. Dic no - bis, Ma - ri - a,
Fa - ther.   Speak, Ma - ry, de - cla - ring,
vi - vus.   5. An - ge - li - cos tes - tes
mor - tal.   Bright an - gels at - tes - ting

4. quid vi - di - sti in vi - a. 5. Se - pul
   what thou sa west way - fa - ring: the tomb
6. su - da - ri - um et ves - tes. 7. Sur - re -
   the shroud and nap - kin rest ing. Yea Christ

14

1. Vic - ti - mae Pas cha - li lau - des
   Christ-ians to the Pas - chal Vic - tim

crum Chri - sti viv - en - tis, et glo - ri -
of Christ who is liv - ing, the glo - ry
xit Chri - stus spes me - a, prae - ce - dit
my hope, is a - ri - sen: to Ga - li -

im - mo - lent Chri - sti - a ni
of - fer your thank - ful prais - es!

am vi - di re - sur - gen - tis.
of Je - sus' re - sur - rec - tion:
su - os in Ga - li - lae - am.
lee____ he goes be - fore you.

2. Ag - nus re - de mit o ves
   A Lamb the sheep re - dee - meth:
3. Mors et vi - ta du - el - lo
   Death and life have con - ten - ded

8. Cre - den - dum est ma - gis so - li
   Hap - py they who hear the wit - ness
9. Sci - mus Chris - tum sur - rex - is - se
   Christ in deed from death is ri - sen,

Chris - tus in - no - cens Pa - tri
Christ who on - ly is sin - less
con - flix - e - re mi - ran - do
in that com - bat stu - pen - dous:

8. Ma - ri - ae ve - ra - ci quam Ju -
   Ma - ry's word be - lie - ving a - bove
9. a mor - tu - is ve - re. Tu no -
   our new life ob - tai - ning. Have mer -

2. re - con - ci - li - a - vit pec - ca -
   re - con - ci leth sin - cers to the
3. dux vi - tae mor - tu - us reg - nat
   The Prince of life who died reigns im -

dae - o - rum tur - bae - fal - la - ci.
the tales of Jew - ry de - cei - ving.
bis Vic - tor rex mi - se - re - re.
cy, Vic - tor King e - ver reig - ning.

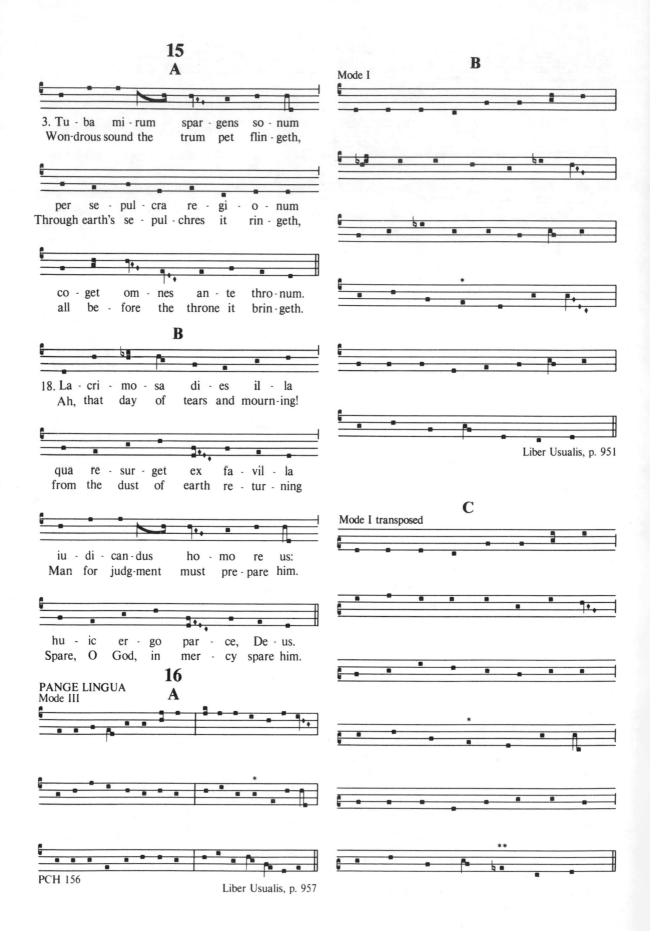

15

A

3. Tu - ba mi - rum spar - gens so - num
Won-drous sound the trum pet flin - geth,

per se - pul - cra re - gi - o - num
Through earth's se - pul - chres it rin - geth,

co - get om - nes an - te thro - num.
all be - fore the throne it brin - geth.

B

18. La - cri - mo - sa di - es il - la
Ah, that day of tears and mourn-ing!

qua re - sur - get ex fa - vil - la
from the dust of earth re - tur - ning

iu - di - can - dus ho - mo re - us:
Man for judg-ment must pre - pare him.

hu - ic er - go par - ce, De - us.
Spare, O God, in mer - cy spare him.

PANGE LINGUA
Mode III

16

A

PCH 156

Liber Usualis, p. 957

B

Mode I

Liber Usualis, p. 951

C

Mode I transposed

17

A

BEATA NOBIS GUADIA

Psalteriolum Chorale, Constance, c.1510

B

AETERNA CHRISTI MUNERA

Cluny ms.

Mode V

C

EH 175: H 132

18

Di - vi - num mys - te - ri - um

Sem - per de - cla - ra - tur.

Et mens in - fi - de - li - um

tu - mens ex - cae - ca - tur,

fir - ma spes cre - den - ti - um

fi - de ro bo - ra - tur.

Di - vi-num mys-te - ri - um

mo-do de-cla-ra - tur, et mens in-fi-de-li-

um tu-mens ex - e - cra - tur

fir - ma spe cre-den - ti - um

fi-des ro-bo-ra - tur.

PCH 155

19

A

En gau-de-at turba fi-de-li-um,

ma-ter vir-go pe-pe-rit fi-li-um

in Beth-le-hem.

B

Con gau - de at

tur - ba__ fi - de - li - um,

Vir - go ma-ter pe-pe - rit

fi - li-um__ in Beth-le - hem.

20

SINGT AUFF, LOBT GOTT

Baeumker I 28, p. 269

21

Mode I

EH 150

LUCIS CREATOR

Lyons Antiphoner, 1738

EH 51

22

JESU DULCEDO
Mode I

AUCTORITATE SAECULI Poitiers Vesperale, 1746

EH 176

23

Mode II

Ut que-ant la - xis   re - so - nar - e   fib ris

mi - ra ges-to - rum   fa-mu-li tu - o - rum,

Sol - ve   pol-lu - ti   la - bi - i

re - a - tum   sanc - te   Jo - an - ncs.

Paris Antiphoner, 1681

EH 191

24

Mode VIII   Beauvais ms. 13th cent.

25

ALTA TRINITA BEATA

26

LAUS TIBI CHRISTE

Nurnberg, 1527
(but older)

Ky-ri-e e-le-i-son.

27

EIN NEUES LIED

Broadsheet, 1523

1.

2.

*

* Thus in 1523 and Erfurt 1524, but in Wittenberg (Walther), 1524 and later, thus:

28

JESU DULCEDO

A

NUN KOMM

B

29

WIR GLAUBEN ALL'

Klug, 1533

30

NUN BITTEN WIR

Walther, 1524

Ky - ri - e - leis.

31

DIES IST DIE ZEHN GEBOT

Enchiridion, 1524

32

NON FREUT EUCH

Achtliederbuch, 1523

* There are no accidentals in the original but almost
certainly they were sung

** F in 1523, but possibly a misprint: D thereafter

33

ES IST DAS HEIL

Etlich Christliche Lieder, 1524

* There are no accidentals in the original, but later usage
makes it clear that the first E and all Bs were flattened.

** Later, E; possibly misprinted in 1524.

34

AUS TIEFER NOTH

Enchiridion, 1524

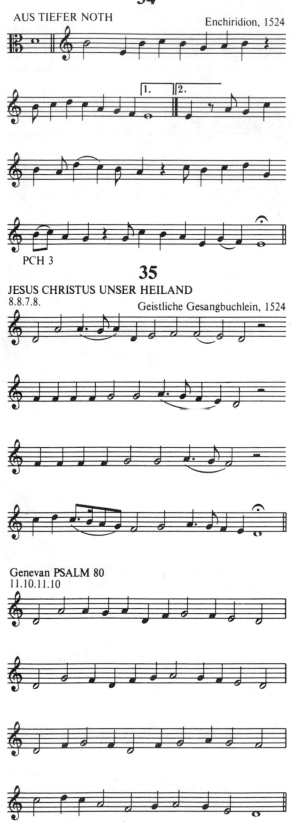

PCH 3

35

JESUS CHRISTUS UNSER HEILAND
8.8.7.8.

Geistliche Gesangbuchlein, 1524

Genevan PSALM 80
11.10.11.10

36

VENI CREATOR

Walther, 1524

(a)

Klug, 1533

37

KOMM HEILIGER GEIST SCHOPFER Enchiridion, 1524

* No flat in key signature in 1524. Later usage suggests the
above distribution of B flats.

** In 1524, F-E-C but this was soon altered and may have
been a 1524 misprint.

Al - le - lu - ia! Al - le - lu - ia!

38

EIN FESTE BURG   Klug 1533

* Walther, 1544, has B hence Bach's version.
** F after 1544
*** F after 1561 Hymnal of the Bohemian Brethren.

PCH 4

39

VATER UNSER   Luther ms.

* (probably misprinted) D (B) in original.

40

VATER UNSER   Schumann, 1539

41

CHRIST UNSER HERR ZUM JORDAN KAMM
8.7.8.7.8.7.8.7.7.
                    1524/1541

47

WAS MEIN GOTT WILL

Erfurt, 1572

Zahn 7568

48

ICH DANK DIR

Magdeburg Gesangbuch

Original final C

49

HERZLICH THUT MICH ERFREUEN

7.6.7.6.D

Walther, 1552

Original final C

50

WIR LOBEN DICH

Wir lo-ben dich ei-mut - ig-lich
Dein kindheit hat die Mis - se that

Herr Je-su Christ_____ der du __ uns bist
da mit wir all_____ durch A - dams fall

ein klei - nes kind ge-bo - ren
ver-dient_ deins va-ters Zo - ren

Ver - soh - net - ganz_____ ein en-glisch ganz

die sel - big Nacht__ gross Freu-den bracht

that uns den Fried ver-kün - den.

Die__ Hir - ten all mit gros-sen Schall

er - furch-ten das ihn selt - sam was

er - le-digt uns_____ von Sün - den.

51

ERSCHIENEN IST

* Later, E - possibly misprinted in original.
** The effective syncopation here appeared later.

52

LOBT GOTT

53

AVE VIRGO

Fine

D.C.

PCH 178

54

MENSCHENKIND

55

NUN LASST UNS GOTT

56

WIE SCHON LEUCHTET

Nicolai, 1597

a

b   ?c

?d

PCH 189

RESONET IN LAUDIBUS

Piae Cantiones, 1582

a

58

EIN FESTE BURG

L. Osiander, 1586

(a)

57

WACHET AUF

PCH 188

PCH 4

59

WACHET AUF

J. Praetorius, 1586-1651

60

ACH BLEIB BEI UNS　**A**

B

PCH 188

61

HERZLICH LIEB HAB ICH
889.889.88.88.44.8   P. Reinigius, 1587

Geistlich Kleinod, 1586

Zahn, 8326

62

Mode II   **A**

EH 61

EIN KIND GEBOR'N   **B**

EH 44

C

63

Ps.130 8.7.8.7.88.7   Kirchenamt, 1525

* Altered 1559 from ♩; ** F in first edition, probably
misprinted E later in 1525

64

Ps. 137 8.7.8.7.8.8.7.8.8.7   Kirchenamt, 1527

Compare ** and * with phrases so marked in Ex. 65.

65

Ps. 36(68)

Final originally F. (a) B♭ (C) in 1551 (b) A♭ (B♭) in 1551

66

Ps. 51, 10.11.11.10.10.11.10.11

70

Ps. 6   G 42

B

PCH 7

71

A

72

Ps. 124   G 51

73

Ps. 141   G 62

cf. Ex. 6

76

Psalm 3   G-51

78

Psalm 107   G 51

(1)

(1) ♩ ♩ in 1547

77

LES COMMANDEMENS   ST 45

rests in 1551

79
A

Psalm 101   G 51

B1

Psalm 101

A-G 1561

(1)

(1) probably misprinted for G's

B2

Parsons, 1563

B3

English, 1570

(1)

(1) Possibly misprint for D

(1)

(1) In 1565 ♩ ♩ as usually sung now.

81

Ps. 23, 11.11.11.11.11.11

G 51

80

Ps. 42, 8.7.8.7.77.88

G 51

82

Ps. 136, 77.77

G 62

83

Ps. 135
G 62

84

Ps. 138, 8.9.8.9.D
G 51

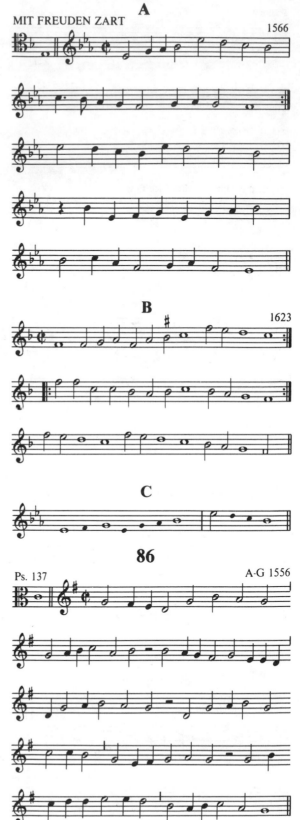

85
A

MIT FREUDEN ZART
1566

B
1623

C

86

Ps. 137
A-G 1556

87

Ps. 23

A-G 1556

88

Ps. 148

(1)

A-G 1558

(2)

(3)

(4)

(1) In later use, from 1592, all rests are omitted. The B at (2) is natural, the note at (3) is full length and that at (4) is half length.

89

Ps. 68

A-G 1558

* almost certainly misprinted for ♭.

90

Ps. 30

A-G 1558

91

Ps. 1

English 1560

95

Ps. 51

English, 1563

97

(Melody in soprano)

TYE c.1553

96

OLD COMMON

Scottish, 1564

* F# in many later versions

* Alto D misprinted B, and corrected in ink, in the British Museum copy.
** Soprano E misprinted D.

100
A

(WINCHESTER OLD) Ps.84

Harm. G. Kirby, Este, 1592

B

Harm. T. Ravenscroft, 1621

101

CHESHIRE (Ps.145)

Harm. J. Farmer, Este, 1592

102

THE STILT (YORK)

Hart, 1615

103

DUMFERMELING TUNE (DUNFERMLINE)

Hart, 1615

104

DUNDEE

Harmonized by T. Ravenscroft
in his Psalms, 1621

105

Nunc Dimittis

A-G 1556, as in Ravenscroft, 1621

(Originally on G)

In A-G 1556 the opening phrase runs (without natural E)

111

OLD 104th

Possibly composed by Ravenscroft, 1621

(1) Ho-nour and ma-jes-ty in thee shine most clear.
(2) That it to a cur-taine com-pa-red may be.

The time signature means ³⁄₁: notes here given at quarter-value.

Later revisions of the last line

Hymns A & M, 1861

Hymns A & M, 1875

English Hymnal, 1906

Hymns for Colleges. & Schools, 1956

112

BON ACCORD

Aberdeen, 1625

O come let us sing to the Lord:

come, let us ev'ry one

a joy-ful

a

a joy-ful noise, a joy-ful

noise make to the Rock, a joy-ful___

joy-ful noise make___ to the Rock make

or (of

noise make to the Rock of our sal -

noise make to the Rock of our sal -

noise make to the Rock of our sal -

to the Rock, the Rock of our sal -

our sal - va - ti - on)

va - ti - on.

va - ti - on.

va - ti - on.

va - ti - on.

Accidentals uncertain here and there.

113

ELGIN   Scottish Psalter, 1625

114

CULROSS   Scottish Psalter, 1634

115

MARTYRS   Scottish Psalter, 1635

* A sharp sign attached to alto F is clearly a misprint.

** Note clash of C and C♯: compare Ravenscroft's version
(1611) of the Coventry Carol (OBC 22) In practice the
alto probably conceded the sharp.

116

WIGTON

Scottish Psalter, 1635

117

GLENLUCE

Scottish Psalter, 1635

118

OLD 137th (in reports)

Scottish Psalter, 1635

Details of underlay remain uncertain: ties or repeated words would cover irregularities. The slurs above indicate the probable allocation of phrases.

Originally in C.

119

LONDON NEW (Ps.50)   Playford, 1671

* In some earlier sources this is D or B. Read small notes
for NEWTOUN, in Scottish Psalter, 1635

120

BRISTOL (Ps. 6)   Playford, 1677

121

A

CHRIST IST ERSTANDEN   Munich ms. 15th cent

Note: The above tune seems to be inexpertly copied in the
Munich ms. It is strictly in the First Mode — Final
D, Dominant A. If the C clef were on the top line
throughout there would be no need for either the
♭ to the B in the above version, or the confusion
caused by its appearance only there, or for the change
of clef, but the initial note of the melody would be on
the third line and the rest would conform.

B

Coverdale, c.1544

Christ   is   now   ris'n   a - gayne

from   his   death   and   all   his   payne

there - fore   will   we   me - ry   be   and   re -

joyse   with   hym   glad - ly   Ki - ri - e - ley - son.

122

Psalm 18   Ainsworth, 1612

I love thee dir, Ie-ho-vah my firm-ness

Ie - ho-vah is my rock and my fort-ress.

and my de - li - ve rer, my God is hee,

my rock in whom I sheltered hope to bee;

my shield and horn, of my sa - va - ti - ō,

my fen-sed hye for - ti - fi - ca - ti - on.

123

OLD DUTCH TUNE   Daman, 1579

DUTCH BASS TUNE   Barton, 1644

124

WINDSOR   Daman, 1591

COLESHILL   Barton, 1644

125

TALLIS III (Psalm 2)   Thomas Tallis, c.1557

* In the original score, written on 4 staves, the bass has a ♮ in the key signature placed on line B, the ten-or on C and the alto on A, with none in the treble.   Bar lines appear where dotted bars are given here.

* misprinted D-E in 1644

126

TALLIS VII (Psalm 52)

Thomas Tallis, c. 1557

* In the original, the treble staff (only) has a ♮ on the B line.

127

TALLIS II (Ps. 68)

129

TALLIS I (Ps. 1)

cf. EH 78

128

TALLIS V (Ps. 42)

WP 34

130

TALLIS IV (Ps. 95)

131

TALLIS VI (Ps. 5)

132

TALLIS IX (ORDINAL)

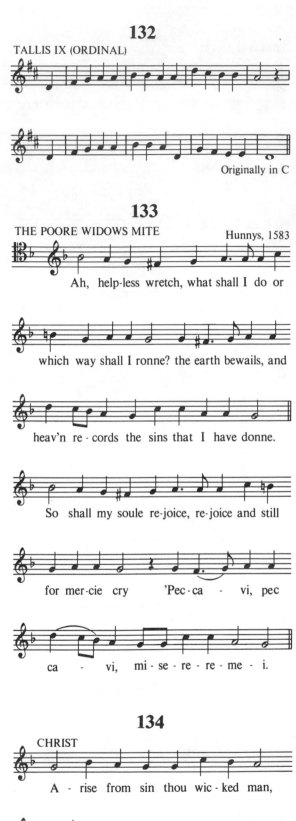

Originally in C

133

THE POORE WIDOWS MITE   Hunnys, 1583

Ah, help-less wretch, what shall I do or

which way shall I ronne? the earth bewails, and

heav'n re - cords the sins that I have donne.

So shall my soule re-joice, re-joice and still

for mer-cie cry   'Pec-ca - vi, pec

ca - vi, mi - se - re - re - me - i.

134

CHRIST

A - rise from sin thou wic - ked man,

be - fore the trump doth sound;

CHRIST

And yet I say, thy ig-no-rance,

shall not thy faults ex cuse.

SINNER

By grace I am re pen-tant made,

wilt thou not mer-cie have? If thou
CHRIST

by grace re pen tant bee, yet thou

must mer-cie crave. O Lord, blot
SINNER

out my fyl-thie deeds, and clense

me from my sinne. A-rise and
CHRIST

walke, thou art made cleane,

as thou be-leev'st there-in.

135

SONG I
O. Gibbons, 1623

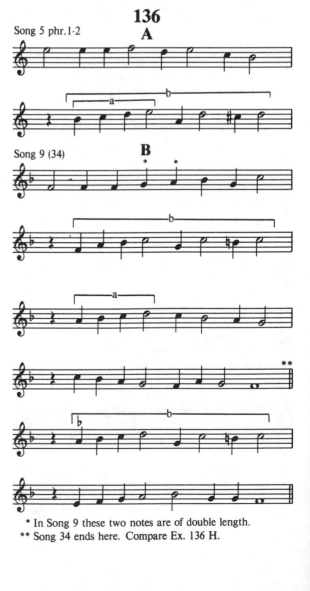

* This bar-line is misplaced by the printer and should stand before the rest.

** In the original the two last phrases are written out again, and a bar line appears, the second time, after the first A.

136

Song 5 phr.1-2
A

B
Song 9 (34)

* In Song 9 these two notes are of double length.
** Song 34 ends here. Compare Ex. 136 H.

Song 13

C

a

* In Farr's edition (1859) this note is misprinted F.

D

Song 14 phr. 1-2

a────c

E

Song 14 phr. 4-5 (6-7)

e

d

F

Song 22 phrases 3-4

d

EH 438: Y 232

G

Song 24 phrase 3(5)

e

H

Song 44

Song 5

137

O prince of peace, who man wast born

that thou might'st die to suc‑cour us,

my foo‑lish tears do thou not scorn,

but be my com‑fort, Christ Je‑sus.

138

Psalm 72   H. Lawes, 1637

d

a

b

145

ST JAMES

R. Courteville, 1697

146

ON THE DIVINE USE OF MUSICK

J. Playford, 1677

We sing to thee whose wis-dom formed

the cu-rious or-gan of the ear:

and thou who gav'st us voi-ces, Lord

our grate-ful songs in kind-ness hear!

147

(DAVID'S HARP) HYMN VII (based on Psalm 101)

R. King

Mer-cy I will and judg-ment sing to

thee, O Lord, from whom they spring;

wis-dom shall all my ways cor-rect,

when wilt thou come and dwell with me?

(My

My whole af-fairs and fa-mi-

whole, my whole)

ly I will with per-fect heart di-rect.

(I will, I will)

EH 378

* Usually thought to be a misprint for A.

** Thus mis-barred in D.C.

148

(TUNBRIDGE) HYMN VI

J. Clarke

E - ver thirs - ty, ne - ver full,

world - ly meat and drink is dull;

souls can ne - ver fit - ly dine

but on heav'n - ly bread and wine.

EH 88

149

(UFFINGHAM) An Evening Hymn
Sett by Mr. Je[remiah] Clarke, 1707

Sleep, dow - ney sleep, come close mine eyes,

Sic.

tir'd with be - hol - ding va - ni - ties.

Wel - come, sweet sleep that driv'st a - way the

toils and fol - lies of the day.

150

(KINGS NORTON) Hymn for Good Friday

J. Clarke

(St.7) If at this sight we don't re -
76

pent, what o - ther sight can move? In -

grate - ful! should we not re -
65   65   #6

lent and pay such love with love!
56

151

BISHOPTHORPE

? J. Clarke II

153

(NEW 100th)

John Blow

* Usually thought to be misprinted for G.

152

(CROFT'S 136th) A Psalm
Set by Mr. William Crofts

154

Hymn XIII SM

Divine Companion, 1707

Let o - thers take their course, and sing _____ what name they please: Let wealth or beau - ty be their theam, such emp - ty, emp - ty sounds as these.

155

Psalm 149

John Church

* In original, F - clearly misprinted.

156

NEW 50th

1708

157

THE CREED, DCM

1708

* The bass note under this is F, so it may be misprinted for C.

158

St. Anne's Tune,   1708

As pants the hart for coo - ling

streams when hea - ted in the chase -

so longs my soul, O God for

thee and thy re - fresh-ing grace.

PCH 15

159

(FOLKINGHAM)   1708

* This note altered to D in EH 558: bass of original being A accommodates either.

160

ILLSLEY (Ps. 100)   J. Bishop, 1711

* Usually now interpreted as tenor C♯ on last beat.

161

CHICHESTER (Ps. 122)   J. Bishop

162

BATH (Ps. 148)   J. Bishop, 1711

163

(OLD 104th)   arr. James Green, 1715

164

A

NUNC DIMITTIS 66.7D

Bourgeois, 1547

B

The same, 66.8.D

J. Green, 1715

165

WALSALL

Anchors, Psalms, 1721

EH 13, Originally in A minor.

166

BANGOR

William Tans'ur, 1734

167

(SURREY) Psalm the 23d Paraphrased by Mr. Addison
Set to Musick by Mr. H. Carey, (1723)

PCH 46

EH 491

168

LONDON (or ADDISON'S) DLM
last line repeated

J. Sheeles, c.1740

169

WIR CHRISTENLEUT 4.4.11.D

Dresden, 1593

170

SELLINGER'S ROUND

16th cent.

171

A

ROWLAND

'Queen Elizabeth's Virginal Book'

PCH 48

EH 297

B

IST GOTT FUR MICH

Augsburg, 1609

172

FÜR DEIN EMPFANGEN SPEIS UND TRANK

Gorlitz, 1599

* These two notes reversed in EH 549.

173

Vulpius, 1609

174

GELOBT SEI GOTT

Vulpius, 1609

175

DAS NEUGEBORNE KINDELEIN

Vulpius, 1609

176

MEIN G'MUTH IST MIR VERWIRRET

Hassler, 1601

PCH 194

177

HERR JESU CHRIST MEINS LEBENS LICHT

As Hymnodus Sacer, 1625

183

Psalm 45

Schütz, 1628

182

Psalm 84

Schütz, 1628

184

LASSET UNS DEN HERREN PREISEN

J. Schop, 1641

Zahn 7886 a

185

CHRISTE DU BEISTAND 11.11.11.5

M. A. von Lowenstern, 1644

PCH 190   EH 160

186

NUN DANKET ALLE GOTT

Cruger ? 1636

PCH 192   cf. EH 533

187

HERZLIEBSTER JESU

Crüger, 1640

PCH 191   Zahn 983 cf. EH 70

188

SCHMÜCKE DICH

Crüger, 1653

PCH 196   EH 306

189

NUN DANKET ALL' UND BRINGET EHR — Cruger, 1653

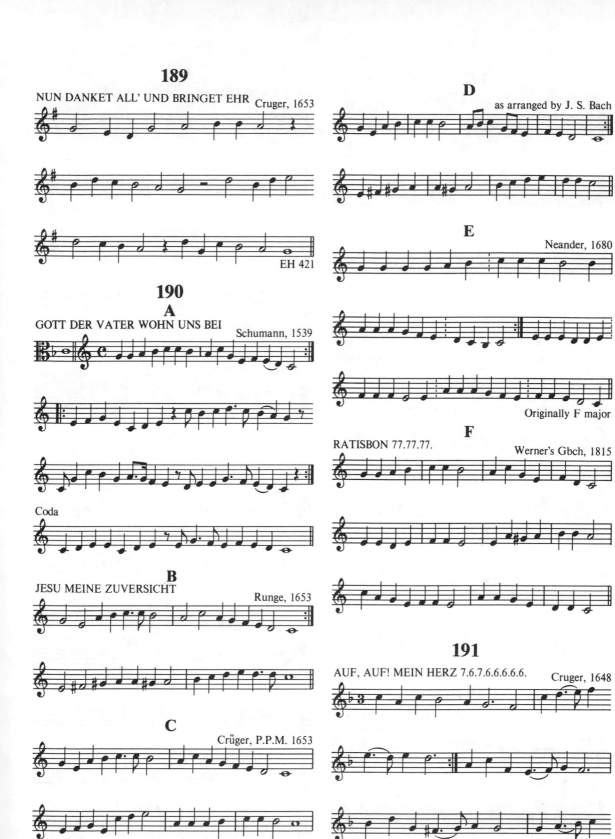

EH 421

190

A

GOTT DER VATER WOHN UNS BEI — Schumann, 1539

Coda

B

JESU MEINE ZUVERSICHT — Runge, 1653

C

Crüger, P.P.M. 1653

D

as arranged by J. S. Bach

E

Neander, 1680

Originally F major

F

RATISBON 77.77.77. — Werner's Gbch, 1815

191

AUF, AUF! MEIN HERZ 7.6.7.6.6.6.6.6. — Cruger, 1648

Zahn, 5243

192

JESU MEINE FREUDE 6.6.5.6.6.5.7.8.6

Peter, 1655

Zahn 8033

193

DAS HERRLICH HÖHE FEST 6.6.6.6.6.6.8.

Peter, 1667

EH 182

194

WARUM SOLLT ICH MICH DENN GRAMEN 8.3.3.6.D

Ebeling, 1666

195

MERKT AUF (DU MEINE SEELE SINGEN) 7.6.7.6.D

Ebeling, 1666

196

DIES IST DER TAG

Söhren, 1668

EH 138ii

197

GEH AUF, MEINS HERZENS MORGENSTERN

8.7.8.7.44.7.44.7. iambic   Joseph, 1657

Zahn, 7612

203

A

HAST DU DENN, JESU

Stralsund, 1665

B

Praxis Pietatis, 1668

PCH 199

204

KOMM SEELE

J. W. Franck, 1681

cf. EH 486

205

O GOTT DU FROMMER GOTT

Hanover, 1646

Hamburg, 1690

* Sharpened in Lüneburg Gbch, 1665

206

O GOTT DU FROMMER GOTT

Meiningen, 1693

207

A

A. Fritsch, 1679

207

B

arr. J.S. Bach

208

WER NUR DEN LIEBEN GOTT LASST WALTEN

Hamburg, 1690

Bracketed portions are extensions in DIR DIR JEHOVA,
Freylinghausen, 1704

209

WAS DER GOTT THUT 4x (4.4.11)

Was dein gott thut ist al-les gut
Dein Küm-mer-nis kann er ge-wiss

blei-ben be-fiehl in al-le dei-
bald en-den und dich wie-der rü-

ne sa____ chen. Ab es gleich scheint,
hog ma- chen.

er sei dein feind, wenn du das

Kreuz-ge wit-ter hör-rest tra - chen

Bei got-tes Hut sei-wohl-ge - nut;

denn sei-ne Kraft ist mach-tig in den Schwa-chen.

(Zahn 8221)

210

MORGENSTERN 7.7.3.3.7

Freylinghausen, 1705

211

DAS IST MEINE FREUDE 7.6.7.6.77.6

Freylinghausen, 1704

EH 97

212

A

FAHRE FORT 6.7.8.7.8.7.6

Freylinghausen, 1704

Zahn 4791

B

O QUAM MUNDUM (8.7.8.7.D)

Piae Cantiones, 1582

213

SOLLT ES GLEICH BISWEILEN SCHEINEN
(STUTTGART) 8.8.7.7.

C. F. Witt, 1715

cf. EH 40

214

GOTT WILLS MACHEN 8.7.8.7.

J. L. Steiner, 1735

EH 253

215

WAS IST, DAS MICH BETRUBT

König, 1738

Zahn, 2207

226

SCHMAL IST DER PFAD 11.6.11.6.

Knecht, 1793

Zahn 870

227

STARK UNS, MITTLER

7.6.7.6.7.8.7.6.6.9.5.6.7.5.

Knecht, 1793

Zahn 8506

228

ZU MEINEN HERREN 11.10.11.10

J. G. Schicht, 1819

Zahn 903

229

TREUER HEILAND 7.6.7.6.7.7.6.

Kocher, 1838

Zahn 4809

230

MORGENGLANZ DER EWIGKEIT

7.8.7.8.3.

Filitz 1847

Zahn 3430

231

AUF, AUF, WEIL DER TAG ERSCHIENEN
8.8.7.7.8.8.8.

Filitz, 1847

Zahn 4921

232

BESCHWERTES HERZ 9.8.9.8.9.8.8.9.

J. Zahn, 1853

Zahn 5999

233

WACHET AUF

PCH 188

234
CHRISTUS DER IST MEIN LEBEN

235
A

WERDE MUNTER

J. Schop, 1641

B

1. Je - sus, name, all names a - bove,
2. Thou didst call the Prod - i - gal;
3. Je - sus, o - pen me the gate

Je - sus, best and dear - est,
thou didst par - don Mar - y:
that the rob - ber en - ter'd.

Je - sus, Fount of per - fect love,
Thou whose words can nev - er fall,
who in that most lost e - state

ho - liest, ten - d'rest, near - est,
love can nev - er var - y:
whol - ly on thee ven - tur'd.

Je - sus, Source of grace com - plet - est,
Lord, to heal my lost con - di - tion
Thou whose wounds are ev - er plead - ing,

Je - sus, pur - est, Je - sus sweet - est,
give (for thou canst give) con - tri - tion;
and thy Pas - sion in - ter - ce - ding,

Je - sus, well of pow'r di - vine,
Thou canst par - don all my ill
From my sins, O let me rise

make me, keep me, seal me Thing!
if thou wilt: O say, "I will!"
to a home in Par - a - dise!

PCH 186

236

PCH 194

237

MACH'S MIT MIR, GOTT   arr. J.S.Bach

cf. EH 138

238

ACH GOTT UND HERR

A

1625

B

1640

C

1655

D

J.S.Bach

E

J.S.Bach Cantata 48

239

ICH HALTE TREULICH STILL

1736 S.466

EH 644

240

DIR, DIR, JEHOVA

1736 S.452

SP 93

241

EINS IST NOTH!

1736, S.453

242

A

SALVE CORDIS GAUDIUM

c.1664

Sal - ve cor - dis gau - di - um sal - ve Je - su!

pec - to - ris in - cen - di - um, sal - ve Je - su!

a - ni - mae prae - si - di - um,

sal - ve Je - su, bo - ne sal - ve Je - su.

B

JESU MEINES HERTZENS FREUD

arr. J.S.Bach

243

Hanover (Ps. 67)

? W. Croft, 1708

AM 367

C

(the same)

arr. J.S.Bach 1736, S.473

244

Lyra Davidica, 1708

PCH 78

245

STROUDWATER

Wilkins's Psalter, 1725

246

WAREHAM (Ps. 36 vv 5-10) LM
W. Knapp, 1738

247

SPETISBURY (Ps. 149 or 104 o.v.)
W. Knapp, 1738

248

MOTTRAM (STOCKPORT) 6x10
J. Wainwright, 1750

PCH 49

249

ST BRIDE SM.
S. Howard, 1762

250

ST BARTHOLOMEW LM.
T. Duncalf, 1762

251

PORTSEA 8.7.8.7.

W. Boyce, 1765

252

DARWALL (Ps. 148) 6.6.6.6.4.4.4.4.

J. Darwall, 1770

253

MAGDALEN COLLEGE 8.8.6.D (Ps.122)

W. Hayes, 1774

Original key D.
EH 457

254

HAYES D.C.M.

W. Hayes, 1770

255

OXFORD CM.

? Coombs, 1770

256

ABRIDGE Watts Ps. 47

I. Smith, c.1780

EH 369

257

Tunbridge 10.11.10.11. Anapaestic

A. Williams Psalmody, c.1785

All ye that pass by, to Je - sus draw nigh.

cf. EH 107

258

UNIVERSITY

C. Collignon (d.1785) 1794

EH 93

Originally in D.

259

ISLINGTON LM.

Foundery, 1742

Bro - ther in Christ and well be-

lov'd to Je - sus and his ser - vants

dear, en - ter and show thy - self ap-

prov'd, en - ter and find, en - ter and

find that God is here.

260

INVITATION (KENT) LM.

J. F. Lampe, 1746

261

HOTHAM 7.7.7.7.D   Butts, c. 1755

O re - ceive, O re - ceive;

O re - ceive my soul at last.

262

FULHAM LMD   Butts, c. 1755

Our Lord is ri - sen from the

dead, our Je - sus is gone up on

high! The powers of hell are

cap - tive led, dragg'd to the

por - tals of the sky.

263

BRENTWOOD LM. 1754

264

SCARBOROUGH 88.88.88. Lock, 1769

265

MANSFIELD LM.

Lock, 1769

A - wake, our, souls, a -

ways, our fears, let ev 'ry

trem bling thought be gone; a -

wake and run the heav'n - ly

a wake and run the

race, and put a cheer - ful

heav'n - ly race and put a cheer-ful

cou - rage on, and put a

cou - rage on, and put a

cheer - ful cou - rage on.

cheer - ful cou - rage on?

PCH 36

266

RONDEAU CM.

Lock, 1769

Sweet is the mem 'ry of thy

love my God, my heav'n - ly King (Sweet

is the mem 'ry of thy love) let

age to age thy right - eous

ness in sounds of glo - ry sing (Sweet

is the mem - 'ry of thy love).

269

MILES LANE — W. Shrubsole, 1779

PCH 84   cf. EH 364

270

CHESTERFIELD — T. Haweis, 1792

dear Lord, remember me, remember me, re-member me, dear Lord, re - mem - ber me.

PCH 103   cf. EH 471

271

EXETER D.C.M. — T. Jackson, 1796

Note: This tune is here scored according to the custom of the time. The top part is the alto, the lower part in the treble staff the tenor, both written an octave above the sung pitch. The people's part in the tenor would be sung at both pitches. Only the bass is where we expect to find it. Ex. 285 was similar.

* From here to the end the down-tail part is for bassoon.

cf. EH 476

273

CANNONS LM.   Handel, c. 1747

EH 66

272

GOPSAL   Handel, c. 1747

274

FITZWILLIAM 8.8.6.D   Handel, c. 1747

PCH 65

275

PCH 82   cf. EH 393

276

ITALIAN HYMN (MOSCOW) 6.6.5.6.6.6.5.

F. Giardini, 1769

cf. EH 553

277

CHRISTE SANCTORUM Sapphic — Paris, 1681

cf. EH 165

* 1-rest understood here   ** 1/2 rest here.

278

UT QUEANT LAXIS Sapphic — Paris, 1681

cf. EH 191

279

AUCTORITATE SECULI LM.

cf. EH 176

280

AD TUUM NOMEM sapphic — Chartres, 1784

cf. EH 188

281

VOS SANCTI PROCERES 6.6.6.6.7.8. — Paris, 1681

AM 37

282

REGNATOR ORBIS Alcaic — Paris, 1681

cf. EH 465

283

THURE FUMANTES Sapphic

Paris, 1681

cf. EH 174

* This tune alone has dotted neums (■·) which appear at these points only.

** Here Pocknee's transcription has a 1-note (■) here interpreted as a 1/2 (♦)

284

REX GLORIOSE LM.

* This seems the most plausible interpretation of diamond - oblong - diamond.

285

PORTUGUESE

as in J. Rippon, c. 1795

Be-gone, un-be-lief, my sa-vior is

(LM)

Lord 'tis a plea-sant thing to

near,— and for my re-lief with

stand — in gar - dens plan - ted

sure-ly ap-pear. By pray'r let me

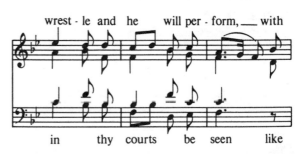

by thy hand. Let me with

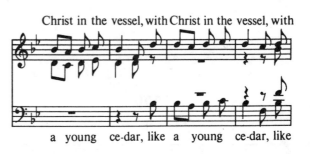

in thy courts be seen like

Christ in the vessel, with Christ in the vessel, with

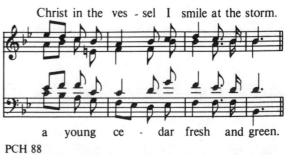

a young ce-dar, like a young ce-dar, like

Christ in the ves - sel I smile at the storm.

a young ce - dar fresh and green.

PCH 88

Transcribed with the parts at sung pitch.
See note at Ex. 269.

292

HIC BREVE VIVITUR CM. (Ps. 42) A. Pettet, 1826

293

BIRMINGHAM LM. F. Cunningham, 1834

294

WARSAW (? Ps. 148) ? T. Clark, 1832

295

ST PAUL Tait, 1749

296

GLASGOW Moore, 1756

297

MONTROSE ? 1746

298

ST. GEORGE'S EDINBURGH. (D.C.M.)

Andrew Mitchell Thomson,
Psalm XXIV. 7-10   1778-1831

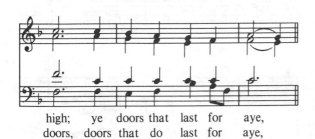

7. Ye gates, lift up your heads on
8. Ye gates, lift up your heads; ye

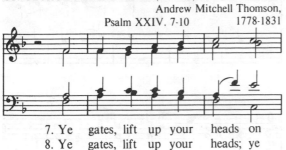

high; ye doors that last for aye,
doors, doors that do last for aye,

Be lift-ed up, that so the King of
Be lift-ed up, that so the King of

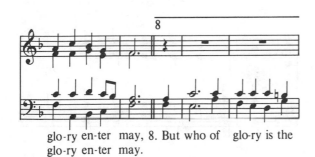

glo-ry en-ter may, 8. But who of glo-ry is the
glo-ry en-ter may.

King? The migh-ty Lord is this;

10. But who is he that is the

King, the King of glo-ry? who is this?

Ev'n that same Lord, that great in might and
The Lord of hosts, and none but he, the

strong in bat-tle is. Ev'n that same Lord, that
King of glo-ry is. The Lord of hosts, and

great in might and strong in bat-tle is.
none but he, the King of glo-ry is.

Coda

Hal - le - lu - jah! hal - le - lu - jah! hal - le - lu - jah!

hal‑le‑lu‑jah! hal‑le‑lu‑jah! A ‑ men,

A ‑ men, A ‑ men.

299

TRIUMPH D.C.M (Par. 20)

Z. Wyvill, 1802
in R. A. Smith, 1820

300

KILAMRNOCK C.M.

N. Dougal, 1831

301

STRACATHRO C.M.

C. W. Hutcheson, 1832

302

ORLINGTON C.M.+

J. Camppell, 1854

303

NORWOOD 7.7.7.7.

arr. T. Attwood

The Psalmist (1835) I 86

304

BAUN 8.7.8.7.

arr. Gauntlett

The Psalmist (1841) III 282

305

PLUMSTEAD L.M.D.

arr. V. Novello

The Psalmist (1843) IV 372

306

PORTLAND 77.77.77.

T. Cooke

The Psalmist (1837) II 180

307

A

See also:
Musical Times Sept. 1966 p. 772, and Nov. 1966 p. 968, on which the reader should on no account miss Professor Temperley's abusive reference to the present author.

PCH 172

BONE JESU

Bo - ne Je - su dul - cis _____ cunc - tis
Te pre - ca - mur pro de - fune - tis

ae - ter - ni Pa - tris fi - li - us
as - sis e - is pro - pi - ti - us.

vul - ne - ra pan - de ci - ti - us

pa - tri pro tu - o fa - mu - lo

ut - fru - a - tur u - ber - ri - us

tu - i per - en - ne gau - di - o.

15th century Processional, Paris Bibl Nat. Fonds Latin ms. 10. 581. The book belonged to a community of Franciscan nuns, and this melody is set to verses which form a Trope on the funeral antiphon Libera me. Hence the setting for two equal voices. The AABA' form of the melody and its very regular pattern suggest an extra - liturgical origin of the form of many French Noels and Welsh hymn tunes.

B

VENI EMMANUEL   Helmore, 1858

308

O LUX BEATA

Helmore, 1852

PCH 327

309

DIVINUM MYSTERIUM

Helmore, 1858

310

DORTMUND

Havergal, 1847

TROCHAIC

DOXOLOGY

311

ST. CHRYSOSTOM CM.

W. H. Havergal, c. 1830

A - men.

312

SMYRNA (Double counterpoint)

Havergal, c. 1836

O God our help in a - ges past,

our hope for years to come,

Our shelter from the stor - my blast

and our e - ter - nal home.

313

CONTEMPLATION

F. A. G. Ouseley, 1889

314

LINDISFARNE

Dykes, 1857

315

A

ST. OSWALD

1857

B

GERONTIUS CM.

1868

PCH 442

318

LUX VERA 10.6.10.6.

J.B. Dykes, 1872

AMS 679

319

GETHSEMANE

J. B. Dykes, 1862

cresc.

f

cresc. *dim.*

PCH 80

320

SANCTUARY 15.15.15.15.

Alla marcia

J. B. Dykes, 1875

Composer's note: First two lines in verses 4 and 5 should be sung in unison.

AMS 436

321

BOSNIA 8.6.55.8. Dykes posth.

322

CEPHAS 6.6.6.6.8.8. W. H. Monk, 1861

323

ST CONSTANTINE 6.5.6.5. W. H. Monk, 1861

AM 194

324

MELTON MOWBRAY 9.6.9.6.4.9.6.9.6.

W. H. Monk, 1889

The voice of God's cre-a-tion found me

per - plex'd midst hope and fear, for

though his sunshine flash'd a - round me, his

Sop.2 Ten. in octaves

storms at times drew near. And I said:

Small notes on org.
without octaves

Oh that I knew where he a -

bi - deth, for doubts be - set our

lot, and lo! his glo-rious face he

*rall.

hi - deth and men per - ceive it not!

AMS 530

* No pause in verses 2 and 3.

325

ST BERNARD

W. H. Monk, 1861

AM 188

326

WELLINGTON LM

H. J. Gauntlett, c. 1835

Psalmist II 168

327

ST ALBINUS

H. J. Gauntlett, 1852

* Last phrase added later.

328

ST ALPHEGE'S TUNE Bold 7.6.7.6.

H. J. Gauntlett, 1852

Al - le - lu - ia!

329

MALDON 8.8.8.6 Tr.　　　　　　　　H. J. Gauntlett, 1865

Lo,____ the storms of life are
Faith - less fears our hearts are

break - - ing
shak - - ing For our

suc - cour un - der - tak - ing, Lord____

____ and Sa - viour, Lord____ and____

sa - viour help - us.

cf. Ps. 475

330

ST BARNABAS 11.10.11.10.　　　　　　　Gauntlett, 1875

PCH 246

331

PILGRIMS 11.10.11.10.9.11.   H. Smart, 1868

333

WRAYSBURY 8.7.8.6.   E. J. Hopkins
Slowly and smoothly

332

ST. HUGH CM.   E. J. Hopkins, 1862

Note: Hopkins in his own manuscripts always insisted on marking the beats between stanzas with the appropriate rests, and on substituting breath-marks for double line bars to mark the ends of phrases. In isometric LM tunes, he wrote a roman figure I at the ends of phrases to indicate a one-beat pause.

334

ST. CHRYSOSTOM 6x8

J. Barnby, 1871

335

LONGWOOD

J. Barnby, 1872

336

THE FOE (St.I)

J. Barnby, 1889

337

VENI SPIRITUS SM.

Slow

J. Stainer, 1898

PCH 253

338

ALL FOR JESUS   8.7.8.7

J. Stainer, 1887

339

REST 6x8

J. Stainer, 1875

Voices in unison

Harmony

340

PER RECTE ET RETRO

J. Stainer c. 1898

341

COELESTIS CURIA

J. Stainer ms.

Collected Hymn Tunes. 8

342

Ballet #2 from
Schubert, Rosamunde, D. 797

Str.

w.w.

343

FALFIELD 8.7.8.7.D

A. Sullivan, 1867

PCH 66

344

Hushed was the Evening Hymn
6.6.6.6.8.8.

A. Sullivan, 1872

Unison

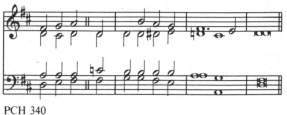

PCH 340

345

ANGEL VOICES 8.5.8.5.8.4.3.

A. Sullivan, 1872

346

BISHOPGARTH 8.7.8.7.D iambic

A. Sullivan, 1897

347

WIGAN 6.6.6.4.8.8.4.

S. S. Wesley, 1872

348

Thou God of Glorious Majesty

CORNWALL 8.8.6.D

S. S. Wesley, 1872

AM 212

AM 195

349

BRECKNOCK 6x8

S. S. Wesley, 1872

PCH 55

350

WHITBY 8.8.8.3.

S. S. Wesley, 1872

PCH 225

351
A

ORISONS (539) 4x10
In unison

S. S. Wesley, 1872

PCH 128

352

WINSCOTT (a) LM.   S. S. Wesley, c. 1862

E. Ps. 370

WINSCOTT (b)   S. S. Wesley, c. 1869

B

ORISONS (540) 4x10
                                 S. S. Wesley, 1872

E. Ps. 589

354

CHRISTCHURCH 6.6.6.6.88

C. Steggall, 1855

353

ELTHAM LM.

Harmonia Perfecta, 1730
Harm. S. S. Wesley, 1872

AM 280

355

CHURCH TRIUMPHANT LM.

J. W. Elliott, 1874

AM 40

356

CRUCIS VICTORIA CM

M. B. Foster, 1889

357

ST. JEROME 6x8

F. Champneys, 1889

PCH 201 B

358

THE INDWELLING SPIRIT 9.8.9.8.   C. C. Scholefield
c. 1903 (1905)

Worship Song 155

359

INTERCESSION
1852

360

REQUIEM 8.7.8.7.8.7.   W. Schulthes, 1816-79

361

A CHRISTMAS CAROL D.C.M. +   from J. M. Haydn

The an-gels sing a - round the stall where

Je - sus cra - dled lies,   the

shepherds hear   the   joy - ful call that

wakes the si - lent skies.   Hark

to   the mu - sic floa - ting by,   ere

yet its e - choes cease!   Poured

forth from an - gels min-strel-sy   is

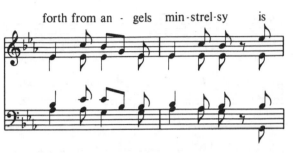

heard the song   of   peace

peace: poured

is

forth   from an - gels   minstrel - sy   is

heard   the song   of   peace.

heard   the song   of   peace.

Arundel Hymns, 1902 #39

362

DEEP HARMONY LM.

H. Parker, 1857-1929

363

RIMINGTON LM.

F. Duckworth, 1862-1941

364

ARIZONA LM.

R. H. Earnshaw, 1856-1929

368

FRESHWATER

C. H. H. Parry, 1893

Sun - set and ev' - ning star, and
Twi - light and ev'. - ning bell, and

one clear call for me! And
af - ter that the dark! And

may there be no moa - ning of the
may there he no sad - ness of fare

bar when I put out to sea,
well when I em - bark:

but such a tide as mo-ving seems a-
for though from out our bourne of time and

cresc.

sleep, too full for sound and foam, when
place the flood may bear me far, I

that which drew from out the bound-less
hope to see my Pi - lot fade to

deep turns a - gain home.
face when I have crossed the bar.

C. H. H. Parry, 1853

369

JERUSALEM

C. H. H. Parry, 1916

370

ALVERSTONE CM.
vv 1, 7

C. V. Stanford, 1924

Praise to the Ho - li - est in the height and in the depth be praise: in all his words most won der ful, most sure in all his ways.

vv 2-6 (originally unit, ♩ = ♪)

PCH 442

371

HAPPY ARE THEY CM.

Charles Wood, ms.

373

GUNDULF 10.4.10.4.10.10.

B. Luard Selby, 1904

372

CAMBRIDGE 66.65.65.

Charles Wood, 1925

374

BATTLE CRY

Alan Gray, 1916

375

CUMNOR 6.7.6.7.

Basil Harwood, 1908

PCH 292

376

RAGLETH HILL CM.

Basil Harwood, 1908

377

CLAMAVI 8.8.8.8.88

E. C. Bairstow, 1904

PCH 429

PCH 55

378

HAMPSTEAD 8.8.8.8.6   H. Walford Davies, 1915

O love that with not let me go.

* In Hymns A & M, 1916, the treble note is B.

PCH 344

379

TEMPLE 6.6.8.4.   H. Walford Davies, 1906

380

VISION   H. Walford Davies, 1915

Mar - ching on   (mar-ching on)

PCH 376

Al - le - lu - ia!

Al - le - lu - ia!

381

RESURRECTION 7.8.7.8.4.   H. Walford Davies, 1923

382

CHRISTMAS CAROL (end)   1905

GOD BE IN MY HEAD   1910

QUINTA   1923

O   Lord our God, a - rise

RESURRECTION   1923

Je - sus   lives!

WENGEN (end)   1916

ETHERINGTON
1923
Hark, the glad sound the Sa - viour comes

SEGENBALM (3rd phrase)
1923

FIRMAMENT (3rd phrase)
1923

WALLOG
1923

383

BRAINT 2.88.8.88.8.

384

A

Can love be con-troll'd by ad - vice? can

mad-ness and rea - son a - gree? O

Ma - ry, who'd e - ver be wise if

madness be lov - ing of thee? Let

sa - ges pre-tend to des - pise the

joys they want spi rit to taste: Let

us seize of Time as he flies, and the

bles-sings of life while they last.

B

CYFAMOD 9.8.9.8.D
from a Welsh folk song, before 1761

390

LLANGEITHO 7.6.7.6.7.8.7.6.

1839

391

CRUGYBAR

1846

Fine

D.C.

392

EIFIONTDD 8.7.8.7.D.

John Ambrose Lloyd, 1848

393

MOAB 6.5.6.5.666.5.

Ieuan Gwyllt, 1869

394

TREWEN 8.8.8.8.D anapaestic   D. Emlyn Evans, 1883

398

PARIS LM.

W. Billings, c. 1776

399

WHEN JUST WEPT

① LM. round

W. Billings, 1770

②

③

④

400

BETHLEHEM

W. Billings

The an-gel of the Lord came

The

The an-gel of the

The an-gel of the Lord came down and

down and glo-ry shone a-round,

an-gel of the Lord came down and

Lord came down and glo-ry shone a-

glo-ry shone and glo-ry shone a-

401

CORONATION CM +

O. Holden, 1793

PCH 84

402

HAMBURG

Lowell Mason, 1824

Tone 1

ending 1

ending 2

PCH 38

403

UXBRIDGE LM.

Lowell Mason, 1830

404

ELTON LM.

Lowell Mason, 1854

405

PARK STREET, LM +

F. M. A. Venua, c. 1810

406

BOYLESTON SM.

Lowell Mason, 1832

413

LOUVAN LM. V. C. Taylor, 1846

PCH 375

414

RATHBUN 8.7.8.7. I. Conkey, 1849

PCH 114

415

BEECHER 8.7.8.7.D J. Zundel, 1870

416

ALL SAINTS NEW DCM

H. S. Cutler, 1872

417

CUSHMAN 11.10.11.10.

H. B. Turner, 1905

418

MOUNT ZION   D.C.M.   Horatio Parker, 1886

H. (U.S.A.) 390

419

KEDRON, LM

Wyeth's Repository II 1813 p. 43
Kentucky Harmony, 1816

420

CONSOLATION C.M.   Wyeth's Repository II 1813 p. 20

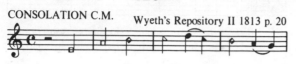

* These 2 bars should have notes of double value.

421

TWENTY-FOURTH C.M.   Wyeth's Repository II, 1813 p. 20

* Tune re-barred: in original these notes are semibreves

422

NEW MONMOUTH 8.7.8.7.D   Wyeth's Repository II, 1813 p. 104

423

ZION'S PILGRIM 11.8.11.8.D   Christian Lyre, 1831

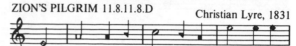

Fine

D.C.

424

BABYLONIAN CAPTIVITY 10.10.10.10.   Wyeth's Repository II, 1813 p. 39

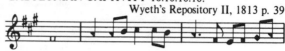

425

A

GANGES 8.8.6.D   Wyeth's Repository II, 1813 p. 98

B

ADVENT 88.6.D   Plymouth Collection, 1855

Teach me some me-lo-dious son-net
Hal-le-lu - jah, hal-le-lu-jah,

sung by fla - ming tongues a-bove: Praise the
we are on our journey home: hal-le -

mount, O fix me on it, mount of
lu - jah, hal-le-lu - jah, we are

God's un - chang ing love.
on our journey home.

426

A

HALLELUJAH 8.7.8.7.D   Wyeth's Repository II, 1813 p. 112

Come thou fount of ev'-ry bles-sing,
Streams of mer-cy ne-ver cea-sing

tune my heart to sing thy grace.
call for songs of lou-dest praise.

B

NETTLETON   modern form of the above

427

PISGAH C.M. +

J. C. Lowry, 1818

Je - sus, thou art the sin-ner's friend; as

O Lord, re - mem-ber me, O

such I look to thee; now in the bo-wels

Lord, re-mem-ber me, now in the bo-wels

of thy love, O Lord, re - mem-ber me.

of thy love, O Lord, re-mem-ber me.

* Misprinted C-G in Wyeth.
** Notes outside the pentatonic scale.

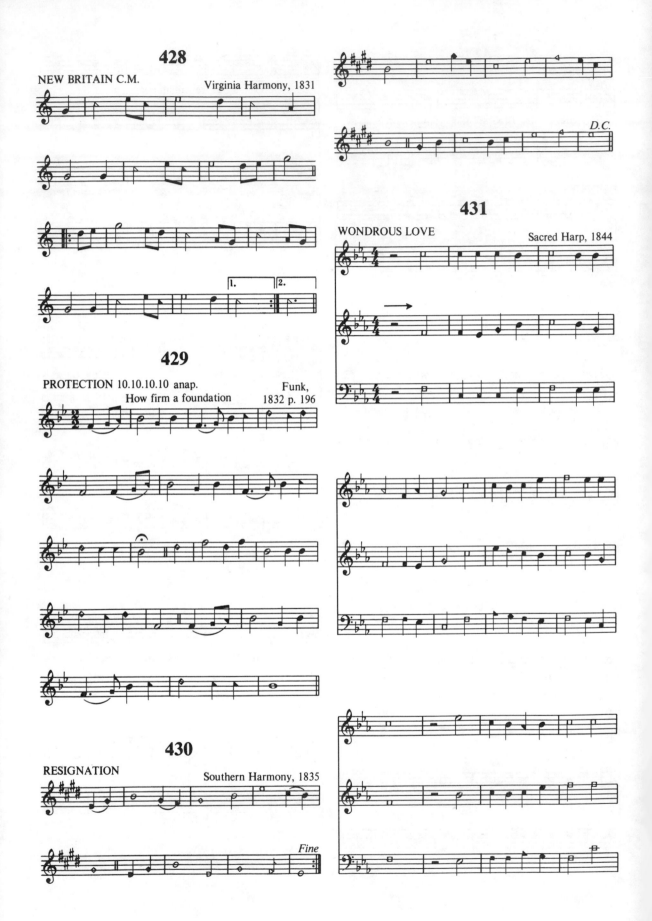

428

NEW BRITAIN C.M.

Virginia Harmony, 1831

429

PROTECTION 10.10.10.10 anap.

How firm a foundation

Funk, 1832 p. 196

430

RESIGNATION

Southern Harmony, 1835

Fine

D.C.

431

WONDROUS LOVE

Sacred Harp, 1844

433

Solo

Swing low, sweet cha - ri - ot

Chorus   S.

coming for to carry me home! Swing low, sweet

Ch.

cha - ri - ot   coming.....

S.

I looked o - ver Jor-dan and what did I see?

Ch.   Solo

coming.....   A band of an-gels

Ch.

coming af-ter me   coming.....

J.Z.

434

Solo

When Is-rael was in   E-gypt's land,

Chorus   S.

let my people go,   op-press'd so hard they

Ch.

could not stand, let my people   go!

Ch.

Go down, Moses, way down in E-gypt land,

tell old Pha-rao, Let my peo-ple go!

432

WINDHAM L.M.

D. Reed, 1785

435

Solo/ Chorus

Roll, Jordan, roll! Roll, Jordan, roll! I

want to go to heaven when I die, to

Solo

hear Jordan roll. Oh brothers, you ought to 've

Chorus

been there! yes, my Lord, a sit-ting in the

D.C.

King-dom to hear Jor-dan roll.

436

Solo

The Gos-pel train is com-ing, I

hear it just at hand, I hear the car-wheels

mov-ing and rumb-ling thro' the land.

Chorus

Get on board, child-ren, get on

board, child-ren! get on board,

1. 2.

child-ren! for there's room for many on board.   J.27

437

Solo

I___ went to the hill side I went to pray, I

know the an-gels done changed my name:

done changed my name for the com-ing day: thank

God, the an-gels done changed my name.

Chorus

Done changed my name for the com-ing day, I

know the an-gels done changed my name, done

changed my name for the com-ing day, thank

God the an-gels done changed my name.
J.104

438

Ga-briel's trum-pet', going to blow by and

by, by and by; yes Gab-riel's trum-pet's going to

blow at the end of time.   J.75

439

Edward Mole, 1707-1874

SOLID ROCK L.M.
William B. Bradbury, 1864

1. My hope is built on noth-ing less
2. When dark ness seems to hide His face,
3. His oath, His cov - e - nant, His blood
4. When He shall come with trum - pet sound,

Than Je - sus' blood and right-eous - ness;
I rest on His un-chang-ing grace;
Sup-port me in the whelm-ing flood;
Oh, may I then in Him be found;

I dare not trust the sweet-est frame,
In ev - ery high and storm-y gale,
When all a round my soul gives way,
Dressed in His right - eous - ness a - long,

But whol - ly lean on Je - sus' name.
My an-chor holds with - in the veil.
He then is all my hope and stay.
Fault - less to stand be - fore the throne.

Refrain

On Christ, the sol - id Rock, I stand; All
oth - er ground is sink - ing sand, All
oth - er ground is sink - ing sand.

440

BLESSED ASSURANCE.   Mrs. J. F. Knapp, 1839-1908
Irregular.

441

WORDS OF LIFE 8.6.8.6.6.6. with Refrain
Philip P. Bliss, 1838-1876   *Philip P. Bliss, 1874*

1. Sing them o-ver a-gain to me,
2. Christ, the bless-ed One, gives to all
3. Sweet-ly ech-o the gos-pel call,

Won-der-ful words of life;
Won-der-ful words of life;
Won-der-ful words of life;

Let me more of their beau-ty see,
Sin-ner, list to the lov-ing call,
Of-fer par-don and peace to all,

Won-der-ful works of life;
Won-der-ful words of life;
Won-der-ful words of life;

Words of life and beau-ty,
All so free-ly giv-en,
Je-sus, on-ly Sav-iour,

Refrain

This is my sto-ry, this is my song,...

Praising my Sa-viour all the day long;...

This is my sto-ry, this is my song,

Praising my Sa-viour all the day long...

Teach me faith and du - ty:
Woo - ing us to heav - en;
Sanc - ti - fy for - ev - er,

Refrain

Beau - ti - ful words, won - der - ful words,

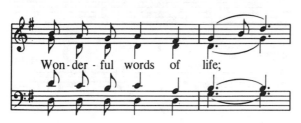

Won - der - ful words of life;

Beau - ti - ful words, won - der - ful words,

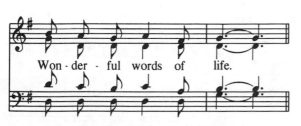

Won - der - ful words of life.

442

ALL THE WAY 8.7.8.7.D
Fanny J. Crosby, 1821-1915
Robert Lowry, 1875

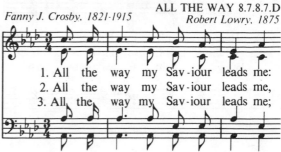

1. All the way my Sav - iour leads me:
2. All the way my Sav - iour leads me,
3. All the way my Sav - iour leads me;

What have I to ask be - side?
Cheers each wind - ing path I tread,
Oh, the ful - ness of His love!

Can I doubt His ten - der mer - cy,
Gives me grace for ev - 'ry tri - al,
Per - fect rest to me is prom - is'd

Who thro' life has been my guide?
Feeds me with the liv - ing bread:
In my Fa - ther's house a - bove:

Heav'n - ly peace, di - vin - est com - fort,
Tho' my wea - ry steps may fal - ter,
When my spir - it, cloth'd im - mor - tal,

443

A
DOWN AMPNEY   Vaughan Williams

B
RANDOLPH   Vaughan Williams

C
SINE NOMINE   Vaughan Williams

D
SALVE FESTA DIES   Vaughan Williams

E
CRANHAM   Holst

F
SHEEN   Holst

G
COME FAITHFUL PEOPLEG   J. Bicknell

H
TUGWOOD   N. Gatty

444

FOREST GREEN

KINGSFOLD

CAPEL C.M.

RODMELL

KINGS LYNN, 7.6.7.6.D

CAMERONIAN MIDNIGHT HYMN, L.M.

MONKS MARCH D.L.M. or 77.77.D

445

MANTEGNA 86.86.888.7. Irreg.

Slow Unison

R. Vaughan Wiliams

Copyright. From *Enlarged Songs of Praise.* by permission of the Oxford University Press, London

PCH 559

446

HILL CREST

G. Holst, 1925

Copyright. By permission of G. Schirmer, Inc.

447

BROOKEND 7.7.7.3.

G. Holst, 1925

PCH 423

Copyright. By permission of the Oxford University Press, London

448

SANYERS 8.6.88.6.

Martin Shaw, c. 1930

Copyright. By permission of G. Schirmer, Inc.

449

PEMBROKE 86.86.88

Patrick Hadley

Broaden slightly

Copyright. From *Enlarged Songs of Praise,* by permission of the Oxford University Press, London

450

CORNHILL C.M.

H. Darke, 1931

PCH 47

Copyright. From *Enlarged Songs of Praise*, by permission of the Oxford University Press, London

451

WELLS L.M.

B. Johnson, 1903

Copyright. By permission of Novello & Co.

452

WOLVERCOTE 76.76.D.

Unison

W. H. Ferguson, 1919

Copyright. By permission of the Oxford University Press, London

453

MIDIAN 65.65.D

Unison

H. P. Allen, c. 1918

1. Chris - tian, dost thou see them On the

ho - ly ground, How the troops of

Organ

Mi - dian Prowl and prowl a - round?

Chris - tian, up and smite them,

Count - ing gain but loss; Smite them by the

me - rit Of the ho - ly Cross.

454

SHERSTON 10.10.11.11.
Unison

W. K. Stanton, 1937

455

COTSWOLD

A. Brent Smith, c. 1925

PCH 62

456

WINTON 10.10.10.10.

G. Dyson, 1928

PCH 128

457

MELLIFONT L.M.

Sun of my soul   P. C. Buck, 1927

PCH 122

458

ALBERTA 10 4.10 4.10 10.

In moderate time. Unison   William H. Harris

PCH 440

459

MICHAEL 87.87.337.

Unison

Herbert Howells

PCH 200

460

HADLOW 84.84.44.44.

John Wilson, 1936

461

PADSTOW 98.98

C. S. Lang, 1949

PCH 552

(A♯ in v.4)

462

MAJESTY 6.6.8.6.6.8.3.3.6.6. William Llewellyn, 1965

PCH 202A

Copyright. By permission of Mr. William Llewellyn

463

HAMBLEDEN 89.89.D Walter K. Stanton, 1951
Unison

PCH 260

Copyright. From *BBC Hymn Book.* by permission
of the Oxford University Press, London

464

ARTHOG 85.85.843.
Unison
G. Thalben-Ball, 1951

Copyright. From *BBC Hymn Book,* by permission
of the Oxford University Press, London

465

CAROLYN 85.85.88.85.
Herbert Murrill, 1951

PCH 453

466

ABBOT'S LEIGH 87.87.D.
C. V. Taylor, 1937

PCH 86

Copyright. By permission of the Oxford University Press,
London

467

FENITON 7.8.7.8. with Alleluias   S. H. Nicholson, 1939
Slow.

After the Last Verse Only

Voices

ff Al-le-lu-ia, Al-le-lu-ia,

Al-le-lu-ia. *ff*

468

ELTON 6.5.6.5.666.5.   J. Dykes Bower, 1950

469

REMISSION 6.6.6.6.6.6.

L. J. Blake, 1950

PCH 242

AM 324

Copyright. By permission of Hymns Ancient and Modern Ltd.

PCH 62

AM 585

Copyright. By permission of Hymns Ancient and Modern Ltd.

470

EMMAUS 6x8

Greville Cooke, 1944

471

MERNLE 7.6.7.6.Ter

D. P. Symonds, 1945

Fine

D.C.

PCH 311

Copyright. By permission of the Royal School of Church Music

472

A

DOWN AMPNEY 66.11.D.

R. Vaughan Williams, 1906

Copyright. From *English Hymnal.* by permission
of the Oxford University Press, London

B

NORTH PETHERTON 6.6.11.D.

W. H. Harris, 1950

Copyright. By permission of the Oxford University Press,
London

PCH 205

AM 235

473

LUCERNA LAUDONIAE 77.77.77.

David Evans, 1927

PCH 235

Copyright. By permission of the Oxford University Press,
London

474

MOVILLE 7.6.7.6.D. (7.6.7.6.7.8.7.6.)

Irish Traditional Melody, 1919

PCH 321

ICH

475

GOD OF MY LIFE L.M.　　　　　　F. L. Wiseman, 1933

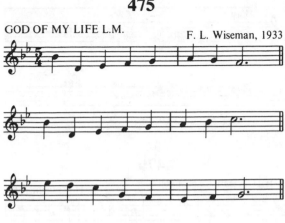

M 429

476

GRANGER C.M.　　　　　　G. F. Brockless, 1887-1957

PCH 210 (sel)

477

ANCHOR 6x8　　　　　　A. Beer, 1933

PCH 58

PCH 277

478

NEARER, MY GOD, TO THEE
(Third Tune)
Unison   6.4.6.4.664.   T. C. Gregory, 1933

verses 1-4

479

MILTON ABBAS 66.4.666.4.
E. H. Thiman, 1951

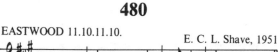

PCH 384

480

EASTWOOD 11.10.11.10.
E. C. L. Shave, 1951

481

TEILO SANT 8.6.8.8.6.   J. P. B. Dobbs, c. 1944

PCH 130

Copyright. By permission of Mr. J. P. B. Dobbs

482

CHESTERTON

Lord, thy word a-bi-deth,

and our foot steps gui-deth; who its

truth be-liev-eth light and joy re - cei-veth.

When our foes are near us, then thy

word doth cheer us. Word of con-so - la - tion,

mes-sage of sal - va - tion.

Copyright. By permission of Josef Weinberger, Ltd.

483

LIVING LORD 45538883   Text and Music by
Patrick Appleford

1. Lord Je-sus Christ, You have

come to us, You are with us,

Copyright. By permission of Mosef Weinberger, Ltd.

484

Geoffrey Beaumont

Ma - ry's Son. Clean-sing our souls from

f   *mf* 1. Hail to the Lord who

C Am Dm G5# C

all their sin Pour-ing your love and

D Bm Em A7

comes, Comes to his tem - ple

Am Em Dm G5#

goodness in Je - sus our love for

Bm B7 Em Gm6

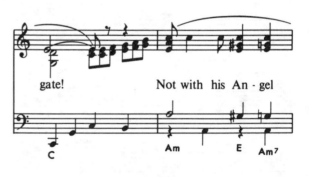

gate! Not with his An - gel

C Am E Am7

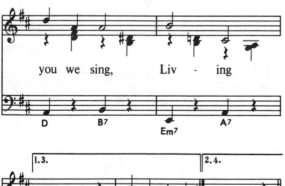

you we sing, Liv - ing

D B7 Em7 A7

host, Not in his king - ly

Dm G G7

1.3.   2.4.

Lord.   Lord.

D G6 A7 D

state; No shouts pro-claim him

C F

nigh, No crowds his com - ing

wait;

be.

PCH 317

485

STAND UP FOR JESUS!

Adam Geibel

Unison 76., 8 lines

Refrain (Harmony)
a tempo

Stand up for Je - sus! Ye

sol - diers of the Cross; Lift

high His roy-al ban - ner, It must not, it

must not suf - fer loss.

486

CHRIST WHOSE GLORY 77.77.77.

Malcolm Williamson, 1961

PCH 61

Copyright. By permission of Josef Weinberger, Ltd.

487

HAIL TO THE LORD

Malcolm Williamson, 1961

PCH 317

Copyright. By permission of Josef Weinberger, Ltd.

488

ANGELS FROM THE REALMS OF GLORY 8.7.8.7.4.7.

Malcolm Williamson, 1963

Copyright. By permission of Josef Weinberger, Ltd.

489

EVERY STAR

Sydney Carter, 1964

PCH 522

Copyright. By permission of Stainer & Bell, Ltd.

490

BRYNLAND 8.4.8.4.8.4.

Peggy Spencer - Palmer, 1951

Copyright. By permission of the Reformed Church,
Publications Dept.

491

David S. Goodall

I want to go out,   I want to go

home,   I want to be   single,

I want to be-long,   I want to grow

up,   I want to stay young,

I want to do both and all at once and anything

else that takes my fan - cy whether it

hurts or helps the time of

day show me the way!

PCH 525

492

CARMICHAEL 86.86.88.886.

Peggy Spencer Palmer, 1900

* See below for Verse 3

493

GLENFINLAS 6.5.6.5.

K. G. Finlay, 1927

Copyright. By permission of the Broomhill Parish Church, Glasgow

494

AYRSHIRE C.M.

K. G. Finlay, 1936

PCH 111

Copyright. By permission of the Broomhill Parish Church, Glasgow

495

CARRICK 7.6.7.6.7.7.7.6.

K. G. Finlay, 1965

Copyright. By permission of the Broomhill Parish Church, Glasgow

496

SALISBURY 8.7.8.7.D.

Organ, before St. 1 only

Herbert Howells, 1964

St. 1 only   Sts. 2-3

Copyright. By permission of Dr. Herbert Howells

497

HILLSBOROUGH S.M.

John Gardner, 1964

PCH 561

Copyright. By permission of Mr. John Gardner

498

WIVETON 11.10.11.10.

Lennox Berkeley, 1967

Copyright. By permission of Sir Lennox Berkeley

PCH 474

499

BISHOPS C.M.

John Joubert, 1967

PCH 437

Copyright. From the *Cambridge Hymnal,* by permission of Cambridge University Press

500

LAUDS 77.77.D.

John Wilson, 1961

Copyright. By permission of the Oxford University Press, London

501

TRINITY

John Wilson, 1961

Three for-ev-er One, for-ev-er

Re-joice with us in God the

Three, Foun-tain of Love, Giv-
Foun-tain of Love, Giv-

Tri-ni-ty, The

er of U-ni-ty!
er of U-ni-ty!

PCH 506

𝄋 All voices, unison

1. We would re - joice a - gain
2. How long and ear - nest - ly
3. So let us all, re - ject -
4. Re - joice with us that man

veils for all to see, in what he
oh, how dead our creeds, un - less they
ills that still di - vide the fold of
man - y live as one, each lov - ing

and yet a - gain that
the Fa - thers strove to
ing none, re - move what -
may yet a - chieve what

St. 1-3

is, what man him -
live in Christ - like
Christ, and all the
each, as

God re - veals his truth to
frame in words a faith we
ev - er thwarts a rec - on -
God him - self has dared us

self may be.   *ANTIPHON D.C.*
aims and deeds!   *ST. 3 D.S.*
world be - side.   *ANTIPHON D.C.*

mor - tal men, un -
can - not prove; but
cil - ing love, all
to be - lieve: the

St. 4   *allarg.*

Fa - ther, Spir - it, Son.

Copyright. By permission of the Oxford University Press,
   London.

NOTE: A later version by the composer sets the verses
   in SATB.

502

BENIFOLD 8.33.7.D.

F. B. Westbrook, 1969

503

SHILLINGFORD

P. W. Cutts, c. 1960 (1976)

504

BIRABUS 8.7.8.7.

P. W. Cutts, c. 1960 (1964)

PCH 504

505

ASKERSWELL L.M.D.

P. W. Cutts, 1975

506

SWITHEN 5.6.5.D.

P. W. Cutts, 1975

Where is God to-day? Shall we find him waiting

when we come to pray? Will he come a-gain ev'-ry

sun-day morn-ing? Do we wait in rain?

Interlude & postlude | Alternate interlude | Ending

Words by David S. Goodall, b. 1922.
Words and music at *New Church Praise* (1975) 108

507

SHRUB END 7.6.7.6.

P. W. Cutts, 1975

stars be‑neath thy feet like leaves on

fo‑rest floor. Man, turn‑ing

All stanzas except last | Last stanza

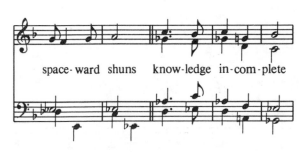

space‑ward shuns know‑ledge in‑com‑plete

508

fe‑vered to ex‑plore.

RODEL 6.5.5.D.

T. C. Micklem, 1976

Christ, burn‑ing past all suns,

PCH 488

Words by Ian Fraser 1964
Copyright Stainer & Bell Ltd.

509

FUDGIE L.M.

A. J. Hutchings, 1962

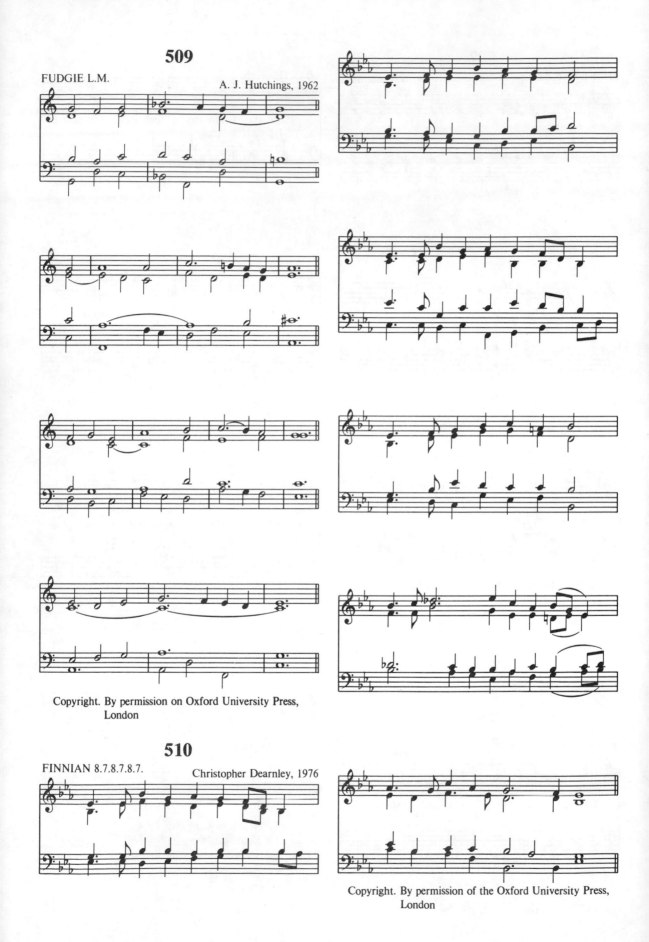

510

FINNIAN 8.7.8.7.8.7.

Christopher Dearnley, 1976

511

ABEL 7.6.7.6.D.

R. Barrett Ayres, 1967

512

TROTTING

Eric Reid, 1967

PCH 503

PCH 532

Copyright. By permission of Stainer & Bell, Ltd.

Copyright. By permission of Stainer & Bell, Ltd.

513

HEADINGTON 11.6.11.6.

Kenneth Leighton, 1973

Copyright. By permission of Professor Frederick Rimmer

515

SOUSTER L.M.

Martin Dalby, 1973

Unison

Copyright. By permission of Professor Kenneth Leighton

514

IONA 8.9.8.7.

Frederick Rimmer, 1973

Copyright. By permission of Mr. Martin Dalby

516

KILVAREE, 11.10.11.10

Sebastian Forbes 1973

PCH-469
Copyright. By permission of Mr. Sebastian Forbes

517

MONIKIE

D. Dorward, 1973

PCH 592
Copyright. By permission of Mr. David Dorward

518

SEARCHING FOR LAMBS C.M.

English Carol Melody, Adapted 1973

PCH 9

519

WELWYN 11.10.11.10.

A. Scott Gatty, 1902

520

HIGHWOOD 11.10.11.10.

R. R. Terry, Before 1933

Copyright. By permission of Search Press, Ltd.

521

HOLCOMBE 87.88.88.77.

A. G. Murray, 1940

Copyright. By permission of Search Press, Ltd.

522

SURREXIT 888 +

A. G. Murray, 1940

Al - le - lu - ia! Al - le - lu - ia!

Copyright. By permission of Search Press, Ltd.

Copyright. By permission of Faber Music, Ltd.

523

VERBUM DEI 8.7.8.7.8.7.

G. Laycock, 1971

524

FELINFOEL L.M.

M. Dawney, 1971

PCH 512

Copyright. By permission of Mr. Michael Dawney

525

PRAISE GOD 10.10.10.10.

Elizabeth Poston, 1971

Organ ped.

Last time

526

TERRY 11.11.11.5.

Paul Inwood, 1972

527

FRANCOIS 7.7.7.7 +

Paul Inwood, 1972

Al - le - lu - ia!

ORA LABORA

528

T. T. Noble, 1918

H576

529

St. DUNSTAN'S 6.5.6.5.6.6.6.5.

Winfred Douglas, 1917

PCH 434 B.

H. (U.S.A.) 563

530

LIGHT 7.6.7.6.D., C.M.D. Or 8.6.8.6.8.8.8.6.

Leavitt, Christian Lyre, 1832

531

MALABAR 8.7.8.7. (Iambic)

D. Mck. Williams, 1941

PCH 181

H. (U.S.A.) 201

Copyright. By permission of the Church Hymnal Corporation

532

SURSUM CORDA 10.10.10.10.

A. M. Smith, 1942

Copyright. By permission of Mrs A. M. Smith

533

TAYLOR HALL S.M.D.

Leo Sowerby, 1941

Copyright. By permission of the Church Hymnal Corporation

534

St. AUGUSTINE 8.7.8.7.

P. Yon, 1939

All of self, all of self,

all of self and none of thee!

536

HINMAN 6.6.4.6.6.6.4.

A. C. Lovelace, 1955

537

RAMWOLD L.M.

R. Warner, 1958

535

FINLAY 7.7.7.7.5.7.3.3.7.

H. W. Friedell, 1953

538

VICAR 11.10.11.10.　　　　　　　V. Earle Copes, 1966

Copyright. By permission of Abingdon Press

539

SOUTH GORE 888.888.　　　　　　Ronald Arnatt, 1967

PCH 465

540

NATIONAL CITY 10.10.10.4.　　　L. P. Schreiber, 1967

Al - le - lu - ia!

PCH 550

541

OREMUS C.M.

Unison

D. Hustad, 1975

PCH 111

542

MORA PROCTOR 11.10.11.10.

W. J. Reynolds, 1974

543

FORTUNATUS NEW 8.7.8.7.8.7.

Carl Schalk, 1967

PCH 156

544

DEXTER 4.5.7.D+

D. N. Johnson, 1969

Sing to the Lord a new song.

sing to the Lord a new song.

He hath done mar - vel-ous things:

I too will praise him with a new song.

545

MARLEE 6.6.6.6.8.8.

L. B. Sateren, 1958

546

WITTENBERG NEW L.M.D.

Jan Bender 1969

PCH 554

547

BOULDER L.M.

Paul Manz, 1973

548

CITY OF GOD 11.10.11.10.   D. Moe, 1957

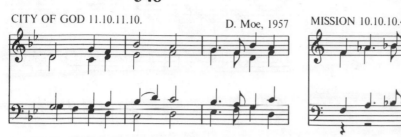

549

MISSION 10.10.10.4.   Richard Hillert, 1967

550

VENERABLE C.M.

V. Persichetti, 1956

Copyright. By permission of Elkan-Vogel, Inc.

551

NEW SONG 6.6.6.6.

L. Burswold, 1970

Copyright. By permission of the Pilgrim Press

552

GROVE STREET 4x12

J. W. Jenkins, 1970

Copyright. By permission of the Pilgrim Press

553

PILGRIMAGE 8.9.10.

J. W. Neely, Jr. 1970

554

NEW DANCE

R. D. Wetzel, 1972

PCH 448

555

ABREU 7.6.7.6.D.

Calvin Hampton, 1975

'The Church's one foundation'

PCH 236

Copyright. By permission of Harold Flammer, Inc.

556

VINEYARD HAVEN   Richard Dirksen, 1974
S. M. with REfrain

557

ARTISTS PROCESSION 11.11.11.5 +
                              Ronald Neal, 1979

558

St. BASIL 11.11.11.11. anap.

H. Willan, 1927

Copyright. By permission of the Executors of the late
Dr Healey Willan

559

BELLWOODS S.M.

J. Hopkirk, 1938

Copyright untraceable.

Copyright. By permission of Mr. Ronald Neal

560

St. JOAN 6.7.6.7.6.6.6.6.

P. E. B. Coller, 1941

Copyright. By permission of the Church Hymnal Corporation

561

THE KING'S MAJESTY L.M.

G. George, 194-

Copyright. By permission of Abingdon Press

562

1940 MASSON 5.6.6.4.

S. L. Osbome, 1971

PCH 496

Copyright. By permission of Dr. Stanley Osborne

563

CARN BREA 8.7.8.7.D.

D. Holman, 1971

Copyright. By permission of Dr Derek Holman

564

CAUSA DIVINA 14.14.4.7.8.

F. R. C. Clarke, 1971

PCH 562

Copyright. By permission of Mr. F.R.C. Clarke

565

DOMINION-CHALMERS 8.7.8.7.

W. France, 1971

PCH 504

Copyright. By permission of Mr. William France

566

SOWBY 8.6.8.6.8.8.8.

G. Ridout, 1971

PCH 322

Copyright. By permission of Mr. G. Ridout

567

PIER PAUL 10.5-3.6-5-6.10

H. B. Cabena, 1971

H 312

Copyright. By permission of Mr. B. Cabena

568

BRUDERSCHAFT 8.8.8.8.7.7.7.

H. Vogel, 1931

Copyright untraceable.

569

HIER IST GEDULD UND GLAUBE

O. Dibelius, 1934

Copyright untraceable.

570

DIE NACHT IST VORGEDRUNGEN 7.6.7.6.D.

J. Petzold, 1939

Sch. 226 CHL 59

© Bärenreiter - Verlag, Kassel

571

HERR DU BIST AN VIELEN TISCHEN 8.7.5.6.6.6.6.6.9.

D. Trautwein, 1964

Sch.118

(PCH 574)

© Burckhardthouse - Verlag, Berlin

572

SINGET DEM HERRN

R. Schweizer, 1963

© Hanssler - Verlag, Neuhausen - Stuttgart

Sch.33

573

SINGET DEM HERRN

O. G. Blarr, 1967

Sch.34

Verses to be spoken over rhythmic accompaniment.

© Gustav Bosse Verlag, Regensburg

574

KOMM SCHOPFER GEIST

O. G. Blarr, 1967

Komm, Schopfer geist,   er - full die

Her-zen deiner glau-bi-ger.

Schalom, 18

© Gustav Bosse Verlag, Regensbufg Hugo Distler

575

(DISTLER) 7.6.7.6.D.

Hugo Distler, 1934

Wea-ry of all trum-pe-ting, weary of all

kil-ling, weary of all songs that sing

promise non-ful-fil-ling: we would raise

O Christ one song, we would join in sing-ing

that great mu-sic pure and

strong where with heavn' is ring-ing.

PCH 555

Copyright untraceable.

576

WILHELMUS VAN NASSOUWE 6.6.6.6.D.
(NETHERLANDS)

Dutch Melody, 1626

577

A. C. Schuurman, 1954

578

ZOLANG ER MENSEN 9.8.9.8.   T. de M. Oyens, 1959

579

ZIJT GIJ WAAROP DE WERELD WACHT   W. Vogel, 1960

8.7.8.8.7. iamb.

580

KERKEN 8.7.8.7.88.7.   L. M. Lindeman, 1840

581

ALTAR L.M.   Carl Nielsen, 1915

Ps. V. 644

© Wilhelm Hansen, Copenhagen

582

TIDENS MATT HAR FYLLTS 8.7.8.5.   I. Milveden

Ps. V.656

© Års Psalmkommitté, Stockholm 1969

583

DE LANADE KRUBBA

T. Kverno, 1972

Ps. V.625

© Norsk Musikkforlag, Oslo

584

11.7.11.7. anap. G. Sodersten, 1970

Ps. V. 642

© Års Psalmkommitté, Stockholm

585

DU SOM GICK FORE OSS 6.6.6.5. dactylic

S. E. Back, 1959

Ps. V. 652

© Års Psalmkommitté, Stockholm

586

BABEL 7.6.8.5.

S. E. Back, 1970

PCH 576

Ps. V. 756

© Års Psalmkommitté, Stockholm

587

DIEU, NOUS AVONS VU

Antiphon

Unison

J. Langlais, 1957

FINE

Verses

D.C.

PCH 570

588

PUISSANCE ET GLOIRE C.M.

C. Rozier, 1974

589

AUJOURD'HUI DANS NOTRE MONDE

(6.6.6.6.D. Troch and lamb)

Arr. C. Geoffroy, 1965

590

CANTATE 48

J. Gelineau, 1970

591

CANTATE 86

Cameroun

592

Leader

Malawi Wedding Song

O praise the king of hea - ven O

praise the king of hea-ven, all ye who are his

Chorus   Leader

peo·ple. O praise the king of heaven. Ye

Chorus

prin · ces! O praise the king of heaven, the

Leader   Chorus

holy gra·cious king: Ye ru - lers! O

Leader   Chorus

praise the king of heaven Al·le - lu - ia! O

praise the king of heaven, the ho·ly gracious king.

Africa Praise 1

593

JESUS WE WANT TO MEET

(Nigeria) A. T. Olajida Olude, 1962

Drum beat pattern:

594

JESU JESU AMEFUFUKA   (Tanzania) Nyaturu Melody

A   B

A   B   A

1.–3.   4.

A   B

Tumshangile Mungu 24

595

CANTATE 11

Malagasy

596

RAKHO PRABHUKI

Preliminary and Refrain

(Bhajan)

North India Tune Book 3

597

MANA MANDIRA

(Bhajan)

end of preliminary.

Verses

North India Tune Book, 18

* This measure is not sung in the preliminary antiphon, in which the singer goes straight to the next measure: but it always concludes the refrain, of which the next four measures are not a part.

598

MAIN TO HUN GUNAHGAR

(Ghazal)

North India Tune Book, 77

605

From an Arabic Hymnal, before 1920

Cantate Domino, 130

Copyright. By permission of Prof. Loh I To

604

CANTATE 35

J. Faustini (Brazil)

© M. J. W. Faustini, Brazil

Selective Bibliography

In order to make this bibliography helpful to readers of other books on hymnology, we include in it certain books which do not deal with the music of hymns. These are distinguished by an asterisk (*). Entries in each section are arranged by date, the most recent books first.

I. DICTIONARIES AND ANTHOLOGIES

1980. Perry, D.W., *Hymns and Tunes Indexed;* Croydon, GB, The Royal School of Church Music and the Hymn Society of Great Britain and Ireland.

1980. Christ-Janer, A., Hughes, C.W., and Sprague Smith, C., *American Hymns Old and New*; New York, Columbia University.

1980. Hughes, C.W., *American Hymns Old and New: Notes on the Hymns and Biographies— of the Authors and Composers;* New York, Columbia University.

1979. Routley, E., *A Panorama of Christian Hymnody;* Collegeville, MN, Liturgical Press.

1979. Routley, E., *An English-Speaking Hymnal Guide;* Collegeville, MN, Liturgical Press.

1977. Hayden, A. and Newton, R., *British Hymn Writers and Composers: A Check List*, (Dates and places of birth and death); as 1980 Perry above.

1957. Connelly, J., *Hymns of the Roman Liturgy* (Latin hymns, texts, translations and notes); London and New York, Longmans Green & Co.

1953. Frost, M., *English and Scottish Psalm and Hymn Tunes, c1543-1677;* London, S.P.C.K. and Oxford University Press.

1907. Julian, J., *Dictionary of Hymnology,* 3rd ed. (1st ed. 1891); London, Murray.

1883 Baumker, W., *Das katholische deutsche*
to *Kirchenlied in seinen Singweisen;* 4 vols,
1911. Freiburg, (I) 1883, (II) 1886, (III) 1891, (V) 1911.

1854 Zahn, J., *Die Melodien dem deutsches*
to *evangelisches Kirchenlieder.*
1893.

II. GENERAL HISTORIES

1980. Routley, E., *Christian Hymns, an Introduction to their Story,* (beginnings to 1900) 6 cassettes in book format, Princeton NJ, Prestige Publications.

1980. Eskew, H. and McElrath, H., *Sing with understanding;* Nashville TN, Broadman.

1978. Reynolds, W.J. and Price, M., *A Joyful Sound;* New York, Holt Rinehart Winston.

1962. Patrick, M., The Story of the Church's Song (orig. ed. 1927), rev. by J.R. Sydnor; Richmond VA, John Knox Press

1952.* Routley, E., *Hymns and Human Life;* London, Murray.

1940.* Foote, H.W., *Three Centuries of American Hymnody;* Cambridge MA, Harvard

1937.* Phillips, C.S., *Hymnody Past and Present;* London, S.P.C.K.

1923. Lightwood, J., *Hymn Tunes and their Story;* London, Epworth

1915.* Benson, L.F., *The English Hymn;* Richmond VA, John Knox Press

1904.* Gregory, A.E., *The Hymn Book of the Modern Church;* London, Kelly

1903. Breed, David R., *The History of Hymns and Hymn Tunes;* New York, Fleming H. Revell.

1889.* Horder, W.G., *The Hymn Lover;* London, Curwen.

III. SPECIAL SUBJECTS

1967. Riedel, J., *The Lutheran Chorale, Its Basic Traditions;* Minneapolis MN, Augsburg

1963. Murray, G., *Gregorian Chant According to the Manuscripts* (new theory of interpretation of rhythm); London, Cary

1962. Pidoux, P., *Le Psautier Huguenot* (Strasbourg and Genevan Psalters critically edited and analysed) 2 vols; Basel, Bärenreiter

1960.* Lowther-Clarke, W.K., *A Hundred Years of Hymns Ancient and Modern;* London, Clowes

1957. McCutchan, R.G., *Hymn Tune Names;* Nashville TN, Abingdon

1955. Taylor, C.V., *The Way to Heaven's Door* (brief broadcast addresses with music exx.) 57 pp; London, Epworth

1956. Chambers, G.B., *Folksong-Plainsong;* London, Merlin Press

1956.* Moore, S.H., *Sursum Corda* (brief studies of German hymn writers), London, Independent Press

1954. Pocknee, C.E., *The French Diocesan Hymns and their Tunes;* London, Faith Press

1949. Patrick, M., *Four Centuries of Scottish Psalmody;* London, Oxford U.P.

1949. Wellesz, E.J., *A History of Byzantine Music and Hymnography,* London, Oxford U.P.

1947. Wellesz, E.J., *Eastern Elements in Western Chant;* Copenhagen, Munksgaard

1945. Bett, H., *The Hymns of Methodism,* 3rd ed. (1st ed. 1913); London, Epworth

1942.* Manning, B.L., *The Hymns of Wesley and Watts;* London, Epworth

1935. Bridges, R., Collected *Essays XXI-XXVI* (ed. M.M. Bridges); London, The Church Music Society.

1929. Terry, R.R., *A Forgotten Psalter, and other Essays* (The Psalter is Scottish 1635); London, Oxford U.P.

1915. Riley, A., *Concerning Hymn Tunes and Sequences;* London, Mowbray

1914.* Mozley, H.W., *Sequences and Hymns;* London, Longmans Green

1899. Marsh, J.B.T. and Loudin, F.J.: *The Story of the Jubilee Singers* (rev. and amplified ed., with music); London, Hodder & Stoughton

1896. Frere, W.H., *Hymn Melodies and Sequences;* London, the Plainsong and Medieval Music Society.

IV. PRACTICAL TREATISES

1965. Lovelace, A., *The Anatomy of Hymnody;* Nashville TN, Abingdon

1960. Sydnor, J.R., *The Hymn and Congregational Singing;* Richmond VA, John Knox Press

1933. Whitley, W.T., *Congregational Hymn Singing in England* (final chapter by Eric H. Thiman); London, Dent

c1885. Curwen, J.S., *Studies in Worship Music* (essays in observation of English customs: second series, c. 1889; both series undated); London, Curwen

V. BIOGRAPHIES &c OF AUTHORS AND COMPOSERS
(Arranged under SUBJECTS)

c1880. Bliss. Grant, W. (ed) *P.P. Bliss, His Life and Work;* London, Morgan & Scott

1897. DYKES. Fowler, J.T., *Life of Dr. Dykes;* London, Murray

1896* ELLERTON. Housman, H. (ed), *John Ellerton, his Life and Writings on Hymnology;* London, S.P.C.K.

1958* ELFED LEWIS. E.W. Parry, *Howell Elfed Lewis* (1860-1953); London, Independent Press.

1955* GRUNDTVIG. J. Knudsen, *Danish Rebel* (Life of N.F.S. Grundtvig); Philadelphia, Muhlenberg

1962* NEALE. Lough, A.G., *The Influence of John Mason Neale;* London, S.P.C.K.

1975. SHAW. E. Routley, *Martin Shaw, A Centenary Appreciation* (with a catalogue of his works); Martin Shaw Trust, Westhorp Ward & Catchpole, 32 Museum St., Inswpch, England, IP 1 1 JB

1929. SHAW. M. Shaw, *Up to Now* (autobiography); London, Oxford U.P.

1974* STERNHOLD. Weir, R.B., *Thomas Sternhold and the Beginnings of English Metrical Psalmody;* Ann Arbor, University Microfilms.

1974* WATTS. Fountain, D., *Isaac Watts Remembered,* paperback; Worthing (England), H.E. Walter

1974* WATTS. Bishop, S., *Isaac Watts, Hymns and Spiritual Songs, A Publishing History and Bibliography;* Ann Arbor MI, Pierian Press

1962* WATTS. Bishop, S., *Isaac Watts, Hymns and Spiritual Songs: A Study in early 18th century Language Changes* (textual study); London, Faith Press

1962* WATTS. Escott, H., *Isaac Watts, Hymnographer;* London, Independent Press

1943* WATTS. Davis, A.P., *Isaac Watts;* Richmond VA, John Knox Press (1948 London, Independent Press)

1972* WESLEY. Nuelsen, J.L., tr. Parry, Moore and Holbrook, *John Wesley and the Christian Hymn;* Calverley, Yorks (England), A.S. Holbrook

1966* WESLEY. Hodges, H.A. & Allchin, A.M. (ed), *A Rapture of Praise* (140 texts with introduction); London, Hodder & Stoughton

1966* WESLEY. Lawson, J., *The Christian Year with Charles Wesley: A Devotional Companion;* London, Epworth

1962* WESLEY. Baker, F., *Representative Verse of Charles Wesley* (texts, with a study of his poetic technique); London, Epworth

1958* WESLEY. Kay, J.A., *Wesley's Prayers and Praises* (transcriptions of less-known Wesley texts); London, Epworth

1953* WESLEY. Flew, R.N., *The Hymns of Charles Wesley: A Study of their Structure;* London, Epworth

1948* WESLEY. Rattenbury, J.E., *The Eucharistic Hymns of John and Charles Wesley;* London, Epworth

1941* WESLEY. Rattenbury, J.E., *The Evangelical Doctrines of Charles Wesley's Hymns;* London, Epworth

1978* WHITING. Cooper, P., *William Whiting, 1825-78;* Southampton, P. Cave

1978* WINKWORTH. Leaver, R.A., *Catherine Winkworth;* St. Louis, Concordia

VI. COMPANIONS TO HYMN BOOKS.

(These are all books associated with particular hymnals, and where the parent book is not shown in the title it is here mentioned after the title).

1981. Stulken, M.K., *Hymnal Companion to the Lutheran Book of Worship;* Philadelphia, Fortress

1979. Barkley, J.M., *Handbook to the Church Hymnary, Third Edition* (CH III); London, Oxford U.P.

1978. Hustad, D.P., *Dictionary-Handbook to Hymns of the Living Church;* Chicago, Hope

1977. Routley, E., *Companion to Westminster Praise* (short); Chapel Hill NC, Hinshaw

1976. Osborne, S.L., *If Such Holy Song* (Canadian United Hymn Book, 1971): Oshawa, Ont., Institute of Church Music

1976. Erickson, J.I., *Twice Born Hymns* (Covenant Hymnal 1973); Chicago, Covenant Press

1976. Reynolds, W.J., *Companion to Baptist Hymnal* (Baptist Hymnal 1975); Nashville TN, Broadman

1970. Gealy, F.D., Lovelace, A.C., and Young, C.R. (ed), *Companion to the Hymnal* (Methodist Hymnal 1964/6); Nashville TN, Abingdon

1970. Wake, A.N., *Companion to Hymnal for Christian Worship;* St Louis, Bethany Press

1969. Wilson, J.W., *A Short Companion to Hymns & Songs* (Hymns and Songs 1969); London, The Methodist Church Music Society

1967. Williams, H., *Tonau a'u Hawduron* (Welsh Calvinist Methodist Hymn Book, 1929: in Welsh); Caernarfon (Wales), Llyfrfa'r M.C.

1966. Ronander, A.C. and Porter, E. (ed), *Guide to the Pilgrim Hymnal;* New York, Pilgrim Press

1964. Reynolds, W.J., *Hymns of our Faith* (Baptist Hymnal 1956); Nashville TN, Broadman

1961. Frost, M., *Historical Companion to Hymns Ancient and Modern* (Hymns A & M Revised, 1950); London, Clowes (revision of FRERE below)

1962. Martin, H. (ed), *Baptist Hymn Book Companion* (English Baptist Hymn Book 1962); London, Psalms and Hymns Trust

1953. Martin, H. (ed), *Companion to the Baptist Church Hymnal Revised* (English Baptist Church Hymnal, 1933; this replaces an earlier Companion ed C. Bonner, 1935); London, Psalms and Hymns Trust.

1953. Parry, K.L. and Routley, E., *Companion to Congregational Praise* (CP 1951); London, Independent Press.

1952. Haeussler, A., *The Story of our Hymns* (Evangelical & Reformed Hymnal 1941); St Louis, Eden

1950. Kelynack, W.S., *Companion to the School Hymn Book of the Methodist Church* (English Methodist School Hymn Book, 1950); London, Epworth

1949. Anon (ed), *The Hymnal-1940 Companion;* Church Hymnal Corp. New York

1936. Dearmer, P. and Jacob, A. (ed), *Songs of Praise Discussed* (SP 1931); London, Oxford U.P.

1935. Moffatt, J. and Patrick, M., *Handbook to the Church Hymnary* (Revised Church Hymnary 1927), with Supplement by M. Patrick including tunes from Scottish Psalter 1929 and additional notes; London, Oxford U.P.

1935. Lightwood, J.T., *The Music of the Methodist Hymn Book* (English Methodist H.B., 1933); 2nd ed. 1955 with supplement and revisions by F.B. Westbrook; London, Epworth.

1934* Telford, J., *The New Methodist Hymn Book Illustrated in History and Experience* (as above); London, Epworth

1909. Frere, W.H., *Hymns Ancient and Modern, Historical Edition* (Hymns A & M 1904); London, Clowes

1901. Cowan, W. and Love, J., *The Music of the Church Hymnary* (CH 1898); Edinburgh and London, Frowde (Oxford U.P.)

1899* Brownlie, J., *Hymns and Hymn Writers of the Church Hymnary* (CH 1898), 2nd ed. 1911; Edinburgh and London, Frowde (Oxford U.P.)

1894* Stevenson, G.J., *The Methodist Hymn Book Illustrated with Biography, History, Incident and Anecdote* (Methodist Hymn Book 1876); London, Kelly.

1891. Love, J., *Scottish Church Music* (various Scottish Free Church Hymnals taken together); Edinburgh, Blackwood

1889.* Moorsom, R.M., *Historical Companion to Hymns Ancient and Modern* (Hymns A & M, 1889), confined to transcriptions of Latin & Greek originals; London, Parker

(Hymn books with biographical notes included)
1958. *Hymns Ancient and Modern,* School Edition; London, Clowes
1956. *Hymns for Colleges and Schools;* New Haven, Yale University
1936. *Clarendon Hymn Book;* Oxford, Clarendon Press
1909. *The Book of Common Praise,* Annotated Edition, ed J.E. Jones; Toronto, Oxford U.P.
1899. *Yattendon Hymnal,* ed R. Bridges; Oxford, Clarendon Press

(Hymn book with historical preface)
1964. *Hymns for Church and School;* London, Novello (later Woking, Unwin).

(Historical works associated with particular hymn books)
1960. Lowther-Clarke, W.K., *A Hundred Years of Hymns Ancient and Modern;* London, Clowes
1928. Kinloch, T.F., *An Historical Account of the Church Hymnary Revised Edition* (CH 1927); Cambridge, Heffer.

VII. HYMN BOOKS
(It is impracticable to include here all hymnals even in current use; the list is confined to those of the major Christian groups which are of significant musical interest to readers of this book.

A1. Hymnals in current use — American: full size
1978. *Lutheran Book of Worship:* Minneapolis MN, Augsburg and St Louis MO, Concordia
1975. *Catholic Liturgy Book* (full music ed. 1981); Baltimore, Helicon
1975. *Worship-II* (Catholic), Chicago, G.I.A.
1975. *Baptist Hymnal* (Southern Baptist Convention); Nashville TN, Broadman (also published as *Broadman Hymnal*)
1974. *Hymns of the Living Church;* Chicago, Hope
1974. *Hymnal of the United Church of Christ;* Philadelphia, United Church Press
1974. *Book of Worship for United States Forces;* US Govt. Publications
1973. *The Covenant Hymnal;* Chicago, Covenant Press
1972. *The Worshipbook* (Presbyterian); Philadelphia, Westminster Press
1972. *The Christian Hymnary* (Mennonite — shape-note); Uniontown, OH, Christian Hymnary Publishers
1971. *Worship Hymnal* (Mennonite Brethren); Hillsboro, KS, Mennonite Brethren Publishing House
1970. *Hymnbook for Christian Worship* (American Baptists and Disciples); St Louis, Bethany Press and Valley Forge, Judson Press
1969. *Mennonite Hymnal;* Scottdale PA, Herald Press and Newton, KS, Faith and Life Press
1967. *Advent Christian Hymnal* (Adventists); Concord NH, Advent Christian Publications
1966. (1964). *The Methodist Hymnal* (later, *The Hymn Book)*; Nashville TN, The Methodist Publishing House
1964. *The Harvard University Hymn Book;* Cambridge MA, Harvard
1959. *Psalter Hymnal* (Christian Reformed Church); Grand Rapids, MI, Christian Reformed Church
1958. *The Pilgrim Hymnal* (Congregationalist); New York, Pilgrim Press

1958. *Service Book and Hymnal* (Lutheran Church in America); Minneapolis MN, Augsburg (and others)
1956. *Inter-Church Hymnal* (ed. Morgan and Howard); Chicago, Biglow-Main-Excell
1956. *Baptist Hymnal;* Nashville, TN, Convention Press (rev. 1975 above)
1956. *Hymnal for Colleges and Schools;* New Haven, Yale University
1955. *The Hymnbook* (Presbyterian); Philadelphia, Westminster Press
1951. *The Brethren Hymnal* (Church of the Brethren); Elgin IL, Brethren Press
1951. *Hymns of the Living Faith* (Wesleyan); Marion IN, Wesleyan Publishing House
1951. *At Worship;* New York, Harper
1943. *The Hymnal-1940* (Episcopal); New York, Church Pension Fund (later, Church Hymnal Corporation)
1941. *The Hymnal* (Evangelical and Reformed Church); St Louis MO, Eden.
1941. *Christian Worship* (American Baptist); Valley Forge, Judson Press (revised 1970 above)
1941. *The Lutheran Hymnal* (Lutheran Church Missouri Synod); St Louis MO, Concordia
1933. *The Hymnal* (Presbyterian); Philadelphia, Westminster Press
1928. *The Oxford American Hymnal;* New York, Oxford University Press

A2. Small Hymnals and Supplements
1980. *Songs for Celebration* (Episcopal — Hymns IV); New York, Church Hymnal Corp.
1980. *Songs of Thanks and Praise,* ed. R. Schulz-Widmar; Chapel Hill NC, Hinshaw
1980. *The Calvin Hampton Hymnal* (music by C. Hampton), Chicago, G.I.A.
1979. *Hymns III* (Episcopal); New York, Church Hymnal Corp.
1979. *Cantate Domino* (Episcopal); Chicago, G.I.A.
1978. *Christian Hymns,* ed. Wetzler; Minneapolis MN, A.M.S.I.
1977. *Ecumenical Praise,* ed. C.R. Young; Carol Stream, Agape
1977. *Hymns II* (Inter-Varsity Fellowship); Downers Grove IL, Inter-varsity Press
1976. *Westminster Praise,* ed. E. Routley; Chapel Hill NC, Hinshaw
1974. *Psalter Hymnal Supplement* (Christian Reformed); Grand Rapids MI, Christian Reformed Church Publications
1973. *Morning Praise and Evensong* (Catholic); Notre Dame IN, Fides Publishers
1972. *More Hymns and Spiritual Songs,* ed. L.H. Bristol; New York, Walton

B. Canadian
1980. *Catholic Book of Worship II* (revision of CB I, 1972); Toronto, G.V. Thompson
1972. *The Book of Praise* (Presbyterian); Don Mills, Ont., Presbyterian Church in Canada
1971. *The Hymn Book* (Anglican Church in Canada and United Church in Canada); no publisher is named; obtainable from publications depts. of the churches. Revised and corrected 1972
1938. *The Hymn Book* (Anglican); Toronto, Oxford University Press

1930. *The Hymnary* (United Church); Toronto, United Church Press (This was published with some hymns substituted by the Baptist Church in Canada for use in Baptist churches, Toronto, Ryerson Press, 1936)

C. Australian
1977. *The Australian Hymn Book;* London and Melbourne, Collins (This was published also in 1978 as *With One Voice,* for use outside Australia)
1973. *Lutheran Hymnal* (Lutheran Church of Australia); Adelaide, Lutheran Church
1967. *The Hymnal* (Baptist); Surry Hills, NSW, Aylesbury Press

D1. British and Irish: full size
(Note: for convenience of the researcher, the editions of HYMNS ANCIENT AND MODERN are placed together beginning at 1950.)

		hymns
1977.	*Christian Hymns;* Cardiff, Evangelical Movement of Wales	901
1977.	*With One Voice;* London, Collins (Australian Hymn Book)	569
1977.	*Grace Hymns;* London, Grace Publications Trust	848
1976.	*Christian Worship;* Exeter, Paternoster Press	716
1974.	*Psalm Praise;* London, Falcon Press	150
1973.	*Church Hymnary, Third Edition;* London, Oxford University Press	695
1972.	*Praise the Lord* (2nd edition: first ed. 1966); London, Chapman	334
1971.	*Gathered Together:* A Service Book for Senior Schools; London, Oxford University Press	151
1971.	*New Catholic Hymnal;* London, Faber	305
1967.	*The Cambridge Hymnal;* London, Cambridge University Press	197
1966.	*Youth Praise;* London, Falcon Press	150
1968.	*The Parish Hymn Book* (Catholic); London, L.J. Cary	249
1965.	*The Anglican Hymn Book;* London, Church Book Room Press	663
1964.	*Hymns of Faith;* London, Scripture Union	659
1964.	*Hymns for Church and School;* London, Novello (now Old Woking, Unwin)	346
1962.	*Winchester College Hymn Book;* London, Oxford University Press	287
1962.	*The Baptist Hymn Book* (revision of 1933); London, Psalms and Hymns Trust	777
1960.	*The* (Irish) *Church Hymnal* (Church of Ireland, Episcopal); Dublin, A.P.C.K.	719
1958.	*Hymns Ancient and Modern, School Edition* (related to 1950); London, Clowes (now Norwich, Hymns A & M Co.)	266
1957.	*Christian Praise;* London, Tyndale Press	401
1958.	*Sunday School Praise;* London, National Sunday School Union	583
1951.	*Congregational Praise* (Congregationalist); London, Independent Press	778
1951.	*BBC Hymn Book;* London, Oxford University Press	542
1950.	*Methodist School Hymn Book;* London, Epworth	647
1950.	Hymns Ancient and Modern Revised; London, Clowes (now Norwich, Hymns Ancient and Modern Co.)	636

The *Hymns A & M* Dynasty in ascending order of date. (Note that in section D2, *100 Hymns for To-day* and *More Hymns for To-day* are part of this continuing project.)

1861.	First Music Edition	273
1868.	1861 edition with Supplement	386
1875.	First Revision (2nd ed.)	473
1889.	1875 edition with Supplement	638
1904.	Second Revision (3rd ed)	643
1916.	Second Supplement to 1875 ed.	141
1922.	Standard Edition (1875, 1889 and 1916 re-set and bound together)	779
1939.	Shortened edition (1922 with many hymns omitted)	
1950.	Hymns Ancient and Modern Revised (4th ed)	636
1949.	*The Public School Hymn Book Revised;* London, Novello	553
1947.	*The Daily Service:* Prayers and Hymns for Schools (Revised)	182
1940.	*The Westminster Hymnal* (Catholic) Revised; London, Burns Oates	275
1937.	*Eton College Hymn Book;* London, Oxford University Press	300
1937.	*The Wellington College Hymn Book* (ed. Stanton); London, Novello	475
1936.	*The Mirfield Mission Hymn Book, Revised;* Mirfield, Yorks, The House of the Resurrection	220
1936.	*The Clarendon Hymn Book* (Charterhouse — School Hymn Book); Oxford, Clarendon Press	300
1933.	*Baptist Church Hymnal Revised;* London, Psalms and Hymns Trust	802
1933.	*The Methodist Hymn Book;* London. Methodist Publishing House	984
1933.	*The Fellowship Hymn Book Revised* (earlier edns 1920, 1909) (Society of Friends and Brotherhood Movement); London, Novello and Allen & Unwin	416
1933.	*The English Hymnal* (revised edn) (1906 texts with additional music, textual alterations only in detail: the *English Hymnal Service Book,* 1962, 336 hymns, is derived from this); London, Oxford University Press	656
1932.	*The Plainsong Hymn Book* (associated with Hymns A & M); London, Clowes	163
1931.	*Songs of Praise,* Enlarged edition (standard); London, Oxford U.P.	703
1927.	*The Church Hymnary Revised* (Church of Scotland and Presbyterian Churches; predecessor of 1973; first ed. 1898; London. Oxford University Press	707
1927.	*Harrow School Hymn Book* (ed. P.C. Buck) London, Oxford U.P.	272
1926.	*School Worship* (Congregationalist); London, Independent Press	402
1926.	*Church and School Hymnal* (Anglican); London, S.P.C.K.	338
1926.	*Golden Bells;* London, Children's Special Service Mission	703
1925.	*Songs of Praise* (original edn); London, Oxford U.P.	470
1923.	*A Student's Hymnal* (200 hymns in English, 123 in Welsh); London, Oxford University Press	323
1922.	*Hymns Ancient and Modern,* Standard edn (see 1950)	779

1919. *The Public School Hymn Book* (revised: 1st ed. 1903, predecessor of 1949); London, Novello 426

1910. *Songs of Syon* (2nd ed., ed. Woodward: 1st ed. music only, 1904) London, Scott 431

1908. *The Oxford Hymn Book* (ed. Harwood); Oxford, Clarendon Press 350

1906. *The English Hymnal* (original ed.) 656

1905. *Worship Song* (Congregationalist) (ed. Horder); London, Novello 803

1904. *Hymns Ancient and Modern* (see 1950) 643

1903. *Church Hymns, with tunes* (last edn: first, 1872); London, S.P.C.K. 658

1903. *Sacred Songs and Solos* (Definitive edition, originally ed. I.D. Sankey); London, Morgan & Scott 1200

1902. *Arundel Hymns* (Catholic), London, Boosey 308

D2. Supplements, Small Hymn Books and Authors' Collections

1980. *More Hymns for To-day* (Hymns A & M: sequel to 1969) 100

1980. *Songs of Worship* (related to Anglican Hymn Book, 1965); London Scripture Union 139

1980. *Mainly Hymns,* by Brian Wren, music ed. Peter Cutts; Leeds, John Paul the Preacher's Press 37

1979. *Partners in Praise,* words ed. F. Pratt Green and B. Braley, music ed. A. Percival and T.B. Coleman; London, Galliard (for Methodist Education & Youth Dept) 175

1978. *Sixteen Hymns of To-day for use as simple Anthems,* ed. J. Wilson, Croydon, Royal School of Church Music 16

1976. *A Song in Season* (Catholic), ed. Walsh, Watson, Bevenot and Cavenaugh; London, Collins 121

1975. *New Church Praise* (supplement to *Congregational Praise* 1951 and *The Church Hymnary* III 1973, for the United Reformed Church) Edinburgh, St Andrew Press 109

1975. *English Praise* (Supplement to the *English Hymnal* 1906, 1933); London, Oxford University Press 120

1974. *Hymns for Celebration,* ed. John Wilson; Croydon, the Royal School of Church Music 28

1974. *Green Print for Song,* by Sydney Carter; London, Stainer & Bell, with author's comments 20

1974. *Praise for To-day* (Supplement to Baptist Hymn Book); London, Psalms and Hymns Trust 104

1973. *The Veritas Hymnal,* ed. J. Threadgold (mainly Catholic); Dublin, Veritas Publications 143

1972. *New Orbit* (for children); London, Stainer & Bell 84

1972. *Songs for the Seventies;* London, Galliard and Edinburgh, St Andrew Press 52

1971. *26 Hymns,* by Frederick Pratt Green; London, Methodist Publishing House 26

1970. *Sing a new Song to the Lord,* ed. K. Mayhew; Southend on Sea, Mayhew-McCrimmon 103

1969. *Sing True,* ed. C. Hodgetts; Oxford, Religious Education Press 100

1969. *Hymns and Songs* (Supplement to Methodist Hymn Book 1933); London, Methodist Publishing House 104

1969. *100 Hymns for To-day* (First Supplement to *Hymns Ancient and Modern:* see also 1980); London, Clowes 100

1969. *New Songs for the Church,* ed. Barrett-Ayres and Routley, Vol. I, Hymns, Vol. II, Canticles; London, Galliard 45

1968. *Pilgrim Praise,* by Fred Kaan; London, Galliard 71

1967. *Gospel Song Book,* ed. M. Stewart; London, G. Chapman (in USA, *Now Songs,* Nashville TN, Abingdon) 62

1952. *Kingsway Hymn Book,* ed. L. Russell (schools) 108

1950. *Rejoice, O People,* by A.F. Bayly (later joined by *Again I say, Rejoice);* published by the author 100

D3. Hymnals and Tune Books of Historical Interest (a small selection)

n.d. (Preface 1902) *Hymn Tunes Composed by Arthur Sullivan,* ed. Anon., London, Novello

n.d. (after 1901), *Hymn Tunes Composed by John Bacchus Dykes,* ed. G.C. Martin, London and New York, Novello

n.d. (Preface 1901) *Hymn Tunes Composed by the late Dr. Edward J. Hopkins,* ed. W.H. Stocks; London, Weekes

n.d. (Preface 1900), *Hymn Tunes Composed by J. Stainer;* London and New York, Novello

n.d. (c. 1897) *Hymn Tunes Composed by Joseph Barnby,* ed. Anon from collections made in 1869 and 1883; London and New York, Novello

(1881.) *The Bristol Tune Book,* complete edition; London, Novello

1877. *The Hymnal Companion,* ed. J.T. Cooper; London, Sampson Low, Marston, Searle and Rivington

1874. *Church Hymns with Tunes,* ed. Arthur Sullivan; London, S.P.C.K.

(1872) *The Hymnary,* ed. J. Barnby; London, Novello

1872. *The European Psalmist,* ed. S.S. Wesley, London, Novello

1863. *The Chorale Book: 1865, The Chorale-Book for England,* Texts tr. by Catherine Winkworth, mus ed. W.S. Bennett and Otto Goldschmidt (1865 edition containing additional English hymns); London, Longman, Green, Longman, Roberts and Green.

1858. *The Church Psalter and Hymn Book,* 16th ed., W. Mercer; London, Nisbet

1857. *The Congregational Hymn and Tune Book,* ed. R.R. Chope (later ed, enlarged, 1862); London, Mackenzie

1852. *The Hymnal Noted* (1851), *with Accompanying Harmonies,* ed. T. Helmore, London, Novello

1847. Old Church Psalmody, ed. W.H. Havergal (enlarged, ed. F.R. Havergal, 1871); London, Cocks

1835-43. *The Psalmist,* ed. V. Novello (issued in 4 parts); London, Novello

1828. *Original Hymn Tunes adapted to every Metre in the Collection by The Rev. John Wesley,* by Samuel Wesley: London, privately published

1821. *Sacred Harmony: A Set of Tunes Collected by the late Rev. John Wesley,* ed. Charles Wesley II; London, J. Mason (re-issue of *Harmonia Sacra,* ed. T. Butts, c. 1755)

n.d. (c. 1820) *Sacred Harmony,* ed. R.A. Smith; Edinburgh

n.d. (c. 1795) *A Selection of Psalm and Hymn Tunes,* ed. J. Rippon; London

1730. *Harmonia Perfecta: A Compleat Collection of Psalm Tunes,* ed. Anon., London

1708. *A Supplement to the New Version of the Psalms,* ed. Anon. London, 1717 (8th ed. 1717)

1701. (1707. 1709) *The Divine Companion, or, David's Harp New Tun'd,* ed. H. Playford. London

E. Foreign or Foreign-Language Hymn and Tune Books: a short list of hymnals of musical interest, or of associated tune books, with texts in non-English languages, or with English texts published outside the USA and the British Commonwealth.

WELSH
1951. *Emynau'r Eglwys* ('Church Hymnal: Episcopal Church in Wales'); Cardiff, Western Mail and Echo Ltd.
1929. *Llyfr Emynau a Thonau* ('Book of Hymns and Tunes': Calvinist-Methodist Church); Calvinist-Methodist Publications

GERMAN
(Note: The 'Standard' Hymnal in German Lutheran Churches is *Evangelische Kirchengesangbuch*, whose first 342 hymns were compiled in 1853 and remain unaltered, with bound-in supplements revised from time to time. Organ books with harmonized versions of the tunes appear also from time to time in different styles, of which the next two entries are examples.
1963. *Spandauer Gesangbuch,* Chorale settings, three to six parts, 2nd ed. Vol. III, *Geistliche Chorgesange,* ed. E. Pepping; Mainz, London and New York, Schott.
n.d. (about 1928) *Vierstimmiges Deutsches Choralbuch* (4-part settings of the 206 tunes in Pt I of EKG) ed. Mauersberger; Berling, Merseburger

(Supplemental modern hymnals)
1971. *Christen Lieder Heute,* Hamburg, Siebenstern Taschenbuch Verlag
1971. *Schalom* (200 modern pieces, with 75 traditional hymns); Berlin, Burckhardthaus

(Swiss Reformed Church, German-speaking)
1953. *Orgelbuch zum Gesangbuch der Evangelisch-Reformierten Kirchen;* Swiss Evangelical Church Publications (no place of publication indicated)

FRENCH PROTESTANT IN SWITZERLAND
1926. *Psaumes et Cantiques,* ed. A. Laufer; Lausanne &c, Librairie Payot et Cie.
1879. *Hymnes et Cantiques a l'usage des Eglises et des Families Chretiennes,* Nancy, Imprimerie Berger-Levrault et Cie.

THE NETHERLANDS
1965. 102 Gezengen; 's-Gravenhage, Reformed Publications
1961. 150 Psalmen; 's-Gravenhage, Reformed Publications
1954. *Oude en Nieuwer Zangen* (Remonstrant Church); Bussum, Voorhoeve

SWEDEN
1975. *Psalmer och Visor* (Supplement to the general hymnal of the Swedish Church); Stockholm: Church Publications
1969. *Andlig Visa* (Free Church in Sweden); Stockholm, Free Church Publications
1961. *Koralbok for Skola och Hem;* Stockholm, Church Publications

ITALY (Waldensian)
1953. *Innario Cristiano;* Florence, Waldensian Church Commission

HUNGARIAN PROTESTANT
1974. *Hozsanna!;* Budapest, Kiadja a Szent Istvan Tarsulat az Apostoli Szentsek Konyvkiadoja

AFRICA
1969. *Africa Praise,* ed. D.G. Temple and A.M. Jones; London, Lutterworth Press

CHINA
1948. (Last edition of) *Hymns of Universal Praise;* Shanghai, Christian Literature Society for China

SOUTH-EAST ASIA
1962. *East Asia Christian Council Hymnal;* Kyoto, Japan, East Asia Christian Conference

POLYGLOT
1974, 1980 *Cantate Domino,* 4th edition; Geneva, World Council of Churches (Previous editions, 1924, 1930, 1950, Geneva, World Student Christian Federation. This edition, 1974 melody edition, Bärenreiter; 1980 full music edition, Oxford University Press).

VIII. Editions of historic books (F — with facsimile)
1964. *John Wesley's First Hymn Book,* ed. F. Baker and G.W. Williams: the Charlestown Hymn Book, 1737 (F) with notes; Charleston SC, the Dalcho Historical Society and London, The Wesley Historical Society
1935. *The Scottish Psalter of 1635,* ed. R.R. Terry: original and modern harmonies, shortened edition of 1864 below; London, Novello
1932. *Calvin's First Psalter,* ed. R.R. Terry: (F) with Preface, and harmonized versions; London, Benn
1910. *Piae Cantiones* (1582), ed. G.R. Woodward; Preface, Texts, melodies (old notation) and notes; London, The Plainsong and Medieval Music Society
1864. *The Scottish Psalter of 1635,* ed. N. Livingston: all the texts and tunes reprinted with extensive essays (original of 1935 above); Glasgow, McLure and Macdonald, folio
1856. (reprint 1895), *Hymns and Songs of the Church, by George Wither,* ed. E. Farr: reprint of all texts with Gibbons's tunes added (these not quite accurately transcribed); London, Reeves & Turner
1845. *A Reprint of all the Tunes in Ravenscroft's Book of Psalms,* with Introductory Remarks, ed. W.H. Havergal: the tunes transcribed in old notation; London, Novello

XI. JOURNALS
The Hymn (Hymn Society of America); Wittenberg University (Sec/T. Smith), Springfield, Ohio, 45501. By Subscription.
The Bulletin of the Hymn Society of Great Britain and Ireland; enquiries in the first instance to The Hymn Society, c/o The Royal School of Church Music, Addington Palace, Croydon, England, CR9 5AD. By subscription.

Index of Hymn Tunes

NOTE: (1) Sometimes a hymn tune is not mentioned by name in the text; but in such a case it is always referred to as an *Example*. To locate it from this index, identify it by its example number.

(2) Example numbers are referred to in this index as 'X103'; page numbers are followed by the letter A or B to distinguish left hand or right hand column.

(3) Occasionally a tune from a non-English speaking source has never been given a name. Such tunes, marked here with a star (*), are given temporary identifications to preserve the integrity of the index.

General Index